Language Variety
in the South Revisited

Language Variety in the South Revisited

Edited by

Cynthia Bernstein

Thomas Nunnally

Robin Sabino

The University of Alabama Press
Tuscaloosa and London

∞

The paper on which this book is printed meets the minimum requirements of
American National Standard for Information Science-Permanence of Paper for
Printed Library Materials, ANSI Z39.48–1984.

Library of Congress Cataloging-in-Publication Data

Language variety in the South revisited / edited by Cynthia Bernstein,
    Thomas Nunnally, Robin Sabino
        p.   cm.
    Includes bibliographical references and index.
    ISBN 0-8173-0882-2 (alk. paper)
    1. English language—Variation—Southern States. 2. English language—
Southern States—Foreign elements. 3. English language—Social aspects—
Southern States. 4. English language—Dialects—Southern States. 5. Afro-
Americans—Southern States—Language. 6. Languages in contact—
Southern States. 7. Black English—Southern States. 8. Americanisms—
Southern States. 9. Southern States—Languages. I. Bernstein, Cynthia
Goldin, 1947– . II. Nunnally, Thomas. III. Sabino, Robin.
PE2922.L37   1997
427'.975—dc21   96-29636

British Library Cataloguing-in-Publication Data available

Dedicated to the memory of James B. McMillan—
1907–1996
Auburn alumnus
Founder of The University of Alabama Press
Dean of Southern Linguistics

Contents

Preface

In 1981 a historic linguistics conference organized by Michael Montgomery and Guy Bailey was hosted in Columbia by the University of South Carolina. That conference, LANGUAGE VARIETY IN THE SOUTH: PERSPECTIVES IN BLACK AND WHITE, produced a lasting effect on the study of Southern American English, especially African-American Vernacular English (AAVE). The conference's concentration upon AAVE and its relationships with other varieties of English served as both compendium of current scholarship and catalyst to a decade of productive research. The value of the conference was multiplied through publication of key papers (Montgomery and Bailey 1986).

In the early 1990s it seemed time to invite scholars together again to assess and reassess what had been accomplished in the study of Southern American language varieties. Responding to this need to see where scholarship had been and where it was headed, Auburn University hosted a second Language Variety in the South (LAVIS) conference, April 1–3, 1993. The culmination of over two years of planning, LAVIS II welcomed an exciting and excited group of researchers—from premier scholars in the field to students in the first stages of graduate studies—who converged for three days of presentation, consultation, and reflection. Like its predecessor, LAVIS II included research into AAVE; however, LAVIS II extended the forum to present findings across a broad spectrum of language topics and issues pertinent to the American South.

This volume of essays, *LANGUAGE VARIETY IN THE SOUTH REVISITED*, disseminates in updated form much of the research presented at LAVIS II. Each essay has undergone a process of revisions that began with the consultation, challenges, and joint reflection that occurred during the course of LAVIS II as an integral part of the conference's design and continued under the supervision of the conference organizers. The four-part organization of this volume reflects the history, prospects, and shape of Southern language study. In the Introduction Michael Montgomery and Guy Bailey look back upon the history of such research and point to the future. Thirty-six essays, organized into three parts, then treat three of the main themes that emerged from the conference. Part One focuses on language contact, including African, European, and Asian influences. Part Two elaborates on Southern dialect features, including discourse along with the more traditional areas of phonology, syntax, and the lexicon. Part Three emphasizes methods of collecting and analyzing data.

We the editors present this volume to our colleagues with this desire: just as the first LAVIS energized a decade of important research in AAVE, we hope this collection will prove fruitful to researchers of language variation, stirring debate, providing guidance, and blazing trails into the next millennium.

Cynthia Bernstein
Thomas E. Nunnally
Robin Sabino

Acknowledgments

This volume of essays and the Auburn conference on Language Variety in the South (LAVIS) that inaugurated it could not have been accomplished without the help and support of many. We wish especially to express our gratitude to the National Science Foundation (SBR–9221890), the Franklin Foundation, the Southeastern Conference on Linguistics, the American Dialect Society, the English Department of Auburn University, and The University of Alabama Press.

Individuals to whom we owe special thanks include Michael Montgomery, Guy Bailey, Elaine Posanka, Jody Abbott, and Nicole Mitchell. We express our great debt to all of the LAVIS participants, who created the congenial and collaborative atmosphere for generating this volume, and most especially to those who took on with us the challenge of creating a volume that would enrich the linguistic understanding of the American South.

We gratefully acknowledge permission to publish the following material:

From BLACK MAJORITY by Peter H. Wood. Copyright © 1974 by Peter H. Wood. Reprinted by permission of Alfred A. Knopf Inc.

From F'SURE: ACTUAL DIALOGUE HEARD ON THE STREETS OF NEW ORLEANS by Bunny Matthews, 1978, Neetof Press. Reprinted by permission.

From THE TRIP TO BOUNTIFUL (screenplay) copyright © 1986, 1989 by Horton Foote, in THREE SCREENPLAYS copyright © 1989 by Sunday Rock Corporation. Reprinted by permission.

From DICTIONARY OF AMERICAN REGIONAL ENGLISH, volume II, D–H edited by Frederic G. Cassidy and Joan Houston Hall. Copyright © 1991 by the President and Fellows of Harvard College. Reprinted by permission of Harvard University Press.

From LINGUISTIC ATLAS OF THE GULF STATES, volume IV, by Lee Pederson. Copyright © 1990 by The University of Georgia Press. Reprinted by permission.

From AMERICAN REGIONAL DIALECTS by Craig Carver. Copyright © 1987 by The University of Michigan. Reprinted by permission of The University of Michigan Press.

From AMERICAN SPEECH, "South Midland Pronunciation in the North Central States," by Timothy C. Frazer. Copyright © 1978 by The University of Alabama Press for the American Dialect Society. Reprinted by permission.

INTRODUCTION

Perspectives on Language Variety in the South

We begin our revisit to Language Variety in the South with complementary essays by the two scholars who organized the original conference on the subject (now LAVIS I) and edited the influential volume of essays that followed (Montgomery and Bailey, 1986). Their own study of language in the American South leaves them well positioned to evaluate the state of the discipline. Both were closely involved with the preparation of the *Linguistic Atlas of the Gulf States*. Montgomery, who has inherited the mantle of bibliographer of the field of Southern English (see McMillan and Montgomery 1989) after the death of James B. McMillan, is working on another important reference work, the *Dictionary of Smoky Mountain English* (Montgomery forthcoming). While continuing his own research on the Scotch-Irish connection with Southern English, he is also editing *Linguistic Studies from the Gulf States and Beyond* (Montgomery and Nunnally forthcoming). Bailey has been influential in the development of survey methods used in the Phonological Survey of Texas (PST), the Grammatical Investigation of Texas Speech (GRITS), and the Survey of Oklahoma Dialects (SOD), projects that have contributed to several of the studies in this volume.

Montgomery presents a retrospective and assessment of scholarship since the 1981 conference, which emphasized "perspectives in black and white." He provides an informative overview of publications that have made available not only new approaches to Southern American English but also a wide range of new data sources. At the same time, he assesses gaps in researchers' incorporation of social, cultural, and historical contexts. Bailey follows with an evaluation of how the themes of the 1993 conference on Language Variety in the South (LAVIS II) signal trends that provide a prospective for research. As Bailey points out, many of the essays reflect a growing concern with the nature of evidence and methods used to evaluate it. Furthermore, they express growing interest in language contact and in an expanded range of linguistic features. The observations of Montgomery and Bailey apply not just to the American South but to research on variation in all regions.

In their assessments of the state of the field, Montgomery and Bailey both acknowledge the ongoing significance of black-white speech relations. As evidenced by the furor initiated by the Oakland, California, school board's 1996 decision to recognize "Ebonics" as a distinct language, there is a great deal of scholarly and public interest in the origins and status of African-American Vernacular English (AAVE). The essays of this volume, especially the ones in Part One, address those issues and consider the interdependence of African languages, creoles, and the varieties spoken by European and non-European settlers.

Together the essays by Montgomery and Bailey prepare the reader for understanding the context leading to LAVIS II and the thirty-six selections derived from it that constitute the three parts of this volume. We recognize that a notable omission here is discussion of Native American languages, a void we hope to see filled once LAVIS III gets underway.

Language Variety in the South:
A Retrospective and Assessment
Michael Montgomery

In 1981 the first Language Variety in the South conference was held at the University of South Carolina (LAVIS I). It was an exciting occasion and, by most accounts, a successful meeting that produced a collection of informative essays (Montgomery and Bailey 1986). It was also an important, even propitious, time for the participants, as it brought together older and younger scholars to begin a conversation, to build bridges, and to bring coherence to a set of issues touching in multiple ways on the fundamental issue of language variation in the American South—that is, the intersection of language and race.

While that first conference focused almost entirely on issues of black-white differences and similarities, many participants sensed that much intellectual energy was being infused into a larger set of issues, and that, if perhaps a new field was not being born, a new sense of the relevance of Southern American English (SAE) to many larger linguistic issues had been established. Whether attributable in part to the 1981 gathering, much important research on Southern American English has been undertaken and published in the more than a decade following the South Carolina event.[1] Scholarly discussion has addressed increasingly diverse and searching questions, making it now timely to synopsize and assess recent progress in the field and summarize the present state of knowledge. This essay attempts to do these things. It also seeks to bring into focus an even broader perspective on language issues in the American South. For a variety of reasons, limiting discussion only to developments since the earlier conference is inappropriate. Not only because LAVIS I dealt with one set of issues, but also because only eight presenters from that meeting were on the program at the LAVIS II conference in Auburn, the latter event signified the gathering of a new generation of researchers. For newcomers, as well as for the field at large, a more general view on the commentary and research on Southern American language patterns may be instructive.

My discussion proceeds as follows: Section one offers a backdrop, with general observations about language and the study of language variation in the American South. This section notes both achievements and shortcomings of the field, even exposing some of its parochial side, particularly as of the mid-to-late 1970s, when this writer entered the profession and can therefore base his commentary on personal experience. Section two identifies areas of research in which significant advancements have been made in recent years. Others could surely be cited, but this coverage shows some of the principal developments and enable us to assess their implications. Finally, section three lays out areas of needed research, each touching on larger issues that command the interest of linguist and non-linguist alike. While my primary tasks are to review and assess the current state of research, this inevitably reveals unanswered questions and needed research.

ACHIEVING A PERSPECTIVE

In 1814 the Reverend Henry Cogswell Knight left his native New England, venturing south on what turned out to be a five-year journey to Philadelphia, Washington City, Virginia, Kentucky, and finally down the Ohio and Mississippi Rivers to New Orleans before he boarded a packet ship and returned home by way of the Gulf of Mexico in 1819. After crossing the Potomac into Virginia, Knight began noticing, as he writes in the account of his travels, that the speech was "peculiar to a northern ear" (1824:81). The pronunciation and usage of English in the Old Dominion, and later in the Commonwealth of Kentucky, seemed foreign to him. "As the New Englanders guess, so do the Virginians reckon" (81), he remarked, and then proceeded at greater length:

> The Virginians use clever for intelligent; whereas we use it for a kind of negative character of weak intellect, but good disposition . . . and what we call afternoon, they call evening, making no quarter divisions of the day. *Tote*, a slave word, is much used, implying both suspension and locomotion, as a slave a log, or a nurse a babe. They say—to grow a crop, for, to raise a crop[2]; [they say] he was raised, for, he was educated, mad for angry. . . . Children learn from the slaves some odd phrases; as, every which way; will you *all* do this? for, will *one* of you do this? and the epithet *mighty* is quite popular with old and young, as, for instance, mighty weak. (82)

> [In Kentucky] the word *great* is sometimes used to signify *little*; as, that lady has a great foot, meaning, without irony, a little foot. Many from habit, like the Virginians, tuck a *t* at the end of such words as onct, twict, skifft. They here call a river, a run; a lot, a section of land; they say to stall, i.e., overload, a horse; and cupping for milking. (106)

Knight was hardly the first American to describe his experiences in the South as if he had been in a foreign land, evoking images of its strange ways and unusual speech. His perceptions were not at all uncommon. Historian Thomas D. Clark, in his *Travelers in the Old South: A Bibliography* (1956), includes others who can just as readily be cited. Down to the present day outsiders traveling in the region have often viewed it, its language, people, habits, and culture as unfamiliar, even exotic, conjuring up an aura of mystery in their accounts. As recently as 1989, the Caribbean-born writer of Indian extraction, V. S. Naipaul, followed the same bent, traversing the South with eyes and ears wide open, making many a personal discovery of the "true South," and presenting his experiences as revelations to the outside world, as we learn from his memoir *A Turn in the South*. On a pilgrimage to find the nature of the South and its people, he too sought answers to the questions posed by the Faulknerian persona in *Absalom! Absalom!*: "Tell about the South. What's it like there. What do they do there. Why do they live there. Why do they live at all."

What is the South linguistically, this strange and foreign land, this linguistic outpost in the English-speaking world? Linguists have known for a long time, of course, that there are many Souths, but that is not the point. Outsiders tend to lump Southerners together on the basis of their speech, and without question there are few, if any, traits that identify Southerners so readily. For better or for worse, how Southerners speak English is often noticed first by non-Southerners, and that draws frequent comment. When Jimmy Carter and, more recently, Bill Clinton made the run for President, the media paid considerable attention to their accents. Carter's drawl was caricatured by editorialists; Clinton, although a Rhodes scholar, was stuck with the label *Bubba* in his campaign because he was from Arkansas and his manners and speech were parodied accordingly. But how Southerners talk has frequently drawn admiration as well: when North Carolinian Sam Ervin chaired the Senate Watergate Investigating Committee some years ago, the nation was spellbound by his adroit, if folksy, manipulation of the English tongue. Southerners have long been well-reputed for their political stumping, their preaching, and their ability to tell a story.

So it comes as no surprise to find that far more has been written about Southern English than any other variety or collections of varieties of American English, as of 1988 nearly four thousand articles, chapters, books, and notes, according to a comprehensive bibliography (McMillan and Montgomery 1989). Americans have been and continue to be fascinated with the region and its speech, and with Southern culture in general. Indeed, a professional phenomenon fit several participants on the second Language Variety in the South program: non-Southerners who take jobs teaching in Southern colleges and universities often find themselves intrigued by and then researching the local language. The fascination is shared by the public and academics.

The attention paid to Southern speech stems, I think, from three realities. First, Southerners are often absorbed with themselves and with their speech. They frequently comment on and study it themselves. This self-absorption sometimes reaches a disposition, or what one historian has even called a "rage," to define and explain themselves (Hobson 1983). This on the one hand can border on defensive-ness because non-Southerners have long viewed the South in terms very different from the region's own residents; on the other it has led to pride, romanticism, and the frequent claim that various Southern varieties of English are "Shakespearean" or "Elizabethan" (in which there is only a small grain of truth), as if the status of the bard can lend prestige to Southern speech across the centuries. For many South-erners, their speech signifies their upbringing, their loyalties, and their roots. It is inseparable, in other words, from a strong regional identity, at least as much a part of them as grits, football, and barbecue. At the same time, Southerners are acutely aware of how conspicuous their speech habits are to non-Southerners and that their speech is often caricatured outside the region, not to mention the extreme and fanciful concoctions that come out of Hollywood. So they are often schizophrenic about their speech, knowing it is part of who they are but uncomfortable about others' attitudes toward it.

The second reality is that both Southerners and non-Southerners identify the South by its language patterns. Everyone knows that Southern speech is, well, different. When Lloyd Bentsen campaigned for Vice President in 1988, he was introduced in the South as being proficient in three languages: English, Spanish, and Southern. Dennis Preston says in *Perceptual Dialectology*, his book exploring how Americans map dialect regions mentally, that "the .94 identification rate . . . of the region here called South is the most significant commonality" (1989a:115) over the course of five studies conducted in disparate parts of the country. Neither the Mason-Dixon line nor any other demarcation has ever distinguished the region from the rest of the country linguistically. Early immigrants to the South were as heterogeneous as those to any other region, and for most of its history the South has been no more isolated than other parts of the country. Yet all Americans, Southerners and non-Southerners alike, perceive the South to be a distinct place.

Drawing from this is a third reality, that Southern language patterns are believed to be disappearing. In the South this is often viewed as unfortunate. There seems to be a continuing interest, even a need, to check the health of Southern language patterns periodically because of the widespread conviction that they are fixing to pass away. Between the mid-1980s (when I began tracking this phenomenon) and 1991, no fewer than five feature stories appeared in newspapers throughout the South with headlines like "Southern accent here to stay," "Don't fret y'all—the drawl isn't dying," and "Southern drawl still going strong." The notion that Southern speech is dying, being wiped out relentlessly by television or drowned out by a horde of Northern migrants or some other alien force, is quite prevalent, and the media give it a checkup from time to time (Montgomery 1993b). Is Southern English fading away? What might research have to say about this?

This broadest of backdrops can frame the rest of our discussion and assist us in seeing how some of the issues being addressed by recent research connect to general, public issues involving language and identity, language status, and language change. To some of these points I return later, but let me first seek a general characterization of scholarly research on SAE, first with reference to the period before the first LAVIS conference.

Following the advice of John Hurt Fisher, a professor of ours at the University of Tennessee, Guy Bailey and I decided in 1979 to organize a conference to tackle one of the larger and more rambunctious questions in the field of American English: how black and white speech were related in the South, synchronically and diachronically. Generating more polemics than empirical research and level-headed discussion, no set of issues in American English in the 1960s and 1970s was more hotly disputed. The temper of the field was such that prominent scholars were often no longer talking to one another because of differences in research paradigms and in basic definitions and assumptions underlying their research (Montgomery and Bailey 1986). Philosophical, personal, even regional animus stymied debate. Scholarly discourse had largely polarized and languished. Arguments frequently centered on unpublished data and were motivated by personal agendas.

At the same time, a new generation of research had developed, a younger class of scholars had quietly done its work, and Bailey and I sensed an imperative to bring them together and assist the profession in fostering a more empirically based and less impassioned discourse on one of the larger questions in the field of American English. We called on scholars who had recently completed fieldwork or had other significant new data concerning black/white speech relations to participate. From all accounts, the resulting NEH-sponsored conference in South

Carolina and the ensuing published collection of essays were successful and helped improve the temperament of the field. Debate opened up on many issues.

The widespread distemper in the 1970s over questions of black and white speech must seem a far cry from today for newcomers, but it must be understood to gauge how much progress has been made, as represented by the papers in this volume. To achieve the fullest appreciation of how far the field has come, I want to characterize more generally the state of research in SAE as of fifteen to twenty years ago. Three broad statements can be made for the overwhelming majority of studies on Southern English until that time. But for space constraints, each could be supported by numerous names, dates, and citations. By no means do the characterizations apply to all research and should not obscure the achievements of linguists like Raven I. McDavid, Jr., of the University of Chicago, James B. McMillan of the University of Alabama, Claude Merton Wise of Louisiana State University, and others (McDavid's, in particular, are impossible to underestimate), but the contributions of these exceptional individuals are beyond the scope of this essay to detail.

First, while publications on Southern English as of a generation ago were numerous and diverse in both regional distribution and topics addressed, most were brief and quite limited in scope. Few formed part of a larger, ongoing research program, and as a result, the field largely lacked coherence. Linguistic atlas work was active across the region by the mid-1970s, with the collecting and editing of data in progress, but research tools were few and standard sources covered only part of the region or only certain aspects of language (e.g., Kurath 1949; Kurath and McDavid 1961; Wood 1971; McMillan 1971). It was quite difficult to attain a larger picture of geographical and social variation in Southern English or to overview the field. It was difficult to recommend where someone might start reading about the subject.

Second, most work on Southern English adhered to a philological paradigm that approached linguistic analysis in terms of individual features and forms, not in terms of related features or grammatical or phonological systems. Much of this work was historically based and paid scant attention to methodology or to describing the instruments used to gather data (personal observations in most cases), much less to the effect of the methodology employed on the data collected. Determining how to replicate most research would have been impossible. Consistent with this philological approach, studies based on historical documents and literary works routinely took those texts at face value rather than seeking a way to assess their validity before analyzing them.

Third, studies often lacked discrimination. Linguistic features were described as if used uniformly in a community or a region, and because most studies observed and classified data rather than comparing them between communities or between or within individual speakers, the quantification of results, much less the interpretation of quantitative findings, was rare. Often reinforced by the historical bias already noted, many studies relied on highly selective citations unattributed to specific individuals. There was little interest in the kind of comparative research for which a quantitative approach might prove useful. While linguistic atlas research had replaced the traditional, philological approach in some academic quarters by midcentury and represented a major advance in many ways, especially for comparative research, by the mid-1970s linguistic geography had only begun to be complemented by other approaches and paradigms, particularly those of synchronic sociolinguistics.

These research tendencies, each of which can be exemplified by hundreds of studies from the McMillan and Montgomery (1989) bibliography, made it difficult, even with the abundance of publications, to summarize fifteen or twenty years ago what was known concerning most issues in Southern English. This was especially true for black/white speech relations, on which research had not proceeded very far, particularly for grammar and pronunciation. Too often linguists in the South (those working on language variation in the region have almost invariably been native Southerners until recently) lacked self-criticism and were satisfied, even a bit smug, with their impressions and intuitions about many matters of language variation, most notably for the general issues of the distinctiveness of black speech in the South. In the face of Northern linguists who were researching Northern urban black speech, which was, after all, largely Southern speech transported to the North, Southerners were often exasperated by statements about features said to be distinctive to black speech, when many whites in the South used them. Yet Southern linguists with rare exception undertook research of their own into black/white speech relations or many other questions. Far more often they, both black and white, accused Northern counterparts of making false claims of what was distinctive to black speakers and dismissed such work, preferring to base their dissent on unpublished data or on the testimony of their own personal experience. Parochialism and rivalry, fueled in part by differences in research paradigms and competition for grant funds, slowed progress in the field for some time.

The lack of communication, mutual respect, and constructive criticism was more endemic than most of us Southerners in previous generations would allow. This researcher can recall innumerable comments on the conference circuit from Southern linguists to the effect that Northern linguists had little idea what "Black English" was and faulting their lack of knowledge of vernacular Southern white English, which had all the allegedly "Black English" features. Ironically, but happily, some of the best studies of Southern white speech since the 1970s (e.g., Feagin 1979) were motivated by the intent to show that in the South many linguistic features were not restricted to black speakers alone.

With these comments in mind, we now examine the significant progress achieved over the past decade or so in the study of language variation in the American South.

PRINCIPAL DEVELOPMENTS

This section is organized around six areas of research and scholarship. First, we can agree that the field has now come of age, as signified by the publication of four reference works or series of works since 1981, each of which requires some commentary.

In 1989 appeared the *Annotated Bibliography of Southern American English*, edited by James B. McMillan and the present writer. The only book-length bibliography of the speech of an American region (much-expanded from McMillan's 1971 bibliography with the same name), this volume catalogs the complete range of scholarly and popular writing on the English spoken from Maryland to Texas, from Kentucky to Florida; it focuses on the grammar, pronunciation, vocabulary, naming practices, word-play, and other aspects of the language that have interested researchers and writers for more than two centuries. Encompassing more than 3,800 items and extensively cross-referenced, this bibliography provided the starting point, the editors hoped, for much research in the field. All entries are annotated, with details of research (location, number and type of informants, etc.) provided where possible. As comprehensive as it may be, however, it covers only English; we have no serviceable bibliography for other languages spoken in the South. A compilation of work on such topics is badly needed, particularly for French and Spanish in the region (interest in these languages is reflected by essays in this volume), but other European languages, such as the German of Virginia, North Carolina, and Texas, and the Gaelic of North Carolina, have played roles in the history of the region but are poorly documented. Perhaps someone in the rising generation will undertake these initiatives. A continuing myth about the South is that its culture and language grew out of contact between only peoples from Africa and the British Isles (usually on a plantation, one might add). The South has long been far more multicultural and multilingual than most know.

DARE, the *Dictionary of American Regional English*, is the monumental, multi-thousand-page compilation of the nation's folk lexicon, pronunciation, and grammar. Conceived in 1889, it came through many dangers, toils, and snares to begin publication in 1985, just four years short of its "centennial," with volume one covering letters A through C, volume two (1991) D through H, and volume three (1996) I through O. Among many other things, *DARE* encompasses within its entries the closest approximation there may ever be to a dictionary of Southern English.

Frederic Cassidy is a cautious man made more cautious by the craft of lexicography, yet I will brave the caveats of Cassidy and his staff to say a few things about the significance and use of *DARE*. The feature that makes *DARE* more important to our knowledge of Southern English than any other is the regional labels like "South Midland" and "chiefly South Atlantic" that it assigns to roughly a quarter of its entries. While *DARE* is a dictionary national in coverage, it actually combines many regional dictionaries. When terms like *gee-haw*, *whimmy-diddle*, *happy pappy*, and *hell's banjer* are labeled "Appalachian," it indicates that, as far as *DARE* can surmise, such terms are rarely to be found outside Appalachia, if at all.

Without perhaps stretching the intention of the editors too far, we can say that, by indicating both where a usage has been found and where it has not, *DARE* provides the best picture of which linguistic usages are restricted to any given region and thus isolates the distinctive vocabulary of Appalachia and many other areas for which labels are used (111 different regional and social labels in all). Identifying the entries assigned a given label in the first two volumes of *DARE* is made all the easier by the appearance of the index to *DARE* recently as a

Publication of the American Dialect Society (PADS) volume (*Index* 1993; see Metcalf, this volume). *DARE* has been justly praised and lauded as a magnificent testament to the diversity of American English, but surely the greatest compliment the profession can pay Cassidy and his team is to *use* the dictionary. Ideas for putting it to student use are badly needed (Algeo 1993 provides a start).

Over the past decade the editing of linguistic atlas materials has progressed in the South in a major fashion. Work on LAMSAS, the Linguistic Atlas of the Middle and South Atlantic States, which encompasses Virginia, West Virginia, the Carolinas, as well as parts of Georgia and Florida, is ongoing under the direction of William Kretzschmar at the University of Georgia. The handbook for LAMSAS is now out (Kretzschmar et al. 1994) from the University of Chicago Press. Publication of other LAMSAS materials on microfiche is in the offing, and access to LAMSAS data by CD-ROM or similar means is foreseen (Kretzschmar et al. 1994).

Publication of the Linguistic Atlas of the Gulf States (LAGS), the most significant research project on Southern English published to date, is now complete. LAGS is undoubtedly one of the half-dozen most important scholarly achievements in American English in the twentieth century. Lee Pederson of Emory University conceived of LAGS, directed it, and deserves the primary credit for it. When LAVIS I convened in 1981, the LAGS Basic Materials (Pederson et al. 1981), a microfiche collection of 1199 cards containing all the transcribed records from 1,121 speakers, were just appearing. By the early 1990s we had a concordance of more than three million items from the LAGS field records (Pederson, McDaniel, and Bassett 1986) and the LAGS Descriptive Materials, a hard-bound series of seven oversized volumes with innumerable maps, displays of data, and the equipment for analyzing the microfiche materials from the University of Georgia Press (Pederson et al. 1986–92).

LAGS surveys the speech of seven Southern states (Alabama, Arkansas, Florida, Georgia, Louisiana, Mississippi, and Tennessee) and part of an eighth (East Texas), comprising a region of nearly a half-million square miles. It surpasses in size and breadth all other studies of Southern American speech and furnishes the most important and most diverse tools for the study of Southern speech in its sociohistorical contexts. The complex picture of speech subregions it outlines strongly counters the simple Upper South vs. Lower South dichotomy so often presented in the linguistic literature: LAGS provides abundant and fascinating evidence for, among others, the Piney Woods of the Lower South and the Mississippi Delta as distinct speech areas.

LAGS makes available more data of more kinds and from a wider range of speakers in eight Southern states than any other source does and, without question, ever will. For exploring social variation within the region, it probably offers more data than all other studies combined. Primary informants for the survey were 197 blacks and 717 whites, permitting comparison of speech patterns on an unprecedented scale and the exploration of countless issues such as the degree of African influence on both blacks and whites. LAGS also offers bountiful data across generational lines for examining sound change in progress; generational differences, particularly in lexis, are more easily charted in LAGS than in any other major database on American English. For innumerable issues involving change and variation in Southern speech, LAGS will provide, or should provide, points of departure for future investigations. Whatever its limitations, LAGS data can be used to explore virtually every major issue in Southern American English, or its varieties, that researchers have identified.[3]

Ironically, LAGS is the past decade's "stealth" project on SAE, given the scant publicity and use it has had. Only the handbook for the project received more than a book notice in the professional journals before a recent comprehensive essay review of LAGS publications appeared in *American Speech* (Montgomery 1993a).

The *Encyclopedia of Southern Culture*, published in 1989, completes the quartet of reference resources. This magnificent volume of 1700 pages, edited at the Center for the Study of Southern Culture at the University of Mississippi, features Language as one of its twenty-four sections of coverage. Here are found popular discussions of twenty-four topics from Southern place and personal names to Outer Banks dialect. When LAVIS I met in 1981, Raven McDavid, newly appointed editor for the Language section, called for suggestions and assistance, and work began in earnest. Today we have a reference work that makes accessible information on several languages in the South, English as well as French, Spanish, German, Amerindian languages, even Amerindian trade languages. The advent of the *Encyclopedia* and *DARE* means that more information on the region's language is now available to a lay audience than ever before.

Generations of researchers have looked to the speech of Appalachia, the Outer Banks, and other relatively isolated parts of the South for keys to the history of SAE. The second in my list of the past decade's developments involves the connections established with even more isolated, or at least more distant, speech enclaves, connections which have raised new possibilities of discerning earlier stages of both black and white SAE. These are exported varieties, what might be called Expatriate or Extraterritorial SAE, carried by descendants of Southerners who left the region in the 18th and 19th centuries and whose descendants now reside in remnant communities abroad. In studies of Liberian Settler English, John Singler (e.g., 1989) has detailed linguistic patterns used by descendants of American blacks, mostly freed slaves from the South, who migrated to Liberia under the sponsorship of the American Colonization Society in the 1830s and 1840s. Two studies of the English of descendants of white Southerners who left the former Confederacy to settle in Brazil in the 1860s and 1870s can also be noted (Montgomery and Melo 1990; Bailey and Smith 1992). A third initiative, description of the English taken in the late 18th century to Nova Scotia by Southern blacks who escaped from South Carolina and other American colonies with retreating Loyalists, is ongoing at the University of Ottawa (e.g., Poplack and Tagliamonte 1991a).

One prominent result of research on expatriate communities has been to counter the popular myth that America is a land of immigrants but not emigrants—people do in fact choose to leave. The reconstruction of 19th-century SAE and understanding its subsequent evolution are much closer to reality, although interpreting late-20th-century recordings of descendants several generations removed from the time of emigration has presented its own challenges. In no case does their speech represent merely a time capsule from an earlier period, and the effects of contact with other languages must always be identified, if possible. For instance, the influence of Portuguese probably explains in part why the ex-Confederates in Brazil are generally *r*-less and never drawl their vowels. Even so, the complete absence of either drawling or homophony of /ɪ/ and /ɛ/ before nasals provides grounds for arguing that some present-day phonological patterns of SAE are innovations. For reasons not yet clear, the findings from contemporary Liberian Settler English and Nova Scotian English suggest very different antecedents, with the former revealing definite evidence of a prior creolized variety of English and the latter none at all.

The minor diaspora of roughly 20,000 ex-Confederate whites from the Lower South after the war not only to Brazil, but also to Japan, Mexico, and Egypt, is indeed a captivating story (see the essays in Dawsey and Dawsey 1995).[4] Research on the speech of their descendants should continue, as should fuller descriptions on other migrated varieties of SAE. One of the latter presented at the 1981 conference was Ian Hancock's work with the Afro-Seminoles (Hancock 1986a), Gullah speakers who went to Oklahoma and Texas a century and a half ago. Another is the migration of Loyalists from mainland South Atlantic colonies to the Bahamas in the late 18th century, some of the linguistic consequences of which are reported in Holm (1983b) and Holm and Shilling (1982).

Although it lacks the time-depth of those situations already cited, the largest question along this line concerns the migration of hundreds of thousands of blacks from throughout the South and of whites from Appalachia to Northern cities in the last seventy-five years. There are now many studies of the children and grandchildren of Southern blacks who moved north or west, and two or three modest ones of Appalachians in Northern cities, but only two investigations, so far as I am aware, actually compare Northern urban speech patterns with their Southern area of origin (for African-American speech, Elizabeth Dayton's dissertation research at the University of Pennsylvania; and for Appalachian speech, Davis 1971). Thus, one of the most significant cases of the exportation of SAE is virtually unexplored for what it can reveal about contemporary language change. Research of this kind is certainly needed to establish an adequate research base for investigating the so-called "divergence" of African-American English from white varieties (see discussion below).

Work on exported varieties actually forms part of a larger and renewed interest of linguists over the past decade in the history of SAE, a third recent development, as historical sociolinguistics has come to the field. One evidence of this interest is the increasing use of manuscript evidence from letters, diaries, and the like in documenting earlier stages of SAE; until recently, excerpts of literary dialect were the only type of written sources routinely employed. While the seminal work in this area is Norman Eliason's *Tarheel Talk: An Historical Study of the English Language in North Carolina to 1860* (1956), the possibilities of quantitative historical research were strikingly demonstrated by the dissertations and subsequent work of two scholars (Brewer 1974; Schneider 1981), who analyzed the WPA Ex-Slave Narratives for evidence of 19th-century black speech patterns, particularly those having a possible creole ancestry. Although not manuscripts but transcriptions by fieldworkers (Schneider, this volume, has most recently called them "note-supported mental protocols"), these narratives were the first written documents to be subjected to large-scale analysis, a process which required Brewer and Schneider to develop an explicit methodology and assess the validity of such texts for linguistic purposes. Other research has examined a variety of questions, most notably the trans-Atlantic evolution of linguistic features that are today characteristic of SAE.

Written documents are indispensable for establishing the input of Irish and British English to American colonies in the 17th and 18th centuries. In a series of papers I have argued that family letters, particularly ones written by emigrants back to the British Isles, offer the best access to vernacular language patterns of the period; and I have detailed the linguistic contributions of Ulster emigrants, people usually called the Scotch-Irish, to contemporary varieties of SAE, especially Southern Appalachian English (Montgomery 1989, 1990, 1992, 1995. See also Schneider 1990a; Montgomery and Nagle 1994). Let us hope that other work on Early Modern English (Bailey 1989; Bailey, Maynor, and Cukor-Avila 1989; Montgomery and Robinson 1992), on Southwestern British English (Hancock 1994), on Ship English (Bailey and Ross 1988), and on Hiberno-English (Harris 1986; Rickford 1986a) also improves our knowledge of earlier vernacular varieties so that no longer will some version of "standard" or textbook English be taken to be the linguistic input of whites to the formation of colonial and other early varieties of American English.

Work on African elements in Southern speech has also witnessed recent progress. Research by Lorenzo Dow Turner (1949) and Mitford Mathews (1948) a half-century ago, as well as that of Dalby, Dillard, and others in the 1960s, led the way on this question. But until a very few years ago there was little interest, or even open-mindedness, among white and black linguists and educators in the South to the deeper questions of African influence on Southern language patterns beyond vocabulary (most work to date has been lexical and etymological). This topic appears now to be completely out of the closet, and there is much catching up to do. Crawford Feagin's essay in this volume argues for phonological and intonational influence on SAE from African languages. Several studies in *Africanisms in Afro-American Language Varieties* (1993), edited by Salikoko Mufwene from a conference he organized at the University of Georgia, contribute to our knowledge on this subject. Mufwene's ongoing work on Gullah, based on his fieldwork of the mid-1980s, has begun to provide the most comprehensive view of the only Anglophone creole on the North American mainland. Along with dissertation work on Gullah over the past generation by Cunningham (1970), Nichols (1976), Jones-Jackson (1978), Mille (1990), and Hopkins (1992), Mufwene's research enables us to move beyond Turner's exclusive concern with Africanisms and to judge not only how African the language is, but also its similarities to Caribbean creoles and mainland African-American English (Mufwene and Gilman 1987; Holm 1991).

Research on Africanisms has turned in many ways to the larger question of the roots of New World Black English. Most scholars today believe that some of these are to be found in earlier creole languages as well as in processes of creolization. Shortly after LAVIS I, William Labov published a well-known essay on the Ann Arbor case in which he announced "a consensus on the nature and origin of Black

English," viz., that "it shows evidence of derivation from an earlier Creole that was closer to the present-day Creoles of the Caribbean" (1982:192). Today the extent of a creole basis for American Black English is not so clear, having been called into question principally by work on exported varieties, by analysis of historical documents (such as 19th-century African-American letters used by Montgomery, Fuller, and DeMarse 1993) and by the fieldwork of Guy Bailey and Natalie Maynor in Mississippi and Texas. The latter show how basic fieldwork in the rural South, in this case cross-generational interviews, can prompt the revision of accepted notions. We must realize that much "knowledge" about the roots of Black English (and probably other varieties as well) is based on inferences from modern data rather than from historical research. The "consensus" that Labov identified drew from comparative research done in Northern cities and in the Caribbean in the 1960s and 1970s. Bailey and Maynor's data argue that some of the best-known and most distinctive grammatical features of black speech, such as the use of the verb *be* to express habituality, may be recent developments. Such research could hardly have been undertaken in the North, where blacks had more recently migrated, and it calls for much more collection of rural speech, black and white, in the South.

A recent volume that deserves special notice is *The Emergence of Black English* by Bailey, Maynor, and Cukor-Avila in 1991. The book is a landmark for reasons beyond the substantive questions its contributors address. What particularly deserve our attention are its format and program. No other publication on SAE, perhaps on American English in general, raises as important, even disconcerting, questions about the notion of "accountability" in our profession nor has more direct implications for it.

Based on eleven recorded interviews with ex-slaves, mostly from the 1930s, *The Emergence of Black English* represents, so far as I am aware, the first collaborative project to make both the tapes and the transcriptions on which it is based completely available to the profession. After the editors had the sound quality of the recordings enhanced and audited them several times to achieve their own best transcriptions, they sent copies of tapes and transcriptions to prospective contributors and anyone else requesting them. In other words, everything the editors did could be double-checked by contributors; everything stated or reanalyzed by contributors could be second-guessed as well. No one else's transcriptions need be trusted. The result was a model of accountability, surpassable only by gathering all the contributors in one room to audit and discuss the tapes at the same time.

If this access model seems commonsense, let us note how few projects in language variation, many financed entirely by public funds, have given full access to their transcriptions or their recordings or have allowed other scholars to analyze the data for themselves. Much of the edifice of knowledge in our own and perhaps other social sciences is constructed on the analysis of privately held data that may not be replicable. While the rights of researchers to first use of material they have collected can hardly be denied, the Bailey et al. book suggests that we should at least begin discussing how to balance personal and professional needs. The matter is pressing when we consider that contributors to *The Emergence of Black English*, who took the same recordings and arrived at conflicting interpretations, had to be totally open about their representation and interpretation of the data at hand. By contrast, how often do we accept, more or less on faith, the reliability both of the data of fellow researchers and of the methodology they use to classify and analyze those data?

Lastly, we know far more now about the grammar of Southern American English than we did a decade ago. Traditional studies of SAE have been historical, phonological, and lexical; grammatical studies are more recent. The "Morphology and Syntax" chapter in the McMillan/Montgomery bibliography, for instance, lists only 70 items pre-dating 1970 (many of the earlier ones short squibs on the use of *you all*). By comparison, there are an even hundred entries from the 1970s and 82 from 1980–1988. Until a generation ago work on grammar was little more than checklists of features; almost none was quantitative, and there were few notions about social variation within communities. Today, although studies of grammatical systems are scarce, we have many studies of single features and some of morphological paradigms.

One reason for this growth has been an emphasis on collecting natural data. Ten years ago Crawford Feagin's *Variation and Change in Alabama English* (1979) featured more citations of multiple modal verbs than all other studies combined, since most examples in the literature came from elicitation rather than observation. Today there is the work of Marianna Di Paolo (1986) and others on multiple modals. In the early eighties citations from speech of the verb *be* in a finite use, whether habitual or not, were almost nonexistent in the literature on Southern English. We have a growing corpus of observed and tape-recorded examples to analyze.

Yet the commentary on too many grammatical features has been based on only intuitions and elicitations. For *you all* and *y'all*, the most trademark of Southern usages, there are no studies at all based on more than a handful of observations; the literature on them still consists almost entirely of testimonies and the elicitations of acceptability judgments. The only source of natural examples of note is the *Concordance* to the *Linguistic Atlas of the Gulf States* (Pederson et al. 1986), which contains by far the largest collection of citations of many grammatical features, 616 of *y'all*, for instance, 248 *might could*, and 45 of *might would* (all of the double modal citations are listed in their sentence contexts).

Each of the principal developments discussed in this section involves a research agenda that should continue. For instance, now that we have the major reference works and resources described above, we must put them to use. There is still nothing approaching a comprehensive grammatical or phonological sketch of SAE or any of its varieties, although work in progress by C.-J. Bailey, Lee Pederson, and Crawford Feagin gives us the promise of such treatments of pronunciation.[5]

NEEDED RESEARCH

While we know much more than in 1981, many important questions and issues have hardly begun to be addressed. The research tools, methodological sophistication, and empirical perspective are at hand to tackle these. As research continues we must challenge ourselves to be self-critical of our methodologies and our findings. Perhaps more than anything else the field of SAE needs to focus on larger questions—comparative and historical ones—and broader issues concerning language and identity, language status, and language change. Issues of needed research arise from the questions we frame.

An event at Auburn University in October 1985 highlighted the importance of questioning. After years of telling his students that Southern English was terminally ill and soon to be a thing of the past, the head of the Auburn Speech and Communication Department, an Alabamian himself, was finally challenged by a linguist from the English Department, Ann Pitts, another Alabamian, and these two squared off in a one-hour public debate on the proposition "The Southern dialect will disappear sometime in the future." The speech professor offered four arguments in support, each of which reflects popular views of the causes of language change: 1) the effect of radio and television; 2) the mixing of people and accents in military service; 3) the fact that more Southerners are getting college educated and even going outside the region for their education; and 4) the supposed influence of immigrants from the Midwest and the Northeast, who had been moving into the South for the last generation or two on such a scale that they were diluting the region's speech patterns. Are these causes of linguistic decline in the South just popular notions? Can linguists provide evidence for or against any of them? How can they be investigated?

While I am not at all sure that popular views can be changed much, they do raise some of the larger questions on which we should be working. Popular and professional interest in language issues in the American South often intersect, showing how linguists may contribute to public understanding and prompting us to continue asking important questions. Let us consider some questions which linguists have hardly begun to address:

What are the linguistic consequences of the large-scale demographic and social events of our time in the South? What is the linguistic effect of immigration—particularly of Northerners moving into the South. To what extent do Northerners shift their speech to accommodate? Do Southerners tend to lose their regional markers in such dialect contact situations or when they move north? I know of only one small-scale study (Montgomery and Epting 1990, based on the members of a university sorority) of the linguistic outcome of this Northern immigration, even though the impression that it is diluting the speech of the South seems to be very widespread.

Then there are the effects of urbanization. What are the linguistic consequences when Southerners, white and black, move to the city? to the suburb? Southern metropolitan areas like Charlotte, Nashville, Jackson, and Atlanta are among the fastest growing in the country, with as much of their increase due to migration from the surrounding hinterland as to migrants from outside the region. Guy Bailey and his team recently began tackling these issues in Texas in their Urban Language and Change project, but this should be only a beginning.

The issues of immigration and urbanization have specific implications for how language change in progress should be tracked. Study of the Southern vowel shift and other sound changes has so far been based almost entirely on natives to the local community. This includes the work of Labov and his associates in Birmingham (Labov et al. 1972; Labov 1991) and Feagin's ongoing research in Anniston. Among suburban teenagers in the South today there is evidence of both the Northern Cities Shift and the Low-back Vowel Merger, and there may be a good case for a modern-day "suburbanization" or "genericization" or even "McDonaldization" of American speech, just as suburban life everywhere is becoming indistinguishable in ways commercial and otherwise. Is this also true of smaller towns in the South? Heretofore the rationale for concentrating on natives to local communities is that they are the speakers who fully participate in local speech norms, and this is appropriate for establishing the baseline internal dynamics of vowel systems and for generating hypotheses. Sooner or later we must broaden this coverage significantly beyond cities to learn much about social dynamics elsewhere in the South as well.

Then there is the matter of racial integration, which over the past quarter century has not only changed the constituency of Southern schools but has also profoundly altered the linguistic interaction, at least during their school career, of millions of white and black youth. To date we know nothing of the effects of integration on any aspect of American English. Particularly needed are longitudinal studies that track the pronunciation, vocabulary, and grammar of middle and high school students as peer influence exerts its pressures, to see who influences whose speech and whether black and white speech are in fact becoming more similar. If we compare their speech to one another and to their parents, this will likely indicate more about the future of SAE than any other type of investigation.

Let me suggest two other directions that the study of sound change in progress can profitably pursue. Both research areas involve seeking a historical perspective on these changes, the research heretofore having usually relied only on apparent-time comparisons. These sound changes cannot be assumed to be 20th-century phenomena.

First, there is an extraordinary wealth of early recordings of Southerners made from the 1930s through the 1960s by various folklore and oral history projects; many of these individuals were born in the third or fourth quarter of the 19th century and the recordings are of sufficient quality to examine spectrographically. For instance, Joseph Sargent Hall recorded a number of elderly Smoky Mountain residents from 1939 to 1941, two of whom were born as early as the 1840s.[6]

The other avenue of research is into early documents. Some elements of the "Southern Shift" identified by Labov et al., as well as vowel mergers, can be identified in 19th-century letters and literary dialect. In letters written by African-Americans from the Lower South in the 1860s, for instance, the /ɪ/ - /ɛ/ merger is frequently evident. Whether such evidence represents unrelated historical residues, incidental features not yet "actualized" into general speech patterns, or a level of fairly stable variation which may still be found among Southern speakers needs to be determined.

Since I have introduced the question of ongoing language change, let me suggest initiatives needed to address other questions. How significant are generational differences in Southern speech? Optimally, research on this question should be family-based, to detect linguistic shifts from parents to children, but much could be discovered by replicating fieldwork conducted a generation ago. Linguistic atlas interviews provide a baseline for many communities, as recent studies by Ellen Johnson (1996) and others have shown. Many researchers have tape recordings from their fieldwork of a generation ago but rarely ask what can be done with them. Many of us need to go back to our data and reanalyze them, whether or not we undertake new fieldwork.

The pressing need in tracking generational shifts is for more real-time comparisons. Nothing illustrates this more than the recent "divergence controversy." Even though the divergence of Northern Black English from white varieties was predicted many years ago by McDavid (1979b) and Dillard (1972), altogether too much attention has been given to this question in relation to a small base of data. The gathering of comparable real-time data is both feasible and appropriate, now that a generation has passed since major projects, especially on black speech, were conducted in the 1960s and early 1970s. Feagin has in fact recently begun to re-interview some of her Anniston, Alabama, informants of twenty years ago.

Another set of issues of considerable significance but hardly touched by research concerns the social status and the social profile of Southern American English, about which we have only vague notions so far. What are the markers of Southern speech? How are they evaluated by Southerners and by Northerners? What is the relationship between the use of such markers and the identity and purposes of Southerners and Northerners when they speak? These are all very broad questions that must be narrowed significantly before they can be investigated. One way to do this is to track how Southern English is maintained when Southerners move north. I have heard over the years of Southerners who maintain, even exaggerate, their regional speech after moving to or visiting other parts of the country—particularly when in the company of other former Southerners; what evidence is there for this? The paradigm of social psychological research based on Speech Accommodation Theory and devised by Howard Giles (e.g., Giles and Powesland 1975) can be fruitfully utilized to investigate many questions about the speech behavior of Southerners.

For research purposes the issue can often be reduced to the how, when, and where of style-shifting. Mike Royko, the *Chicago Tribune* columnist, made some observations relevant to this issue. He wrote,

> a dialect . . . has crept into American speech. I call it yuppabilly, because it is often spoken by white Northern yuppies who, for whatever reason, want to sound like Southerners or blacks. I first noticed yuppabilly dialect when I heard a former yuppie co-worker of mine speaking it. If you didn't know him, you would have thought he was from Arkansas or some such rustic place. In fact, he was from a wealthy New England suburb and had attended Ivy League schools. But he developed his yuppabilly dialect because he was single and discovered that he could impress more females in singles bars if he spoke with a drawl. It provided him with a more rakish, macho, good old boy personality than did his Yale background. (Atlanta *Journal and Constitution*, September 29, 1985, D-6)

The 19th-century New Englander Henry Cogswell Knight would today need to go only to Bennigan's or a country and western club in Boston to have his ears twitched by Southern voices. On the serious side, Mr. Royko provides evidence that Southern speech continues to have a mystique and prestige even in our postmodern age. But who adopts a Southern style, and for what reasons? How well are Northerners doing in mimicking Southern speech? Are we witnessing covert prestige in action here, or maybe something more profound?

What is Southern politeness, linguistically speaking? Closely related to issues of style are questions about discourse and interactional patterns in SAE, which Barbara Johnstone and her research team have begun to address (see Johnstone, this volume). But there has been little work on politeness (one of the most durable stereotypes of Southern behavior), on terms of address, and on numerous other questions involving the pragmatics of Southern speech (but see Davies, this volume). What is Southern hospitality, linguistically speaking? A few suggestions have been made, but there is much we do not know. In terms of the Brown and Levinson (1987) framework, how do Southerners typically express positive and negative politeness?

Finally, beyond the modest advances cited earlier, we need much more attention to the historical derivation of SAE. Researchers have begun to tackle 19th-century data sources, but barely. The 19th century remains as important a frontier as any other for the study of SAE. Students of American English have done a poor job of ferreting out, much less analyzing, manuscript documents, and they have mined only the tiniest fraction of published historical (not literary) documents in their institutional libraries. The *Annotated Bibliography of Southern American English* lists only one or two studies drawing on the accounts of travelers like Henry Cogswell Knight, none at all on slave and ex-slave letters or on the innumerable, often vernacular Civil War letters and diaries in local historical libraries (these sources—especially the ones written by privates—offer the greatest potential for a 19th-century sketch of American English in general, including its regional varieties), and only three on the wealth of overseers' letters in many Southern archives (Boyette 1951; Williams 1953; Hawkins 1982—all on the same corpus). As I have already said, it is premature to characterize grammatical and phonological features of SAE and other varieties of American English as twentieth-century innovations. While I am actively collecting emigrant letters and other materials in order to piece together the general picture of Colonial American English and have examined the usefulness of Ulster emigrant letters as linguistic documents (Montgomery 1995), there are many other lines of research to be pursued if we want an adequate reconstruction of earlier Southern American English. A history of SAE is probably still at least a decade away. Let us hope its celebration will be one of the themes of a third LAVIS.

This essay presents one linguist's views of the study of Southern American English and its course over the past generation or so and suggests where it should go in the future. Many important and fascinating questions deserve continued or initiated attention. Because of the labors of several generations of scholars, including many of the individuals represented in this volume, far more is known about the varieties of SAE than about the English of any other American region, and the field appears to be in very good hands. The existing linguistic literature, and not just that produced in more recent years, reveals much about the history and dynamics of Southern speech, serving as a point of departure for future work, prompting us to discover what it cannot tell us, and reminding us of the inseparability of speech patterns from the region and its people.

NOTES

1. This essay will deal with only the English language in the South.

2. This transitive use of the verb *grow* may foreshadow Bill Clinton's usage of the verb; his promise during the 1992 Presidential campaign to *grow the economy* drew media comment.

3. Although LAGS has received little attention from scholars so far, two impending developments should help correct this neglect. One is that complete recordings of all LAGS interviews have been put on deposit for consultation both at the University of Georgia and at the Special Collections Department of the Woodruff Library at Emory. In connection with this, Lee Pederson has arranged for Emory to copy recordings of interviews on cassette for individual researchers. The second development is that Pederson will be making arrangements to donate the entire collection of LAGS microcomputer files and programs to the American Dialect Society and to authorize ADS to distribute copies of them at the cost of blank diskettes. It should soon be possible to have all the LAGS materials at hand for both our research and that of our students.

4. The special collections department at the Auburn University library is actively collecting material on this little-known chapter in the nation's history.

5. Bailey has been at work for more than two decades on his *Southern States Phonetics*, early installments of which were published in the *University of Hawaii Working Papers in Linguistics* (see chapter 4 of McMillan and Montgomery 1989 for citations). Lee Pederson (1993) has projected the composition of a *Pronunciation of English in the Gulf States* volume, based on LAGS data.

6. As presented in Hall's (1942) monograph, there is evidence of certain components of the Southern shift: the lowering of /ɪ/ to /e/ in words like *real* and the centralization of the stressed vowel in *steady*. Whether these represent isolated forms, the basis for some type of analogical sound change, or something else remains to be determined; the tapes are in the public domain for analysis.

Southern American English: A Prospective

Guy Bailey

INTRODUCTION

No variety of English has received as much attention as Southern American English (SAE), but attention is not always a good thing. Much of the early work on SAE, and especially on its relationship to African-American Vernacular English (AAVE), was anecdotal, speculative, and polemical. This massive literature produced little hard evidence on even the most basic characteristics of that variety. Moreover, the few scholars who were doing empirical research on SAE and related varieties worked from a number of different perspectives and often did not communicate with one another. Michael Montgomery and I designed the first conference on language variety in the South (in 1981) in part to rectify these problems. LAVIS I was a forum for bringing together researchers from a wide variety of perspectives to focus on a single problem: the relationship between black and white vernaculars in the American South. The papers were all to be based on hard linguistic data. We felt that such an approach would help us reach some consensus on the problem of black-white speech relationships—one of the most controversial issues in the field at that time. LAVIS I was quite successful but not exactly in the way that we thought it would be. It focused attention on the need for empirical evidence, on the need for researchers to respect and to consider work from other perspectives, and on the importance of SAE as a locus for the study of language variation and change. A quick scan of the tables of contents of *American Speech*, *English World-Wide*, *Journal of English Linguistics*, and *Language Variation and Change* for the last fifteen years suggests that SAE has become a major focus of empirical research and that the research is informed by a variety of perspectives. As a result of LAVIS I and the research inspired by it, we know much more about SAE than we did in 1980, but no consensus emerged on the black-white speech issue. In fact, the work that grew out of that conference inspired new controversies—the divergence controversy, for example.

Such unintended consequences make writing a prospective tricky, but they also suggest that the results of LAVIS II will be much richer and its impact more far-reaching than anyone can anticipate. Although the prospects for the study of SAE looked good after LAVIS I, they look even better after LAVIS II. Part of my optimism comes from where the conference was held—Auburn University. Auburn is the alma mater of James B. McMillan, the dean of Southern linguistics (and the primary reason I am in the field), but in 1981 Auburn had only one linguist, and his research was not on SAE. By 1993 not only did Auburn have three linguists, all of whom do work that contributes to our understanding of SAE, but rapid increase had occurred in the number of sociolinguists and dialectologists at Southern universities, which, like Auburn, have Ph.D. programs: the University of Georgia, the

University of South Carolina, Texas A&M University, and Oklahoma State University all have strong linguistics programs now. Both the research of faculty at these institutions and the work of the students they have produced have greatly expanded our knowledge of SAE. The number of LAVIS II participants (including two of the organizers of the conference) who are products of these programs is especially encouraging. The growing interest of non-Southern linguists (some of whom are now at Southern universities) in SAE also bodes well for the field. Non-Southerners often see things that native speakers overlook (note Wolfram's "Resolving Dialect Status" in this volume for an example), and their interest is frequently more dispassionate. Their contributions are crucial.

The primary reasons for my optimism, however, are the papers presented during LAVIS II and at the concurrent sessions of the Southeastern Conference on Linguistics (SECOL). The themes that emerge provide both a microcosm of current research on SAE and a glimpse into the future. Three major themes emerge from these papers: the importance of methods, the role of language contact (especially as it affects historical developments), and the expansion of the object of study to include discourse and pragmatics. A closer look at these three themes provides us with our best prospectus for the study of language variation in the South.

THE IMPORTANCE OF METHODS

The papers presented at LAVIS I treated a wide range of phonological, morphological, and lexical problems, but they had little to say about research methods, and the methods they employed were conventional ones. Most of the papers used either linguistic atlas data or evidence gathered through conventional sociolinguistic interviews, and with one exception (John Rickford's use of VARBRUL), the papers that analyzed data quantitatively used simple frequency counts. The social variables used to explain linguistic behavior were also conventional: age, ethnicity, gender, geography (and settlement history), and social class dominated the discussion in LAVIS I. Only the ethnographically influenced work of Shirley Brice Heath and Boyd Davis (who has an interesting follow-up essay in this volume) pointed toward the kinds of methods that have developed in the last ten years. The primary contribution of LAVIS I, then, lay in the large amounts of linguistic data that the papers provided.

The papers presented during LAVIS II also included a significant amount of new linguistic data, but the variety of new research methods they discuss is surely among the most significant contributions of this conference. As Wolfram points out in his discussion of camouflaged structures in AAVE (this volume), casual observations are no substitute for hard evidence and methodological rigor. The early history of the study of SAE was plagued by just the kind of casual observation and personal testimony that Wolfram confronted when he first discussed AAVE structures like "you call yourself dancing." This research strategy of personal testimony is why so little is known about SAE in spite of the fact that so much has been written about it.

One frequently discussed feature, the alleged use of *yall* as a singular will illustrate my point. Although more than 30 articles have debated the use of *yall* as a singular, only one article (Richardson 1984) has presented anything like hard linguistic evidence on the issue. In order to counter non-Southerners' casual observations of apparent singular uses of *yall*, Southern linguists had simply "testified" that the form could not be as a singular. In other words, the evidence on *yall* consisted of haphazard, undocumented observations on the one hand and personal testimony on the other. This situation is further complicated by the fact that many apparent instances of *yall* singular can easily be given plural readings. For example, several months ago I called the grants officer at the University of Memphis to ask her if she had a form that I needed. She replied yes, and I responded that *I* would be right over to pick the form up. She then said, "I'll put it in a pick-up tray for yall." Now this seems like a straightforward singular use of *yall*, but it is certainly possible to give it a plural reading. It may be that the grants officer, knowing that I was a department chair, assumed that even though I said that I would come over and pick up the form myself, I would actually send someone else. Then again, maybe not; the only way to know would be to ask her what she meant.

Although my intuitions were like those of most other Southern linguists, at the insistence of Jan Tillery (a Southerner whose intuitions were different) I included a question in a Survey of Oklahoma Dialects (SOD) that asked respondents if they could use *yall* for just one person. To my surprise, about a third (34.4%) of the *yall* users in Oklahoma said that they could. Many of the respondents elaborated on their responses, explaining why and when they could or could not use *yall* as a singular —the use of *yall* singular is an issue of some debate among the general public as well as among linguists. The replication of these results in a similar survey conducted by an independent source (the Southern Focus Poll, a random sample telephone survey conducted twice a year by the Institute for Research in Social Science at the University of North Carolina) provides strong evidence that a solid minority, 30.9%, of Southerners can use *yall* as a singular.

Based on this and other evidence, Tillery and Bailey (forthcoming-b) conclude that a substantial minority of Southerners can use *yall* as a singular. We further suggest that there actually are two sets of norms regarding this form: for a majority of Southerners, *yall* is only a plural, but for many other Southerners, *yall* can be a singular too. That is not what Southern linguists had testified (nor what I originally thought), but to borrow the title from the biography of Alton Delmore (of the Delmore Brothers, one of the most important groups in early country music), "truth is stranger than publicity." Because we relied on our intuitions and our testimonies, we failed to understand a rich, complex sociolinguistic situation. The papers presented during LAVIS II detail a number of innovative methods that can help us sort out such complex sociolinguistic situations. These fall into two types—those for analyzing existing evidence and those for gathering and evaluating new data.

Innovative Methods of Analysis

The recent completion of the Linguistic Atlas of the Gulf States (LAGS), the availability of the workbooks of the Linguistic Atlas of the Middle and South Atlantic States (LAMSAS) on microfilm, and the continuing progress of the *Dictionary of American Regional English* (*DARE*) mean that a substantial body of empirical evidence on SAE already exists. The essays in this volume by Kretz-schmar, Johnson, Cassidy, Hall, Metcalf, and von Schneidemesser all illustrate ways that this data can be used; the essays by Kretzschmar and Johnson also make use of some innovative analytical techniques. Kretzschmar uses spatial statistics such as spatial autocorrelation and density estimation to provide a new perspective on LAMSAS data. These techniques enable him to establish clusters of locations that are linguistically similar, to show the density of occurrence of features, to show the probability that a feature will occur in a given area, and to predict where a feature might be expected to occur in a survey region. Johnson uses LAMSAS data as a source of real-time evidence. She interviewed informants in 39 communities where LAMSAS interviews had been done some 60 years earlier using a protocol that included 150 of the items elicited in the earlier survey. She then compared the relative effects of a number of social variables such as age, race, region, and rurality on linguistic variation in the two samples using the GLM (General Linear Models) procedure in SAS, a procedure popularized in sociolinguistics by Bernstein (1993). Johnson's results reveal an interesting contrast: in LAMSAS, region was the most important variable affecting linguistic variation; in the follow-up survey, it was the least important. At the same time, the effect of rurality has remained constant, while that of race has increased somewhat. Perhaps more surprising is the fact that the six social variables Johnson considers account for only 30% of the explained variation in the earlier sample and 10% of the explained variation in the latter, results similar to those reported in Bernstein (1993) for data from a Phonological Survey of Texas (PST) and in Bailey, Wikle, Tillery, and Sand (1993) for a Survey of Oklahoma Dialects (SOD).

The stock variables of age, education, ethnicity, gender, and social class explain a relatively small amount of linguistic variation. As a number of essays in this volume point out, we need to expand our range of explanatory variables. Tillery's analysis of data from PST and SOD shows that social processes such as urbaniza-tion (operationalized as rurality in both her study and Johnson's) and in-migration (operationalized as nativity) are more important than the conventional social categories in explaining linguistic variation in the Southwest. She also shows that group identity (in this case identity with the state of Texas) is a crucial factor in explaining some kinds of variation, a theme echoed by Coles's discovery of solidarity cues in New Orleans speech. Coles shows that the English of the Ninth Ward in New Orleans, a nonstandard variety that is achieving increasingly overt prestige, functions within a strategy of accommodation to indicate solidarity. While we still do not know exactly what kind of role that symbolic factors such as group identity and solidarity play in linguistic variation, Preston's work on folk linguistics clearly shows that SAE has considerable symbolic importance as perhaps the main foil to other varieties of American English. This kind of symbolic significance, of course, is a prerequisite for using language to achieve solidarity.

Innovative Means of Gathering and Evaluating Data

Discovering the precise role of identity and solidarity in linguistic variation requires new ways of gathering data: neither linguistic atlas interviews nor conventional one-on-one sociolinguistic interviews provide the kind of evidence we need. In order to ferret out the role of identity factors, we need to know how different audiences affect linguistic usage. At LAVIS I, Davis presented an approach to fieldwork that enabled her to identify how adolescents' shifts in linguistic register were keyed to shifts in locale and shifts in interlocutors—just the kind of evidence we need for exploring the role of linguistic identity in language variation (see Davis 1986 and her follow-up essay in this volume). Over the last ten years ethnographically inspired approaches to fieldwork such as Davis's have enriched our understanding of the role that group identity plays in language variation and have developed sophisticated techniques for studying language in its social contexts. The work of Wolfram and his research team on the speech of Ocracoke (in the Outer Banks area of North Carolina) illustrates how fieldworkers can immerse themselves in a community to record language in a variety of private and public functions. As reported in this volume, their fieldwork suggests that the speech of "isolated" areas like Ocracoke is far more complex sociolinguistically than we have previously thought. The work of Cukor-Avila and Bailey (1995) in Springville, Texas, develops research strategies (especially the site study) for recording a wide range of people talking to each other, rather than to fieldworkers, and thus for ameliorating the observer's paradox. As Cukor-Avila's essay shows (this volume), fieldwork that records the everyday life of a community offers linguistic insights that cannot be garnered in other ways. The Springville study is interesting in one other way as well: the study has been ongoing for nearly a decade. As one of the few longitudinal studies in linguistics, it provides a unique opportunity for observing the acquisition and evolution of individual vernaculars (see Cukor-Avila 1995 for an example).

Although ethnographically inspired research is our best hope for ameliorating the observer's paradox and for obtaining the deepest vernacular, it cannot provide evidence on the distribution of linguistic variables in a large population: for this we need linguistic surveys. The large investment of time and money that traditional linguistic surveys require means that few surveys are begun and even fewer completed. Several recent studies, however, demonstrate that the telephone can be used to conduct large-scale, tape-recorded surveys quickly and (relatively) inexpensively. Telephone surveys also offer one other advantage: they enable researchers to obtain probability samples so that a wide range of statistical procedures can be applied to the data. The surveys discussed in this volume by Wikle and Tillery (PST and SOD) both use the telephone to gather data on a variety of linguistic features from a large, representative sample of people (1000 Texans and 632 Oklahomans respectively), but they differ in other ways. PST was "piggy-backed" on a pre-existing telephone survey (the Texas Poll), while SOD was organized and conducted by Bailey, Wikle, Tillery, and Sand. Using a computer-generated list of all possible telephone numbers in telephone exchanges in Texas, the Texas Poll surveys a simple random sample of telephone households in the state and uses the "last birthday" method (in which the interviewer asks to speak with the member of the household who most recently had a birthday) within each household to control for gender differences in telephone answering practices. SOD also uses a computer-generated list of possible telephone numbers and the last birthday method, but it uses a proportionate stratified random sample to insure better spatial coverage in Oklahoma. Random samples such as these allow us to apply a variety of statistics and cartographic techniques (see Wikle, this volume) that are inappropriate for other kinds of data and to make inferences, with a known sampling error probability, about the distributions of linguistic features in a defined population. In other words, random samples allow us to generalize the results of our studies to a larger population, a basic goal of sociolinguistics and dialectology.

While random sampling is crucial to the development of our discipline, it is certainly not the only kind of sampling that is appropriate: different research questions require different research methods. For instance, Johnson's resample is entirely appropriate for her real-time study (this volume): her informants are matched with the informants in the original sample. In Oklahoma we found that a proportionate stratified random sample was not effective in exploring linguistic diffusion. To study diffusion in Oklahoma, we devised a field survey that uses the 33 township and range divisions, illustrated in the figure below, that were used in the original settlement of the state (by Anglos) as primary targets for interviews.

Figure: Grids for SOD Field Survey
Township/range divisions of Oklahoma

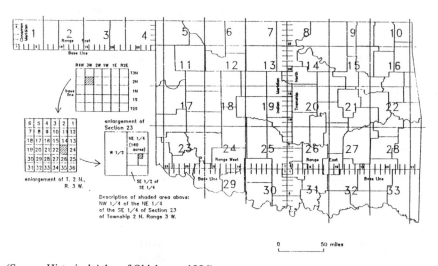

(Source: Historical Atlas of Oklahoma, 1986)

Within each township and range division, we interviewed four natives of the area: someone about 80, someone about 60, someone about 40, and someone about 20. Although this survey does not allow us to make inferences about the distribution of linguistic features in the population of Oklahoma, it provides an evenly distributed sample of matched informants that allows us to track the spread of linguistic innovations in space and time. Like Johnson's sample, it is the best one for answering the research question that was posed. While we can choose from a variety of sampling approaches to answer our research questions, what we can never afford to do again is to resort to haphazard observation or samples of convenience.

Surveys and ethnographic fieldwork are not the only ways of gathering useful linguistic data, of course. Papers in this volume explore a number of other interesting sources of data. Coles tape-recorded telephone interactions in a veterinary clinic and on a call-in radio talk show to explore New Orleans English, while Davies uses an enacted movie script to explore address terms in SAE. Wilmeth finds linguistic data in the recitations of Luke the Drifter, a pseudonym for Hank Williams. These sources complement more systematic methods and are especially useful for discovering variation. We should not ignore them.

Neither should we ignore problems inherent in even the most rigorously gathered data. In spite of their differences in aims and methods, sociolinguistics and dialectology are essentially text-based disciplines: the most basic function in each is the description of linguistic texts. Although the character of the linguistic texts may vary quite a bit, ranging from phonetic transcriptions of tape-recorded interviews to orthographic transcripts of interviews to archival records, we typically assume that these texts are objective entities, independent of their compositors. A number of recent developments, however, remind us that the texts we describe are shaped by the biases and limitations of those who compose them. Twenty years ago, the publication of the WPA ex-slave narratives (written down by WPA field-workers, presumably, as they were spoken) seemed to offer data that could resolve the debate over the origins of AAVE. A decade later we became aware that many of these documents had been edited at state offices and that some of the dialect features had been added after the fact by people not present at the interviews (see Maynor 1988). This editing might seem to invalidate the narratives as linguistic evidence, but Schneider's essay (this volume) suggests that the situation is not so simple. He finds that data from the edited narratives is quite similar in many ways (but not in every way) to data from a series of mechanically recorded interviews that were conducted as part of the same WPA project. The data from the mechani- cally recorded interviews is, in turn, quite similar to data from sociolinguistic interviews with African-Americans born a generation later. Thus while the written ex-slave narratives cannot be regarded as faithful transcripts of the speech of former slaves, Schneider's work shows that they are not simply artifacts of interviewers' fancies either. They are clearly a step closer to actual speech than literary dialect, but exactly what their status is remains unclear.

While the ex-slave narratives might seem like a unique textual puzzle, they are actually just a special case of a larger problem—the status of linguistic texts. An example will illustrate this problem. Once we learned of the existence of mechani- cally recorded interviews with former slaves, two colleagues and I decided to try to resolve the debate over the origins of AAVE by giving copies of and rough transcripts of these tapes to scholars representing a wide range of perspectives on the issue. Each scholar was to write an essay on these texts; we also asked each of them to audit the tapes closely and edit the transcripts so that we could publish the most accurate transcripts possible. Although all of these scholars were working with the "same" texts, the conclusions that the contributors reached and the emendations that they made to the transcripts differed remarkably. A naive observer might conclude that the contributors were actually working with different texts. To some extent, of course, they were. Linguistic texts are not "objective" entities; they are products of the interaction between a speech event (or a writing event) on the one hand and the scholar who transcribes and analyzes that event on the other. (Yes, Stanley Fish, there *is* a linguist in this text.) As we pointed out in the preface to *The Emergence of Black English*, the volume that publishes these transcripts and essays, "the creation of a linguistic text is an interpretative act, just as the analysis of a text is. The crucial question involves the extent to which our analyses are simply artifacts of the texts we have created" (Bailey, Maynor, and Cukor-Avila 1991:ix).

It is not just transcriptions that are textual problems, though; tape-recorded interviews pose them too. Over a quarter of a century ago Labov (1966) pointed out that the observer's paradox poses an inherent barrier to recording the unmonitored vernacular. Although linguists have developed ways to ameliorate the observer's paradox, Brewer's essay (this volume) is one of the first to look at the kinds of problems that make recording the vernacular difficult. Confronting textual problems such as these, and determining how they affect our results, is a major task not just for the study of SAE but for sociolinguistics and dialectology in general.

THE IMPORTANCE OF LANGUAGE CONTACT

It is no accident that a number of the methodological innovations discussed above were developed to address problems that arose in the study of AAVE. AAVE has been a major topic of research for a quarter century. While that research has generated a remarkable amount of controversy, the controversy has been a driving force in the evolution of American sociolinguistics. The concept of the variable rule (see Labov 1972a), a wide range of sophisticated field methods, and a number of important textual discoveries are all outgrowths of work on AAVE. Work on AAVE, of course, is primarily concerned with issues of linguistic diversity and language (or dialect) contact. Although much of the early work on SAE looked at linguistic diversity in the region in terms of black-white speech relationships, during the last 15 years scholars have begun to explore other instances of linguistic diversity and language contact in the South, have begun to expand the kinds of research questions they address, and have uncovered a variety of new sources that bear on these questions. All of these trends are reflected in the papers presented at LAVIS II.

The essays by Klingler on Louisiana Creole, by Picone on Louisiana French, by Ching and Kung on Chinese in Memphis, and by Bayley on Tejano English illustrate the examination of other kinds of language contact. These papers demonstrate that black-white speech relationships are only part of a rich tapestry of language diversity and contact in the American South. The essays also show how complex the results of language contact are. Ching and Kung suggest that, contrary to what most linguists believe, language is not always the primary locus of ethnic identity, while Picone's work shows that code switching can have important morphological consequences. The expansion of the Spanish-speaking population in Florida and the Southwest and the rapid growth of the number of people who speak southeast Asian languages in Southern cities like Houston suggest that linguistic diversity is in many ways increasing in the American South. Examining this diversity will be a major task for future work. Other non-English languages spoken in the South, such as French in Louisiana and German in Texas, are important topics for research for different reasons: their futures are uncertain. The precise impact of languages like Spanish, French, and German on local varieties of SAE is also a major research need in the study of SAE.

The extent to which the speech of African-Americans has contributed to the overall development of SAE is also still unknown. Much of the early work on black-white speech relationships simply focused on how much alike or how different those varieties were. Differences were usually attributed either to the creole origins of AAVE (see Dillard 1972, for instance) or to the conservative nature of that variety (see Kurath 1949). Similarities were attributed to "decreol-ization" (see Mufwene's essay in this volume for an alternative perspective) or to the fact that African-Americans had simply learned the language of their white peers. Comparisons to a hypothetical standard English further complicate the study of black-white speech relationships (see Montgomery, this volume). Over the past decade it has become clear that these scenarios cannot account for the complexity of black-white speech relationships. The relationships differ somewhat from one place to another, and they suggest a history both of mutual influence and of independent development. Although recent work on the divergence controversy provides clear evidence of independent development, the influence neither of white vernaculars on AAVE nor of AAVE on white vernaculars has been documented in any detail. Feagin's essay (this volume) on the African contribution to SAE is particularly important in this regard and expands an avenue of research first suggested in McDavid and McDavid (1951) and touched on in Wolfram (1974). She presents evidence which suggests that r-lessness, a hallmark of the speech of the lower South, is the result of African-American influence.

Our evolving recognition of the complexities of black-white speech relation-ships is in large part the result of the availability of new sources of data. Both the written ex-slave narratives and the mechanical recordings with former slaves have enhanced our understanding of earlier AAVE, while new in-depth studies of African-American communities in Philadelphia (see Labov and Harris 1986), East Palo Alto (see Rickford 1992), and Texas (see Bailey 1993; Cukor-Avila 1995) have produced surprising evidence on current developments. The additional sources of historical evidence discovered by Cooley, Mille's reconsideration of a well-known historical source, and the real-time evidence on current developments in Edwards's work in Detroit (all in this volume) will help us begin to sort through some of those complexities, as will the rigorous considerations of sociohistorical contexts in the essays by Klingler and Mufwene. Mufwene suggests that Gullah actually emerged from a gradual restructuring of nonstandard English and was never a homogeneous variety. He argues that synchronic variation in present-day Gullah is an artifact of its historical variation, not of decreolization. His re-examination of an old issue from a different perspective is precisely the kind of approach we need in diachronic studies.

Diachronic studies, both of AAVE and of SAE, are also in need of convergent data. The convergence of data from a number of different sources enabled scholars to describe the structure of present-day AAVE with some confidence. Montgomery's (1989) work on Appalachian English outlines clearly the kind of chain of evidence that we need in order to make historical connections between two varieties and provides a paradigm for such historical work. In doing diachronic work, we should also remember Popper's metaphor for the study of history: it is like looking at the ocean on a dark night with a searchlight. We see only a small part of a vast area. Making accurate generalizations based on what is illuminated by a small searchlight is a difficult task. Convergent results from different kinds of diachronic data represent our best hope for making accurate historical statements. Brown's (1990, 1991) work on the history of the merger of /ɛ/ and /ɪ/ before nasals provides a model of how this can be done. She uses LAMSAS data, early mechanical recordings of Southerners, and evidence from a "sister" dialect of SAE (the English of the descendants of ex-Confederates who migrated to Brazil) to validate the historical documents that she uses in establishing the history of this merger. The convergence of all of these sources allows her to say with some confidence that until the last quarter of the 19th century, the merger of /ɛ/ and /ɪ/ before nasals was a stable, low frequency feature. After 1875 the merger began to expand rapidly until by World War II it had gone almost to completion. Brown (1993) shows, however, that the same documents she used to study the merger of /ɛ/ and /ɪ/ before nasals (the *Tennessee Civil War Veterans Questionnaires*) are much less useful for studying relative clauses. She attributes an unexpectedly low number of nonstandard relative clauses to a skewed set of data: a small group of the veterans uses a disproportionate number of relative clauses (7% of the veterans use 37% of the relative clauses), and some veterans do not use relative clauses at all, possibly because those veterans who are uncomfortable with writing may avoid complex grammatical structures like these. Thus, Brown concludes that any generalizations about relative clauses in earlier SAE based on this source would be suspect and that historical documents that are useful for studying one feature may not be reliable for examining another.

THE EXPANSION OF THE OBJECT OF STUDY

Except for a set of papers on educational implications, the papers at LAVIS I dealt almost exclusively with lexical, morphosyntactic, and phonological features. Similarly, many papers at LAVIS II dealt with these same features (note, for instance, the essays by Southard; Lance and Faries). All of these papers contribute substantially to our knowledge of SAE, and some of them, like Maynor's analysis of the evolution of *ain't*, treat features that have been frequently noted but rarely studied. From the decade between the two LAVIS conferences, however, there emerges a dramatic expansion in the kinds of linguistic features that researchers analyze. Within this volume, for example, Catherine Davies explores the use of terms of address in the South, while Weatherly looks at the holographic complexity of discourses of "Southernness." Johnstone not only examines discourse features, but she examines them from a different perspective. Whereas most of the papers at LAVIS II look at social factors in explaining linguistic variation, Johnstone's looks at individual factors. She points out that it is the individual who mediates between the social and the linguistic: individuals select and combine the linguistic resources available to them in a given environment to create individual voices. Johnstone's focus on the individual takes on added meaning in light of the recent work which shows that standard social categories account for a relatively small proportion of explained variation.

It is interesting to note that the person who is most responsible for bringing the role of social factors in linguistic variation to our attention, William Labov, is also one of the people most responsible for expanding the object of study. His essay with Sharon Ash (this volume) looks not at how Southerners talk but at how they (and speakers of other dialects) use and understand their own vowel systems in the coding and decoding of linguistic information. In other words, Labov and Ash focus on the cognitive consequences of linguistic diversity. In refocusing the object of study, they make use of a variety of innovative methods. They use spectrographic analyses of vowel systems to establish patterns of vowel shifting and then develop a set of controlled vowel identification experiments to determine how these vowel shifts affect perception.

CONCLUSION

In many ways, the work of Labov and Ash illustrates in microcosm the range of themes that emerged at LAVIS II. Their refocusing of the object of study from production to perception required them to develop innovative methods for measuring people's ability to decode linguistic information, and their results have important implications for the study of dialect contact. In finding that linguistic diversity has cognitive as well as social consequences, Labov and Ash also point to new directions for research on SAE and demonstrate how the vitality of a field comes not from calls for research by those who write prospectives but from the creativity of scholars who have the insight to apply new methods to old problems and expand the object of study. The fact that many of the papers at LAVIS II demonstrate this kind of creativity makes me optimistic about the future of the study of SAE, and those papers are themselves the best prospective on the field.

PART ONE

Language Contact with Emphasis on the African Diaspora

This section carries forward two concerns from the first LAVIS volume (Montgomery and Bailey 1986)—commitment to solidly grounded, empirical research and continuing interest in the diachronic and synchronic relationships between African-American and European-American Englishes. However, as our field has grown, so have our concerns, as Bailey highlighted (this volume). Although the papers in this section are dedicated to understanding the linguistic and social ramifications of language contact in the American South, the topics range from the validity of historical corpora to the relationship between ethnic identity and maintenance of a non-English mother tongue in a Southern community.

The first author brings the accumulated knowledge of a decade of research on African-American Vernacular English (AAVE) to the question of the validity of two important corpora: The WPA Ex-Slave Narratives (ESN) and the Archive of Folk Song (AFS) recordings. Schneider explores five sources of contamination of the ESN, specifically considering several linguistic features which appear to have been subject to editing. He concludes that inaccuracies in the representation and editing of the ESN resulted in distortion mostly of quantities rather than forms. With this in mind, Schneider then subjects the AFS to multivariate analysis in order to expand the comparison of this corpus with the ESN. Although he concludes that AAVE contains both English-influenced features and "putative creole" features, he rejects the hypothesis of a Plantation Creole.

Brewer addresses the validity of the ESN, AFS, and the Hyatt Foundation interviews, providing detailed information on the nature of these corpora. In particular, she points to the need for researchers to be mindful of the lack of uniformity in the ESN and thus their need to control for interviewer, topic, setting, and individual speaker variation.

Cooley's paper presents a fascinating examination of the history of a play first performed in London in 1768. One of the central characters in the play is an African-American whose language was based on Caribbean Anglophone varieties—especially Jamaican. Like Schneider and Brewer, Cooley illustrates the importance of knowing the history of the corpora we use. Additionally, she demonstrates how rewarding careful historical research can be.

The paper by Johnstone affords us the privilege of encountering Mattie Blair. Wishing to reveal how Mrs. Blair, how all of us, use linguistic resources to "perform identity," Johnstone reaches beyond quantitative sociolinguistics to "discourse analysis in the philological tradition." In doing so, Johnstone reminds us that linguistics as a discipline extends from perception and comprehension to appreciation.

The next two papers in the volume focus on Gullah. Mille's paper considers variation in the Gullah tense-mood-aspect (TMA) system as it is represented in the literary texts of Ambrose Gonzales. Her analysis demonstrates, on the one hand, the usefulness of the Gonzales corpus for studying 19th-century Gullah. On the other hand, though recognizing stereotyping in his later texts, Mille is able to use the TMA data to counter claims of a homogeneous Gullah basilect.

Mufwene looks further back in time to provide a "sociohistorical scenario" of Gullah's development. For those unfamiliar with early 20th-century notions of AAVE origins, Mufwene's overview of these "myths" is a necessity. In addition to considering how demographic factors such as black/white ratios and the changing nature of the agricultural base impact our assumptions about creolization as a linguistic process, Mufwene proposes considering how markedness mediates between superstrate and substrate influences.

Feagin shows that consideration of the historical record is equally useful for examining African contributions to European-American Southern English. Like Mufwene, she considers how black/white population ratios and the social relationships between African- and European-Americans may have impacted language change—here three distinctive phonological features of Southern English: r-lessness, the drawl (i.e., syllable intonation), and the use of falsetto.

The next two papers shift our attention to French-influenced varieties. Klingler uses a recently published reconstruction of the sociocultural matrix of colonial Louisiana to inform his discussion of Chaudenson's theory of creolization. Like Mufwene, Klingler considers the distinction between small-scale agriculture and the "agro-industrial complex," concluding that despite the formation of African linguistic and cultural groups, "colonists, and later, Creole slaves" provided the primary linguistic input for newly arriving Africans.

The paper by Picone scrutinizes the use of uninflected forms in modern-day Louisiana French in order to further our understanding of code switching. By introducing the notion of a "code-neutral buffer," Picone convincingly argues for a resolution to the "controversy swirling around the universality of the Equivalence Constraint and the Free Morpheme Constraint." He cautions that relying on data that might have been prejudiced by the assumption of a binary model can lead to distorted analysis.

The final paper in Part One considers the relationship between language and ethnic identity from the perspective of language loss. Ching and Kung demonstrate that although language is a major aspect of ethnic identity in the Chinese-American community, it is not the most important one. Their subjects reported that "the most devastating blow to their ethnicity would be loss of [Chinese] values and traditions."

Language contact continues as an important theme throughout this volume. Particularly relevant are the essays in Part Two by Bayley, Coles, Weatherly, Maynor, and Butters and the essays in Part Three by Cukor-Avila, Wolfram, and Labov.

Earlier Black English Revisited

Edgar W. Schneider

INTRODUCTION

More than a quarter century has elapsed since the beginnings of the discussion of the genesis of Vernacular Black English (BE)—since the publication of Stewart's ([1967] 1975b, [1968] 1975a) seminal papers on the subject; since the final report of the large-scale Harlem project by Labov et al. (1968); since Wolfram's (1969) dissertation on Detroit BE; and more than twenty years since Dillard's provoking and successful book of 1972. But the topic is still on the agenda of linguistic research and discussion—or rather, it is here again and has regained new topicality over the last few years, after the apparent closure of the first phase of the debate, marked by the Ann Arbor court decision and Labov's 1982 paper on "Objectivity and Commitment." The renewed interest in the historical side of the matter has arisen in the shadow of the "divergence controversy" (Butters 1989), which has attracted more attention than the diachronic question—a fact which, luckily, leaves the latter less encumbered with politically motivated tension. Another reason for the calmer atmosphere in the quest for the past of BE may be that a younger generation of scholars refuses to accept and continue the old affiliations to well-defined linguistic camps which characterized so many of the earlier battles.

Perhaps the most characteristic aspect of the discussion of the origins of BE in the 1960s and 1970s was its lack of original data. With the exception of very few pieces of anecdotal and questionable evidence, statements on the history of BE were mostly based on inferences drawn from the results of synchronic studies and general considerations. Dialectologists read Linguistic Atlas data as historical records; sociolinguists viewed present-day variation as a mirror of past structures; and creolists viewed scarce structural parallels between BE, Gullah, and Caribbean creoles as traces of an earlier decreolization process. However, none of these groups had access to a sufficiently large and trustworthy body of historical records as first-hand evidence. That, I think, has changed to a considerable extent in recent years. The study of BE has again followed the lead of creole studies, where the search for historical records has constituted a major research trend (see Rickford 1987 on Guyanese Creole; D'Costa and Lalla 1989 on Jamaican Creole; or Fields 1992, Rickford and Handler 1994, and Roberts 1992 on Bajan). Creolists, however, have been more successful in this search than scholars looking for records of earlier BE. This is probably not a chance product but a consequence of the typical routes of early travelers, which would have led them to seaports and areas of commercial or military interest, many of which were locations where creoles were spoken, while the rural interior of the American colonies with its small-scale farming structure attracted fewer foreign visitors. Remarkably, Cooley (this volume) shows that due to specific historical circumstances in the 18th century, even the representation of BE in literary dialect, one of the standard sources for the history of the variety, was based upon Caribbean rather than Southern U.S. speech. Given the patterns of communication and the fact that the speakers of the variety we are interested in were held in forced illiteracy, it may turn out to be difficult indeed to get hold of the kind of evidence one might wish to see—authentic BE texts of, say, the 18th or the early 19th century from the rural South, although valuable new sources are disclosed from time to time, as shown by Montgomery, Fuller, and DeMarse (1993). Recent studies have brought to light other specimens of BE which are at least a few steps closer, in terms of their historical, geographical, and cultural development, to "early" BE than the speech of inner-city adolescents of the late 20th century. In the present paper, I will be concerned with two of these, the so-called ex-slave narratives (Rawick 1972, 1977, 1979), and the tape recordings made for the Archive of Folk Song (AFS) published and analyzed by Bailey, Maynor, and Cukor-Avila (1991). The following section will provide another discussion of the ex-slave narratives, especially of the question of their linguistic reliability. Subsequently, I will present analyses of the AFS tapes that go beyond the material in Bailey, Maynor, and Cukor-Avila (1991), using them both for an evaluative comparison with the written records and as a source for additional analysis.

THE EVIDENCE OF THE EX-SLAVE NARRATIVES

The term "ex-slave narratives" mostly refers to the collection published by George Rawick (1972, 1977, 1979), some thousand life-stories told by aged black Americans to professional interviewers sent out in the 1930s by the FWP, a division of the WPA (see Yetman 1967; Brewer 1980). This material has been widely used for linguistic research (e.g., Brewer 1974 and this volume; Fasold 1976; Oomen 1985; Oomen and Lissewski 1989; Pitts 1986; Schneider 1983a, 1983b, 1989; Viereck 1989), but its reliability has recently been questioned by Maynor (1988), Wolfram (1990), Montgomery (1991a), and Dillard (1993). The point raised by Maynor is indeed well taken and deserves serious consideration. How trustworthy are the slave narratives as records of the language of the people interviewed?

The FWP slave narratives are not verbatim records. The fieldworkers were instructed to provide records "as nearly word-for-word as is possible" (Rawick 1972,1:173), but there are additional instructions as to specific usages to be avoided; there is the question of whether they were able and willing to follow these instructions; and there are warning voices among the editors of the collection not to accept the records as close linguistic transcripts. As to the willingness of the interviewers, I think it is possible to rule out those that did not even try to provide a realistic rendering (which I did by means of a "pre-test"—see Schneider 1989), but still this does not leave us with texts that are as accurate as transcriptions or recordings, as argued reasonably in Wolfram (1990) and Maynor (1991).

We may assume that most of the texts were written down soon after the interview from field notes. Although some writers may have used shorthand, a procedure which may have increased reliability, it is not likely that many of them did, and we have no way of now knowing which these were. What can be our assumptions in this situation, or, in other words, what kinds of text, in terms of their reliability levels, are the narratives composed of? I assume we have to distinguish at least four different textual strata with respect to the accuracy of the linguistic record. First, some expressions and passages, forming a basic framework throughout the discourse, would indeed consist of verbatim notes taken on the spot during the interview. That portion would secure factual information and would consist of a high proportion of lexical material, not necessarily including much syntactic and grammatical detail.

The second textual layer would consist of those statements that were not taken down on the spot but remembered and written down accurately afterwards, when the fieldworker sat down to expand his or her field notes into a full interview text. Depending on how soon after the interview this was done and how good the fieldworker's notes and memory for detail were, we can expect a fairly high to average degree of correspondence between this part of the record and the words as originally spoken. In fact, this is probably the layer most important for our linguistic analyses, and I dare hypothesize that we need not be too pessimistic as to the quality of this portion of the text. Consider how much detail we often remember of a conversation that interests us; assume that, in addition to memory, the fieldworker has a substantial framework of notes representing the course of the conversation, and assume also that the fieldworker is trained and experienced in such a procedure and instructed to pay attention to linguistic detail: the result will not be a verbatim record, but it will be a mixture of a wholly accurate and a reasonably close rendering of what was said.

The third layer would consist of the "filling material" invented by the writer. For example, the interviewer has a note or memory of what was said but not of how it was said, and so would rephrase the meaning in what would be presumed to be the speaker's (possible) words. That is, of course, not what we as linguists prefer. Notice, however, that such text still will have to be rated better than literary dialect: even if it is imagined language, it is language tied to a specific individual, conversation, and topic meant to be rendered, as reflected in the interviewer's mind; it does not build upon just a general stereotype but is based upon a single historical experience and is therefore not fully fabricated.

Finally, there may be portions of the text for which none of these relatively optimistic assumptions hold, portions created by a fieldworker who perhaps did not care or could not do any better, writing down things that were never said. At this level we get a stereotype—what the writer believes to be possible statements by a member of the speaker's social group. Here we are close to literary dialect (which may of course vary greatly in quality—see Mille, this volume), and here we are also with the language that is produced by linguistic editing.

The problem is, of course, that we will have no chance of knowing which portion of a given interview has to be assigned to which of these four levels of credibility. Nevertheless, I insist that this is not a cause for too much pessimism. There is no reason to assume that the whole text would be of the fourth type, and therefore of highly restricted linguistic value. Even if indirect and presumably distorted in details, the slave narratives are renderings of real ex-slave speech.

There are two further considerations that may be applied to the assessment of individual linguistic structures. First, there is the momentum of consensus across fieldworkers and regions. If we find a more or less consistent linguistic rendering of some structure in texts written by dozens of different fieldworkers from various regional backgrounds, then we have to credit this observation with the status of reflecting reality, as no consensus to forge some linguistic detail consistently is conceivable. Frequencies may be inaccurate and unreliable in such cases, but the phenomena as such cannot be discarded. It is of course possible to postulate that certain phenomena in the speech of the interviewees were not understood properly and therefore not recorded or mistakenly recorded; but if we consider the size of the undertaking, the number of people involved in both roles, the individual differences between the many interviewers and their approaches and attitudes, then I think it is highly unlikely that some core linguistic phenomenon in ex-slave speech went totally unrecorded or that the character of the variety was completely misrepresented. Second, it seems reasonable to assume that the reliability of the rendering of specific linguistic features correlates with their morphological and syntactic "heaviness," as longer constructions and meaningful and phonetically heavy morphemes are certainly more easily noticed and memorized than, say, a phonetic detail or a morpheme that is realized by a single sound (cf. Wolfram 1990). In other words, I would place greater trust in whether a speaker formed an indirect question with inversion or used a double modal than whether he did or did not use a particular plural -*s* or verbal -*s* ending. Also relevant is whether or not a particular feature is generally associated in the public mind with a particular dialect; if so, it is likely to show up frequently without substantial justification; if not, no writer would insert it to improve the apparent authenticity of the narrative.

The other problem for the reliability of the narratives, apart from the limitations of the interview context, is the impact of deliberate linguistic editing—a factor which probably has to be judged to have an effect comparable to that of the level four text passages mentioned above, that is, a reinforcement of nothing but stereotypical notions about the dialect in question. Maynor (1988) was the first to point out that some of the interviews collected in regional headquarters of the FWP were heavily edited before being submitted to the Washington headquarters. The amount of editing varies greatly from one state to another—for instance, we have evidence of massive changes with Texas and Mississippi narratives, while the Georgia records seem to have remained relatively unaltered. It has been shown that the versions published in 1977 and 1979, consisting mostly of material drawn from regional archives, often appear to be more reliable than the Library of Congress collection published in 1972, as in many instances these are the earlier, unedited versions, the originals produced by the interviewers which for some reason some regional secretary did not feel were adequate for submission to the headquarters. In fact, often we can find two versions of the same story in the two series, one edited and one original, which gives us a chance to assess the impact and consistency of such editing. The question is: How did this editing affect the linguistic reliability of the narratives, and, in particular, are there any particular structures which are more liable to being edited in or out, or others which are hardly affected?

An answer to this question can be sought by comparing two versions of identical narratives, an approach which was followed by Maynor (1988) and by two graduate students of mine (Ariane von Orlow and Julia Brueggemann) in term papers at the Free University of Berlin in 1992 analyzing about a dozen narratives from Texas.[1]

The results indicate that it is indeed possible to detect some consistent lines of modification, whether resulting from a conscious or subconscious editing policy. In general, the major motivation behind the editing process seems to have been a rewriting of the contents of the narratives. For submission to Washington, the Texas interviews were reduced to about half their size, and very frequently sensitive material—reports of whippings and other cruelties, the suppression of religious activities, the slaves' hatred of slavery and desire for freedom, and disparaging remarks about whites—was omitted, thus producing a relatively more positive view of antebellum life in line with its patronizing interpretation by white historiography. However, these deletions and changes did not have a consistent effect upon the rendering of the speakers' language. Linguistically, a number of changes were more or less randomly introduced in the various rephrasings, the overall effect of which was to render the narratives more dialectal: earlier versions are frequently closer to Standard English (Maynor 1988:113).[2] There are at least three cases in which the evidence is strong enough to document a noticeable linear effect upon the representation of the respective features.

First, the verb form *am* with subjects other than the first person singular is frequently inserted. The effect is very strong; it seems that the vast majority of all *am*'s in the 1972 versions are products of editorial interference. See, for instance, (1) to (5), in which the (a) sentences are as published in Rawick 1972, while the (b) versions are from the older originals of the 1979 Supplement.

(1) (a) when the field hands come in, it am the same way (Will Adams, p. 2)
     (b) when the fiel' hands come in, it was the same way (Will Adams, p.12)
(2) (a) my nigger am comin' to you place (Will Adams, p. 3)
     (b) My Nigger is coming to your place (Will Adams, p. 13)
(3) (a) This gal am free and has papers (Mary Armstrong, p. 29)
     (b) this gal is free an' has papers (Mary Armstrong, p. 73)
(4) (a) de rope am cut (Harrison Beckett, p. 56)
     (b) de rope was cut (Harrison Beckett, p. 228)
(5) (a) Dey claim dey gwine kill everybody what am Repub'can.
         (L. Ezell, p. 30)
     (b) Dey claim dey gwine kill eb'rybody claim Republican
         (L. Ezell, p. 1326)

This type of editing was also observed by Maynor (1988:116–17). It seems to be exceptional in the *be* paradigm, as she found that the uses of the forms *are* and invariant *be* do not seem to be affected greatly by editing. This is an important observation with respect to Jeutonne Brewer's (1974) finding that nonagreeing *am* occurs specifically in the Texas narratives and her claim that *am* in Earlier BE served as a habitual marker, to be replaced later by invariant *be*. This particular relexification process was an unconfirmed postulate with little further evidence in support of it; the present findings, I think, render this position untenable.

A second feature that apparently was systematically affected by editing was the use of verbal -*s* endings, which were introduced readily in nonstandard positions but deleted in the third singular. It is less dramatic than the case of *am*, as there are both a number of non-third singular suffixes and third singular zero endings in the original narratives, but the effect is quite consistent and certainly highly relevant at least for the frequency of the respective phenomena in the records from Texas. That, of course, affects the validity of some of my own results and claims on the nature of verbal -*s* in Earlier BE (Schneider 1983b). I will come back to this point in the next section.

The third form to have been affected by consistent editing is the first person plural pronoun: According to Maynor (1988:112), *we* seems to have been replaced more or less routinely by *us* in the Mississippi narratives. That, I think, solves a puzzle which I noted in my 1989 book (171, 178), namely the discrepancy between the fairly general use of *us* to be observed in the narratives and the fact that even if this is a creolism it does not really fit, given that the invariant pronoun form in Gullah is not *us* but *we*.

To assess the quality of literary dialect, it would have to be compared to real life records of the dialect in question. For the slave narratives, the same line of argumentation holds and, thanks to Guy Bailey and his associates, we now have tape recordings of speakers whose sociohistorical background matches that of the written records almost perfectly.

THE EVIDENCE OF THE AFS TAPE RECORDINGS OF EX-SLAVES

There is no doubt that the AFS tape recordings (Bailey, Maynor, and Cukor-Avila 1991) constitute a source of primary importance, despite the fact that, as is conceded by the editors, they do not provide a solution to major questions for a variety of reasons that I will not go into here (see Rickford 1991; Schneider 1994). Rather, I would like to scrutinize some of the linguistic evidence of these texts. The material will be used for three purposes: first, for a comparison with the written ex-slave narratives, in order to continue the assessment of the reliability and possible directions of modification of the latter; second, for a detailed analysis in its own right; and third, for a survey of possible evidence for creole elements.

The Tape Recordings as a Test Case for the Written Narratives

Studying the tape recordings as a test case for the validity of the written records is a relatively obvious way of using them. As audio recordings they possess the authenticity and reliability which the latter, due to the problems in the written recording and editing process discussed before, generally lack; yet, on the other hand, the tape sample is quite small, especially as opposed to the thousands of extant written records. Thus, if the former can teach us what is or is not trustworthy and worth studying about the latter, that could be a major step forward.

Direct comparisons of corresponding samples from the ex-slave narratives and the AFS tapes have been carried out and published in two earlier papers, Maynor (1988) and Montgomery (1991a). Maynor's results (1988:116–17) on forms of *to be* can be summarized as follows: In the first person singular, the written narratives predominantly show the form *is* (about 50% to 75% of all instances), which she does not find on the tapes at all, and they also raise the frequency of zero from 3%

to about 20% while decreasing the representation of *am* from 94% (based upon the tapes) to 28% (1977/79 texts) and even 4% (1972 versions). In the third singular, the tapes show mostly *is* (88%) and some zero (12%), while in the narratives the frequency of zero is increased to slightly over 30% and some *am* forms are introduced (mostly in the 1972 texts) at the expense of *is*, which falls between 50% and 60%. In the plural and second singular the tapes show zero predominating (59%) with *is* and *are* as strong alternatives (slightly below 20% each). In the written texts *is* is quantitatively overrepresented (at a rate of over 60%), and zero (slightly over 20%) and *are* (4% and 15%) occur less frequently. Montgomery (1991a) compared left dislocation and relative pronoun choice and also observed a lack of congruity between the two samples: left dislocation and subject relative pronoun deletion occur significantly more frequently in the sound recordings, while the relative *what* is more common in Rawick's texts. Consequently, he concludes that the value of the written narratives is only equivalent to that of literary dialect. In my view, however, he is too pessimistic, as there are also a number of substantial parallels between both varieties, which he does not discuss. For instance, the proportion of restrictive clauses out of all relative clauses is 69% in the written narratives and 79% in the taped corpus; of relative zero out of all relative pronouns, 56% as against 54%; of relative *that*, 19% vs. 30%—figures too subtle and too close to each other to be chance products from totally unrelated samples; and even in the case of *what* (14% vs. 6%) the discrepancy is not dramatic. Also, some of the constraints operating on left dislocation are also remarkably similar: out of all instances of the phenomenon in either corpus, 76% in the written narratives and 73% in the tapes move a subject, 15% in both groups move direct objects, 8% as opposed to 5% move prepositional objects—again, I think, justification to assume that the two varieties compared are at least closely related, despite all differences.

Table 1 compares another crucial area of morphology, verbal inflection. The data for the written narratives are from my (1983b, 1989) studies of Rawick (1972); those for the tape recordings are taken from Poplack and Tagliamonte (1991b:295).

Table 1: Verbal -*s* endings in written ex-slave narratives
and the AFS tape recordings

	written narratives			*tape recordings*		
	% -*s*	n	rank	% -*s*	n	rank
1st singular	52	737	4	3	173	4
2nd singular	37	167	6	0	59	5.5
3rd singular	72	211	1	71	42	1
1st plural	71	41	2	29	7	2
2nd plural	44	9	5	0	1	5.5
3rd plural	58	184	3	5	92	3

There is no question that the two series of figures are considerably different and that therefore verbal -*s* in the narratives must be regarded as a feature which is not represented accurately. That confirms Maynor's statement referred to before, and it is in line with my earlier remarks on the effect of the phonological heaviness of a feature on the quality of its representation: a single-consonant suffix cannot be expected to have been heard and noted accurately. Obviously, many of the suffixes recorded in the narratives are the products of scribal or editorial interference, and the real figures of use were considerably lower. This invalidates much of the factual basis of my (1983b) analysis of verbal -*s* in Earlier BE. However, there remains some support for the views presented there.

First, even the distorted representation of the narratives is not wholly mistaken: At least in the third person singular, the percentages of -*s* usage are remarkably similar (72% vs. 71%); and if we check the rank order of frequencies of the suffix in the grammatical persons, we find that it is identical in both samples, so the written material has retained some truth. Second, Rickford's (1991) argument on representativeness can be used in my favor: if it is true that, as I argued and supported with some data (1983b:106–7), the zero form in the verbal paradigm was the prestige form in the earlier black community, then the formality of the interview situation might explain some of the lower frequency of the verbal suffix. Thirdly, my thesis was not based upon the ex-slave data alone but was also supported by several related statements and observations (see 1983b:103–4), as well as by recent results by Poplack and Tagliamonte (1991b:314). Finally, in my earlier analyses (1983b:105–6; 1989:23–5) I observed a consistent regional distribution, showing that the very high frequencies of -*s* occurrence are characteristic of the early-settled eastern states and not of the later settlement areas of the western part of the South—a pattern (1) which in its large-scale consistency is hard to see as a product of chance, (2) which made sense in the light of its historical explanation, and (3) which, given that almost all the speakers on the tapes are from further west, might also account for some of the quantitative difference.

Thus, while I concede that a considerable proportion of the database of my (1983b) paper is flawed, I still hold that the basic claims are right: namely, that verbal -*s* was used more freely and more frequently in earlier phases of black speech than today, that this particular subsystem is to be explained by its descent from a mix of British dialectal systems, and that within the black speech community zero was the innovative, prestigious, and quantitatively increasing form.

In tables 2 and 3, comparisons are set up along the same lines for two morphological features which are, on the one hand, not phonologically heavy and thus, as discussed earlier, prone to inaccurate representation and, on the other, less conspicuous and therefore less subject to deliberate modification than the verbal suffix, namely, the past tense formation of verbs and the plural formation of regular nouns.[3]

Apart from the same tendency noted before, that of introducing verbal -*s* endings (which obviously also works in past contexts), the similarities between the two samples shown in table 2 are remarkable. The proportion of irregular verbs marked for past tense is 79% in the tape recordings and 81% in the written texts; with regular verbs, the corresponding figures are 57% vs. 67%; with *have*, 99% vs 92%, and with *say*, 50% as opposed to 30%. Note that the greatest discrepancy occurs with the verb *say*, presumably because it is more salient and thus more subject to conscious modification.[4] On the whole, however, this table confirms that the written narratives *can* be fairly accurate in their representation of linguistic phenomena, and apparently the degree of trustworthiness correlates indeed with the saliency and the phonological weight of the respective phenomenon.

Table 2: Verbal past tense formation in written ex-slave narratives
and the AFS tape recordings

	written narratives				*tape recordings*			
	% -ed	% -0	% -s	n	% -ed	% -0	% -s	n
regular verbs	67	26	8	2678	57	42	1	394
irregular verbs	81	13	6	4203	79	21	0	766
have	92	6	2	943	99	1	0	140
say	30	53	17	403	50	43	7	95

In the case of the plural formation of regular nouns, compared in table 3, the results are also far from disappointing. Again, there is one remarkable discrepancy: whereas the tapes show a certain amount of zero plurals in all environments, the written records do so only if a numeral premodifies the respective noun. Counter-examples exist but are relatively rare; redundancy of the plural marking is represented as almost a prerequisite for the deletion process to take effect. This is not confirmed by the tape samples: while a preceding numeral certainly promotes the deletion of the plural marker, the process operates also outside this constraint.

Table 3: Plural formation of regular nouns in written ex-slave narratives
and the AFS tape recordings

	written narratives			*tape recordings*		
	% -s	% -0	n	% -s	% -0	n
(a) all nouns (incl. b)	98	2	5999	90	10	548
(b) with numerals (incl. c)	86	14	502	82	18	105
© NUM year(s)	76	24	156	82	18	34

I concede that this difference should not be underestimated because in effect the written data suggest a structural condition which is mistaken. Apart from that point, however, the other figures are again remarkably close. Following a numeral, 14% of the nouns in the written sample and 18% of those in the tapes are uninflected. In the most characteristic collocation of this type, the phrase *NUM year(s)* (mostly followed by the word *old*), the respective rates are 24% and 18%. In the cases of the latter two distributions, a chi-square test of significance leads to a nonsignificant result (at the 5% level), so the assumption that both series of data were drawn from the same sample is not rejected.[5]

Thus, the comparisons of detailed analyses of tapes and narratives can be summarized as follows:

- There is evidence of substantial inaccuracies in representation in the written texts, but there are also structures which seem to be fairly accurately rendered, even in terms of quantitative proportions.

- The basic problem in using the slave narratives for linguistic purposes, then, is to differentiate the structures that are recorded relatively reliably from those that deserve less credibility. It is possible to make estimations based upon the morpho-phonological "heaviness" and the stereotypical saliency of individual structures, and in some cases it is possible to establish reliability estimates on the basis of comparisons with other sources, in particular the AFS tapes. Such comparisons suggest, for instance, that
  - among the forms that did occur in the narratives with greatly increased frequency due to the effect of editing are *am* as a form of *to be* outside the first person singular and *us* for *we* as the first person plural personal pronoun;
  - among the forms whose frequency is exaggerated in the narratives are *is* and *zero* as finite forms of *to be*, *what* as a relative pronoun, and the verbal suffix *-s* in persons other than the third singular;
  - among the forms which are recorded less frequently in the narratives are left dislocation, zero subject relative pronouns, and nonredundant zero plurals of nouns (a rare feature under any circumstances, though); and
  - among the features which appear to have been represented accurately, in terms of both form and frequency, are *be* and *are* as finite forms of the copula; relative pronouns, apart from those listed above; the structural properties of left dislocation; the use of the verbal suffix in relation to grammatical person, especially in the third singular; the past tense marking of verbs; and noun plural formation, especially after numerals.

Basically, it is worth noting that in most cases the effect of inaccurate representations and editing resulted in a modification of quantities, not in fundamental qualitative distortions of the speech represented. Thus, despite all the problems involved, I am convinced that the language of the ex-slave narratives is linguistically more useful and trustworthy than purely fictitious literary dialect. Let me call it "note-supported mental protocol," a category not unique in its own right but rarely needed and thus rarely found in other contexts.

Variation in Past Tense Marking and Plural Marking

Apart from using the tape recordings as a test case for the written narratives, they can and should of course be used as linguistic evidence in their own right. This is exemplified in tables 4 and 5, which present VARBRUL analyses of past tense marking and plural formation in this variety to determine which factors are responsible for the deletion of past tense and plural morphemes, respectively.

In table 4, the factors analyzed as constraints on the nonmarking of past tense are the individual idiolects of the informants, the types of verbs, and the preceding and following phonological environments. According to the step-up / step-down routine of VARBRUL, all four of these factors exert a statistically significant influence upon the shaping of the observed distribution, with the type of verb being strongest in effect, the preceding phonological environment ranking second, idiolectal differences third, and following sound type fourth. Regular verbs lack past marking much more frequently than irregular ones[6] (with a probability of .80

versus .61), which is due to the additional phonological effect of final consonant cluster simplification. *Have* is almost always inflected for past and absolutely inhibits nonmarking (.04), while with *say* the unmarked form for past is promoted more strongly than any of the other factors (.81); in this case, even the -*s*-inflected form, *says*, occurs more regularly than with other verbs. Factor group 1 in table 4 shows the effect of idiolectal differences upon the lack of past tense marking. The probabilities vary between .25 (Celia Black) and .80 (Billy McCrea).[7] However, most are close to the neutral effect of .50. Thus, there is some individual variation along a continuum, variation that might be attributable to a speaker's proximity to a creole or to English.

Table 4: Past tense formation in the ex-slave tapes

GROUP	APPS	TOTS	PERCENT	VARBRUL probability
Informants				
(Fountain Hughes)	39	175	22	.48
(Billy McCrea)	23	44	52	.80
(Bob Ledbetter)	10	56	18	.34
(Joe McDonald + woman)	14	50	28	.47
(Isom Moseley)	10	52	19	.51
(Alice Gaston)	9	30	30	.61
(Laura Smalley)	126	332	38	.65
(Harriet Smith)	36	228	16	.34
(Celia Black)	10	117	9	.25
(Charlie Smith)	90	280	32	.54
Total	367	1364	27	
Verb Type				
(regular)	167	394	42	.80
(irregular)	158	735	21	.61
(have)	1	140	1	.04
(say)	41	95	43	.81
Total	367	1364	27	
Preceding Phonological Environment				
(consonant except d/t)	135	233	58	.73
(vowel)	19	120	16	.28
(dental stop)	13	41	32	.49
Total	167	394	42	
Following Phonological Environment				
(consonant)	126	247	51	.64
(pause)	12	46	26	.45
(vowel)	28	100	28	.41
Total	166	393	42	
TOTAL	367	1364	27	

Regarding the phonological nature of the process of deletion of the past suffix with regular verbs, the effect of preceding environment is strong, ranking second among the four constraints, whereas the nature of following sound exerts the weakest influence of all constraints. The role of consonant cluster simplification becomes apparent in that preceding and following consonants promote (at a rate of .73 and .64, respectively) and neighboring vowels inhibit (.28 before, .41 after) the deletion of the dental suffix. Preceding dental stops enhance the phonological weight of the suffix, making it syllabic, and thus do not support its deletion as other consonants do; their overall effect, however, is practically neutral (.49). A following pause is equivalent to a following vowel, having relatively little impact (.45).

Table 5 shows the factors that promote the deletion of the noun plural marker with regular nouns.[8] In this case, it is the premodification of the noun phrase that constitutes the primary constraint, followed by the influences of the phonological environment (with the following environment ranking second and the preceding one third) and, as the factor fourth in rank, individual proclivities. The impact of different lexemes is not significant.

As has been shown in studies of comparable varieties, the presence of a numeral in the noun phrase, which renders the suffix redundant, promotes the deletion of the plural marker (.58). Remarkably, however, the impact of non-numerical quantifiers (*some, many, all of,* etc.) is even stronger (.65), an effect which, to my knowledge, has not been documented before. An explanation for this may be that, cognitively speaking, quantifiers carry the notion of plurality per se even more saliently than numerals, in which the focus of information may be on the precision of the figure rather than the baseline fact of multitude.

Considering the following phonological environment, it is remarkable that a pause more than anything else promotes the nonrealization of the plural suffix (.66, as opposed to .45 with consonants and .38 with vowels). The impact of phonological clustering becomes apparent again in the role of a preceding consonant (.72). A preceding sibilant strengthens the weight of the plural suffix and thus inhibits its deletion almost as strongly as a vowel (.40 and .36, respectively). Again, there are individual differences of a moderate kind. Half of the informants have -*s* absence rates between 12% and 14% and effects around .5 that can practically be ignored. Four of the speakers rarely lack plural marking and two not at all (these two were eliminated from the final VARBRUL run). Only Billy McCrea has a strong favoring tendency (.78) towards zero plural. Interestingly, with the exception of Laura Smalley, who favors the zero past (.65) but avoids the nonmarking of plural (.30), speakers who typically delete past tense markers also typically delete the plural suffix. This suggests that individuals occupy a fairly consistent position on a linguistic continuum.

Earlier studies have suggested that nouns of measure allow zero plural. Factor group 3, although statistically not significant, is consistent with this observation: nouns of measure (i.e., *year, dollar, mile*) favor zero plural when compared with other nouns.

Table 5: Plural formation in ex-slave tapes

GROUP	APPS	TOTS	PERCENT	VARBRUL probability
Informants				
(Fountain Hughes)	12	101	12	.49
(Billy McCrea)	12	44	27	.78
(Bob Ledbetter)	2	16	13	.42
(Joe McDonald + woman)	2	14	14	.56
(Isom Moseley)	6	48	13	.57
(Laura Smalley)	3	68	4	.30
(Harriet Smith)	5	130	4	.29
(Charlie Smith)	11	89	12	.57
[(Alica Gaston)	0	9	*KNOCKOUT*]	
[(Celia Black)	0	29	*KNOCKOUT*]	
Premodifier in Noun Phrase				
(numeral)	19	105	18	.58
(other)	22	395	6	.28
(quantifier)	12	48	25	.65
Individual Nouns				
(*year*)	6	35	17	.67
(any other)	37	422	9	.35
(*dollar*)	6	26	23	.70
(*mile*)	1	3	33	.50
(*folk/s*)	3	62	5	.28
Preceding Phonological Environment				
(vowel)	18	212	8	.36
(non-sibilant consonant)	32	266	12	.72
(sibilant)	3	70	4	.40
Following Phonological Environment				
(vowel)	10	150	7	.38
(pause)	33	217	15	.66
(consonant)	10	181	6	.45
TOTAL	53	548	10	

The Speech of the Tape Recordings: An Overall Assessment

Some phenomena in the recordings are found also in various other dialects of English. The examples below confirm the mixed but basically English nature of Earlier BE. The perfective (6), the progressive (7), and the genitive (8–9) are constructed as in standard English:

(6)   That the way I've done. If I've wanted . . . (FH, 18)
(7)   you folks are leaving here (CB, 246)
(8)   somebody's house (FH, 309)
(9)   master's home (BMcC, 55)

There are also nonstandard English forms such as *yourn* (10) and *them there* (11), a double modal (12), and inverted indirect questions (13–14):

(10) if it's yourn (FH, 13; also 38)
(11) on them there . . . cannon (BMcC, 10)
(12) I used to could sing (FH, 388)
(13) they ask him could he, did he know . . . theology (BL, 183)
(14) and ask her did she want to go with him (HS, 239)

However, the recordings also provide evidence of constructions which are, or have widely been claimed to be, creole or creole-derived in character: the zero copula before stative predicates, especially adjectives (15), preverbal *done been* (16), *ain't* used as a preverbal negator (17).

(15) They Cheap. (FH, 22)
(16) eight o'clock he done been all aroun' (IM, 98)
(17) you ain't want to eat (LS, 528)

The most interesting case in point is preverbal *been* (18–19). Example (19) is creole in character, whereas in (18) a derivation from an English perfect by way of the deletion of an unstressed preceding *have* is conceivable:

(18) the white folks all been treating me nice ever since (AG, 20)
(19) . . . that I brought from Texas. Been have it all my days. (CS, 122)

The stress, weight, and semantics of the verb phrases, in which continuity back to a remote past is emphasized, suggest a creole reading as reasonable even to a skeptic like me (see Schneider 1983a).

The interpretation and source of some structures leave room for discussion. Two of these, preverbal *done* (20–22) and habitual *be* (23–24), have been widely discussed. Both are infrequent in this sample. In examples 20–22, the semantic feature [+completive] of *done* is clear. As for habitual predicates, ordinarily they are unmarked in the present or expressed by *used to* or *would* in the past. In example 24, however, *be* has the semantic features [+habitual] and also [+*irrealis*], referring to a typical, perhaps repeated series of events in the past (meaning something like "whenever there was A, there was also B").

(20) I done forgot now (HS, 503)
(21) I done show it to you (CS, 327)
(22) I done showed it to you (CS, 331)
(23) Sometimes they be passing by all night long (FH, 262)
(24) If you be do the wrong thing, an' they sen' me after you, only reason I won't get you, I won't see you. (CS, 233)

Another structure which deserves attention is the use of *did* before full verb predicates (25–26). The grammar of Standard English requires an emphatic reading in such cases. In examples 25 and 26 such a reading is conceivable, but the element of emphasis is not particularly strong. What is remarkable (and, as far as I can see, has not been noted before in any potentially related variety) is that the presence of *never* (as in example 25) triggers the *did+verb* sequence in the predicate, an effect which can be observed across the whole sample and is thus fully grammaticalized.

(25) I never did buy nothing on time (FH, 75)
(26) The colored people always did hate me (CS, 47)

Finally, there are two features which may be creole in origin but whose status in this corpus is doubtful. Both have been mentioned in the context of creoles but not, to my knowledge, in connection with BE. The first of these is the nonoccurrence of an indefinite article, as in examples 27 and 28. Both can be subsumed under a common semantic reading: "X is a representative of class Y," with the "Y" noun phrase lacking a determiner. This is consistent with both the individuated-nonindividuated distinction proposed by Mufwene (1986) for the Gullah noun phrase and Bickerton's (1981) creole specific-nonspecific distinction, thus providing a new link of BE with creole languages. However, at this point the evidence is scant. The other possibly creole construction used by the ex-slaves is the iteration of adjectives for semantic intensification as in 29 and 30. Reduplication is characteristic of creoles (Holm 1988:88, 141); here, however, the repetition for emphasis is a marginal mechanism. Still, it may be evidence of a creole link with BE.

(27) I was good, big boy (BMcC, 75)
(28) He was regular church man (BL, 25)
(29) a big, big boy (BMcC, 43)
(30) a good, good person (FH, 154)

CONCLUSION

Despite some reservations, I think the slave narratives and the AFS tapes provide possibilities for fruitful research. But there are other sources, some of which are still largely untapped. The recent work of Shana Poplack and associates on speech islands of descendants of earlier BE speakers on the Samaná peninsula and in Nova Scotia, whose dialect survived in non-English speaking environments, is of primary importance (Poplack and Sankoff 1987; Tagliamonte and Poplack 1988; Poplack and Tagliamonte 1991a, b). The Hyatt corpus (see Viereck 1988) may provide further data, as might slave letters (e.g., Bailey, Maynor, and Cukor-Avila 1991). It is possible that comparable material still rests unearthed in some archives. The biography of Silvia Dubois (Larison 1883), a quasi-phonetic transcript of 19th-century black speech, has remained unanalyzed so far (apart from extensive but unpublished comments on it by William Stewart in personal communication).

The picture that emerges on the basis of the available evidence is complex. The work of Poplack and her colleagues has disclosed linguistic variability which corresponds to that found in dialectal varieties of English. The Dubois text contains little that can be interpreted in a creole light. The slave narratives and the slave tapes do contain some creole forms and structures, although the evidence is considerably stronger for English and English dialects shaping their grammar. It can be reasonably stated for Earlier BE as a whole that it was predominantly English in nature, although it includes creole structures and remnants of an African past. It is related in some ways to the creole languages of the Caribbean and to Gullah, but there is no serious empirical support for the assumption that black speech in earlier periods, outside coastal South Carolina, was a full creole language or that there was a uniform, supraregional Plantation Creole.

Creole theory has been increasingly concerned with notions of "differential creolization" (Cooper 1979), "clines of creoleness" (Schneider 1990b), and "creoloids" or "semi-creoles" (Holm 1988, 1:9–10). Holm (1992) classifies American BE, Afrikaans, Popular Brazilian Portuguese, Réunionnais, and others as semi-creoles. It would be a mistake, however, to let the classification of BE or Earlier BE as a semi-creole lead us back to a uniform view of the varieties. It is more likely that from the very beginning black speech was characterized by the same degree of variability, contigent upon the speaker's sociolinguistic circum-stances, that we observe today. It is more reasonable to posit Black (or African-American) English*es* than to insist on an idea of linguistic homogeneity and thus a single explanation for the African-American linguistic past.

NOTES

1. These unpublished papers are based on 1972 and 1979 versions of interviews with the following speakers: Will Adams, Sarah Allen, Andy J. Anderson, Mary Armstrong, Stearlin Arnwine, Isabelly Boyd, Lorenza Ezell, Carey Davenport, Agatha Babino, Harrison Beckett, and Rosanna Frazier.

2. The strong evidence for this observation indicates that the difference between Standard English and Earlier BE is even smaller than the 1972 versions suggest. Thus, the evidence for editing does not imply support for the view that Earlier BE was heavily creolized.

3. The data for the narratives are from my earlier study; those for the tapes are based upon the texts as transcribed and published in Bailey, Maynor, and Cukor-Avila (1991). Wallace Quarterman is excluded as a speaker of Gullah rather than of Black English.

4. Wolfram (p.c. 1993) suggests that the unmarked occurrence of *say* in these contexts may be a result of the creole *tell se*.

5. The respective figures are as follows: for numeral + N, 19 times zero and 86 cases of -s (tapes) as opposed to 68 zero and 434 -s (narratives); chi-square = 1.12; for NUM *year(s)*, 6 zero/28 -s vs. 38 zero/118 -s; chi-square = .38.

6. The verbs *cut, hit, hurt, put, quit*, and *set*, which never take a past tense marker and thus cannot be categorized for the application value, are excluded from the analysis.

7. Probabilities of less than .50 are disfavoring; probabilities greater than .50 are favoring.

8. See Singler (1991:264–66), who analyses some different factors, chooses the suffix rather than zero as the application value, and uses a slightly different corpus (Wallace Quarterman is not considered here).

An Early Representation
of African-American English
Marianne Cooley

In the absence of written evidence by speakers of African-American English, literary dialect and other secondary sources have provided evidence of the earliest structure and development of this variety (Read 1939; Stewart [1967] 1975b, [1968] 1975a; Dillard 1972, 1975a, b). Travel commentary from the 16th to early 19th centuries and literary representations of African-American speech, particularly in American drama, have been cited. But early attestations in English plays have not been as fully researched, likely in order to prevent charges that the dialects represented in those plays would not have been native to or known in the colonies. However, during the late 18th and early 19th centuries until the independence of the American colonies, English literature encompassed works authored by both American and English writers, the same books were printed both in England and in the colonies, and English acting companies regularly presented English plays throughout the colonies. To identify a distinctly American tradition within general English culture is rather difficult until after the War of 1812; Nathan (1962) and Damon (1934) also mention this period as distinguishing an earlier Anglo-American conjoint tradition from a later American one regarding African-American songs. Thus, though one might initially overlook representations of African-American English in English plays of this time, such dismissal is unfortunate because it prevents the recognition of possible literary dialect influence and the acknowledgment of the importance of West Indian sources for both English and American representations of African-American speech.

One such source includes an African-American character named Mungo in a major role. First produced in London in 1768 and just eight months later in New York in May 1769, *The Padlock* has special importance in the development of African-American literary dialect because of its great popularity and the consequent likelihood that it was imitated by later writers. In 18th-century Philadelphia, *The Padlock* had thirty-two productions compared with fewer than twenty for any other non-tragedy and fewer than ten for most similar plays (Pollock 1933). In New York City between 1769 and 1794, *The Padlock* had at least fourteen productions (Odell 1927: vol. 1), and they continued through 1813 (Odell 1927: vol. 2). Indeed, its 18th-century productions blanketed the colonies—Savannah, Charleston, Richmond, Washington (Kentucky), Baltimore, Newport, and Boston, in addition to Philadelphia and New York (Brown 1870; Clapp 1853; Hill 1971; Hoole 1946; Ireland 1866–7; Patrick 1953; Pollock 1933; Seilhamer 1888–1891; Shockley 1977; Willard 1891; Willis 1924). Furthermore, the play was printed in Boston in 1795 and in New York in 1805 in addition to its several London and Dublin printings between 1768 and 1789, quite a testimony to its popularity since many plays were never published and very few in both England and the Colonies. Further attesting to the play's popularity and public knowledge of its dialect representation, one of

Mungo's songs independently appeared in the *American Songster* published in New York in 1788 (Damon 1934). Another bit of evidence for its familiarity may be cited from the years of the Revolution. Although the Continental Congress closed the theaters from 1774 to 1784, both British and American officers produced plays for the entertainment of the troops and of the citizens of towns where they were stationed. Quinn (1943:60) quotes a letter from a soldier at Valley Forge during May 1778 about a performance of Addison's *Cato* (a play with two African characters speaking standard English that represents either Latin or their native language) and about a probable performance of *The Padlock* as the letter continues, "if the Enemy does not retire from Philada soon, our Theatrical amusements will continue—The fair Penitent with the Padlock will soon be acted."

The *Padlock* was written by Isaac Bickerstaffe with music by Charles Dibdin, both Englishmen never in the Americas. But apparently the artistic force initiating the play was an actor named John Moody, who had established a successful professional theater in Jamaica before returning to England to join David Garrick's company. The play's dialect is generally attributed to Moody's knowledge of African-American English in the West Indies, primarily Jamaica and Barbados. It can thus be identified as based on Caribbean varieties, including pidgin and creoles, with an actor's consideration for stage presentation and audience perception. In his autobiography, Dibdin, a career actor known for his imitative ability, stresses Moody's role in the invention of Mungo's African-American dialogue declaring that "the part would never have been written as it is but for Moody's suggestions, who had been in the West-Indies, and knew, of course, the dialect of the negroes" (Dibdin 1803: vol. I, 70). Dibdin is additionally connected to the West Indies, and perhaps also to maritime English varieties, by his brother, a sailor who shipped to the West Indies among other places. Like many plays of its time, *The Padlock* seems to have been written as an acting vehicle. Mungo, the most interesting and unusual character, is an excellent acting part. Besides sometimes having the stage to himself, an actor can exhibit his command of dialect, his singing ability, and his acting versatility in portraying both sober and drunken states. Moody was first listed as playing Mungo, but in actual performance as listed in the play's early printed copies, Dibdin assumed the role (Hutton 1891:93; Stone 1962:1356).

In the continental colonies' productions of the play by the American Company of Comedians, Mungo was acted by Lewis Hallam the Younger. The American Company had resulted from a merger of Moody's Jamaican company with an earlier Hallam-Douglass company that had toured the continental colonies from 1752 to 1754 before removing to Jamaica (e.g., Quinn 1943; Wright 1937). As Hallam's most famous role, along with that of Hamlet, he continued to play it until the year before his death in 1808. His success, like Moody's role as adviser, was attributed to his study of the dialect and manners of African-Americans in Jamaica, where the Company had stayed from 1754 to 1758 and where he had married a West Indian (Dunlap 1832; Odell 1927: vol. I; Rankin 1960).

Because we know the sources of Mungo's dialect and of the story, we can better evaluate the language variety it represented. The "Advertisement" prefacing the play's original printing cites its source as a story by Cervantes, claiming that "the characters are untouched from the inimitable pencil of the first designer; unless the dialogue with which the English writer supplies them has done them an injury. The chief addition to the fable is the circumstance of the Padlock" (Bickerstaffe 1768). Cervantes's *El Celoso Extremeño* 'The Jealous Husband' has the same major characters, though most were renamed in the play—"el negro Luis" (Mungo), the elderly merchant Carrizales (Don Diego), who made his fortune in the West Indies, his young wife Leonora (the same), her duenna Marialonso (Ursula), the young lover Loaysa (Leander). The story is narrated with little dialogue and no dialect representation of Luis's speech either in the original Spanish or in Mabbe's 1640 English translation. Thus, African-American dialect in *The Padlock* as originally written and as presented on the American stage for over forty years was historically based on African-American English as spoken in Jamaica, yet it seems to have constituted a prototype for other early African-American literary representations regardless of provenance.

Significantly, all the characteristics of Mungo's dialect are found in later examples of African-American literary dialect, and only a few characteristics found in other 18th- and early 19th-century literary texts do not occur in *The Padlock*. The list below summarizes the features of Mungo's individual dialect.

Phonological Features

1. θ, ð → t, d   tanks, dem, noting (var.: Thursday, nothing)
2. absence of postvocalic *r*   youself, you (var.: yourself, your)
3. loss of final consonant   kine (var.: mind, last)
4. s → ∅ / #___t   trike (var.: string)
5. absence of palatal glide   moosic
6. paragogic vowels   worky, closee, scruba
7. l → r   insurance 'insolence'
8. loss of unstressed   imperance 'impertinence'
   medial syllables

Grammatical Features

1. invariant *be*   I must be stay in a cold all night
2. zero copula   me very good servant
3. invariant verb stem   you lick me last Thursday, he sing for bit
4. no "do support" in questions   what you say, massa
5. negation by *no*   me no savee
6. undifferentiated pronoun case   *me* subj; *him* subj & poss; *you* poss
7. double comparative   more merrier
8. double negative   no tanks neither
9. a-prefixing participle   a-sinking
10. ∅ infinitive marker   you teach me play
11. *for* complementizer   What she say, I want for ___
12. ∅ article   noting here but poor man

Lexical Features

1. axe/ax	6. savee
2. massa	7. missy
3. neger	8. sirrah
4. lila/lilly	9. by gog
5. tief	10. Gad

Mungo's dialect includes the characteristics which subsequently designate African-American speech in both more accurate and more stereotypical representations. Phonologically, the absence of postvocalic *r*, the substitution of stops for the interdental fricatives, and the simplification of final consonant clusters are changes that most often represent literary African-American characters. Other phonological characteristics in this text, also associated with pidgins or creoles, include paragogic vowels and loss of word-initial *s* before *t*. On the other hand, some phonological features do not occur in *The Padlock* that have been noted elsewhere. These include the loss of initial unstressed syllables, the addition or deletion of word-initial *y* before vowels, and the following sound substitutions: /ʧ/ → /ʃ/; /ʃ/ → /s/; /(h)w/ →/w~v~f/; /ŋ/ → /n/; /v/ → /b/. Of these latter changes, the substitutions of *b* for *v* and *n* for *ng* are the ones absent that are widespread among other literary representations.

Interestingly, grammatical features are more extensively represented than phonological ones. Perhaps those were easier to represent without necessity of respellings that changed the standard textual representation, or perhaps they were more salient. These include verb and pronoun morphology and syntax along with other syntactic structures characteristic of African-American literary dialect. Some features, such as undifferentiated pronouns, have been cited as being pidgin- and creole-based while others such as *a*-prefixing have been cited as being based on British dialects. African-American grammatical features not represented here, but occurring later or in nonliterary texts include nonredundant pluralization, headless relative clauses, pleonastic subjects (subjectivizers), and perfectives with *been* or *gone*.

Mungo's distinctive vocabulary appears regularly in later African-American literary dialect, with the exception of three forms from traditional British theater. Individual words may have originally resulted from the operation of phonological rules (e.g., *tief* from *thief* or *massa* from *master*), but they appear so often in literary representations that they seem to have been restructured as lexical markers to identify African-American speech even when the character was not otherwise identified. Of other lexical markers in early American literary dialect, *The Padlock* is missing only *learn/larn* 'teach' and *bimeby* 'by and by'. A few other words have some interest. *Sirrah*, of course, was traditionally used as a form of address in British drama, perhaps most often by and to comic relief servant characters. *By gog* and *Gad* come from the same tradition, with euphemistic or phonological alteration. *Imperance* apparently for 'impudence/impertinence' and *insurance* apparently for 'insolence' likely represent phonological changes of /l/→/r/ and loss of unstressed syllables, but they also seem to share lexical characteristics related to malapropisms used to effect humor for the audience's interpretation. Such word substitutions or misformations would be intended to exemplify Mungo's lack of education and to individualize his character. Together, these phonological, grammatical, and lexical features evoke the perception of an African-American speaker.

It is also notable that rather than being consistently invariant, several of these characteristics alternate whether from different printings or acting copies, from authorial intention, or from real-life model. Variation in Mungo's dialect seems more prevalent than in other early representations of African-American speech perhaps also because of its greater length and Mungo's position as a central character. Appearing in both acts, Mungo speaks about a quarter of the lines in the play, whereas African-American characters in other 18th-century plays usually had fewer than ten. His dialect varies in several kinds of structures. For instance, *noting* occurs along with *nothing*, the loss of postvocalic *r* seems restricted to pronouns, *lila* varies with *lilly* and *lily*, *to* appears as the infinitive marker as well as *for*, negation by prefixed *no* varies with negative contractions in noun phrases, and articles and the copula are variably present. In any case, variation better reflects real language. It also shows that literary representations of dialect rely on audience perception that a character speaks a certain dialect, without the text necessarily being completely consistent or accurate. In fact, too consistent a representation may be distracting or stereotypical while too accurate a representation may be unintelligible. Perhaps the more important principle is that, given audience reaction to the play, Mungo's speech did not contrast with what the audience accepted or expected an African-American to sound like.

Furthermore, variation may have been more frequent in theatrical performances than in printed texts. In the 18th century, the two were not always identical because of the power that actors exercised in adapting the texts as personal vehicles for aggrandizement or for political reasons. Presumably, speeches in one performance could vary from another, as when Hallam was sober performing and when he was drunk performing. Given this situation, the dialect representation likely occurred more in performance than in text. Since more people saw performances than read scripts, the performances became a primary means to spread knowledge of dialect representation, though only the printed texts survive for our analysis except for anecdotal reports about performances from contemporary observers.

Although the length of Mungo's role makes selecting a short but representative passage difficult, the following scene illustrates the context and some of the characteristics of his speech.

> Mungo: Ah! massa! You brave massa, now; what you do here wid de old woman?
> Leander: Where is your young mistress, Mungo?
> Mungo: By gog, she lock her up. But why you no tell me before time, you a gentleman?
> Leander: Sure I have not given the purse for nothing.
> Mungo: Purse! what, you giving her money den? Curse her imperance; why you no give it me? You give me something as well as she. You know, massa, you see me first.
> Leander: There, there, are you content?

Mungo: Me get supper ready, and now me go to de cellar. But I say, massa, ax
de old man now, what good him watching do, him bolts, and him bars, him
walls, and him padlock?
Leander: Hist! Leonora comes.
Mungo: But, massa, you say you teach me play. (Act II, scene 1)

The Padlock's African-American dialect is important for our understanding and
use of literary dialect in historical study. Because of contemporary reports of its
creation and presentations (Dibdin 1803; Dunlap 1832), as well as its linguistic
structures, it seems clear that Mungo's language was based on African-American
English from the West Indies as interpreted by an Englishman. Neither Mungo nor
his language were originally modeled on continental native African-Americans, but
his dialect does not greatly differ from that of other African-American literary and
stage characters in the late colonial and early federal periods. On the contrary, it
was generally accepted and enjoyed great popularity through extensive presentation. For members of the audience without personal knowledge of African-
Americans, it may have provided an introduction to those language varieties, and
for those with knowledge, it may have adequately represented the varieties they
knew. This acceptance of a Caribbean model may suggest that the language of 18th-
century African-Americans in the continental colonies was indeed very similar to
that of Caribbean African-Americans, i.e., the Plantation Creole that Dillard (1972)
has proposed. Or, it may suggest that a literary dialect tradition was operating, very
likely with *The Padlock* playing a role in such an establishment.

Apparently, this dialect portrayal of an African-American became part of early
American popular culture, a starting point for two traditions: one in legitimate
American drama and one in low comedy minstrelsy and vaudeville. *The Padlock*
played in reputable theaters and was presented by a serious professional troupe,
attaining some degree of respect as well as popularity. Consequently, audiences,
which likely included other playwrights, would accept Mungo's dialect as
representative in the absence of other negative evidence, a situation leading to the
development of a literary tradition.

Knowledge of *The Padlock*'s history and dialect representation necessitates
reconsideration of previous critical commentary. Its earlier 1769 presentation in
New York and subsequent popular presentation throughout the colonies casts doubt
on two of Walser's assertions that "the dialect as written [in 18th-century American
plays] was uninfluenced, at least in the earliest efforts, by literary tradition; and
there can be little doubt that most of the Negro characters were drawn from life"
(1955:269) and that "this Negro dialect [of Priscilla and Banana in *The Yorker's
Stratagem*] was the first to be heard from an American stage, for the comedy was
acted in New York early in 1792" (1955:273). Similarly, this evidence challenges
Krapp's assertion that "Negro dialect characters as they appear in early American
plays and novels do not owe anything to imitation of similar characters in British
writing. They are apparently the result of direct observation" (1960 rpt.:263). His
other assertion that "the barbarous Gullah was the customary form of negro dialect
for use in literature until after the middle of the nineteenth century" (1960 rpt.:254)
may be closer to the truth in that Caribbean models with pidgin and creole

characteristics, like Gullah, provided origins for at least some African-American literary characters, whether of English or American authorship.

By its nature, literary dialect is a tertiary representation of speech with the conventional writing system being itself manipulated to represent variant speech patterns. Except for more folkloric texts and random instances, literary dialect suggests or corroborates rather than directly records language varieties. Literary dialect also serves purposes internal to the literary concerns of the text such as establishing authorial tone or the story's setting as well as representing the character's language. Like individual literary works, literary dialect may be more or less realistic, depending upon the author's decisions. These purposes affect how the dialect is represented. For instance, if the purpose is to effect humor, then the dialect may be exaggerated in ways more deviant or distracting from the standard forms, and puns and malapropisms that produce humorous images become more frequent. But if the purpose is realism, then the dialect may more closely reflect the actual language variety. In the case of Mungo, the internal situation suggests comedy with the play's title page also identifying it as a "comic opera" or "farce." But since Dibdin, the actor-composer, writes that the language was based on first-hand description, it seems that some degree of portraiture was intended just as contemporary reports also suggest some reality in Lewis Hallam's American stage presentation.

Nevertheless, in view of the nature of literary dialect, one legitimately questions the extent to which it can be validly used as historical evidence. Both the validity of literary dialect and its use as historical evidence have been much debated (Downer 1958; Foster 1971; Ives 1954, 1955; Pederson 1966, 1968). Nineteenth-century American literary dialects such as those of Twain, Harris, Eggleston, and others have been shown to accurately reflect corresponding Linguistic Atlas data (Craigie 1938; Dillard 1977; Ives 1950; Krapp 1926; Stewart 1970), but that time period was also especially devoted to types of realistic modes and folklore research with authors explicitly stating their intentions to represent the language of their characters as accurately as they could. Literary dialect may additionally provide suggestive material for language attitudes study since it portrays language in specific social and psychological settings, and it may show internal variation related to different contexts. On the other hand, many literary representations are quite imperfect and stereotypical, instances of eye dialect and stage traditions with little basis in real language. Others like *The Padlock* have different geographical origins in spite of being widely accepted by audiences. It seems preferable, therefore, to treat literary dialect as suggestive or corroborative evidence, not as definitive historical evidence.

Considered along with its chronological precedence, its continuing popularity, and its widespread geographical dissemination, the close resemblance between *The Padlock*'s linguistic features of African-American literary dialect and those in all the other early plays suggests its pre-eminence for study of early African-American literary dialect. Mungo's dialect includes characteristics found in Caribbean creoles because that was its source, but it also was filtered through perceptions of white nonnative speakers to serve purposes of theatrical performance. The represented dialect includes enough African-American features to be distinctive but just enough in order to remain easily intelligible to a standard speaking audience. Audiences would recognize characters talking like Mungo as being African-American, and authors would have an easily accessible model to imitate and to embellish. When later authors personally knew African-Americans, they could represent additional linguistic features they had noticed. The dialect in later plays could combine direct observation and literary tradition or use either alone. As long as the dialect represented on the stage or in the literature did not directly conflict with audience preconceptions, the dialect would be accepted as "real." Thus, without evidence in addition to that culled from literary dialect and other indirect sources, we cannot confidently write accurate language history. Sociocultural, historical, and ethnographic information about a text or genre is necessary before accepting its use for linguistic history as being appropriate.

Challenges and Problems of Recorded Interviews
Jeutonne P. Brewer

The data from the Archive of Folk Song (AFS) ex-slave interview recordings, the Works Projects Administration (WPA) Ex-Slave Narratives, and the Hyatt Foundation interviews are of different types, collected at different places with different purposes and procedures. Researchers tend to focus on one of these sources while neglecting the other two. Researchers also tend to assume that the mechanically recorded AFS interviews are valid representations of the dialect and that other sources like the WPA narratives are unreliable. Moreover, in spite of Viereck's (1988) informative introduction, researchers seem to overlook the Hyatt Foundation interviews.[1] Some researchers use the ex-slave recordings as if they are equivalent to current sociolinguistic interviews. Few researchers use the recordings as carefully as Schneider, Rickford, Bailey, and Maynor. Problems for researchers are similar in some ways for all three sources: possible bias of the interviewer, social and economic racism prevalent at the time, use of white interviewers, and representativeness of any or all of the oral and written sources.

The AFS recorded interviews have generated excitement and high expectations about examples of early Black English. Although the recordings are limited in quantity and present their own particular challenges and problems, some studies have left the impression that this source of data is representative of the ex-slave population and that the findings about their linguistic features can be generalized. Actually, AFS recordings provide only a few hours of recorded speech; the material is limited to a 30,000-35,000-word sample collected from 11 ex-slaves in less than ideal circumstances. (For transcripts, see Bailey, Mayor, and Cukor-Avila 1991.) The interview situations were typically rather formal. The interviewers varied widely in their abilities to elicit casual forms of speech, with the untrained interviewer sometimes performing more effectively than the trained interviewer. For example, the interviews collected by John Henry Faulk, an untrained interviewer, demonstrate better technique and more effective results than some of the interviews collected by the more experienced John Lomax.

When I say that researchers too often use the mechanically recorded interviews as if they are equivalent to current sociolinguistic interviews, I mean that most studies have assumed or projected a consistent and uniform use of language by the ex-slaves. Important differences in language use have been obscured by lumping all the examples together to present a particular grammatical feature as folk speech. Noting significant differences, both qualitative and quantitative in the *transcriptions of linguists*, Rickford (1991) reminds us that "we cannot abandon the alternative sources of evidence," including written texts.

Scholars' findings differ even more than we thought. Because the narrative collection is very large, to say that we are working from the narratives is not enough. In fact, we have not all worked with the same data set. Reported findings may be true for a particular data set and not be true for the whole. We must all pinpoint, as Rickford (1991) noted, which narratives are examined, how they were recorded, and how they were transcribed. In the end we should be in a better position to select narratives, spoken or written, with greater confidence in our analysis and a greater awareness of the peculiar challenge each data set presents. The first three sections of this paper review previous studies: the first study dismisses the written text to focus only on the spoken; the second examines written sources; the third draws a comparison among features in both spoken and written materials. The fourth section analyzes data from three sources: the AFS oral interviews with former slaves, the written WPA accounts from the Rawick collection, and a set of ex-slave interviews with John Henry Faulk.

FOCUS ON SPOKEN DATA

Poplack and Tagliamonte (1991b) compare AFS recorded interviews with 21 speakers of Samaná English, spoken by the descendants of ex-slaves in the Dominican Republic. Observing that Brewer and Schneider present widely different percentages for concord -*s* forms as in *I knows* and *He know*, they assume that this difference between investigators proves the WPA narratives to be unsuitable for linguistic analysis. As a result they dismiss the WPA narratives and focus on the AFS recordings. What Poplack and Tagliamonte seem not to take into account is that widely different percentages are not unusual in data based on small samples drawn from a large and diverse corpus.

Schneider (1983b, 1989) found 28.8% occurrence of -*0* for the 3rd person singular in South Carolina and Texas WPA Ex-Slave Narratives while Brewer (1986b) reported 69.8% occurrence of -*0* for the 3rd person singular subjects (see table 1). What accounts for the difference? Basically, it is a matter that the two studies used two different sets of narratives for analysis. Although the narratives for both studies came from the set of 3500 WPA Ex-Slave Narratives, the two researchers independently selected different texts with practically no overlap in the narratives selected. Taken together, all the narratives studied by Schneider (1981, 1989) and Brewer (1973, 1974, 1979, 1986a), excluding duplicates, come to 276, or 8% of the 3500 narratives available in Rawick (1979). Furthermore, sociolinguistic field studies have also reported widely divergent findings for -*0* for 3rd person singular. The studies listed in table 1 show a range of 0% to 78% for the use of -*0* forms.

Even in the small data set provided by the AFS recordings, researchers report different findings for this linguistic feature. Table 2 compares the findings of Schneider (1989:70) and Poplack and Tagliamonte (1991b:295).

Although the findings are different for verbal -*s* use for nearly all grammatical persons, the major differences are for the occurrence of -*s* with first person singular (57.1% and 29%) and with the third person plural (10.5% and 5%) respectively. More importantly, as Schneider points out, more than three-fourths of the inflections in the AFS recordings are provided by three ex-slaves—40.5% by Fountain Hughes (Baltimore, MD), 21.8% by Laura Smalley (Hempstead, TX), and

14.1% by Harriett Smith (Hempstead, TX). In addition, more than a third of the examples come from a particular locality in Texas. Researchers should ask how representative these findings are of an earlier period of Black English, how comparable the findings are to those of present-day sociolinguistic fieldwork, and how generalizable the findings are.

Table 1: Verbal *-0* and *-s* for third person singular

	% -0	% -s	Comments
Brewer 1986b (Pronoun Subjects)			
SC	93.0	7.0	31 WPA narratives
Texas	56.2	43.8	32 WPA narratives
Total Occurrences	69.8	30.2	
Schneider 1989 (All Subjects)			
SC	29.5	70.5	12 WPA narratives
Texas	25.0	75.0	12 WPA narratives
Total Occurrences	28.8	71.2	
Selected Studies for Comparison (Adapted from Schneider 1989:74)			
Wolfram 1969	71.4		12 LWC blacks, Detroit
Henrie 1969	72.5		3 five-year-old black children
Fasold 1972	65.3		LC blacks, Washington, DC
Wright 1976	17–78.0		5 LC black preachers, preaching style
Wright 1976	0–23.0		5 LC black preachers, talking style
Baugh 1983	75.3		overall sample of black street speech
Butters and Nix 1986	51.6		LWC blacks, Wilmington, NC
Butters and Nix 1986	10.8		LMC blacks, Wilmington, NC

Table 2: Verbal -*s* for WPA narratives and AFS recordings

	WPA[a]	AFS 1[a]	AFS 2[a]
1 sg.	52.4	2.8	3.0
2 sg.	37.1	2.0	0.0
3 sg.	72.0	67.6	71.0
1 pl.	70.7	57.1	29.0
2 pl.	44.4	0.0	0.0
3 pl.	58.2	10.5	5.0
Total %[b]	54.9	11.8	not available
Total Number [c]	1349	348	374

[a] WPA = Schneider (1989:70); AFS 1= Schneider (1989:81); AFS 2 = Poplack and Tagliamonte (1991b:295).

[b] AFS 1: 40.5% of inflections from Fountain Hughes; 21.8% from Laura Smalley; 14.1% from Harriet Smith (Schneider 1989:72). Poplack and Tagliamonte do not discuss the differences between their findings and Schneider's (1989) findings.

[c] AFS 2: 265 examples from 3 AFS2 narrators: 140 from Fountain Hughes, 76 from Laura Smalley, 49 from Harriet Smith (derived from Schneider 1989:72). Poplack and Tagliamonte do not provide any analysis of individual variation.

FOCUS ON WRITTEN DATA

Maynor (1988) matched thirteen WPA ex-slave interviews with the thirteen AFS recorded interviews in her comparison of the occurrences of present tense forms of *be*; she included WPA narratives from both Rawick (1972) and (1979). She reports that in both the written and the spoken data sets, invariant *be* is rarely used, a finding similar to Brewer (1979) and Bailey and Maynor (1987). *Are* occurs almost exclusively with plural subjects and the second person singular. Differences in the written narratives were the uses of nonconcord *am* and the different distribution of *is* and zero in the plural and second person singular, as Schneider (this volume) also points out. She concludes that the WPA Ex-Slave Narratives should not be considered as equivalent to "verbatim records of speech" and adds an appropriate warning that the limitations of the written narratives must be considered.

However, it is also appropriate to note that the thirteen narratives used in this study account for .4% of the 3500 WPA Ex-Slave Narratives available. Clearly the points Maynor raises about the editing of the narratives are important. However, such a small sample does not call into question all the historical material available.

We have long known the questions and problems researchers encounter in working with the WPA narratives (Brewer 1973, 1986b; Schneider 1981, 1983b, 1989). We also know that the Ex-Slave Narratives are "superior in quantity and quality" to such indirect sources as literary attestations and travelers' brief notes about early Black English (Schneider 1989:45). However, no one has ever claimed that the WPA interviews are equivalent to present-day sociolinguistic tape recorded interviews or to the acetate records of the AFS interviews of ex-slaves. In fact, researchers have frequently noted the differences and explained in detail the nature of the Ex-Slave Narratives.

The Ex-Slave Narratives collected by the WPA cannot be viewed as having the same linguistic reliability as tape recordings collected in present-day linguistic field research. Their significance is as historical material; they are a large corpus of the elderly ex-slaves' autobiographical statements about their experiences during slavery, Reconstruction, and post–Civil War racial isolationism. The ex-slaves were asked during the late 1930s and early 1940s to tell about what happened to them and their families, topics charged with emotion. Although we would certainly prefer to have mechanically recorded interviews, there are few of those available. Of the 31 records listed by the Archive of Folk Song, 7 are of poor recording quality or unintelligible. It is important to understand that those recordings are also not equivalent to recent sociolinguistic interviews. The recording equipment was obtrusive, and the interview setting was formal.

Both Maynor (1988) and Montgomery (1991a) raise the issue of editing in the state WPA offices. Maynor (1988:112) quotes from a letter in which one of the interviewers in Mississippi "protests some of the instructions from Washington on the handling of dialect in the narratives." This information should first be balanced with another letter from the state and then be placed in a larger context. Burnette Yarbrough, Mississippi Supervisor of Assignments and Files, sent ten narratives to the Mississippi State Director with a memorandum commenting on his editorial view: "All of these are in the same phraseology as recorded by the fieldworkers. . . . Consistent spelling throughout one manuscript has been attempted so far as it seemed feasible. . . . We have tried to avoid too consistent spelling lest we destroy the personality of the story. . . . The sequence of a narrative has not been altered in an effort to produce a more interesting or readable story." (See Brewer 1980 for the complete text of the memorandum.) South Carolina sent two versions of a narrative when questions arose about the accuracy of an interviewer's material. Both versions were included in the 1941 Library of Congress collection of Ex-Slave Narratives; these materials are reproduced in Rawick 1972. (The texts and correspondence are reprinted in Brewer 1980). Examples like these point out that researchers must think of editing policies instead of a single editing policy. (See Brewer 1980 for a discussion of editing policies.)

The researcher is faced with challenges and problems. How effective were particular WPA interviewers? What were the situations faced by the workers?

Maynor (1988:115) noted that "the interviewers for the WPA project were for the most part neither linguists nor stenographers." People who needed jobs were hired to help with the project. Organizers in Washington, DC, sent directions to the untrained interviewers, who collected narratives and prepared typed versions to send to Washington. Supervisors at the state and local levels, like the interviewers themselves, had different levels of interest in the assigned work and different levels of ability. The subject matter was socially sensitive and politically controversial.

In some areas, material was stored within the state rather than sent to Washington, effectively censoring what state material would appear in the national narrative collection. Certainly, the WPA interviewers were at a disadvantage in trying to record characteristics of Black English without benefit of mechanical recording devices. However, this disadvantage does not mean that the interviewers were totally unsuccessful in trying to record the dialect features.

COMPARISON OF SPOKEN AND WRITTEN DATA

Montgomery (1991a:178) matched eleven WPA narratives with eleven AFS recordings, stressing the regional backgrounds of the individuals interviewed. He analyzed two linguistic features in the two data sets—left dislocation, "more a conversational device than a dialect feature" (187) and relative pronouns. Finding that left dislocation occurs more frequently in the AFS ex-slave recordings than in the WPA Ex-Slave Narratives, he concludes that the WPA Ex-Slave Narratives "are not transcripts of natural conversations" (187).

Again, it is important to note that no one who has studied the Ex-Slave Narratives has ever claimed that they represent verbatim records. From the earliest study (Brewer 1973) to the latest studies (Schneider 1989; Brewer 1991), readers have been informed that the Ex-Slave Narratives are not verbatim records, that they were hand-written and not mechanically recorded, and that there are important differences between the Ex-Slave Narratives and recent sociolinguistic field recordings. Like most of the historical records used in language research, the WPA Ex-Slave Narratives are renderings of language use. The WPA Ex-Slave Narratives try to present a written record of the ex-slaves' autobiographical comments about their experiences during slavery.

In his study of the patterning of relative pronouns, Montgomery focuses on the occurrence of *what* and the absence of a relative pronoun, the zero form. Montgomery (1991a) shows that the use of *what* occurs more frequently in the WPA narratives than in the AFS recordings. Noting that half the uses of relative *what* in his sample of WPA Ex-Slave Narratives come from one narrator, Montgomery suggests that the use of *what* in the one narrative appears to be "excessive, and possibly introduced by the interviewer" (184). There is another possibility of course. The narrator is not a categorical user of *what*; half of her relative pronoun uses were *what*. Her number of uses of *what* may appear to be large in relation to the small number (24 of all 167 relative pronoun uses) of examples. Individual variation is not unusual in sociolinguistic studies.

The occurrence of the zero form is essentially the same for both data sets—56% in the WPA narratives and 54% in the AFS recordings. However, the zero form occurs as subject only 2% (N=3) of the time in the WPA narratives; it occurs 12% (N=19) of the time in the AFS recordings. Assuming that the WPA narratives are transcripts, Montgomery concludes that the WPA narratives underrepresent this feature because they have been subjected to editing. It should be noted, however, that the number of examples is small in both data sets. Also, in this case, there is no discussion of individual variation, so it is not possible to determine which individuals in which regions used the zero form in subject position.

As Montgomery pointed out, this is not a salient feature of Black English. More importantly, there is nothing to indicate that the feature is particularly salient as a test of the reliability of a transcription. In any case, it is not surprising that the written data in the WPA slave narratives, which are not verbatim transcripts of interviews, show some differences from tape-recorded interviews. What is notable is that the WPA ex-slave interviews show some patterns similar to those reported for the AFS recordings. Also, as pointed out above, there can be differences in the transcriptions of linguistic features in different data sets in the AFS recordings as reported by Rickford (1991) and in the reported use of -0 and -s forms in recent studies as shown in table 1. Even using the same recordings and the same set of data, researchers reported differences as shown in table 2.

Other researchers propose a quite different reason for a high frequency in the use of relative clauses. In their studies of variation across speech and writing, Finegan (1992) and Biber (1988) have shown that relative clauses signal the use of elaborated, more careful, use of language rather than the use of language characteristic of face-to-face, or everyday, conversation. The background and dialect of the individual could determine which particular relative form would be used more frequently. A higher level of occurrence of relatives may be an important discourse marker that indicates more formal or more guarded use of language.

Montgomery's analysis, in which narratives are matched on the basis of geography, is also flawed by choosing at least one WPA narrator, Julia Banks, who was not a match for the AFS recorded interview, Laura Smalley. In a study of 22 narratives from Texas and Mississippi, Brewer (1973) reported that Julia Blanks, whose narrative was identified as TX029, was "the youngest narrator" of the group studied and that her "dialect differs from the dialects of the other narrators in more closely approximating standard English" (8, 18). In terms of the Linguistic Atlas classifications, Julia Blanks might well be equivalent to a better-educated subject; Laura Smalley, who would have been a more rustic, equivalent to a less-educated subject. Other factors can be as important as geography.

As Montgomery notes, Rawick (1979:vol. 11) cautions that the narratives should not be used to study black speech patterns, to do a quantitative study of the narratives, or to illustrate or buttress a predetermined theory. However, as Brewer (1986b) points out, Rawick immediately modifies each of these claims, noting that narratives may be useful in some language studies, some quantitative studies, and to some theoretical concerns. Rawick seems to be primarily concerned with controversies in historical studies during the 1970s, particularly Fogel and Engerman's (1974) cliometic studies and Genovese's (1974) theory of "paternalism as the dominant nature of the master-slave relationship."

COMPARISON OF DATA FROM THREE SOURCES

In this section, I first look at similarities and differences in the patterning of relative clauses in the AFS oral interviews with former slaves, the written WPA accounts from the Rawick collection, and a set of ex-slave interviews with John Henry Faulk. Then I present an analysis based on the type-token ratio, a measure of the number of unique words used in relation to the total number of words.

Table 3 shows the relative frequency with which the relative pronouns are used in each data set. If we compare all three data sets, we see more similarity than difference. *That* is the relative pronoun used most frequently. It is in effect the universal relative pronoun. The WPA Ex-Slave Narratives include slightly more frequent use of *what* than the AFS recordings, less frequent use of *which*. The WPA Ex-Slave Narratives are more like the Faulk interview in the use of *who*; the AFS recordings are similar to the Faulk interview in the use of *which*. The pattern of relative pronoun use is similar for all three data sets. The noticeable variation is that John Henry Faulk used *what* less frequently than either the WPA narratives or the AFS recordings.

Table 3: % of relative pronouns used, three data sets

Data Set	That		What		Who		Which		Total
	N	%	N	%	N	%	N	%	N
WPA Narratives	166	70	56	24	14	6	1	0	237
AFS Recordings	41	73	12	21	1	2	2	4	56
John Henry Faulk	240	80	2	1	32	11	27	9	301
Total	447	75	70	12	47	8	30	5	594

Table 4 shows relative pronoun use by WPA narrative, table 5 by AFS interview, and table 6 by Faulk interview tape.[2] There is only one use (Stearlin Arnwine) of *which* in this set of narratives. Two narrators, Harrison Beckett and Parilee Daniels, account for half of the uses of *what* (28 of 56 uses). The relative *that* is the only relative pronoun used by all the WPA narrators. Two WPA narrators, Jacob Aldrich and Harrison Beckett, account for 52% of the uses of relative pronoun *that*. Two relative pronouns account for 94% of the relative pronouns used—70% were *that*, 24% were *what*.

Table 5 shows relative pronoun use by AFS interview. The relative pronouns *which* and *who* are rarely used; Laura Smalley and Charlie Smith account for the 3 uses of these relative pronouns. Two relative pronouns account for 94% of the relative pronouns used—73% (41 of 56 uses) were *that*, 21% (12 of 56 uses) were *what*, a distribution like that for the WPA narratives.

Table 6 shows relative pronouns use by Faulk interview tape. His use of *that*, at 80%, is similar to the pattern of use in both the WPA narratives and the AFS interviews. Faulk uses *what* only two times, but he uses *who* and *which* more frequently than either the WPA narratives or the AFS interviews.

These figures show a macro view of the presence of relative pronoun forms and their frequency of use in relation to each other. The frequent use of *that* is similar in all three sets of data. *What* is the next most frequently used pronoun in both the WPA narratives and the AFS interviews; the form occurs rarely in the Faulk interview. *Who* and *which* occur infrequently in the WPA narratives and the AFS recordings; these forms occur more frequently in the Faulk interview than in the other two data sets. Interestingly, the WPA narratives and the AFS interviews are more similar to each other than to the Faulk interview. In both the WPA narratives and the AFS interviews, a small number of individuals account for a significant portion of the variation reported.

Table 4: Four relative pronouns, WPA narratives

Narrator	That		What		Who		Which		Total by Narr.
	N	%	N	%	N	%	N	%	N
Will Adams	4	2	0	0	1	7	0	0	5
Jacob Aldrich	40	24	9	16	0	0	0	0	49
Nora Armstrong	3	2	1	2	0	0	0	0	4
Stearlin Arnwine	3	2	1	2	2	14	1	100	7
Hattie Austin	1	1	1	2	2	14	0	0	4
Harrison Beckett	46	28	15	27	0	0	0	0	61
Sam Bush	23	14	6	11	2	14	0	0	31
Jake Compton	19	11	1	2	2	14	0	0	22
Laura Cornish	16	10	9	16	2	14	0	0	27
Parilee Daniels	11	7	13	23	3	21	0	0	27
Total	166	70	56	24	14	6	1	0	237

Table 5: Four relative pronouns, AFS recordings

Ex-Slave Interviewed	That		What		Who		Which		Total by Int.
	N	%	N	%	N	%	N	%	N
Celia Black	1	2	0	0	0	0	0	0	1
Alice Gaston	1	2	0	0	0	0	0	0	1
Fountain Hughes	9	22	0	0	0	0	0	0	9
Bob Ledbetter	0	0	1	8	0	0	0	0	1
Bob McCrea	2	5	1	8	0	0	0	0	3
Joe McDonald	0	0	0	0	0	0	0	0	0
Isom Moseley	0	0	0	0	0	0	0	0	0
Wallace Quarterman	3	7	0	0	0	0	0	0	3
Laura Smalley	7	17	5	42	1	100	1	50	14
Charlie Smith	10	24	5	42	0	0	1	50	16
Harriet Smith	8	20	0	0	0	0	0	0	8
Total	41	73	12	21	1	2	2	4	56

Table 6: Four relative pronouns, John Henry Faulk interview

Tape	That		What		Who		Which		Total by Tape
	N	%	N	%	N	%	N	%	N
1	50	21	0	0	10	31	4	15	64
2	42	18	0	0	9	28	8	30	59
3	42	18	0	0	1	3	2	7	45
4	46	19	0	0	5	16	7	26	58
5	34	14	2	100	5	16	4	15	45
6	26	11	0	0	2	6	2	7	30
Total	240	80	2	1	32	11	27	9	301

Another interesting comparison is the type-token ratio for the data sets. The type-token ratio is a measure of the number of unique words in relation to all the words in a narrative or interview. In conversation analysis, the measure can be used to indicate where subjects shift to more careful use of language. In more careful speech, subjects will tend to use unique words more often; that is there will be less repetition of words. Another way of looking at the measure is in terms of repetition. More repetition of words within a sample, that is, the lower the percentage of unique words, indicates a less formal or a less guarded use of language (Carpenter 1990). Figure 1 shows the type-token ratios for the WPA narratives, figure 2 for the AFS interviews, and figure 3 for the John Henry Faulk interview tapes.

Figure 1: WPA Narratives, % of unique words by narrative

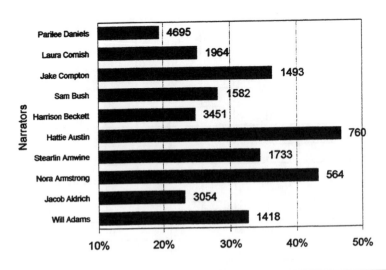

Figure 2: AFS Recordings, % of unique words by interview

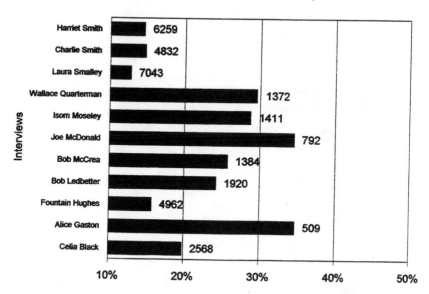

The WPA Ex-Slave Narratives in figure 1 show a range of 19% to 47%; the AFS interviews in figure 2 show a range of 13% to 35%. Interestingly, these two data sets show essentially the same range. The type-token ratio shows that the WPA narrators divide into two groups of 5 narrators: those with a ratio of less than 30% and those with a ratio of more than 30%. The 5 narrators (Aldrich, Beckett, Bush, Cornish, and Daniels) with a ratio less than 30% account for 93% (52 of 56 uses) of the uses of *what* as a relative pronoun. The AFS interviews also divide into two groups: 5 interviewees (Black, Hughes, Smalley, C. Smith, and H. Smith) with a type-token ratio of 20% or less and 6 with a type-token ratio greater than 20%. Two individuals (Laura Smalley and C. Smith) with a ratio less than 20% account for 83% (10 of 12 uses) of the uses of *what* as a relative pronoun.

The John Henry Faulk interview tapes show essentially the same pattern for the first four tapes, an increase in the number of unique words in the fifth tape, and a slight decrease in the sixth tape. The range for his type-token ratio, 18% to 23%, is lower than the range for either the WPA narratives or the AFS interviews. The interview began on the first day with a type-token ratio of 18% for the first tape. The increase to a ratio of 23% for tape 5 and 22% for tape 6 occurred on the second and last day of interviewing. After Faulk explained that we would have to conclude the interview earlier than we had planned because he had to go out of town that afternoon, he explained what he considered important in his experiences and answered questions. The two uses of relative pronoun *what* occur in a saying that he remembered; the second use occurs in a repetition of the saying. The relative pronouns *that*, *who*, and *which* occur in all the tapes. Interestingly, the patterns in the WPA narratives and the AFS recordings are more similar to each other than to the Faulk interview.

Figure 3: JHF Interview, % of unique words by tape

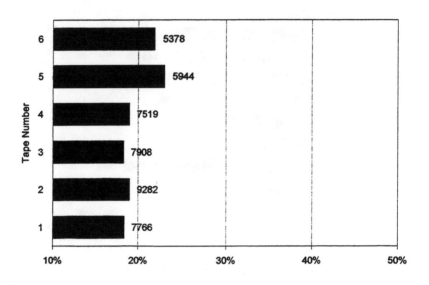

When viewing ex-slave narratives as discourse, we must take into account competing factors: subject and situation. The subject of slavery encourages talk about events that are emotionally charged. This context should encourage casual, natural speech. However, the situation encourages more careful speech because

1) Interviewers are strangers, usually white outsiders.
2) The bulky recording machinery is intrusive.
3) Interviewers sometimes use questionable interview techniques.

Montgomery (1991a:187) concludes that the black speech in the WPA narratives showed "greater similarity to Southern white folk speech" than to Gullah, as reported by Mufwene, or to the AFS recordings. I suggest that his point also applies to the AFS recordings. If 2 and 3 are factors, as they must have been at the time of the recordings, then we can expect an upward shift in style. The next higher level might be Southern white folk speech.

Montgomery (1991a:188n1) has questioned the influence of the recording equipment in the context of the interview situation of the 1930s. Even the modern tape recorder in its small, easily transportable form can influence the language used in the interview. Part of the effort to overcome the observer's paradox involves overcoming the unnatural effect of using recording equipment, even the modern, small box version. It is not natural for someone to bring a tape recorder to the table, the den, or the community center. Imagine, then, the effect of bringing a 250-pound recorder with two 75-pound car batteries to the interview. During the 1930s the equipment was not only large, it was novel. I think it would be a mistake to dismiss the recording equipment as a minor aspect of the 1930s interview situation. Some interviewers were able to overcome these effects; others were not.

Faulk and the other interviewers used huge "suitcase-size" recorders that "would take up the entire back seat" of the car. Batteries were large and heavy. John Lomax (1937) reported that there had been major improvements by 1937; the equipment weighed only 250 pounds instead of 500. The recorders were awkward to operate and required constant attention to assure a good recording—checking the depth of the cutting head, sweeping the shaving cut from the groove, making sure the cutting head did not move too far toward the center of the record. Of course, like Faulk, the interviewer could ignore the equipment, set it up as inconspicuously as possible with the microphone in front of the ex-slave, and hope for a good recording (Brewer 1991).

Further support for this view comes from the number of times the interviewer and the ex-slave refer to the recording equipment in the AFS recordings. For example, at the beginning of the Fountain Hughes interview collected by Hermond Norwood, Fountain Hughes begins to talk about himself and then suddenly says, "Tha's enough." When the recording begins again, he has evidently started about a different subject:

My name is Fountain Hughes. I was born in Charlottesville, Virginia. My grandfather belong to Thomas Jefferson. My grandfather was a hundred an' fifteen years ol' when he died. An' now I am one hundred an', an' one year old. Tha's enough. [recording stops and starts again] She use' to work, but what she made I don' know. I never ask her.

At the end of the recorded material, the fieldworker asks:[3]

FW: You rather not have this on? You rather not tell me or you rather not have this on when you tell me?
INF: It don't make any difference. I ain' gonna say nothing wrong. I ain't gonna [unintelligible]. If I, I, I say

At this point the recording ends; the needle has reached the end of the acetate disc recording area.

Isom Moseley begins his recorded interview, collected by Robert Sonkin, with a few comments about his mother, his master, and mistress. Then he stops and asks, "Well, are you ready for me to talk?" Clearly, he was aware of the process of setting up the cumbersome equipment:

INF: My name is Isom Moseley. Raised up in ol' time without a mother. My ol' master an' mistress raised me. My master was named L. M. My mistress was name B. M. Well, are you ready for me to talk?

At the end of this record the needle gets stuck; note that this is not the end of the interview. After the fieldworker goes through the process of starting the needle on another record, he asks, "You ready?"

> INF: Yes sir, I've explain that. Now I was large enough to tote water to the soap maker, put on ash hopper. They had a barrel, uh . . . . [needle gets stuck]
> INF: You ready?
> FW: You were telling about the soap making.
> INF: Huh?
> FW: You were talking about the soap.

Billy McCrea seems to have forgotten about the recording equipment, however. Evidently, the interviewer, John A. Lomax, notices that the recording needle is nearing the end of the recording area and says, "That'll be enough." After a slight pause, Billy McCrea says, "Now I see all of that I was a boy," after which the needle gets stuck or reaches the end of the record.

At times the interviewers urged the ex-slaves to talk louder. For example, John Henry Faulk gently reminded Harriet Smith twice during the interview:

> FW: "Born to Die." How did that go, you know?
> INF: [mumbles]
> FW: Yes, a little louder.
> INF: Yeah, yeah.
> FW: How'd it go?
> INF: Yeah. They'd sing "Are We Born to Die?" [unintelligible] I was little. I would sit back.

Later in the interview, Faulk again reminds Harriet Smith to talk louder:

> FW: Well did you and he, did he try to whip you one time?
> INF: Yes, yes. He couldn' whip me.
> FW: Speak a little louder Aunt Harriet.
> INF: No, he couldn' whip me. He tried, but he couldn'. I put him [FW interrupts]

At the beginning of his interview with Bob Ledbetter, John A. Lomax refers to the equipment:

> FW: What was that you said, uh? What was that you said, uh, Uncle Bob?
> INF: What about?
> FW: Uh, then. I, the machine went off I didn't hear you.
> INF: I said I'm glad N. got acquainted with you because I believe you's a good man an' I want him to be with a good man.

About two-thirds of the way through the interview, other people enter the room. After trying to find more chairs, Lomax asks, "Well is it still running here?" and then tells Ledbetter:

FW: Well go ahead. Talk to Nora. So you never went to . . .
INF: I, I say, he can tell you, I never went to school a hour in my life. Not a hour.

It is clear that John A. Lomax is at times trying to retrace their steps through earlier conversation that was not recorded. For example, Lomax wants Ledbetter to sing a song and says, "Well now say it just like you did to me in the car and say it louder." After Ledbetter sings a song, Lomax continues:

FW: Well how, how did you tell me you used to call your sweetheart out at night?
INF: Let me see, I'm near forgot what I was to holler, what sort of holler . . . . [FW interrupts]
FW: And holler.
INF: Jus' tell me one word of it so I'll know what you talking about.
FW: You said you didn't have any starch or soap.
INF: Yeah. [starts to sing]
No soap.
FW: *LOUDER.* [Emphasis added to the written transcript to represent the difference in level of loudness.]

Additionally, some interviewers almost certainly affected the content of the recorded interview when they used poor techniques. Even more significant are the condescension and inappropriate joking. For example, John Lomax emphasizes Bob Ledbetter's apparent inability to calculate his age:

FW: And how old are you?
INF: Well now uh, I told you 'bout, oh, they say I'm seventy something, two or three. My daddy tol' me I was un, nineteen years ol' on eight, on the eighteenth, of, uh, December. An' tha's all I can go by.
FW: Eighteenth of Decem, December when?
INF: Well, 1880.
FW: Yeah. And you, you don't know to figure how much that is, that makes you now?
INF: No sir. I'm a poor figurer.

Near the end of the recorded interview, Lomax asks Bob Ledbetter how he learned to read and then adds his own joke about a "colored boy":

FW: And how you learn to read?
INF: Well he learn me at night. He said he, he wasn' no educated man. He could jus' read printing. An' he set up at night and teach his children. Tha's the way we learned
FW: I heard a story about, uh, a judge asking a colored boy on the witness stand, he said, uh, "Jim, can you read writing?" He said, "No sir, Judge. I can't even read reading." [all laugh] But you can read reading and writing both.
INF: Yes sir. [coughing in background]

The AFS recordings are an important source of data, but they are not equivalent to present-day sociolinguistic interviews. They must be analyzed in relation to the context and the interaction between the participants. As discourse, they provide limited but very interesting examples of the exchanges between interviewers, most of them white, and the ex-slaves. In every case except Harriett Smith, the interviewers evidently did not know the ex-slaves before the interviews took place. We still need studies that will take into account individual variation in relation to the social and interview context.

CONCLUSION

The three data bases discussed above constitute the most extensive records of African-American English currently available. However, they are not verbatim records. They do not reflect the strategies of contemporary linguistic interviews. Therefore, linguists who study these texts must cope with data of inconsistent quality. We should not reject these sources because they evidence the "Li'l Abner Syndrome" (Preston 1985). Those who study them should also be aware of the danger of looking at small numbers of narratives and isolated features. Otherwise, the researcher falls into the trap of searching for confirmation of a preconceived idea. Continuing study of these materials should add many interesting and significant findings.

Maynor (1988) and Montgomery (1991a) claim that because the WPA Ex-Slave Narratives are not verbatim transcriptions, they are closer to literary examples than to linguistic examples. I have argued that this dichotomy is simplistic. (See Schneider, this volume.) It is more useful to think of them in terms of a continuum. It is possible, for example, to think of the narratives as oral history, which moves from recording—written or mechanical—to rough transcript, to some type of finished version. To adapt a statement from Finegan (1992:110), it is not accurate to claim that the WPA narratives exist "for the eyes to read, not for the tongue to utter." The WPA narratives were not presented in a literary style removed from the everyday experience of English speakers in the area.

The importance of enhancing published transcripts with taped recordings, when available, has been pointed out by Bailey, Maynor, and Cukor-Avila (1991). Researchers should also take into account individual and geographical variation in the data. Additionally, analyzing the forms by individual interviewed is important. With these goals in mind, I am preparing a computer-based index for the WPA narratives with such social factors as age, sex, education, occupation during slavery, and interviewer. It will then be easier to analyze such factors as the recording and editing of particular interviewers.

Although research is still needed into the history of Black English in this country, we have more information available than ever and many useful studies on which to build. However, we need to give due consideration to our methods of construction. I am reminded of my dad repeating a story that warned about such pitfalls:

A man who was searching for truth and guidance searched the scriptures for answers. This busy man did not have much time for the effort, so he picked up his Bible and read whenever he could. One day he picked up his Bible and read about Judas' betrayal of Jesus for 30 pieces of silver. "And then Judas went and hanged himself."

A few days later, this busy man and desultory reader of the Bible, opened his Bible. His eyes fell upon these words: "Go thou and do likewise."

Too often this is the way linguists have studied historical sources of African-American English.

NOTES

I wish to acknowledge the research support of the Department of English, University of North Carolina at Greensboro. During the semester in which my teaching load was reduced, I was able to continue my work on the data sets included in this study.

1. The Hyatt interviews were "recorded between 1936 and 1942 on over 3,000 Ediphone and Telediphone cylinders and then transferred into normal orthography" (Viereck 1988:292). The transcriptions contain variant spellings, including eye dialect such as "wus" for "was."

2. The WPA narratives included in the data set are taken from the Texas narrative collection: Will Adams, Jacob Aldrich, Nora Armstrong, Stearlin Arnwine, Hattie Austin, Harrison Beckett, Sam Bush, Jake Compton, Laura Cornish, and Parilee Daniels. The AFS interviews included in the data set are: Celia Black, Alice Gaston, Fountain Hughes, Bob Ledbetter, Bob McCrea, Joe McDonald, Isom Moseley, Wallace Quarterman, Laura Smalley, Charlie Smith, and Harriet Smith. I interviewed John Henry Faulk in Madisonville, Texas, in July 1979.

3. Underlined text indicates doubt or disagreement on the part of the editors (Bailey, Maynor, and Cukor-Avila 1991).

The Variable Persistence of Southern Vernacular Sounds in the Speech of Inner-City Black Detroiters

Walter F. Edwards

INTRODUCTION

Among the pronunciations that have been traditionally associated with southern vernacular speech are the monophthongization of /ay/ in *crime*; the raising and diphthongization of /ɪ/ in *kids*; the raising of /ɛ/ to /ɪ/ in *then*; and the deletion or vocalization of postvocalic, preconsonantal, and word-final /r/ in *certain* and *poor*, respectively. Researchers have shown that these forms also occur frequently in the vernacular speech of working-class African-Americans in northern cities such as Detroit, but that they hardly occur in the speech of working-class northern Whites, even in very informal contexts. The ultimate linguistic provenance of these so-called southern forms is in some dispute, but most linguists agree that African-Americans in northern states learned their speech behavior from their forebears who migrated from the South. In other words, these immigrants did not leave their language habits behind.

This paper will examine the variable incidence of these four southern pronunciations in the vernacular speech behaviors of working-class African-Americans from an inner-city neighborhood in Detroit. I will first show that the quantitative incidence of these forms among this population differs from form to form, and I will suggest linguistic and sociolinguistic explanations for these differences in their frequency of occurrence. I will then compare the levels of frequency for the vernacular variants of these variables with figures given by other linguists for groups in the South to see whether northern and southern populations share similar quantitative values for these forms. Finally, I will examine my data to see how language choice varies with sex and age and to show that the survival of these pronunciations in the North is sometimes correlated with these variables. Much of this paper, then, will be like bringing southern folk news of their family and friends who moved away to northern climes to seek their fortunes.

THE DATA

The data on which my conclusions are based consist in part of transcriptions of sociolinguistic interviews with 114 informants from a working-class lower east side Detroit neighborhood. These interviews were used for two studies. The first study involved 48 African-American and white residents who volunteered to be interviewed in 1987 and 1988 for a pilot study to identify linguistic and social variables for the second, larger study. The second study involved 66 African-American informants selected through a scientific random sample and interviewed in 1988 and 1989 for my East Side Vernacular Language Project (EVLP) that was funded by the National Science Foundation. The main purpose of that second study was to see whether or not central ideas and analytical instruments associated with social network theory were useful in explaining linguistic variation in this neighborhood.

FREQUENCY OF SOUTHERN VARIANTS OF LINGUISTIC VARIABLES

Table 1 shows the average percentages for the vernacular (i.e., southern variants) in the ELVP. By far the most frequently occurring vernacular variant is the monophthongization of [ay] to [a:]. This variant averaged 58.3% across the sample of 66 respondents. The second most frequent vernacular variant among the four variables is the deletion or vocalization of postvocalic, preconsonantal [r], either word internally or word finally when the underlying [r] occurs in a stressed syllable. This very salient linguistic feature, which is stigmatized in the white community, occurs 37.8% of the time over the entire sample. The vernacular variant that occurred least frequently is the diphthongization of underlying [ɪ] to [iy].

Table 1: Linguistic choices for four variables by respondents participating in the EVLP by sex (% of vernacular variants)

Variable	Mean %		
	F	M	Total
/ay/→ [a:]	58.3	58.3	58.3
/r/→ V, zero	38.6	36.9	37.8
/ɛ/ → [ɪ]	35.5	26.6	31.1
/ɪ/→ [iy]	13.0	8.7	10.9

Variable (ay)

The southern variant of (ay) occurred frequently in all environments in the EVLP data. Crane (1977) identified three phonetic environments that influenced the occurrence of what he called "broadcast /aɪ/" in the vernacular speech of Whites in Tuscaloosa in 1971–1972: 1) word-final and preceding voiced sounds, 2) preceding voiceless fricatives, and 3) preceding voiceless stops. However, Crane acknowledged that /aɪ/ preceding voiceless fricatives patterns like /aɪ/ in the first environment. We also notice in Crane's figure 1 (reproduced below) that lower-class informants within the three age groups produced very few tokens of /aɪ/ in either environment. Thus, at least for this subsample, environmental effect was negligible in Crane's data.

Figure 1: Percent of /aɪ/ by class in all environments

Socio-economic class	[aɪ]	[aɛ]	[a] *or* [aˀ]
62+ upper class	32	49	19
62+ middle class	7	44	49
62+ lower class	0	56	44
23+ upper class	33	37	30
23+ middle class	10	48	42
23+ lower class	2	39	59
22- upper class	18	64	18
22- middle class	13	51	36
22- lower class	0	47	53

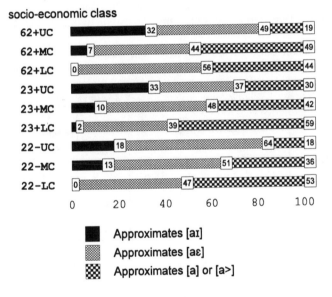

(Redrawn from Crane 1977:192.)

When we compare the overall incidence of /aɪ/ in Crane's data with the incidence of the form in the EVLP data we see that /aɪ/ occurs substantially more frequently in my data than in Crane's: 43% to 6.25%, if the production of the middle and lower classes are aggregated in Crane's figure 1. The difference between the incidence of /aɪ/ in the two data sets becomes less dramatic (43% to 26.25%) if we combine Crane's figures for /aɪ/ and /aɛ/, considering them both instances of the diphthongal pronunciation. It seems to me that this admittedly strained comparison shows that the putative vernacular southern habit of producing monophthongal [a:] where northerners use [ai] was less frequently found among African-American working-class residents of inner-city Detroit in 1987–89 than it was among white middle- and lower-class speakers in Tuscaloosa in 1972. If we assume that in 1972 [ai] production in Tuscaloosa was an innovation from the North that middle-class Whites were more likely than other populations to embrace, then we might speculate that for working-class African-American Tuscaloosans the incidence of monophthongal [a:] was higher than Crane's figures indicate. What is clear is that this so-called southern feature persists among working-class African-American speakers in Detroit but that, not unexpectedly, the incidence is lower in Detroit than in Tuscaloosa. We should bear in mind that the monophthongization of underlying /aɪ/ is a stigmatized linguistic feature in the wider linguistic culture of the Detroit metropolitan area. In the pilot study the vernacular feature was not found in the speech of any middle-class white respondent and only sporadically in the speech of working-class Whites.

Variable (r)
    The overall incidence of the vocalization or absence of postvocalic, pre-consonantal and word-final /r/ in the EVLP data was 37.8%. This level of incidence is quite high in view of the fact that northern speakers typically have constricted [r]'s in these environments. The r-less pronunciation is a southern feature, according to the findings of several linguists. Raven McDavid, Jr. ([1948] 1978:180) has pointed out that in South Carolina the unconstricted pronunciation is the prestige variant: "In the communities where post-vocalic /r/ occurs . . . normally the more education an informant has, the less constriction; and within the same cultural level, younger informants generally have less constriction than older ones, and urban informants less than rural ones." In the same article, McDavid claims that unconstricted [r] was propagated in South Carolina and throughout the Deep South by the spread of the plantation culture, in which African-Americans played a central role. In fact Feagin (this volume) strengthens McDavid's claim pointing out that many West African languages are r-less and that the non-rhotic pronunciations spread from southern areas where the plantation system was established. Juanita Williamson (1968:23) also showed that in Memphis, Tennessee, constricted [r] was rare, occurring only sporadically in word-final positions. Levine and Crockett (1971:444) discussed the ubiquitousness of unconstricted [r] in the South: "Pronouncing these final and pre-consonantal r's with little oral constriction or with none at all is characteristic of Eastern New England, New York City, and of the South Atlantic States . . . ; for example *guard* sounds like *god*." A more recent example of the southern claim to this feature is recorded in Brooks (1985:5): "These two early settled regions do agree . . . in dropping the consonant *r* when it occurs finally, or before a consonant. Thus, the Southerner pronounces *never* as *nev-uh* and *barn* as *bahn*. The man from Massachusetts Bay agrees in dropping the *r*, but he pronounces *barn* as *ba:n*."
    Even though /r/ vocalization or deletion is ubiquitous and prestigious in the South, it is stigmatized in the North. In the pilot study in Detroit we found that the feature occurred only 5.6% of the time in the speech of working-class Whites and 2.2% of the time in the speech of middle-class Whites. Thus, the relative frequency

with which the feature is found in the speech of African-Americans in this Detroit neighborhood is strongly indicative of a southern provenance for the pattern.

Variable (ɛ)

The raising of /ɛ/ to [ɪ] has been mentioned by Jaffe (1973) as a characteristic of the speech of Carteret County in North Carolina. She claims that in this lect "/ɛ/ also displays a raising and fronting tendency: before /n/ it is raised toward and often to /ɪ/." In the EVLP data the raised allophone occurred almost exclusively in the word *get* and when the sound was followed by an anterior nasal (i.e., [n] or [m]). Consequently, the count for this variable was limited to these environments. The fact that in the EVLP data this variant had a fairly high incidence (i.e., 31.1% of possible tokens) might suggest that it is a feature of the inner-city African-American speech culture. However, the feature is also prevalent in the speech of white working-class residents of the area and also in the speech of the African-American middle class. This is also a feature that is not as strongly stigmatized in the area as are monophthongal /ay/ and /r/ deletion. This variable was not selected for investigation in the pilot study but was included in the EVLP because, interestingly, working- and middle-class white respondents in the area identified the raised /ɛ/ as a feature of African-American speech.

Variable (ɪ)

The diphthongization of short vowels, such as the glide that produces the [iy] allophone of /ɪ/, is also typical of southern speech. The feature was investigated both in the pilot study and in the EVLP. In both studies the occurrence of the diphthongized allophone was encouraged by a following nasal sound and by /d/. The count for this variable was limited to these two environments. This feature is clearly not part of the speech culture of the general Detroit metropolitan area. The middle-class white speakers sampled in the pilot study did not have the feature, and the working-class Whites used it only 6.2% of the time. The working-class African-Americans in the pilot study diphthongized the /ɪ/ 25.3% of the time. This is a much higher percentage of usage of this feature than the 10.9% usage (table 1) we found in the EVLP. The reason for this difference remains an issue for further research but is in part explained by our decision in the EVLP to limit the number of counted tokens of the word *kid* and all other words to ten. We had noticed in the pilot study that the diphthongized variant was almost categorical in *kid(s)* when used as a noun and that the word occurred very frequently in the data. My view is that /ɪ/ diphthongization is a lexicalized feature of the speech behavior of African-Americans in the neighborhood studied.

The story I wanted this brief review of the frequency distribution of these forms to tell was that these four putative southern phonological variants persist in the speech of African-Americans living in inner-city neighborhoods of Detroit but that their incidence varies from form to form. The healthiest variants are /ay/ monophthongization and /r/ deletion and vocalization. All four of these variants occur with less frequency in the speech of African-American working-class Detroiters than they probably do in the speech of African-American working-class southerners, but that is predictable given the principle of sociocultural accommodation and acculturation. That principle holds that individuals and groups will adjust their social behavior, including their linguistic behavior, in the direction of the dominant individuals or groups in their social environment. (See Giles, Taylor, Lambert, and Bouris 1973.)

We shall now further consider why monophthongal /ay/ and /r/ deletion and vocalization might have persisted as robustly as they did. To do that we will focus on the patterns displayed in tables 2 and 3. Table 2 shows the variation in the choice of the vernacular variants of the (r) and (ay) variables in the pilot study. In the sections immediately below I will argue that the persistence of these forms is related to their sociolinguistic functions as a sex and group marker respectively in the African-American neighborhood studied.

Table 2: Linguistic choices of nonstandard variants of
variables by African-Americans in East Side Detroit
/r/ → zero, vowel; /ay/ → [a:]

Postvocalic, preconsonantal and word-final /r/ Vocalization/Deletion
/r/ → <V,ø> / # V___(C) # (#) <- central V >
<+ central V,-stress>
<+ central V,+stress>

Groups	% of Vernacular variants
MMAA	19.6
FMAA	20.9
MWAA	66.2
FWAA	29.7

Vowel laxing /ay/monophthongization
/ay/ → <[a]> / ___   <nasal C>
<##>
<d>

Groups	% of Vernacular variants
MMAA	28.8
FMAA	31.7
MWAA	81.8
FWAA	60.9

SEX, GROUP IDENTITY, AND LANGUAGE CHOICE

In table 2 we see that by far the most frequent users of the vernacular variant of the (r) variable are working-class African-American men (MWAA). While the other groups—middle-class men (MMAA), working-class and middle-class women (FWAA, FMAA)—use the vernacular pronunciation between roughly 21% and 30% of the time, the working-class men delete or vocalize their [r]'s over 66% of the time. This suggested to the pilot study team that something sociolinguistically special was indicated. The same was indicated in the pattern for /ay/ monophthong-ization in this data since the working-class males used the vernacular variant much more frequently than the working-class women. In the latter case there was a clear social class stratification: the middle-class informants monophthongized /ay/ much less frequently than the working class. In this case, however, the difference between the incidence of the vernacular pronunciation for the male and female working-class respondents is much less than it is for the (r) variable (20.9% versus 36.5%) indicating that sex is a more significant factor for the (r) variable in the working-class sample than it is for the (ay) variable. The fact that among the working-class respondents the vernacular variant of (ay) averaged 71.35% in the pilot study and 57.0% in the EVLP—compared to 47.95% and 36.3% respectively for the vernacular variant of (r)—suggests that monophthongal [a:] is a marker of group identity for working-class African-Americans in this neighborhood.

The information in table 2 might lead one to suspect that sex is an inherently diagnostic sociolinguistic variable in this neighborhood. However, when we look again at table 1, which presents the EVLP average occurrences for the vernacular variants of the four variables under discussion, we see that, overall, the male and female respondents chose almost the same percentages of vernacular variants of the variables. In fact, one of the most interesting results of the linguistic analysis of the data for EVLP was the finding that there was no significant difference between the sexes in their choice of vernacular variants of linguistic variables. This is unusual since in most sociolinguistic surveys men have been found to use more vernacular variants than women. This is such a strong expectation that Fasold in his text *The Sociolinguistics of Language* (1990) refers to it as the "sociolinguistic gender pattern." Labov (1990) also has pointed out that "in stable sociolinguistic stratification men use a higher frequency of non-standard forms than women" (his Principle 1). We should remember, however, that Eckert (1989b) and Rissel (1989) have pointed out that the biological category of sex is not directly related to linguistic behavior; rather, for them, it is the social category of gender that often correlates with language choice. Labov (1990:218) has also pointed out that "the mechanism of change is . . . not linked to sex differences in any clear and simple way. Either sex can be dominant." Recall, too, that Fasold (1990) showed that sociolinguistic gender pattern did not always hold. The variation observed in table 2 was caused by the tendency for older males in this neighborhood to use higher frequencies of the vernacular variants of variables than the other groups. This is captured in table 3 below.

Table 3: Comparison of overall mean percentages of choices of vernacular
variants of selected variables by respondents in the EVLP
with choices made by respondents in the 60+ age group

Variables	60 + (mean %)		All age groups (mean %)	
	F	M	F	M
/ay/→[aː]	64.0	82.8	58.3	58.3
/r/→ zero,V	45.7	59.4	38.6	36.9
/ɛ/→[ɪ]	30.8	32.4	35.5	26.6
/ɪ/→[iy]	5.8	8.2	13.0	8.7

Note that males in the oldest age group (60+) chose more vernacular linguistic variants than older females, especially in the cases of variables (ay) and (r). In the case of the (r) variable the men in the 60+ age group chose the vernacular variant 59.4% of the time compared to 45.7% for the females. This result was consistent with the finding of the pilot study, partially reproduced in table 2, where it was shown that for the (r) variable working-class men chose the vernacular variant 66.2% of the time compared to 29.7% for women. A similar disparity between men and women was noted for the vernacular variant of (ay) in the pilot study. In the EVLP, because, for the (r) and (ay) variables, males in the 60+ age group used many more vernacular variants than females, there was a significant difference (p < 0.05) between the male and female respondents in terms of their average percentage of vernacular linguistic choices.

We should note in table 3 that of the other two variables presented—i.e., (ɪ) and (iy)—the percentage means for men and women are not substantially different. I take this as additional evidence that sex is influencing the choice of the variants of (ay) and (r). The information in table 3 would suggest that the so-called sociolinguistic gender pattern still holds but only for selected variables and principally in the oldest age group.

This brings us to the problem of explaining why the older males in the EVLP sample adopted the vernacular variants of (r) and (ay) for culturally symbolic use while the older females did not. Part of the explanation might be that the older males in this neighborhood generally have a more focused linguistic experience (in the sense of Le Page and Tabouret-Keller 1985) since they were the residents that interacted least with people outside the neighborhood (see Edwards 1992). One would expect that the retention of southern linguistic forms would be facilitated by the continual reinforcement of frequent and exclusive intragroup interactions among people who learned their dialect from southern folk or were themselves from the South. Since the oldest males in the sample came into contact least frequently with Whites and middle-class African-Americans living outside the neighborhood, they were most likely to retain southern speech characteristics, including the vernacular variants of (ay) and (r). This notion is supported by Myhill's findings in New York and Philadelphia. Myhill (1988:212) found that African-American residents who had very little contact with Whites used the BEV /r/ deletion rule much more frequently than African-Americans who interacted frequently with Whites. This finding essentially corroborated the conclusions of Labov and Harris (1986) in which it was argued that, generally, the increasing isolation of working-class African-Americans in the inner-city areas of northern cities is leading to increasing linguistic differences between that group and Whites.

AGE AND LANGUAGE

I now wish to explore interaction of the independent variable AGE GROUP with choice of linguistic variant and to see how this interaction affects the retention or disappearance of southern linguistic forms.

Table 4: Results of Scheffe Post HOC tests done on ANOVAs
(shaded areas link pairs of groups significantly different at the p < 0.05 level)

Mean Percentages		*26–39*	*18–25*
Vernacular variant of (ay)			
39.5	26–39		
56.8	18–25		
59.2	40–59	▓	
73.5	60+	▓	
Vernacular variant of (r)			
21.6	26–39		
26.3	18–25		
45.0	40–59	▓	▓
52.6	60+	▓	▓
All vernacular variants			
27.8	26–39		
28.1	18–25		
32.3	40–59		
39.1	60+	▓	▓

For the EVLP the random sample of 66 informants was grouped in the following age ranges: 18–25; 26–39; 40–59; 60 and above. When respondents were grouped in this way the independent variable AGE correlated significantly ($p < 0.01$) with average percentage of the vernacular variant of the (ay) variable. Table 4 gives the results of a Scheffe Post HOC Procedure indicating that respondents in the 40–59 and 60+ age groups used significantly higher percentages of the vernacular variant of this variable than respondents in the 26–39 age group. Table 4 also shows that for variable (r), respondents in the two oldest age groups (40–59 and 60+) used a significantly higher percentage of the vernacular variant than respondents in the two younger age groups and that respondents in the oldest age group averaged a significantly higher percentage of vernacular variants than respondents in the 18–25, and 26–39 age groups.

The independent variable AGE was also re-coded into the following ranges: 18–35, 36–39, and 50+. When grouped in this way AGE was again significantly correlated with choice of the vernacular variants of (ay) and (r). In this case respondents in the 50+ age group used significantly higher percentages of the vernacular variants of the variables than respondents in the two younger age groups.

The figures in table 4, therefore, indicate that younger people are less inclined than older people in this neighborhood to use vernacular variants of linguistic variables. Thus, younger people are learning the new northern norms while the older people are manifesting the old southern linguistic habits.

IMPLICATIONS FOR LINGUISTIC CHANGE

What does all this imply for language change? The data given in tables 1–4 suggest that in a general way, and for the linguistic variables I analyzed, the incidence of the southern linguistic features African-Americans brought with them when they migrated north to Detroit are becoming quantitatively more like that of Whites in the Detroit area. That general finding has, perforce, to be taken with a number of caveats, which I mentioned above. One is that some features appear to have become linguistic symbols of community culture. In this study /r/ deletion seems to have this status for the older working-class African-American males.

Information in tables 2 and 3 shows that in Detroit some traditional southern linguistic features are moving more rapidly than others toward quantitative values that resemble those of the general population and that the most linguistically conservative individuals are males who are 60 years or older.

Table 4 indicates that in some linguistic features younger people are consistently choosing fewer vernacular variants. Thus, it seems that, over time, these young speakers will change (for these features) the character of the linguistic culture in the neighborhood to make it resemble more closely that of the general linguistic culture of the Detroit metropolitan area. The reasons for this linguistic difference between younger and older respondents in this neighborhood are complex but results from the Vernacular Language Project suggest that what Milroy and Milroy (1992) might refer to as "loose network ties" to the neighborhood is the main principle. The Milroys argue that individuals who have loose ties with their communities are less likely than those with strong ties to use vernacular linguistic norms. In the EVLP, younger respondents were more likely than older respondents to have social or occupational contact with Whites and middle-class African-Americans and therefore to have linguistic models for acculturative behaviors, if they choose to acculturate linguistically. Expressed in terms of the Milroys' position we could argue that younger people in the Detroit neighborhood studied had looser ties with their community than older residents, both physically and psychologically, and thus were less likely than their parents and grandparents to conform to the neighborhood linguistic norms. This hypothesis seems to receive support from the information in table 4. There we see, somewhat surprisingly, that respondents in the 26–39 age group consistently used fewer vernacular linguistic variants than members of the 18–25 age group. This pattern could be explained by the observation made by EVLP fieldworkers that the members of the 26–39 age group were generally more geographically mobile, less bound to the neighborhood than their younger peers. Most members of 18–25 were unemployed and were forced by that status to interact with their parents and grandparents.

Southern Speech and Self-Expression in an African-American Woman's Story

Barbara Johnstone

In overviews of the current state of scholarship on Southern American English, both Guy Bailey and Michael Montgomery (this volume) encourage us to explore new modes of explanation for variability in the speech of particular southerners and among groups of southern speakers. Referring to work done by Bernstein (1993), Bailey points out that at most 27% of the phonological variability uncovered in his own large study of Texas speakers turned out to be accountable for with reference to the most commonly adduced social categories such as ethnicity, age, and gender. (Only 9% of the variability in one set of variables correlated with such social facts.) To understand the rest of the variability we must, Bailey urges, pay increased attention to new explanatory variables. Montgomery suggests what some of these variables might be, wondering about how southerners' uses of the markers of southern speech might be related to "the identity and purposes of Southerners and Northerners."

Several contributors to this volume explore, in one way or another, how the "identity and purposes" of southern speakers are connected with how they talk. Cukor-Avila shows how supplementing traditional sociolinguistic interviews with ethnographic techniques can lead to a deeper understanding of what it is about themselves and their relationships that people in a community use their linguistic resources to express. Davis uses ethnographic method, too, in exploring how adolescents understand what they do with language and how speech and setting are related. Johnson adduces cultural and psychological explanations for the persistence of lexical variation between town and country, when regional differences are disappearing. Preston examines the symbolic importance of southern speech, using various techniques to discover how people conceive of Southern ways of talking.

This essay is also about how "identity and purpose" help in understanding how southern linguistic resources are used in talk.[1] Part of my aim is also to illustrate how the particularistic focus of discourse analysis in the philological tradition helps clarify reasons for variation that can be blurred in work done from a more holistic, social-deterministic perspective. I suggest that some familiar ways of explaining why utterances and texts take the shapes they do result in incomplete explanations, because they take only the social into account and not the individual. My text is a bit of discourse I have been studying for some time: part of the life story of an African-American woman in her late 50s.

It should be clear from the fact that I am talking here about a single text that what I am reporting on is neither a quantitative study nor a study, except in its implications, of variation among different speakers or groups of speakers. My approach to linguistic variation is based in the close-reading techniques of discourse analysis, or "the linguistics of the particular" (Becker 1984, 1988). Discourse analysts sometimes attempt to explain particular utterances and texts solely in terms of the social categories that have proven useful in understanding large-scale patterns of variation—class, gender, region, and so on. When we do this, we are failing to take advantage of what is precisely the main benefit of our research methodology and the main way our methodology can contribute to dialectology and quantitative sociolinguistics. This is the usefulness of discourse analysis for uncovering the mechanisms of variation among individual speakers and texts. In ways quantitative modes of analysis cannot, careful searches for patterns in particular texts and their correlations with purposes can help us understand the actual reasons why a particular person talks a particular way on a particular occasion.

THE STORY AND ITS AUTHOR

Mattie Blair[2] was born in Georgia; she spent her childhood there and her adulthood in Michigan, Indiana, and California. Blair told her story to me (a white woman then in my early 30s) several months before her death, from brain cancer, in 1985. She was then a patient in a church-sponsored convalescent home in Fort Wayne, Indiana. When the home's Activities Director asked what she would like to do with her time, Mrs. Blair said that she would like to tell her "story" and have someone write it down and publish it. She had led an interesting life, she said. Comparing her story to that of the author of the recently televised *Roots* series, she told me that what she had to tell was "as good as anything Alex Haley wrote about." I agreed to record Mrs. Blair's story. I listened to her talk about her life for ten or twelve hours during the summer of 1984, and I have been trying ever since to find ways to understand why she said what she did and why she said it the way she did.

It was clear to both Mrs. Blair and me that aspects of her history and her language had to do with her shaping by race, ethnicity, gender, and socioeconomic status. She mentioned variations in skin color often in descriptions of people and made references to African-American ways of doing things. She was clearly aware of connections between language and ethnicity, too, stopping, for example, to explain African-American slang to me. She very often attributed troubles in her life to her being poor and female and, in her childhood, rural and southern. But it was also clear to both of us that Mrs. Blair's life, and her telling of it, were not generic. This was *her* story, not the story of a type, and she wanted it treated as a particular biography, not as a representative case study. In treating it that way—looking for Mattie Blair's particular reasons for saying what she did—I respect her wishes. I also become able to illuminate aspects of the language of the story that I would miss if I thought of the text simply as an example of African-American women's narrative, or of southern speech, or of the speech of the generation of the 1920s, or some other combination of demographic facts like these.

The moment I started the tape recorder on our first visit, Mrs. Blair began her story: "Well as you know, my name is Mattie Margaret Blair, born December the

20th, 1926, in Chester, Georgia." She insisted, especially during the first of our eight meetings, that her story not be interrupted except for relevant reasons. She sometimes referred to the story as a book and gave thought to possible titles. On the basis of the ten or twelve hours of tape I made, I could not provide a complete chronology of Mrs. Blair's life, but I could piece together most of it. "Sonny" is from the second of our sessions. The text is transcribed in lines corresponding to breath groups (Chafe 1980, 1987); line spaces separate episodes, which I discuss below. In addition to conventional punctuation, ellipses (of one or more periods) represent short silences; colons represent lengthened syllables. Parentheses enclose parts that I and many other listeners have been unable to figure out. My back-channeling and nonverbal noises are in angled brackets.

SONNY

Uh, he was an entertainer.
I met him at . . uh (   ) out there, at Fontana,
and uh, his name was Sonny.
And him and Doc became good friends.
5 And uh . . . Sonny was . . real nice.
He had a . . new car, first car I ever rode in had a record player in it, a tape
    or whatever.
<Um-hm>
And him and Doc was very good friends.

So he has . . he eh, eh got, carried me someplace with him that day,
to the insurance company,
10 t– to to take out insurance on his car.
And while he was in there,
eh the man was out,
and he tore <(cough)> a bunch of checks out of the back of the checkbook,
insurance checks.
15 Well you know those type of checks,
it's checks like you can write 'em any amount, like you have an accident.
<uh-huh>

So uh, he goes around cashing checks, buying me, uh,
'cause I've always I'monna be truthful with you,
always been a clothes freak.
20 I l:ove pretty clothes, here I am blind.
And the first time he give me a piece of . a dress or something I bit it!
<Uh-huh>
You know, you know how you feel everything?, I don't know.
I said "Yeah, this is good material!"
And I used to be fond of Lili Ann suits.
25 But anyway, this Sonny cashed all of them checks,
and I found out about it,
that he had made about . . seven eight hundred dollars, they–

I don't never known that, I always been kind of a dummy, 'cause I was
     brought up that way, old *country* old dumb country girl.
If I hadda been brought up hip like the little city girls, I'd have some sense.
30 But I was raised down there in them cotton fields, you know I ain't had no
     sense, anybody could use me.
So he goes to work and uh cash them checks that day,
and he e– he showed me all this money.
And he carried me in the store,
and all I got out of it was he said . to cash another check,
35 (*I bought?*) all them groceries see.
And (*I just got?*) "Get anything you want. Get anything you want." [mimics
     whispered voice]
And I was putting that stuff in the, in the uh . . buggy,
and he just wrote this check and give it to the woman and she'd give him
     back the change.

And then uh, . . so he, I said "What are you . . ooo?"
40 And he had wa– a:ll that money.
And so he told me "Honey, you be doing that all today with me?"
And he said oh we'd buy, oh we would need to buy something, a little
     something, not too much,
and people'd give him back money, and he'd give them a piece of paper.
<Uh-huh>
And so I said "Ohh my God." [disbelieving semiwhisper]
45 And he said "Yeah, you didn't know I was a paper-hanger, baby?"
I said "What– who you hang paper for?"
I thought he meant hang paper on the walls!
<(laughter)>
I told you I wasn't nothing but a dumb– old *country*– ignorant Georgia girl.
<(cough)>
50 And he meant hang paper write checks.
And he said "Hey."
Said he was gonna go with me,
to this place, where he was gonna take me,
he– he'd give me some money.
55 I said "Uuu uh-hn, no:, uh-hn,"
I said "I ain't going no place with you."
And uh, he just caught me by the arm and pushed me and shoved me in the
     car,
said "Oh yeah, you're going."
And they told me . he was smoking marijuana, he was you know he was a
     dope addict.
60 And I said "No: uh-un."
So he taken me to this here here here motel,
and I crawled through the window and got out the window and run and went
     to the motel office.
And that's what saved me from him.

So, soon as I got back and could find Doc, I told Doc.

65 So Doc got his gun,
   and went looking for his rump.
   And when Doc– uh uh everybody told Doc,
   say eh "I seen him. Oh he– I seen him over there."
   He went to every big tavern in in in in in in– San Bernardino.
70 Finally, we didn't find him so we went on home.

   So he was so ignorant,
   he (*goes to work?*) and gets in his pretty car,
   and come over there and knock on my door,
   on 30th Street, and say "Hey, I know that that old– that man of yours was
      looking for me."
75 And here Doc say "Yeah man, I sure was."
   I didn't know he was look– listening, I thought he was in there watching
      television.
   But he gon always peek to see who at the door, don't want nobody come in,
      think it's some man come looking for me.
   And so Doc say "Yeah, man" say "I sure was looking for you." [mimics high
      whiny voice]
   And he said "Well here I am, big man, what you want?"
80 And so Doc say he's "Aww, man."
   And next thing I know *pumm*.
   Shot him right through the head,
   right there in my doorway.
   And I said "Oh my God" my kids went to running went to hollering went to
      screaming,
85 I run and went to hollering, run across,
   uh them old little stickers that (*put?*) in your feet,
   and went to running went to run–
   I told you about he hid in the church.
   You know he hid in the church when he killed that boy.

90 So he went on to the penitentiary, and uh . . .
   They had me accessory to the fact, but he pleaded guilty,
   you know 'cause I didn't pull no trigger,
   but you know they had to go through the whole procedure.

In what follows, I examine three aspects of the language of the "Sonny" story. For each of the three, I ask "Why did Mattie Blair do this rather than doing something else?" And each time I ask that question I provide two explanations, one having to do with the general social determinants of variation and one having to do with more individual, particular determinants. The three things I look at are

1) one element of the story's syntax: Mrs. Blair's use of negative concord and the negative auxiliary *ain't*,
2) one fact about the vocabulary in the story: her use of the verbs *take* and *carry*, and
3) the overall structure of the story: how it is divided into parts and how the parts fit together and flow into each other.

USES OF SOUTHERN SPEECH IN "SONNY"

Negative Concord and *Ain't*

Mattie Blair's speech is nonstandard in a number of ways. She uses verb forms such as *he taken, he cash*, and *he give* in the preterit; *them* as a demonstrative pronoun; the expression "him and Doc" instead of "Doc and he." She also employs negative concord, the repeated expression of negation throughout a negative clause. And she uses *ain't* to mean several things, among them the equivalent of *did not*, as, for example, in line 30: "But I was raised down there in them cotton fields, you know I ain't had no sense, anybody could use me."

Thinking about this fact from the *social* perspective, one explanation is clear: Blair uses double negation and *ain't* this way because she is relatively untrained in standard English; this has to do with social oppression related to being poor and African-American. This feature of Blair's speech could be used as an example of socially constrained variation.

But the social mode of explanation does not provide the whole picture. Thinking about Blair's nonstandard speech from the perspective of the *individual* provides an additional layer of understanding of her uses of *ain't*. The negation patterns which mark Mattie Blair's as nonstandard were part of her repertoire of linguistic resources, and she used socially marked, nonstandard forms variably as symbolic tools in the depiction of herself as a character in the story. Though negative concord is consistent throughout the story, and thus cannot be said to reflect the result of choice, Blair's use of *ain't* as an equivalent for *did not* in the first person singular is not consistent. Describing herself as an incompetent country girl, she used the lower-status form, "I ain't had no sense," in line 30. But describing herself as being in the right after the murder, she used a more standard form: in line 92, she said "you know 'cause I didn't pull no trigger" (instead of "I ain't pulled no trigger"). Blair's use of nonstandardness in the depiction of versions of herself results on one occasion in overreaching the mark, in the ungrammatical (that is, inconsistent with her own grammar), hyper-nonstandard form in line 28: "I don't never known that, I always been kind of a dummy."

Focusing on the individual speaker and the particular utterance here encourages us to think about creative use of resources rather than socially determined behavior and provides, in this case, a way of understanding inconsistency that makes more sense than most ways of understanding inconsistency (as performance error or free variation) in more holistically oriented sociolinguistics.

Take and *Carry*

Mattie Blair chose among two verbs, *take* and *carry*, where some speakers of English would have only one choice, *take*. In the Sonny story, *carry* seems to signify willing accompaniment: Sonny "carries" her to places she wants to go, as in line 8, "So he has . . he eh, eh got, *carried* me someplace with him that day," and in line 33, "And he *carried* me in the store" to pick out clothes and groceries. *Take*, on the other hand, appears when Mattie does not want to accompany Sonny. Sonny "takes" her to the motel, as in line 52,

51 Said he was gonna go with me,
52 to this place, where he was gonna *take* me,
53 he- he'd give me some money.

or in line 61, "So he *taken* me to this here here here motel."

Why did Mattie Blair use *take* and *carry* in these ways, and what did she mean by doing so? The obvious social explanation has to do with regional variation. *Carry* can mean, for speakers of southern varieties, something close to what *take* means: "to escort, accompany; to take, bring," according to the *Dictionary of American Regional English* (Cassidy 1985:550). Her knowledge of southern possibilities provided Blair with a way of creating meaning that someone who was not a southerner would have to create another way.

But the contrast Blair set up with her uses of *carry* and *take* between willing accompaniment and forced accompaniment is not one suggested by the *DARE* entry on *carry*. Blair had two choices available because she spoke a Southern variety, but what the two verbs mean in this story is a result of their juxtaposition in this story, which is tinged with but not solely a result of their meaning in the abstract. This is one approach to thinking about Blair's choices of *take* and *carry* from the perspective of the individual, and it results in our being reminded that the meanings of words a person chooses are not dictated by the variety he or she is speaking when choosing them. The variety provides resources, but the use of those resources is an individual matter.

We might also think about the meanings of *take* and *carry* in this story from the perspective of another individual, the original audience to the story. Except in listening to children and to people whose ways of speaking are very different from ours, we do not often hear true linguistic novelty: familiar forms being used for the very first time to express unfamiliar meanings, or brand-new forms or meanings. This is because most of the things we hear are not new and because our theories of language, both folk and scholarly, do not provide us with ways of incorporating newness. But I did notice something new when I listened to this story for the first time, in May 1984: it was the first time I had ever heard anybody use *carry* to mean anything like *take*. (At that time I was completely unfamiliar with Southern and African-American ways of talking, having lived only in nonindustrial university towns in the Northeast and Midwest.) So my decisions about the meanings of *take* and *carry* in the story and the contrast between them was the result of regional variation only in a negative way. To me, what Blair was doing sounded idiosyncratic, a creative choice made by her, entirely individual.[3]

Discourse Structure

The plot of Mattie Blair's story is the plot of tragedy. The story involves slowly but inexorably rising tension leading to a climax made inevitable by a tragic flaw in the protagonist's character: "ignorance," as Mrs. Blair would have called it, by which she meant not just lack of knowledge of certain facts, but an almost willful naiveté, an inability to deal quickly or smartly with the world.[4] The structure of the story reflects its plot. The outcome of Mrs. Blair's story seems inevitable. There are no clues about the ending before it happens and thus no reason to think about alternatives to it, so there seem at first to have been no options. Blair's long, relatively complex verbal lines, the relatively unpredictable criteria for scene-setting that force her hearer simply to follow rather than anticipate, her consistent use of the result-toned transition marker *so*, and her unevaluated, emotionless summaries throughout all contribute to the tragic effect of her story.

In the first scene, Mattie and Sonny go to the insurance company (lines 8–16). Mrs. Blair announces the beginning of the scene with *so*. "So he has . . he eh, eh got, carried me someplace with him that day, to the insurance company, t- to take out insurance on his car." *So* is a discourse marker (Schiffrin 1987) that is often used for the purpose of showing when a new "paragraph" of spoken discourse starts. *So* is consistently enough used as a boundary-marker in discourse to be defined that way in at least one desk dictionary (*Webster's Ninth New Collegiate Dictionary* 1983). However, *so* has a dual effect; it is also a marker of result. Connecting two clauses with *so* is thus ambiguous. To say, as Mrs. Blair does, "so he carried me someplace with him that day" suggests that Mattie's going off with Sonny is the inevitable result of knowing him, or of his being Doc's friend. Mrs. Blair's story continues to present new events as being connected to previous ones in this quasi-causal way, and the effect is to suggest that the events of the story flowed inexorably out of one another.

In the next episode, Sonny "goes around cashing checks" (lines 18–38). Like the first, this episode begins with *so*.

> So uh, he goes around cashing checks, buying me, uh,
> 'cause I've always I'monna be truthful with you,
> always been a clothes freak.

Sonny's check-cashing is presented three times in this segment:

> So uh, he goes around cashing checks (line 17)
> But anyway, this Sonny cashed all of them checks (line 25)
> So he goes to work and uh cash them checks that day (line 31)

In between, Mrs. Blair talks about her character in the story, about how Mattie had "always been a clothes freak" and why she didn't understand sooner what Sonny was up to: "I always been kind of a dummy, 'cause I was brought up that way." After the third mention of the only real action in this section, she tells how the scam worked. The structure of the narration perfectly fits the developing understanding of the Mattie character, first unthinkingly accepting pretty clothes, then wondering why Sonny has so much money but still not citified or hip enough to know why, then finally catching on. At the end of the segment, Mrs. Blair summarizes: "And he just wrote this check and give it to the woman and she'd give him back the change."

In the third part of the story (lines 39–63), Mattie realizes what is happening and finds out exactly what her role is to be. This scene portrays a new state of knowledge. It is signaled by the summary before it, and by *then*—here not indicating a temporal shift, but rather a rhetorical one—and, again, *so*: "And then uh, . . so he, I said 'What are you . . ooo?'" The aside in this segment about the "dumb old *country* ignorant Georgia girl" echoes the one in the previous scene. As she did in the preceding scene, Mrs. Blair ends this one with a summation: "And that's what saved me from him."

The next scene starts, as have previous scenes, with *so*. A new character comes into play here, namely Doc, and the temporal framework changes, the change marked with a subordinate modifying clause. "So, soon as I got back and could find Doc, I told Doc." A summary marks the end of the scene—"Finally, we didn't find him so we went on home," and character and point of view shift into the next, the initial *he* ("So he was so ignorant") now having to be taken as referring to Sonny rather than Doc. The new scene, beginning at line 71, is marked at the beginning (not surprisingly) with *so*. As have others, this scene ends with a summation, "he killed that boy." Not having been foreshadowed in any way, this event comes as a surprise. Sonny's "ignorance" leads him blindly into trouble, as Mattie's ignorance did her. The final segment of the story presents its aftermath, in a flat, reportorial way:

> So he went on to the penitentiary, and uh . . .
> They had me accessory to the fact, but he pleaded guilty,
> you know 'cause I didn't pull no trigger,
> but you know they had to go through the whole procedure . . .

Unlike many of the spontaneous storytellers sociolinguists have studied, Mrs. Blair provides no moral for her story. She ends the story without commenting on its significance in any way. Instead, she simply mentions the final result, "so he went on to the penitentiary," and the part of it that was most relevant to her: "they had me accessory to the fact." She goes on, in subsequent talk, to a different episode of her life involving a different man and a different place.

The way Mrs. Blair's story is structured contrasts sharply with the way many white Americans organize narratives of personal experience, as sets of temporal episodes (often there are three such episodes), each building on the one before, so that hearers can anticipate possible outcomes before the end.[5] This way of structuring a story is strongly reminiscent of the structure of many less spontaneous and more consciously performed genres of talk. American jokes, for example, very often have this structure, as do many Euro-American folk tales: there are three main characters, or something happens three times. In all these cases, and others, the third episode provides the resolution or completes the pattern.

Why is Mrs. Blair's story structured as it is? A social answer might refer to ethnicity. With the exception of some work by Etter-Lewis (1991a, 1991b, 1993), there is little published work about African-American women's discourse style in narrative. It has been suggested, though, that factual recountings of personal experience (i.e., recountings meant to be taken as factual) may occupy a different place in the set of things African-Americans do with talk than in the set of things white Americans do. Work by Kochman (1981) suggests that personal information of the sort Mattie Blair was giving me is less freely or comfortably given by Blacks than by Whites. Heath (1983) contrasts the factual norms by which working-class white southerners evaluate personal anecdotes—such stories have to tell the truth and have clear morals involving lessons the teller learned—with the requirement among working-class African-American southerners that stories be entertaining above all, a requirement that may give rise to overtly fictional versions of personal experience. McLeod-Porter (1991) shows that one reason adolescent African-American boys are, as a group, often evaluated as nonfluent, immature writers is that the narrative writing tasks used as diagnostics violate cultural constraints on divulging personal information.

But there is also a more particular, individual answer to the question, "Why does this story have the structure it does?" It has to do with the most basic reason for personal narrative, namely, the creation and expression of a unique self. When people transform personal experience into stories, they create meaning on three levels. In the first place, people tell stories to create and share knowledge about the world. Second, people tell stories to evoke and create interpersonal relationships; stories shape, and are shaped by, the interactions in which they occur, and stories reflect and mold the social relationships they tell about, too.

A third sort of meaning in stories is personal. Stories express people's individuality; "acting yourself" is speaking yourself, telling your own stories. People perform their identities as they act and talk (Goffman 1959), calling attention to who they are as they call attention to the ways they choose for creating meaning and coherence in their stories. This involves showing that one is a person at all, that is, an autonomous member of the species with a temporally continuous history (Hallowell 1955). Creating a human self in discourse is the most basic reason for narrative; this is what accounts for what Harold Rosen has called the "autobiographical impulse" (Rosen 1988). Children differentiate themselves from others when they notice that different things happen to them than to others, that they can, in other words, have different life stories than anyone else (Bruner 1986). When there are temporal holes in people's life histories, people can lose their sanity, and sanity can sometimes be regained, in therapy, by constructing a new, complete life narrative (Schafer 1981). Speaking oneself also involves showing what kind of person one is, both explicitly and implicitly. Speakers create selves in narrative via choices of theme (you are the history you create) and via choices of language (you are how you talk). Stories are always covert performances of self, and sometimes they are overt ones.

This function of narration sheds light on the most basic facts about Mrs. Blair's life story. The themes of her narratives, their structures, and their sounds and syntax are all relevant to the self she is creating in her discourse. Mrs. Blair's story is an explicit attempt to create a meaningful life—part of her "book." This is serious business, and the story has the serious structure of tragedy, a structure that allows for reflection and revision and in which the meaning emerges slowly. This illuminates, for example, the digressions about the young "country" Mattie, which are syntactically more complex than the rest of the story and uttered in longer breath groups. In creating her life, Blair drew on the linguistic resources available to her. But she also, as we have seen in connection with each aspect of the story we have examined, used available resources to create new ones.

Different speakers tell different stories about themselves, and they tell them differently. More generally, language is variable from individual to individual. This is a familiar fact; we would be astonished, in fact, to hear two different people speak exactly the same way. Discourse analysts sometimes try to account for facts about the particular texts they examine purely with reference to demographic categories that have helped account for variation among groups of speakers. But such explanations leave out part of the process. People talk differently because they are creating different selves in discourse. To do this, they use the resources available to them, reshaping the "prior texts" (Becker 1994) provided by things they have heard, read, and said before. These resources vary, depending on people's language, dialect, gender, and so on, but we need to remind ourselves that an utterance does not take the shape it does *because* its teller is black, poor, or female; or because her audience is captive; or because she is uninhibited. The influence of society, situation, and psychology on language is indirect: the role of social, rhetorical, and psychological differences is that they provide differential resources for talk. Social, psychological, and rhetorical facts are mediated by the individual, who selects and combines linguistic resources available in his or her environment to create a voice, a voice with which not just to refer to the world or relate to others, but a voice with which to be human.

NOTES

1. I am grateful to Judith Mattson Bean and A. L. Becker for helpful critiques of a draft of this essay. I have expanded upon the discussion in this essay in chapter 2 of Johnstone 1996.

2. The name has been partly changed, in case Mrs. "Blair's" family might object to its use. Mattie herself very much wanted her story identified with her name, so I have kept that part of it.

3. Not being able to tell the conventional from the idiosyncratic, the mundane from the creative, is both an advantage and a disadvantage for the linguistic outsider. It means extra work for the fieldworker—I would never have been able to talk about Mrs. Blair's story without lots of research into African-American language and ways of speaking—but it also brings extra opportunities to notice differences and wonder about them.

4. The specific tragic genre I have in mind here is Greek tragedy of the sort described by Aristotle in the *Poetics*. It is a kind of tragedy that crucially involves predestination and fatal god-given character flaws.

5. See Polanyi (1985) and Johnstone (1990).

Ambrose Gonzales's Gullah:
What It May Tell Us about Variation

Katherine Wyly Mille

As an outgrowth of my historical study of Gullah (or Sea Island) Creole (Mille 1990), this paper conveys the importance of the literary dialect writing of Ambrose Gonzales (1857–1926) as a resource to the study of Gullah's history and a background against which to evaluate present-day variation in the creole. My conclusions are based on an analysis of the tense-mood-aspect system of Gonzales's Gullah and of the variation present in his texts.

Arguments that variation in Gullah speech communities is evidence of decreolization (Bickerton 1975) assume that an earlier stage in the life-cycle of the creole contained little or no variation but rather had a more uniformly basilectal system (Mufwene 1987). Mufwene (1987, 1991a) argues that there exists no evidence to support this assumption. Nichols (1989:4) has pointed out that 18th-century newspaper ads for runaway slaves occasionally describe their language—sometimes as "good English," sometimes as "good Black English" (seeming to indicate a distinctive variety), with those considered "new" to the country described as speaking little or no English.

Nevertheless, historical analysis of Gullah has been hampered by the absence of early records. Except for the WPA Ex-Slave Narratives, which reflect a "careful style of speech" (Brewer 1986b:132) and which, according to Montgomery (1991a), are of questionable reliability, and for data from Turner's.(1949) informants, an historical record of the language exists mainly through literary and popular representations, anecdotal comments, and short linguistic commentaries by white observers who themselves displayed varying competencies in Gullah and used an abundance of eye-dialect. Bickerton (1975) and Rickford (1987) have, however, found the historical literary texts from Pinckard, McTurk (alias Quow), and others to be of use in reconstructing Guyanese Creole's past. Similarly, in the case of Gullah, the historical literary dialect writing of Ambrose Gonzales can provide particularly helpful clues.

However much literary dialect writers desired to record Gullah for posterity, some also made erroneous linguistic claims, and passed on for the amusement of their readers disparaging and damaging racial stereotypes, all the more insidious for their being presented with paternalistic affection for Gullah speakers. Gonzales (1922) has often been quoted from his Foreword where he—or someone writing on his behalf (Stewart p.c.)—makes disturbing, racially based claims for Gullah's distinctiveness. This view reminds today's reader of the prevailing assumptions of Gonzales' time and prepares the reader for caricatures based on race, social class, and gender that pervade the stories. Mufwene (1991a) suggests that Gonzales' caricature of the Gullah people might falsify his version of Gullah by relying on a caricature of its linguistic features. In any case, Gonzales frequently portrays Gullah speakers using malapropisms and what he undoubtedly considered comic twists on English multisyllabic words.

Gonzales did, however, inspire strong endorsement from most of his contemporaries for what they saw as an authentic use of Gullah. After the success of his Gullah sketches published in *The State* newspaper in 1892 (Columbia, SC) and, after a long hiatus in his dialect writing, Gonzales received in 1916 a widely circulated petition from his friends, urging him to write again (Smith 1977). In a time when Gullah-inspired tales were fashionable, Gonzales was singled out as being exceptional in his ability as a white man to write the language in a manner faithful to its models.

His fluency in Gullah was acquired at an early age. Born in 1857, Gonzales spent his childhood on family plantations near Edisto and Hilton Head, reared by and among Gullah-speakers, hunting and fishing with young black companions (Smith 1926a). The family home having been burned during the Civil War, the Gonzaleses lived for a time in reduced circumstances in an outside kitchen left standing, neighbors to the newly freed African-Americans.

Gonzales's version of Gullah as he remembered it from his youth has been considered by some present-day Gullah scholars, Stewart chief among them, to be the best source available from that period (Stewart 1988; see also Cassidy 1978). Reinecke et al. (1975:468) state, "Writers such as Gonzales have represented Negro speech with an accuracy approaching transcription; others have knowingly or unwittingly distorted it almost beyond recognition." Haskell (1964:238–41) compares Gonzales's phonological representation of Gullah with the dialectal phonology of single-word entries from the field records of the *Linguistic Atlas of the Middle and South Atlantic States*, finding Gonzales's particularly subtle shades of phonological variation to be substantiated in the Atlas. Gonzales is also sometimes cited by scholars referring to the use of specific forms in Gullah (e.g., Nichols 1976; Mufwene and Gilman 1987; Cassidy 1978). Indeed, prior to the advent of creolistics, Gonzales displayed competency in the grammatical features linguists would later inventory in attempts to describe creole languages. The point to be made is that it is Gonzales's syntax and grammar, despite his characterization of Gullah people, that is worthy of inquiry.

I undertook analysis of the tense-mood-aspect (TMA) system in three of Gonzales's books, *The Black Border* (1922), *The Captain* (1924a), and *Laguerre* (1924b). When scanned into computer memory, they yielded a total of 10,222 lines (85,388 words) representing Gullah. A preliminary analysis of approximately 700 lines, with passages selected from various parts of the three texts and hand-coded, yielded an inventory of forms marking the Verb Phrase (VP) as well as zero tense marking. Gonzales's consistent orthography made it possible then to search for VP markers in the larger corpus with the help of the Oxford Concordance Program. Virtually all tokens with their immediate environments and locations were identified in the analysis; each valid token was examined in its full context and then coded for semantic content and structural contexts.

Importantly, if one shifts from hunting basilectal TMA features, one also finds features in Gonzales's texts which are usually identified as mesolectal and acrolectal. In other words, features uniquely creole as well as features shared with local English speakers are present, often in the same phrase. In the charts that follow, the distinction will be made between non-English Gullah forms (GUL) and the intersection of Gullah and local English (GUL/LENG) in order to represent the continuum as it appears in Gonzales's Gullah.[1]

The line-numbering in the concordance also provided a means of examining intratextual variation. It became predictable, for example, that a higher incidence of acrolectal TMA markers would occur in those lines coming from the last fourteen stories of the first book, *The Black Border*. That section consists of the stories written and published in *The State* newspaper in the spring of 1892, when Gonzales was thirty-five years old. The remaining twenty-eight stories were written and published in 1918 and later combined with the earlier stories to create *The Black Border*, published during the year 1922.

Further analysis of Gonzales's texts reveals the same kind of variation between non-English features and those shared with local English speakers that one has come to expect in modern samples of Gullah speech, not only in lexical items but also in the grammatical categories mapped out by the TMA system of Gullah. This finding calls into question, on the one hand, any assumption that a literary account of Gullah would necessarily fail to provide a useful corpus for historical analysis, and, on the other, the assumption of Gullah's earlier uniformity as a basilect. If one assumes that Gonzales probably exaggerated the frequency of those features not shared with local English speakers (and one of his contemporaries claimed he did) in order to create a Gullah stereotype, then an even higher percentage of shared features can be inferred for the period. Indeed, one of his contemporaries, the Reverend John G. Williams (1895) commented on Gonzales's 1892 publication in the following terms: "Mr. Gonzale's [sic] Gullah is as perfect as it can be written, and he is easily the first honor man in that school. The lowcountry negro's [sic] description of a jackass to a negro who has never seen a jackass, 'E look same like a mule, only mo'so,' is almost true of Mr. Gonzale's Gullah."

The early text to which Williams refers, in fact, exhibits a greater number of grammatical features shared with local English speakers than Gonzales's later publications exhibit. This discrepancy suggests a tendency by Gonzales increasingly to codify his representation of Gullah, giving fuller play to the marked, and thereby more stereotypical, non-English features for the entertainment of his audience and at the same time providing copious documentation of those forms which most distinguished Gullah from English.

In view of the fact that his later writing was in response to popular demand, it is easy to see how he might attempt to focus on that which most intrigued readers of his earliest publications—the basilectal features of the creole—thus stereotyping Gullah. Stewart (p.c.) takes issue with this position and asserts that Gonzales may have deliberately "decreolized" his early text for a Columbia, SC, readership unfamiliar with Gullah, using a more accurate, basilectal version in later years. However, the continuum of TMA forms in the early text does not render the basilect more transparent, although it does reflect the kind of variation one routinely finds in modern-day Gullah. Thus it seems likely that his earlier representations, fresher in his experience, were produced less self-consciously than those of thirty years later when he set out to record the language for posterity.

ANTERIOR AND PAST TENSE

In Gullah, as in many West African languages, the tense system tends to be relative rather than absolute or absolute-relative as in English (for a broad view of TMA, see Singler 1990). This is true of Gonzales's Gullah although one finds the co-occurrence of anterior tense markers and English-like past-tense markers. Some English-like forms no doubt result from borrowing with reanalysis; these Gonzales is careful to make obvious by their placement in incongruent contexts. Others, however, suggest the possibility of access by some Gullah speakers to the English system of past marking—speakers' straddling two systems and selecting morphemes as interactions require. The co-occurrence of the two systems GUL and LENG (in conventional terms, representing the entire continuum) is noticeable primarily in the early text, as soon will become apparent.

GUL zero tense marking is one of the most salient features in Gonzales's work as a whole, accounting for nearly 85% of all [+past] VPs. Instances of zero tense marking are overwhelmingly (93%) dynamic or action verbs as opposed to stative. Once an event is established as past by some clue early in the narrative, subsequent VPs may be unmarked for tense and yet interpreted consistent with the past tense (see Le Page and Tabouret-Keller 1985:149). For this reason, every VP token had to be viewed in its larger context in order to note preceding clues of pastness. The following is an example of zero tense marking in Gonzales:[2]

(1) *I lib on Mass Kit FitzSimmun' plantesshun, w'ich'n 'e jus' done **buy** 'um de Chuesday een week befo' las' mek six munt' done gone, en' I glad 'e **buy** 'um, too, bekasew'y jis' ez soon ez 'e **buy** 'um 'e **run** dat las' husbun' w'ich I **marry** een augus' off de place . . .*
'I live on Master Kit FitzSimmon's plantation which he just finished buying six months ago Tuesday before last, and I'm glad he bought it too, because just as soon as he bought it, he ran that last husband which I married in August off the place . . .' (B2361)

Nichols (1991) has found verbal patterns of present-day blacks and whites in coastal South Carolina reflect different preferences for past-tense marking with the black community revealing zero marking for past tense, while the white community uses the traditional English system of marking tense through ablaut and -*ed*, albeit with occasional non-standard forms. In the Gonzales texts, in the case of dynamic verbs, tense is usually marked for an action or state prior to the point of reference, what Bickerton calls Anterior Tense (Bickerton 1974). Otherwise, it is typically unmarked. In the case of stative verbs, marking indicates simple past. Particularly in the early text, however, there occur instances (10.3%) of English-like marking of past through the use of inflected auxiliaries and, to a very limited degree, main verbs. Otherwise, *bin* is the most common [+anterior] marker in those VPs that are marked and occurs either as a preverbal morpheme followed by an uninflected V-stem or as a precopula morpheme followed by a zero-copula. The examples below set out the variation one finds in Gonzales from creole tense formation to English-like past tense:

(2) Anterior to another action:
     *W'en I yeddy 'bout all 'e **bin** eat . . .*
     'When I heard about all that he had eaten . . .'

(3) Anterior/dynamic verb:
     *I **ketch** (**bin ketch**) cootuh een me time.*
     'I caught (have caught) cooters in my time.'

(4) Past/stative verb:
     *I **had** (**bin hab**) um een me pocket.*
     'I had it in my pocket.'

(5) Anterior zero-copula:
     *dem buckruh' t'row me fibe dolluh bill same lukkuh dem **bin** dime.*
     'the buckras threw me five dollar bills just like (as if) they were dimes.'

(6) Strong verb inflection:
     *I **t'awt** you was a juntlemun.*
     'I thought you were a gentleman.'

(7) Strong inflection of auxiliary:
     (a) *ef him **hadduh** ketch you . . .*
          'if she had caught you . . .'
     (b) *Uh **didn'** hab chance fuh fen' fuh meself.*
          'I didn't have chance to fend for myself.'

(8) Weak verb inflection:
     *W'en I **marri'd'** um I t'aw't 'e could specify.*
     'When I married her I thought she could measure up.'

In the early text, zero tense marking occurs twenty-seven times for every *bin* and more than five times for every VP that has an overt tense marker. Based on its percentage (84.9%) of all VPs counted in the early text, one might project a minimum of 3,905 tokens of zero tense markings throughout the rest of the corpus, by holding that percentage constant, a minimum considering the frequency of other basilectal features increases in the later texts. Likewise the appearance of LENG weak inflected forms (1.6%) in the early text might be projected to be no greater than 1.6% in the later texts.[3] This allows us to speculate at least on the relative presence of anterior and past tense markers in the later texts (see table 1), using actual counts of creole *bin* and English-like strong verb inflection. The relationship between GUL *bin* and GUL/LENG strong inflected forms across the corpora illustrates the change in Gonzales's emphasis in the later texts (table 4).

In the early text, *bin* alternates more with English-like features than in subsequent writings. The eighty-four tokens of *bin* in *The Black Border* (0.3% of a corpus of 27,683 words) increase to 163 tokens in *The Captain* (0.7% of a corpus of 22,824 words) and to 331 tokens in *Laguerre* (0.9% of a corpus of 34,881 words), suggesting that Gonzales eventually tripled its frequency because he became aware of the stereotypical value of the creole marker.

Table 1: Distribution of anterior and past tense markers

	Early Text		Later Texts	
GUL	#	%	#	%
zero marker	428	(84.9)	~3,905	(84.9)
bin	16	(3.2)	562	(12.2)
GUL/LENG				
strong*	52	(10.3)	59	(1.3)
-ed	8	(1.6)	~74	(1.6)
Total	504	(100.0)	~4,600	(100.0)
(~ projected; * including inflected auxiliary and main verbs)				

There is also contrast between the early text and later texts when comparing *bin* as a preverbal anterior marker and as a precopula anterior marker (where there is a zero copula). Preverbal *bin* goes from 31.3% of 16 *bin* tokens in the early text to 64.2% of the 562 tokens in the later texts (see table 2). The more English-like precopula *bin* goes from 68.7% in the early text to 35.8% in the later texts.

Table 2: Anterior marker *bin*

	Preverbal		Precopula	
	#	%	#	%
Early Text (N = 16)	5	(31.3)	11	(68.7)
Later Texts (N = 562)	361	(64.2)	201	(35.8)

The shifting emphasis from precopula *bin* to preverbal *bin* is consistent with Gonzales's intent to reflect a more basilectal Gullah in his later texts. If the early text reflects more accurately the variety that could be heard in Gonzales's youth, then we must note a strong use of English-like precopula *bin* in conjunction with the distinctly creole preverbal anterior marker.

I have eliminated from the count (tables 1 and 3) irregular verbs which are indistinguishable in present and past tense forms (*put, hit, set*) and tokens of *lef'* and *bruk* which are problematic in that they occur in present tense, *irrealis* and past contexts with the same form and no present-tense variant. Gonzales himself glossed *lef', bruk,* and *loss* as verb stems. This is consistent with evidence in modern data from other creoles of ungrammaticalized borrowing (Bickerton 1975). Holm (1989) points out that *brok* 'break' in Jamaican Creole English seems to come from Scots and Irish English *bruck* 'break', while the creole *lef'* 'leave' and *las* 'lose' may come from regional British *leff* and *loss*. Nonetheless, *lef'* is mainly used by Gonzales in the English sense with a past context in the early text. The distribution of non-past *lef'* suggests that as Gonzales began giving greater exposure to basilectal features in later writings, he likewise introduced a greater frequency of seemingly past-inflected verb forms in non-past contexts in order to illustrate more dramatically the difference between GUL and LENG tense marking.

Taken as a whole, Gonzales's use of inflected verb forms is consistent with Nichols's finding in present-day speech: they rarely if ever occur (with the exception of ungrammatical *lef'*, N=53). However, in the early text, they are more likely to be grammatical, consistent with the notion that some of Gonzales's models may have had limited access to the LENG verb inflection system.

Table 3 represents the inventory of strong-inflected auxiliary and main verb forms in both the early text and later texts. A form's percentage of each respective inventory reveals the comparative prevalence of certain forms over others, as well as some fluctuation in use between the two corpora. While the numbers and distributions of inflected forms in both corpora are very similar, we must remember that the much smaller early text has a higher concentration of those tokens in alternation with creole zero-tense and anterior marking (see table 1).

Table 3: Distribution of strong-inflected auxiliaries and main verbs

	Early Text		*Later Texts*	
	#	%	#	%
aux *hadduh*	3	(5.8)	19	(32.2)
mv *had*	17	(32.7)	7	(11.9)
aux *didn't*	18	(34.6)	23	(39.0)
aux *was*	2	(3.8)	1	(1.7)
mv *was*	8	(15.4)	4	(6.8)
t'awt	4	(7.7)	5	(8.5)
Total strong	52	(100.0)	59	(100.0)

Of the 15 tokens of aux/mv *was* (all [+past]), 66% occur in the early text as in:

(9) *When she conclude eatin' my peas, she lie down, and, Missis, she **was** so full that she could not rise!* [referring to a cow]
'When she finished eating my peas, she lay down, and, Miss, she was so full . . .' (B707)

In the early text, where there are 4 instances of [+past] *t'awt*, they are in opposition to 11 tokens of [-past] *t'ink* as in the following:

(10) *Me shum duh bu'n fuh true, Unk' Ebbrum, but oonuh binnuh sleep en' uh **t'awt** 'e would bex you fuh wake.*
'I saw it burning for sure, Uncle Abram, but you were sleeping and I thought it would vex you to wake up (be awakened).' (B1186)

(11) *You mus'be **t'ink** you is buckruh, enty?*
'You must think you are white folk, right?' (B40/36)

There are an additional 4 tokens of ungrammatical [+past] *t'ink*, which mitigate against this being part of the English past-tense system. However, Gonzales maintains the *t'ink/t'awt* opposition somewhat in the much longer, later texts where only one token of *t'awt* is markedly ungrammatical Gullah (see example 13 below), and 5 more tokens of [+past] *t'awt* occur in alternation with 17 tokens of [-past] *t'ink*. Predictably, Gonzales also increases the incidence (14 tokens) of ungrammatical [+past] *t'ink* in the later text signaling the incompatibility of grammatical strong verb inflection with a purely basilectal Gullah. The extent of the opposition between *t'awt* and *t'ink*, nonetheless, leaves open the question of whether it was indeed possible in Gonzales's day to hear an English-like past-tense distinction made with verb inflection by some speakers conversant in GUL and LENG.

Gonzales uses *hadduh* to distinguish the past-inflected auxiliary from main verb *had*. The former is always part of an if-clause, and *bin* follows *hadduh* 50% of the time.

(12) *Yaas, suh, Uh know dat 'cause ef you **hadduh bin** home Uh woulduh git ketch.*
'Yes sir, I know that because if you had been home I would've gotten caught.' (C139)

This combination indicates ambiguity between the surface relation of *bin* to the lexifier and its creole function to mark anteriority. One can only speculate as to whether this ambiguity existed for some speakers in Gonzales's day, or existed simply in Gonzales's mind. A disproportionately high number (71%) of Gonzales tokens of main verb *had* occur in the early text, suggesting that Gonzales suppressed its use in the later texts. Its use is generally English-like throughout Gonzales, though it may occur in close proximity to basilectal features.

(13) *Oonuh **had** no bidness fuh t'awt nutt'n' !*
'You had no business thinking anything!' (B188)

(14) *De only fau't I **had** wid'um is 'cause 'e gone en' dead een June!*
'The only fault I had with her is that she went and died in June!' (B2750)

Other inflected auxiliaries include *didn't* and *was* as distinct from main verb *was*. *Didn't* is the most prominent strong inflected auxiliary in all of Gonzales and occurs only as a negative.

(15) *'E **didn'** hab nutt'n' een 'e mout.*
'He didn't have anything in his mouth.' (B2491)

All instances of auxiliary *was/wuz* in Gonzales are tokens with a passive.

Weak verb inflection barely exists in Gonzales, and yet its appearance (N=8) in the handcoded early text is usually in the form *marri'd*. Gonzales places these forms in [+past] contexts as one would expect in English. The absence of a variety of other weak-inflected forms suggests, however, that these few are not grammaticalized (Stewart p.c.). Holm (1989) indicates that many basilectal Atlantic creoles contain fossilized remains of European inflections such as *marid* 'to marry.'

Table 4 displays the dramatic jump in creole *bin* and equally dramatic reduction in English-like inflected forms when moving from Gonzales's early to his later texts. Clearly, Gonzales considered these strong forms to be English-like in character when compared to creole *bin*.

Table 4: Distribution of tense markers

	GUL bin		*GUL/LENG strong*		*Total*	
	#	%	#	%	#	%
Early Text	16	(23.5)	52	(76.5)	68	(100)
Later Texts	562	(90.5)	59	(9.5)	621	(100)
Total	578	(83.9)	111	(16.1)	689	(100)

MODALITY

In the Gonzales texts, *irrealis* and conditional moods are marked by fifteen different forms, ranging from basilectal *fuh* to *haffuh, gots fuh* and *mus'be* to English-like modals such as *could* and *oughtuh*. Importantly, one finds here alternation of forms from all points on the creole continuum. In contrast to the tense system where zero tense marking is the rule, non-indicative mood in Gonzales is nearly always marked. Thus, distinguishing the factual from the nonfactual is a fundamental attribute of Gonzales's Gullah system. The examples below illustrate Gonzales's diverse ways of marking mood in Gullah.

(16) Future:
    (a) *fuh*   *ef you ent watch'um, 'e sho **fuh** lef some een de quawt cup*
    (b) [+aspect]*gwine*   *ef you ent watch'um, 'e sho **gwine** lef some een de quawt cup*
    (c) will   *ef you ent watch'um, 'e sho **will** lef some een de quawt cup*
                          'If you don't watch him, he surely will leave some in the quart cup.'

(17) Obligation:
    (a) *fuh*   *Uh **fuh** do alltwo.*
    (b) *haffuh*   *Uh **haffuh** do alltwo.*
    (c) *got(s) fuh*   *Uh **got fuh** do alltwo*
    (d) *have ta*   *Uh **have ta** do alltwo.*
    (e) *had ta*   *Uh **had ta** do alltwo (yesterday)*
    (f) *got(s) to*   *Uh **got to** do alltwo*
    (g) *must*   *Uh **must** do alltwo*
    (h) *supposed to*   *Uh **supposed to** do alltwo*
    (i) *oughtuh*   *Uh **oughtuh** do alltwo*
                        'I should do both.' 'I must do both.'

(18) Possibility:

    (a) *fuh*   *Oh Jedus! We **fuh** hab snow!*

    (b) *might*   *Oh Jedus! We **might** hab snow!*

                         'Oh Jesus! We might have snow!'

    (c) *kin*   *Oonuh **kin** gone.*

                         'You can go.'

(19) Likelihood:

    mus'be   *'E **mus'be** hab some berry 'pawtun' bidness.*

                         'He must have some very important business.'

(20) Conditional:

    (a) *fuh*   *'E know suh ef him ent kill da' t'ing dead, da' lion **fuh** nyam him*

    (b) *would*   *'E know suh ef him ent kill da' t'ing dead, da' lion **would** nyam him*

                         'He knew that if he didn't kill that thing, that lion would eat him.'

(21) Ability:

    (a) *fuh*   *ebb'rybody **fuh** see how 'e stan.*

    (b) *kin*   *ebb'rybody **kin** see how 'e stan.*

                         'Everybody can see how he is.'

    (c) *cyan'*   *Uh **cyan'** shum.*

                         'I can't see it.'

(22) Volition:

    would   *Uh **wouldn'** go een.*

                         'I would not go in.'

(23) Intensifier:

    done fuh   *'e strong; 'e **done fuh** strong!*

                         'It's strong! It's really (excessively) strong!'

Overall, Gonzales's work is marked by an abundance of basilectal modal *fuh*. It completely overshadows all but two other modals: *haffuh, kin/cyan'*. Beyond *fuh*, however, one finds in limited numbers a full repertoire of modals. The English-like forms occurring in Gonzales are sometimes distorted by eye-dialect, but phonologically, they are no different than the local English usage.

The construction *done fuh* intensifies the effect of the VP. Gonzales explains the phrase with the gloss 'done for—meaning excessively, as *Da' 'ooman done fuh fat'*. Interestingly, Turner (1949:14) interprets Gonzales as inferring that a Gullah speaker thinks one is 'done for' if one is fat. Turner asserts, alternatively, that *dafa* is the Gullah word for 'fat' reminiscent of the Vai word $da_3 fa_1$ 'mouth full/fat'. The Gullah speaker, Turner says, is merely adding the English word for clarification. A problem with this explanation is that Gonzales uses the construction with verbal adjectives besides 'fat' as in *'e done fuh schemy* and *'e done fuh sporty*. He also uses it before a verb-stem as in *'e done fuh fool 'um*. The combination of the perfective/completive *done* with *irrealis fuh* seems to accentuate the extraordinary degree of the attribution. Gonzales understood its use in Gullah to be one of intensification.

Basilectal *fuh*, in its several meanings, clearly dominates the 19th-century modal system, as portrayed by Gonzales's overall corpus. When compared to rare modern instances of modal *fuh*, this decrease in frequency and narrowing of function is consistent with an assumption of decreolization in the intervening century. However, Gonzales's early text shows no token of *fuh* encoding *irrealis*, although 152 tokens of complementizer *fuh* or benefactive *fuh* do occur, as in examples 24 and 25 below:

(24)   *'E lub **fuh** eat . . .*
      'He loves to eat . . .' (B236)

(25)   *but Paul nebbuh buy no frock **fuh** Diana*
      'but Paul never bought any frock for Diana' (B1518)

Table 5 shows the dramatic difference in the use of modal *fuh* in the early and later texts.

Table 5: Distribution of modals

	GUL *fuh*		GUL		GUL/LENG		Total VPs	
	#	%	#	%	#	%	#	%
Early Text	0	(0.0)	5	(4.7)	102	(95.3)	107	(100)
Later Texts	715	(48.0)	324	(23.0)	464	(29.0)	1503	(100)
Total	715	(44.0)	329	(20.0)	566	(36.0)	1610	(100)

It appears that by the time Gonzales writes the later texts, modal *fuh* has been resurrected to constitute 48% of 1503 modals. He clearly knew how it worked, given his abundant examples in the later texts, but he had ignored it when constructing his first articles as a young man. If Stewart's (p.c.) line of reasoning is correct, Gonzales presumably thought modal *fuh* would be incomprehensible to readers and thus left it out. Also possible, however, is that the large inventory of GUL and GUL/LENG modals caused Gonzales to ignore modal *fuh* until he focused on its distinctive nature during his later efforts to codify a stereotypical, basilectal Gullah.

From Gonzales's early text to the later ones, the English-like modals were diminished substantially. Yet, while the relative frequency of *fuh* 130 years ago can be debated, other basilectal and English-like modals were clearly in place then as now. In the early text, *kin*, its negative *cyan'*, and their related forms *could, coulduh*, and *couldn't* together account for 95% of all modals in the early text. They comprise 29% of modals throughout the later texts—after the rise of *fuh*. Future marker *will* and its contraction are greatly diminished in the later texts. Nearly half of its 20 tokens make up 20% of all modals in the early text, dropping in the later texts to 2%. While Mufwene (p.c.) finds no future tense in Gullah, Gonzales uses *will* to mark the *irrealis* of future as well as present conditional, alternating with basilectal *fuh* and with prospective aspect marker *gwine*. The following is an example of *fuh* to mark future:

(26) *Missis, ma'am, uh nebbuh tek de ansuh wuh you sen' to da' juntlemun todduh side de Ilun', 'cause uh nebbuh git dey, Missis; en', ef Jedus yeddy me, uh nebbuh **fuh** gone to da' place no mo' duh night-time!*
'Missis, Ma'am, I never took the answer that you sent to that gentleman the other side of the island, because I never got there, Missis; and, if Jesus hears me, I never will go to that place any more at night!' (B1950)

Gonzales uses *will* or -*'ll* to mark both future (N=18) and present conditional (N=30) as in the following:

(27) *Maussuh, no rain nebbuh fall 'pun Phibby een dis house! Ef you ax'um, him **will** tell you so, too.*
'Master, no rain ever fell upon Phoebe in this house! If you ask her, she will tell you so, too.' (C2391)

English-like modals account for 36% of the [+modal] VPs counted throughout Gonzales. Since basilectal *fuh* is not found at all in the early text as a VP modal, English-like modals account for 95.3% of [+modal] VPs in Gonzales's earliest writing. A look at Gonzales's modals elaborates our notion of the creole VP: we see a rich variety of contexts and functions for the GUL modal *fuh* and can better appreciate its versatility. At the same time, we're struck by the large inventory of other GUL and GUL/LENG modals in hundreds of contexts. Gonzales illustrates how much closer Gullah's modality system is to English than are its tense and aspect systems.

ASPECT

While tense is often unspecified in Gullah, aspect, like mood, plays an important role in conveying the speaker's impressions of a referenced action. In Gullah, aspect is marked by periphrastic preverbal lexical forms. GUL *V-in* with its grammaticalized ending is the exception; it marks the continuative aspect of the verb as its English *v-ing* counterpart but needs no auxiliary. Ranging from basilectal to English-like forms, 1146 tokens of aspect markers are identified in the Gonzales corpus. The examples below set out the system of distinctions which was devised during the preliminary line-by-line analysis:

(28) Progressive/continuative aspect:
    (a) *duh*   *I **duh** eat*
    (b) *V-in'*   *I **eatin'***
                  'I am/was eating'

(29) Anterior continuative aspect:
     binnuh   *I **binnuh** eat*
                    'I had been/have been/was eating (when)'

(30) Perfect/completive aspect:
     done   *I **done** eat*
                    'I have/had eaten; I already ate'

(31) Habitual/iterative aspect:
     does   *I **does** eat*
                    'I regularly eat/ate'

(32) Anterior habitual aspect:
     (a) *nyuse fuh/to*   *I **nyuse fuh** eat*
     (b) *blan*   *I **blan** eat*
                    'I used to eat'

(33) Prospective aspect:[4]
     gwine   *I **gwine** eat um now*
                    'I'm going to eat it now'

If *blan* was ever prominent in Gullah, it may have already been relexified as *nyuse fuh* or *nyuse to* by the 19th century. Only six tokens of *blan* occur throughout Gonzales, none in the early text. The form may have only occurred to Gonzales as he scanned his inventory for basilectal forms for the later texts. It has been suggested that *blan* is one of the oldest forms and may have been almost gone from the language when Gonzales was acquiring Gullah. Alternatively, *blan* was just a scant, occasional feature even in the early days of the creole. In his glossary, Gonzales interpreted *blan* (. . . *wunnah blan blonx to po buckruh* [B5] 'you used to belong to poor whites') to mean 'belong/belongs/belonged/belonging' and thought it was being used redundantly with *blonx* to mean 'used to belong'. However, only one of his tokens outside of the glossary occurs in this combination. Other uses (*blan push, blan hab, blan go*) include the following:

(34) . . . *en 'e **blan** quile da' tail 'roun' de limb*
     ' . . . and it used to coil that tail around the limb' (C1065)

One token is interesting for its redundant iterative markers:

(35) . . . *en' buh alligettuh **blan does** kill buh deer*
     ' . . . and brother alligator used to (regularly) kill brother deer' (C2187)

Hancock (1969) compares the Gullah form with Krio habitual marker *blant*, pronounced *blan* in Gambia Krio, and suggests that it may have been brought to Sierra Leone by American Blacks. He also cites *The English Dialect Dictionary* (Wright 1898–1905), where *belong to, belang,* and *belangt,* 'be accustomed, be in the habit of', occur in the dialects of Lincolnshire and Cornwall. In Virgin Islands English Creole, *belong(s)* = 'supposed to/should (be)': *He belongs going home* = 'He should be (is supposed to be) going home'.

Contrasting the early text and the later texts (table 6) reveals the forms Gonzales used more extensively in his more stereotyped writing of the later years. In fact, he favored use of the distinctive *duh* and *gwine* enough to have doubled their incidence in the later texts. However, iterative *does*, which Gonzales uses true to creole form in the early text, may have seemed too English-like in print to interest him in his later more basilectal Gullah. In his glossary, Gonzales fails to describe iterative *does*. Its occurrence in 17% of the [+aspect] VPs of the early text suggests, however, a fully developed use 130 years ago. Gonzales's aspect system, unlike that for mood, is clearly distinct from English.

Table 6: Distribution of aspect markers

| | Early Text | | Later Texts | |
	#	%	#	%
GUL				
blan	-	-	6	(0.6)
duh	12	(14.6)	300	(28.0)
binnuh	15	(18.3)	155	(14.5)
done	21	(25.6)	260	(24.3)
gwine	7	(8.5)	221	(20.7)
V-in'	7	(8.5)	98	(9.2)
does	14	(17.0)	13	(1.2)
nyuse fuh	-	-	2	(0.2)
Total GUL	76	(92.7)	1,055	(98.6)
GUL/LENG				
nyuse to	6	(7.3)	15	(1.4)
Grand Total	82	(100.0)	1070	(100.0)

CONCLUSION

The contrasts between Gonzales's early and later texts are striking and together establish a pattern in his selection of Gullah forms. The smaller early text exhibits a greater mix of acrolectal TMA markers with distinctly creole variants: Gonzales's use of strong inflected auxiliary and verb forms alternates more frequently there with his use of GUL *bin*; those instances of past-inflection are more likely to be grammatical than when they occur in the later texts. In the early text, he also favors the more English-like precopula *bin* while the preverbal *bin* predominates in the later texts. GUL modal *fuh* is absent from the early text, where English-like modals make up 95% of all modals, yet modal *fuh* becomes the most salient modal in the later texts, while GUL/LENG future marker *will* and its contraction are greatly diminished. Gonzales eventually doubles the incidence of GUL aspect markers *duh* and *gwine*. However, GUL *does* decreases in frequency in the later texts, perhaps because it seemed too English-like in print and thus did not fit with Gonzales's fastidious construction of a basilect. The circumstances of Gonzales's work make it highly plausible that the later texts are in fact an archetype, artfully designed to provide a key to the language before Gonzales died. Meanwhile, the early text, written by the young Gonzales, seems to be a sampling of the kind of speech one is likely to encounter today among Gullah people—speech that is less rule-bound, more varied. My sense is that the early text provides a clue to the presence of variation in the Gullah speech communities Gonzales knew so well in the third quarter of the 19th century.

Gonzales's texts hold considerable value in their numerous and diverse illustrations of grammatical constraints on TMA marking. These, when compared with modern samples, establish that Gonzales had a competency in the Gullah of 130 years ago that we cannot ignore despite the interference of racist caricatures conveyed through his stories. Gonzales's work suggests that a wide range of usage in Gullah—beyond a putative basilectal system—was in place over a century ago. The early text, in combination with the comprehensive basilect of the later texts, provides us with an impressive inventory of Gullah features together with the implications of Gonzales's differing emphases.

NOTES

I am grateful to Michael B. Montgomery, Salikoko Mufwene, Patricia C. Nichols, Carol Myers Scotton, Dorothy Disterheft, and Alice Kasakoff for their valuable guidance in my initial project. I am also grateful to John Singler and William Stewart for their subsequent close readings of my original study and their critical comments and suggestions. I have attempted to address their comments to the extent possible here. Any errors remaining are my own.

1. See Mille 1990 for a proposed model of intersecting grammar spheres (GUL and LENG) that avoids the unidimensional and unidirectional implications of the linear creole continuum model. The spheres intersect to varying degrees in the tense, mood, or aspect systems. The model allows speakers to orient themselves, selecting as their linguistic virtuosity permits, and allows the variation present within the speech of an individual and a community, as illustrated by Gonzales and much modern data.

2. Examples taken directly from my corpus are identified by a code letter and number. In order to facilitate comparison, I also present examples which, though possible, do not necessarily occur verbatim in the text. All translations are mine.

3. The *-ed* markings are usually written *'d* and are typeset with such inconsistent spacing before or after the apostrophe or after the word (from crowding) as to prevent the formation of a comprehensive computer concordance.

4. I have used Comrie's (1976) classification of "prospective aspect" in order to describe the most common use of *gwine* in Gonzales's Gullah. The form is also used in alternation with future markers *fuh* and *will* when the context is more remote than immediate, i.e., *I gwine eat um nex' week.*

Gullah's Development:
Myth and Sociohistorical Evidence

Salikoko S. Mufwene

INTRODUCTION

The term *myth* in the title of this paper is intended to be provocative, not disparaging, although I sometimes dwell on the nonfactual nature of the evidence adduced in some accounts of the development of African-American speech. The word *myth* underscores the assumption that historical discourse is not a report of facts but an interweaving of fact and fiction, often with ideologically induced distortions.

Writing about the development of a language variety is also writing a historical myth, as facts may be distorted to suit the ideology of authors in their attempt to explain phenomena that interest them. As in any historical discourse, the balance between facts and ideological distortions is a delicate one. Therefore, an important question for scholarship is: what is the degree of fit between fact and interpretation?

In this paper, I discuss my working assumptions, review some sociohistorical evidence concerning the development of colonial South Carolina, and assess its interpretation in some accounts of the development of Gullah. After highlighting shortcomings and strengths of competing analyses, I propose an alternative, which, I claim, distorts the facts the least and makes obvious some questions. The questions still need plausible answers. This paper continues my articulation of the sociohistorical ecology in the context of which the formation of Gullah must be interpreted. It outlines a research agenda more than it answers some of the thorny research questions that it raises, questions that should be at the center of the debate on creole genesis.

WORKING ASSUMPTIONS

First, according to the ideological background that molds my account, I will call a variety a creole if it was associated at some point in its genesis with a creole population. Current research on structural features of creoles and the sociohistorical conditions of their development has made it difficult to determine which contact-generated language varieties are creoles and which ones are not. As languages are typically identified in relation to the ethnicity of their speakers, characterizing a new class of creole language varieties in relation to creole populations may do no harm as long as no typological-structural claims are made a priori.

Second, regarding the origin of the structural features of creoles and other contact varieties, I see only two competing influences: lexifier (or superstrate) and substrate. The lexifier is the primary source of the lexical material, what Robert Chaudenson (1979, 1989, 1992) calls "*matériaux de construction*," and probably of an important component of the grammatical principles of the new language varieties.[1]

I consider the substrate element as one of the factors accounting for differences among new varieties lexified by the same language, keeping in mind that lexifiers themselves were not homogeneous and may not have been represented in the same makeup in different colonies. The definition of substrate influence needs to be expanded beyond the sense of the French term *apports*, features brought from substrate languages that may not be present in the lexifier, to include the determination of what features of the lexifier are selected into the contact variety. Substrate influence may thus account for structural alternatives among creoles which may equally be traced back to the lexifier, for instance, in the different ways the new varieties express the progressive, the habitual, or the perfect. For example, English contact varieties in the Atlantic and Pacific Oceans have resorted to different strategies for marking the progressive/durative aspect, the perfect, and even relative clauses. Definiteness and plurality are not expressed in identical ways in Jamaican and Gullah.

I look at the bioprogram as a body of principles and constraints which, in part, guarantees that the outcome of the restructuring of the lexifier will be a language (Mufwene 1989). Contrary to Bickerton (1981, 1984, 1988, 1989, 1992), who claims creations almost *ex nihilo* from the point of view of syntax, I see the bioprogram as regulating how selected features get integrated into the new system, sometimes as competing variants. In other words, the bioprogram is not a factor of the same kind as the substrate and lexifier in the development of new contact varieties.

Third, contrary to Thomason and Kaufman (1988), I assume that the populations that developed Gullah and similar contact vernaculars had access to the lexifier. What makes the creole-development situation different from second language acquisition is that the lexifier varied and must have diverged substantially from anything spoken in the British Isles by the time the basilects emerged.

Fourth, I am assuming the model for the formation of contact vernaculars presented by Chaudenson (1979, 1989, 1992) and Baker (1990, 1993; Baker and Corne 1986) for French colonies in the Indian Ocean and the New World, and by Mufwene (1992) for South Carolina. According to the model, Europeans settled in and peopled their colonies in phases. In the first phase, lasting from ten to fifty years, they lived in small homesteads, made their living primarily farming and trading, and developed a technological infrastructure. Europeans generally outnumbered non-Europeans, integrated the latter in their homesteads, and often mated with them. These living conditions produced a sizable creole population, with several mulattoes, who spoke colonial varieties of the lexifier. These varieties differed minimally from those spoken by European colonists and may have reflected variation in the latter.

As colonization moved into the second phase, characterized by agricultural and mining, non-Europeans far outnumbered Europeans. Segregation was institutionalized, newcomers were seasoned by the creole or previously seasoned slaves, and plantation vernaculars emerged more and more different from the colonial varieties of the lexifiers spoken by the creole populations. Because no large plantation was peopled overnight to produce the population disproportions ratios typically associated with creolization, we must assume that the new vernaculars diverged gradually from the European models toward the basilectal constructs often assigned to them. Since infant mortality was high during the second phase and the slave population increased mostly by importations from Africa, it is implausible that children formed the new vernaculars (Mufwene 1996a, b). The basilect may have stabilized by the time slavery was abolished. Or perhaps, with some variation in timing from plantation to plantation, the development of the new vernaculars may have stabilized when a permanent critical mass was reached.

The abolition of slavery marks the third phase, which was characterized for some communities by importation of non-European indentured labor. This period saw the formation of new African communities, such as those in Trinidad (see Warner-Lewis 1996), which preserved some of their African languages intact. Based on Lalla and D'Costa (1990) and Baker (1990), it may be assumed that since cross-plantation interactions among slaves were not regular during the earlier stages, some cross-plantation leveling must have taken place during this third, post-formative phase, especially toward the end of the 19th century. This factor may account for the relative regional uniformity of Gullah, despite claims by Smith (1926b) and Bennett (1908) for cross-plantation variation.

MYTHS ABOUT GULLAH'S GENESIS AND THEIR SHORTCOMINGS

With the above working assumptions, I now assess diverse interpretations of the genesis of Gullah and indirectly of AAVE. The oldest myth about Gullah's genesis lies in the now defunct claim that its structural peculiarities are due to the physiological features of its primary speakers, especially to what is characterized as their indolence, their clumsy tongues, and their fat lips.

Adam (1882) and Vinson (1882) are reported by (Baggioni 1988) to have spoken of Africans' inability to learn the allegedly "superior" IE languages:

Le créole diffère de nos patois précisément par son caractère artificiel: le patois est un langage naturel antérieur, latéral, secondaire au langage littéraire; le créole est l'adaptation d'une langue, et surtout en fait d'une langue indo-européenne, au génie pour ainsi dire phonétique et grammatical d'une race linguistiquement inférieure. (Vinson 1882; qtd. in Baggioni 1988:87)
'A creole differs from our patois precisely by its artificial character: a patois is a natural language anterior, lateral, and secondary to literary language; a creole is the adaptation of a language, and especially in fact of an Indo-European language, to the phonetic and grammatical genius, so to speak, of an inferior race'. (my translation)

This position is echoed in Bennett's (1908, 1909) account. What he describes as distorted retentions of English archaic dialectal features are:

... the natural result of a savage and primitive people's endeavor to acquire for themselves the highly organized language of a very highly civilized race [and] . . . the endeavor of untutored Africans, deficient in sound-appreciation and delicate vocalizations, to acquire English through a Scotch medium, produced the singular inflections and enunciations which characterize the pure Edisto *Gullah*. (1908:338)

In *Gullah*, intellectual indolence, or laziness, physical and mental, which shows itself in the shortening of words, the elision of syllables, and modification of every difficult enunciation, results in phrases so disguised that it is difficult at times to recognize them, or, at sight, to comprehend the process of their derivation, so great has been the sound-change and so complete the disintegration. (1909:30)

The general attitudes held then toward the black race made this physiological explanation irresistible (see also Mille, this volume).[2] The determinative influence of the substrate languages set aside, it did not matter that many of the structural features of Gullah were in fact European.

Up to the 1930s, the Baby-Talk Hypothesis, according to which pidgins and creoles developed from child-like attempts by non-Europeans to speak European languages, seems to have been popular. It was invoked not only by Schleicherians such as Adam (1882) and Vinson (1882) to account for the genesis of French creoles, but also by Bloomfield (1933). Jespersen (1922) is a remarkable exception.

Krapp (1924) did not see the contradiction between the Baby-Talk Hypothesis and the English Dialect Hypothesis he substitutes for it:

The Negro speaks English of the same kind and, class for class, of the same degree as the English of the most authentic descendants of the first settlers in Jamestown and Plymouth [in Virginia].

The Negroes, indeed, in acquiring English have done their work so thoroughly that they have retained not a trace of any African speech. Neither have they transferred anything of importance from their native tongues to the general language. A few words, such as *voodoo, hoodoo*, and *buckra*, may have come into English from some original African dialect, but most of the words commonly supposed to be of African origin, e.g., *tote, jazz*, and *mosey*, are really derived from ancient English or other European sources. (190)

Krapp's position is repeated by Johnson (1930) and Crum (1940:101), who notes, "Gullah is predominantly English, a true English dialect; in fact more truly English than much of the English spoken in America today." While making allowance for the Baby-Talk Hypothesis (8), Johnson (1930) observes:

The most numerous class in the colony before the slave trade began to flourish was composed of indentured servants, laborers, and artisans. They worked side by side with the Negroes and came into contact with them in various other ways, and it was from them that the slaves learned most of their English.[3] (7)

The Negro took over the English of the whites with whom he was associated, and he did it remarkably well. White speech has undergone some degree of change, moving a little nearer, perhaps, toward a standard American English, but, because of cultural isolation, the Negro lags behind, thus conserving the white man's linguistic past. (11)

Rebutting claims which attribute several of Gullah's peculiarities to African linguistic influence, he writes:

He [the Gullah speaker] has merely responded to the speech patterns with which he was confronted in the low-country by assimilating them in practically every detail. His speech comes nearer being a duplicate of eighteenth century English dialect to which he was exposed than the speech of some of our immigrant groups, say the Germans and the Scandinavians, comes to being a copy of nineteenth century English. (51)

It does not seem to have bothered proponents of the English Dialect Hypothesis that there was no native white dialect of English identical to either Gullah or AAVE. That is, even though the African-American is supposed to have preserved a variety that the European American has outgrown, no evidence is adduced to support the claim that there was a time in the development of American English when poor whites and the vast majority of African-Americans spoke the same language variety. Neither do they show how poor white Americans outgrew that variety which most African-Americans putatively preserved. Although this myth is not totally fictitious (assuming the English origin of most of Gullah's and AAVE's vocabulary and part of their grammars), its implausibility comes from its denial of the contribution of African languages to, at least, African-American speech itself.

With *Africanisms in the Gullah Dialect*, Turner (1949) responds to both the English Dialect Hypothesis and the position held by Bennett and Gonzales. His position was that Gullah, which he identified as a "dialect" of English, "is indebted to African sources" (254). Having cited Sylvain (1936), he also resuscitated her position that Haitian Creole consists of Ewe grammar with a French vocabulary. It did not matter to most of his followers that he was not as specific as Sylvain in identifying a specific African language as the provider of Gullah's grammatical substratum, nor that he actually discussed little of Gullah grammar and focused more on its vocabulary. They created the myth of dominant African grammatical influence in Gullah.

The soundest critique regarding Turner's lexical evidence is Cassidy's (1983) observation that very few of the regular items, i.e., those that are not proper names, occur in the spontaneous narratives at the end of the book. Like Cassidy (1983), Mufwene (1985) concluded that the basket names studied by Turner (1949) are post-formative additions, as their phonologies reflect distortions imposed by an established English-like system. This finding is consistent with the positions of the present essay that Gullah developed gradually and in the direction of basilectalization, having started with closer approximations of colonial English.

Since Turner, there has been little debate on the development of Gullah, except for Cassidy (1986), discussed in Mufwene (1992). Most of the literature has been on the hypothesis that Gullah decreolized (i.e., debasilectalized) presumably in comparison with its Caribbean kin.[4] Mufwene (1987, 1991a, 1991c, 1994) argues against this position, citing the sociohistorical evidence discussed below, asserting that early and late 20th-century Gullah texts do not differ.[5]

GULLAH'S DEVELOPMENT: WHAT SOCIOHISTORICAL EVIDENCE SUGGESTS

The Spaniards had settled in several places on the South Carolina coast since 1526. The British colonization of South Carolina began in 1670 with colonists and slaves from Barbados. They raised cattle and pigs, and a few traded meat and fur with the Indians (Wood 1974; Ver Steeg 1975). Their typical dwellings were homesteads (not plantations), which they shared with their African slaves, who remained a minority until 1700. Population was estimated by the Spanish governor in 1671 to be 30% African. A year later in the British colony it was "800 English and 300 Negroes," or 27% (Wood 1974:25). In 1700, the colony counted 3,000 (descendants of) Africans against 3,800 (descendants of) Europeans, showing a more rapid growth of the black population, due both to natural reproduction and to importations mostly from the West Indies. There were a handful of plantations then but not many, nor were these large enough to make South Carolina the rice plantocracy it became in the 18th century. Africans barely outnumbered Europeans in 1708, when 4,100 Africans were counted, against 4,080 European. In 1720 Africans became an important majority, totalling 11,828 against 6,525 Europeans (see also the table below). From this year to 1740, the population increased significantly, growing to 39,155 Africans against 20,000 Europeans. The following table, excerpted from Wood (1989:39), illustrates part of what he terms "the changing population" of the colony from 1685 to 1790:

	Year							
	1685	1700	1715	1730	1745	1760	1775	1790
White	1,400	3,800	5,500	9,800	20,000	38,000	71,000	140,200
Black	500	2,800	8,600	21,600	40,600	57,900	107,300	108,900

These figures reflect an increase both in the size and number of plantations, corresponding to the industrialization of rice culture on primarily the coastal plantations. After the first 50 years, however, the population grew more by importation from Africa and Europe. Indentured labor was imported from Europe in part to counterbalance, if not to offset, the African population. In 1720, South Carolina became a crown colony. The year also marked the institutionalization of segregation, barring regular social interaction between Africans and Europeans. Ver Steeg (1975:131) mentions the increasing "fear of black power" among the white colonists, which "led to the political response of the 1720s to propose and execute a township system to contain the territorial limits of slavery [to the coastal area], thereby attempting to moderate its social-economic effect." The creole slaves, including several mulattoes (the epitome of racial creolization), lived with the new African slaves in separate quarters from the Europeans. With this, the creoles' speech, the counterpart of Chaudenson's (1979, 1989, 1992) *français approximatif* in the sense that it is not drastically different from white colonial speech—became the model and lexifier for the noncreole slaves.

Institutionalized segregation thus marks an important turning point, which led to the development of Gullah as an African-American variety distinct from European-American varieties. Abolition of slavery did not bring the *de facto* segregation of the populations to an end; to date African-Americans and European-Americans have remained basically separate communities. Although the less powerful group accommodates the more powerful one in switching to what creolists have called the acrolect, separate linguistic communities that follow different norms have emerged, even though they overlap in some respects.

Between 1745 and 1760, growth rates were reversed in favor of the European population. Elsewhere I argue that this shift makes the period between 1720 and 1750 the critical stage in the emergence of Gullah as a distinct African-American variety (Mufwene 1992).

Without more specific information, the above demographics, applied uniformly to the whole colony, might still lead to incorrect conclusions on the restructuring of language during the first half of the 18th century. To begin with, when coastal South Carolina switched to the naval stores and rice field industries between 1710 and 1720, this switch did not mark the discontinuation of trade and farming by some Europeans, nor did plantations replace homesteads. According to Ver Steeg (1975:112), trade especially "contributed to capital accumulation, providing one means of obtaining money and credit to buy land and slaves." As far as Gullah is concerned, we are dealing with a partial and uneven transformation, even though, according to Joyner (1991:218), rice fields of 100 slaves or more account for about half the slave population in 1790 and for 80% by 1810. Wood (1974:55) notes that "as late as 1720 there was probably more labor engaged in the production of meat exports and naval stores than in the growing of rice." As becomes clearer below, Gullah may have developed slowly and more or less separately, though not completely independently on each major plantation throughout the 18th century.[6]

The plantations which developed were more or less self-contained estates whose populations were not in regular contact with each other (e.g., Smith 1926b). Also, though it is generally reported that in coastal South Carolina the average disproportion of Africans to Europeans by the beginning of the 19th century was ten to one (e.g., Joyner 1989), the actual ratios varied from plantation to plantation (e.g., Joyner 1984). If the regular population disproportions that creolistics has relied on are taken seriously, the African-American plantation vernaculars that emerged must have varied from one estate to another, as suggested recently by Lalla and D'Costa (1990). That the variation is less obvious today suggests that some cross-plantation leveling must have taken place after the Civil War or the abolition of slavery (Mufwene 1991b).[7]

Gullah seems to have developed with different degrees of restructuring on large, naval store and rice plantations. This raises the question of what social and demographic factors correlate with a particular linguistic output. Why did Gullah develop on the naval store and rice plantations and not on mainland tobacco and cotton plantations?

Coastal South Carolina is not a continuous piece of land on which European and African populations were more or less uniformly distributed during different phases of the colony's development. Historical sources suggest that plantations of different sizes existed at different times, in different places, with different population ratios, and often at a distance from one another. While one group could influence the linguistic development of another, especially whenever a new plantation started, there was also a lot of room for independent development. Cross-plantation contacts were not regular enough after initial development to influence further linguistic development. Meanwhile, in places where the homestead system was not discontinued and where small farmers outnumbered plantocrats, leading to a higher ratio of whites to blacks, it is unlikely that anything close to Gullah developed.

The above demographic data suggest that children may not have played as central a role in the development of Gullah as claimed by some hypotheses of creolization, including such less partisan analyses as Cassidy (1986). The birth rate was highest during the first forty to fifty years, a period during which the typical dwellings consisted of homesteads, in which the Africans were a minority and well integrated with the Europeans. The Europeans depended for their survival on Indians' and Africans' familiarity with the new subtropical ecology, in the same way Chaudenson (1992) posits the scenario for French colonies around the same time. Adult slaves needed to develop a full-fledged language variety from the first days of the colony, regardless of the extent of restructuring from the lexifier. Even if African parents developed a pidgin—as unlikely as this assumption is—their children during the first forty to fifty years of the colony must have spoken the kind of English spoken by the white children they grew up with. I surmise that the reason why no creole evidence has been reported from the 17th and early 18th centuries is that the language spoken by descendants of Africans sounded like that spoken by the descendants of Europeans.

The onset of the development of Gullah as a distinct African-American variety coincides with the adoption of the naval store and rice industries as lucrative investments, the massive importation of slaves directly from Africa, the high infant mortality among black creole and African labor, the growth of the population mostly by continuous importation of slaves, institutionalized segregation and—borrowing terms from Chaudenson (1989, 1992)—the "autonomization" and "normalization" of the new African-American vernacular.

Gullah must have developed gradually throughout the 18th century, since the plantations did not reach their critical population disproportions suddenly. The land-development scenario proposed here suggests that over the years the lexifier must have been restructured again and again, becoming increasingly different from its original shape as more and more new slaves arrived from Africa while more and more seasoned slaves died, and as the original lexifier became less accessible. That is, Gullah must have started in a form closer to the lexifier and developed in the direction of its basilect.

Thus, what creolists have characterized as creolization amounts to no more than the basilectalization of the new vernacular, a process that ended with the fall of the rice plantation industry. Since segregated life patterns for descendants of Europeans and Africans still exist, we have reason for treating hypotheses of decreolization with skepticism. First, inter- and intra-individual variation, commonly invoked to support claims of decreolization, must have started with the inception of Gullah and other new language varieties that emerged in similar contact settings.

The gradual development of Gullah would have made African linguistic influence on its structure(s) possible at any time during its formation. However, in order to determine the nature of specific African influences, one must take several factors into account, including the diverse forms of English that were brought to North America as well as the diverse languages that the Africans brought with them.[8] As representatives of the different African ethnolinguistic groups did not all arrive at the same time nor in the same proportions on the different plantations, the scenario of language contact in South Carolina is now much more complex than previously assumed in the literature on creolization. We wind up with a wide pool of features, characterized by a lot of variation, to which a sophisticated selection model should be applied to account for the features that distinguish Gullah from other 17th-century language varieties (Mufwene 1996a, b). The English lexicon in Gullah is only part of the story. Other things to consider are how Gullah made choices from among lexical and grammatical options available in the lexifier and substrate languages and how some meanings were redefined. Future work is needed also to determine whether Georgia Gullah should be considered an extension of South Carolina Gullah and why these varieties should be considered one regional-ethnic variety in contrast with AAVE.

CONCLUSIONS

The sociohistorical scenario proposed here is clearly at odds with myths surrounding Gullah's origins, but it is consistent with the history of settlements in South Carolina. It highlights several questions which call for more research. It also points out that the process of language formation was more complex than the literature has shown. The question is not whether Gullah is primarily English or African but what principles regulated the selection of its structural features. Since neither the English nor the African elements were homogeneous, research must address how selection operated both within the lexifier as a combination of several varieties and within the diverse substrate languages.

Myths based on African physiology, English dialects, baby-talk, and dominant African influence inadequately explain Gullah's genesis. I suspect that in the end it will have become irrelevant to speak of creole genesis as a special phenomenon. Rather, it will have helped us understand better how new language varieties develop in contact situations. We will have more adequate pictures of the development of varieties such as Gullah and AAVE only through carefully considering social history.

NOTES

1. Lexifiers may vary in this respect from one setting to another. In addition, the interactional dynamics which obtain between speakers of the lexifier and those of the substrate languages determine the relative accessibility of variants in the lexifier.

2. Though I know of no linguist who has used such an explanation to account for the genesis of Gullah, it perpetuates a view that Baggioni (1988) characterizes as Schleicherian, which sees non-Indo-European languages as inferior.

3. This claim is similar to Chaudenson's (1989, 1992) explanation for the formation of "le français approximatif" in the first phase of colonization.

4. The latest publications on this subject matter are Jones-Jackson (1986), Nichols (1986), and Rickford (1986b).

5. Mille (1990) shows similarities between late 19th-century texts and contemporary texts recorded by Mufwene and by Jones-Jackson and corroborates Mufwene's position, which prompted her quantitative investigation.

6. Some plantations were offshoots of others, developed earlier by the same plantocratic family. Creole and seasoned slaves from the previous plantation helped start the new one, in part by training the unseasoned slaves.

7. In contrast, striking differences have been reported by Bennett (1908) and corroborated by native speakers, but I have found these difficult to detect.

8. Details of how to address these questions on Gullah's development are discussed in Mufwene (1992), with ample references to the relevant literature.

The African Contribution to Southern States English

Crawford Feagin

INTRODUCTION

Language change through language contact is mentioned in all discussions of linguistic change. However, whether we look at classical neogrammarian studies or at recent sociolinguistic studies, phonological change is often discussed as if the only source of change were to be found within the phonological system itself. One important exception is the work of C.-J. N. Bailey, which has consistently emphasized the importance of language contact in triggering linguistic change (Bailey and Maroldt 1977; Bailey 1973, 1982, 1996). Another is Thomason and Kaufman (1988), which also discusses a wide range of languages. More narrowly, Thurgood (1996) has shown that changes in register and tone, triggered by language contact, have developed in the Chamic language family of Southeast Asia. The most fine-grained discussions of the mechanisms of such change can be found in Trudgill's (1986) *Dialects in Contact*, which explores contact situations in English and other languages. Kerswill (1994) explores the impact of an urban variety on speakers of a nearby, but extremely different, rural variety who move to the city, and the possible development of a koine there. Chambers's (1992) study of the acquisition of the English of Southern England by the children of two families of Canadian English speakers provides extensive discussion of principles of dialect acquisition in regard to lexical, phonetic, and phonological features. Payne's (1976, 1980) study reports on how young speakers of one dialect adopt the phonological features of another. Payne's work, however, does not go beyond the immediate neighborhood. The only study of whole communities regarding contact-induced language change in the United States, for English, seems to be Herold (1990), which argues that Slavic was the likely source of the merger of low back vowels in Eastern Pennsylvania.

In a somewhat more ambitious program, I hope to demonstrate how one large ethnic group in the American South influenced the speech of the other main group: that is, how African-American English (AAE) affected the development of Southern States English (SSE) as spoken by the white community, so far as phonology is concerned.[1] While the question of whether and if so, how, AAE influenced Southern States White English (SSWE) is of regional interest, such a discussion can contribute to a more general understanding of language change. More information is becoming available about both SSWE and AAE. The origins of AAE, though not agreed upon, have been examined extensively. Furthermore, a deeper understanding of both the historical and linguistic factors involved in the creation of the Atlantic creoles is developing. (See, e.g., Arends 1995a; Singler 1995; McWhorter 1996.) In conjunction with linguistic information about varieties of AAE and SSWE, we also have access to personal histories which provide insight into what took place in the South under slavery and thereafter.

Since this topic is complex, it is important to state carefully what the questions are and how far we can go on each point toward answering them. I have selected three features of Southern speech—black and white—to explore: R-lessness, the Southern drawl, and the use of falsetto. The questions to be addressed are:

1) What is the current situation in regard to R-lessness, the Southern drawl, and falsetto for SSWE and AAE?
2) What is known of the historical situation in regard to each feature for each community?
3) What was the proportion of Blacks to Whites in the South between 1617 and 1870?
4) What would be the necessary and sufficient conditions for innovation, retention, and transmission of linguistic features brought into SSWE from AAE? What is the documentary evidence for such an influence? What about the Post-War/Reconstruction situation, or the situation up to World War II?

Unfortunately, despite the research discussed earlier, information available to address these questions is uneven. What we need is information about current Southern White and AAE, about those varieties during the last century and earlier, about the situation in regard to British and Irish English of the 17th and 18th centuries, about Atlantic creoles of those years, and about African languages of those same years. Many of these areas have received very little attention from the research community. For example, while some information in regard to segmental phonology is available, information about intonation is very difficult to find, and mention of falsetto is virtually nonexistent. However, these topics are worth exploring as far as possible.

LINGUISTIC FEATURES COMMON TO SSWE AND AAE

R-lessness

One of the most salient features of traditional SSWE is R-lessness—that is, the pronunciation of R as schwa, extra length, diphthong, or zero when it occurs as a syllabic or in postvocalic tautosyllabic position. What makes this so noticeable to non-Southerners is that, except in Eastern New England and the New York/New Jersey area and among speakers of AAE, the rest of the U.S. "pronounces their R's," to use everyday terms. Moreover, in those Northern areas R-less speakers are today generally labeled as working class, while in the South the social evaluation for Whites has been the complete opposite.

My own interest in R pronunciation until recently was limited to documenting and explaining the change from R-less to R-ful in the speech of Whites in Anniston, Alabama, a change which can be observed going on across the South among white speakers born after World War II (see Feagin 1990). As the table below shows, in Anniston, old-fashioned, upper-class white speech (as exemplified by informants RK and HH1) was almost completely R-less, while that of their working-class contemporaries (HB, MJ, SC, and MB) had high proportions of R. However, the proportions of R for the grandchildren of the upper-class informants (HH2 and BK) match those of the working class regardless of age. This is a massive reversal of the situation which existed over the last two centuries.

Table: Percent pronunciation of R in all vocalic and postvocalic tautosyllabic positions by age, sex, and social class

Urban Upper Class		Rural Working Class		Urban Working Class	
m	*f*	*m*	*f*	*m*	*f*
RK b.1883 3% N=292	HH1 b.1890 0% N=320	HB b.1907 63% N=296	MJ b.1911 84% N=464	SC b.1899 87% N=300	MB b.1895 87% N=311
HH2 b.1955 91% N=242	BK b.1953 65% N=282			BH b.1956 86% N=164	CS b.1957 92% N=275

(From Feagin 1990)

During the 19th century, a great contrast developed between the North and the South. R-lessness spread from Virginia and Maryland to Texas, from Central Kentucky to the Gulf of Mexico, as the population moved West, but not across the North and Midwest. Moreover, it is notable that R-lessness in the South was limited to the plantation regions of each state, while R-ful speech was characteristic of hill folk from Virginia to Arkansas and of small farmers around the edges of the plantation areas in Texas, the piney woods, and other marginal areas across the South. White oystermen of the Chesapeake Bay are also R-ful, as are white natives of the Outer Banks of North Carolina. Neither group played a part in plantation culture.

The "received" explanation, which can be found in Kurath and McDavid's writings (e.g., McDavid 1948; Kurath and McDavid 1961; Kurath 1972)—and the many secondary references to their work—is that the plantation South maintained its connections with England to a greater extent than did the rest of the country, during all phases of its history, from colonial times up until recently. Consequently, the prestige of R-less Standard British speech (RP) influenced upper-class SSWE, which in turn influenced the pronunciation of the middle and lower classes of Whites.

There is support for this. Indeed, some well-to-do Southern families did send their sons to England for their education. Occasionally, they even sent their daughters. William Byrd I of Virginia, for instance, sent his four-year-old daughter to England in 1685 to be educated, joining her older brother and sister there. As he wrote to his English father-in-law who was looking after the children, "I confess she could learn nothing good here in a great family of Negroes" (Byrd [March 31, 1685] 1977, I:32). Over a hundred years later, South Carolina families were still sending their sons to England. Meanwhile, English clergy filled pulpits across the Southern colonies; English tutors educated the children of the planters.

However, not all Southern families, even among the aristocracy, could—or wanted to—send their children to England, certainly considering the loss of markets for tobacco, indigo, and rice after the Revolution and the general depression which that brought about. Even earlier, there was reluctance to send children to England for fear of smallpox, so many sons were sent instead to William and Mary College in Williamsburg, Virginia. Also, tobacco wore out the soil in Virginia and North Carolina, while cotton did the same thing in South Carolina and Georgia, so that by 1830 many planters headed West—to Kentucky and Tennessee, Alabama and Mississippi. So an English education was an exception, not the normal state of affairs. Besides, the universities of Virginia, North Carolina, South Carolina, and Georgia were all in existence by the early 1800s. Their students, of course, were the sons of planters or of professional people living in towns across the South. So the London argument seems weak.

One of the points of controversy centers around whether the settlers were already R-less when they arrived or whether it was a London innovation which became fashionable and hence a consciously acquired status symbol in the coastal cities which then spread into the countryside. Hill (1940) argues convincingly from changes in place names that R-lessness before apicals (as in *cart, court*) began, variably, all over England about 1300. According to Wyld (1920), the general loss of postvocalic R in all environments reached the upper classes of London by 1650, after originating in Essex and Suffolk.

There is general agreement about the isogloss for folk speech in England, with constricted R in the Southwest and R-lessness in the Southeast. To the north there were trilled and uvular R's. Obviously, the people who arrived in the colonies varied in their pronunciation of R. We know that the Scots-Irish settled in considerable numbers to the west of the plantation areas, in the hills and mountains, and in marginal areas. They had constricted R's then, and their descendants do to this day. However, the whites who settled the plantation areas were from all parts of Great Britain and Ireland, not just the R-less Southeast of England.

It is clear that R-lessness was completely established in the Deep South among the middle and upper classes by 1860. The Brazilian Confederados, English-speaking descendants of Southerners who left the South after the War between the States and who set up a colony near São Paulo, are R-less (Montgomery and Melo 1990; Bailey and Smith 1992). Even as early as 1789, Noah Webster commented, "Some of the southern people, particularly in Virginia, almost omit the sound of *r* as in *ware, there*" ([1789] 1951:110). Eliason (1956), in his study of North Carolina letters, diaries, and other documents up to 1860, reports that the R-less variant is frequent in early spellings in North Carolina, more so in the eastern part of the state than in the west, as it is today. Among his examples are "foe" for *for*, "noth" for *north*, "Shalotte" for *Charlotte*. Using sources dating from 1861 to 1864, Faust (1988:11) presents a summary of Confederates' attitudes toward their own speech which is revealing in the open attribution of certain features to African-American influence, including R-lessness. Substitution of "pooah" for *poor* or "mattuh" for *matter* was attributed to influence from black speech.

In an 1879 travel account, Edward King, a Massachusetts journalist writing for *Scribner's,* reports, "It may be said without exaggeration that all classes of Southerners find it impossible to pronounce the letter 'r'. . . . Such words as 'door' and 'floor' and 'before' are transformed into 'do', 'flo', and 'befo' by the lower class, while some educated and refined people pronounce them as 'doah', 'floah', and almost invariably allude to our late unpleasantness as the 'waw'"(King [1879] 1972:785).

In the American South, Southern R-lessness was taken West, as far as East Texas, as outlined in Linguistic Atlas of the Gulf States (Pederson et al.1986, 1991, 1992) and spread as a prestige pattern, as outlined in Stephenson (1968). The question then becomes, why did Whites in the South, unlike those in New England and New York, take the R-less speech west? In other words, why was R-lessness so closely tied to plantation speech?

It seems to me that the obvious—and crucial—difference between the plantation area and hills, and between the North and the South, was the large African-American population in the plantation areas of the South. This is in direct contradiction to Kurath (1972:128) who avers, "Any notion that the 'weakening' of postvocalic /r/ to /ə/ could be attributed to the Negro majority in the plantation country is untenable on two grounds: (1) /ə/ is clearly a prestige pronunciation in the South; (2) it appears in New England and Metropolitan New York, areas that had few Negroes."

R-lessness as characteristic of the black community has been documented over the past 25 years.[2] In these studies, in informal conversational tape-recorded data, the proportions of syllabic or postvocalic tautosyllabic R range from a low of 2.2% to a high of 17%. As among Whites, there seems to be a movement from R-lessness to R-fulness, though this change is less advanced, perhaps by as much as two generations. What about the situation during slavery? If the accounts of Black English in Central Georgia as depicted in *Uncle Remus* (Harris 1883) and in Mississippi as presented in *Diddie, Dumps and Tot* (Pyrnelle 1882) can be taken as valid, then these show that Blacks in the middle of the last century were indeed R-less.

One issue which has not been settled is whether today's AAE is a decreolized version of an earlier Gullah-like language. Research on Samaná in the Dominican Republic (Poplack and Sankoff 1987), on Liberian Settler English in West Africa (Singler 1984, 1989), and on AAE (Mufwene, this volume) suggests that AAE never had a Gullah-like ancestor. Hancock (1986b:265) writes, "most of the principal characteristics that each creole is now associated with were established during the first twenty-five years or so of the settlement of the region in which it came to be spoken: Black English has always looked much the way it looks now. . . ." On the other hand, Dillard (1975b:96) notes that "the earliest Plantation Creole in the United States . . . spoken by the field hands on the big plantations was closer to Saramaccan. . . ." Quantitative comparison of AAE copula deletion with that of Gullah and Jamaican Creole, however, clearly displays some sort of historical relationship between those creoles and AAE (Holm 1984; Baugh 1980; Rickford

1996). Baugh concludes that his and Holm's work "established the creole ancestry of contemporary BEV beyond any doubt" (1980:103). Rickford carries the parallelism even further, in a reanalysis of the Jamaican data, while a comparison of AAE and European-American contraction and deletion data (Fasold and Nakano 1996) shows an even greater contrast between the two. Winford (1992:329), comparing AAVE and Trinidadian past tense marking, proposes that while BEV was never necessarily a creole, "it may have arisen from a process of shift away from a Gullah-like creole toward the English dialects that made up the superstrate during the 17th–19th centuries." Hannah (1995) refutes the claims of Poplack and Sankoff (1987) as being a result of skewed data collection; Rickford (1995) emphasizes that the origin of Samaná, Nova Scotia, and Liberian African-Americans was not the Deep South, where Blacks were either a majority or a very high proportion of the population, and were more likely rural, but rather from the Upper South (Maryland and Delaware) and Mid-Atlantic states, where blacks were a smaller presence, and more urban, with a resulting dilution of the strength of any creole residue because of greater exposure to the language of Whites. Pardoe (1937) points to amount of contact with Whites, opportunities for education, and geographical location (urban/rural; North/South; East/West) as providing parallel continua for the amount of creole or African influence remaining in black speech.

One obvious problem here is that AAE is not monolithic today and never was. Bailey and Maynor (1987, 1989) point out differences between present-day urban and rural AAE in Texas. Butters (1989) continues in this vein in regard to the black community of Wilmington, North Carolina. We know also that on the plantations there was individual variation in orientation toward white culture which would have been reflected in language. This may have been observed in linguistic distinctions between house servants and craftsmen, and those who worked in the fields.

In the early colonial days—up to the middle of the 17th century—white indentured workers outnumbered black workers in Virginia. The same could be said for the first decade of settlement in South Carolina. Wood (1974:175) points out that "whatever their theoretical status, in practice it was difficult to separate African slaves from English servants on the early settlements, and this *de facto* integration reduced the base upon which African survivals could rest. . . ." But late in the 17th century, the numbers of Blacks grew rapidly in both colonies, outnumbering first the white indentured servants, then the earlier Blacks, and finally overtaking the total white population. Most of the new Blacks were brought in directly from Africa. In 1737 a Swiss newcomer commented, "Carolina looks more like a negro country than like a country settled by white people" (Samuel Dyssli quoted in Wood 1974:132).

Did this change in population have a swamping effect on AAE? Was an earlier, more English-like speech among Blacks overwhelmed by a later more creole-like speech? (See Bickerton 1996 for such a development in Guyana.) Or did the later arrivals learn their English directly from the earlier arrivals? Writing in 1713, a clergyman in South Carolina reports that "the Negroes born and brought up in South Carolina were civilized and spoke English as well as himself, whereas those newly brought from their own country seldom attained good command of English" (Klingberg 1941:31). Ten years later, a Virginia clergyman wrote, "The planters and even the native Negroes generally talk good English without idiom or tone" (Jones [1724] 1956:80). Latrobe [12 May 1796] 1977:125) makes a similar remark concerning Virginians—common people and slaves—in his journal seventy years after that.

Whichever way we interpret the development of AAE—whether we assume that AAE has not changed noticeably over 350 years (which seems doubtful), or whether we assume that Early AAE resembled one of the Atlantic Anglophone creoles, we still are dealing with an R-less variety.

If indeed Early AAE was a creole, Charles Gilman (1985) makes a case that 17th-century Proto-Creole was variably R-less, like the 17th-century English it sprang from. He shows that the three families of Anglophone creole—West African, Surinam, and the joint Guyana and Caribbean family—vary in their R-lessness from totally R-less in the West African and Surinam branches—for different reasons—to variably R-less in the Guyana-Caribbean branch. More relevant to the U.S. South, Gullah itself is an R-less variety, though questions remain as to whether Gullah is the surviving isolate of a general plantation creole which was spoken throughout the Southern States.

Initially, Africans brought to the New World were from West Africa, though later, most were from Angola. In fact, 70% of the Africans brought into South Carolina between 1735 and 1740 were from Angola—that is, 7,000 Africans out of more than 11,000. The second largest contingent was from the Senegambia area, but that was only 6% (Wood 1974). Between 1733 and 1807, nearly 40% of the imported slaves were from Angola, nearly 20% from Senegambia, 16% from the Windward Coast, 13% from the Gold Coast. As for Virginia, between 1710 and 1769, 38% came from the Bight of Biafra, 16% from Angola, with 15% from Senegambia, 16% from the Gold Coast (Curtin 1969).

In the major West African language groups—Mande, Kru, Gur, Kwa—the syllable structure is mainly CV (Welmers 1973; Westermann and Bryan 1952). This eliminates tautosyllabic postvocalic R as a possibility. As for the larger, later group from Angola, they would have been Bantu speakers, whether they were from the coastal areas or transported from Central Africa. Here, too, CV is the main syllable structure (Gregersen 1977; Welmers 1973; Turner 1949). Nevertheless, it is useful to look at the realization of R in these languages. Ladefoged (1964) says that for Sierra Leone Krio, "the voiced uvular fricative occurs . . . whenever the corresponding English words have **r**"(28). He is referring to RP English here, which is R-less where SSE is R-less, so this uvular R occurs only in prevocalic position. He goes on to report that in his investigation of 61 West African languages, 20 had "[n]o phonemic contrast between **l** and some form of **r**. Some languages have only one articulation of this kind (usually **l**). Many others have **r** and **l** in free variation . . ." (1964:29). Similar variation in L and R has been reported for Bantu languages in the Congo and in Angola and for Gullah (Turner 1949).

The likelihood of AAE having any remnants from Africa in its phonology is not as remote as earlier researchers might have thought. In fact, Pardoe (1937), Williams (1993), and Gilbert and Spiegel (1996) suggest an African impetus to AAE R-lessness. As more scholars search for African sources for various linguistic features of Atlantic creoles, it is becoming progressively more evident that phonology will prove to be a fertile field for inquiry. Even Bickerton (1981:2) acknowledges that creole phonologies can have substratum influences, though Mühlhäusler (1986:208–210) advises caution, concluding on the basis of both Atlantic and Pacific creoles that "claims as to strong substratum influence in creole phonologies appear to be dangerous," suggesting phonological naturalness as a better source for similarities among creoles. (See also Singh and Muysken 1995, who urge a more careful examination of both argumentation and facts.)

Nevertheless, Alleyne (1980) and Sabino (1990, 1993a, 1993b) have shown how substrate phonotactic constraints have contributed to the evolution of creole phonology, while Holm (1993) presents evidence for the African origin of coarticulated stops in Saramaccan, Ndjuka, Príncipe Creole Portuguese, Krio, Liberian, Nigerian Pidgin English, and Gullah; and of palatalization in São Tomé Creole Portuguese, Papiamentu, Negerhollands, Caribbean Creole French, Surinam creoles, and Gullah. Carter (1993) argues for Jamaican Creole as having double (rather than long) vowels because of the African substrate. (See also Rickford's 1993 comment on the Holm and Carter papers.) Brousseau (1994) discusses the Fongbè influence on Haitian Creole phonology, concluding that the phonological processes of Haitian Creole phonology have come down intact from Fongbè. (See also Bilby 1993 on intervocalic liquids in Aluku, a Guyanese Maroon people.) From these reports it is evident that R-lessness is not the only African phonological feature to be passed on to daughter creoles; furthermore, all the Atlantic creoles, regardless of the lexifier language, appear to have certain phonological features derived from substratum African languages.

Between the African substratum and whatever variety of creole (or AAE) was spoken, R-lessness in the black population was the obvious result. As for the earliest Whites in the South, their speech was variably R-less, depending on their personal histories—where they were from, what social class, etc. The R-lessness which developed in the speech of Whites came as a result of contact with speakers of AAE. The same phenomenon has been noted in Brazilian Portuguese and in Caribbean Spanish (Megenney 1978; Guy 1981a, b).

Southern Drawl

The *Southern Drawl* will here refer to the elaboration of vowels which interacts with a wide intonational drop. Elsewhere, I have divided the drawl into two entities, the lengthening and gliding of individual vowels, which I call the basic drawl, and the emphatic drop in pitch on those vowels when occurring in particular contexts, which I call the extended drawl (Feagin 1985). The connection between the black community and the white community in regard to the vowel-gliding aspect of the drawl is uncertain. Work by Dorrill (1986a, b) using Linguistic Atlas data along the Atlantic Coast shows that in corresponding linguistic environments and social categories, Blacks have much less gliding than Whites. It is certainly the case in the Atlantic creoles, including Gullah, that vowels are much less glided than in other varieties of English. However, using extensive field data from rural Louisiana in the 1930s, Pardoe (1937) shows that while AAVE speakers have more "pure" unglided vowels than other speakers of English, they also have the extended drawl, with epenthetic w and y. I have reported on this feature among Southern Whites in Feagin (1996).

On the other hand, the wide pitch range characteristic of Southern Whites in contrast to other white Americans does indeed seem to be connected with the long association with the black community. The spread of suprasegmental features through substrata or language contact can be seen in Indian English, and in Irish English. Less well known in the English-speaking world is the spread of suprasegmental features around the Baltic Sea described by Jakobson (1931) and more recently and more extensively by Lehiste (1988), who reports contact-induced change involving tone in some dialects of Finnish, Swedish, and Polish. Similarly, as mentioned earlier, Thurgood (1996) reports two Chamic languages independently developing tone through language contact. Given these changes, the development of a distinctive intonation in the English of Southern Whites from long contact with AAE should not be surprising.

Very little research has been done on variation of intonation across varieties of English. Most of the better-known work on intonation has been done on RP in Britain and on unspecified American English, often so-called "General American." However, N. Bailey (1930:68) compares white Southerners and white Easterners, showing that Southerners have "a wider pitch range, . . . more pitch changes within phonations, . . . greater average pitch rises and pitch falls within phonations, . . . more pitch rises, . . . more pitch falls," and "a greater tendency to change the pitch within a phonation from rising to falling, and vice versa, as evidenced by the markedly greater number of circumflex and compound circumflex inflections."

In the course of discussing English intonation in general, C.-J. N. Bailey differentiates between patterns characteristic of SSE and of Northern States English, as well as other varieties of English (1978, 1985). He points out that "Northern States and Southern States varieties of English use different tunes [contours] for plain questions," and that a particular SSE contour for yes/no questions "may strike other speakers as exaggerated and out of place" (1978:36, 37). Also, in regard to yes/no questions, "Southern States and Irish patterns convey enough surprise . . . to make a hearer who speaks another lect feel one's veracity is being doubted" (1985:37).

Meanwhile, Ching (1982) initiated the discussion of the final rise—or "high-rise"—in SSE statements which make them seem like questions to non-Southerners. This was extended considerably by McLemore (1990, 1991a) in the most thorough study yet of the intonation of one variety of SSE. Basing her conclusions on 25 hours of tape-recorded speech collected during weekly chapter meetings of a University of Texas sorority (i.e., white, upper-middle-class Texas women), McLemore demonstrates that phrase final rise is used, not for uncertainty or deference, but to highlight new information for listeners or to connect the speaker to the listener. However, before concluding that this is necessarily characteristic of SSWE, it should be noted that "high rise" or "uptalk" not only seems to be a feature of Australian English (Guy et al. 1986), but is suddenly spreading throughout U.S. speech, enough to be noted in the *New York Times Magazine*. This new intonation is said to be used as a probe to see whether the hearer has understood or to indicate "more is coming" (Gorman 1993).

It is frequently reported that the intonation of AAE in the U.S. is very different from that of "General American." Studies covering a wide range of speakers—

children and teenagers, middle-class college students, and adults, in the Mid-Atlantic, South, and Northwest—demonstrate that this is true. For instance, research done among black children and teenagers in Washington, D. C., and observations of African-American speech in Clinton, Tennessee, and in Jackson, Mississippi, suggest that "the constant shift between [mid and high] pitch levels . . . may constitute the 'musical' character of the Negro dialect—especially as [those mid and high] pitch levels have a somewhat different distribution in the dialect as compared with standard American pronunciation" (Loman 1975:242).

In a preliminary study of the identification of ethnicity, Rickford (1972, 1977) showed that American Blacks and Whites can indeed be identified by their speech, mainly by suprasegmental features. Four college-age middle-class speakers (2 black—m,f; 2 white—m,f) were correctly identified 85.7% of the time by 20 college-age listeners (10 black, 10 white). The black speakers were from Kentucky and from Washington, D.C./ Baltimore; the white speakers, from the Detroit and Washington suburbs and from the Bronx. Spectrographic analysis and narrow phonetic transcription revealed that "both black speakers used higher pitch levels and more varied intonation than the white speakers" (1977:205). A more elaborate contrastive study compared the vernacular (working-class) English of blacks in Seattle to the vernacular English of whites there (Tarone 1972, 1973), demonstrating that (Seattle) Black Vernacular, in contrast with (Seattle) White Vernacular, had "a wider pitch range, extending into higher pitch levels than in white English or formal Black English, and often shifting into a falsetto register" (1973:35).

A study comparing Black Vernacular and White Vernacular in the South would undoubtedly show much less difference between Blacks and Whites than found in either the Rickford or Tarone studies so far as pitch range and falsetto are concerned. I believe that the wide pitch ranges would extend across the entire SSE community, black and white. However, it seems to be women who use the wide pitch ranges rather than men, as a general rule, and Blacks more than Whites.

The "high rise" intonation mentioned in connection with Southern white speech may also be a characteristic of black speech, a matter worth investigating. Turner (1949) claims that this is a feature of Gullah, while Alvarez Nazario (1974) makes similar comments about the Spanish of Puerto Ricans of African descent. Ryan (1973) mentions this as a feature of the speech of Whites on the Bay Islands of Honduras. For these reasons, "high rise" may have Caribbean roots as well.

Reliable information about earlier intonation of Whites is not available today. However, it is possible that the suprasegmental drawl came to the American South from Africa or the Caribbean through contact with speakers of African languages or Anglophone creoles.

One report from Jamaica around 1800 says, "The Creole language is not confined to the Negroes. Many of the ladies who have not been educated in England speak a sort of Broken English, with an indolent drawling out of their words" (Nugent [1839] 1934:132). So apparently the Caribbean Whites, especially the women, were influenced by local creole languages, not surprising under the circumstances. This can certainly be extended to the mainland. A report from Low Country South Carolina specifically says of one planter that "his language was like a Negro's, not only in pronunciation but even in tone" (G. M. 1831:250). By "tone" we can be confident that intonation is intended, and that a distinctive black intonation could be perceived at that time.

King's (1879:788) account of the South says, "The negro in South Carolina and in other adjacent States shows a tendency to render the English language more musical than it is when spoken by Anglo-Saxons. He gives an extra syllable to words which end abruptly, and puts a kind of rhythm into all that he says."

Assuming AAE is the remnant of a creole, evidence from creoles would explain such a distinctive intonation. In *Africanisms in the Gullah Dialect*, Turner makes a point that Gullah intonation is quite distinct in comparison with other types of English. He attributes this to the African substratum of tone languages. A number of studies have reported on Jamaican Creole as a possible tone language (Lawton 1963, 1968, 1982, 1984; Carter 1979, 1982; Sutcliffe 1982). These linguists suggest that Jamaican is a creole which resembles West African languages in its prosody, rather than English. Referring only to intonation, DeCamp (1960:138) reports that in Jamaican "[a]ll [pitch] levels are much more widely spaced than in American English. The tonal range of an animated speaker often astonishes the stranger to Jamaica." In an extensive comparison of suprasegmentals (vowel length, syllable structure, pitch systems) of Guyanese with English (RP), Twi, Yoruba, Kongo, and West African Pidgin English, only Pidgin yielded enough "resemblances which can be interpreted in terms of a genetic relationship" (Carter 1987:258). Moreover, she reports that while "superficially, Guyanese can sound similar to English . . . the resemblance is spurious; the two systems are different in kind" (226). In his discussions of Saramaccan, Ndjuka, Sranan, Principe, Papiamentu, Guyanese Creole, and Nigerian English and English borrowings in Yoruba, Edo and Hausa, Devonish (1989) shows that European (mainly English) word stress is converted into high tone. That is, all these languages can be shown to have West African rather than European prosody. While the status of Jamaican Creole as a tone language is not yet resolved, other sources regularly refer to Caribbean intonation as conspicuously different from that of so-called "General American" and British English (Wells 1982). Similarly, while Haitian Creole does not have tone, "the accentual system . . . appears to be very different from that of French" (Lefebvre 1986:298).[3] The similarity between these reports and the discussion of AAE intonation as distinct from that of (non-Southern) white intonation merits investigation.

If we assume a substratum effect, a look at the languages of West Africa turns up a bewildering variety of languages with tone, some without tone, though tone and length can be considered areal features of African languages (Welmers 1973; Gilman 1986). Tone in African languages can be lexical, grammatical, or a combination of these. On top of tone, of course, is intonation. In regard to the many African tone languages, "intonational contrasts . . . usually seem to be restricted to intonations for statements, yes-no questions, and non-final clauses" (Welmers 1973:100). Using Kpelle as an example, Welmers says, "in terms of English intonation, Kpelle questions sound astonished or rude. . . . [In questions] high tone . . . is extremely high and tense, often falsetto. Mid tone is a sharp rise to a similar level" (Welmers 1973:101). Another problem is that one can question whether there can be any historical connection between tone languages and a later creole with extreme intonation range. Westermann and Ward (1933) mention that a number of African languages are in the process of changing from tone to non-tone languages, possibly due to their use as lingua francas. If this happened in Africa in non-colonial lingua francas, perhaps it also happened in AAE.

Herskovits (1941:291), for example, speculated: "That the peculiarly 'musical' quality of Negro English as spoken in the United States and the same trait found in the speech of white Southerners represent a non-functioning survival of [tone in] African languages is entirely possible, especially since the same 'musical' quality is prominent in Negro-English and Negro-French everywhere." What lends credence to this idea is the fact that it is not only found in varieties of English and French spoken by Blacks, but in the Puerto Rican and Cuban Spanish of Blacks and in Palenquero Spanish as well as in Portuguese spoken in the majority black areas of Brazil (Alvarez Nazario 1974; Megenney 1978; Guy p.c. 5/89).

Evidence from Tây Bôi (Vietnamese Pidgin French), which kept the five tones of Saigon Vietnamese without keeping their distinctive function, lends more support to this hypothesis (Reinecke 1971). Studies of Chinese learners of French go even farther in relating the development of Atlantic creole intonation to African tone languages: when Chinese speak French as a second language, they tend to have a wider pitch range and higher overall pitch level than native speakers of French (Shen 1988).

Falsetto

Falsetto defines one of three pitch ranges (or registers, in the acoustic phonetic sense) in the human voice: *falsetto*, with tensed vocal cords, at the top; *modal*, the normal pitch range for speech or singing, in the middle; and *creak* or *vocal fry*, with laxed vocal cords, at the bottom. While falsetto does not seem to be used in any language for linguistic purposes, it often has a paralinguistic function in a number of cultures, with conventions of usage for that culture.

Among white speakers in Anniston, I found use of falsetto among teenagers, both working-class and upper-class, male and female, usually for emphasis, especially in protests. Women use falsetto in greetings to express pleasure and surprise, particularly in situations involving long absences or unexpected appearances. The emphatic aspect of falsetto shows up among men discussing such subjects as football and hunting and in joke telling. Falsetto is used by white Southerners in addressing babies and sometimes pets, as in the rest of the United States for Whites. In contrast to the white community, working-class African-Americans in the South do not use baby talk, according to Heath (1983). However, Tarone (1972, 1973) and Loman (1975) do identify falsetto as characteristic of AAE in Seattle and Washington, D.C., respectively, for contrast, emphasis, or in emotionally laden contexts.

There is little available information on falsetto in Africa, although Singler (p.c. 3/15/93) indicates that its use is widespread in West Africa. Moreover, while not mentioning falsetto specifically, Nketia (1971:736) reports that different levels of pitch and other qualities of voice are associated with "mode of recital" in Akan and Hausa trickster tales. Falsetto may have been brought to the American South by Africans, maintained by African-Americans, and borrowed into white SSE.

SOCIAL AND DEMOGRAPHIC SETTING

It is useful to examine the social and demographic setting in order to understand language contact. One point to consider is the relative status of the speech varieties involved in the contact setting. It is often assumed that the direction of borrowing is from the higher status language or variety to the lower. Why, then, would Whites adopt features of AAVE in the American South of the 18th and 19th centuries? Language attitudes have been the focus of research since at least Lambert et al. (1960). Using the term "covert prestige," Trudgill (1972) reports that British working-class speech is perceived as more masculine and standard speech as more feminine. Labov (1966) and others have observed similar phenomena in the United States. As noted by Edwards (1982), speakers of the more standard variety are perceived as more competent and intelligent, but speakers of regional or lower-class varieties are frequently seen as more friendly and warm (Edwards 1982:30). Moreover, Blacks and black culture fascinated white children in the antebellum South (Harris 1883; Pyrnelle 1882). Consequently, the influence of the speech of slaves on the speech of white children living in proximity should not be surprising.

A second consideration is the proportion of Whites and Blacks. The main discussion here is limited to Virginia and South Carolina, since these were the earliest centers of colonization in the South, with settlements radiating out from them. Moreover, both Virginia and South Carolina kept their leading positions in Southern culture throughout the antebellum and Reconstruction periods.

What is now Virginia was first settled by Whites in 1607; it was just over a decade later when 20 Africans were brought to the colony. At that time, there were about 1,000 English in Virginia. By 1671, Blacks still made up only 5% of the population. By 1770, they constituted 45% of the population. As elsewhere in the South, the populations were not uniformly distributed, however. Hemphill et al. (1957:231) show the distribution of African-Americans for 1860 for Virginia:

Southside Virginia (south of Richmond, east of the Piedmont)	57% black
Other Tidewater & Piedmont counties	44%
West of Blue Ridge (Valley of Virginia, mountains, W. Va.)	10%

The large proportion of retroflex R west of the Blue Ridge is undoubtedly related both to the low proportion of Blacks there and to the Scots-Irish ancestry of the white population. In contrast, Southside Virginia, where Blacks constituted the majority, was R-less (Stephenson 1968).

South Carolina was settled in 1670, with Blacks and Whites arriving on the same ships from Barbados. The ratio of Blacks to Whites from 1670 to 1695 was much higher than in Virginia. By 1710, Blacks outnumbered Whites; by 1740, the ratio was two to one. The graph below demonstrates that dramatic shift. In a study of the 1726 population of St. George's Parish on the Ashley River near Charleston, an examination of 108 households shows an overall average of 2.4 Blacks to each White in the parish, including children (Wood 1974).

Population trends in colonial South Carolina, 1700–1740

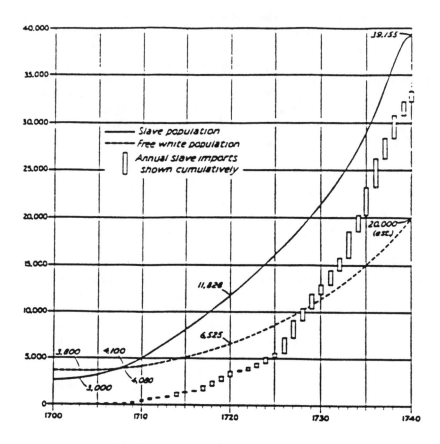

Clinton (1980) details the isolation of plantation families, especially the women and children. In Virginia, Anna Daniel wrote her sister Jane Lewis in March 1816, "I have very little worth while writing about for I have not been off the land since some time before Christmas, and I see very little company" (Clinton 1980:234). Fox-Genovese (1988:39) reports,

> In 1853 Mary Kendall, a transplanted New Englander, wrote to her sister of her special pleasure in receiving a letter from her, for "I seldom see any person aside from our own family, and those employed upon the plantation. For about three weeks I did not have the pleasure of seeing *one white female face*, there being no white family except our own upon the plantation." [Georgia Department of Archives and History, Hamilton/Kendall Family Letters]

The rural isolation of middle- and upper-class Whites should not be exaggerated. Nevertheless, Southern cultural life, even among the elite, was much more rooted in rural rather than urban surroundings. Opportunities to associate with other Whites were limited, especially for children. In the antebellum South, white children of the middle and upper classes were brought up by black nurses. On plantations, they were allowed to wander in the slave quarters and to play with black children until adolescence. As William Byrd pointed out, white children were surrounded by Blacks as early as the late 17th century, and the Marquis de Chastellux had the same observation a century later. Letitia Burwell, writing in 1895 about her childhood, reports, "Confined exclusively to a Virginia plantation during my earliest childhood, I believed the whole world one vast plantation bounded by negro quarters" (1895, I:8). Many travelers commented on the fact that wealthy families had an extraordinarily large number of house servants. Each child was assigned a same-sex, same-age personal servant who often continued in that position for life.[4]

Going beyond the era of slavery, in South Carolina, Mississippi, and Louisiana, Blacks constituted more than half the population in 1870. In Alabama, Florida, Georgia, and Virginia, they were close to half the population and between 30% and 40% in North Carolina, Texas, and the District of Columbia. Upper-class informants in Anniston born between 1880 and 1900 reported extensive contacts with Blacks in their childhoods and into their adult lives. An older upper-class woman in Anniston (the person labeled HH in the table above), who had no R in vocalic and postvocalic tautosyllabic environments, provides an example of contact between Whites of her class and Blacks. Born in 1890, she grew up in a household with four black servants: a nurse for the children, a cook, a maid, and a yard-man/driver. As a child, she enjoyed spending the day with an old couple who had been slaves in her grandmother's household. Examples such as this are typical of her generation and social class (Sledge 1991).

What is relevant to the linguistic development of SSWE is that such an intimate association at an impressionable age accounts for phonological similarities between AAE and SSWE in the pre–World War II South. Diaries and family papers show that slave-holding parents were concerned about the cultural influence of the slaves. "They worried about—and were not charmed by—their children's imitation of what was considered black speech" (Fox-Genovese 1988:112). Roberts (1993) has shown the profound effect that a child's caretakers can have on the transmission of sound changes from generation to generation. Such sharing of phonological features—as well as morphosyntactic features—is reported in the American South as early as 1736, continued through the 19th century, and was observed into the 1950s in Alabama (King 1879; R. Shuptrine p.c. 10/5/83; and references in Sobel 1987 and Joyner 1984). Joyner, for instance, points out that in Low Country South Carolina, the planters learned to talk like their slaves, rather than vice-versa.

There is far less information about the contact between the white working class and Blacks. What little is said about working-class children in the South in colonial days refers to apprentices, often small children. Colonial records, vestry books, and local histories from Carolina to Maryland show children bound out as young as age two (Spruill 1938). Such children may have worked alongside slaves and have been influenced by their speech. In the 19th century most Southerners lived in rural households, laboring on farms under an adult male tenant or landowner. Sharecropping and tenancy became increasingly common (McDonnell 1993). White tenants were concentrated in the piedmont, while black tenants were concentrated in the old plantation areas. Even where Blacks and Whites were tenants on the same property, they tended to cluster according to race.

A telling contrast exists in two quite different accounts from older women of the same age, growing up in Anniston, Alabama, in the 1890s. In both cases the mother had died young, leaving little children to be cared for. The mother who was a doctor's wife entrusted her children on her death bed to the black nurse. The elderly sisters then recounted happy childhood days of playing with her children. The sisters were completely R-less. In contrast, when the wife of a railroad man died, the oldest daughter cared for her three young siblings—dropping out of school herself at age 14. When asked whether as an adult she had ever had any black help, the daughter, then in her seventies, laughed and asked rhetorically how a barber's wife could have had a maid! This woman had 87% R in her speech.

Perhaps the working-class stories—and the quality of the R—would have been different if those informants had grown up in the Black Belt of Alabama, the Mississippi Delta, or the Tidewater areas of Virginia, the Carolinas, or Georgia. According to an African-American woman in her seventies, living near Augusta, Georgia, the children of tenant farmers played together, walked to their (separate) schools and churches together, visited in each others' homes, worked in the cotton fields together, watched adults of either race at their crafts. However, little children mainly stayed with their nuclear family (Mathis p.c. 3/29/94). Without more information about the social interaction between Blacks and working-class Whites, we can only speculate on the ways each group influenced the speech of the other.

The most important contact, so far as SSWE is concerned, was that between Blacks of all ages and white children. Payne (1976) documents that children from other areas acquired the nonprestigious Philadelphia lect. Trudgill's work (1986) on contact between lects shows that influence of one on another is not always direct, but that it does take place. Moreover, he shows that children can be facilitators for linguistic change—often away from a local prestige variety. Although the situation in the South differed demographically, it would be consistent for white children to acquire features of AAE.

In South Carolina in the 1940s palatalization of velar stops as in [kʲar] and [gʲardn̩] was considered prestigious by the upper class but was ridiculed by lower-class white children. Upper-class children attending the public schools acquired the unpalatalized forms, providing another example of how nonprestigious forms can wipe out prestigious forms. As Labov (1972a) and Trudgill (1972) have pointed out, overt prestige is not the only criterion for change, certainly not for children.

CONCLUSION

I have argued that three remnants of the antebellum South remain in white SSE: R-lessness, the Southern drawl, and falsetto, all of which have been influenced by AAE. The social relationship between speakers of those varieties over ten generations—over 300 years—is well known from diaries, letters, travelers' reports, and, more recently, from tape-recorded interviews. While the social mechanisms described therein are of local interest, the relationships and the resulting linguistic outcomes have broader implications showing phonological borrowing across a caste barrier which nonetheless permitted intimate relationships.

Similar social dynamics and linguistic outcomes in regard to R-lessness and exaggerated intonation have been noted for Portuguese and Spanish in the Americas (in contrast to Peninsular Portuguese and Spanish) where African and European cultures and peoples have also coexisted for 300 years. Such parallels among three languages across three European-based cultures cannot be accidental. What these cultures and languages had in common was a large population of people and languages which originated in Africa. Obviously, this is the source of such similarities, whether directly, from African languages, or indirectly, from Atlantic creoles based on African and European languages. For this reason, these same linguistic traits in the SSE of Whites can be attributed ultimately to African influence by way of whatever history AAVE may have had, whether decreolization from an African-European creole, as suggested by Holm and Baugh, or through language shift away from an earlier Gullah-like creole toward SSWE, as suggested by Winford. Regardless of the directness of transmission, SSWE was profoundly affected by these African-derived features, as were all the languages of Europeans between the Potomac and the Rio de la Plata.

NOTES

I am grateful to C.-J. N. Bailey, James McMillan, James Sledd, Michael Montgomery, and James W. Stone for comments on earlier versions of this paper. It is important to point out that none of these colleagues agrees completely with all of my conclusions.

1. Here, Southern States English (SSE) refers to the speech of both the black and white communities of the American South. Elsewhere (Feagin 1990), I have used SSE for the speech of the white community since I was discussing the results of my research among that sector of the population of Anniston, Alabama. This is also the term consistently used by C.-J. N. Bailey (1978, 1985). Here, SSWE will be used to refer to the speech of Southern Whites and AAE to the speech of Blacks.

Among those who have discussed the possibility of AAE's effect on SSWE are McDavid and McDavid ([1951] 1971), C.-J. N. Bailey (Bailey and Maroldt 1977; Bailey 1996), and William A. Stewart ([1968] 1975a). Holm (1980) and Ryan (1973) provide concrete discussions of it in the Bahamas and on the Bay Islands of Honduras, respectively.

2. See Anshen (1969, 1970) and Butters (1989) for North Carolina; Bailey and Maynor (1987) for Texas; Labov for Harlem (Labov et al. 1968; Labov 1972a); Wolfram (1969) for Detroit; Baugh (1983) for Los Angeles; Pederson et al. (1991) for the Gulf States.

3. Mufwene (p.c. 4/2/93), a native of Zaire, tells me that when he first heard Papiamentu, he thought it sounded like his native tonal language.

4. See Clinton (1980, 1982), Sobel (1987), Fox-Genovese (1988), and McCollie-Lewis (1994) for detailed accounts of plantation life based on letters, diaries, journals, and oral histories.

Colonial Society and the Development of Louisiana Creole

Tom Klingler

INTRODUCTION

In his recent book on linguistic and cultural creolization, Robert Chaudenson, long known for the importance he places on sociohistorical context in creole studies, reiterates his view that a "rigorous and meticulous approach to the history of the societies concerned" is an "absolute necessity" for the study of all forms of creolization (1992:53).[1] At approximately the same time that this quote appeared in print, the desideratum it expresses was in large part fulfilled for Louisiana Creole (LC) by the appearance of an historical study providing impressively detailed information on demographic trends and social relations in colonial Louisiana. Thanks to historian Gwendolyn Hall's (1992a) *Africans in Colonial Louisiana*, Louisiana now ranks among those creole-speaking regions whose sociocultural matrix during the formative years of the creole has been reconstructed in considerable detail.

The subtitle of Hall's book, *The Development of Afro-Creole Culture in the Eighteenth Century*, is an early clue to her thesis that in colonial Louisiana, not only did African ethnic communities and cultural practices thrive, but, moreover, they had a profound influence on culture in the colony as a whole and, eventually, on American culture in general. With regard to language, predictably, Hall comes down squarely on the side of the substratists, those creolists who believe that significant portions of the grammar of creole languages may be traced to African languages spoken by the slaves who contributed crucially to the creoles' development. While I believe that Hall's claims about the language are excessive, I wish to show that what her study reveals about social structure and language use in colonial Louisiana conflicts with Chaudenson's characterization of French colonial society in general and necessitates a revision of certain elements of his theory of creolization.

CHAUDENSON'S THEORY OF CREOLIZATION

Surely one of the most useful contributions Chaudenson has made to creole studies has been to draw our attention to the distinction between two basic stages in the development of colonial societies, the stage of the *habitation*, or small farm, and the stage of the much larger plantation, a veritable agro-industrial complex. In the first stage, characteristic of the early years of a developing colony, agriculture tended to be limited to subsistence crops and was carried out on small farms where a colonist and his family lived and worked in direct and constant contact with their slaves, who were generally few in number and often constituted a minority in relation to the members of the colonist's family. Resources were scarce and conditions for masters and slaves alike were harsh, which tended to reduce the social distance between the two groups. Relations between slave and master were in fact very often intimate, a circumstance to which the early appearance of a population of mixed race attests quite clearly. The physical as well as social proximity of the two groups led to intense linguistic exchange, and because the slaves had direct and sustained access to the French of their masters, they began early on to speak what Chaudenson calls "approximate varieties" of this language (1992).

Once an economic foundation had been laid in the new colony, it was possible to establish plantations devoted primarily to the production of export crops such as tobacco, cotton, and sugar. On these agricultural units slaves far outnumbered their masters, who no longer had direct contact with the masses of field slaves, though they continued to have contact with the smaller number of slaves who worked in the house and yard. These tended to be Creole slaves who, having been born in the colony, were acculturated to colonial society. In the social hierarchy of slavery Creoles occupied a significant position and served as the primary agents of socialization of the newly arrived *bossales*, most of whom were placed in the fields. Linguistically, the essential feature of plantation society was that the newly arrived slaves now had as their target language, not the French of the colonists, but the approximate varieties of French spoken by the Creoles. According to Chaudenson, it was at this point when the *bossale* slaves began speaking their own approximate varieties of the approximate varieties of French already spoken by the Creoles—or, put another way, when they began speaking approximate varieties of French once removed—that the development of creole languages which were structurally autonomous from French became possible (1992).

CONDITIONS IN LOUISIANA

Thus far, Chaudenson's characterization of French colonial society in general corresponds quite well to what we know about conditions in the specific case of Louisiana. In the first decades following the founding of Fort Maurepas, near present-day Biloxi, Mississippi, in 1699, France's primary interest in Louisiana was as a military counterweight to the British and Spanish presence on the North American continent, not as a producer of goods for export. Furthermore, the colony's first rulers, whom Hall calls "a military-bureaucratic clique," were more interested in lining their own pockets through smuggling and piracy than in providing for the colony's long-term development (1992a:9). Although there were a few early examples of estates possessing several hundred slaves, subsistence agriculture on the scale of the small farm clearly predominated in the early period. In the Pointe Coupee post, for example, of the thirty-three households listed in a 1731 census, six had no slaves, one had nine black slaves and one Indian slave, and the rest had between just one and five slaves (Hall 1992a). It was not, in fact, until the invention of the cotton gin and the discovery of a suitable method for making sugar from Louisiana cane, both of which occurred in the 1790s, that plantation society truly began to take hold in Louisiana (Klingler 1992).

It seems likely that linguistic relations on the colony's farms and plantations were very similar to those Chaudenson describes: on the small farms, slaves began speaking approximate varieties of French based on their direct and regular contact with the French of the colonists, which was itself quite heterogenous and marked by regional features as well as by features typical of what may be called popular French (a tendency toward analytic rather than synthetic constructions, the frequent use of tonic pronouns for emphasis, the prevalence of the adverb *-là* used postnominally with demonstrative value, etc.); on the plantations, in contrast, the masses of newly imported slaves were largely removed from direct contact with the white colonists and were exposed primarily to the approximate French spoken by the Creoles, whose role it was to socialize them. I am inclined to agree with Chaudenson that it was in the *bossales'* attempts to learn the approximate French of the Creoles that LC came to be a relatively stable, though certainly not invariable language, structurally distinct from the French of the colonists.[2]

EVIDENCE FROM EARLY LC DOCUMENTS

The few known attestations of LC from the colonial period, most of which have only come to light in the last few years thanks to archival research by Hall (1992a), Ricard (1992), and Marshall (1989), support the notion that in the early and mid-18th century the language had not yet fully stabilized and was in some respects closer to French than it would be by the time additional written texts began to appear in the mid-19th century (for a collection of these texts see Neumann-Holzschuh 1987). The most substantial attestations of LC from the 18th century come from the transcript of a 1748 trial in New Orleans of a slave accused of murdering a French soldier. This transcript, uncovered by Hall (1992a), contains testimony from several slaves recorded in direct discourse. Great caution must be exercised in interpreting these texts, since they were transcribed by a Frenchman who may have inadvertently introduced French forms not actually used by the slaves in their testimony. Nevertheless, he clearly intends to show that the slave witnesses were speaking something other than Standard French, and these portions of his transcript merit close examination for the clues they provide as to what early LC may have been like, at least in the New Orleans area.

The relevant passages from the transcript are listed below in order of appearance:[3]

(1) Vu! laisser la notre trapes. Pourquoi tirer vois sous notre trapes? 'Hey you, leave our traps alone. Why are you firing under our traps!'

(2) Ce que pour esta a toy ne ree pas a M. Raquet? 'Is it that they belong to you, not to M. Raquet?'

(3) Ou toy courir Charlot pendants que nous diner? 'Where did you go, Charlot, while we were eating?'

(4) Qui toy tuer, Charlot? 'Who did you kill, Charlot?'

(5) Moy na rien tué. 'I did not kill anyone.'
(6) Comment, Bougre, pourquoy tourner ton chemise comme ça? 'Hey, fellow, why do you turn your shirt that way?'
(7) Et quelle manière est cela, travaille donc! 'What are you doing, work, then!'
(8) Bougre, si je te revois je le tireray un Coup de fusil. 'You guy, if I see you again I'll shoot you with my gun.'
(9) Est-ce je ne suis pas sur moy terrain à mon maître? 'Am I not on my land of my master?'

In (1) the feature of greatest interest is the interrogative inversion of the subject *vois* ('vous') and the verb *tirer*, a structure typical of written and formal styles of French but relatively rare in the spoken language and unknown in contemporary LC. The fact that inversion in French is generally restricted to formal styles makes it unlikely that this construction was ever characteristic of LC across registers. Rather, its use here—unless it is simply to be attributed to the transcriber—suggests that the slave giving testimony commanded a range of styles and was able to invoke the one most appropriate to the formal context of a court proceeding.

A second feature of interest in this sample is the French interrogative adverb *pourquoi* 'why'. This form is rare in the 19th-century LC texts analyzed by Neumann-Holzschuh (1987), and it is entirely absent from 20th-century descriptions of the language. Instead, this adverb takes the form [kofɛ] or some variant thereof. However, the four remaining speakers of the LC of New Orleans I have been able to locate use [pu(r)kwa] exclusively and are unfamiliar with [kofɛ],[4] which suggests that [pu(r)kwa] is an early acrolectal LC form which was eventually replaced by [kofɛ] in most parts of the colony but survived in the urban speech of New Orleans. It is possible, in fact, that a number of the French-like features of this transcript continued to be used in New Orleans where, as Mercier observed in 1880, LC was generally more acrolectal than in the rural areas: "Il y a une différence sensible entre le langage créole de la campagne et celui de la ville; ce dernier se rapproche davantage du français, surtout quand la personne qui le parle sait lire et écrire" (1880:381). ('There is a noticeable difference between the creole speech of the country and that of the city; the latter is closer to French, especially when the person who speaks it knows how to read and write.')

The text in (2) is difficult to interpret.[5] Perhaps the easiest feature to comment on is the use of the preposition *a* to express possession *(a toy, a M. Raquet)*. This construction is found, albeit rarely, in 19th-century texts as well as in the contemporary language (Neumann 1985; Klingler 1992). Its occurrence here is significant primarily because it argues against Mercier's (1880) claim that it was imported to Louisiana by émigrés from St. Domingue—an impossible scenario, given that these refugees of the colony's slave revolt did not begin arriving in Louisiana until well after the time of this trial. The rest of the sentence is quite confusing, particularly since it appears to lack a subject. It would be possible to interpret *ce* as a pronoun subject if we were to assume that *ce que* were equivalent to French *ce qui* 'what, that which' and did not represent a shortened form of the interrogative marker *est-ce que*. In this case the meaning of the question would be something like 'What is yours is (it) not (also) M. Raquet's?' The form *ree* is also perplexing, though it appears to be related to the French combination of the future/conditional marker -[r]- and the conditional ending -[ɛ] of the third person, probably of the verb *être* in this case (*serait*). The most literal French rendition of the question might thus be something like *Ce qui est à toi ne serait(-il) pas à M. Raquet?* which, translated literally into English, means 'What is yours would (it) not (also) be M. Raquet's?' If this interpretation of *ree* is correct, then the form is related to the modern-day LC conditional marker [se], which has the rare variant [sre] and clearly comes from French *serait* (Neumann 1985:220n1).

This explanation is not wholly satisfactory, in part because it involves a good deal of conjecture, but also because it fails to account for the appearance of *pour*, whose function remains opaque. These difficulties in interpreting (2) have several possible sources, the most obvious being my own unfamiliarity with the LC of the mid-18th century. It is also possible, however, that the sentence itself is not fully coherent, which could have at least three explanations. One is that the transcriber failed to render faithfully the slave's testimony; a second is that the slave, who was reporting the French soldier's own words, was only able to reproduce them approximately; finally, a third—and more intriguing—explanation is that (2) reflects a stage in the development of LC when the language had not yet stabilized, so that variation was especially great and regular relationships between specific forms and specific functions had not yet been clearly established.

The questions in (3) and (4) correspond perfectly to modern-day LC, except for the form of the second-person singular subject pronoun, which today is [to] rather than the form [twa] suggested by the spelling *toy*, and the form of the verb *courir* 'to go', which would rarely show a final [r] today. Of course we cannot assume that the transcriber's French-based spelling represents such phonological detail, and it may be that the forms actually used by the witnesses matched those of modern-day LC.

The statement in (5) is structurally closer to French (*Je n'ai rien tué* 'I didn't kill anything', or *Je n'ai tué personne* 'I didn't kill anyone') than is its equivalent in modern-day LC, [mo pa t͡ʃwe arjɛ̃] or [mo pa t͡ʃwe pærsɔn], preserving as it does the negation with *n(e)* but not *pas*, and the placement of the adverb *rien* before the non-finite verb (but after the finite verb, if we take the *-a* of *na* to be an auxiliary corresponding to first-person singular *ai* of the French translation).[6]

Sample (6) contains little that is noteworthy; aside from the French interrogative adverb—previously seen in (1), but here spelled *pourquoy*—and the representation of the final [r] of *Bougre*, its forms and structure match those of later LC.

Sample (7) also conforms to modern-day LC, particularly as it is spoken in Breaux Bridge (in Pointe Coupee, the interrogative adjective [kɛl] and the demonstrative pronoun [sila] are very rare; see Klingler 1992:131, 216). Of particular interest is the verb *travaille*, which appears here in its 'short' form, without the final vowel -[e] (i.e., [travaj] rather than [travaje]). While this truncated form of verbs whose full form ends in -[e] is found systematically in the second-person singular imperative (as well as in the habitual/universal present and after the impersonal expression [(l)fo]) in the LC of Breaux Bridge today, in 19th-century texts such verbs have a single, invariable form in -[e] which appears in all contexts

(Neumann 1985). Neumann attributes this relatively more complex verb morphology in modern-day Breaux Bridge Creole to recent decreolization, but the appearance of the short form *travaille* [travaj] here suggests that a more complex morphology than is found in 19th-century texts was already a feature of LC in the 18th century.

Like (2), (8) is uttered by the accused slave who is reporting the speech of the murdered French soldier. This may explain the appearance in this sample of numerous French-like features, such as the first-person singular subject pronoun *je* (rather than *moy*), the second-person singular direct object pronoun *te* (rather than the tonic pronoun *toy* [twa] placed after the verb, as is typical of LC), and the synthetic future of the verb *tirer* 'shoot', which is not found in modern-day LC.[7] However, in (9) the same slave is reporting his own response to the soldier's threat, and yet we find again the use of *je* for the first-person singular subject instead of *moy* as in (5).[8] Also worthy of mention in (9) is the French form of the first-person singular copula, *suis*; in later LC the copula never takes this form and frequently does not appear at all before a prepositional phrase (Neumann 1985).

To summarize, the features I have highlighted in the course of this analysis can be grouped into three categories:

1) those which match or closely resemble 19th-century and modern-day LC
2) those which are closer to French than their counterparts in later LC (the interrogative adverb *pourquoi*, interrogative inversion of subject and verb, the pronouns *je* and *te*, etc.)
3) seemingly anomalous forms and structures which do not fall clearly into either of the first two categories and whose meaning or function are difficult to interpret

As noted earlier, the questionable reliability of the transcription weakens the force of any conclusions we might want to draw from these samples. Nevertheless, unless we assume that the features of categories two and three were not in fact uttered by the slave witnesses but were instead introduced by the court transcriber, these features taken together lend support to the hypothesis that in 1748 an early form of LC was already being spoken (shown by the features of category one) which was as yet unstable and highly variable (shown by the features of category two) but, as a result of the intimate social relations and intense language contact characteristic of the small-farm period of colonial development, was in many respects closer to French than it would become in the 19th and 20th centuries, particularly in rural areas (shown by the features of category three).

According to Chaudenson's theory, the French-based creoles became relatively stable, autonomous language systems when vast quantities of new slaves were imported to work on the plantations which were established during the second phase of colonial development, after the initial phase of the small farm. The large-scale development of plantations and the concomitant re-Africanization of slave society took place in Louisiana towards the end of the 18th century, during the period of Spanish rule (1763–1800). While noting the difficulty of accurately determining Louisiana's population during this period, Hall (1992a:278) calculates that the number of slaves rose "from 5,600 in 1766 to 9,649 in 1777 and 20,673 in 1788," an increase which, she emphasizes, could not have been due simply to "natural increase [or] the importation of slaves from other parts of the Americas" but must be attributed in large part to the arrival of *bossales* from Africa. If Chaudenson's scenario for creolization is correct, we would expect that LC should have begun to stabilize during this period. While little evidence exists to test this hypothesis, it does gain some support from a few short samples of LC written in 1791, which conform almost perfectly to later LC. These samples, which, like the previous ones, come from testimony given during the murder trial of a slave, are provided below as they appear in Hall (1992a:253–54), accompanied by her English glosses:

> (10) C'est moi! C'est moi moi-même, Latulipe! Toi fini, moi aussi. C'est ton dernier jour aujourd'hui, mon tienne aussi. 'It is I! It is I myself, Latulipe! You are done for today, and so am I.'
>
> (11) Moi crois toi pas besoin moi encore. 'I believe you do not need me anymore.'

The only features of these samples which diverge from the LC of the 19th and 20th centuries are the forms *moi, toi,* presumably representing the pronunciations [mwa], [twa] instead of today's [mo], [to] for the first- and second-person singular subject pronouns (*toi fini; moi crois toi pas besoin moi encore*); the possessive pronoun *montienne,* pronounced [mokɛn] or [motšɛn] today;[9] and the French *aujourd'hui,* which today takes the form [ʒo(r)di]. While it would be imprudent to try to draw any firm conclusions from these two short samples, when compared to the samples from 1748 they nonetheless suggest that by 1791 LC had stabilized considerably and, in Pointe Coupee at least, had come to more closely resemble LC as it is represented in 19th-century texts and as it continues to be spoken today.

This fragmentary linguistic evidence from colonial Louisiana combines with the sociohistorical evidence seen earlier to support Chaudenson's linking of the development of creole languages to the successive stages of the small farm and the plantation in French colonial society generally. The samples from 1748, when small farms were the principal agricultural units, are not inconsistent with a version of LC which is variable and unstable, and yet in many respects is closer to French than LC would come to be. In contrast, the (admittedly short) samples recorded under similar conditions in 1791, when large plantations were becoming more common and disproportions between the white and black populations had grown, match later LC very closely, suggesting that the language was already stabilizing as a result of the new linguistic situation created by re-Africanization.

AFRICAN ETHNIC GROUPS IN LOUISIANA

Chaudenson makes another significant claim about French colonial society, however, which is contradicted by conditions in Louisiana as described by Hall and others. His claim is that African ethnic and linguistic communities could not have reestablished themselves in the colonial setting, and this for essentially two reasons. First, as is supported by a number of historical accounts of plantation colonies which Chaudenson examines (1992), the slaves constituted a very heterogeneous group, particularly on individual estates where their owners purposely separated them according to ethnicity to prevent conspiracy. Second, the slaves were bound to their particular farm or plantation and were utterly denied the freedom of movement which might have allowed them to seek out other members of their ethnic and language groups on distant estates or in commercial centers of the colony. Clearly, if conditions were as Chaudenson describes them, this would have served to dilute African cultural influence in colonial society, including the possible influence of African languages on the incipient creole.

Hall's research suggests, however, that among the slaves brought to Louisiana there were in fact large numbers who came from the same or closely related ethnic groups, and that it was not uncommon for these slaves to be grouped together on the same estates.[10] Furthermore, her research supports that of other historians in showing that slaves in Louisiana, contrary to Chaudenson's characterization of colonial society in general, enjoyed surprisingly great freedom of movement which allowed them to go well beyond the confines of their masters' property to engage in social as well as commercial activities on other plantations or in other parts of the colony.

Regarding the ethnicity of Louisiana slaves, Hall notes that fully "two-thirds of the slaves brought to Louisiana by the French slave trade [3945 of 5987] came from Senegambia" (1992a:29), a region which, according to the historian Philip Curtin, has "a homogeneous culture and a common style of history," and whose primary languages—Sereer, Wolof, Pulaar, and Malinke—are closely related (Curtin 1975:6, quoted in Hall 1992a:29). Among the Senegambian slaves, Hall claims that one group in particular, the Bambara, were numerically and culturally dominant. Although she gives no figures showing what proportion of the population they represented, she cites a report by Louisiana officials according to which, in 1731, "four hundred Bambara slaves speaking the same language were involved" in a conspiracy to revolt. While the officials' ability to accurately identify West African languages may be questioned, this nonetheless suggests, as Hall (1992a) points out, the existence of a significant African language community in the early years of the colony.

During the massive re-Africanization of Louisiana's slave population that took place under Spanish rule in the last decades of the 18th century, the Bambara and other Senegambian slaves continued to make up a substantial portion of that population, though they no longer formed a majority as increasing numbers of slaves were brought in from the Bight of Benin, Central Africa, and the Bight of Biafra (Hall 1992a). In the Pointe Coupee post, slaves from the Bight of Benin during this period rivaled in number those from Senegambia. The Mina, in particular, were a numerically significant group who successfully functioned as a community even in slavery. This is made clear in an account of their well-planned, though abortive, conspiracy to revolt against the whites at the post in 1791. Of the seventeen slaves implicated in the conspiracy, fifteen were Mina (Ricard 1992). The record of the trial of these slaves shows that they spoke a common language, which according to Hall (1992b) must have been a dialect of Ewe closely related to Fon.[11] The record is less clear on the question of whether or not the defendants also spoke Creole. A court interpreter proficient in Creole insisted that they were perfectly competent in this language, but the defendants themselves claimed total ignorance of it (Ricard 1992). It may be, however, that this was a calculated lie on the part of the accused to help protect them from conviction. Regardless of whether or not the Mina could in fact speak Creole in addition to their native language, we have here a clear case of an African language community which was able to function successfully within colonial Louisiana.

This was possible in large part because, as the trial records show, despite living on separate plantations, the Mina were able to travel with relative ease to the plantations of their co-conspirators in order to attend dances at which they planned their revolt. That this kind of mobility among Louisiana's slaves was common is confirmed by other historical accounts. The French traveler C. C. Robin describes in the following manner the liaisons many slaves maintained with lovers on distant plantations:

Sometimes their mistresses live several leagues away. The fatigues of the day do not prevent them from going to stay the night with her to be back in time for work the next morning. It is no little astonishing that these men enfeebled by difficulty and poor nutrition, are able to continue these nocturnal carouses. Misfortune indeed, for the masters or neighbors who have horses in charge of these gallants. . . . I used to hear the galloping of the horses of these lovers all night; coming and going. (Robin 1966:245, cited in McGowan 1976:133)

In some instances the slaves did not need to borrow their masters' horses, for they possessed their own. An example comes from Pointe Coupee, where in 1774 the *commandante* of the post, concerned about the slaves' unrestricted nighttime movements, declared such ownership illegal and confiscated the horses of several slaves, which he then put up for sale. Three of the dispossessed slaves secretly made their way to New Orleans to protest the *commandante*'s action and to claim the money from the sale of their horses (Hall 1992a).

But not all slave movement was unsanctioned. At times, in fact, travel was required of slaves by their masters. Records from 1739 show that this was the case for a group of twenty of the king's slaves, stationed at Balize, who "made voyages to serve the needs of the post, cutting wood, going fifteen to twenty lieus up the river during seven months out of the year to get provisions for the garrison." Another group were required to go as far as Illinois for stays of up to eight months (Hall 1992a:135).

Freedom of movement among slaves became so widespread that the white colonists eventually felt their security threatened, and as the example from Pointe Coupee illustrates, official actions were taken to restrict it. McGowan (1976) notes that Governor Vaudreuil's police code of 1750 was designed in part to put an end to unchecked slave movement. Severe penalties were to be inflicted on planters who failed to confine their slaves to their own plantations or to prevent outside slaves from making visits to their property for assemblies of any kind. In spite of these provisions, the gatherings continued. While not all slave movement beyond the confines of the farm or plantation resulted in contact with slaves of the same or related ethnic groups, it is clear that, as in the case of the Mina, such contact did occur often and provided the means by which these groups could continue functioning as such in the colonial setting.

The historical evidence from Louisiana, then, presents a picture of colonial society which differs radically from Chaudenson's in that it shows significant numbers of slaves from similar ethnic and linguistic backgrounds who, thanks to a surprising degree of mobility, were able in some measure to regroup themselves along lines of language and ethnicity. It is Hall's (1992a) contention that, as a result, African culture left deep traces on Louisiana society in particular and on American society in general. Not only does she consider lower Louisiana to have had a more thoroughly Africanized culture than any other part of the country, she also believes it to have been "the most significant source of Africanization of the entire culture of the United States" (157).

AFRICAN INFLUENCE ON LOUISIANA CREOLE

As noted earlier, one aspect of culture where Hall (1992a) seeks to locate African influence is in the Creole language. As she puts it, "The cultural impact of the Africans brought to Louisiana during the French slave trade is engraved upon the very structure of language as well as in the history of its use" (187). She goes on to state that the "vocabulary of Louisiana Creole is overwhelmingly French in origin, but its grammatical structure is largely African" (188). While the first part of this claim is uncontroversial, the second part concerning grammar should raise serious questions in the minds of all but the most fervent adherents to the substratist position. For anyone familiar with a variety of French-based creoles would likely recognize that LC's structural proximity to French makes it a poor candidate for African grammatical influence as compared, for example, to Haitian Creole, which is structurally more distant from its lexifier and, indeed, has often been at the center of the debate between proponents of the substratist and superstratist points of view. Furthermore, while LC does have some features for which possible African models have been cited, such as postposed definite determiners and the widespread agglutination onto nouns of syllabic elements having their origin in a French determiner ([ɛ̃ lamezɔ̃] 'a house', [ɛ̃ gro lefej] 'a big leaf', [ɛ̃ gro dife] 'a big fire', etc.), its possessive determiners, in contrast to those of the Caribbean creoles but like those of French, are preposed, and it appears to lack true serial verbs, a feature common to many creoles and one for which perhaps the strongest arguments for substratal influence have been made.[12] In short, while African origins for portions of LC structure cannot be ruled out, they remain to be demonstrated, and doing so promises to be a difficult task, requiring meticulous comparative work on African and creole languages. It is a task which Hall, as an historian, cannot be expected to undertake, but it is nevertheless surprising that she offers no linguistic evidence for her claim that LC grammatical structure "is largely African."

CONCLUSION

The conclusion to be drawn from this comparison of Chaudenson's model of creolization to the specific case of Louisiana is dual in nature. On one hand, it would appear that Chaudenson's model must be revised to allow for the possibility that as Hall shows was the case in Louisiana, African ethnic and language groups were in fact able to reform and continue functioning in the context of slavery. At the same time, however, admitting the existence of these groups is by no means tantamount to admitting that there must have been significant substratal influence on the incipient creole's grammatical structure. Chaudenson may exaggerate the extent to which African slaves were culturally isolated on their farms or plantations and the rapidity and thoroughness with which they were simultaneously deculturated of their African heritage and acculturated to the ways of colonial society. But in the end it appears that he is right to emphasize what he calls the fundamentally *centripetal* nature of this society, in which the language and culture of the colonists and, later, the Creole slaves served as the primary models for the *bossales*, the center towards which they would eventually gravitate. For the Louisiana experience shows that though peripheral ethnic and language groups did exist among the slaves, they most likely disintegrated shortly after the last arrival of new slaves from Africa, at which point their members were inevitably drawn into the orbit of the highly original systems of Creole language and culture. If their African languages did, in fact, leave structural traces on LC, these traces remain well hidden, and the kind of careful linguistic research which would be required to uncover them remains to be done.

NOTES

I wish to thank Salikoko Mufwene for helpful comments on earlier versions of this essay.

1. ". . . l'absolue nécessité, pour l'étude génétique de toute forme de créolisation, d'une approche rigoureuse et minutieuse de l'histoire des sociétés concernées."

2. This is not to say that creolization occurred abruptly with the advent of the plantation society, which itself developed slowly over a period of years. On the contrary, it seems more reasonable to assume, as do a growing number of creolists (e.g., Singler 1986; McWhorter 1992; Mufwene 1992), that creolization took place gradually and was characterized by a good deal of individual as well as regional variation.

3. In the interest of saving space I have not supplied background information to the proceedings, so that these excerpts appear out of context. For a detailed account of this fascinating trial, see Hall (1992a), which is also my source for the excerpts and their English translations. Although each of the speech samples comes from slave testimony, it is not always clear from Hall's account which of the several slaves interrogated is speaking. The original documents are part of the Records of the Superior Council of Louisiana, which are kept at the Louisiana Historical Center of the Louisiana State Museum in New Orleans.

4. The speakers are two males and two females, all of whom were born and raised in New Orleans. I am indebted to Gwendolyn Hall, Gloria Harris, and James Viator for their help in locating these speakers.

5. This question was reportedly asked by the French soldier, who would later be murdered, to a group of slaves belonging to Raquet.

6. If Hall is correct in translating *rien* as '(not) anyone' rather than '(not) anything' (the latter being its meaning in French), then this sample of LC shows a semantic difference with French which does not characterize modern-day LC. The proximity to French of the structure of the negation in the sample holds regardless of which translation is correct, however.

7. I am unable to suggest an explanation for the anomalous appearance of *le* before the verb *tireray*.

8. It may be significant that, in contrast to (9), where Charlot himself is reporting his own words, sample (5) containing *moy* was uttered by another slave supposedly quoting Charlot.

9. While it is doubtful that the court transcriber would have used the spelling *tienne* to represent the pronunciation [kɛn], it is conceivable that he used it to represent the palatalized pronunciation [ʧɛn], in which case this feature does not differ from later LC.

10. In making this claim, Hall relies primarily on designations of slave *nations* (a term which she equates with ethnic group) found in the voluminous historical documents she consulted, although historians of the slave trade have often warned that such designations are vague and inaccurate (see, e.g., Chaudenson 1992, who cites a number of those historians and challenges the notion that *nations* referred to ethnic groups in 18th-century French usage). Hall notes several factors which argue in favor of the reliability of the designations in the documents she uses. First, in court transcripts, slaves who testified during the proceedings apparently identified their own nations. Second, regarding the use of the term *Bambara*, Hall says that, while it later came to have a "generic meaning" (as noted by Debien 1961), during the French slave trade of the early 18th century it referred to truly ethnic Bambara, as is evidenced by early documentary reference to a large community of speakers of the Bambara language in Louisiana (see below). Finally, in an appendix the author notes that the designations used to indicate the origins of Louisiana slaves are much more varied and specific (and therefore, presumably, more accurate) than those used in other colonies.

11. It is Hall's belief that the Mina slaves came from the Bight of Benin rather than from the post of El Mina, as some historians have claimed.

12. For a discussion of possible African influence on creole determiner systems see Valdman (1977) and Holm (1988); for attempts to trace agglutination to African influence see Baker (1984) and Baker and Corne (1986). LC verbs in serial-like constructions are described by Klingler (1992) and Neumann (1985); McWhorter (1992) amasses considerable comparative linguistic evidence in support of his theory that serial verbs in Saramaccan are attributable to African influence.

Code-Switching and Loss of Inflection in Louisiana French

Michael D. Picone

BORROWING OR SWITCHING?

The determination of the proper classification for linguistic material that has been transferred from one language to another is often problematic. There is not always a sufficient amount of transparent criteria for determining whether a particular transferred item constitutes an instance of borrowing or of code-switching. One looks first to the phonological profile of the transferred form(s) as an indicator of the degree of assimilation. Phonological indicators alone, however, will not suffice.

Some bilingual speakers may retain an accent when articulating their non-dominant language (L2), and, consequently, transferred material, though phono-logically altered, might still constitute an instance of code-switching (Poplack 1980:583–84). Conversely, an L2 phonological signature characterizing a particular transferred utterance does not always guarantee that the speaker of the utterance is in even partial possession of the L2 code, and this, in turn, makes it difficult to claim that the speaker is actually switching codes. For stylistic reasons and not by constraint, a highly fluent bilingual may purposely subject a switch to the phonology of the recipient language. In still other cases, owing to the closeness of the phonological attributes of the two languages, either fortuitously or due to convergence phenomena, phonological indicators are not contrastive enough to efficiently differentiate between codes (as is sometimes the case for Louisiana French).[1] In attempting to minimize these kinds of problems, strategies arrived at have privileged morphosyntactic and/or sociolinguistic phenomena as indicators of the type of processing to which the transferred material has been subjected, be it borrowing or switching (Hasselmo 1970; Shaffer 1978; Lipski 1978; Poplack 1981).

Even use of these strategies, however, does not always guarantee a clear result. Problems surface particularly in relation to the filling of a single lexical slot with a transferred item. Poplack (1988:96) illustrates this with the following example, extracted from the Ottawa-Hull Franco-Ontarian corpus. Since the morphosyntactic environment that normally accompanies the italicized forms is similar in both English and French, and in the absence of any sociolinguistic information about the degree of community acceptance of these forms, there is no immediately available contrastive criteria, other than the phonological, to determine whether these words are being processed as borrowings or as switches:

> (1) Il y avait une *band* là qui jouait de la musique *steady*, pis il y avait des games[2] de *ball*, pis . . . ils vendaient de *l'ice cream*, pis il y avait un grosse *beach*, le monde se baignait.

'There was a band there that played music all the time and there were ball games, and . . . they sold ice cream, and there was a big beach where people would go swimming.'

This problem crops up continually in attempting to determine the status of English-origin lexical transfers in Louisiana French. While it appears that in the Ottawa-Hull corpus the problem is far more characteristic of nouns than verbs, since the latter tend to conform to the dictates of the inflectional morphology of the recipient language (Poplack, Sankoff & Miller 1988), this is not the case for Louisiana French, where both transferred nouns and verbs, being uninflected, defy immediate categorization.

Though examples appear, this phenomenon goes unanalyzed in Conwell and Juilland (1963:24), the most comprehensive—though now outdated—descriptive grammar of Louisiana French, and in Griolet (1986:18). Brown (1986:402), in a general study of code-switching, independently provides corroborating examples, but no specific analysis, of uninflected nouns (pluralized only by virtue of the preceding determiner), as in example 2a, and uninflected verbs, as in example 2b.

(2) (a) Il oubliait comment mettre les *brake*.
        'He would forget how to put on the brakes.'
   (b) Puis ils ont *settle* à Lafayette.
        'Then they settled in Lafayette.'

In what is to follow, the principle topic of investigation and discussion is the analysis of such uninflected forms and the resulting ramifications for code-switching theory. I will begin with the nouns, demonstrating how the analysis is fraught with difficulty until a comparison with the verbs allows for a more satisfactory reanalysis, one that views inflectional loss for both word classes as a unified phenomenon.

FILLING LEXICAL SLOTS WITH TRANSFERRED NOUNS

Data obtained from speakers of Louisiana French show that single lexical slots are frequently filled with English-origin items, sometimes for stylistic reasons, sometimes out of necessity (Picone 1994a). In the following, there is no contrastive morphosyntactic information to determine if the italicized nouns belong to L1 or L2.

(3) (a) un *truck* seconde main
        'a second-hand truck'
   (b) Il était après dire ça ce matin sur le *radio*.
        'He was talking about that this morning on the radio.'

The italicized forms in 3a–b were processed according to Cajun English phonology: the presence of the retroflex /r/ rather than the apical, stress placement, and so on. In the absence of contrastive morphosyntactic environments, then, one is tempted to fall back on the purely phonological criteria and to class these forms as switches.[3] This solution becomes unsatisfactory, however, when one considers the following data in which the italicized nouns are pronounced according to the attributes of Cajun English, but, in apparent obedience to the morphology of French, the task of marking plurality is left to the preceding determiner or quantifier.

(4) (a) J'ai deux *truck*.
      'I have two trucks.'
   (b) . . . le monde qui halle l'huile pour eux dans les   gros *tank truck.*
                                                  DET+PLUR
      . . . 'the people who haul the oil for them in the big tank trucks'
   (c) Lui, le plus jeune, il a été à l'école ici, tu connais, avec les   *big shot.*
                                                         DET+PLUR
      'Him, the youngest, went to school here, ya know, with the big shots.'

Consider this "s-less" plural in relation to Poplack's (1981:174) well-known Equivalence Constraint. According to that constraint, "codes will tend to be switched at points where juxtaposition of . . . elements does not violate a syntactic rule of either language, i.e., at the point where the surface structure of the languages map onto each other." Plurality representation in Louisiana French, as in other dialects of French, generally takes place in conjunction with the preceding determiner, whereas this is never the case in English. Even in those rare cases where plurality is phonologically manifested in the noun-final position in French (*animal* [animal] > *animaux* [animo]), the representation takes the form of a phonological alteration rather than English-style adjunction of /-s/. In any event, such cases involve the presence of a discontinuous morpheme, since pluralization of the determiner is not thereby obviated. Consequently, the Louisiana French speaker who transfers an English-origin noun into a context calling for plurality has the following matrix of hypothetical choices (examples 5a–5d): as in 5a, retain the entire noun phrase in English; as in 5b, use an uninflected French determiner with an inflected English noun; as in 5c, use double representation of plurality where both the French determiner and the English noun are inflected; and as in 5d, use an inflected French determiner with an uninflected English noun.

(5) (a) *the truck[s]
   (b) *le truck[s]
   (c) ?les truck[s]
   (d) les truck

Examples 5a–b are starred because there is no evidence that they occur. Examples such as 5c may be found but are of exceedingly low frequency compared to 5d, which is the norm. Examples 5a and, arguably, 5c would not have violated the Equivalence Constraint and could have qualified as switches. However, 5b and 5d clearly do violate the constraint. Since only 5d systematically obtains in actual speech, in accordance with the Equivalence Constraint, one is forced to conclude that these are instances of borrowing rather than switching, perhaps to be viewed as "nonce" borrowings as per Weinreich (1953) and Poplack, Wheeler & Westwood (1987). That is, since the loss of the "s-ful" plural violates English morphosyntactic rules, these forms cannot constitute switches and must be considered to be borrowings.

This, however, creates an obvious contradiction. Singular English-origin nouns cannot be classed as code-switches, appealing to phonological criteria by default, while, at the same time, the plural versions, sometimes of the same nouns, are classed as borrowings, based on morphosyntactic criteria. In order to avoid this unwanted inconsistency, one might simply use extrapolative reasoning to extend the analysis formulated for the transferred plural nouns so that it encompasses all transferred nouns. In other words, on the strength of the morphological treatment that plurals receive, and to maintain parallelism, it is inferred that all transferred nouns, be they singular or plural, are instances of borrowing. This solution would have the advantage of posing no challenge to Poplack's Equivalence Constraint. Furthermore, it would seem to connect well with Poplack's other general constraint, the Free Morpheme Constraint (see below for more discussion), by disallowing the union of a "converted" noun—which, by definition, is to be viewed as an integral part of L1—with a bound morpheme from L2, in this case the English noun-final pluralizer /-s/. These advantages notwithstanding, this solution is problematic for three reasons.

First of all, as previously stated, based on informal observation, the processing of transferred English-origin nouns is highly systematic in Louisiana French, admitting of few exceptions. Consequently to assign all such nouns to the "borrowed" category, is to all but eliminate any possibility of code-switching for lexical nominals. This would indeed be a strange state of affairs for a language where code-switching is both demonstrable and frequent at other levels. This contradiction is especially significant if noun incorporation in Louisiana French is to be viewed as a common variety of "emblematic" switching, as Poplack (1980:589) posits for Puerto Rican Spanish, whose speakers regularly incorporate English nominals.[4]

Second, the following metalinguistic comment made by a Louisiana French speaker, in which the whole point of the utterance is to compare codes, shows that a phonologically assimilated borrowing and an incontestable nominal code-switch undergo identical processing when it comes to the s-less manifestation of the plural at the phonological level (accents indicate stress placement).[5]

(6) Un rein *is backbone*, et les [kidnɛ́] *is* [kɪ́dnə].
    '*Rein* is backbone and *kidneys* is kidneys.'

Finally, the processing to which nouns are subjected does not exist in a vacuum and must be reconsidered in light of a similar phenomenon whereby English-origin verbs, retaining Cajun English pronunciation, are also transferred into Louisiana French.

FILLING LEXICAL SLOTS WITH TRANSFERRED VERBS

As examples 7a–e show, loss of inflection is also systematic in the processing of virtually all transferred verbs and deverbal adjectives. This is not simply a case of word-final [t,d] loss, which exists variably in normal Cajun English discourse as it does in virtually all other dialects of English (Labov 1989a:89), for it is no longer variable but is categoric when verbs are transferred into French discourse. Furthermore, loss of inflection occurs not only word finally, as in examples 7a–b, but also word internally in those cases where the normal English vowel alternations for PAST do not obtain, as in 7c–d. Nor are infinitives marked in any way, as exemplified in 7e. Example 7b demonstrates that past participles converted to predicate adjectives are subject to the same treatment. The consequences of this must be carefully considered.

(7) (a) Je l'   ai   bien *convince.*
        I   him PAST   really ———
        'I really convinced him.'
    (b) Il   est *retire.*
        He is   ———
        'He's retired.'
    (c) On a   *drive* en ville.
        We PAST ——— in city.
        'We drove to New Orleans.'
    (d) J' ai   *ride* sur le *bike.*
        I   PAST   ——— on   the ———
        'I rode the bike.'
    (e) Ça   voul'ait   *americanize.*
        they want IMPERF   ————————
        'They wanted to Americanize.'

The surface manifestation of these verbs transgresses the morphosyntax of both English and French and, therefore, is not working in compliance with the Equivalence Constraint in these cases. English participial inflections are missing, as is the prepositional introduction that sometimes serves to mark an infinitive. None of this has been replaced by the normal Louisiana French participial and infinitival inflections that accompany native verbs, as in examples 8a–c. Instead, the verbs in 7a–e have been stripped of all inflectional representation, be it English or French.

(8) (a) J' ai   travaill[e]   en ville.
        I   PAST$_1$ work PAST$_2$ in city
        'I worked in New Orleans.'
    (b) Ils   ont   appr[i]   un tit brin parl[e]   en anglais.
        they PAST$_1$ learn PAST$_2$ a little bit speak INF   in English
        'They learned to speak a little bit of English.'

(c) Tu peux voi[r] pour écri[r] mon *check.*
You can see INF for write INF my —
'You can see to write my check.'

Thus, since the verb forms in 7a–e violate the morphosyntax of both languages, it could be argued that they deviate from both codes and cannot be properly classified as either true borrowings or as true switches to L2. They might be considered to be code neutralized (Picone 1994b). But before returning to consider this possibility more carefully, let us first approach the verbs in relation to Poplack's constraints.

On the surface of things, the English phonological signatures that the transferred verbs bear argue for their classification as code-switches, but, as previously noted, that possibility seems to fly in the face of the Equivalence Constraint. This violation would normally argue for their classification as borrowings, but in this instance, the simultaneous transgression of both French and English morphosyntax admits to no comfortable solution in the direction of borrowings. Some reconciliation between these seemingly divergent analyses, however, is obtainable. Their opposition can be minimized by turning to Poplack's Free Morpheme Constraint, the only other constraint that Poplack has postulated for the constraining of permissible code-switching (Poplack 1981:174), and assigning it a new functional role. This constraint states that switching may occur at any point "at which it is possible to make a surface constituent cut and still retain a free morpheme." Consequently, what appears to be a violation of the Equivalence Constraint may actually be the transparent use of the Free Morpheme Constraint, or some constraint akin to it, as an empowered device for operating switches: by dint of not adjoining any native morphemes, these forms are being flagged as switches. The assumption is that for Louisiana French, though not for every language, the Free Morpheme Constraint takes precedence over the Equivalence Constraint in the management of switches and borrowings. The reason that this same end could not have been achieved simply by retaining the English-origin inflections can be best illustrated by first turning to examples 8a–b.

These examples make clear that the PAST morpheme has discontinuous representation at the surface level in French. To retain English inflection in the place of $PAST_2$, as in hypothetical 9a, would constitute an unacceptable intrusion into the morphosyntactic integrity of the base language; this, indeed, is in accordance with the Equivalence Constraint. Hypothetical 9b, on the other hand, would result in the unintended (if the intention is to flag it as a switch) integration of the verb form into the base language. The solution is to drop all inflection and rely on the phonological signature and the transparency of the operation of the empowered Free Morpheme Constraint to flag the transferred material as a switch, as in 9c, even if, in so doing, the transparency of the Equivalence Constraint is somewhat compromised because the morphosyntax of neither language is fully respected and does not receive full representation at the surface level.

(9) (a) *Je l' ai *convinc·ed.*
      I him $PAST_1$ $PAST_2$
         French   English

(b)	*Je	l'	ai	*convinc ' é.*	
	I	him	PAST₁		PAST₂
			French		French
(c)	Je	l'	ai	*convince ' Ø.*	
	I	him	PAST₁		PAST₂
			French		Neutral

A similar argument can be marshaled to explain the loss of the infinitival inflection. Lack of inflection is a flagging device, along with the English phonological signature, to signal a switch, and it does so with less affront to French morphosyntax than the inclusion of the English *to* would have incurred. Again transparent use of the Free Morpheme Constraint in preference to, but not incongruously with, the Equivalence Constraint provides an appropriate explanation.

INFLECTIONAL LOSS AND FUNCTIONAL SHIFT

Returning now to the case of the nouns, although as an isolated phenomenon it was shown that it is possible to analyze them as a class of borrowings, in the fuller picture of things it can be argued that they are undergoing the exact same treatment as the verbs. That is, in what constitutes a general functional shift for the entire language, the suppression of inflection in Louisiana French is an operator for creating and manipulating switches. In keeping with this, the suppression of plural inflection enhances the phonological signature of nouns that are to be flagged as switches.

Such a functional shift is not entirely without precedent in Cajun English and French. Though infrequent, uninflected native verb roots occur in Louisiana French. Compare examples 10a and 10b. Both utterances belong to the same individual and occurred within a few minutes of each other.

(10)	(a)	Ils	ont	appris		un tit brin.
		they	PAST AUX	learn PAST PART		a little bit
		'They learned a little bit.'				
	(b)	Ils	ont	apprend	les	chansons.
		they	PAST AUX	learn	DET + PLUR	songs
		'They learned the songs.'				

It is not yet clear whether there is any regularity or generality to this phenomenon. However, inflectional loss is attested in Ditchy (1932:29) and Conwell and Juilland (1963:92) of the following type: *gonflé* 'swollen' > *gonfle*. Furthermore, variable inflectional reduction, not loss, is attested regularly in past participles of the following type: *répondu* 'answered' [repõdy] > [repõd] (Ditchy 1932:29; Conwell and Juilland 1963:107). The presence of the word-final [d] alone still serves to differentiate the past participle from present tense forms: *répond* [repõ].

Instances of inflectional reduction and loss co-occurring with native French items, however rare, allied with the existence of variable word-final [t,d] deletion in Cajun English as a generalized phonological phenomenon, may have provided some precedent for the functional accommodation herein proposed. Other dominated languages and languages in contact situations have generalized available but underused features (Hill and Hill 1986:162–63) or have resorted to various innovations for the purposes of managing imported materials as part of an overall strategy of vocabulary expansion (Picone 1994a).

It should be pointed out at this juncture that native inflection can occur with an English-origin verb root in certain limited contexts, such as 11a, showing the imperfect inflection, but these, too, are relatively rare. In fact, 11a does not come from my own corpus of spoken data, but from a transcription of a radio presentation (Arceneaux 1991:2–3) in what might well have constituted a "language playful" register. It seems that the Louisiana French speakers prefer to let auxiliaries and modals accompany the verb, as much as possible, in order to permit the uninflected flagged version in the output to identify it more clearly as a switch. In cases such as 11b, the present tense verb form, bearing the English phonological signature, can still constitute a switch because in the present tense in Louisiana French there is usually an absence of morphological inflection and so no classificational conflict will ensue.

(11) (a) Il a eu pour appeler un *wrecker* parce que plus il *back-up* · ait,

                                                                          IMPERF

           plus le sable *cave-in* · ait.

                            IMPERF

           'He had to call a towtruck because the more he backed up the more
           the sand would cave in.'

      (b) Ça *advertise* plus sur *Donahue show* que ça parle.

           'They advertise more on the Donahue show than they talk.'

Based on the foregoing, one can conclude that the general tendency in Louisiana French is to fill lexical slots, be they nominal or verbal, with transferred forms that are emphasized as switches not only as a consequence of their English phonological signature but also by virtue of special morphological processing—namely suppression of inflection—thereby reconciling the testimony of phonology and morphosyntax. A possible reason for such a functional shift will be proposed in the final section. It should be pointed out, however, that such functional accommodations are not unique.

Independent evidence for the apparent violation of the Equivalence Constraint to achieve a particular functional objective is found among Korean-English bilinguals. According to Yoon (1992), the adjunction of Korean "operating verbs" to English roots (variously verbs, adjectives, and nouns in the language of origin) allows for orally articulated recognition and negotiation of social position. This is owing to the fact that operating verbs, in turn, permit adjunction of the appropriate honorific inflections. Yoon (1992) notes that, irrespective of lexical need, speakers use such forms more frequently in socially mobile contact situations than in fixed relationships.

A sociolinguistic connection is implicit in the Yoon study because frequency in the use of such forms changes when speakers change social registers. However, even if the elements are difficult to untangle, frequency of use cannot be evaluated independently from their pragmatic function. This is all the more evident given the surprisingly unconstrained choice of available word classes from which English-origin materials are adopted. In this case, morphosyntax is subservient to communicative function, even if it can be shown that these forms are also used to mark prestige.

BILINGUAL PROFICIENCY

Further circumstantial evidence for the view that most transferred nouns and verbs are switches rather than borrowings in Louisiana French can be drawn from the informal observation that it is the proficient bilinguals who are the most adept at manipulating vocabulary across languages in the ways exemplified above, especially in relation to the verbal constructions. This conforms to Poplack's (1980) concluding statement: "Code-switching, rather than representing deviant behavior, is actually a suggestive indicator of degree of bilingual competence." Preliminary observations resulting from the analysis of the Louisiana French sampling indicate that the most intrasentential switching does indeed obtain among the balanced bilinguals. Age was not a factor in Poplack's sampling of Puerto Rican Spanish speakers in New York City. Superficially, it appears to be a factor in Louisiana French. This is owing to the fact that the younger speakers (30–45 years) are uniformly English dominant, not having acquired full competence in their parents' vernacular, which typifies the condition of a language in serious decline. While one might naively expect to find more, not less, crossover from English into the weaker French of the younger speakers, in actual fact, in what surely constitutes a striking confirmation of Poplack's hypothesis, one finds greater reluctance to switch codes at the intrasentential level. King (1991) makes note of a similar phenomenon: loss, not increase, of the use of adverbial *back* among young, English-dominant speakers using Acadian French in Saint-Louis, Canada.

In the case of Louisiana French, the fact that there is an age differential in the use of verb transferral[6] but much less so for noun transferral gives some pause to reconsider the amalgamation of both phenomena with respect to the younger speakers. Presupposing, as I have, that there is liberty to shift constraints to achieve desired functional ends, it is entirely possible that younger speakers, whose diminished use of French does not seem to include extensive use of verbal transfers, are processing nouns differently. Surface similarities in the speech production of the younger and older speakers with regards to the transfer of nouns may, therefore, be misleading. This scenario is plausible given the wide linguistic discrepancy that can exist even between contiguous generations for a language community in decline. Laudable attempts at renewal aside (Ancelet 1988; Brown 1993), Louisiana French still qualifies unequivocally as a declining speech community.

CODE NEUTRALITY

To conclude, I will return to the notion of code neutrality. Views according to which there is a continuum mediating between borrowing and outright switching to L2 (Weinreich 1953; Haugen 1956) have not met with favor by Poplack and Sankoff (1984:103), who entertain them only as hypothetical constructs to be overthrown. Nevertheless, the data from Louisiana French suggest the possibility that switching is not always a binary proposition. That is to say, a switch does not necessarily invoke the full grammatical apparatus of L2 but might, in some instances, invoke a third set of conditions forming a buffer code separating the full grammatical apparatus of L1 and L2. This would still constitute a code-switch, but of a different order and subject to different constraints. There would be functional justification for this, especially in the case of a declining, heavily dominated language like Louisiana French. It would allow for use of the necessary lexical resources of L2 and yet simultaneously keep dominant L2 at a desirable distance. If a language community, for whatever reason, eschews borrowings and the assimilation of elements from the dominant code, perhaps owing to purism (Dorian 1994) or perhaps finding such procedures to be unacceptably superfluous due to increased bilingualism, an appropriate strategy can be arrived at by establishing the type of buffer code herein proposed. By virtue of the buffer code, the dominant language becomes less invasive but can still be utilized for needed lexical expansion (see Drapeau 1993). Such functional necessities could serve to explain the motivation for reconfiguring the operational constraints in a particular dominated language as part of a strategy for arriving at appropriately adaptive, language preserving measures.

Introducing the notion of a code-neutral buffer would obviously call for a radical departure from the present view of code-switching processes. It is entirely possible, however, that the controversy swirling around the universality of the Equivalence Constraint and Free Morpheme Constraint exists in part because these constraints, while valid in their appropriate domains, are being applied to the analysis of language-contact situations that diverge from the binary configuration that has been presupposed. In fact, in some instances analysis of language-contact situations may have been inadvertently prejudiced by using data that have been refined based on judgment criteria that have been formulated in accordance with binary presuppositions. The possibility that code-neutral phenomena exist should, I contend, be seriously considered (Picone 1994b). The data provided from Louisiana French supply substantive support for such consideration.

Ultimately, functional factors like the ones suggested above, that seek their resolution in the creation of intermediary codes, will have to take their place alongside of formal and sociolinguistic factors in order for researchers to arrive at an accurate understanding of the complex assortment of elements that shape code-switching.

NOTES

Except where noted, the Louisiana French data are from recordings from summer 1992, as part of an ongoing project conducted primarily in the St. Landry, Lafayette, and Evangeline parishes. This fieldwork was made possible by the Research Grants Committee of the University of Alabama (grant no. 1630). I extend my gratitude to all those in Cajun Country who welcomed me unselfishly and participated enthusiastically in this project. I am indebted for their input to Barry Jean Ancelet, Carl Blyth, Becky Brown, and Kevin Rottet. I also thank Connie Eble for her inspirational support. Finally, thanks go to Robert Bayley for his insightful comments subsequent to the initial presentation of this paper at LAVIS II.

1. For example, there is insufficient phonological contrast to determine the status of *pop* or *show* in the following utterances:
   (i)   Bois ton [pɑp]
         'Drink your pop.'
   (ii) Il était dessus un gros [ʃo]
         'He was in a big show.'
Even if *show* is classed as a borrowing in ii, it must temporarily shed that status, based on syntax, not phonology, in iii.
   (iii) Ça *advertise* plus sur *Donahue show* que ça parle.
         'They advertise more on the Donahue show than they talk.'

2. Poplack apparently does not deem *games* to be ambiguous in status (no italicizing was provided in her account) because the phonological realization (English) or nonrealization (French) of the word final /-s/ denoting plurality is decisive (Poplack, Sankoff, and Miller 1988:67–68). In what follows, however, it will become evident that using "null realizations" of morphemes (French plurality in this case) is inherently problematic and that using this criteria alone may lead to an erroneous conclusion. In fact, evidence shows that Poplack herself succumbs to ambivalence on this very point: in the French-language version (Poplack 1989:133) of Poplack (1988), *games* is found italicized along with all the other forms whose "forme superficielle est an accord avec la morphologie ou la syntaxe des deux langue." This directly contradicts the assignment that *games* was given in Poplack (1988:96).

3. Some variation between an apical (French) and retroflex (English) /r/ has been noted for *truck*. The unassimilated version is the majority pronunciation, but due to the variation noted, one might conjecture that *truck* is somewhere midstream in its process of lexicalization into the community code.

4. Labeling nouns as emblematic, however, is somewhat problematical. Other types of emblematic switches are less tightly woven into the fabric of the sentence. Typically they take the form of tags, as in (iv), or are accompanied by a flag, as in the sentence break in (v).
   (iv) *But really,* en français c'était tout le temps "pépère."
         'But really, in French it was always "pépère" (for Grandpa).'
   (v)   C'était si différent de les autres musiciens violoneurs que j'avais attendu que c'est
         . . . *just blew my mind.*
         'It was so different from the other fiddler musicians that I had heard that
         . . . just blew my mind.'

5. Compare the remarks of Hill and Hill (1986:348) with regards to Malinche Mexicano and switches to Spanish: "Shaffer (1978) proposes that individual lexical items should always be considered cases of borrowing, never of code-switching. Unfortunately, in Mexicano, as in any syncretic discourse, the possibility of placing an individual lexical item in 'oral quotation marks' through so-called metalinguistic commentary is always available."

6. The accuracy of this observation was subsequently corroborated by Blyth (1993).

Ethnic Identity, Americanization, and Survival of the Mother Tongue: The First- vs. the Second-Generation Chinese of Professionals in Memphis

Marvin K. L. Ching and Hsiang-te Kung

> "Cannot be helped," my mother said when I was fifteen and had vigorously denied that I had any Chinese whatsoever below my skin. . . . All my Caucasian friends agreed: I was about as Chinese as they were. But my mother had studied at a famous nursing school in Shanghai, and she said she knew all about genetics. So there was no doubt in her mind, whether I agreed or not: Once you are born Chinese, you cannot help but feel and think Chinese.
>
> "Someday you will see," said my mother. "It is in your blood, waiting to be let go."   —Amy Tan, *The Joy Luck Club*

INTRODUCTION

In real life, professional Chinese in Memphis of the first generation have had to decide whether their sense of ethnicity would be lost if future generations were to lose their language, especially since speaking Chinese in the home contributes heavily to their sense of ethnicity and uniqueness. This threat of loss of the ethnic language is real in Memphis, Tennessee. Of a city of roughly 1,000,000, there are only 1,275 Chinese in the city proper, and 1,896 in all of Shelby County, which includes Memphis (U.S. Department of Commerce 1990:Table Race).

This study ascertains the perceptions of professional Chinese of the first generation and of a corresponding group of children of the second generation concerning the degree to which ethnic identity is affected by loss of their native language. It does not attempt to predict the validity of these opinions for subsequent generations. However, this study does report the attitudes of the informants concerning fundamental questions: What does it mean to be Chinese? Can one be Chinese without knowing the native language?

Sixteen of the 24 first-generation Chinese faculty members at the University of Memphis who have children born in the U.S. responded to a written questionnaire designed to ascertain 1) the adults' identity, 2) their opinion about the importance of having their children maintain the Chinese language for ethnic identity, 3) their own definition of what it means to be Chinese, and 4) the successful attempts to preserve fluency in the second generation. The questionnaires proved an invaluable tool as a springboard to the 10 in-depth personal interviews, which gave a clearer and more thorough picture of how the adults felt and thought about language, ethnicity, and the Chinese dialect(s) used in their homes.

Of the 16 adult informants, 3 were women, and 13 were men. Informants' length of stay in the U.S. ranged from 8 to 28 years. All but 4 respondents were employed in mathematics, the hard sciences, or engineering. Eight were born in Taiwan; 4 in Mainland China; 2 in Hong Kong; and 2 in Vietnam. All reside in affluent or middle-class communities.

To compare first and second generations, a similar but not identical questionnaire was administered to 29 students, aged 6 to 16, at a church school whose clientele are the children of Chinese professionals and where Sunday School is used for Chinese language instruction. These children were used instead of faculty members' own children in order to preserve independence of the children's judgments. Like the children of the University of Memphis Chinese faculty, most of these children attended prestigious private schools.

QUESTIONS ON IDENTITY

To ascertain cultural and social identity, both adults and children were asked,

Do you consider yourself
a. more Chinese than American
b. more American than Chinese
c. exactly half American and half Chinese

Table 1 shows a distinct difference between the two groups:

Table 1: Cultural and social identity

Identity	*16 Adults**	*29 Children*
a. More Chinese	81.2% (13)	20.6% (6)**
b. More American	0.0% (0)	37.9% (11)
c. Exactly half American / half Chinese	12.5% (2)	41.3% (12)

* The 16th wrote that the answer depends upon the area of life under consideration.

** All 6 were born outside the U.S. In comparison, all faculty members' children were born in the U.S.

For the entire sample, $\chi^2 = 18.10$, $p < .0001$. For adults only, $\chi^2 = 19.6, p < .0001$. For the children only, the χ^2 test was not significant.

To ascertain degree of conservatism or liberalness in politics, the populations were asked,

For whom would you vote for President of the U.S.?
a. the Democratic candidate
b. the Republican candidate
c. an Independent candidate

Table 2 shows some difference in political orientation, although the majority in each case indicated they would vote Republican.

Table 2: Political leaning

Political Leaning	13 Adults*	24 Children**
a. Democratic candidate	0.0% (0)	29.1% (7)
b. Republican candidate	61.5% (8)	58.3% (14)
c. Independent candidate	38.4% (5)	12.5% (3)

* Only 13 adults answered this question.
** Of the 5 children who did not answer the question, 3 were aged 6–7, apparently too young to answer the question. The others were between 8 and 11.
For the entire sample, $\chi^2 = 6.44$, $p = .04$. For adults only, $\chi^2 = 8.92$, $p = .02$. For children only, the χ^2 test was not significant.

Probably, this tendency to vote Republican is influenced by Chinese valuation of success and achievement through individual initiative and self-help. That both adults and children considered themselves successful or able to succeed in the U.S. was evident from their answers to questions on success in the U.S. The adults were asked,

Can Chinese succeed in the university tenure and promotion system and be appointed like all other ethnic (racial) groups?
a. strongly agree　*b.* agree　*c.* neutral　*d.* disagree　*e.* strongly disagree

Children were asked,

Do you believe that Chinese can succeed in American life—in their occupations, the world of work—like all other ethnic (racial) groups?
a. strongly agree　*b.* agree　*c.* neutral　*d.* disagree　*e.* strongly disagree

Both groups answered positively, as revealed in table 3, with no significant difference between them.

Table 3: Ability to succeed

Ability to Succeed	15 Adults	27 Children
Strongly Agree or Agree	80% (12)	92.5% (25)
Neutral	20% (3)	7.4% (2)

Interestingly, one of the faculty members who chose neutral said in his interview that Chinese can succeed but must be superqualified to receive rewards in the university system. Personal interviews with two faculty members also revealed that they felt the possibility varied with the fairness of individual university departments and the individual departments' tenure and promotion committees.

THE IMPORTANCE OF MAINTAINING THE MOTHER TONGUE FOR ETHNIC IDENTITY

There is no doubt in this case that the mother tongue—Chinese—helps strengthen ethnic identity and bonding. Those married to Chinese spouses stated that they spoke to their spouses in Chinese either all of the time or most of the time; the only person who did not speak in Chinese to her spouse had married a Korean. All 14 adults answering the question about what language they used with their children stated that it was Chinese. One of the two adults who did not answer the question of home language used with children was the same woman who indicated she did not speak Chinese to her spouse. In interview, however, she said that she taught her son Chinese until he started going to school. The other person said in interview that although he and his wife always spoke to each other in Chinese, they spoke to their children in English. This informant also reported that he came to the U.S. to be a part of it. Unlike the others, he did not send his children to the Chinese church language school; his family attends an American church in the city. Because both he and his wife were fourth- or fifth-generation Chinese Christians, they did not feel that Christianity was incompatible with Chinese philosophy. His Western orientation was evident not only in his fluent communication in English but also in his knowledge of popular culture, in such realms as movies, sports, politics, and social problems.

The loss of the mother tongue typically begins in the second generation. Five of the responding 14 adults stated that their children seldom or never responded to them in Chinese. As one parent explained in interview, the children see no need to use Chinese because their parents understand English. Another parent explained that one of her daughters pronounced Chinese like a Taiwan foreign missionary. Only the need to speak to monolingual Chinese grandparents over the phone and on vacations, says this parent, demands that both her children speak Chinese.

Many parents evaluated the comprehension skills as poor and said that the subject matter of their children's Chinese is restricted to small talk and general subjects. In fact, four said that when conflicts, arguments, and emotional tension arise in the home, English is the language used for quick, efficient communication. They found it difficult to discuss serious matters in Chinese because of their children's limited vocabulary. Moreover, one of the four said using English loanwords is easier in certain situations because a compound word in Chinese does not describe accurately the meaning of the corresponding English word: a hardbound book in English is a *high-quality book* in Chinese; a paperback is an *ordinary-quality book*.

But does this loss of the language affect ethnic identity? To discover the adults' opinions, these questions were asked:

What is lost if your children do not use the Chinese language? What are your concerns or fears? Check as many as applicable.
  a. They will not be Chinese.
  b. They will be like any other racial group in America.
  c. They will lose Chinese values.

    d. They will lose Chinese traditions.
    e. Their identity might very well get lost in intermarriage.
    f. I have no concern. They can be Chinese without speaking the Chinese
      language.

The children's question was similarly worded. Responses for both groups are presented below in Table 4.

Table 4: Consequence of loss of language

Consequence of Loss of Language	16 Adults	26 Children
a. Not be Chinese	37.5% (6)	0.0% (0)
b. Be like any other racial group	25.0% (4)	37.5% (6)
c. Lose Chinese values	50.0% (8)*	69.2% (18)
d. Lose Chinese traditions	68.7% (11)	69.2% (18)
e. Lose identity in intermarriage	37.5% (6)	7.6% (2)
f. Not have any concern	31.2% (5)	42.3% (11)

* In oral interviews conducted with various family members concerning this question, the word *values* was often interpreted as *traditions*.
For the entire sample, $\chi^2 = 14.17$, $p = .01$. For adults only, the χ^2 test was not significant. For children only, $\chi^2 = 751.35$, $p < .001$.

Interestingly, neither group indicated that loss of ethnic language meant loss of ethnicity. Of much greater concern was loss of values and traditions, as seen in responses *c* and *d*. Personal in-depth interviews revealed why this was so and led to the next item of discussion: what does it mean to be Chinese?

DEFINITION OF BEING CHINESE

    Personal in-depth interviews revealed that even though their children or their future grandchildren might lose their ethnic language, the adults believe their offspring will still be Chinese because of the values and traditions they have received either through direct teaching or through example in the home: respect for elders and teachers; marital fidelity; strong familial and intergenerational ties; a sense of responsibility for the members of society as opposed to extreme individualism; hard work and sacrifice; self-discipline; thrift; perseverance; a regard for education; an adherence to action based upon long-term results and goals; dedication to the cultivation of talent and training in learning, in contrast to the American belief that talent is in-born so that cultivation and training are not required in the onerous task of learning difficult subjects.
    Indeed, to show that language does not necessarily a Chinese make, one informant stated that one can be more Chinese in Memphis than in Hong Kong or Taiwan today, when he explained the loss of traditional Chinese values in those places, as evidenced in the way modern Chinese youth in the East treat their elders

with disrespect as when they push and shove to get on crowded buses. Another respondent said that there are Americans who are more Chinese than the Chinese, indicating that these Americans adhere to the Chinese values named above. A third informant said that the close relation between grandparent and grandchild, such as a grandfather allowing his grandchild to sip coffee from his cup, is much more Chinese than learning Chinese phrases. Moreover, says this last informant, there is a negative effect in forcing children to use Chinese. He pointed out, however, that when they go to college, they begin to see a need to take Chinese and to use the language, as his daughter did. Another informant agreed that the children's desire or need to develop their mastery of Chinese often arises later when they are asked questions about the Chinese language or about Chinese culture and history because of their Chinese ancestry. Two informants also said that even though one may not use the Chinese language and may speak English fluently, other people will respond to a Chinese person as a Chinese because of his/her physical features. Most, even one of the informants who checked "They would not be Chinese," believed that some time sooner or later, their children would return to their Chinese roots, although right now they may feel totally American and believe their parents are prejudiced about their Chinese ancestry.

Parents said that they preferred their children to marry within their own ethnic group but that they have no control over the outcome. Some expressed the view that even if their children should intermarry, they would retain their ethnicity. One said that Americans interested in dating Chinese do so in the first place because they are often attracted to Chinese values and traditions. This person, who spoke to his children only in English, believed traditional American values to be consonant with Chinese values.

Parents, with their pragmatic outlook of succeeding in American life, believe that they can perform a delicate balancing feat in rearing their children to become westernized enough to succeed in America, but Chinese enough in what matters—values and traditions. As one parent quipped, "You don't have to cook in a wok to make Chinese food. There is a more efficient way of knowing about Chinese culture, history, and geography than having to use the Chinese language as the only tool for such knowledge." To this person, what is really important is to pass on Chinese stories conveying values. For example, the Chinese tale of one who draws feet on a snake in a contest illustrates the point that it is important to simplify life by avoiding extraneous acts.[1]

THE MOST IMPORTANT FACTORS FOR CHILDREN'S USE OF THE LANGUAGE

From questionnaire responses and from personal interviews, the important factors for children's language use seemed to be 1) whether they visited their grandparents, either here or abroad; 2) whether they attended language immersion summer camps; or 3) whether the parents tolerated the use of English in the home.

Personal interviews revealed interesting matters about these points. A researcher in the Center of Earthquake Studies could afford to send his children yearly to Taiwan. Not only did his children communicate with grandparents there, but the children were placed in Chinese schools for the months of May and June. Although they could not keep up with the reading and writing at their respective grade levels, they could socialize with their peers in Chinese.

Concerning Chinese language school as a factor in language maintenance, parents said they believed that the school's effectiveness was limited for several reasons: 1) time spent in class was minimal, i.e., classes were held only during the time the adults worshiped on Sunday mornings; 2) there was no reinforcement in the home concerning what was learned in school; and 3) children's attitudes about having to go to school, as borne out by our personal observation of classes, were poor. However, parents felt that attendance at Chinese school was important as a healthy social outlet for their children, an exposure to other Chinese youth so that they would feel it is all right to be Chinese. This orientation is consistent with Wong (1988:7), who stated that Chinese schools' main function is not primarily linguistic. Instead, nonlinguistic functions, such as promoting cultural and ethnic pride, have become the focus.

The interviews also revealed that the adults want their children to study Mandarin at Chinese school because of this dialect's importance. Although conversation in another Chinese dialect might be used between spouses, most of the time parents used only Mandarin with their children because Mandarin is the standard prestigious dialect and the lingua franca throughout the People's Republic of China and Taiwan. However, one parent spoke both Mandarin and Taiwanese to his children because he intends to return as a Christian missionary to Taiwan. Cantonese is also used in the home if relatives know only this dialect.

Interviews also revealed that instilling ethnic pride to motivate language learning occurs through the telling of family history. One family can trace its heritage, through the family book of genealogy, for 120 generations. Another traces its origins to Confucius, 75 generations back. Chinese television programs, transmitted via satellite from Los Angeles, provide another means of motivating children to like the Chinese language.

CONCLUSION

Although the Chinese parents in this study try to have their children learn Chinese because it is part of their heritage, the majority see language as just one facet of their culture. Far more important, many seem to believe, is the preservation of values and orientation toward life for ethnic identity. For all adults interviewed, even though their children might not use Chinese in speaking to their parents, the parents felt their children were Chinese because of their orientation toward life.

For some ethnic groups—dialect speakers of Filipino and Catalan speakers—maintenance of language preserves ethnic identity (Gonzalez 1991; Woolard 1991). However, loss of language does not necessarily mean de-ethnicization. For the Amish and Mennonites in Pennsylvania, for example, religion rather than language provides the common bond (Huffines 1991; Enninger 1991). This seems to hold true for many, though not all, of the Chinese population in this Memphis study.

Although there is some shift in identity among the children concerning political leanings and feelings of being more American or half Chinese and half American, nonetheless, the queries on the questionnaire concerning the consequence of loss of language revealed that this loss itself did not necessarily cause loss of ethnicity. Although there is some change in what constitutes their identity, the children felt, much like the adults, that the most devastating blow to their ethnicity would be loss of Chinese values and traditions. There is among the children a strong sense of tradition preserved, of being Chinese, which has been instilled by the first generation.

Interviews with the first generation show their pragmatism. To succeed in American life, their children must be well grounded in the English language. Although the parents in general try to encourage use of Chinese, they have faced the reality of their children losing the ethnic tongue. Many feel confident, however, that loss of the ethnic language does not have to mean loss of ethnicity.

NOTES

We wish to thank John Nickey for his assistance with statistical analysis.

1. The Chinese story is from the *Guo Tse*, an ancient history of the Chou dynasty (500 B.C.):

Once there was a master in a temple in Chu Guo in Hubei Province who gave a jug of wine to his temple keepers. But there was not enough wine for all of them to drink, so they agreed to let only one person enjoy it. The problem was to determine who should have the privilege. They decided that the one who could draw a snake on the ground first would be the winner. The contest began. The person who finished drawing first picked up the jug and started drinking while the others were still busy drawing snakes on the ground. Proud of his accomplishment, this person who finished first added feet to the snake. As he continued drawing more feet, the person who finished second said that snakes did not have feet. So if feet were added, then the creature drawn was no longer a snake. So the second person who finished should be the winner. The first person admitted his error and stared at the second person, who helped himself to the jug of wine.

Since then, the idiom *hua she tian zu* 'drawing feet on a snake' means that we should not make simple things complicated; we should do things just right and not overdo what is required.

PART TWO

Phonological, Morphosyntactic, Discourse, and Lexical Features

Part Two both widens and narrows the scope of Part One and also moves toward the focus on methods of Part Three. Some essays reach out from the geographical South for comparative purposes; others focus on specific features within Southern subdialects. While illuminating features of the Southern linguistic landscape, these studies offer theoretical insights, visions of artistry, and even calls for linguistic social action. Although every essay in this volume concerns linguistic features to some extent, the essays in Part Two place the study of particular linguistic phenomena at center stage. As a whole, this section demonstrates the energy that an areal approach lends to linguistic investigation and speculation when the many subdisciplines of linguistics are brought to bear upon the topic of language variety in the South.

The papers by Wolfram et al. and Southard concern linguistic features associated with the Outer Banks of North Carolina, so-called "Hoigh Toider" speech. Wolfram, Schilling-Estes, Hazen, and Craig study the English of the island Ocracoke to identify a constellation of features that match as well as contrast with other Southern and non-Southern varieties; they go on to show the sociolinguistic complexity involved in analysis of even the most salient features. The depth of analysis generates personal involvement in the community, spawning a sense of stewardship toward the community studied. Southard, combining historical development and linguistic atlas materials, investigates the features of general "maritime English" and the relation of those features to mainland speech characteristics. He examines the fate of relic area features facing pressures such as mainstream linguistic change that moves toward the marked relic features and language contact occasioned by tourism.

The phonological studies by Bayley and Taylor both address theoretical issues. Bayley's research into /-t,d/ deletion in Tejano English in San Antonio, Texas, incorporates lexical phonology and provides empirical support for an exponential model of morphological constraints. Using as data some under-documented features of Alabama and Georgia speech, Taylor's study challenges contemporary sociolinguistics to pay renewed attention to the ordering of underlying phonological rules, illustrating their importance with his analyses.

The next two essays consider dialect features in relation to discourse, a relatively new area for the investigation of regional diversity (as Bailey notes, this volume). Coles investigates the ability of New Orleanians to quickly develop solidarity through linguistic accommodation based upon their shared knowledge of the features of the *Yat* dialect. Davies, a non-Southerner dependent upon her Deep South students for guiding her understanding, discovers an enlightening range of discourse functions associated with honorific *Ma'am* (with some attention to *Sir*) as presented in the screenplay of *The Trip to Bountiful*. Davies' analysis is notable, too, for its use of fictionally represented, rather than naturally occurring, Southern English.

The essays by Weatherly and Wilmeth also consider artistic data sources in analyzing Southern discourse features. Incorporating the physical and metaphoric power of the mighty/muddy Mississippi, Weatherly locates the South in a holographic confluence of time, cultures, and space. She layers our critical understanding of Southern fiction and its chief practitioners of the fictive grotesque. Wilmeth then transports us to Hank Williams honky-tonk, illustrating how that performer and songwriter artistically manipulated his regional linguistic resources. Wilmeth argues that in spite of Williams's proud regionalism, the artistry of his pseudonymous Luke the Drifter songs effects universal appeal.

Universally known but historically unappealing to many, the shibboleth *ain't* is the subject of Maynor's paper. Maynor's preliminary research into the history and ethnic parameters of *ain't* usage begins a set of six essays exploring lexical questions.

Butters discovers disjunction in the face of presumed connection between Caribbean *auntie(-man)* (an effeminate, possibly homosexual, male) and North American English *auntie* (an older, effeminate homosexual). Butters's careful investigation, illustrating what might be considered an underground lexicography, argues for parallel development without clear influence.

Metcalf serves up the next question and begins a subset of four essays based on the research of the vast lexicographical project, Dictionary of American Regional English (DARE): just how prominent is the South as a region within DARE? Metcalf illustrates that the American Dialect Society's *Index* (1993) to volumes I and II of *DARE* allows a comparison of the regional labels of terms used by DARE. Though he proposes caveats to his findings, the labeling suggests that the South is indeed linguistically distinctive. Next, Cassidy, the Dean of DARE, discusses seven etymological puzzles in the DARE data, mainly of Southern occurrence, that illustrate some of the problems and challenges faced by DARE lexicographers. Von Schneidemesser, drawing from DARE field records, then explores the hypothesis that the speech of Southerners may be more genteel and euphemistic than the national norm. She compares Southern DARE informants' rates of profane, obscene, and euphemistic terms with the national rates. Finally, ending Part Two and pointing the way to the study of methods in Part Three, Hall explores the symbiosis of DARE and The Linguistics Atlas of the Gulf States and shows how these two major research projects have benefited from each other.

The Sociolinguistic Complexity of Quasi-Isolated Southern Coastal Communities
Walt Wolfram, Natalie Schilling-Estes, Kirk Hazen, Chris Craig

INTRODUCTION

As Labov's (1963) vanguard study of Martha's Vineyard demonstrates, the changing status of island communities makes them ideal for examining the socially situated dynamics of language change and variation. Whereas each island community has a unique history, there is little doubt that important generalized sociolinguistic principles may be derived from such situations.

Given the sociolinguistic significance of isolated communities, it is somewhat surprising that the traditional Linguistic Atlas surveys conducted in the Atlantic States tended to ignore the Outer Banks, a set of barrier islands approximately 20 miles from the North Carolina coast. Furthermore, the restricted descriptive accounts of these communities (e.g., Howren 1962; Shores 1991) minimize the sociolinguistic situations that contextualize these varieties in deference to the description of traditional dialect traits that set these islands apart from contiguous mainland varieties.

In an effort to give these island communities the sociolinguistic attention they deserve, we present some preliminary findings from our current study of Ocracoke, an island community on the Outer Banks of North Carolina. Ocracoke is a prototypical Eastern seaboard island community. It is not accessible through driving but is reached primarily through state-operated ferries. As with a number of the island's counterparts along the Eastern seaboard, a vibrant but now controlled tourist industry has developed, largely since World War II but in existence to some extent for a century. This situation has changed the economic, sociopolitical, and sociocultural dynamics of the island community.

As part of the North Carolina Language and Life Project, we conducted interviews with 45 island residents, aged 10 to 82, who represent several diverse social networks within the community. Most of the postadolescent interviews were conducted with *ancestral islanders*, residents who can trace their genealogy as islanders at least several generations back. We also interviewed some *new islanders*, first-generation lifetime residents whose parents moved to the island.

Interviews were conducted based on a set of island-appropriate sociolinguistic interview modules; subjects were selected using a modified social network procedure (Milroy 1987a). Some of the interviews also were conducted by pairs of interviewers in a home visit format. (For example, the husband and wife team of Walt and Marge Wolfram might make an after-dinner visit to a home for an interview, thus fitting into a fairly natural and recognized type of social occasion). The paired-interviewer technique, not traditionally used in sociolinguistics, proved to be an especially effective procedure for eliciting natural language. Both individual and limited group (two to three islanders) interviews were conducted.

There are two major sociolinguistic issues that become immediately apparent in a situation like the one in Ocracoke. First, there is the issue of dialect affinity. Given the surrounding dialects, the long-standing history of relative isolation, and the various migrations affecting the island, where does the Ocracoke dialect fit in? In what direction is this variety changing, who is leading the change, and why? The second issue involves sociolinguistic description. What are the socially diagnostic variables in island speech and the relevant social interactional, demographic, and psychological factors that correlate with language variation?

As an essential addendum to our sociolinguistic study, we include a brief discussion of a collaborative research model in which sociolinguists return to the community information and linguistic artifacts that preserve the island's rich linguistic heritage (see Appendix, this essay).

THE AFFINITY ISSUE

The constellation of structures that defines the traditional Ocracoke dialect, or *brogue* as it is sometimes referred to by islanders, certainly sets this island apart from mainland Southern varieties. The Ocracoke brogue combines a distinctive set of dialect features that makes it appear, at various points, related to highland varieties such as Appalachian English, mainland Southern dialects, and Northern varieties. At the same time, it manifests a few unique characteristics that reveal some relics of its historical roots and migratory past.

The earliest Euro-American settlers on Ocracoke were English ship pilots who arrived in 1715 to inhabit land claimed by the English throne. Various land ownership acts in the mid-1700s apparently brought in upperclass English settlers from Southeast England, as well as settlers who migrated from settlement sites in the Maryland and Virginia colonies. Several island families trace their lineage to these early settlers of English origin, though one of Ocracoke's oldest and largest families, the O'Neals (the current generation had 11 sons), claims Irish ancestry. In 1850, there were as many as 104 African-Americans on the island, according to Alton Ballance, local historian and author of *Ocracokers* (1989). Today there is only one African-American family, the descendants of freed slaves who moved to the island after the Civil War. What must be stressed, in contrast to popular stereotypes of island speech, is the fact that no residents speak or ever spoke Elizabethan English, though phonological, grammatical, and lexical relics are still attested in Ocracoke (e.g., the nucleus of the /ay/ diphthong, in EModE [ʌ¹]; vestigial [h] retention in *hit* 'it'; a-prefixing; *weren't* generalization, as in "She *weren't* there"; and *mammick* 'harass').

Migration and travel patterns must not be obscured as we unravel the island's sociohistorical linguistic mystery. Ocracoke saw heavy ship traffic for many decades, whether for lawful trade, pirating, or military purposes. The commercial ship trade also took natives, especially men, to such Northern ports as Philadelphia and Wilmington, Delaware. In fact, an estimated 75% of the older generation spent some time in these Northern seaports. These men would return to Ocracoke after periods ranging from a year to decades. Even today, islanders often make shopping, business, and social trips up the coast.

War also affected the sociohistorical context of the island. Ocracoke was strategically important in the Revolutionary War, the War of 1812 and the Civil War, when it was occupied by Union soldiers. In addition, a naval base was established on the island in World War II.

The population demographics have changed significantly since the island became a popular tourist spot, producing a classic love-hate relationship between *dingbatters,* the name islanders use for outsiders, and *O'cockers,* the island term for native residents. At present, it is estimated that about half of the 600 year-round island residents are ancestral O'cockers. During the height of the tourist season, the population may swell to 4,000, with summer homes, island motels, and National Park Service campgrounds housing overnight dingbatters.

Notwithstanding outside influences, the Ocracoke dialect retains distinctive traditional structures. In order to address the question of dialect affinity, we present in tables 1 and 2 a broad-based comparison of traditional island dialect features with several other major varieties. It is important to understand that we use as our basis for comparison the more traditional version of the Ocracoke dialect. The major dialects compared with it are Highland Southern (found in Appalachia and the Ozarks), non-Highland Southern (found in the North Carolina Piedmont), and non-Southern, which includes Midland and Northern varieties of American English.

Tables 1 and 2 reveal a unique constellation of structures for Ocracoke. Some structures set this Outer Banks dialect apart from all surrounding dialects. For example, Ocracoke displays /ay/ raising in [tʌ'd] 'tide' and [aw] raising and fronting in [sɛ^{U}θ] 'south' not shared by inland Southern varieties, although some of these features are present to a degree in some Southern coastal varieties, including the Cartaret County area of North Carolina. Grammatical features that occur with high frequency in Ocracoke speech (and to a lesser degree in mainland coastal North Carolina) but not elsewhere include *were/n't* generalization (e.g., "I *weren't* there") and use of *to* as static locative (e.g., "She's *to* the store"). Additionally, lexical items unique to Ocracoke (and the North Carolina Outer Banks) are *meehonkey,* a term used in the Ocracoke version of hide-and-seek, and *mammick* 'harass'.

While some features are unique or shared only with contiguous coastal Southern varieties, the Ocracoke brogue has many features in common with isolated Highland varieties such as Appalachian English and Ozark English (Wolfram and Christian 1976; Christian, Wolfram, and Dube 1988). Such features include *a*-prefixing (e.g., "Rex went *a-fishin'*"), absence of -*Z* plural with nouns of weights and measures (e.g., "four *mile*"), singular verb concord with collective noun phrases (e.g., "People *is* nice") and with conjoined noun phrases (e.g., "Candy and Melinda usually *takes* them"), [æ] lowering (e.g., [ðar] 'there'), <ire> syllable reduction before *r* (e.g., [tar] 'tire'), schwa raising (e.g., [ɛkstri] 'extra'), and intrusive *r* in unstressed final syllables (e.g., [skitr] 'mosquito').

Table 1: A comparative overview of selected phonological structures

STRUCTURE	Variety of English			
	Ocracoke	Highland South	South	Non-South
/ay/ raising, backing e.g., [tʌˈd] 'tide'	x			
/aw/ raising, fronting e.g., [sɛᵁθ] 'south'	x			
[h] retention in 'it', 'ain't' e.g., [hɪt] 'it'	(x)	x		
/æ/ lowering preceding /r/ e.g., [ðar] 'there'	x	x		
intrusive *t* e.g., [wʌnst] 'oncet'	x	x		
/ayr/-/awr/ reduction e.g., [tar] 'tire'	x	x	(x)	
stressed interdental fric. del. e.g., [ær] 'there'	x	x	(x)	
expanded unstressed syl. del. e.g., [tetrz] 'potatoes'	x	x	(x)	
intrusive *r*, unstressed final /o/ e.g., [fɛlr] 'fellow'	x	x	(x)	
/šr/ fronting e.g., [srɪmp] 'shrimp'	x		(x)	
Cr [V+rnd] reduction e.g., [θo] 'throw'	x	x	x	
unstressed initial /w/ deletion e.g., [yʌŋ ənz] 'young ones'	x	x	x	
/ɪ/-/ɛ/ prec. [+nas] merger e.g., [pɪn] 'pin'/'pen'	x	x	x	
front lax vowel gliding e.g., [fɪˑš] 'fish'	x	x	x	
/ay/ ungliding e.g., [tam] 'time'	(x)		x	
back vowel fronting e.g., [bo<ᵁt] 'boat'	(x)		x	
/a/-/ɔ/ merger e.g., [kat] 'cot'/'caught'				x
postvocalic /r/ loss e.g., [ka] 'car'			x	(x)

Table 2: A comparative overview of selected grammatical structures

STRUCTURE	Variety of English			
	Ocracoke	Highland South	South	Non-South
Were/n't Generalization e.g., She *weren't* here	x			
to stative locative e.g., She's *to* the store	x			
a-prefixing e.g., He was *a-fishin'*	x	x	(x)	
measure N plural absence e.g., twenty mile	x	x	(x)	
collective NP concord e.g., *People gets* upset	x	x	(x)	
have concord e.g., My nerves *has* been bad	x	x	(x)	
completive *done* e.g., She *done* messed up	x	x	x	
double modals e.g., He *might could* come	(x)	(x)	x	
embedded rel. subject del. e.g., The man ø come down was nice	x	x	x	
irregular verb (1) generalized past/part. e.g., She *had came* here	x	x	x	x
(2) generalized part./past e.g., She *done* it	x	x	x	x
(3) bare root as past e.g., She *give* him a dog	x	x	x	(x)
(4) regularization e.g., She *knowed* him		x	(x)	
(5) different irregular e.g., He *retch* up the roof		x		
2nd plural *y'all* e.g., *Y'all* come again	x	(x)	x	
intensifying *right* e.g., He's *right* silly	x	x	x	
positive *anymore* e.g., We watch T.V. *anymore*	x	x		x
was/is generalization e.g., We *was* there	(x)	x	x	x
Preverb indef. Neg. concord e.g., *Nobody didn't* go	x	x	x	x

In comparing Ocracoke speech with other varieties, we must keep in mind that many structures are inherently variable. Table 3, for example, compares the incidence of nonstandard subject-verb concord for three different classes of noun phrases as found in Ocracoke, Appalachian English, and Ozark English, namely, a conjoined plural (e.g., *She and I does this*), a collective noun phrase (e.g., *People likes them*), and a pronoun (e.g., *They likes them*). The figures for Ozark and Appalachian English (from Christian, Wolfram, and Dube 1988:116–117) exclude *be*, *have*, and *don't*, which operate independently in their effect on nonstandard concord. The preliminary figures for Ocracoke are based on only six subjects (Hazen) and include several tokens of *have*; nonetheless, they suggest certain dialectal affinities with respect to subject-verb concord patterns.

Table 3: Nonstandard concord for three noun phrase types in
Highland Southern and Ocracoke English

NP TYPE	Ozark	Appalachian	Ocracoke
Conjoined NP	33.3%	52.9%	12.5%
Collective NP	26.9%	25.9%	28.9%
Pronoun	0.1%	0.2%	2.6%

Although the figures for Ocracoke are still preliminary, the increased incidence of nonstandard concord for collective and conjoined noun phrases and the low incidence of nonstandard concord with pronouns is a pattern shared across the varieties. Of course, it is necessary to compare these figures with those from other varieties as well to get a picture of how the variable dimensions of structural affinity position Ocracoke within the full complement of American English varieties.

It is important to note that classic Southern features such as /ay/ ungliding and postvocalic *r*-lessness are not typically found among ancestral islanders in Ocracoke, although some selective Southern features occur, such as plural *y'all* and some lax vowel gliding, as in [fɪ˅š] 'fish'. By the same token, traditionally non-Southern structures such as positive *anymore* (e.g., "Anything that hits me puts a mark on me *anymore*") are found in Ocracoke. The overall profile of Ocracoke speech that emerges from such a comparison highlights the unique constellation of structures that comprises this Outer Banks variety.

SOCIOLINGUISTIC COMPLEXITY

Although our detailed analysis of phonology and morphosyntax is in the incipient stage, the complexities involved in describing even the most salient feature of Ocracoke speech—the raising, backing, and slight rounding of the nucleus vowel in the diphthong /ay/ of [hʌˈ tʌˈd] 'high tide'—present a substantial linguistic and sociolinguistic challenge. The analysis we have so far undertaken reveals that the incidence of /ay/ raising is variable, affected by such external factors as social network, gender, and style (even perhaps an "island quaintness quotient"). This systematic variability also appears to be affected by internal linguistic factors such as following phonological environment. However, some linguistic contexts prohibit /ay/ raising. For example, in the sequence /ayr/ of words like *fire* and *tire*, the production is categorically [ar], as in [tar] for *tire*. This restriction suggests a straightforward qualitative phonological condition on the operation of a regular phonological rule. Other cases are not so simple. For example, a single speaker was recorded as invariably producing unglided /ay/ in the word *Carolina* ([kærəlanə]), although he does not typically use Southern ungliding to any extent elsewhere. This is an interesting lexicalized pronunciation of the term for the state whose mainland region is often viewed by islanders as far more distant symbolically than the 20 miles of water that separate it from Ocracoke.

The distribution of a selection of diagnostic dialect structures for three ancestral islanders in tables 4 and 5 shows the complexity of the sociolinguistic situation in Ocracoke. It reveals how traditional indices may not correlate directly with incidence of diagnostic Ocracoke English features.

Table 4: Comparison of selected phonological structures for
three ancestral islanders in Ocracoke

PHONOLOGICAL STRUCTURE	*49-year-old male*	*82-year-old female*	*29-year-old female*
/ay/ raising, backing e.g., [tʌˡd] 'tide'	x		(x)
/aw/ raising, fronting e.g., [sɛᵁθ] 'south'	x		(x)
/æ/ lowering prec. /r/ e.g., [ðar] 'there'	x		x
/ayr/-/awr/ reduction e.g., [tar] 'tire'	x		x
intrusive *r*, unstr. final /o/ e.g., [fɛlr] 'fellow'	x		
unstressed initial /w/ del e.g., [yʌŋ ənz] 'young ones'	x		
front lax vowel gliding e.g., [fɪˡš] 'fish'	x	(x)	x
back vowel fronting e.g., [bo<ᵁt] 'boat'	x		x
postvocalic /r/ loss e.g., [ka] 'car'		(x)	

Table 5: Comparison of selected grammatical structures for
three ancestral islanders in Ocracoke

GRAMMATICAL STRUCTURE	49-year-old male	82-year-old female	29-year-old female
Were/n't Generalization e.g., She *weren't* here	x	(x)	x
to stative locative e.g., She's *to* the store	x	x	x
a-prefixing e.g., He was *a-fishin'*	x		
measure N plural absence e.g., twenty mile_	x		x
collective NP nonstandard concord e.g., *People gets* upset	x	(x)	x
double modals e.g., He *might could* come	x		x
irregular verb (1) generalized past/part. e.g., She *had came* here (2) generalized part./past e.g., She *done* it (3) bare root as past e.g., She *give* him a dog (4) regularization e.g., She *knowed* him (5) different irregular e.g., He *retch* up the roof	x x x	x x	x x x
2nd plural *y'all* e.g., *Y'all* come again	x	x	x
intensifying *right* e.g., He's *right* silly	x	(x)	x
was/is generalization e.g., We *was* there	x		x
postverbal multiple negation e.g., They *didn't* do *nothing*	x		x
Preverb indef. Neg. concord e.g., *Nobody didn't* go	x		

The speakers include a 49-year-old male ancestral islander and two women aged 82 and 29. The 49-year-old male, both a prominent community leader and a college graduate, is regarded as a "classic" brogue speaker. Both the 82-year-old and the 29-year-old women are high-school graduates. Structures represented in the speech sample, variably or categorically, are indicated by x; structures represented to a limited variable extent, by (x).

Tables 4 and 5 suggest that the distribution of dialect structures does not fit neatly into a simple generational, educational, or gender-related pattern. The 82-year-old female high school graduate whose heritage goes back to one of the original island families hardly uses any of the traditional dialect features, while the 49-year-old male college graduate uses a full set of these structures. At the same time, the 29-year-old female high-school graduate maintains a core of the traditional structures but not to the extent of the 49-year-old male. Nevertheless, there does appear to be a curvilinear relationship between age and use of the classic brogue, especially when the intersecting effect of social network is considered. Fieldwork suggests that middle-aged men who are part of the "poker game network" (a relatively exclusive male islander group that meets several times a week and interacts in relatively dense, multiplex networks) show a higher incidence of some traditional island features than some of their older cohorts.

In the following sections, we discuss briefly two of the diagnostic structures under investigation in Ocracoke, illustrating the sociolinguistic and linguistic challenge involved in providing an authentic description of this variety.

Were/n't Generalization

The case of past tense concord for finite *be* (Schilling-Estes and Wolfram 1994) illustrates the type of sociolinguistic challenge we face in describing the speech of an island such as Ocracoke. The use of *were* regularization patterns, particularly with the negative *weren't*, is quite well attested historically and currently in vernacular speech in England (Trudgill 1990; Cheshire 1982). However, even the most limited descriptive dimensions of the *were* regularization alternative have apparently been ignored for American English varieties, although *were/n't* regularization, as well as the *was* regularization more commonly noted in U.S. varieties, does occur in relic areas such as Ocracoke. In fact, a single speaker may regularize both *was* and *were*, as in sentence (1):

(1) Then one time I *were* looking through the dictionary and there *was* both words, "shipwreck" and "shipwrack."
(80-year-old male, native of Ocracoke)

Were/n't regularization does not appear to be receding in Ocracoke; it has been observed in the speech of young islanders, even in formal elicitation frames, as the exchange given in (2) illustrates:

(2) FW: If I said, "Was that you I saw on the point yesterday and you said, 'No, it _____
SUBJ 1: *Weren't.*
SUBJ 2: *Wasn't. Weren't* is what I would more use. *Weren't.* It *weren't* me, it *wasn't* me, whatever, whatever I say at the time.

SUBJ 1:　I think I'd probably end up saying it *weren't* me.
(16-, 18-year-old males)

Since both *was* and *were* regularization are variable phenomena, we are investigating the internal linguistic constraints on this pattern, as well as its role as a socially diagnostic linguistic variable. A preliminary analysis of *was/n't* and *were/n't* generalization in Ocracoke speech was conducted based on conversational interviews with two native islanders, a 70-year-old female and an 80-year-old male. The internal factor groups examined are subject person and number including the type of noun phrase (e.g., *The duck were there*; *I were there*); regular pronoun versus existential subject (e.g., *They were down by the docks*; *There were ducks*); and positive and negative polarity (e.g., *She weren't here*; *She were here*).[1] The results of a limited preliminary analysis are summarized in table 6.

Table 6: *Were/Weren't* regularization patterns
Preliminary data from two ancestral islanders

	Were (vs. Was)		Weren't (vs. Wasn't)	
Singular				
Pronoun				
1st person	3/54	**5.6%**	1/4	**75.0%**
2nd person	2/2	**100.0%**	1/1	**100.0%**
3rd person	2/85	**2.4%**	9/16	**56.3%**
Existential *there*	1/9	**11.1%**	1/1	**100.0%**
NP	1/36	**2.8%**	1/1	**100.0%**
Plural				
Pronoun				
1st person	8/8	**100.0%**	1/1	**100.0%**
2nd person	—	—	—	—
3rd person	18/20	**90.0%**	2/2	**100.0%**
Existential *there*	4/10	**40.0%**	—	—
NP	9/11	**81.8%**	—	—
Total	48/235	**20.4%**	16/26	**61.5%**

Some interesting hypotheses arise from this preliminary examination. For example, the above figures indicate that first and third person singular *weren't* is more common than positive *were*, especially with non-existential pronoun subjects. Note also that, while third person plural past tense positive *be* is sometimes regularized to *was* (e.g., *The men was*; *They was*), the negative *be* is never regularized to *wasn't*. Such findings suggest that Ocracoke speakers tend to generalize past tense *be* to *was* in the positive paradigm and to *weren't* in the negative, although further quantitative analysis is necessary to strengthen this tentative conclusion. Our limited data reveal, however, that the linguistic and sociolinguistic complexity of *weren't* distribution extends beyond the simplistic observation that islanders sometimes use *weren't* for *wasn't*.

Our investigation of *weren't* has so far been limited to internal constraints. As mentioned previously, associations with such external constraints as age and gender are complex. For example, the 82-year-old female included in our comparison in tables 4 and 5 used *were/n't* generalization only once during an hour-long interview (and not at all in several hours of nonrecorded conversation with fieldworkers), although it is a relatively widespread Ocracoke dialect structure. Although this speaker attributed her lack of traditional dialect features (a subject which arose naturally during the course of the conversation) to the fact that, when she was growing up, her father owned a general store frequented by customers from all over the country, her speech patterns are perhaps more accurately explained by her several years of high school education on the North Carolina mainland (at the time of her schooling, high school education for islanders was only available on the mainland), as well as the reputation of her family as prestigious, well-traveled members of the island community.

/ay/ Raising

Our investigation of /ay/ raising illustrates the complexity of both external and internal constraints on Ocracoke speech. Preliminary tabulations based on conversational interviews with two male islanders and one female islander (ranging in age from 39 to 60) suggest that /ay/ raising may be influenced by such features of the following segment as voicing and position within the sonorancy hierarchy as outlined by Selkirk (1982). Of special interest is the fact that /ay/ raising in Ocracoke speech occurs with greater frequency before voiced segments than voiceless. This finding runs counter to the pattern we find in Standard American English and many vernacular varieties, where [ay] is often slightly raised before voiceless segments but not before voiced sounds (e.g., write→ [rʌ¹t], ride→ [ra¹d]).

The results of our /ay/ raising analysis are summarized in table 7. The number raised out of the potential cases of /ay/ raising (with *I* excluded as a lexical exception) and percentage of raising are given in each environment for the three speakers.

Table 7: Potential internal constraints on variability in /ay/ raising

Speaker	##	V	Liq	Nas	Vd Fr	Vl Fr	Vd St	Vl St
49-year-old male	2/2 **100**	3/5 **60.0**	5/12 **41.6**	28/36 **77.7**	18/19 **94.7**	1/5 **20.0**	17/29 **58.6**	38/66 **57.6**
47-year-old female	0/2 **0.0**	4/7 **57.1**	9/17 **52.9**	12/18 **66.6**	13/15 **86.6**	7/12 **58.3**	19/21 **90.4**	27/48 **56.3**
39-year-old male	17/21 **81.0**	7/7 **100**	6/9 **66.7**	12/17 **70.6**	4/8 **50.0**	2/6 **33.3**	7/7 **100**	30/44 **68.2**
N/Total %	19/25 **76.0**	14/19 **73.7**	20/38 **52.6**	52/71 **73.2**	35/42 **83.3**	10/23 **43.5**	43/57 **75.4**	95/158 **60.1**

= word-final position (e.g., *high*), V = vowel (e.g., *buying*), Liq = liquid (e.g., *file*), Nas = nasal (e.g., *time*), Vd Fr = voiced fricative (e.g., *five*), Vl Fr = voiceless fricative (e.g., *nice*), Vd st = voiced stop (e.g., *tide*), and Vl St = voiceless stop (e.g., *bike*)

An external constraint that appears greatly to influence the incidence of /ay/ raising, as well as select other features of the Ocracoke dialect, such as the raising and fronting of [aw] in words such as *south*, is speakers' awareness of these features as markers of stereotypical island speech. In fact, there exists a set of "soap box" phrases that include a concentration of stereotypical island dialect features such as /ay/ raising. Example (3), elicited from a 39-year-old male in reference to meeting Walt Wolfram at the poker game, illustrates:

(3) Came out there and said, "I'm studying speech." I said, well, it's high[1] tide[1] on the sound[2] side[1], last night[1] the water fire, tonight[1] the moon shine[1], no fish[3], no fish[3]. (39-year-old male, fisherman)

[1][ay] raising, backing
[2][aw] raising, fronting
[3]front lax vowel gliding ([ɪ] → [ɪ[i]])

These caricatures of island speech are used frequently by both islanders and outsiders. We find such fairly typical representations of island speech as example (4), an excerpt from a newspaper column written by an outsider:

(4) On Hatteras and Ocracoke and in the fishing village of Wanchese, you will occasionally hear an Outer Banks accent. It sounds something like this: "What toime is it hoigh toide on the sound soide?"
(Ford Reid, "Outer Banks resists homogenization of the American voice," *The Coast*, May 23, 1993)

While both islanders and nonislanders are aware of such highly marked features, islanders manipulate their incidence of dialect features in response to an array of interactional variables. For example, /ay/ raising appears to be sensitive to stylistic variation. The 39-year-old male included in the tabulation in table 7 was interviewed in the natural context of working outside on his crab pots, by a fieldworker with whom he had become good friends in the course of the research visit. During the interview, the subject's brothers arrived and engaged in an animated conversation about a hole in a duck pen. At this point, the fieldworker became an auditor (according to Bell's 1984 model of audience design), and the subject's style shifted toward the brogue.

Table 8 reanalyzes the data from table 7 to show the effect of the two conversational contexts on /ay/ raising. While there is a dramatic increase in the use of /ay/ raising in the two interactions, a tabulation of a second variable, /æ/ lowering before /r/ (e.g., *there, wear*), for the same passages reveals no significant stylistic variation. The difference between the two shows the highly marked social nature of diagnostic variables such as /ay/ and makes principled consideration of linguistic, situational, interactional, and sociopsychological factors critical for understanding the complexity of Ocracoke English.

Table 8: Audience-related stylistic differentiation in /ay/ raising

Context	##	V	Liq	Nas	Vd Fr	Vl Fr	Vd St	Vl St	Total
Brothers Included	11/12 **91.7**	6/6 **100**	3/3 **100**	2/3 **66.7**	2/3 **66.7**	—	7/7 **100**	18/20 **90.0**	49/54 **90.7**
F.Worker Alone	6/9 **66.7**	1/1 **100**	3/6 **50.0**	10/14 **71.4**	2/5 **40.0**	2/6 **33.3**	—	12/24 **50.0**	36/65 **55.4**

= word-final position (e.g., *high*), V = vowel (e.g., *buying*), Liq = liquid (e.g., *file*), Nas = nasal (e.g., *time*), Vd Fr = voiced fricative (e.g., *five*), Vl Fr = voiceless fricative (e.g., *nice*), Vd st = voiced stop (e.g., *tide*), and Vl St = voiceless stop (e.g., *bike*)

NOTE

1. Internal factor groups for future study include tag versus non-tag structure (e.g., *The duck was there, weren't it?*), and the type of clause in which *was/n't* or *were/n't* occurs (e.g.; matrix versus embedded clause: *Rex weren't the fisherman*; *The man who weren't there was fishing*).

APPENDIX
APPLYING THE PRINCIPLE OF LINGUISTIC GRATUITY IN OCRACOKE

Sociolinguists have been conducting community-based studies for some years, but the benefit has mostly been unidirectional in terms of linguistic profit and education. We would like to suggest that there is a level of social commitment that investigators should adopt toward the language communities who have provided them data, a level that is more positive and proactive in that it actively pursues ways in which linguistic favors can be returned to the community. The *principle of linguistic gratuity* maintains that investigators who have obtained linguistic data from members of a speech community should actively pursue positive ways in which they can return linguistic favors to the community (Wolfram 1993a).

Several follow-up activities involved in our Ocracoke research project aim to apply the principle of linguistic gratuity. First, we are writing a popular account of the language history of Ocracoke that is intended to be useful to Ocracoke residents. Ocracokers are conscious of some unique island or Outer Banks lexical items, and some of these items have, in fact, become symbolic tokens of island quaintness. Thus, a simple, relatively superficial vocabulary-based exercise such as the one that follows is rooted in islander's pride in their unique historical lexical heritage.

Second, we are compiling representative speech samples from our interviews to share with the Ocracoke Historical Preservation Society. Language is, in many ways, the most sacred of all cultural traditions and is the rightful property of its users. We hope to be sensitive to this role of language and to preserve this unique artifact that has been shared with us by archiving for present and future generations of Ocracokers the current state of Ocracoke English and the apparent time changes that are represented in the current population of the island.

Third, with the cooperation of the educational system, we are developing a modified Dialect Awareness Program Project appropriate for Ocracoke. School children will be exposed to a unit on language in which they explore the socio-historical circumstances that have molded the development and maintenance of Ocracoke language and culture in particular, and the coastal culture of North Carolina in general, in the context of dialect development in the United States (Wolfram 1992). In the best of all scenarios, we hope to involve students not simply as passive observers of language variation but as student ethnographers in the active collection and description of Ocracoke speech.

AN OCRACOKE IQ TEST, or
HOW TO TELL A DINGBATTER FROM AN O'COCKER*

1. *dingbatter*
   a. baseball player in a small boat
   b. a husband
   c. a wife
   d. an outsider
2. *winard*
   a. a poker-playing wino
   b. moving into the wind
   c. a person who wins a game
   d. a piece of equipment used in crabbing
3. *meehonky*
   a. a call used in hide and seek
   b. a call made to attract ducks
   c. the call of an angry person
   d. an island marsh plant
4. *quamish*
   a. an upset stomach
   b. a fearful feeling
   c. a bad headache
   d. an excited feeling
5. *pizzer*
   a. a small boat
   b. a deck
   c. a porch
   d. a small Italian pie with cheese
6. *mammick* (also spelled *mommuck*)
   a. to imitate someone
   b. to bother someone
   c. to make fun of someone
   d. to become close friends with someone
7. She's *to* the restaurant.
   a. She ate at the restaurant twice.
   b. She's been to the restaurant.
   c. She's at the restaurant.
   d. She's going to the restaurant.
8. *fladget*
   a. gas in the alimentary canal
   b. an island men's game
   c. a small island bird
   d. a small piece of something
9. *puck*
   a. a small disk used in island hockey games
   b. a sweetheart
   c. a kiss on the cheek
   d. a mischievous person
10. *O'cocker*
    a. a derogatory term for an Ocracoker
    b. an outsider's mispronunciation of the term Ocracoker
    c. an island term for a native Ocracoker
    d. an island term for bluefish
11. *token of death*
    a. a coin needed for admission to Hades
    b. a sickness leading to death
    c. a fatal epidemic
    d. an unusual event that forecasts a death
12. *louard*
    a. lowering an anchor
    b. an exaggerated exclamation, as in "louard have mercy"
    c. moving away from the wind
    d. a fatty substance
13. *Russian rat*
    a. a unique island rodent
    b. an island gossip
    c. a vodka-drinking narc
    d. a mink
14. *Hatterasser*
    a. a storm that blows in from Hatteras
    b. a ferry ride from Ocracoke to Hatteras
    c. a person from Hatteras
    d. a fishing trip in Hatteras Inlet
15. *skiff*
    a. a large boat
    b. a small boat
    c. a strong wind
    d. a light wind

OCRACOKE IQ SCORE
0–4 = a complete dingbatter
5–8 = an educable dingbatter
9–12 = an average O'cocker
13–15 = an island genius

Answers:
1. d   4. b   7. c   10. c   13. a
2. b   5. c   8. d   11. d   14. c
3. a   6. b   9. b   12. c   15. b

*Thanks to James Barrie Gaskill of Ocracoke for his input on this test.

Pronunciation Variation in Eastern North Carolina

Bruce Southard

The barrier islands off the Atlantic coast have attracted a great deal of attention because of the language of their inhabitants. Historically isolated from mainland communities, the natives of these islands exhibit language forms believed to represent early stages of the speech of an area; such islands represent classic relic areas—areas settled early in a region's history but bypassed by the surrounding communities because of their isolation. Thus, we have such important speech forms as the Gullah found on the sea islands off the coasts of Georgia and South Carolina, as well as the language found on the barrier islands that constitute the Outer Banks of North Carolina.

Typically, but incorrectly, described by newspaper and television reporters as exemplifying "Elizabethan" speech, the inhabitants of the Outer Banks have become increasingly unwilling to model their unique language in the presence of strangers (see Wolfram et al., this volume). The Bankers often display to visitors only a hint of their native dialect, for they clearly have become bidialectal. For example, Morgan (1960) comments on the efforts by natives of Ocracoke, one of the most isolated of the Outer Banks islands, "to conceal the very deviations we wished to hear" (315). Perhaps because of the Ocracokers' reticence to model their unique speech forms, Morgan finds "no striking difference between their speech and that of the inhabitants of the mainland" (322).

In contrast, Howren (1962) offers a detailed study of the language of Ocracoke which finds a number of differences between the speech of Ocracoke and that of the mainland. Noting that the Outer Banks were not included in any surveys for the Linguistic Atlas of the Middle and South Atlantic States (LAMSAS), Howren was motivated to study the speech of Ocracoke by the fact that in 1960 an independent ferry operator had initiated a ferry service between Ocracoke and Hatteras, making possible a relatively easy connection to the mainland. Howren wished to record the speech of Ocracoke, fearing that outside contact would lead to linguistic interference and eventual "leveling" of the dialect—that is, the Banks dialect would come to resemble the language of the area surrounding it.

Howren presents a comprehensive analysis of the vowel phonemes of Ocracoke speech and discusses lexical and grammatical differences between the language of Ocracoke and the mainland. He concludes his article by noting three phonological differences which help distinguish the speech of Ocracoke from that of the rest of North Carolina (1962:174–175):

1) retention of postvocalic /r/, in contrast with the mixed patterns of r-retention in eastern North Carolina;
2) the quality of the /aɪ/ diphthong in such words as *tight*, *tide*, and so on;
3) the diphthong of /oʊ/, which has a nucleus approaching a mid-front rounded position in Ocracoke.

Jaffe (1965) examines the language found in the Core/Bogue Banks islands, which lie to the south of Ocracoke. Closer to the mainland than the other barrier islands, they are not considered to be part of the "Outer Banks" though they were settled in much the same manner as the Outer Banks and even became one of the favorite relocation areas for some Outer Bankers who apparently found life more hospitable closer to the mainland and resettled there. Jaffe notes in her introduction that although Bankers are not unfriendly, strangers from the outside (dingbatters) are kept at a polite distance. Indeed, Jaffe found it so difficult to locate willing respondents for her survey that she made arrangements to have the interviews conducted by a resident of the Bogue Sound area, and even he found it difficult to locate people willing to be interviewed. Eventually, twelve residents of Carteret County were interviewed, but two of those were born outside the area. Jaffe states that the most notable pronunciation differences from the rest of eastern North Carolina are as follows (1965):

1) "a marked retroflection of postvocalic /r/, very striking in a region where 'r-less' speech is universal" (5);
2) a single allophone for the phoneme /aɪ/, which she identifies as a raised low central vowel with a high-central glide [ɑ̈ɨ];
3) /u/, /ʊ/, and /ʌ/ tend to be fronted;
4) "the vowel /o/ is characteristically, though not always, pronounced [ɜʊ]" (6).

In her introduction, Jaffe notes that several of her informants were of families which had moved down the coast from the Outer Banks. She offers the opinion that the speech of the Core and Bogue Sounds would not differ in any significant way from that of the Outer Banks, though she makes no reference to Howren's study. Obviously, the two have identified three common features by which coastal North Carolina differs from the "South"—postvocalic /r/, a central or back /aɪ/ diphthong, and a fronted /o/.

Shores's (1984) study of the speech of Tangier Island, Virginia, is also of relevance here, for the Banks' first settlers apparently came down from Virginia around the Albemarle Sound. At the time English settlers were first coming to these shores, the Outer Banks formed a barrier preventing direct settlement on the mainland; thus, North Carolina was settled by overflow from its neighbors and was one of the last of the thirteen colonies to be settled. By 1722 a sufficient number of settlers had found their way to Carteret County for it to be established as a "precinct," and many of the names from that early settlement can be found among the residents of coastal Carteret County today. From 1725 on, the settlement history is somewhat obscure, though settlers were typically of English stock, with perhaps an Irish admixture.

Located in Chesapeake Bay, off the east coast of Virginia, Tangier Island is accessible only by water, even today. And like the speech of the Outer Banks, its speech is frequently described by off-islanders as "quaint, old-fashioned, and Elizabethan" (Shores 1984:40). Shores states that Tangier Island speech does not share with eastern Virginia speech the loss of postvocalic /r/; he further notes that /ɛɪ/ tends toward a back and higher position than its usual low-central position and glides toward a high central [aˆɨ]; and /o/ almost without exception is [oːu], a lengthened mid-back rounded vowel with a glide to the tense high back rounded position (39–47).

Shores concludes his article by stating that Tangier "has a communal solidarity and cohesiveness that will allow it to move well along into the twenty-first century relatively undisturbed. I say this because they can and do keep things and outsiders at a distance and because they are tied to the water for their sustenance" (48).

These various studies suggest a commonalty of maritime language along the Virginia/North Carolina coastal areas and lead to three questions:

1) Does current language usage show a resemblance between the language of the Outer Banks and that of the Core/Bogue Banks?
2) Do other mainland coastal communities share the speech characteristics of these barrier islands?
3) Has the speech in these areas changed? That is, is "leveling" taking place, with the language becoming more like that of the mainland, or are the communities retaining their distinctive language in the face of the hordes of tourists descending from other areas?

These three questions lead to a fourth question of theoretical interest: What happens when the area surrounding a relic area is itself in the process of undergoing language change, a change which moves in the direction of the sounds of the "relic" area? For example, in describing the Southern Vowel Shift, Labov reports that /ow/ tends to be fronted, while /ay/ is either monophthongized or backed and "raised along the back peripheral path" (1991:23–25). Thus, the Southern Vowel Shift has vowels moving in the direction of the relic sounds of the speech reported for the Outer Bankers. Will such change in the surrounding community support retention of these vowels by current Bankers? And, in regard to postvocalic /r/, what happens if that sound comes to be retained in the surrounding area? In other words, is it possible that the sounds of a relic area will be retained while the sounds of the neighboring area become more similar because of factors having nothing to do with the relic area?

To answer these questions, and to avoid the problems associated with obtaining reliable dialect samples from the Outer Banks, I turned to the Folklore Archives of East Carolina University.[1] Using the archive material has a number of advantages— the data are typically acquired by natives of an area or even a close relative of the informant; the informants are aware that the student interviewers are interested in folk ways, not language, and are apt to give a much more naturalistic speech. Moreover, the students constitute a statewide network that can gain access to even the smallest communities—there are interviews with people from crossroad communities of 15 to 20 inhabitants, in addition to farmers living in rural areas. A stranger to these areas would be unlikely to receive the sort of participation that the students do.

On the other hand, there are a number of disadvantages—tape quality is sometimes poor, though generally the students are sufficiently technically oriented that they produce high-quality recording. Even then, however, there are variables introduced by a lack of control over the recording equipment. For example, even a slight change in recording and playback speed may affect the researcher's perception of the recorded sound. Topics also vary widely, as do interview lengths. This is of less importance for a phonological study than for a lexical study, but some forms may simply not appear in a brief interview. Finally, missing biographical data meant that several tapes could not be used in this study.

Within North Carolina, I-95 is generally perceived as dividing eastern North Carolina from the rest of the state. Moreover, within North Carolina, eastern North Carolina is generally considered the poor relative of the more prosperous western three-fourths of the state. Its income has traditionally been based on farming and fishing rather than industry; it is the section of the state with the highest death rate among newborns and the greatest number of outhouses. With the possible exception of Wilmington, there are no large metropolitan areas. Listed below are the communities for which data are presented (numbers in the list correspond to numbers on the maps which follow).

Towns of eastern North Carolina

1 Rich Square	14 Dudley	26 Sea Level
2 Elizabeth City	15 Newton Grove	27 Atlantic
3 Windsor	16 Mount Olive	28 Morehead City
4 Columbia	17 Oriental	29 Salter Path
5 Manteo	18 Ocracoke	30 Burgaw
6 Williamston	19 Fayetteville	31 Ash
7 Wilson	20 Roseboro	32 Calabash
8 Greenville	21 Clinton	33 Ocean Isle
9 Simpson	22 Beulaville	34 Henderson
10 Washington	23 Havelock	35 Durham
11 Lowland	24 Newport	36 Chapel Hill
12 Buxton	25 Beaufort	37 Raleigh
13 Goldsboro		

Four communities west of I-95 were included in order to help delineate the area where loss of postvocalic /r/ is common; these are communities 34–37. The Outer Banks communities included are numbers 5, 12, and 18. It might be objected that community 5, Manteo, is actually on Roanoke Island, which is on the "sound side" of Bodie Island, one of the true Outer Banks islands. Manteo's history, however, links it closely with the true Banks islands. Carteret County communities are numbers 25 through 29. Of these, only number 29, Salter Path, is actually on the Banks island helping to form Bogue Sound; Morehead City, number 28, is on the mainland side of Bogue Sound. Communities 25 through 27 have historically been fishing communities; they are located on the mainland adjacent to Core Sound. The Banks islands to the east of Core Sound are uninhabited.

In *The Pronunciation of English in the Atlantic States* (*PEAS*), Kurath and McDavid (1961:170–71) discuss the distribution of postvocalic /r/ in North Carolina, noting that it "is preserved . . . to a considerable extent in coastal North Carolina." *PEAS* map 156, which shows the distribution of postvocalic /r/ in *door*, clearly shows /r/ as the only form along the North Carolina coast from the Virginia border to as far south as Morehead City. It is virtually the only form occurring in the western part of the state and is present with a lesser degree of constriction from the central part of the state to the coastal communities. Indeed, /r/ is deleted primarily only in the north-central portion of the state.

Map 1 shows the distribution of /r/ in the Folklore Archives data; each symbol adjacent to a community number stands for a separate informant. For the purposes of this study, I indicate an informant as having /r/ if the sound occurs more than 90% of the time in such words as *four, for, before, more, forty* and so on. Map 1 shows the area of loss of /r/ to be even more circumscribed than *PEAS* describes, the north central portion of the state being the only "r-less" area. Thus, /r/ seems not to be fading away but to be expanding and is retained in the maritime communities.

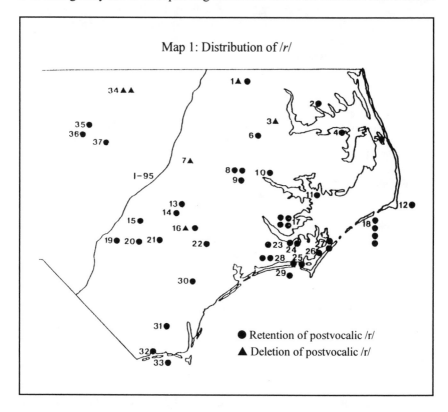

Let us now consider the distribution of /aɪ/.[2] *PEAS* map 26 (showing the low front and low central nuclei of the diaphones for *nine*) indicates broad distribution throughout the state. Map 27 (for *twice*) shows a higher low-central nucleus tending to cluster along the Virginia border, though it has some limited distribution throughout the east central portion of the state. A low back nucleus is not indicated.

Map 2 indicates a low-back rounded ([ɒ]) or unrounded ([ɑ]) nucleus to be common to the Outer Banks and Core/Bogue Sound areas. [aɪ] is found throughout the central portion of the state, though [ɑɪ] shows up among a number of the younger informants in the central portion of the state. It may be informative to look at the informants for community 18, Ocracoke, in the summary data presented in the table below. The two oldest informants have [ɒɪ]; the next younger one, an unrounded low back vowel alternating with a low central vowel ([ɑ̈ɪ ~ ɑɪ]); and the youngest, a low front nucleus. The area around Carteret County (e.g., communities 25, 26, 27, 28, and 29) shows a similar flux, with the oldest inhabitant having a low-back rounded nucleus and the youngest a low-front. The informants between these age extremes show either a higher low-central nucleus ([ɐ]) or a low back vowel. Perhaps these data indicate a movement toward a low central nucleus, but the sound is being raised to differentiate it from the centralizing movement of the low front nucleus.

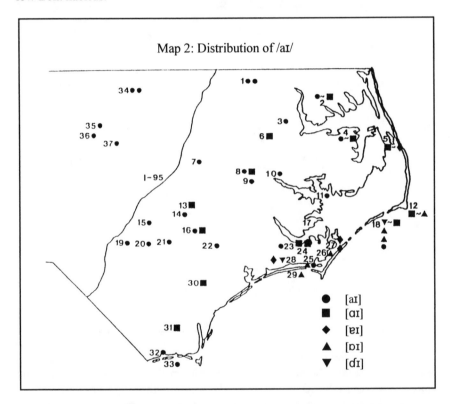

Map 2: Distribution of /aɪ/

Finally, *PEAS* maps 20 and 21 (of the vowels in *ago* and *coat*, respectively), show an [oʊ] diphthong throughout North Carolina, with a few instances of [ɝʊ], a "more or less open mid-central rounded beginning" (106) being recorded in northeastern North Carolina, basically from Morehead City northward along the coast. Map 3 illustrates that this fronted [ɝʊ] is now found throughout North Carolina, while the extremely fronted, indeed, mid-front rounded, nucleus ([œ]) can still be found in Ocracoke and the Bogue/Core Sound areas.

Once again, however, these data show a lack of fronting by the younger Ocracoke informants. In contrast, even the youngest informant in the Core/Bogue Sound area shows fronting. If we look at age and gender, we see that 11 of the 18 female informants below the age of 30 front this vowel, while only 4 of the 11 males do. Of the 14 informants in the Outer Banks and Core/Bogue Sound communities (5, 12, 18, 25, 26, 27, 28, 29), half have retained the rounded mid-front nucleus, five have a rounded mid-central nucleus, and only three have a rounded back nucleus. These data seem to suggest that fronting may be retained in the Banks dialect and that pressure from the vowel shift is supporting that retention.

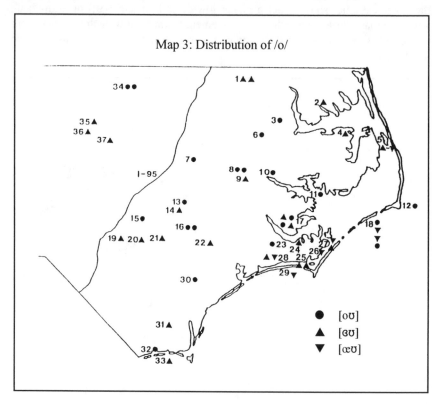

In answer to the four research questions posed above, then, it does seem that recent data confirm the similarities of speech which help make the Outer and Core/Bogue Banks dialect so distinctive. However, with the exception of some of the coastal Carteret County communities, it does not seem that other mainland communities of eastern North Carolina clearly match the four specific characteristics of the Banks dialect examined in this study. Though numerous eastern North Carolina communities now retain postvocalic r, none has the distinctive back nucleus for /aɪ/ and none has the front nucleus for /o/. The data are mixed as to whether the Banks dialect is disappearing. /aɪ/ seems to be in considerable flux, but retention of [œʊ] may be benefiting from the fronting of /o/ outside the Banks area. Thus, language change in the surrounding area may lead to retention of those distinctive language characteristics which mark relic areas.

Table: Summary of data

Community/ Informant	Age	Sex	/r/	/aɪ/	/oʊ/
la	50	M	ø	aɪ	ɤʊ
1b	21	F	r	aɪ	ɤʊ
2	24	F	r	aɪ ~ ɑɪ	ɤʊ
3	21	M	ø	aɪ	oʊ
4	22	M	r	aɪ ~ ɑɪ	ɤʊ
5	22	M	r	ɐɪ ~ ɑɪ	ɤʊ ~ œʊ
6	48	M	r	ɑɪ	oʊ
7	41	F	ø	aɪ	oʊ
8a	27	F	r	aɪ	oʊ
8b	30	M	r	ɑɪ	oʊ
9	70	F	r	aɪ	ɤʊ
10	22	F	r	aɪ	oʊ
11	55	M	r	aɪ	oʊ
12	40	M	r	ɑɪ ~ ɒɪ	oʊ
13	20	F	r	ɑɪ	oʊ
14	46	F	r	aɪ	ɤʊ ~ oʊ
15	22	M	r	aɪ	oʊ
16a	25	M	ø	aɪ	oʊ
16b	29	F	r	ɑɪ	oʊ
17a	22	M	r	aɪ	ɤʊ
17b	86	F	r	ɒɪ	oʊ
17c	67	F	r	aɪ	oʊ
17d	42	F	r	aɪ	ɤʊ
18a	35	M	r	ɑ́ɪ ~ ɑɪ	oʊ
18b	52	M	r	ɒɪ	œʊ
18c	49	F	r	ɒɪ	œʊ
18d	25	M	r	aɪ	oʊ
19	22	F	r	aɪ	ɤʊ
20	22	F	r	aɪ	ɤʊ
21	22	F	r	aɪ	ɤʊ
22	70	F	r	aɪ	ɤʊ
23	22	F	r	ɑɪ	oʊ
24a	20	M	r	ɑɪ	—
24b	27	F	r	ɑɪ	ɤʊ
25a	89	M	r	ɒɪ	ɤʊ
25b	21	F	r	aɪ	ɤʊ
26	50	M	r	ɒɪ	œʊ
27a	69	M	r	ɐɪ	œʊ
27b	69	F	r	ɐɪ	ɤʊ
28a	44	M	r	ɐɪ	ɤʊ
28b	66	M	r	ɑ́ɪ	œʊ
29	35	M	r	ɒɪ	œʊ
30	21	F	r	ɑɪ	oʊ
31	23	M	r	ɑɪ	ɤʊ
32	22	F	r	aɪ	oʊ
33	20	F	r	aɪ	ɤʊ
34a	20	M	ø	aɪ	oʊ
34b	20	M	ø	aɪ	oʊ
35	19	F	r	aɪ	ɤʊ
36	23	F	r	aɪ	ɤʊ
37	21	F	r	aɪ	ɤʊ

NOTES

1. Begun in the late 1970s, the Archives contain materials collected by folklore faculty and students within the English Department of East Carolina University. Material collected ranges from ghost tales to folk medicine/remedies, from hog-killing to shrimp fishing, and from quilting practices to guitar making and other of the folk arts. While most of the material exists only in written narratives, there are a substantial number of tape-recorded interviews—well over two hundred. It is from these interviews that the data presented here are drawn.

2. The vowel symbols used here in general follow Kurath and McDavid (1961:1):

[ɪ]   high front tense unrounded
[œ]   mid front rounded
[ɜ]   mid central rounded
[a]   lower low front unrounded
[ɐ]   higher low central unrounded
[ɑ]   lower low central unrounded
[ɒ]   low back rounded
[ɑ̇]   low back unrounded
[o]   mid back tense rounded
[ʊ]   high back lax rounded
[ɨ]   high central lax unrounded
[ɨ]   high central tense unrounded

Variation in Tejano English: Evidence for Variable Lexical Phonology

Robert Bayley

A classic sociolinguistic variable, consonant cluster reduction, or /-t,d/ deletion, has received renewed attention (e.g., Santa Ana 1991, 1992) as a result of Guy's (1991a, b) suggestion that linguistic variables that are subject to both morphological and phonological conditioning may be accounted for by incorporating a variable rule into lexical phonology (Kiparsky 1982). Guy hypothesizes that the greater incidence of final consonant cluster reduction in monomorphemes (e.g., *past*) than in bimorphemes (e.g., *passed*) may be explained if /-t,d/ deletion is treated as a variable rule that applies at each level of the derivation. Such a model predicts an exponential relationship among rates of deletion from monomorphemes, semiweak verbs (e.g., *leave, left*) and regular past tense verbs. The exponential hypothesis offers a more powerful explanation for observed patterns of variation than the traditional rank-ordering of constraints within a factor group because it allows for precise quantitative predictions of rates of consonant cluster reduction in words belonging to different morphological classes

This paper tests the exponential hypothesis with data from a relatively neglected dialect, the English spoken by working-class Mexican Americans in San Antonio, Texas, or Tejano English (TE).[1] Analysis of /-t,d/ deletion in the speech of working-class Hispanic adolescent and young adult residents of a San Antonio housing project supports the predictions of an exponential model of morphological constraints. This study also attempts to situate TE in relation to other dialects of English, at least with respect to the patterning of constraints on consonant cluster reduction, by comparing the TE pattern with /-t,d/ deletion in dialects of English that have not been influenced by contact with Spanish. Results of multivariate analysis with Rousseau and Sankoff's (1978) variable rule program show that TE generally follows the pan-English pattern summarized by Labov (1989a). Finally, the paper compares constraints on /-t,d/ deletion in TE with the Los Angeles Chicano English (CE) pattern examined by Santa Ana (1991). The comparison indicates that working-class Mexican American English spoken in widely separated cities exhibits strikingly similar patterns of variation.

EXPLANATIONS OF /-t,d/ DELETION

Numerous studies of /-t,d/ deletion in a wide variety of English dialects have shown rule application is constrained by the grammatical category of the word which contains the final /-t,d/ cluster, resulting in the following likelihood of cluster reduction: monomorpheme (Mm) > semiweak verb (SwV) > regular past tense or past participle (Pt/Pp) (see Labov 1989a; Santa Ana 1991). That is, /-t,d/ is most likely to be deleted from monomorphemes (e.g., *mist*) and least likely to be deleted from regular past tense forms (e.g., *missed*) with semiweak verbs (e.g., *lost*) occupying an intermediate position. The regularity of the patterning of morphological constraints has led to several attempts at explanation from both functionalist and formalist perspectives. The following sections summarize those explanations, briefly discuss their limitations, and outline the features of lexical phonology that are most relevant to the present study.

A Functionalist Explanation

Kiparsky (1972) offers a functionalist explanation of the effect of a word's morphological class on the likelihood of final consonant cluster reduction. He proposes the "distinctness condition," defined as the "tendency for semantically relevant information to be retained in surface structure" (195) and further suggests that grammars tend to block rules "in environments in which their free application would wipe out morphological distinctions on the surface" (197). Such a condition would account for the relative infrequency of /-t,d/ deletion from past tense forms where /-t,d/ serves as a unique grammatical marker, as in (1):

(1) He talked all night long.

The distinctness condition also accounts for the somewhat higher incidence of /-t,d/ deletion from semiweak verbs in which the past tense is marked by an internal vowel change and, in some cases, regressive voicing assimilation (e.g., *leave, left*), in addition to the affixation of /-t,d/. That is, while final /-t,d/ in semiweak past tense forms contains grammatically relevant information, the information it contains also is recoverable from other segments or features. In addition, a functionalist explanation provides for the relatively high incidence of /-t,d/ deletion from monomorphemic words in which the final segment conveys no essential information. The phrase *jus' me*, for example, contains the same semantic information as the phrase *just me*.

Despite its appeal, however, a functionalist explanation cannot account for all of the results of empirical studies of /-t,d/ deletion. For example, it cannot explain empirical results (e.g., Guy 1980) that show that /-t,d/ is as likely to be deleted from a regular past participle, where it serves as a redundant marker, as from a past tense form, where it serves as a unique tense marker. Little information is lost, for example, if the final segment is deleted from *missed* in (2a) below. In (2b), however, the final consonant in *missed*, as a unique tense marker, carries information that is not recoverable elsewhere in the sentence:

(2) (a) Carmen was missed by all.
     (b) We all missed Carmen.

A second failure of the functionalist explanation is that it cannot account for empirical results that show a greater likelihood of /-t,d/ absence from regular past tense forms than from participles in the speech of learners of English as a second language (Bayley 1991). In fact, a functionalist explanation would predict exactly the opposite result.

Formal Explanations

Chomsky and Halle's (1968) framework offers an alternative explanation for the patterning of morphological constraints on /-t,d/ deletion. Within this framework, the grammatical categories subject to /-t,d/ deletion are characterized by different internal morphological boundaries. For purposes of rule application, mono-morphemes have no relevant internal structure. Semiweak verbs are characterized by a formative boundary (+) that leads to changes in the stem. Regular past tense forms and past participles are characterized by a "word" boundary (#) between the stem and the past tense morpheme. The factors in the grammatical category group, then, have the following structures:

Monomorpheme: just
Semiweak Verb: lef+t
Past Tense, Participle: walk#ed

Final /-t,d/ may be freely deleted from monomorphemes, subject only to lower level constraints such as the preceding and following segments, voicing, stress, and cluster length. A formative boundary constrains rule application to some extent and accounts for the intermediate rates of deletion for semiweak verbs. Participles and preterits, having the same internal structure, which is characterized by the still more formidable word boundary, undergo approximately the same rate of deletion, despite their different functional loads.

The ordering of grammatical constraints, then, including the similar patterning of past tense and participial forms, can be accounted for within an *SPE* framework. An explanation that relies on internal boundaries to inhibit /-t,d/ deletion from semiweak and regular past tense verbs, however, offers no way of explaining the *quantitative* results of empirical studies. It can only account for the relative ordering of morphological classes; it does not enable us to predict rates of /-t,d/ deletion from words of different grammatical categories. To account for the quantitative results of empirical studies, Guy (1991b) has proposed that Kiparsky's (1982) model of lexical phonology be modified to include a variable rule that applies at each level of the derivation. The features of lexical phonology that are relevant to the present study are summarized by Guy:

1) multiple levels of lexical derivation;
2) interleaving of morphological and phonological processes;
3) phonological rules may apply at more than one level; and
4) bracket erasure occurs at the end of each level. (1991b:6)

In lexical phonology, then, morphological derivation is a multilevel process, with phonological processes, including cluster reduction, alternating with morphological processes at each derivational level. Moreover, internal boundaries of the types + and # are assumed not to exist. Rather, within a derivational level, morphemes are bracketed. Bracket erasure occurs at the end of each level (Guy 1991b:6–7).

In this framework, the three morphological classes that are most relevant to /-t,d/ deletion have distinct derivational histories. Monomorphemes have -*t* or -*d* present from the beginning of the derivation. Semiweak verbs, like other forms character- ized by irregular inflection, undergo affixation of /-t,d/ at the second level (corresponding to Kiparsky's level 1), and past tense forms and participles, like other regular inflectional forms, undergo affixation of /-t,d/ at the third level (corresponding to Kiparsky's level 2) before surfacing. Thus, monomorphemes are subject to phonological processes three times, semiweak verbs twice, and past tense forms and participles only once.

If, as Guy suggests, lexical phonology may be modified to include variable rules that apply at a fixed rate at each derivational level, we can predict relative rates of /-t,d/ deletion (or retention) from words with different derivational histories. Thus, past tense forms and participles, which are subject to one pass of a variable /-t,d/ deletion rule, would have a probability of retention Pr. Semiweak verbs, which are subject to two passes of the rule, would have a probability of retention Pr^2, while monomorphemes, which are subject to three passes of the rule, would have a probability of retention Pr^3. That is, there should be an exponential relationship among rates of /-t,d/ retention for past tense forms and past participles, semiweak verbs, and monomorphemes. For example, based on a hypothetical 25% fixed rate of /-t,d/ deletion, a data set containing 100 tokens each of past tense forms, semiweak verbs, and monomorphemes, should yield the results shown in table 1. As table 1 outlines, with a fixed rate of /-t,d/ deletion of 25% and 100 tokens in each morphological class, an exponential model predicts surface /-t,d/ retention in 75 regular past tense verbs or participles (one pass), 56 semiweak verbs (two passes), and 42 monomorphemes (three passes).

Table 1: Quantitative consequences of an exponential model
of /-t,d/ deletion (hypothetical data)

Grammatical Category	Tokens	Probability of /-t,d/ Retention	N /-t,d/ Retained
Monomorpheme	100	$Pr^3 = .4219$	42
Semiweak Verb	100	$Pr^2 = .5625$	56
Past tense/Past part.	100	$Pr = .7500$	75

Guy's model of variable lexical phonology, then, offers very explicit empirical predictions. Moreover, it accounts for the fact that forms in which /-t,d/ carries different functional loads (e.g., regular past tense verbs and participles) are subject to the same rate of cluster reduction and for the relative ordering of grammatical categories, as well as for observed quantitative results. In the following sections, I report on a test of the exponential hypothesis on TE data and compare patterns of /-t,d/ deletion in the English spoken by Mexican Americans in Texas with /-t,d/ deletion in other English dialects.

METHODS

The Community

The data reported here were collected in Buena Vista Courts (BV, a pseudo-nym), a housing project operated by the San Antonio Housing Authority (SAHA) in the overwhelmingly Hispanic southwest quadrant of the city. BV reflects the ethnic composition of the neighborhood. Of the 483 families in residence at the beginning of 1992, 98% were Hispanic and 82% were headed by single women. Owing to SAHA residency requirements, BV residents are all classified as low income, and all are U.S. citizens or permanent residents.

Speakers

Although not a random sample, the eighteen speakers included in the present study represent a reasonable cross section of the young people living in Buena Vista. Their social and demographic characteristics are summarized in table 2.

Table 2: Speaker social and demographic characteristics

Speaker ID	Age	Sex	Birthplace	Years in SA	First Lang.	Current Home Lang.	Ed. Level
001	15	F	Laredo	2	Sp	Eng/Sp	7
002	17	M	Chicago	6	Eng	Eng/Sp	9
003	16	F	San Ant.	16	Sp	Eng/Sp	9
006	17	M	San Ant.	17	Sp	Sp	11
007	15	F	Chicago	15	Eng	Eng/Sp	8
009	18	F	San Ant.	18	Sp	Eng/Sp	12+
011	19	F	St. Louis	5	Eng	Eng/Sp	8
012	18	M	San Ant.	18	Sp	Sp	8
013	18	F	San Ant.	18	Sp	Eng/Sp	9
016	18	M	San Ant.	18	Sp	Sp	10
017	15	F	San Ant.	15	Eng	Eng/Sp	9
018	18	M	San Ant.	18	Eng	Eng	9
019	16	F	Pied. Neg.	13	Sp	Eng/Sp	7
021	19	F	San Ant.	19	Eng	Eng/Sp	8
022	20	M	Los Ang.	12	Eng	Eng	12+
024	16	M	San Ant.	9	Sp	Sp	7
026	19	M	San Ant.	19	Sp	Sp/Eng	10/GED
057	26	F	San Ant.	26	Sp	Eng/Sp	11/GED

Most speakers have lived their entire lives in San Antonio or south Texas. All have lived in south Texas for at least five years and only one was born outside of the United States, just across the border in Piedras Negras.[2] Eleven speakers claim Spanish as their first language. Four use Spanish at home nearly exclusively. Twelve speakers use both English and Spanish at home, usually with frequent code-switching. Only two speakers, one of whom was born in Los Angeles and moved to San Antonio at the age of six, are English monolinguals.[3]

Data Collection

The sociolinguistic interviews from which the data for the present paper have been extracted were conducted between February and August 1992. Interviews, which followed standard sociolinguistic methods, were conducted by fieldworkers who shared ethnic and linguistic backgrounds with consultants. In fact, one of the fieldworkers had grown up in Buena Vista and later worked as a manager of the project. Although their university affiliation resulted in some social distance between interviewers and consultants, the fieldworkers' familiarity with the neighborhood, including its folklore and immediate concerns, enabled us to obtain a great deal of highly vernacular speech.

Data Reduction

Words containing final /-t,d/ clusters were transcribed, along with enough of the surrounding context to indicate the grammatical category of the word in which the cluster occurred. The word *and* and tokens followed by neutralizing homorganic stops (*e.g., talked to, calmed down*) were excluded from the corpus (cf. Neu 1980). Tokens followed by interdental fricatives (e.g., *called them*) were also excluded because nearly all speakers in this study, like working-class speakers of other dialects (Wolfram 1991), frequently pronounced initial interdental fricatives as corresponding stops. Tokens with a preceding nasal and a following vowel, which in some dialects are subject to nasal flap formation (Labov 1989a), were retained, a practice followed in other studies of Mexican American English (e.g., Hartford 1975; Santa Ana 1991).

RESULTS AND DISCUSSION

The results conform closely to the predictions of the exponential hypothesis. Moreover, a comparison of VARBRUL results with previous studies of /-t,d/ deletion in other English dialects shows that TE approximates the pan-English pattern for a great majority of linguistic constraints. Finally, a comparison of /-t,d/ deletion in TE and Los Angeles CE indicates that, on the dimension examined here, San Antonio and Los Angeles varieties exhibit very similar patterns of variation, although there are minor differences.

A Test of the Exponential Hypothesis

As shown above, Guy's (1991b) exponential hypothesis predicts a precise quantitative ordering of /-t,d/ deletion by morphological class. Expressed in terms of /-t,d/ retention, the hypothesis predicts that given a base probability of retention Pr, equal to the surface rate of retention for regular past tense forms (assuming a sufficiently large corpus so that statistical fluctuations are neutralized), the probability of retention for semiweak verbs will equal Pr^2. For monomorphemes the probability of surface retention will equal Pr^3. As table 3 shows, the results for monomorphemes conform to the predictions of the exponential hypothesis at an accuracy rate of 98.66%.

Table 3: Tejano English /-t,d/ retention by grammatical category

Gram. Cat.	N	Predicted Retention	Observed Retention	N Predicted	N Observed	Token Error	Error Rate
Mm	2012	$Pr^3 = .4309$	.4175	866.97	840	27.0	.0134
SwV	204	$Pr^2 = .5705$	.6471	116.38	132	15.6	.0765
Pt/Pp	568	$Pr = .7553$	.7553	429.01	429	—	—

Exclusions: *and*, tokens in the environment of a following homorganic stop. No weighting of the Pr; N = 2784.

That is, assuming that the retention rate for regular past tense forms represents one application of a variable rule and that the morphological categories Pt/Pp, SwV, and Mm occupy different levels in the multilevel architecture of lexical phonology, we can predict the actual number of /-t,d/ retentions in monomorphemes with an error rate of only 1.34%.

Table 3 also shows, however, that semiweak verbs exhibit considerable deviation from the predictions of the model, with an error rate of 7.7% (.0765). This may be due to sampling error, since semiweak verbs occur much less frequently than either monomorphemes or regular past tense forms. In the present corpus, the number of semiweak verbs is relatively small (N=204) compared to monomorphemes (N=2012) and regular past tense forms and participles (N=568).

A question arises, however, concerning the proper treatment of semiweak verbs by the speakers studied here. Guy and Boyd (1990), in a study of several northeastern dialects, found that speakers under the age of 30 tend to analyze semiweak verbs as monomorphemes, a finding that has subsequently been confirmed by Santa Ana (1992) and Roberts (1994). Santa Ana found age-grading among Los Angeles Chicanos,[4] and Roberts found that children in a south Philadelphia preschool treated semiweak verbs like monomorphemes. To test whether a similar age effect holds for the San Antonio speakers, all of whom were younger than thirty when interviewed, I combined the Mm and SwV classes. Table 4 compares the prediction of the exponential model with the Tejano results for the remodeled data. Note that I have assumed that the Mm + SwV class is still subject to three passes of the rule.

Table 4: Tejano English retention by grammatical category
(monomorphemes and semiweak verbs combined)

Gram. Cat.	N	Predicted Retention	Observed Retention	N Predicted	N Observed	Token Error	Error Rate
Mm, SwV	2216	$Pr^3 = .4309$	.4386	954.87	972	17.1	.0077
Pt/Pp	568	$Pr = .7553$	.7553	429	429	—	—

Exclusions: *and*, tokens in the environment of a following homorganic stop. No weighting of the Pr. N = 2784.

As the results in table 4 show, the data conform substantially better to the prediction of an exponential model of morphological constraints when monomorphemes and semiweak verbs are combined. The accuracy rate for the combined category improves from 98.66% to 99.33%.

/-t,d/ Deletion in TE and Other English Dialects: VARBRUL Analysis

As a widely studied sociolinguistic variable, /-t,d/ deletion offers a convenient locus for comparing variation in TE with variation in other English dialects. This section summarizes previous multivariate analyses of /-t,d/ deletion, presents the results of VARBRUL analysis of /-t,d/ deletion in San Antonio TE, and compares those results with the pan-dialectal pattern summarized by Labov (1989a) and with the Los Angeles Chicano pattern examined by Santa Ana (1991).

More than twenty years of research have established the grammatical and phonological constraints on /-t,d/ deletion. According to Labov, /-t,d/ deletion is constrained by the following factors (adapted from Labov 1989a:90):[5]

a)   syllable stress (unstressed > stressed)
b)   cluster length (CCC > CC)
c)   the phonetic features of **the preceding consonant**, yielding the segmental order /s/ > stops > nasals > other fricatives > liquids
d)   **the grammatical status** of the final /t/, with the order: part of *-n't* morpheme > part of stem > derivational suffix > past tense or past participle suffix
e)   the phonetic features of **the following segment**, yielding the order: obstruents > liquids > glides > vowels > pauses
f)   **agreement in voicing** of the segments preceding and following the /t,d/ (homovoiced > heterovoiced).

Some studies differ in details from the pattern above. Guy (1980), for example, shows that a following pause has different effects on cluster reduction in the speech of New Yorkers and Philadelphians. Nevertheless, the main outlines of the pattern Labov summarizes apply to the great majority of English dialects in which the /-t,d/ variable has been systematically investigated. The results of variable rule analysis with GoldVarb 2.0 (Rand & Sankoff 1990), a Macintosh version of the VARBRUL 2 program, indicate that TE generally follows the pan-English pattern, although there are several important differences between TE and other dialects.

To examine the relationship between /-t,d/ deletion in TE and other English dialects, I coded the data for the six factor groups outlined by Labov as well as for four additional groups: speech style (conversation, reading passage, word list); reported first language (Spanish, English); current home language(s) (English, English and Spanish, Spanish); and speaker gender. The data set was expanded to include tokens of *-n't* and tokens from the reading passage and word list, resulting in a total of 5022 tokens. VARBRUL analysis indicates that seven of the tested factor groups significantly affect realization of final /-t,d/ ($p < .05$): 1) the grammatical category (or morphological class); 2) the phonetic features of the preceding segment; 3) the phonetic features of the following segment; 4) syllable stress; 5) voicing agreement of the preceding and following segments; 6) speech style; 7) current home language. Cluster length (CC, CCC), speaker gender, and reported first language proved not to be significant. Statistically significant results are summarized in table 5. Factors within groups that did not differ significantly from one another have been combined.

Although space does not permit a full discussion of all of the factor groups in table 5, results for a number of the factor groups do require explanation. The Grammatical Category factor group combines monomorphemes and semiweak verbs because the log likelihood test for significance of the differences between factors within groups showed that the difference between these two categories was not significant at the .05 level ($\chi^2=3.048$, df=1, $p >.05$). This result is consistent with the interpretation that the speakers in this study do not analyze semiweak verbs as a separate morphological class.

Table 5: /-t,d/ deletion in Tejano English, results of VARBRUL analysis

Factor Group	Factor	p_i	% Deletion	N
Grammatical Category	*n't*	.70	78	1400
	Mm, SwV	.46	50	2643
	Pt/Pp	.30	20	979
Preceding Segment	/s/	.75	67	1258
	stop, nasal	.48	65	2964
	fricative	.27	12	349
	/l/	.17	16	451
Following Segment	obstruent, /l/	.66	70	2338
	glide, /r/	.52	57	651
	pause	.39	32	949
	vowel	.26	28	1084
Syllable Stress	unstressed	.56	65	830
	stressed	.49	49	4192
Voicing Agreement	homovoicing	.55	58	2760
	heterovoicing	.44	45	2262
Style	conversation	.56	59	4155
	reading	.40	25	583
	word list	.05	2	284
Current Home Lang.	Eng & Sp, Sp	.51	53	4391
	English	.44	43	631
TOTAL		p_o=.49	52	5022

Exclusions: *and*, words followed by homorganic stops or interdental fricatives. All factor groups significant at $p < .05$.

The results for the Following Segment factor group, which show the pattern of obstruent, /l/ > glide, /r/ > pause > vowel, also require attention. As Labov's (1989a) summary of previous work on /-t,d/ deletion indicates, the usual practice has been to combine following /l/ and /r/ under the more general category of liquids. Guy, however, suggests that this procedure is in error and hypothesizes that "word-final stops may, when they satisfy possible-onset conditions (i.e., before vowels and certain glides and liquids), be syllabified as the initial segment in the following syllable . . . and consequently become ineligible for deletion" (1991b:18). This hypothesis predicts that /t/ and /d/ should be blocked from rightwards resyllabification before /l/ because *dl* and *tl* are not possible syllable onsets in English. Resyllabification should be possible before /r/, however, because *dr* and *tr* onsets are very common. Quantitatively, the hypothesis predicts that following /l/ should have a factor value similar to following obstruents that fail to satisfy syllable onset conditions (e.g., *db, *dn, *ts) while following /r/ should have a factor value similar to following segments that do satisfy onset conditions (e.g., *tw*). The results in table 5 indicate that the San Antonio data confirm the resyllabification hypothesis, as can be seen even more clearly in table 6, which shows the values for /l/ and /r/ before they were combined with obstruents and glides and the data remodeled to group factors that did not differ significantly from one another.

Table 6: Tejano English /-t,d/ deletion by following segment
(no significance tests)

Following Segment	VARBRUL Weight
obstruent	.66
/l/	.60
glide	.52
/r/	.49
pause	.39
vowel	.26

The effect of the speaker's current home language also requires attention. As shown in table 5 above, speakers who report exclusive use of English at home are less likely to reduce final clusters ($p_i = .44$) than those who use Spanish exclusively or a combination of Spanish and English ($p_i = .51$). This result, which would seem to lend support to an interference hypothesis, should be treated with caution, particularly in view of the fact that VARBRUL's step-up step-down procedure did not select reported first language, as distinct from current language use, as a significant contributor to /-t,d/ deletion. Only two speakers reported exclusive home use of English. Moreover, one of the English monolinguals, #22, had fewer close ties within Buena Vista than any of the other consultants in the study, even though he had lived in the project for twelve years. Unlike many neighborhood young men, Keith (a pseudonym) had completed high school at the age of eighteen, was attending a local community college, and had aspirations to attend a university. He was dating an Anglo woman from Minnesota and even taking golf lessons from her father. Data are needed from more English dominant Tejanos before any generalizations can be made about the effect of home language use on cluster reduction.

Although most of the results for this study are similar to those reported for other dialects, there are important differences from the pan-English pattern and from results reported for Los Angeles CE. The first of these differences concerns the effect of syllable stress. As Labov's (1989a) ordering of constraints on /-t,d/ deletion suggests, in some dialects stress strongly constrains cluster reduction, with unstressed syllables being much more liable to /-t,d/ deletion than stressed syllables. Even though the San Antonio results show a significant effect in the expected direction, syllable stress is the least prominent among the significant factor groups, with a range of only .07. (Compare this very small range with, for example, the range of .40 between the most and least favorable factors for deletion in the grammatical category factor group.) A full explanation of this divergence from other dialects awaits further investigation. For the present, however, suffice it to say that there is considerable evidence that Mexican American vernacular varieties exhibit different patterns of stress and intonation than do other dialects of English (Penfield 1984; Penfield & Ornstein-Galicia 1985). Such differences offer potential explanations of the divergence found here.

A second difference between the San Antonio and pan-English patterns of /-t,d/ deletion concerns the effect of cluster length, listed second by Labov (1989a). In the San Antonio data, cluster length does not significantly affect deletion, a surprising finding since articulatory constraints would seem to favor greater reduction of triclusters than of biclusters. The lack of significance of this factor may, however, be a consequence of the extreme imbalance in the token distribution. Of the tokens analyzed here, 94% were biclusters and only 6% triclusters, a distribution which resulted in too great an overlap between the factor value for biclusters and the input probability to achieve reliable VARBRUL results. (See Guy 1988 for a discussion of problems associated with unbalanced data sets.)

The third difference is between the San Antonio speakers and speakers of Los Angeles CE. In contrast to other studies, where preceding /r/, like preceding vowels, results in near categorical retention, Santa Ana (1991:87) reports a 13% rate of /-t,d/ deletion following /r/. A model which attributes a substantial influence to Spanish would predict just such a result because Spanish /r/ is [+consonantal –vocalic], in contrast to general American /r/, which is [+consonantal +vocalic]. The 263 examples of /rt/, /rd/ in the San Antonio data, however, contain no instances of /-t,d/ deletion. They were therefore excluded both by the VARBRUL program (as a knockout factor) and from the percentages used to test Guy's exponential model. While the reasons for this difference between the speech of Mexican Americans in Los Angeles and San Antonio require further investigation, with respect to this factor, TE exhibits less substrate influence than does Los Angeles CE.

With some important exceptions, then, consonant cluster reduction in the speech of San Antonio Tejanos follows the pattern found in other dialects, as can be clearly seen in table 7, which compares /-t,d/ deletion in Mexican American English in San Antonio (TE) and Los Angeles (CE) with Labov's pan-dialectal pattern.

As table 7 shows, fifteen of twenty factors tested in the San Antonio corpus and sixteen of twenty factors in Santa Ana's Los Angeles corpus match the pan-dialectal pattern. Moreover, of the five factors that do diverge from the pan-English pattern in the San Antonio data, two diverge in ways that have been documented in studies of other English dialects. The TE divergence from the widely documented factor ordering of Mm > SwV > Pt/Pp can be explained as a consequence of the relative youth of the San Antonio speakers and a following pause having different effects on cluster reduction in New York and Philadelphia English (Guy 1980). Moreover, although additional work on a range of variables is necessary before any firm conclusions can be reached, the patterning of /-t,d/ deletion in Mexican American speech in the San Antonio and Los Angeles studies suggests that Chicano/Tejano English has some of the characteristics of a supraregional ethnic dialect, with only minor regional differences in areas such as final stop deletion in the environment of a preceding /r/.

CONCLUSIONS

The results presented here suggest several conclusions about the exponential hypothesis and the treatment of the grammatical category and following segment factor groups in studies of /-t,d/ deletion, as well as about the status of Mexican American varieties of English. First, this study adds to the growing evidence for an exponential model of morphological constraints. Second, it provides additional evidence that younger speakers do analyze semiweak verbs as monomorphemes.

Table 7: Comparison of /-t,d/ deletion in Mexican American English dialects (San Antonio Tejano English and Los Angeles Chicano English) with English pan-dialectal pattern

1. Syllable Stress

Pan-English	unstressed	>	stressed
LA CE	.53		.49
*SA TE	.56		.49

2. Length of Consonant Cluster

Pan-English	CCC	>	CC
LA CE	.57		.48
SA TE	*.48*		*.50*

3. Agreement in Voicing of Preceding and Following Segments

Pan-English	same	>	different
LA CE	.55		.45
*SA TE	.55		.43

4. Grammatical Category

Pan-English	-*n't*	>	Mm	>	SwV	>	Pt/Pp
LA CE	.58		.55		.43		.28
*SA TE	.70		.46 (+SwV)		—		.30

5. Preceding segment

Pan-English	/s/	>	stop	>	nasal	>	fricative	>	liquid
LA CE pattern	/s/	>	*nasal*	>	*stop*	>	fricative	>	liquid
LA CE	.56		*.56*		*.38*		.28		.23
SA TE pattern	/s/	>	stop	>	nasal	>	fricative	>	liquid
*SA TE	.67		.47		.46		.22		.16

6. Following Segment

Pan-English	obstruent	>	liquid	>	glide	>	vowel	>	pause
LA CE pattern	obstruent	>	*glide*	>	*liquid*	>	vowel	>	pause
LA CE	.62		*.60*		*.57*		.33		.32
SA TE pattern	obstruent	>	liquid	>	glide	>	*pause*	>	*vowel*
*SA TE	.67		.55		.49		*.36*		*.26*

Notes: To allow for a clearer comparison across studies, tokens occurring in reading passages and word lists have been excluded from the San Antonio data and following segments /l/ and /r/ and have been combined. Monomorphemes and semiweak verbs are also combined in the San Antonio data. Factor values that diverge from the pan-English pattern are in italics. Los Angeles N = 5049, average /-t,d/ deletion 61%; San Antonio N = 4155, average /-t,d/ deletion 59%; * Factor group significant at $p < .05$. (Sources: Pan-English, Labov 1989a:90; Los Angeles, Santa Ana 1991:82.)

Because all of the speakers in the corpus were under thirty, however, the results provide no information about whether older working-class Tejanos assign semiweak verbs to a separate morphological class. In addition, the results of VARBRUL analysis, which show that following /l/ patterns with obstruents and following /r/ with glides, confirm the hypothesis that resyllabification is at least partially responsible for the following segment constraint on /-t,d/ deletion. Finally, this study provides evidence that TE should be treated as a dialect of English rather than as an imperfectly mastered interlanguage. Without multivariate analysis, the high incidence of final cluster reduction (59% in conversation) might be attributed to the influence from Spanish, which lacks final clusters (see, e.g., Penfield & Ornstein-Galicia 1985; González 1988). The VARBRUL results, however, clearly show that /-t,d/ deletion in TE operates much as it does in other English dialects. Although the speakers in this study do exhibit speech patterns which are most likely attributable to a Spanish substrate (e.g., *ch-sh* alternation, the effect of syllable stress and cluster length on /-t,d/ deletion), such influence does not account for the patterning of the majority of constraints on the /-t,d/ variable.

NOTES

The research reported here was carried out under a grant from the Committee on Faculty Research of the University of Texas at San Antonio (UTSA), whose support is gratefully acknowledged. Interviews were conducted by Nohemí Torres and José Zapata, both UTSA graduate students in Bicultural-Bilingual Studies. I have also benefited from discussions with Gregory Guy, William Labov, Julie Roberts, and Tom Veatch. Faults that remain are, of course, my own.

1. The question of the name of the dialect spoken in working-class Mexican American communities in Texas raises a number of issues of ethnicity and self-identification. All except two speakers in this study, like most San Antonio Mexican Americans, identify themselves as Hispanic. In addition, speakers accept the term *Tejano* and all but two speakers object to the term *Chicano*. Hence, I have chosen to refer to the variety of English spoken natively by working-class *barrio* residents as Tejano English (TE), a term which respects speaker preferences while avoiding the confusion of the more generic Hispanic English.

2. Data from the one Mexican-born speaker (#19) were included because his family moved to Texas and settled in the neighborhood of Buena Vista when the speaker was only three years old, well before the end of any version of the critical period for second language acquisition.

3. Language use information represents responses to interview questions and conforms to what interviewers observed in consultants' homes. More detailed ethnographic study is needed to determine actual patterns of home language choice with confidence.

4. Santa Ana also found that speakers born before World War II, who spoke Spanish as often as English when they were growing up, never analyzed semiweak verbs as a separate morphological class. In San Antonio, older speakers, who are more likely to be Spanish dominant, show a different pattern. As shown in Bayley (1994), for older Spanish-dominant speakers the grammatical status of a word does not significantly constrain /-t,d/ deletion.

5. Labov's summary is based on studies by Labov, Cohen, Robins, and Lewis in Harlem (1968), Wolfram in Detroit (1969), Fasold in Washington (1972), and Guy in Philadelphia (1980). Although recent work by Bayley (1991) on Chinese learners of English in California, Patrick (1991) on mesolectal creole speakers in Jamaica, Santa Ana (1991, 1992) on Chicanos in Los Angeles, and Roberts (1994) on preschool children in Philadelphia has added refinements to the analysis of the /-t,d/ variable, Labov's (1989a) summary holds for most native English dialects that have been systematically investigated.

Rule Ordering in the Phonology of Alabama-Georgia Consonants
William C. Taylor

Recent phonological research demonstrates that accurate description of phonetic forms by spectrographic analysis and computer-drawn statistical comparisons over time, between regions, and by age, sex, and other social variables is a highly developed analytic technique. Computer programs like those described in the collection by Kretzschmar, Schneider, and Johnson (1989) and Kretzschmar (this volume) can analyze large databases of words and speakers. Much of the research, however, de-emphasizes a distinction between underlying structure (phonemic or lexical form) and surface structure (phonetic form). An examination from that theoretical perspective of consonants and consonant sequences from selected Southern areas shows that many differences—between Standard American English (SAE) and regional speech, and between one region and another—are differences of neither lexical nor phonetic form alone, but of phonological rules and of rule ordering. A description of a language variety—like that of a language—is incomplete without a description of its phonology. My primary purpose is to show the necessity of an accurate phonology for an adequate description of the speech of one region—and of subgroups within the region.

A number of works on Southern English have dealt with some aspects of the phonology of consonants without citing specific rules or have stated rules without discussing their order. Wolfram and Christian (1976) cite many examples of cluster simplification in white Appalachian speech and occasionally attempt to refine the rules and justify a particular order. Wolfram and Fasold (1974) indirectly deal with phonological rules by showing that a given substitution or deletion may be stigmatized in certain phonetic environments. Several contributors to Montgomery and Bailey (1986) make statistical comparisons—number of tokens, number of speakers, classification of speakers by age, sex, socioeconomic status—based primarily on surface structures. This is the approach taken by some writers on language teaching methodology as well. But Scott (1986:346) points out that "the contrastive approach to language instruction . . . emphasizes the matching of surface structures, rather than the learning of rules, and that treats language learning as an imitative rather than a generative process." My intention in this paper, then, is to illustrate an integration of the approaches of sociolinguistics and generative phonology.

In doing so, I examine some Deep South speech phenomena which have not been widely reported elsewhere—forms that are common either in middle Georgia or in much of the Deep South. Most of my examples are from an area that Cleanth Brooks (1935) attempts to establish as a distinct dialect area in the Alabama and Georgia counties around Auburn, Alabama, and Columbus, Georgia. Wood (1967) also shows the Auburn-Columbus region to be a distinct dialect area in that numerous congruent isoglosses—lexical, grammatical, and phonological—appear on his Alabama and Georgia maps as a result of this early computer-analyzed data. My examples are drawn from personal interactions with college students and business and trades people or from TV and radio broadcasts involving both prominent and obscure citizens of the region.

PHONOLOGICAL RULES AND RULE ORDERING

Although one hears one group of Southerners say [sku] instead of [skul], [bo] instead of [bol], etc., it is not necessarily true that these words are stored in the speakers' mental lexicons without /l/. For example, in the intervocalic context of *school-age* and *schooling*, the /l/ is normally retained, while in *school book* and *school teacher* it is deleted. The presence of /l/ in *feeling* suggests that it is present in the underlying structure of *feel* and is deleted only in contexts such as *feels* and *feel good*. Similarly, final /d/ of *red*, which sometimes becomes voiceless in the African-American Vernacular English pronunciation of *redness*, is not devoiced in *reddish*. The same is true of the final /d/ of *did, could, should*, and *would* in some speech varieties: normally pronounced [d], it is devoiced (becoming [t]) before *n't*. Variation in the pronunciation of a given lexical item within a dialect should not be assumed, therefore, to be based solely on register, social situation, stress level, age, sex, etc., and scholarship citing a particular pronunciation for a specific group should be considered incomplete unless a representative number of tokens in a variety of phonetic contexts has been examined. Moreover, both rules and rule order vary among dialects.

Chomsky and Halle (1968:18) make two statements about phonological rule ordering that are especially important:

> It is always possible to order rules in a sequence and to adhere strictly to this ordering in constructing derivations without any loss of generality as compared to an unordered set of rules or a set ordered on a different principle.

> Such linear ordering makes it possible to formulate grammatical processes that would otherwise not be expressible with comparable generality.

Kenstowicz and Kisseberth (1979:291–327) have more recently argued in favor of at least partial ordering and against the direct-mapping and free-reapplication hypotheses. The data examined here, from Standard and Alabama-Georgia English, tend to support ordering.

Let us look first at three rules of SAE that also apply to Alabama-Georgia speech:

nasalization: Nasalize a vowel that precedes a nasal.

nasal deletion: Delete the nasal consonant itself if it is followed by a voiceless stop or affricate and the preceding vowel is stressed and the vowel following the voiceless consonant is unstressed.

tap substitution: Change intervocalic /t/ to a tap ([ɾ]) under the following conditions: (a) medially or initially if the second vowel is unstressed, or (b) finally regardless of stress.

The above ordering of the rules is necessary for correct derivation of *winter* (see below). As written, **tap substitution** "bleeds" ('prevents the application of') **nasal deletion** and **nasal deletion** bleeds **nasalization**:

$$/\text{wɪntər}/ \rightarrow [\text{wĩntər}] \rightarrow [\text{wĩtər}] \rightarrow [\text{wĩɾər}]$$

Nasal consonant deletion applies also to /mp/ and /ŋk/ clusters. In some Southern speech, however, an even more general rule deletes the /n/ before any voiceless fricative or stop and applies to *consequence* ([kãsəkwə̃s]), *institute* ([ĩstətyut]), etc. The same ordering of vowel **nasalization** and **nasal consonant deletion** is needed to account for these forms.

The Order of /l/ Deletion and Other Rules

One of the most prevalent phonological rules in Deep South English (as in some northern British dialects) is **/l/ deletion** where no vowel follows.

/l/ deletion: Delete /l/ when preceded by a vowel and not followed by a vowel.

A rule of SAE also inserts schwa if /l/ is preceded by a front vowel.

Much variation within the region can be accounted for only by the ordering of /l/ deletion with respect to other rules. One example is an unusual pronunciation of *vulnerable*. If **nasalization** produces a nasalized vowel in such words as *pen*, and /l/ deletion produces [sku] from /skul/, what effect would the two rules have on the first syllable of *vulnerable*? The answer depends on the order of the two rules in the speaker's phonology.

In fact, the most common nonstandard Deep South pronunciation of *vulnerable* deletes the first /l/ (or both), but since **nasalization** precedes **/l/ deletion**, **nasalization** does not apply. Subsequently, the first vowel remains non-nasal (derivation A).

Derivation A of *vulnerable* (more common):
Underlying form:	/vəlnərəbəl/
nasalization (not applicable):	[vəlnərəbəl]
/l/ deletion:	[vənərəbəl]

In a less common derivation, however, **/l/ deletion** precedes **nasalization** (derivation B). After the /l/ is deleted, the first vowel directly precedes /n/ and is nasalized.

Derivation B of *vulnerable* (rare):
Underlying form:	/vəlnərbəl/
/l/ deletion:	[vənərəbəl]
nasalization:	[və̃nərəbəl]

Associated with /l/ **deletion** in nonstandard speech is **schwa insertion** in SAE, which can be stated as follows:

schwa insertion: Insert [ə] before /l/ preceded by a front vowel.

Schwa insertion preceding /l/ **deletion** produces the [ə] where it is expected: in *feel good*. If /l/ **deletion** applied first, **schwa insertion** would not apply, which explains why *[fi gʊd] is not attested. The derivation of *feel good* follows:

Underlying form:	/fil gʊd/
schwa insertion:	[fiəl gʊd]
/l/ **deletion**:	[fiə gʊd]

With **schwa insertion** preceding /l/ **deletion**, the pronunciation of *Alma* is [æəmə], not [æmə] or [æ̃mə]. But a subset of speakers with /l/ **deletion** does not always insert schwa. These in turn can be divided into two groups: those that never insert schwa, omitting it even when /l/ is intervocalic as in *feeling* and *Alabama*, and those that include it in those words but omit it before syllable-final /l/. The latter group apparently has **schwa insertion**, but it follows /l/ **deletion**, so that *Alma* first undergoes /l/ **deletion**, producing [æmə], after which **schwa insertion** is not applicable.

When /l/ **deletion** precedes **schwa insertion**, the latter may also precede vowel nasalization. The first vowel of [æəmə], with schwa, is not normally nasalized. But when /l/ **deletion** precedes **schwa insertion**, **schwa insertion** is thus prevented from applying, and **nasalization** is possible. The result is [æ̃mə].

Schwa Deletion

One variety of Alabama and Georgia English has the following rule for deletion of schwa (or unstressed vowels such as /ə/ and /ɪ/):

schwa deletion: Delete /ə/ when it is preceded by a voiced continuant and followed by only one consonant, if the schwa is in the first of two or more unstressed syllables following a stressed syllable.

Some results of **schwa deletion** (also accompanied by vowel lengthening) are the following:

Derivations with **schwa deletion**:			
Underlying forms:	/prɛzədənt/	/kalənɪ/	/ɛvələn/
schwa deletion (and lengthening):	[prɛ:zdənt]	[ka:lnɪ]	[ɛ:vlən]

/l/ Deletion and Tap Substitution

A rule ordering that does not vary in Southern English, as far as most data show, is that **tap substitution** (an SAE rule mentioned earlier) precedes /l/ **deletion**. By **tap substitution**, /hat + ər/ becomes [harər]. However, /hɔltər/ does not become *[hɔrər]. The derivation of *halter* is as follows:

Derivation of *halter*:
Underlying form:	/hɔltər/
tap substitution (not applicable):	[hɔltər]
/l/ deletion:	[hɔtər]

The derivation of *bolder* is similar, never producing a homophone for *boater*.

Schwa Deletion and Tap Substitution

That **schwa deletion** precedes **tap substitution** is suggested, given some speakers' pronunciation of *ready to*. The most common pronunciation of *ready* in Standard and Southern English is with the *d* pronounced as a tap, [rɛɾɪ] . However, among speakers who delete schwa according to the above rule (as in the three-syllable *ready to*) the *d* is a stop, not a tap. The derivation of *ready to* is shown below:

Derivation of *ready to*:
Underlying form:	/rɛdɪ tə/
schwa deletion:	[rɛd tə]
tap substitution (not applicable):	[rɛd tə]

Thus, **schwa deletion** bleeds the tapping rule, prohibiting *[rɛɾ tə].

/l/ Deletion and Schwa Deletion

Words such as *colony*, *felony*, and *Eleanor* demonstrate that **/l/ deletion** precedes **schwa deletion**. The derivation of *colony* as [ka:lnɪ] is as follows:

Derivation of *colony*:
Underlying form:	/kalənɪ/
/l/ deletion (not applicable):	[kalənɪ]
schwa deletion:	[ka:lnɪ]

In the opposite order **schwa deletion** would first produce [ka:lnɪ], which would then undergo **/l/ deletion**, the result being *[ka:nɪ] or *[kã:nɪ], depending on when vowel **nasalization** occurred. Since neither of these pronunciations occurs, this is not a possible order.

Stopping

There is a tendency among some Deep South speakers to change /z/ to [d] when followed by /n/ as in *doesn't, wasn't,* and *isn't*. When **schwa deletion** is applied to *business* and *reasonable*, a /zn/ sequence occurs in which /z/ also becomes [d]. The derivation of *business* as [bɪ:dnɪs] leads us to conclude that **schwa deletion** precedes **stopping** and that **tap substitution** occurs late in the derivation so as not to convert [d] to a tap.

Derivation of *business*:
Underlying form:	/bɪzɪnɪs/
schwa deletion:	[bɪ:znɪs]
stopping (/d/ for /z/):	[bɪ:dnɪs]
tap substitution (not applicable):	[bɪ:dnɪs]

For some speakers **stopping** may actually be one result of a more general rule applying to the affricate /ǰ/ and the palatal fricative /ž/, as well as /z/, and in environments other than before /n/.

Such a broader application would account for **stopping** (/d/ substitution) in *regional* and *emergency* and in one pronunciation of *register*. In Deep South English there are at least three possible pronunciations of *register*. Apparently among speakers who delete schwa, there are some who substitute [d] for /ǰ/, some who delete the following /s/, and some who do neither, but there are none that do both—no examples of *[rɛdtər] have been found. One subset of speakers ends the derivation after **schwa deletion** (derivation A):

Derivation A of *register*:
   Underlying form: /rɛǰɪstər/
   schwa deletion: [rɛ:ǰstər]

The more general **stopping** accounts for derivation B:

Derivation B of *register*:
   Underlying form: /rɛǰɪstər/
   schwa deletion: [rɛ:ǰstər]
   stopping: [rɛ:dstər]

A third group of speakers does not substitute [d] for /ǰ/ but instead (also after **schwa deletion**) simplifies the cluster [ǰst] by deleting [s] (derivation C):

Derivation C of *register*:
   Underlying form: /rɛǰɪstər/
   schwa deletion: [rɛ:ǰstər]
   /s/ deletion: [rɛ:ǰtər]

The rule that changes /ǰ/ to [d] could be made more general (by omitting reference to voicing), so as to change /č/ to [t]. At least one example suggests that for some speakers a more general form exists—a case where /č/ follows /s/ and becomes [t] in *exchange*—pronounced [ɪkstenǰ].

Are Deletion and Vowel Laxing

Several phonological rules whose order is found to be crucial in the Auburn-Columbus area are mentioned or suggested in Wolfram and Christian's (1976) *Appalachian Speech*. One affects the pronunciation of *they* (and possibly *we* and *you*) when the following *are* or - *'re* (realized as [ar] or [r]) is deleted, as in their examples (41):

   They __ afraid.
   They __ good and straight.

Since Wolfram and Christian's (1976) examples are given in conventional spelling, one cannot tell whether the phonetic form is [ðe] or [ðɛ]. In SAE, tense vowels become lax before /r/ in *they're/there/their*, *your/you're*, etc. But if the pronunciation of their informants is [ðɛ], then **vowel laxing** must precede /r/ **deletion**. If it is [ðe] (the pronunciation heard most often in Middle Georgia), then /r/ **deletion** comes first (unless -*'re* deletion is syntactic).

Pre-Syllabic Vowel Deletion and Substitution of [t] for /θ/

What Wolfram and Christian (1976:49, 50) say about /θ/ in Appalachian English is also true for Middle Georgia. It "may be pronounced as a *t* next to a nasal segment" as in "*aritmetic, mont'*, or *nutt'n.*" According to their derivation of *nutt'n*, the vowel between /θ/ and /n/ is deleted, leaving a sequence [θn], to which the rule /θ/ → **[t]** applies. They say the vowel deletion "must take place before the rule changing *th* to *t* can operate, since it is dependent on the nasal segment immediately preceding or following the sound."

But in the Deep South this may not be the case. The change of /θ/ to [t] may instead provide the environment for the deletion of the vowel. The **vowel deletion** rule is then similar to that of SAE, where, for example, the vowel is deleted from the participial -*en* of *written* and other /ən/ forms such as *cotton*, with /t/ and /n/ at the same point of articulation. Casual SAE also deletes /ə/ between /z/ and /n/ as in *chosen* and between other stops and nasals, as in casually pronounced *open* ([opm]). But deletion does not occur (at least as a result of this rule) in the Deep South between dissimilar points of articulation such as /kən/ of *spoken* (though the previously discussed schwa deletion rule may apply).

Initial /ð/ Assimilation, Tap Substitution, and Aspiration

Wolfram and Christian (1976:55) also mention a few cases of initial /ð/ assimilation and more numerous cases of initial /ð/ deletion in West Virginia. In most cases in the Deep South the absence of /ð/ can be considered an assimilation rather than a deletion. There are two reasons for this conclusion, both related to what happens when /ð/ **assimilation** occurs in conjunction with other rule applications.

First, *in air* and *in [th]ere* do not sound the same. The [n] is longer in the second. Either /ð/ becomes [n] or the /n/ doubles when /ð/ is deleted, the result being the same—[ɪnnɛr].

Second, the single intervocalic /t/ of *hot air* becomes a tap, while there is no tap in *not [th]ere*. Either tap substitution precedes /ð/ deletion or *not [th]ere* is the result of /ð/ assimilation.

The order of /ð/ **assimilation** and **aspiration** is also crucial. Deep South *not [th]ere* (with assimilated *th*) is not phonetically identical to *not tear*. **Aspiration** must precede **assimilation**. Otherwise the assimilation rule would change /nat ðɛr/ to [nat tɛr] and the aspiration rule would change [tɛr] to *[tʰɛr].

First Fricative Assimilation

In Alabama-Georgia speech a rule assimilates the *first* of two fricatives similar in voicing (both voiced or both voiceless) within words and across word bound-aries. Some examples are *breathes* (/ðz/ → [zz]), *life saver* (/fs/ → [ss]), and *fourth string* (/θs/ → [ss]). This too is not a case of deletion, as can be seen by comparing *four-string* ([for strɪŋ]) and *fourth string* ([forsstrɪŋ]), the latter having a longer (or double) [s]. The order of the two assimilation rules determines the pronunciation of *live there* ([vv] and [ðð] both occur), since the second rule in either order would apply vacuously.

> Derivation A of *live there*:
> | | |
> |---|---|
> | Underlying form: | /lɪv ðɛr/ |
> | /ð/ assimilation: | /lɪv vɛr/ |
> | **first fricative assimilation** (vacuous): | /lɪv vɛr/ |

> Derivation B of *live there*:
> | | |
> |---|---|
> | Underlying form: | /lɪv ðɛr/ |
> | **first fricative assimilation**: | /lɪð ðɛr/ |
> | /ð/ assimilation (vacuous): | /lɪð ðɛr/ |

The derivation of *behave as he* in the sentence "He's gonna behave as he pleases" is evidence that **first fricative assimilation** precedes **schwa deletion**. To the form /bɪhev əz ɪ/ **first fricative assimilation** does not apply, and **schwa deletion** produces [bɪhev z ɪ]. The reverse order would produce the nonexistent *[bɪhez z ɪ].

Glottal Stop Substitution and *-ed* Pronunciation

In the Auburn-Columbus region, the rule that produces [t] as the pronunciation of the *-ed* ending applies only after voiceless continuants (and not after stops) when the next segment is a vowel. Otherwise the /d/ is retained. By another rule /p/ and /k/ before /d/ become [ʔ]. Some examples are *locked up* ([laʔdəp]), *hopped on* ([haʔdon]), *knocked out* ([naʔdaʊt]), and *camped out* ([kæʔdaʊt]). Thus *knocked out* and *not doubt* are identical, and *camped out* and *can't doubt* differ only in the pronunciation of the first vowel.

> Derivation of *locked up*:
> | | |
> |---|---|
> | Underlying form: | /lak d əp/ |
> | **[t] substitution** (not applicable): | [lak d əp] |
> | **[ʔ] substitution**: | [laʔ d əp] |

PHONOLOGICAL RULE ORDERING IN THE STUDY OF LANGUAGE VARIATION

A number of conclusions can be drawn about English as spoken in Alabama and Georgia south of Appalachia from the discussion above:

1) Several rules of Alabama-Georgia English do not occur in SAE.
2) A few rules of SAE do not occur in Alabama-Georgia English.
3) Rules shared by both dialects generally share the same ordering.
4) For a few pairs of rules, the ordering in some subdialects differs from that in most varieties of Alabama-Georgia English.
5) The ordering of many pairs of rules is essential to producing correct output.

Are sociolinguists and theoretical descriptive linguists needlessly failing to shed light on each other's work? Followers of Chomsky and Halle (1968) often limited themselves to SAE, disregarding as nonstandard anything that cluttered the system, while specialists in regional and social dialects cited the number and percentage of speakers old and young, male and female, who produced a given surface structure, without precisely stating the rules and their orders.

Available technology is being extensively utilized to study language variation, as it should be. But when computer studies of language variation are based solely on surface structures, the equipment is being underutilized. Programs do exist that could lead to a deeper understanding of the grammars of language varieties. Machines that read a conventional text and synthesize human speech (e.g., the Kurtzweil reading machine) function by applying a set of phonological rules to an underlying structure. Commercially available software for mainframe computers is sophisticated enough to make fairly idiomatic translations of extended passages from one language to another. (The first two 1985 issues of *Computational Linguistics* are devoted to machine translation, and translation was demonstrated at the summer 1986 meeting of the Association for Computational Linguistics and the 1995 meeting of the American Translators Association.) String analysis programs like SNOBOL can operate a series of rewriting rules forward or backward and show whether a given surface structure could be derived from a given underlying string. In a more time-consuming way, even the search-and-replace function of a word-processing program could do the same. Hypotheses about the phonological rules and rule order—of a language or of a dialect—can be tested using such technology. Statistical study of rule order differences may produce a deeper insight into language variety than analyzing surface structures alone.

Solidarity Cues in New Orleans English

Felice Anne Coles

In the territory investigated by the Linguistic Atlas of the Gulf States (LAGS), New Orleans, the largest city represented, is considered a probable focal area for the Gulf Southern dialect (Pederson 1986:70; Malmstrom and Ashley 1963:43). However, it is the site for relatively few LAGS informants. It may be that the social complexity of the city makes it less desirable as an area of investigation for traditional linguistic atlas methodology; indeed, Wolfram and Fasold (1974:78) separate it as a special urban area. Nevertheless, the social complexity of New Orleans makes it ideal for investigation into the pragmatic function of dialect features.

Blanton (1989:780) notes that a number of dialects within Greater Metropolitan New Orleans differentiate the population according to race (black or white), ethnic heritage (Cajun, Creole, or immigrant populations), and neighborhood affiliation (Uptown, Downtown, any of the political wards, or suburbs like Gretna and Metairie). One dialect of English, "Yat" (from the traditional greeting "Where *y(ou) at?*"), also called "Ninth Ward," originally represented the speech of residents within the political boundary of that voting district. The rough boundaries of the Ninth Ward in the metropolitan area encompass most of east New Orleans, from Franklin Street down to Almonaster Street, including the suburb of Gentilly. Whereas the nouveau riche live on the Lakefront and the Old Money of the South live in the Garden District, the Ninth Ward is considered to be composed of lower middle-class neighborhoods.

Lemotte (1985:5–6) states that, in reality, Yat is now spread throughout the city and has become a social indicator:

> Fact is, most human beins [sic] in the New Orleans area talk some form of Yat. Virtually all working class and lower middle class whites grow up speaking it. . . . Many Downtown Blacks also talk Yat, particularly in the Creole Seventh Ward. Yat is the dominant speech in suburban Jefferson Parish [southwest of the Ninth Ward] , and suburban St. Bernard parish [to its south] is now more Yat than the Ninth Ward itself.

Speaking Yat has become a symbol of identity with increasingly overt prestige. It marks those who are "real" New Orleanians without pretensions of wealth: "those folks dat talk normal" (Lyman 1978:ii). Because of the special social significance it has developed, this dialect may be thought of as New Orleans English (NOE).

As a result of gains in prestige for NOE, evidenced by its increased use in the media by local people in positions of authority (such as politicians) or with local popularity (such as radio/TV personalities), I predicted that the discourse strategy of upward convergence would be apparent in local conversations. For data sources

I chose telephone conversations of a radio talk show host and a clinic receptionist because they are professional communicators who are employed to present a friendly and knowledgeable voice to callers with whom they interact and wish to identify as partners in solidarity. Here I am adapting Williams's (1992:193) definition: "Solidarity is a feature not of an allegiance to some norm whose source or origin is unspecified, but of a socioeconomic unity which must have political dimensions."

Below I present an overview of some of the linguistic features of NOE and examples and conclusions from my research that illustrate the use of some of these features as cues for attempts at solidarity through upward convergence.

DIALECT FEATURES OF NEW ORLEANS ENGLISH

The most salient dialect feature of NOE according to Lemotte (1985) and Lyman (1978) is the phonological system combining features of Southern American English with New York City English. Lyman (1978:iv) quips, "For those who have never heard it, you must begin by imagining all of Brooklyn on Quaaludes." Common phonetic variations of NOE include Southern features discussed in Pederson et al. (1986–1992) and Wells (1982):

monophthongal /aɪ/	*outside*	[awtsad]
	time	[tam]
vocalization of postvocalic /r/	*sister*	[sɪstə]
	board	[boəd]

This r-lessness is also a feature of working-class New York City English (Labov 1966). Due to the large number of Italian and Irish immigrants from the Northeast—the Irish arriving after 1820, the Italians between 1890 and 1914 (Conklin and Lourie 1983)—who fit easily into the predominantly Catholic New Orleans neighborhoods, NOE has other pronunciation features shared with New York City English:

replacement of fricative interdentals with stops	*that*	[dæt]
	nothing	[nʌʔn]
replacement of /ɚ/ with diphthongal [ɔj]	*girl*	[gɔjl]
	worse	[wɔjs]
corresponding replacement of /ɔj/ with [ɚ]	*toilet*	[tɚlət]
replacement of /ɑ/ with [ɔ]	*darling*	[dɔlɪn]
	doll	[dɔl]
	Mardi Gras	[madɪ grɔ]

Although in New York City English these features represent working-class and lower middle-class speech, the extent to which this distinction carries over into NOE is not yet known. As to their origin, Liebling (1980:v) states:

There is a New Orleans city accent . . . associated with downtown New Orleans, particularly with the German and Irish . . . that is hard to distinguish from the accent of Hoboken, Jersey City, and Astoria, Long Island. . . . The reason, as you might expect, is that the same stocks that brought the accent to Manhattan imposed it upon New Orleans.

Pronunciation features are not the only indicators of NOE. Lexical items and idiomatic phrases peculiar to New Orleans include the following:

throw	'souvenir of Mardi Gras parades thrown off floats into the crowd'
mirliton/melliton	'a fruit'
making groceries	'to shop for groceries'
to dress	'to put the fixings and garnishes on a sandwich'
po-boy	'a submarine sandwich'

The features of NOE are not limited to the register of personal conversation. Commercials on local TV and radio stations feature NOE speakers, and a popular single-frame newspaper cartoon (see figure) explores daily life and speech in New Orleans:

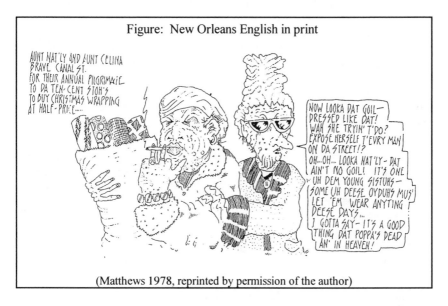

Figure: New Orleans English in print

(Matthews 1978, reprinted by permission of the author)

Local authors also recognize and represent NOE in literature, as in this passage from Toole (1980:4):

> "Oh, Miss Inez," Mrs. Reilly called in that accent that occurs south of New Jersey only in New Orleans, that Hoboken near the Gulf of Mexico. "Over here, babe."
> "Hey, how you making?" Miss Inez asked. "How you feeling, darling?"

"Not so hot," Mrs. Reilly answered truthfully.

"Ain't that a shame." Miss Inez leaned over the glass case and forgot about her cakes. "I don't feel so hot myself. It's my feet."

"Aw, no!" Miss Inez said with genuine sympathy. "My poor old poppa's got that. We make him go set himself in a hot tub fulla berling water."

ACCOMMODATION IN NEW ORLEANS ENGLISH

Because NOE is a nonstandard linguistic variety indicative of residential affiliation, its use in interactions is a strategy of accommodation indicating solidarity among the conversational participants. The concept of accommodation, as set forth by Giles, Taylor, Lambert, and Bourhis (1973:170), proposes that "a speaker makes linguistic adjustments depending upon such perceived characteristics of the listener as social status." Upward convergence is the process by which individuals adapt their speech to reduce certain dissimilarities between them in order to gain a favorable evaluation (Giles 1973). In the case of NOE, solidarity represents residential and social-class affiliation of the "real" New Orleanian.

In order to test my prediction that NOE features would function as cues of solidarity in a strategy of upward accommodation, I gathered 272 opening segments from 52 hours of tape-recorded telephone conversations in a veterinary clinic and on a call-in radio talk show. Each segment consisted of the initial exchange, if any, through the pre-sequence exchange. As Schegloff (1979) observed, most initial exchanges over the telephone are identification and recognition sequences designed to ascertain the appropriate interactants before embarking upon the conversation:

Receptionist: Good morning, Gretna Animal Hospital.
Caller: Good morning, it's me.
Receptionist: Good morning, Mrs. Echrell, how're you?

A pre-sequence is defined by Levinson (1983) as a distinctive kind of turn built to set up or make a transition to the actual business of the conversation. The example below consists of an initial exchange followed by a pre-sequence (in **bold**) setting up a narrative (a recipe):

Host: Rosalyn, how ya doin, gal?
Caller: Fine, thank you. How're you?
Host: I am doin excellent.
Caller: Uh, you ready for the King Cake recipe?
Host: I am ready for the King Cake recipe.
Caller: Well, you take a cup of sugar . . .

Both the call-in radio talk show host and the clinic receptionist can be considered to be in positions of power, as they both control the flow of conversation over the telephone. Therefore, I predicted that callers would accommodate their speech towards these NOE speakers in order to achieve the social recognition of solidarity as a fellow native New Orleanian. Measures of accommodation included the following:

1) traditional NOE greetings (lexical and/or phonologically distinct)
2) terms of endearment like *babe* (in reference to women or men) or *darling*
3) exaggerated phonological features of NOE (impressionistically measured)
4) direct questions or other strategies

Within the 272 conversational exchanges I discovered 121 bids for solidarity, tokens indicating that the caller is also a NOE speaker who wishes to be identified as such. The results to be discussed are shown in the table below.

Table: Solidarity cues in conversational samples			
method of *establishing solidarity*	*# of tokens*	*%*	*example*
standard greetings	65	54	"Where you at?"
terms of endearment	33	27	"Hey, doll . . ." [dɔl]
phonetic cues alone	21	17	"Charlie, . . ." [čɔlɪ]
direct questions/other	2	2	"Who's this? Frank?"
Total	121	100	

These 121 examples observed within the 272 conversational exchanges are bids for solidarity, indicating that the caller is also a NOE speaker who wishes to be identified as such. Predictably, the callers on the radio who phone in to talk about Mardi Gras anecdotes are by far the most accommodating in upward convergence, due to the specialized regional nature of the conversational topic. By contrast, the more mundane conversations in the clinic provoke fewer callers to seek solidarity. The callers on the radio show are also "performing" for the audience and therefore adopt in their speech characteristics of a performance, including exaggeration of accent.

The predominant means of negotiating social distance is the use of distinctively New Orleans greetings, which constitute 54% of the solidarity tokens, as in these examples:

Host: Shirley, how ya doin, girl?
Caller: Where ya at, darlin?

Host: Elvira, how y'all doin?
Caller: Oh, hi, Frank, how y'all doin?

Another popular strategy (27%) is the use of terms of endearment like *darling* or *doll* (with the /ɔ/ pronunciation) or *babe*, often tagged to a greeting:

Receptionist: Good morning, Gretna Animal Hospital.
Caller: Good mornin, darlin.
Receptionist: Oh, how ya doin?

Less frequent at 17% were phonetic cues alone, used mostly in response to stress or intonation patterns by the radio host, who often reintroduces topics of conversation with every caller without providing an opportunity for the standard greeting-and-response exchange:

> Host: I remember when Mardi Gras—*when what*, Louise?
> Caller: —*when* Alla had one float . . .

Finally, callers rarely use actual direct questions (2%) such as "Is this Frank?" or even "Who's this?" to establish that the answerer is a recognized NOE speaker who acknowledges that the caller has encountered the appropriate conversational participant in charge:

> Host: ((beep)) Charlie, I remember when Mardi Gras—*when what*?
> Caller: Who's this? Frank?
> Host: Yes, it is.
> Caller: Aw, hey, where ya at?
> Host: Where ya at, babe?
> Caller: Right here, babe. Listen, I remember 1927 . . .

The attempt to negotiate solidarity is accomplished within the first four turns of the conversation. Due to the relatively short nature of the clinic telephone conversations in which the receptionist serves mainly as the "gatekeeper," the callers quickly have to accommodate their speech before either stating their business or being transferred to the appropriate veterinarian, groomer, kennel manager, or other employee:

> Receptionist: Gretna Animal Hospital, good morning.
> Caller: Miz Cole?
> Receptionist: Yes, dear?
> Caller: It's Bernice, how ya doin?

On the call-in radio talk show, in which the callers have a little more time to pre-sequence the business of their conversations, these callers still accommodate their speech quickly, perhaps as a validation device to demonstrate that their anecdotes are truly New Orleans experiences. Whatever their motivations, the callers negotiated their social positions within the first moments of conversation.

In conclusion, the upward convergence of speakers of NOE is accomplished in the opening exchanges of conversation. This rapid accommodation is possible because NOE has features that are readily apparent in even brief casual interactions. The fact that speakers accommodate their speech indicates that NOE (with its origins in the Yat dialect of the Ninth Ward) has prestige within New Orleans communities and is gaining recognition as a symbol of being truly native to the city.

Social Meaning in Southern Speech from an Interactional Sociolinguistic Perspective: An Integrative Discourse Analysis of Terms of Address

Catherine E. Davies

"Linguistically speaking, what is Southern hospitality?" is the question posed by Montgomery (this volume) in noting an area of needed research: the discourse patterns and pragmatics of Southern American English. An essential development allowing such research was noted by Bailey (this volume) as an expansion of what we consider our object of study. A theoretical orientation based in interactional sociolinguistics offers a perspective on variation as a systematic result of speakers' use of linguistic phenomena as resources in the mutual construction of situated social identities.

This paper examines how Southern politeness is linguistically enacted, focusing in particular on use of address terms. Tracking an individual speaker across a range of situations in the 1985 movie *The Trip to Bountiful* (VanWagenen; screenplay, Horton Foote 1989), this study identifies prototypical uses of *Ma'am/Sir* for deference and emphasis, and demonstrates how speakers draw on these core meanings to convey a range of social messages in discourse. Such an approach to understanding variation stands in contrast to a methodology which isolates individual features of pronunciation, lexical items, or grammatical forms and correlates them with demographic categories characterizing speakers or with components of a pre-existing context. An interactional sociolinguistic orientation demands an integrative discourse analysis; intensive examination of videotaped interaction from participants' perspectives allows identification of interpretive processes, highlighting the role of prosody in situated communication.

INTERACTIONAL SOCIOLINGUISTICS

The theoretical orientation to the study of face-to-face interaction presented here is based in Gumperz's (1982a, b) theory of conversational inference. A basic premise is that all communication is in some profound sense indirect; therefore, we need to focus on the study of situated interpretive processes whereby people make sense out of the conversations they participate in. This cognitive focus on situated interpretation of communicative intent has fostered an interdisciplinary stance, drawing on linguistics for pragmatic analysis (in the broadest sense which necessarily includes grammatical, phonological, and prosodic analysis), anthropology for the ethnography of speaking, and sociology for ethnomethodology and conversational analysis. The cross-disciplinary work of Bateson (1972), Goffman (1974), Erickson and Shultz (1982), and Brown and Levinson (1987) has developed our understanding of nonverbal aspects of communication, the framing of messages, and the relationships between such framing and individual presentations of self as negotiated representations of cultural and social identity.

A core interdisciplinary theme in this theoretical orientation is the elaboration of our understanding of what is meant by "context" (see Duranti and Goodwin 1992). The basic tendency is away from a notion of context as a static background against which interaction unfolds, and toward a conceptualization of context as dynamic and emergent, both constraining interaction and created through it. An ultimate goal is to understand how society "is being reanimated or creatively reaffirmed from day to day by particular acts of a communicative nature which obtain among individuals participating in it" (Sapir 1968:104) while at the same time accounting for the fact that the links between language and social organizational patterns are usually mediated (see Ochs 1992) as well as potentially ideologically masked in various ways. In this paper terms of address, which might be assumed to represent a straightforward linguistic encoding of social information, are shown to be used by speakers in more complex ways.

An "integrative discourse analysis" allows a broad range of phenomena to be taken into account in analyzing the process of conversational inference in the situated interpretation of face-to-face communication (Tyler and Davies 1990). Basic analytical constructs which serve as heuristics, listed roughly from most inclusive to most specific, include: schema, discourse strategy, conversational management strategy, interpretive frame, and contextualization cue. These analytical constructs are illustrated through the analysis of the data. It should be noted that the relationships among these constructs are complex, e.g., that a schema will include expectations concerning all other constructs but that a shift in contextualization cue could, in principle, invoke a different schema. The analytical focus in this paper is on the identification of contextualization cues (see Gumperz 1992) which channel situated interpretive processes. Such cues involve more than just aspects of the linguistic code as narrowly defined, and in this study the importance of prosody or "tone of voice" is highlighted as one of a constellation of cues which channel inferences. The emphasis on combinations of cues represents continuity with Ervin-Tripp's (1972) identification of the sociolinguistic importance of co-occurrence expectations.

This study presupposes the existence of "areal discourse patterns" (see Emeneau 1964; Johnstone 1990), which represent shared schemas concerning politeness. Thus Southerners from Texas and Alabama may differ in their use of lexical items or particular phonological features, but they may share—over against non-Southerners—a basic schema for the production and interpretation of a particular style of politeness. In addition, a shared interpretive schema may obtain, for example of "the way Grandma used to do it," even when usage is changing. Southerners and non-Southerners may share address terms such as *Ma'am* and *Sir* which form part of different schemas for each group. Those schemas may partially overlap, but they can also differ in essential ways which cannot be captured by traditional approaches to variability. This is a classic scenario for pernicious cross-cultural miscommunication, where no allowances are made for potential differences in production and interpretation because the assumption is made of linguistic and cultural homogeneity (for example, we all speak English and call ourselves "Americans"; see Ervin-Tripp 1972; Gumperz 1982b). An instructive study illustrating such a problem is Tannen's (1981) analysis of New York Jewish conversational style.

In the case under consideration we can think of terms of address as part of a schema which linguistically enacts an ethos that is expressed through particular discourse strategies. I draw on Brown and Levinson (1987) for conceptualizing the terms of address as part of a system expressing deferential politeness, one of the strategies of which is direct grammatical encoding of relative social status between participants in an interaction (what for some languages are called *honorifics*). On the face of it, this might appear to be a relatively straightforward calculation predicting who is going to say *Ma'am* or *Sir* to whom, given certain basic knowledge of the speech situation. And, in fact, if a positivist view of language were accurate, and speakers' usages were determined by certain identifiable features of a separate social context, then speakers' behavior would be utterly predictable and consistent (see Rabinow and Sullivan 1979).

In fact, there does appear to be a consistent pattern in certain circumstances that we might conceptualize as prototypical uses to which conventional interpretations of deference/respect attach and that we might call the "core social meaning" (Ochs 1992:341) for these terms. However, when we look at usage in discourse context, we find that there is variation, which brings us back to the theoretical position that language must be conceptualized as a resource that speakers use strategically as part of the process of social action and interaction and to a recognition that an integrative discourse analysis of situated usage is needed to understand the signaling and interpretation of social meaning in discourse. The shared conventional expectations are precisely what allow speakers to deviate for particular effect, and this resource of variation is an essential feature of human communication. Brown and Levinson's (1987) model, although limited in certain ways in accounting for variation (as will be discussed below), provides just such an unmarked schema against which speakers use *Ma'am* and *Sir* as a resource to contextualize and recontextualize.

This theoretical framework allows us to study the process of conversational participants' mutual construction of social identities. Speakers are not only signaling an assessment of the addressee and of their relationship in the situation; they are also presenting themselves as particular kinds of people through such things as choice of terms, frequency of use, strategic omission. They are presenting themselves as a dutiful son, a well-brought-up young woman, a man in authority; and such representations are being ratified, challenged, and negotiated in the ongoing process whereby social organization is recreated and transformed moment by moment in interaction.

PREVIOUS STUDIES OF TERMS OF ADDRESS

Linguistic subsystems which encode social information have attracted the attention of scholars of language because they appear to offer a clear point of linkage between language and sociocultural systems. Classic studies in the field are

Brown and Gilman (1960) and Brown and Ford (1964). The particular case of *Ma'am/Sir*, in effect a form of title without last name, receives minimal attention from Brown and Ford. Their characterization (1964:237) is that it represents a "minimally intimate and maximally deferential form." In another classic study, Ervin-Tripp (1972:222) captures her (non-Southern) "rules of address" in a flow chart showing the effects of social factors on the selection of a term. She also comments in passing that *Sir* and *Ma'am* "are either not used or used only to elderly addressees in this system."

The original impetus for this paper came when I, a non-Southerner operating with a basic system as described above, saw the movie of Horton Foote's screenplay *The Trip to Bountiful*. I found the usage of *Ma'am* by grown son to mother in an intimate setting strangely formal; I found the usage of *Ma'am* from young woman stranger to elderly woman readily interpretable but then was surprised to hear the older woman use *Ma'am* once to the younger woman (I was familiar with the idea that *Yes, Ma'am* could be used in an emphatic way but was unprepared for it in a context in which the deference *Ma'am* had been used exclusively in the other direction); I could understand the initial use of *Ma'am* and *Sir* between an elderly woman and a man in the role of sheriff, and could see that change in usage of the terms was somehow an index of a change in their relationship, but then I could not understand why the sheriff used *Ma'am* twice more in the course of their conversation; I was completely mystified not only by the consistent usage of *Ma'am* from the older to younger woman (from the mother-in-law to the daughter-in-law) but especially by the fact that the only time the daughter-in-law produced *Ma'am* to the mother-in-law she appeared to be trying to be rude to her!

Fortunately, studies such as Friedrich (1972), Parkinson (1985), Braun (1988), and Duranti (1992) allow us to view the kinds of variation described above in usage of terms of address as a linguistic resource rather than as simply a reflection of independent social variables which speakers produce apparently involuntarily. Specific studies of honorifics in Southern speech, Simpkins (1969) and Ching (1988), identify a core social meaning of deference for *Ma'am* and *Sir*. Simpkins (1969:24) specifies usage for the "*Ma'am* of Deference" from younger to older person, and from child to adult, as well as between strangers. Ching identifies other uses for the conventionally deferential terms: to convey hearty emphasis, and among younger people to show solidarity between peers and to younger addressees. Simpkins observes that the same person will receive different terms (from among a range of terms, not simply restricted to *Ma'am* and *Sir*) in different settings depending on how that person's social identity is assessed by interlocutors.

Prosody or tone of voice is mentioned by Friedrich, Parkinson, and Braun as crucial to accurate interpretation in particular instances but is not represented other than by means of lexical description—due to the limitations of the methodologies used, which will be discussed in the next section of the paper. Work on prosody in Southern speech includes Ching's (1982) work on question intonation in assertions, and McLemore's (1991b) work on conventional intonation contours associated with greetings among Texas sorority girls. Although not concerned with the terms of address under study here, McLemore's work is particularly relevant because she emphasizes the symbolic significance of conventionalized prosodic dimensions of speech for situated interpretation. In this paper I demonstrate how conventional prosodic contours associated with terms of address convey social meaning, serving as one of a constellation of contextualization cues to channel interpretive processes.

METHODOLOGY

The studies referred to in the preceding section of this paper have made use of a range of methodologies: self-report questionnaires (Brown and Gilman 1960; Brown and Ford 1964; Ching 1988; Parkinson 1985; Braun 1988), participant observation (Brown and Ford 1964; Ching 1988; Simpkins 1969; Parkinson 1985; Duranti 1992), interviews (Ching 1988; Parkinson 1985; Braun 1988), and the analysis of literary texts (Brown and Ford 1964; Friedrich 1972). Several have used a range of methodologies (Brown and Ford 1964; Ching 1988; Parkinson 1985); one of the main points of Ching (1988), which appeared in a volume on methods in dialectology, is the importance of using a range of methods to triangulate the data. If Ching had not combined several methods (and, crucially, personal observation) to cross-check, he never would have confirmed the use of *Yes, Sir* and *Yes, Ma'am* to show close bonding toward peers and younger addressees. Interviewees had mentioned this usage, but self-report questionnaires had actually disconfirmed it.

Friedrich (1972) emphasizes the importance of situated, contextualized interpretation and points out that certain kinds of literary data provide key ethnographic insights into the thought processes of the speakers. Friedrich clearly appreciates the importance of prosody and tone of voice, as well as nonverbal dimensions of communication such as gesture. He mentions that as contextualization cues interpreted jointly with pronouns, they may have significant power to transform messages. His data, however, limit his investigation to lexical descriptions of tone of voice.

This study attempts to provide a means of incorporating the kinds of dimensions identified as important in previous work. As such it provides a supplement to methods already in use, another point of view on a text, and thus a further means of triangulation. The methodology is a natural expression of the theoretical orientation I described earlier, a form of close reading in the discourse analysis tradition (see Johnstone, this volume) designed to get at schemas, discourse strategies, conversation management strategies, interpretive frames, and con-textualization cues. It is consistent with a vision of language as embedded in context, with interpretive processes signaled by a wide range of face-to-face interactional dimensions. This means more ethnographically oriented methods and taking advantage of new technologies, especially video. I have imported the basic methodology from interactional sociolinguistics where it is used for studying cross-cultural communication in particular. An essential feature of the analytical process is that audio or videotapes of interaction are played back either to the participants (as in Tannen's 1984 study of conversational style) or to members of the partici-pants' sociocultural group (defined in terms of shared interpretive conventions and norms) to listen and identify contextualization cues and generally provide insider information on interpretive processes. This inevitably creates a cross-cultural research team, with members of the different cultural groups collaborating, and providing insight into the multiple perspectives involved from which the analyst is able to discern patterns. In this case, the outsider analyst is able to notice patterning which the insiders experience as unmarked and thus take for granted.

My refinement to the methodology is that I am using an enacted screenplay (*The Trip to Bountiful* 1985; Foote 1989) as the video data which I ask Southern speakers to interpret. (As we have seen, there is a tradition of the use of literary idealizations as a source of data, notably in Brown and Ford 1964 and Friedrich 1972.) In contrast to the scripts of contemporary American plays used by Brown and Ford as sources of data, a film of an enacted script provides the missing prosodic and nonverbal dimensions of the communication. In effect, actors and director bring their communicative competence to bear in producing a text which will be experienced as authentic.

The playwright Horton Foote is a native Southerner (born in Texas in 1916), and the play is set in Houston and east to the Gulf coast in about 1950. Even though I had assumed some areal discourse conventions in the use of *Ma'am* and *Sir*, I was prepared for my native Alabamian consultants to reject the usage in the film; in fact they judged it to be authentic.

Each of my consultants, a range of young Southerners, separately has watched the film intensively enough to be able to 1) draw intonation contours on the script for each occurrence of *Ma'am* and *Sir*, 2) give a commentary on each *Ma'am* and *Sir* trying to explain the social meaning and what the contextualization cues are (some examples of their comments will be included in the analysis section of the paper), 3) comment on anything else that struck them. Then each of these consultants has been interviewed by me for several hours, probing what they had written and asking other questions designed to get at implicit sociocultural knowledge: e.g., Why doesn't *Ma'am* occur in this slot? Could Mrs. Watts conceivably have used *Sir* to her son? Give me a scenario and dialogue. How could Ludie have said the same *Yes, Ma'am* sarcastically? Such ethnographic interviewing also inevitably yields commentary on the evolution of consultants' personal use and experience of the terms of address.

Videotaped data offer tremendous advantages over other kinds of data when we want to be able to do a fine-grained transcription and a close, integrative discourse analysis based on insiders' commentary on interpretive processes. Limitations include the possibility that because of the out-of-awareness nature of signaling, even with the best of intentions consultants may not in fact be able to tell us what cues they are using as a basis for their interpretation; the best they may be able to do is give an account after the fact which makes sense to them.

A further critique of these data is that consultants' judgments of authenticity may be conditioned by their late-20th-century media literacy: they are literate enough in film that literary idealizations presented according to the conventions of that genre are perceived as virtually identical with natural interaction. On the other hand, it could be argued that literary idealizations are a valuable source of information about interaction because they capture some essential truths about language as a sociocultural phenomenon (see Lakoff and Tannen 1984).

ANALYSIS

The analysis that follows begins with a brief integrative discourse analysis exemplifying analytical constructs used in demonstrating how speakers use address terms as a resource in mutually constructing situated social identities. Although the focus has been on *Ma'am* and *Sir*, all terms of address need to be taken into consideration (see Friedrich 1972; Parkinson 1985), and I indicate the points at which it became obvious that other terms needed to be considered (see sections E1 and E4 below). The excerpts from the film, E1–E6, illustrate: 1) the prototypical usage of *Ma'am* for deference; 2) how a shift in the nucleus of the prosodic contour in relation to the address term serves to convey different social meanings; 3) the emphatic use of the address term, both as separate from and in conjunction with the deferential use; 4) how the usage of address terms may indicate situated power relations which override the polite fiction of conventional deference; 5) how *Ma'am* may be used to convey sarcasm; and 6) how usage of terms of address may be a subtle index of the evolution of a relationship.[1]

In this play the central character, Mrs. Watts, is an elderly woman who lives with her son, Ludie, and her daughter-in-law, Jessie Mae, in an apartment in Houston. The play is about how she accomplishes, on her own initiative and against the adamant wishes of her relatives, an important spiritual goal in the form of a trip to her hometown of Bountiful on the Gulf coast. She interacts with middle-aged male ticket agents in train and bus stations, a young woman stranger on the bus, and the middle-aged male sheriff in the Bountiful area who agrees to drive her out to her abandoned home, where her son and daughter-in-law find her to take her back to Houston.

E1: Prototypical Usage of *Ma'am* for Deference

Deferential usage of *Ma'am* occurs in the film from the young woman stranger, the middle-aged male ticket agent, and the middle-aged male sheriff to Mrs. Watts, as well as from Ludie to his mother. I have chosen the excerpt below, an interaction between adult child and elderly parent in the initial scene in the film, because it also offers an opportunity to illustrate the analytical constructs and their relation to one another.

The intonational contours over the terms of address represent composites of what my Southern consultants hear. The nucleus, defined as the combination of change in pitch direction (here the highest point from which the pitch then falls) and greatest intensity, is in **boldface**. Selected written commentary from my Southern consultants is in brackets.

FADE IN. A field of bluebonnets in the Texas countryside. A young boy is seen running through the bluebonnets, followed by his mother, who is also running. [A woman's voiceover is singing a hymn.] INTERIOR: THE FRONT ROOM OF THE WATTS' HOUSTON APARTMENT. NIGHT. Mrs. Carrie Watts is seated in a rocking chair looking out the window and quietly humming the same hymn to herself. . . . Her son, Ludie, comes into the room from the interior bedroom. He has a book in his hand. He opens the book as he stands near the bedroom door and begins to read.[2]

1 Mrs. Watts: Don't try to be quiet, Sonny. I'm awake.

2 Ludie: Yes **Ma**'am.
["Normal *yes*." / "Normal tone, slight rise on initial part of *Ma'am* then falls off. This is a simple affirmation and the *Ma'am* merely makes it polite. The *Ma'am* is necessary and important because he is addressing his mother. Ludie uses this absent-mindedly/habitually."]

3 Mrs. Watts: Couldn't you sleep?

4 Ludie: No **Ma**'am.
["Normal *no*." / "Same as line 2 above."]

At line 2, Ludie utters his first *Ma'am*. There appears to be a conventional prosodic contour in which pitch starts at midpoint on *yes* or *no* and rises to a nucleus on the start of *Ma'am* and then falls to a low point (if nothing more is to be uttered). An interesting feature of this contour, which consultants describe as "simple affirmation," is that the nucleus coincides not with the affirmative particle *yes* but rather with the address term *Ma'am*. In line 4's "normal no" the nucleus again falls on *Ma'am* rather than on *no*. It seems that prosody is used to foreground the social meaning of deference or politeness encoded in the address term. (And in the next example it will be shown how a prosodic shift in the contour of *yes/no Ma'am* has pragmatic effect in foregrounding different dimensions of social meaning.) It seems to me that this prototypical contour may be another example of what McLemore (1991b) has identified as "situated symbols," i.e., conventional prosodic contours which serve as contextualization cues.

In terms of the immediate discourse context, this prototypical usage of *Ma'am* for deference is produced in line 2 as acknowledgment of uptake (as in "speak when you're spoken to") and in line 4 as an initial response to a form of yes/no question. *Mama* is the other term used, in a slot at the end of a question. This usage could be thought of as part of a conversation management strategy whereby responses are appropriately placed and constructed, which is part of a discourse strategy for conveying appropriate role behavior as a respectful and loving son toward his elderly mother. One consultant comments that "the *Ma'am* is necessary and important because he is addressing his mother." Ludie's "habitual/absent-minded" production could be conceptualized as part of such a discourse strategy. The discourse strategy, in turn, could be thought of as subsumed within a schema which is part of a shared repertoire representing a complex structure of expectations in the culturally defined situation at hand. The schema would include appropriate role behavior for both son and mother, expressing a particular ethos (which includes a preferred mode of politeness).

This is the first point at which it becomes important as part of the analysis to consider the other terms of address which are being used. The choices made by speakers (here, of course, the playwright and also the director) in the situation allow us to see how the analytical constructs of contextualization cue and interpretive frame come into play. A schema can be thought of as representing expected behavior and interpretive conventions, within which there may be a range of options. In the context of this play, the range of options which appear to be available to Mrs. Watts in addressing her son, based on her usage, are *Ludie* (apparently his first name, or perhaps a nickname), *Son* and *Sonny*. Her typical usage is *Son* (and interestingly, in the film this has been modified from the script, where *Sonny* is used more frequently under everyday circumstances). *Ludie* is used in one case where she is clearly appealing to him as the one having power to grant her wishes. *Sonny* is obviously the term which is typically used to a boy, i.e., most clearly associated with usage from parent to child.

In the setting described at the beginning of the play, Mrs. Watts addresses her son as *Sonny*. The fade in and the continuity of the hymn being sung and then hummed suggests that in fact she has just been thinking about the past, when Ludie was a child. Thus her choice of address term can be thought of as a contextualization cue which in this case is an unconscious importation of the past of her memories into the present moment. *Sonny* as a contextualization cue here invokes the relationship between her as a young mother and Ludie as her child. The contextualization cue here can be conceptualized as the signaling of a potential interpretive frame: "let's collaborate in recreating a version of the relationship indexed by my contextualization cue." Such collaborative activity would constitute the mutual construction of situated social identities.

Ludie's response and the next nine turns represent an interesting negotiation as the participants signal indirectly to each other that they are both interested in sharing the proffered interpretive frame. Ludie's "Yes *Ma'am*" response is ambiguous because as Simpkins (1969:24) noted, the "*Ma'am* of Deference" is customarily used from younger to older person, as well as in the specific subset of child to adult. My Southern consultants pointed out that the *Ma'am* here is "necessary and important because he is addressing his mother," but a special childhood address term for his mother (more specialized than Mama) would have constituted, in contrast, an unambiguous acceptance of the interpretive frame signaled by his mother's contextualization cue of *Sonny*. Ludie uses *Ma'am* very frequently in this interaction with his mother and also uses *Mama* once, as noted above. The frequency of use may also index the child's respect for the parent, but the use of the term *Ma'am* here illustrates how an address term serving as a contextualization cue may potentially convey more than one social meaning, the interpretation of which is channeled by the constellation of cues in the context.

Ludie's ambivalence in accepting the frame offered by his mother is also represented in his handling of topic in the conversation (a part of conversational management/discourse strategy). On the one hand he is minimally cooperative in his mother's indirect offer to discuss his potential preoccupation with his work as he steers the conversation back to her reasons for being awake. On the other hand he then denies remembering the events from his childhood that she is describing. In fact, we know from later in the play that he does remember and has been trying not to because the memories serve to remind him that he has somehow failed in living up to his childhood expectations. But after denying memory of what she is describing, he discloses that he has been unable to sleep because he has been trying to remember a song that she used to sing to him when he was a child. She then sings it to him in a true reenactment of the mother/child relationship. Her philosophical commentary after singing the song leads up to her switch to *Ludie* as an address term, as she is about to appeal to him as an adult male to take her back to the childhood setting in the town of Bountiful. But she breaks off the appeal before she has uttered more than the vocative and slips back into the mother/child frame by offering to get her son some hot milk, an offer which he accepts politely ("Yes *Ma'am*. If you don't mind.").

This brief integrative discourse analysis has shown how speakers use address terms in mutually constructing and maintaining situated social identities, while it has focused on identifying the prototypical usage of *Ma'am* for deference.

E2: How a Shift in the Nucleus of the Prosodic Contour in Relation to the Address Term Serves to Foreground Different Social Meanings

The evolution of the relationship between Mrs. Watts and the sheriff will be discussed in more detail in E6 below. For purposes of illustration here, it should be noted that when these two characters first meet, they exchange formal *Ma'am* and *Sir*, with the conventional contour on *Ma'am* as described in E1. After their relationship has changed to one of situated solidarity, the nucleus is shifted within the prosodic contour from *Ma'am* to *yes/no*:

---

1 Mrs. Watts: I thought that was a redbird, but it's been so long since I heard one I couldn't be sure. Do they still have scissortails around here?

2 Sheriff: **Yes** Ma'am. I still see one every once in a while, when I'm driving around the country.

3 Mrs. Watts: You know, my father was born on this land and in this house. Did you know my father?

4 Sheriff: **No** Ma'am. Not that I can remember.

The shift of nucleus in the prosodic contour in relation to the address term has pragmatic significance in terms of what dimension of the message is being foregrounded. As the characters come to an understanding, they treat each other more like peers, dropping the deference markers (except in this case) and focusing on the content of the conversation (by putting the nucleus on yes and no) rather than on the social meaning related to deference. The sheriff is here using the "habitual *Ma'am*" noted by the consultants in E1 which is part of his discourse strategy in interacting with an elderly woman.

Thus far in E1 and E2 we have seen a prototypical discourse use signaling deference with a conventional prosodic contour which is then modified, that modification conveying a subtle shift in foregrounding of social meaning.

E3: The Emphatic Use of the Address Term, both as Separate from and in Conjunction with the Deference Use

E3a. Pure Emphasis

This excerpt is taken from near the end of the extended interaction between Mrs. Watts and Thelma, the young woman she met on the bus. Up to this point all

Ma'am's have been uttered by Thelma to Mrs. Watts. And now suddenly one is directed from Mrs. Watts to Thelma. My consultants say that this is an example of pure emphasis. Ching (1988) also reports that his interviewees claim a "hearty affirmation" use of *Ma'am* and *Sir*. The prosodic shape is the same as the conventional contour, but it is perceived as having more energy and higher pitch. Thus the greater energy in speech production stands for greater emotional intensity invested in the communication. It should be noted that intensifications of prosodic contours are necessarily situated calculations; they are relative to an individual's voice, personality, and the general intensity of the interaction.

In terms of immediate discourse context, this *Yes Ma'am* is an acknowledgment of an acknowledgment. Mrs. Watts has offered an "abstract" of a story as an initiatory move toward producing a narrative. Thelma has offered encouragement in the form of her own acknowledgment, "Did you?"; Mrs. Watts is responding to that encouragement when she produces her emphatic *Yes Ma'am* before beginning her narrative.

---

1 Mrs. Watts: You know, I came to my first dance in this town.

2 Thelma: **Did** you?

3 Mrs. Watts: Yes **Ma'am.** It was the summertime. . . .

E3b. Emphasis Use in Conjunction with Deference Use

This excerpt continues the conversation of the opening scene discussed in E1 between Mrs. Watts and Ludie. The focus of the analysis here is on two pairs of contours: in lines 4 and 8, and in lines 12 and 14.

---

3 Mrs. Watts: Couldn't you sleep?

4 Ludie: No **Ma'am.**
["Normal *no.*" / "Same as line 2 above."]

5 Mrs. Watts: Why couldn't you sleep?

6 Ludie: Just couldn't. Couldn't you sleep?

7 Mrs. Watts: No, I haven't been to bed at all. You're not worrying about your job, are you, Sonny?

8 Ludie: No **Ma'am.** Everybody seems to like me there. I'm thinking about asking for a raise.
["Emphatic." / "Sharper rise and fall on *Ma'am*. His tone indicates that he is surprised by the question—as if to say, 'Why would you think that?' He also looks puzzled and his movement slows indicating that he is thinking about *why* the question was asked."]

9 Mrs. Watts: Oh, you should, hard as you work.

10 Ludie: Why couldn't you sleep, Mama?

11 Mrs. Watts: Because of the full moon. I never could sleep when there
     was a full moon. Even back in Bountiful when I'd been working out in
     the fields all day, and I'd be so tired I'd think my legs would give out
     on me, let there be a full moon and I'd just toss the night away. I
     remember once when you were little and there was a full moon, I woke
     you up and dressed you and took you for a walk with me. Do you
     remember?

12 Ludie: **No** Ma'am.
["Why *Ma'am* and not hun unh?" / "This is very flat and there is a gravelly quality to
his voice indicating he is tired and possibly that he doesn't want to remember. His eyes
seem to show that he doesn't want to think about this event—or that he is simply not
interested."]

13 Mrs. Watts: You don't?

14 Ludie: No **Ma'am.**
["He adds a slight rise and fall on *Ma'am* to emphasize his previous response—as if
saying '*No, I really* don't remember.'"]

As we saw in E1, the *No Ma'am* in line 4 is a "normal no" with a conventional
contour. In line 8, affect is conveyed by exaggerating the conventional contour: the
pitch is raised more sharply and there is an increased intensity. In line 12, the
nuclear shift to *no* is another example of what was discussed in E2; he is responding
directly to a positive yes/no information question. Then in line 14 he is responding
to another negative question (in effect) which challenges his previous response. He
escalates by shifting the nucleus back to *Ma'am* and exaggerating the contour
slightly, in effect, possibly attempting to compensate for his lack of politeness in
line 12.

E4: How the Usage of Address Terms May Indicate Situated Power Relations Which Override the Polite Fiction of Conventional Deference

According to Brown and Ford (1964), we would expect to see the deference
terms being used in the excerpt below from younger to older woman, since the only
superseding factor is occupational status and neither woman works outside of the
home. Thus either relative age or generational status within the family group would
predict the use of the *Ma'am* of respect from the daughter-in-law to the mother-in-
law. In fact, the older woman says *Ma'am* to the younger without reciprocation
(except in the special case discussed in E5 below).

The background to this excerpt is that Jessie Mae has asked Mrs. Watts to find
a recipe that she claims to have given to her, and Mrs. Watts has gone into her son
and daughter-in-law's bedroom to find it. She returns with the recipe and a very
tense episode ensues:

1 Mrs. Watts: Jessie Mae, here's your recipe.

2 Jessie Mae: Thank you. Where did you find it?

3 Mrs. Watts: In your room.

4 Jessie Mae: In my room?

5 Mrs. Watts: Yes **Ma**'am.
["Mrs. Watts says this in a quiet unassuming manner. Her tone indicates that she means 'yes ma'am, in your room.'" "Subtle challenge being conveyed here."]

6 Jessie Mae: Where in my room?

7 Mrs. Watts: In your dresser drawer. Right-hand side.

8 Jessie Mae: In my dresser drawer?

9 Mrs. Watts: Yes **Ma**'am. I looked on top of the dresser and it wasn't there and something said to me . . .
["Mrs. Watts speaks louder indicating impatience. The rising tone at the end of *Ma'am* shows she is not through speaking." "Moving in the direction of impudence."]

10 Jessie Mae: Mother Watts!

11 Mrs. Watts: **Ma**'am?
["She says this timidly, almost childlike, because she knows Jessie Mae is angry. The fall-rise tone indicates a question." "Subtle challenge."]

12 Jessie Mae: Ludie. How many times have I asked her never to look into my dresser drawers?

13 Mrs. Watts: I thought you wanted me to . . .

14 Jessie Mae (interrupting): I did not want you to go into my dresser drawers. I'd like a little privacy if you don't mind.

15 Mrs. Watts: Yes **Ma**'am.
["She says this with the normal rise-fall tone on *Ma'am*. Her stern expression and direct eye contact indicate that she is just going to stand there and take her 'punishment.' Her tone is somewhat defiant though." "Subtle sarcasm."]

This interaction shows the characters using (or avoiding) address terms to reflect the true power relations in the situation. The film provides evidence that the daughter-in-law is the one of the two women who wields direct power in the situation: twice by means of Jessie Mae's comments (that this is her house, and Mrs. Watts has to do as she's told, and that she has directed the grocer not to cash

Mrs. Watts's own pension check); and once by means of Mrs. Watts saying to the sheriff that Ludie has to do whatever Jessie Mae tells him to do. When a power struggle emerges, the daughter-in-law receives the deference terms from her mother-in-law, as we have seen. The prosody also reinforces the deference interpretation through conventional contours.

This is another point in the analysis when it becomes obvious that other terms of address needed to be taken into account. As Brown and Ford claimed, we prefer to maintain a "polite fiction" which denies the actual power relations; but to see this we need to consider the other address terms. Usually Jessie Mae calls her mother-in-law *Mother Watts* (Title Last Name [TLN]) and receives First Name (FN) from Mrs. Watts. This usage meets the requirements of the conventional schema. When tension arises, in the form of Jessie Mae's rising anger, Mrs. Watts signals deference through use of *Ma'am* with conventional contour. Thus conflict triggers a surfacing of the actual power relations, which are clearly represented linguistically, with *Ma'am* emerging as a key indicator serving as a contextualization cue (cf. Friedrich's 1972 "pronominal breakthrough").

My Southern consultants had mixed reactions to Mrs. Watts's utterances here and difficulty in describing exactly what was going on. The general feeling was that she was "playing the edge" in overtly giving deference but subtly challenging Jessie Mae, the classic strategy of the resentful subordinate. One consultant described her utterances as not really "impudent" but possibly moving in that direction. Thus, Mrs. Watts's anger toward Jessie Mae is also expressed in the ambiguous and therefore deniable manner in which she produces the overt linguistic markers of deference.

E5: How *Ma'am* May Be Used to Convey Sarcasm

Sarcastic *Ma'am* poses a particular problem for an approach which correlates social categories with usage; from younger to older woman it would appear to be used deferentially, especially if prosody is not taken into account. The excerpt precedes the interaction discussed in E4.

---

1 Jessie Mae: Mother Watts, where did you put that recipe that Rosella gave me on the phone yesterday?

2 Mrs. Watts: Jessie Mae, I don't remember you having given me any recipe.

3 Jessie Mae: Well, I did. This morning, right here in this very room, and I asked you to please put it on my dresser and you said I will and went out holding it in your hand.

4 Mrs. Watts: Did you look on your dresser?

5 Jessie Mae: **Yes Ma**'am.

["The sarcasm is almost totally in the intonation." / "Jessie Mae puts a slight rise and fall on *Ma'am*. She also shakes her head, tilts it down looking at Mother Watts. Her tone and actions indicate sarcasm—'Well of course I did, why the hell would you ask such a stupid question.'"]

6 Mrs. Watts: And it wasn't there?

7 Jessie Mae: **No Ma**'am. I looked just before I went to bed.

As discussed in E4, the two women operate within a "polite fiction" schema in which Jessie Mae and Mrs. Watts use nonreciprocal TLN/FN, and the only one who uses *Ma'am* is Mrs. Watts under conditions in which she has to signal her subordinate position to her daughter-in-law; therefore, Jessie Mae's use of *Ma'am* becomes interpretable as marked, producing a paradoxical situation in which the usage is interpretable as the opposite of its usual social meaning (if the opposite of showing deference/respect is to show contempt and hostility). Both Friedrich (1972:280) and Braun (1988:47) cite comparable usages with formal second-person pronouns in other languages and emphasize the importance of tone of voice in interpretation of these phenomena. In fact, my consultants perceive the contextualization cue to be primarily the prosody (as noted in the comments cited above), together with nonverbal dimensions of the communication. There appear to be two distinct nuclei in the contour, with a slight break between them, together with an exaggeration of the contour on *Ma'am*.

My consultants were quite upset by Jessie Mae's behavior toward Mrs. Watts, one describing it as "incredibly disrespectful." In terms of the immediate discourse context and interpretive frame that the women are working within, given the true power relations, Mrs. Watts's questions in 4 and 6 could have been interpreted by Jessie Mae as inappropriately challenging her in some way. This could be the frame within which she produces her strong sarcasm, trying to reassert her authority as well as her anger and hostility toward her mother-in-law.

E6: How Usage of Terms of Address May Be a Subtle Index of the Evolution of a Relationship

Finally, we see *Ma'am* and *Sir* usage serving as a sensitive indicator of the evolution of the brief but important relationship between Mrs. Watts and the sheriff in the Bountiful area. The terms are initially used reciprocally as markers of deference (to an elderly woman on the one side, and to the authority of the position of sheriff on the other).

1 Sheriff: Mrs. Watts?

2 Mrs. Watts: **Yes** Sir. Are you the sheriff?

3 Sheriff: Yes **Ma**'am.

4 Mrs. Watts: I understand that my son will be here at seven-thirty to take me back to Houston.

5 Sheriff: **Yes** Ma'am.

6 Mrs. Watts: Then listen to me, **Sir** . . .

The sheriff's offer to drive Mrs. Watts out to Bountiful serves to reframe the relationship. Initially it is a formal and adversarial one in which the sheriff, as the representative of authority, is responsible for holding Mrs. Watts, thus limiting her autonomy. But once Mrs. Watts has appealed to him emotionally, he treats her in a very different way. He chooses to do a kindness which is not only not required of him in his role of sheriff, but which in fact constitutes stretching the directive to hold her there until her son arrives. The sheriff chooses to respond to Mrs. Watts as a person entitled to some autonomy, which her personal circumstances and the society at large would otherwise deny her. He drives her out to her abandoned house in Bountiful, sits and talks with her a bit about birds, and listens to her feelings about being there, and then tactfully distances himself so that she can be alone and yet feel protected by his presence.

Once the relationship has been reframed, the deferential terms of address are dropped. The only occurrences are in the cases analyzed and discussed in E2 above (and repeated below), in which the shift of nucleus in the prosodic contour in relation to the address term has pragmatic significance in terms of what dimension of the message is being foregrounded. In these responses to yes/no questions the focus shifts to the content of the conversation (by putting the nucleus on *yes* and *no*), backgrounding the social meaning related to deference. The sheriff is here using the "habitual *Ma'am*," noted by the consultants in E1, which is part of his discourse strategy in interacting with an elderly woman.

---

1 Mrs. Watts: I thought that was a redbird, but it's been so long since I heard one I couldn't be sure. Do they still have scissortails around here?

2 Sheriff: **Yes** Ma'am. I still see one every once in a while, when I'm driving around the country.

3 Mrs. Watts: You know, my father was born on this land and in this house. Did you know my father?

4 Sheriff: **No** Ma'am. Not that I can remember.

In this instance we see that cessation of use can itself serve as a contextualization cue of a different sort from the ones we have discussed so far. Dropping of the deferential address terms could be seen as showing a loss of respect or simply as a move away from formality. I suggest that the usage after the reframing of the relationship by the sheriff represents a situated solidarity based in compassion. This analysis provides an example of the instantiation of Brown and Levinson's (1987:231) programmatic statement that "the linguistic realization of politeness strategies may be a very revealing index of the quality of social relationships and the course of their development."

CONCLUSION

In this examination of how Southern politeness is linguistically enacted, we have seen variation from the point of view of interactional sociolinguistics, as a systematic result of speakers' use of linguistic phenomena as resources in the mutual construction of situated social identities. We have also seen how the links between language and social organization are mediated rather than direct. This theoretical orientation demands an integrative discourse analysis which fosters the close reading of discourse at the same time that it emphasizes the role of context in interpretive processes and the negotiation of meaning. Analyses of excerpts have been presented which illustrate 1) the prototypical usage of *Ma'am* for deference; 2) how a shift in the nucleus of the prosodic contour in relation to the address term serves to foreground different social meanings; 3) the emphatic use of the address term, both as separate from and in conjunction with the deference use; 4) how the usage of address terms may indicate situated power relations which override the polite fiction of conventional deference; 5) how *Ma'am* may be used to convey sarcasm; and 6) how usage of terms of address may be a subtle index of the evolution of a relationship.

This paper has focused on *Ma'am* (and, to a lesser degree, *Sir*) although it has become clear in the course of the analysis that all terms of address need to be taken into consideration. Such an elaboration of this study would also allow a more extensive critique of the theoretical framework provided by Brown and Levinson (1987). Another extension of the study, of interest in light of American egalitarian ideology, would be to examine trends in honorific usage (see Simpkins 1969; Ching 1988). Interviews of Southern consultants for this study revealed wide variation in attitudes toward and self-reported usage of the terms of address.

NOTES

I wish to acknowledge Horton Foote for the beauty and spiritual inspiration of his work and for his graciousness in encouraging me to undertake this project; the scholars of Southern American English for their welcome and encouragement in pursuing research in this area, in particular, Marvin K. L. Ching, Barbara Johnstone, and Michael Picone; and my Southern consultants for their patience in answering a Yankee's sometimes obtuse questions, their generosity in sharing their cultural schemas, and their pride in their linguistic distinctiveness.

1. Pages of the screenplay (Foote 1989) corresponding to the excerpts from the video are as follows: E1, 153–54; E2, 207; E3, 195 and 154–55; E4, 158–59; E5, 156; E6, 202 and 207.

2. I have modified the description slightly from the way it appears in Foote (1989:153–54).

That Muddy Mississippi of Falsehood Called "History"

Joan Weatherly

> "It's disgusting," he said, pointing to me. "Our new brother has succeeded by instinct where for two years your 'science' has failed, and now all you can offer is destructive criticism." (Ellison 1952:265)

Descriptions of Southern English, whether collected by dialectologists or savored by literary critics out of the mouths of characters in Southern literature, are best seen as holograms, which record all stages of an activity simultaneously, at the same time that the "viewer's changing perspective . . . provides the illusion that it is unfolding [irreversibly] in time" (Talbot 1991:201). Only the hologram can compress the multiple senses of time, of history, and of natural balances for a region on which as many preconceptions have been laid as the Mississippi has deposited alluvial dirt on its way to the Gulf. The literary genre called Southern grotesque, for example, presents characters and situations defined by their language and by their efforts in discourse to recreate the hologram of time and nature.

The genre is overlaid by reactions of outsiders to the real people as well as to the fictional characters who make up the other-defined grotesque landscape. Evil characters in television cartoons speak in their animators' notions of Southern English, not unlike Dickens's Putnam Smif in *Martin Chuzzlewit*; Elvis Presley wind-up dolls mimic and replicate its parameters. But like the Mississippi, changing its character as it roils through successive Southern states, there is more than one Southern language, even more than one Southern English. To sample any portion, without being aware that it is only a portion, is to stand on a shaky levee. The speech in the mouths of Southerners holds words and sounds and syntax from African, Romance, Native American and Germanic languages, an alluvial deposit from travelers, visitors, those who came willingly to stay, and those brought without consent. Taking the Mississippi as both guide and metaphor, this essay presents some of the dimensions, some of the contexts, for studies of Southernness.

VOICES OUTSIDE OF TIME

Time is not so much annihilated by Southern mythtorians as relativized (opened futureward), impressionistic tapestries with cubist angles. Welty was a photographer; Faulkner and O'Connor serious dabblers in painting—as was poet Roderick Usher. Hear the theory of Poe's omnipresent scientist narrator: "the paradoxical law of all sentiments having terror as a basis" is that "rapid increase" in superstition serves "mainly to accelerate the increase itself"; or the omniscient narrator whose sparse stage directions in Welty's "Petrified Man" are limited to an occasional remark of action-based rhetoric. Through speech acts, Southern writers reveal "unconscious motivations, which *manifest themselves linguistically*"; they are interested in "*psychological* as well as *sociological parameters* and categories" (Menz 1989:230).

These writers tell the stories of how and why, as Conron (1973) puts it, we now recognize both a cultural and a biological symbiosis between people and land: a way of perceiving landscape as an interplay of "the natural processes by which land and the living things upon it have achieved their characteristic forms (evolution) and by which they maintain their existence (ecology)" (478).

Ecospeak is coined by Killingsworth and Palmer (1992:11) for their environmental rhetoric describing a "continuum of perspectives on nature," which moves from Nature as Object through Nature as Resource to Nature as Spirit. Postman (1992) would teach the history and meaning of three stages: tool users, technocracy (in Leo Marx's 1963 terms, the machine could be fused into the garden), and technopoly (the machine in control). Postman uses Twain to exemplify technocracy, that stage between tool using and technopoly when the old truths—"verities" as Faulkner calls them in his Nobel Prize Speech—can exist alongside technology. And it may be that Southern speakers, Southern writers still work extensively within this stage, as they certainly did in the second half of the 19th century.

Both the 19th-century explorer-investor William Gilpin and the *Harper's* article with which Twain opens *Life on the Mississippi* call the Mississippi Valley "the body of the nation" and herald the triumph of Manifest Destiny which we here call technocracy. Gilpin (1973) touts the land he wants to sell or settle as "geographical centre at once of the North American Continent" and of "the American Union," indeed of the world:

> . . . equidistant from, and exactly in, the middle between the two halves of the human family . . . one half Christians, occupying Western Europe, to the number of 259,000,000 of population; the other half Pagans, occupying Oriental Asia and Polynesia, to the number of 650,000,000. . . . When, therefore, this interval of North America shall be filled up, the affiliation of mankind will be accomplished, proximity recognised, the distraction of intervening oceans and equatorial heats cease, the remotest nations be grouped together and fused into one universal and convenient system of immediate relationship. (Gilpin 1973:375)

> Behold, then, rising now and in the future, the empire which industry and self-government create. (377)

Behold reflects the view of nature as separate object: yet it is, say Southern writers, as impossible to separate time, the landscape, and language in the American South as to channel its rivers or the grotesquerie in its fictional portrayals.

THE RIVERSCAPE OF FREAKS

Observing that the grotesque is neither as antibourgeois as Thomas Mann counts it, nor so sentimental as Americans think, O'Connor (1969) argues that Southern grotesque emphasizes intellectual and moral judgments. Says O'Connor:

> Whenever I'm asked why Southern writers particularly have a penchant for writing about freaks, I say it is because we are still able to recognize one. To be able to recognize a freak, you have to have some conception of the whole man, and in the south the general conception of man is still, in the main, theological. . . . Ghosts can be very fierce and instructive. They cast strange shadows, particularly in our literature. In any case, it is when the freak can be sensed as a figure for our essential displacement that he attains some depth in literature. (44–45)

Amused that Southern writers are usually considered a cross between Poe and Erskine Caldwell, O'Connor traces the evolution of the Southern grotesque from Frontier humor, through more serious, absurd mid-20th-century versions, to Elvis Presley (1969:28, 33). Yet all the media and all the king's men can't unravel this weird web of Southern "Mystery and Manners," though Warren's reading of Huey P. Long as Willie Stark in *All the King's Men* is a good start.

The Bible Belt's weirdness is often attributed to "foreign" influence: French and Spanish are but two. "Ever'body in New Orleans believes ever'thing spooky," declares Welty's (1980:525) Leota. Twain appends the accounts of English travelers Basil Hall and Frances Trollope to *Life*, and more recent travelers Hall and Wood (1992) verify the desolate view of the river's "end" begat by technopoly: "She saw a mighty river pouring forth its 'muddy mass of waters and mingling with the deep blue of the Mexican Gulf.' She wrote that she had never beheld a scene so utterly desolate; 'had Dante seen it he might have drawn images from its horrors'" (275).

Driving out of New Orleans beyond Elysian Fields on down the German Coast, past Empire, Triumph, and the road's end at Venice, sojourners Hall and Wood reach the point at which La Salle and his party planted the cross for France. They are unsurprised that the water is neither "pouring" nor "blue," told that just off this shore, out there where the oil rigs sit, the water is "probably forever" a hypoxic region (274): "How odd that Mrs. Trollope would have Dante on her mind when she first saw the mouth of the Mississippi; we had an image from Dante in our minds too, but we were thinking of that dead zone [killed by technopoly] out there" (275). In fiction and in place names (Faulkner's Frenchman's Bend) throughout the Valley, French influence is still traceable, aerated.

French Camp, on the Natchez Trace Parkway, today houses two relics once belonging to the great Choctaw chieftain Greenwood Leflore: his restored (neon lights almost hidden) Council House, brought from Leflore county for the Bicentennial, and the carriage used for his trips to Washington during the Jackson era. The "historic" Lodge specializes in the new money crop of catfish, which de Soto's men observed, Mrs. Trollope hated, Twain liked, and a lot of which Hall and

Wood found belly up from poison used on an old money crop. A few yards away the carriage stands behind the glass window of a box, not unlike the cage in which the heroic Black Hawk was exhibited like a freak.

Visible Spanish influence, which plays out roughly with Spanish moss, is harder to find in and out of fiction, beyond chronicles of trading and surveying, but Hall and Wood comment, "Unlikely as it seems, de Soto's brief touch on this country-side influenced its way of life for centuries," leaving after the Civil War "a morass of peonage worse than slavery" (169). Gertrude Stein (1969) quipped, "Spaniards did not mistrust science they only never have recognized the existence of progress" and adds, "While other Europeans were still in the nineteenth century, Spain because of its lack of organisation and America by its excess of organisation were the natural founders of the twentieth century" (12).

The American South is not usually linked to excess organization, though Poe and Twain are clearly associated with modernism. Poe, pioneer in detective stories and science fiction, had marked influence on French Symbolism, itself an influence on Faulkner. Twain, whose *Life on the Mississippi* parallels *Don Quixote* in structure and theme, praises Cervantes as the greatest of writers though he insists that Southern chivalry, cause of both the South's Civil War and its inflated language, was "caught" from reading Sir Walter Scott. Later, a comment on Flannery O'Connor, by Paul Engle, her Iowa professor, that "Flannery spoke a dialect beyond instant comprehension but on the page her prose was imaginative, tough, alive" (Giroux 1971:vii) at once locates the setting and the sound of her grotesque fiction and highlights its modern tone and content.

Engle's remark helps to answer the perennial question Southerners are asked: where does that Southern Gothic—as it is usually called instead of the closely related grotesque which O'Connor prefers—literature come from? His comment exposes the fact that the South is still considered a kind of subculture, a strange, barely literate anomaly, but it points toward a lesser known fact: under the surface veneer of its backwardness and conservatism, there lies rich diversity in folk language and culture such as Mikhail Bakhtin (1982:471–2) notes for the Northern Mediterranean region where the tradition of the formal grotesque first arose and flourished. Twain, O'Connor, Faulkner, and Poe employ the grotesque to dramatize the divisions between comedy and tragedy, as well as their ancient and modern connections, and both the distances and connections between medievalism and modernism. Grounded in grotesquerie, gnosticism, and traditional religion, the South may also be associated with modernism and postmodernism. Here is the rich "intertextuality," typical of writers, readers, tellers, and listeners in much Southern fiction and metahistory.

MYTHOGRAPHY AS METAHISTORY

One of Melany Neilson's autobiographical stories related in *Even Mississippi* (1989) recalls some of the myths about Southern English, giving new depth to Florian Menz's (1989) argument that myth binds social groups "to represent their interests and to create a common basis of identification" (233). Neilson's homesickness evokes the holographic, simultaneous synthesis of past and present, hereness and thereness: "It is common that annoyances in a new place—foul weather, stalled traffic, the rudeness of strangers—bring out thoughts of the familiar. . . . Pennsylvania and Mississippi, were beginning gradually to exist in separate realities, one meaning everyday things, the other, something to return to, to remember" (133).

Neilson's epiphany of difference echoes Ellison's Jack-the-Bear whose quest for form in *Invisible Man* is marked by contrasts between New York and the South he finds by leaving. Freedom is everywhere associated with language for Jack; here, his ellipses show his epiphany unfolding in his first Party speech: "I feel that I can see sharp and clear and far down the dim corridor of history and in it I can hear the footsteps of militant fraternity! No, wait, let me confess . . . I feel the urge to affirm my feelings . . . I feel that here, after a long and desperate and uncommonly blind journey, I have come home . . . Home!" (262).

Jack analyzes his speech from several angles, sure that Party "science" will cleanse his old-fashioned style. Both James Meredith (1966), the first African-American to integrate Ole Miss, and Anne Moody (1969), a Civil Rights activist who moved to Germany, describe this same time-subsuming, paradoxical homesickness in their autobiographies. Positive memories of home triggered by homesickness—for the former of a lush landscape and for the latter of a speech pattern—holographically encircle even injustice. Such homesickness is at the holographic heart of Twain's metahistory in *Life*, which sets the old and new times of Twain's life alongside that of the Valley and the Western world, and which, like Faulkner's *Old Man*, is discourse about discourse.

Noting that "all art is linked to a set of artistic conventions," some general and some imposed by nationality and the time, Jakobson (1987) says: "The artist's revolt, no less than his faithfulness to certain required rules, is conceived of by contemporaries with respect to the code that the innovator wants to shatter"; hence, the "attempted confrontation between arts and language may fail if this comparative study relates to ordinary language and not directly to verbal art, which is a transformed system of the former" (451). The revolt of Ellison's artist figure Jack-the-Bear is illuminated by his correct analysis of this confrontation. He finds the key to his quest for form (ultimately his grandfather's irony) in the old woman's definition of freedom: "I guess now it ain't nothing but being able to say what I got up in my head" (14).

Autobiographies such as Neilson's, or Moody's *Coming of Age in Mississippi*, also effect Jakobson's comparative study, and such a confrontation is at the center of Faulkner, O'Connor, and Twain. O'Connor (1969) dramatized the "working of grace on evil," sure that writers "will have, in these times, the sharpest eyes for the grotesque, for the perverse, and for the unacceptable" (33). Simultaneously, she insisted on realism: dislocation of the familiar is needed to expose the irrational. Writers from, of, and about the South have consistently found in myth strength as well as language for their visions of the familiar and the irrational. That myth, which survived the "new objectivity" of the late 19th century, became in itself the new landscape superimposed on the physical, familiar one:

During this period of psychic and physical change, the cultural and natural history of landscape spanned several dimensions of time. In landscape one could see the past of one's childhood, the regional or national past, the past of Indian civilizations . . . that of the Moundbuilders . . . and even the past of geological change and of evolution. These visible records of history gave landscape a dynamic quality: it was not inert or dreamlike but changeful and pulsing with dynamic and vitalistic energies. (Conron 1973:449)

Such dynamism of landscape seen through time is Twain's focus in *Life*, dramatized in the history of Napoleon, Arkansas, located at the point where the Arkansas river flows into the Mississippi. How much alluvial deposit here: this is the site of de Soto's "entry" into Arkansas; the southernmost point of Marquette and Joliet's exploration; the key stop for La Salle en route to the Gulf of Mexico; the setting for Twain's hearing news of his brother's fatal injury; the setting of real and imagined Gothic tales, the "Lynching Bee" and the Royal Nonesuch scenes of *Huck*. Twain the metahistorian muses:

These performances [La Salle's sign giving] took place on the site of the future town of Napoleon, Arkansas, and there the first confiscation cross was raised on the banks of the great river. Marquette's and Joliet's voyage of discovery ended at the same spot—the site of the future town of Napoleon. When de Soto took his fleeting glimpse of the river, away back in the dim early days, he took it from that same spot. . . . Therefore, three out of the four memorable events connected with the discovery and exploration of the mighty river occurred, by accident, in one and the same place. It is a most curious distinction, when one comes to look at it and think about it. France stole that vast country on that spot, the future Napoleon; and by and by Napoleon himself was to give the country back again—make restitution, not to the owners, but to their white American heirs. (20)

Curious joins "look" and "think" (at once), bending space and curving time toward the future. Place subsumes time in the name, so the metahistorical reader enfolds person and place into Twain's musings on, in, and at layered Napoleon(s). Musing *upon* diachronic "history" and "historical history" *makes* what White terms *metahistory*. Twain's book opens upon the 19th century, but it enfolds more than five centuries; his fractal, changing river evokes Lévi-Strauss's (1966) concept of history as myth inseparable from language.

THE GROTESQUE IN OTHER MOUTHS

In August 1992, I was standing before the Pyramid in Memphis, by the new Hernando de Soto Bridge connecting Memphis with West Memphis, Arkansas, a few miles north of the Spaniard's discovery point. Waiting for the Clintons and the Tennessean Gores to appear at the Homecoming '92 Rally, I felt enfolded in history and myth, in the sense of the hologram, which is there all at once while seeming to materialize over time.

Elvis's last name, pronounced by a Northern photographer who asked for directions to the press area, attested to the survival of the "Greasy Line" marking a river-deep division between /s/ and /z/ speakers. He seemed unable to understand either me or a black Arkansan waiting to give the Clintons a jar of peach pickles: it was our dialects, "stupid," not our directions. A secret service man crisply directed the photographer—the latter shaking his head hopelessly in our direction.

The Arkansan said, "He's a-seein' freaks," to which I replied, "And hearin' 'em, too," thinking of the "Monsters be here" inscription on Renaissance maps and the assertion of Ralph Ellison's *Invisible Man* (1947:3) narrator that he is neither an Edgar Allan Poe "spook" nor an "ectoplasm," although as a stereotype he is invisible. The Arkansan and I agreed with a Mississippi self-acknowledged carpetbagger couple that Hilary's Yankee background and language could come in handy in the forthcoming November election. In the oppressive heat, with Secret Service personnel serving iced water, we talked about the quality of Southern newspapers, water, language, and education: on the last three counts the Arkansan assured us, Clinton and Gore were "way yonda ahead" (speaking exactly as my white Mississippi grandmother did) of the other two, though he "kinda liked the ol' clown wi' the *sahn*tific chah'ts in a Southern drawl" (referring to Ross Perot) better "anyhow than listnin' to somebody soundin' like J.R.'s cousin."

An older white urban Tennessee man—using *it* in place of *there*, a feature limited to no one Southern group—was sure "*It* wudn' much diff'rance between none of 'em but Gore who might hep save the land" (here, read "environment" not "country"). "And that'll take some educatin'," we all agreed, to which a new voice, that of a stylish young woman (part Cherokee she told us), added, "To fix this old leaky *house*." She pointed out—observing the slogan greeting Clinton and Gore on the Pyramid, *Homecoming '92*— that *eco-* means 'house' in Greek. "Then it must mean 'econ-*omee*' too," the Arkansan surmised. Before she was lost ("kinda ghostlike," thought the Arkansan) in the crowd, she said, "It's kyurse, the only ones that come home are them that never left." The urban carpetbaggers had never before heard that odd pronunciation of *curious*.

FRACTAL MEANDERINGS

To his titular question *Is Literary History Possible?* David Perkins (1992) answers: "My opinion is, then, that we cannot write literary history with intellectual conviction, but we must read it. The irony and paradox of this argument are themselves typical of our present moment in history" (17). Ellison and White would answer, "Yes": Jack, whose boomerang theory of history leads him to reject dialectical materialism (386, 435), clearly dramatizes White's belief that recognition of the "Ironic perspective provides the grounds for transcendence of it," thereby freeing the historian for other "moral and aesthetic" stances (434). Whether Perkins is right or wrong about literary history, O'Connor's Southern grotesque vision remains as (im)pertinent as ever "for the continuance of a vital Southern literature": "I hate to think that in twenty years Southern writers too may be writing about men in gray-flannel suits and may have lost their ability to see that these gentlemen are even greater freaks than what we are writing about now. I hate to think of the day when the Southern writer will satisfy the tired reader" (1969:50). The quest (not quite *search* in our fractal meanderings) for balance between inner and outer ecologies, often through a deconstructed laugh, is shared by these writers, fictive and nonfictive. Facing the Hell created by gray-flannel-polyester types at the end of the river, Hall and Wood embrace Big Muddy's paradoxes and ask if the river's very size makes comprehension of its problems impossible, but they conclude with a weird hope—not quite optimism—arising from a new sense of "connectedness" confirming Gore's (1992) vision of ecology and the human spirit. This holographic sense of connectedness was enunciated to the iron-suited de Soto by an Indian chief–master ironist within hours of de Soto's "discovery" of the Mechesebe: "My Lord, I and mine are yours; therefore if you had [destroyed us], you would have destroyed your own country, and your own people" (reported by Elvas [{1542} 1939] 1986:11). This chieftain would surely smile at Matthew Arnold's "muddy-missi-history" metaphor of my title.

"Pictures from Life's Other Side": Southern Regionalism in Hank Williams's Luke the Drifter Recordings

Thomas L. Wilmeth

Of the more than 150 songs that Hank Williams recorded, 14 were released under the pseudonym of Luke the Drifter. These recordings are unique to Williams's work, for they contain recitations, spoken sections filled with Southern dialect forms and strong lexical regionalisms which rarely, if ever, appear in the rest of his canon. I suggest that through his specific lexical selection and his unabashed use of Southern working-class vernacular Williams is able to vividly and positively affirm his Southern regional identity.

These 14 recordings act as linguistic snapshots of Williams's own era, and are also useful as aural fingerprints that demonstrate the Southern language patterns from which this artist emerged. The utterances discussed here are authentic and linguistically rich resources, similar to the WPA slave interviews or the Tennessee Civil War Veteran Questionnaires. The content of the Luke the Drifter recordings reaffirms Williams's Southern regional identity and demonstrates how he successfully addresses themes which transcend simple regional portraits, speaking to the universality of the human condition.

Hank Williams's brief recording career began in December 1946 and ended in the fall of 1952. During this time he sold millions of records and provided both country music and the South with one of its best known performers and song writers (Williams 1980:157). His popularity was so great that record store owners and juke box operators would unquestioningly order large quantities of any song that MGM Records released under the Hank Williams name (Caress 1979:129). This placed Williams in a financially enviable, yet artistically uncomfortable, position. Soon after achieving nearly unprecedented fame in country music, Williams was forced to produce consistent records that would not disappoint his established audience and would, in essence, sound like a Hank Williams record. I suggest that it was this pressure to produce somewhat uniform-sounding or recognizable material which led, in part, to the creation of a persona Williams called Luke the Drifter. Using this pseudonym, Williams could record songs of a different tenor and experiment with various types of material without fear of risking his established reputation (or economic situation).[1]

In the Luke the Drifter recordings, Williams usually offered recitations reflecting upon broken relationships, societal wrongs, and death. And while much of the material Williams released under his own name dealt with heartbreak and loneliness, it is the overall *feeling* which these Luke the Drifter recordings evoke in the listener that differs from his major country hit singles, with the Luke recitations often trading a strong melody for a strong message. For example, "I Saw the Light" is one of Williams's most powerful affirmations of faith, but this is not a Luke the Drifter selection. It has the *sound* of a Hank Williams record, containing a memorable melody and a musical drive that can rise above (or at least not be at odds with) a typical barroom atmosphere.[2]

This too was a reason for the creation of the Luke the Drifter persona, as Williams did not want his heartfelt and low-keyed recitations having to compete with the potential rowdiness (and perhaps the godlessness) of a saloon environment (Williams 1980:128). In the role of Luke, Williams further developed his art as writer and performer, with special emphasis given to his recitations (Escott 1994:125).[3] And by employing this pseudonym, Williams solved two potentially troublesome problems: he would disappoint neither the local retailer, who had to sell what records he ordered from MGM, nor the bar patron who punched the juke box numbers expecting to hear a familiar Hank Williams sound.

It is this strange but fascinating Luke the Drifter subset of the Williams's canon which is examined here, for it is in this less restrictive context that the artist most vividly depicts his native landscape and the culture from which he emerged—a regional portrait accomplished by means of expressive Southern vernacular and spoken pronunciation traits. The distinction between utterances sung and utterances spoken is an important one, for in the Luke the Drifter recitations Williams demonstrates speech mannerisms less hindered by the strict song meter and rhyme patterns present in traditional song structures.

At the heart of the Luke the Drifter recordings are the speaker's recitations, which act as a centerpiece for many of the selections. The structural paradigm for most of these performances follows an A B A pattern: a sung verse is followed by a recitation and then a concluding sung verse (which now carries far greater meaning since the narrator has placed it in a proper context for the listener). The tone (or mood) presented in these 14 recordings is usually, although not exclusively, that of a concerned speaker gently lecturing the listener on love gone wrong or family upheavals. One typical selection ("Help Me Understand") effectively demonstrates this characteristic by describing a marriage which has dissolved due to harsh words that "never should-a been said." The stubbornness and selfishness of the couple is criticized by the speaker, but the recitation focuses on how this divorce affects their little daughter Sue, who is now left to wander "from pillar to post."[4]

Inseparable from the usually somber tone of these admonitions is Williams's distinctly Southern regionalism, as evidenced by his speech patterns. Phonologically, for example, Williams uses final consonant cluster simplification in words such as *hones'*, for *honest*; *groun'* for *ground*, which Williams rhymes with *down*; and *durn* for *durned* when recounting how the "*durn* rabbits got the turnip greens." Other deletions include the absence of [w] in the speaker's reference to his "young 'uns" and the dropped medial syllable in *usual* [južəl] in reference to a "usual dad." Williams repeatedly pronounces *picture* as *pitchure* [pɪčɚ] in "A Picture From Life's Other Side," monophthongizes /aɪ/ as in *time* [tam] and *while* [wal], and raises /ɛ/ before nasals to /ɪ/ (the "pin/pen merger") as in *expense* and *went*. "Luke" refers to his *maw-in-law*, exploiting internal rhyme. Williams rhymes the color *yeller* with *umbreller*, and the epenthetic *r* found in these words is also used when the speaker collapses *sort of* not into *sorta*, but into *sorter*. He inserts an epenthetic *d* when he discusses a "stern'd old man" in the song "Too Many Parties and Too Many Pals." He repeatedly adds an *a-* prefix to the word *living* (and replaces /ŋ/ with /n/), turning *living* into *a-livin'*, and uses *chimbley* for *chimney*.

Function words are often used in interesting ways in the Luke the Drifter material, such as when the speaker explains that his "cow broke in the field and ate up the beans." The image of a broken cow is intriguing in itself, but what the speaker obviously means is that the cow broke *into* the field. Also, Williams often omits the subject pronouns *we* and *I*, such as in the line, "Got nuthin' to put in the smoke house," and uses perfective *done* when Luke laments that his hogs have "done died."

One Luke the Drifter selection must be singled out for its variety of distinctly Southern articulations and for its unusual structure. "The Funeral," set in a named Southern location, Savannah, Georgia, contains no singing, but only recitation. This aural portrait is placed against the backdrop of a mourning Hammond organ. Williams employs a double mask of character narration for most of the recitation, as Luke vividly recounts the words of an African-American preacher at a child's funeral service.

In many ways, this selection acts as a concise summation of the speaker's Southern articulations. Although there is not a radical style shift when Luke begins to quote the preacher in "The Funeral," this section recounting the sermon includes several features also associated with working-class African-American speech of the era. Williams changes the ending of *desk* and *grotesque* by substituting a *t* for the concluding k, uttering [dɛst] and [grotɛst]. We also again hear repeated consonant cluster simplification, including *interes'* for *interest*, and *chil'* for *child*. The perfective *done* is again employed here, as is the pronunciation *pitchure* [pɪčɚ], and initial syllable deletion is evident in the line, "He *'ppreciates* your love."

Other Southern characteristics of "The Funeral" include *very finely* used as an adjective, a reference to God as the child's "*sho' nuff* Father," and a nonstandard relative pronoun in place of *who* in the line "the one *what* knows the best." Plurals are usually uninflected in this recitation, and the *be* verb is left unconjugated. Past tenses also remain uninflected, or are regularized, as in the line, "Then the angel's chief musician *teached* that little boy a song."

Many lexical items found throughout these numbers are also specifically regional. For example, while mules are not uniquely Southern, such lexical denotations are indicative of specific regional references found throughout the entire Luke the Drifter canon. *Mule* here conjures up images of Southern field labor, thanks to its long association with this geographic area (Wilson and Ferris 1989:512). Writers from William Faulkner to Alton Delmore so frequently discuss the importance of the mule to the region that the animal becomes a motif of sorts for Southern prose. Similarly, *weevils* (for *boll weevils*), while not confined to the South, helps to provide another link in the lexical chain of association which sets these pieces so firmly in a Southern landscape. *Corn meal, smokehouse, preacher* and *billy goat* are also not unique to the region but, taken in context and tightly clustered within a few lines, combine to portray a distinctly Southern scene.

While "The Funeral" provides an excellent summation of Williams's articulation, "Everything's Okay," its thematic inversion, is unusually rich in Southern lexical information. As the title suggests, "Everything's Okay" has an upbeat mood and attitude rare to the Luke the Drifter canon, exhibiting an optimism which is retained even while listing numerous personal problems and setbacks. Williams, as Luke, tells this tale from the point of view of "my Uncle Bill." Although again employing a double mask of character narration, it is still Williams who employs lexical items like "rotted down" and "tote the water." The speaker is almost Job-like in listing the troubles that have recently visited him. And like Job's initial reaction to suffering, Uncle Bill refuses to curse his bad situation. It is important to the regional analysis to note that in spite of all the ills recounted in this aural portrait, Williams is not playing upon the stereotypical image of the unhappy poor Southern farmer who laments over his unfair situation. Instead, after each list of life's problems and irritations, the verse ends with the spoken repetition, "But we're still a-livin', so everything's okay." Uncle Bill even stresses at the song's end, "I guess things are in pretty good shape."

This upbeat attitude is noteworthy for several reasons. Williams's ability to communicate so effectively with his audience was due, in part, to the sad and mournful tone of his most powerful works, both as Hank ("I'm So Lonesome I Could Cry") and as Luke ("The Funeral"). Because of this reputation for songs of melancholy, he could have easily portrayed a scene of desperation on an economically failing farm, more along the lines of the destitute and suicidal South Dakota farmer in Bob Dylan's "Ballad of Hollis Brown." Yet Williams uses his unfortunate farmer's various plights to illustrate the most confident and optimistic of his Luke the Drifter portraits.

"Everything's Okay" neither presents a bleak view of the South, nor condemns the living situation of the lower agrarian classes of the region. Instead, here is a depiction of a survivor. This song represents an insider's understanding of one who may be in rough shape at present but who is determined to take the long view.

It could be argued that because Luke the Drifter is a persona that Williams creates, he might also be adopting some purposefully affected speech for his role as compassionate lecturer. This might be seen as especially possible with some of the multi-layered narrations discussed here. I indicated earlier that there are no recitations in the Hank Williams canon with which the Luke recitations can be compared.[5] Still, there are enough recorded samples of his speech and conversation to identify the utterances in the Luke the Drifter recitations as accurately depicting Williams's unaffected and unaltered linguistic patterns.

Examples of Williams's speech come primarily from his introductions to songs. In addition to spoken utterances recorded during concert performances and radio broadcasts, tapes exist of interviews and an interesting "Apology" which he recorded for missing a concert engagement in Baltimore. During none of these instances is he evoking the Luke persona, yet the linguistic patterns he exhibits on these tapes are identical to those found in the Luke the Drifter recitations. Especially important to this comparative study is the 1993 release of the complete *Health and Happiness Show* recordings, which contain numerous and varied examples of Williams's speech characteristics. These eight syndicated radio programs date from October 1949—more than three months before Williams's first recording session as Luke the Drifter (Escott 1993:7).[6] The similarity of the linguistic forms on these broadcasts to his later recitations further verify the genuine Southern pronunciations uttered by Williams in the Luke the Drifter recordings.[7]

The regional characteristics of the utterances, the lexical selection, and the scenes portrayed in these songs all speak to the Southern background of the artist. Yet these Luke the Drifter numbers are in some ways reminiscent of other American writers—those in the school of local color. Sarah Orne Jewett's *Country of the Pointed Firs* is very New England in tone yet communicates with people who have never visited her locale of Maine. Kate Chopin's *The Awakening* has a readership and impact far beyond its Louisiana bayou setting. Like these local color artists of literature, Hank Williams also is unapologetic and seemingly instinctive about presenting this regional tone. And like Chopin and Jewett, Williams's themes of humanity transcend the locale about which they were written and speak of the human condition. Williams is a regional artist, but like Faulkner before him and Garrison Keillor since, Williams is able to demonstrate the universal aspects of humanity which connect a diverse audience with the specific region being portrayed.

The fact that this unusual subset of Williams's canon retains its artistic merit makes these selections more than just oddities to analyze as Southern aural artifacts. The Luke the Drifter recitations operate as meaningful works of art, since the world is still plagued with the situations that they discuss.[8] Whether one finds "The Funeral" sad, hokey, sentimental, or chilling, a child's death and the parents' subsequent sense of loss is a universal human topic. The timeless themes of suffering and questioning are subjects that Williams addresses in this brief vignette. Similarly, personal upheavals conquered through faith and optimism, such as Uncle Bill's situation in "Everything's Okay," also conjure universals of human endurance.

Hank Williams's Luke the Drifter material is strikingly and unashamedly Southern in content and delivery. By examining these recitations, one can gain insights into the linguistic patterns not only of Williams, but of the region which produced this artist. However, perhaps the larger reason to examine his fiercely Southern terminology and pronunciation is to see how Williams uses these vivid portraits while simultaneously transcending their specific regional attributes. Through Luke, Williams shows listeners the universality of his own *pitchures* from life's other side.[9]

NOTES

1. Williams's business managers were also very much in favor of this separate moniker so as not to confuse the public with the two different types of music that this artist was offering. They did not want to risk alienating an audience apparently willing to buy most any record with the Hank Williams name attached to it (Cusic 1993:xx). MGM Records also had an interest in distinguishing the different musical styles that Williams was pursuing. If a record store ordered a large quantity of atypical Williams records that did not sell, it would decrease immediate profits for MGM and probably depress orders for the next release.

2. In spite of some confusion generated by his recording company, these 14 Luke the Drifter recordings, I stress, should not be considered interchangeable with the rest of the Williams canon. Although the Luke the Drifter selection "Ramblin' Man" was reissued under the Hank Williams name after the artist's death, this was done by the record company for the economic reasons of attempting to secure an additional hit single from their finite cache of recordings. And while Williams recorded "Help Me Understand" as an early demo (now available on the compact disc *Rare Demos: First to Last,* Country Music Foundation 067) the song was not then meant for release. It was not until Williams later created the Luke the Drifter persona that he re-recorded "Help Me Understand" and commercially issued this later version.

3. This Luke the Drifter subset should not be seen as merely a dumping ground for random songs or various experimental oddities which did not adhere to Williams's recognizable image. Bob Pinson, of Nashville's Country Music Foundation, notes that while several hours of Williams radio broadcast transcriptions remain unreleased, at no time does Williams introduce any but these selections as belonging to his Luke the Drifter repertoire (Pinson p.c. 1993). It is also clear that Williams did not have a cavalier attitude toward this material but took these recordings seriously. Several sources indicate that Williams was especially proud of these performances as they "required a special kind of showmanship to put across . . . some serious thoughts" to an audience (Caress 1979:129; Williams 1980:128).

4. Williams's Luke the Drifter persona often returns to the theme of words better left unsaid, such as in "Be Careful of Stones You Throw." Given my analysis of silence as an uncooperative speech act (Wilmeth 1992), I find it interesting that Williams urges a married individual to silence all complaints, or the "stones you throw" at your partner.

5. Although it contains no recitation, "Fly Trouble" provides an exception. It is a spoken selection recorded under the Hank Williams name, and is very close to the tenor of the upbeat Luke the Drifter material. "Fly Trouble" has the spoken structure of "Everything's Okay" and "No, No, Joe."

6. The five recording sessions that produced all of the Luke the Drifter material were held 1/10/1950, 8/31/1950, 12/21/1950, 6/1/1951, and 7/11/1952. It is again worthwhile to note that Williams did not begin to assume this persona until well into his recording career—not until after he was already a huge success and associated with a specific sound.

7. Among the principle sources for Williams's spoken articulations are *Hank Williams, Sr., Live at the Grand Old Opry* (MGM 1 5019), *On the Air* (Polydor 827 531), and *Rare Takes and Radio Cuts* (Polydor 823 695). The spoken "Apology" track is on *I Won't Be Home No More* (Polydor 833 752), and the *Health and Happiness Shows* are available on Mercury 314 517 862-2. In addition, a handful of unreleased radio interviews have circulated among audio recording collectors which shed further light on Williams's linguistic traits. None of these recordings indicates that Williams was, at any time, altering his natural speech for the Luke the Drifter performances.

8. These numbers continue to strongly influence performers in the country music genre as well. Dwight Yoakam, in a 1992 television interview, spoke about the specific influence of Williams's Luke the Drifter material on "Lonesome Roads," a song he wrote for his 1993 release, *This Time* (Reprise 45241-2).

9. The complete Luke the Drifter recordings can be assembled from the compact discs *Long Gone Lonesome Blues* (Polydor 831 633), *Hey, Good Lookin'* (Polydor 831 634), and the previously mentioned *I Won't Be Home No More*. One should obtain these audio recordings if interested in further study and not rely on published transcripts of Williams's lyrics. Curious inaccuracies exist in most printed versions of the recitations, particularly within transcribed copies of "The Funeral."

The Evolution of *Ain't* in African-American Vernacular English

Natalie Maynor

In spite of its status as one of the most easily recognized shibboleths in Modern English, *ain't* remains one of the least studied verb forms in the language. Language historians are still not sure whether *ain't* developed independently from *am not, are not, is not, have not,* and *has not* or whether it grew out of only one of these forms and then spread to the others. E. Payson Willard wrote in a 1936 letter to *Word Study,* "The word *ain't* is certainly a linguistic puzzle. It seems to have just popped up in the language out of nowhere in particular, with practically no recorded history" (2). The editor forwarded Willard's letter to Harold H. Bender, who responded in some detail but without claiming a definitive etymology of the word (2–3). Other brief discussions of the murky history of *ain't* include Raven McDavid's (1941) article in *Language,* Martin Stevens's (1954) article in *American Speech,* and Archibald Hill's (1965) article in *College English.* In spite of these useful discussions, however, the etymology remains unclear.

One problem in attempting to trace the history of *ain't* is, of course, its status as a form that is primarily colloquial. Dictionaries, including the *OED,* of necessity rely heavily on written documents. Thus, a clear picture of the evolution of a form like *ain't,* whether in its earliest stages or more recently, is hard to draw. Pointing out in his (1954) article that "very little work has been done to determine the origin of *ain't*" (196) and that "historical records have unfortunately not yet yielded any conclusive evidence of the origin of *ain't*" (201), Stevens adds, "There must be a rich field for research in the diaries and letters which record informal and colloquial English from the Middle English period on. I believe that these are the documents which may eventually provide us with the antecedent of Modern English *ain't.* But until such positive proof is found, if ever it will be, we must be satisfied with answers involving probabilities" (201). As far as I know, no one has done much with this potentially "rich field for research" yet. Because I already had tapes available for three generations of speakers of African-American Vernacular English (AAVE) in the Southern U.S., I decided to start with recent history and move backwards in an attempt to fill in some of the data gaps in the history of the use of *ain't* by various groups of English speakers. This paper is a very limited first step in the project.

The oldest generation I have looked at for this paper is represented by a group of former slaves, born between 1844 and 1861 and interviewed between 1935 and 1974. Most of the interviews were done in the early 1940s. Transcriptions of these tapes constitute the texts published in Bailey, Maynor, and Cukor-Avila's *The Emergence of Black English: Texts and Commentary* (1991). The second set of tapes contains interviews with African-American adults recorded in Texas and Mississippi in the early 1980s. Most of these speakers are elderly and have little formal education. The final tapes are of African-American twelve- and thirteen-year-olds, also recorded in Texas and Mississippi in the early 1980s. The socio-economic level of these speakers is roughly equivalent to that of the older speakers.[1]

All three groups of speakers used *ain't* for negative *be*, negative *have*, and in a few cases negative *do*. I have limited this paper to negative *be*, although I plan to examine negative *have* and *do* in a later study.

Table 1 shows the percentages of *ain't* for expected *is not*, *am not*, and *are not*. In counting the standard forms, I include both full forms and contractions but omit the few instances of full forms containing intervening words (e.g., "I am really not happy") since these do not provide a possibility for contraction. I similarly omit the relatively small number of negatives with zero forms.

Table 1: Negatives of *be* among three generations of AAVE speakers

1st person singular subject

	am not	is not	are not	isn't	aren't	ain't
slaves	3	0	0	0	0	9 (75%)
adults	36	0	0	0	0	44 (55%)
children	11	0	1	0	0	30 (71%)

3rd person singular subject

	am not	is not	are not	isn't	aren't	ain't
slaves	0	0	0	0	0	13 (100%)
adults	0	33	0	15	0	123 (72%)
children	0	13	0	3	0	89 (85%)

plural or 2nd singular subject

	am not	is not	are not	isn't	aren't	ain't
slaves	0	0	1	0	0	2 (67%)
adults	0	3	8	3	2	94 (85%)
children	0	0	1	0	0	33 (97%)

Totals: slaves 24/28 = 86%
         adults 261/361 = 72%
         children 152/181 = 84%

The person-number distribution of *ain't* among children in these tapes follows the same pattern exhibited by the children in the Washington, D.C., data published by Loman in his *Conversations in a Negro American Dialect* (1967). In Loman's transcripts, the children used *ain't* with first person singular subjects 75% of the time (9/12), with third person singular subjects 80% of the time (12/15), and with plural or second person singular subjects 100% of the time (4/4). Although the limited number of data from Loman's transcripts makes the specific figures of questionable value, his 75%, 80%, and 100% are strikingly similar to the 71%, 85%, and 97% I found in the taped speech of the Texas and Mississippi Children.

The small number of tokens for the former slaves also makes it impossible to reach any definite conclusions about the use of *ain't* in that generation. Most of the *ain'ts* used by the former slaves were for expected *hasn't* or *haven't*, a finding not unlike that made by other studies (e.g., Schneider 1989). Ignoring the slaves because of the limited number of tokens and looking at the other two groups, it appears that the use of *ain't* as negative of *be* is increasing and that it is the most frequently used negative of *be* in all person/number contexts. In every case, children use *ain't* more frequently than do adults. Age-grading is probably not a factor since the children are all at least twelve years old.

Nor is stylistic emphasis a factor. Speakers who used *ain't* most often tended not to use the contracted standard forms. If they alternated, it was usually between the full form and *ain't*. Those who used *isn't* or *aren't* seldom used *ain't*. It appears, then, that *ain't* is not used often in these groups of speakers for stylistic effect. There was no indication of a switch to *ain't* for emphasis by speakers who used standard forms more often than *ain't*; nor was there a switch to standard forms for emphasis by speakers who preferred *ain't*. Most speakers who used both forms switched between them smoothly. The following sentences from an elderly African-American female in Texas are typical of the kind of variation I found in all of the tapes: "Our prayer service now is not like it used to be. . . . It ain't like that now." Even in tag questions, a position that often favors *ain't*, standard forms alternate freely with *ain't*: "That's your heater, ain't it? . . . This is a porch, isn't it?"

One interesting point is that the Mississippi children used *ain't* more often than did the Texas children. Table 2 separates the children by state. Table 3 is included to show that the differences by state did not show up with the adult speakers.

Table 2: Use of *ain't* by African-American children
in Mississippi and Texas

1st person singular subject

	am not	is not	are not	isn't	aren't	ain't
MS	3	0	0	0	0	18 (86%)
TX	8	0	1	0	0	12 (57%)

3rd person singular subject

	am not	is not	are not	isn't	aren't	ain't
MS	0	0	0	2	0	38 (95%)
TX	0	13	0	1	0	51 (78%)

plural or 2nd singular subject

	am not	is not	are not	isn't	aren't	ain't
MS	0	0	0	0	0	8 (100%)
TX	0	0	1	0	0	25 (96%)

Totals: MS 64/69 = 93%
              TX 88/112 = 79%

Table 3: Use of *ain't* by African-American adults
in Mississippi and Texas

			1st person singular subject			
	am not	is not	are not	isn't	aren't	ain't
MS	7	0	0	0	0	4 (36%)
TX	29	0	0	0	0	40 (58%)

			3rd person singular subject			
	am not	is not	are not	isn't	aren't	ain't
MS	0	9	0	6	0	26 (74%)
TX	0	24	0	9	0	97 (75%)

			plural or 2nd singular subject			
	am not	is not	are not	isn't	aren't	ain't
MS	0	0	2	2	0	17 (81%)
TX	0	3	6	1	2	77 (87%)

Totals: MS 47/73 = 64%
TX 214/288 = 74%

The observed difference between the children must be approached with caution, however. Although both sets of children were interviewed in a variety of settings, including individual and group interviews, the Mississippi interviews included a larger percentage of time with no interviewer present. The children were given the tape recorder to carry with them to lunch and recess. How much they remained aware of the tape recorder during this time is not clear. It is likely, however, that these "unchaperoned" settings produced more natural speech. Such a circumstance would be similar to what Crawford Feagin noticed with her taping of teenagers in Anniston, Alabama. Feagin found a much higher percentage of *ain't* in conversations among a group of girls who were "chatting with each other during a sewing class while [she] stayed in a different part of the room" than she did in the more formal interviews with the same seven teenagers (1979:216).

Feagin's work in Anniston provides some comparable data on the use of *ain't* among white speakers.[2] Feagin's data, like mine, showed use of *ain't* for negative *be* by both children and adults in all person/number environments. There are, however, some differences in frequency of *ain't* usage. Feagin presented no data on or examples of the contexts favoring *ain't*.

In order to make Feagin's Alabama data more appropriately comparable with mine from Texas and Mississippi, the data below exclude her figures for upper-class speakers and present just working-class teenagers and adults. Interestingly, the older speakers Feagin recorded used *ain't* for negative *be* slightly more often than did the teenagers (48% compared with 41%). In her table of "Language change in Anniston area among working class" *ain't* is labeled "erratic," used 42% of the time by rural men over 60, 50% by rural women over 60, 41% by urban men over 60, 47% by urban women over 60, 61% by urban teenaged boys, and 19% by urban teenaged girls (1979:290). It is the large discrepancy between the use of *ain't* by the teenaged boys and teenaged girls that led to the label "erratic," of course. Although it is not surprising that teenaged girls would use fewer nonstandard forms than teenaged boys, a well-established pattern, the difference Feagin found between the boys and girls is surprisingly large. Feagin suggests that it is perhaps the association of *ain't* with masculinity and the desire of these teenaged girls to emphasize femininity that might have influenced their speech. Presumably the women over 60 would be less concerned with the issue of femininity.

Although I have not yet tabulated my data by sex, a partial analysis does not reveal significant differences between the males and females, especially the children. Part of the difference may be that the children in my taped speech samples were a few years younger than those in Feagin's study. Perhaps the girls have not yet reached the stage of emphasizing their femininity linguistically. Or perhaps this is a cultural difference between Feagin's white Alabamians and the African-American Texans and Mississippians. To my knowledge, the relationship between nonstandard forms and masculinity has not been identified as clearly in the culture of African-American working-class speakers as it has been among white working-class speakers. That is one area for future research.

Other gaps in the history of *ain't* remain to be filled. Resources such as *LAGS* and other atlas materials will help in completing the analysis of *ain't* for negative *be* and extending the analysis to its other uses in 20th-century U.S. speech. For earlier periods, examining records as close as possible to colloquial speech, such as diaries and journals, will help to depict the evolution of *ain't*.

NOTES

1. I wish to thank Guy Bailey for his help in collecting the examples of *ain't* in all of these tapes. We collected the tokens of *ain't* while working on other verb forms several years ago.

2. Although I plan to continue my project by analyzing tapes of white speakers in Texas and Mississippi and by looking at *The Tennessee Civil War Veterans' Questionnaires* for data from an earlier generation, I have compared my findings from the African-American speakers in Texas and Mississippi with Feagin's findings from white speakers in Alabama.

Auntie(-man) in the Caribbean and North America

Ronald R. Butters

Ten years ago, at the first LAVIS conference, Ruth Nix and I presented a paper on phonological and morphological variation in Wilmington, North Carolina (Butters and Nix 1986). I plan to return to this type of study to do real-time examination of linguistic change that Michael Montgomery stressed the need for in his presentation to open LAVIS II (see Montgomery, this volume). Nevertheless, the topic of the present paper raises important issues which I hope to see more prominently discussed among variationists, particularly those working on English in the South. First, unlike most of the other papers, mine is essentially Caribbean in subject matter, thus emphasizing the important fact that Southern English does not stop in Key West and Coral Gables nor is the language and culture of New-World slavery confined, even primarily, to the North American continent alone. Moreover, I take up a lexicographic topic unconnected with the *Dictionary of American Regional English*; DARE is a project of immense importance, but it should not be the exclusive focus of current attention for lexicographical study in the American South. Finally, my paper examines a historical linguistic question within the larger framework of social and cultural meaning and both involves and reflects the persistent repression of and discrimination against gay men and women throughout our history and our culture. In this sense, the paper reflects, in part, the growing new field of Gay Studies (or Queer Studies, as it is increasingly called). I hope that, ten years from now, at LAVIS III, even more papers on these topics will emerge.

Several years ago, when I was visiting St. Croix, United States Virgin Islands, Francis Smilowitz, a transplanted white New Jerseyite who earns his living as a charter-boat captain, said to me, "You know, down here they call you guys *anti-man*."

"Huh?" I said.

"*Anti-man*. You know. That's the term here for *gay*. Like *anti-aircraft* or *anti-Christ*. That's what they think about homosexuality in the Islands."

However right my friend may have been about the place of homosexuality in traditional Caribbean cultures, he was doubtless wrong in his folk etymology: the /anti/ of /antiman/ is clearly not the Greek prefix *anti-*; rather, it derives from *aunt* 'mother's sister' or 'father's sister'. The spelling of the following entry in Valls's Virgin Islands dictionary (1981) makes the etymology clear: "*auntie-man*: An effeminate man." A similar definition is found in Collymore's Barbados dictionary (1970): "*aunti-man* (Rare). A fussy, effeminate man. Perhaps better expressed by the patois *mamapoule*." Collymore does not have an entry for *mamapoule*, apparently because it is not found in English; cf. French *maman* 'mother' + *poule* 'hen'. However, Lise Winer (p.c. 8/9/93) reports that, in Trinidad and Tobago, *mamapoule* "is still reasonably common but means . . . [something] closer to today's U.S. *wuss*—I have never heard it used for a homosexual." The definitions, moreover, do not in themselves encompass the meaning that Smilowitz had in mind: at least from his cultural perspective (and mine) 'an effeminate man' is not the same thing as a homosexual man, and vice versa. Of course, neither Valls nor Collymore intended their works to be full-scale scholarly dictionaries. More important, neither of these two Caribbean lexicographers—and, for the most part, this would be true of their linguistic sources as well—was necessarily concerned with or knowledgeable about the subtleties of North American gender politics. It would be fair to conclude that no sharp semantic distinction existed for most speakers who had *auntie-man* in their vocabularies: homosexuality would be seen as a logical (though by no means inevitable) extension of the identity of an effeminate man, and general effeminacy of manner would be viewed as a likely quality of those men who are strongly inclined towards receptive same-sex sexual intercourse. In this respect, *auntie-man* is no different from such general English terms as *sissy* or *pansy*. 'Effeminacy', as the outward, constant, publicly visible behavioral trait, would be the primary semantic feature from which the secondary feature of 'homosexuality'—covert, intermittent, and private—could be suspected and hence derived. From such a cultural perspective, in fact, it is generally quite possible for an individual to commit overt acts of homosexual penetration without "being" homosexual himself, so long as 1) he is not effeminate in manner and 2) he is the sexual penetrator, not the one penetrated. The forbidden nature of such acts and the taboo nature of discussion of them further obscure any mental distinction between 'effeminate male' and 'homosexual'. Though homosexual acts historically must inevitably have taken place in the Caribbean as frequently as elsewhere in the world, the recent Western European and North American social construct 'homosexual person'—Francis Smilowitz's conception (and mine)—would scarcely have existed for most speakers.[1]

To date, the published scholarly record for *auntie-man* in the Caribbean virtually ends with Valls and Collymore (though see Yansen 1975, mentioned below). Stymied by the lack of published resources, I decided to poll a number of eminent scholars of Caribbean linguistics concerning their knowledge of the term and its provenience. As with Winer above, their personal responses (p.c.), with dates, are cited within my text. Surprisingly, of all the English-speaking locales I surveyed in this way, only Liberia remains as a place where it is reasonably certain that *auntie-man* is unknown, according to John Singler's report (p.c. 10/19/92); there *punk* (n.) and *sweet* (adj.) are the common colloquial terms for 'gay'.[2] Allsopp (p.c. 8/19/93) attests to its use throughout the Caribbean, though he says that *auntie-man* or *anti-man* is used to refer to "a man who behaves in effeminate ways . . . mainly in the East Caribbean" speech area; he cites the following from the files of the Caribbean Lexicography Project, of which he is the director:

> He well knew that they laughed at him behind his back and called him 'Auntie-man'. His wife had done that work until the fever which swept through the valley in 1855 had taken her away from him.
> [*Tales of Trinidad & Tobago*, C. R. Ottley, 1962, p. 37]

Holm (p.c. 12/16/85) acknowledges that *auntie-man* occurs in the Bahamas, even though he and his co-author left the term out of their Bahamian dictionary (Holm and Shilling 1982), perhaps because of its derogatory connotations and culturally sensitive nature. Holm also says that *auntie-man* occurs in Nicaragua (citing his own fieldwork there; see Holm 1978, 1983a) and in Guyana (citing Yansen 1975). According to Lise Winer (p.c. 8/9/93), *auntie-man* is known in Trinidad, but such a person "is usually a fussy, effeminate man. . . . It is rarely used for 'homosexual' and is in any case now dated, mostly used by people at least 60 years old." *Auntie-man* is not found in Cassidy and Le Page's Jamaica dictionary (1967), and Cassidy says (p.c. 2/86) that he has never heard the term in Jamaica, "though that doesn't prove more than that it is not common."[3] Ian Hancock (p.c. 1/17/86) also believes that "it is not [used] in Jamaica," asserting further that it is generally "not [found] in areas not influenced by French Creole." He cites *mamapúl* as the most common form for 'homosexual' in Creole French, but he lists "also *tantí* in, e.g., Trinidad." However, Allsopp (p.c. 8/19/93) reports that *auntie-man* in the sense 'male homosexual' "occurs in Jamaica and Belize (i.e., Western Caribbean) as well as in the Eastern Caribbean." He cites the following important evidence from the files of the Caribbean Lexicography Project (his source is given only as "Labour Spokesman, St. Kitts, June 1965"): "I read in your columns how the British House of Lords have legalised the disgusting act between consenting males. I hope our government will never recognize anty-men here." Considering the spelling, one wonders if this particular speaker does not share Smilowitz's etymological connection of *auntie-man* with the Greek prefix *anti-*. Further elaboration awaits the publication of Allsopp (forthcoming).

In sum, *auntie-man* with the meanings 'homosexual' and/or 'effeminate male' seems widespread in the English-speaking Caribbean, despite its absence from some of the published dictionaries and its marginalization in others. The survey evidence all suggests strongly that *auntie-man* began in the East Caribbean English-speaking area as a general term for 'effeminate male' and spread more recently into the rest of the Caribbean with the later sense 'homosexual'.

But what about *auntie-man*'s earlier etymological history in the Caribbean? The possibility that the term had origins in England itself seems very slim: the form *auntie-man* is not recorded anywhere outside the greater Caribbean. According to the *Oxford English Dictionary* (2nd ed.), the only early usage for *auntie* with any kind of relevant meaning was in the Renaissance sense 'prostitute', obsolete in England since the 18th century but in use at the time of the slave trade. It would certainly not be impossible for a term for 'prostitute' to evolve into a term for 'homosexual': some scholars have suggested a similar if questionable evolution for the term *gay* 'homosexual' from 'prostitute' to 'male prostitute' to 'homosexual male'; see, for example, Rawson (1981), s.v. *gay*.[4] But against this etymology is the fact that 'homosexual' seems to be only a secondary, later meaning for *auntie-man*, with 'effeminate male' being the older, primary meaning: the hypothetical psychological progression from 'prostitute' to 'effeminate male' (and THEN to 'homosexual') does not seem very likely. Ian Hancock (p.c. 1/17/86) sees *auntie-* as most likely a calque from French creole, citing *tanti* (from French *tante* 'aunt') with identical meaning(s) in Trinidad and "elsewhere" in French creoles. Lise

Winer (p.c. 8/9/93), however, reports having heard *tanty* in Trinidad only "as a widespread respectful term for an older woman . . .; I have never heard it used for a homosexual." Hancock's argument is etymologically powerful, in that *tante* has long had the slang meanings 'effeminate male' and 'homosexual' in France (see, e.g., DuBois 1960, s.v. *tante, tantine*). Although the presence of *auntie-man* in the Virgin Islands, Barbados, Nicaragua, and especially the Bahamas might be seen as running somewhat counter to the hypothesis of a French creole origin, Hancock's argument also has the virtue of explaining the apparent absence of the term in Liberia and its seeming recentness in Jamaica and the West Caribbean area.

As for 'homosexual' meanings for *auntie* in the 20th century elsewhere in North America, the story is probably something like this. According to a number of slang dictionaries, especially Lighter (1994–), the term *auntie* evolved from the basic 16th- and 17th-century meaning 'prostitute' into a more specialized 18th-century sense of 'procuress' and/or 'woman who keeps a brothel', ending up in the 20th century as a relatively rare slang term with the additional further specialized meaning 'prostitute up in years'. Furthermore, according to Lighter (1994–) the term developed in the 20th century, at least in the United States, in "disparaging" usage as a term for a 'middle-aged or elderly effeminate male homosexual'— "probably influenced" by the earlier set of meanings 'prostitute/procuress/ madame/ prostitute-up-in-years'. It seems to me that the French slang usage for *tante* (referred to above) may well also have been influential here.

The lexicographical entry given by Legman (1941) sums up this 'homosexual' usage: "*auntie : A derogatory term for a middle-aged or elderly homosexual. Also: *aunty*." Legman's asterisk indicates that this is a term which was a part of the gay subculture language—only members of the subculture would have understood it in this sense in the 1930s and 1940s. In fact, so it has probably remained, from the 1920s on into the 1970s. The term is, by the way, apparently dying out. At last report, according to Jesse T Sheidlower (p.c. 1/21/93), Lighter has been unable to find other than a dictionary citation for *auntie* in this sense after 1972. My own polling of young American gay men indicates that they are unfamiliar with the term today.

And there the story ends. So far as the current evidence indicates, the evolution of *auntie* 'elderly homosexual' has no connection to African-American Vernacular English (AAVE) in North America. The only nonstandard use of the term *auntie* in AAVE is one found in Southern States English in general: a kind of term of respect for any woman who is one's elder. In this sense, *auntie* is listed in the standard unabridged dictionaries and is particularly associated with 19th-century usage. Thus the possibility certainly seems remote that *auntie(-man)* should be listed with other terms (*goober, jazz, cooter, juke*) that indicate the influence of Caribbean language on the English of North America; the far greater likelihood is that the colloquial uses of the term *auntie* had a totally independent development in the two locales, even though it ended up with very similar semantic features.

So what have we learned from *auntie-man* and *auntie*? Two things.

First, the rather well-known principle is reinforced: not every pair of terms of highly similar meaning and form, however specialized, necessarily points to a common origin. *Aunti-man* in the Caribbean and *auntie* in homosexual subculture in the United States seem to be two completely independent developments.

Second, the term *auntie-man* and its creole French counterpart *tanti* are widespread in the Caribbean and may well be related, with the hypothesis that the former is a calque from the latter being most attractive. *Auntie-man* seems to have begun in the Eastern Caribbean with the general meaning 'effeminate male' and spread throughout the rest of the English-speaking region in recent times. Moreover, the semantic range of *auntie-man/tanti* is today somewhat fluid, dependent in part upon the beliefs and conceptions which the individual speaker has with respect to effeminacy, homosexual acts, and homosexual identities. In most cases, the term appears to be derogatory and denotes 'effeminacy'—or it at least connotes 'effeminacy' where 'effeminacy' is not central to its semantic domain. However, the extent to which *auntie-man* directly signifies 'homosexual male' is problematical, given that the subject itself is relatively taboo and generally associated culturally, although of course not scientifically, with effeminacy. Thus *auntie-man/tanti* is not merely of etymological and lexicographical interest, but the analysis of the terms should be helpful to those seeking a clearer picture of the construction of queer identities.

NOTES

1. Words such as *buggery* 'anal intercourse' and *bugger*, which lack connotations of effeminacy, have existed in English since medieval times to denote specific sexual acts and persons who perform them; but while such terms are today often associated with the social construct "homosexual person," the fact that they existed prior to the 20th century of course does not mean that the modern social construct "homosexual person" also existed in previous eras.

2. Cf. Holm and Shilling (1982), s.v. *fonk* 'to undergo anal intercourse; a male homosexual' and *punk* 'a male or female homosexual'.

3. According to Cassidy (p.c. 6/23/93), in Jamaica "the 'standard' patois (=creole) word is *batty-man*. *Batty*, hypocoristic for *bottom*, [ranges] from childhood usage to jocular and indecent adult use." Genevieve Escure (p.c. 7/28/93) likewise reports that [bate] and [bateman] are frequent in the Stann Creek area of Belize. See Cassidy and Le Page (1967), s.v. *bati-man*; see also Holm and Shilling (1982), s.v. *batty* 'buttocks', *batty-hole* 'anus', *boungy* 'to have anal sex'. Lise Winer (p.c. 8/9/93) reports that *batty-man* is rare in Trinidad and Tobago and "more likely now to be a recently imported Jamaicanism than a Tobago 'retention'." According to her, "the common straightforward local term for homosexual male is *buller*, verb *to bull*." (Cf. *bull-dike* 'lesbian' in the U.S.)

4. For a detailed analysis of the history of the term *gay*, see Butters 1995.

The South in *DARE*

Allan Metcalf

As a conference named Language Variety in the South bears witness, the South looms large in the American mind when we think of dialect. Now there is new evidence that this is not just the layperson's imagination, not just the revanchist pride of the defeated Confederacy or the literary effect of Uncle Remus, Faulkner, and Zora Neale Hurston. We can report that the South looms over the *Dictionary of American Regional English* as well.

Word by word, volume by volume, *DARE* (Cassidy and Hall 1985–) is confirming and challenging preconceived notions of the dialect regions of the United States, including the South. The first two volumes (I, A–C; II, D–H) contain some 21,700 headwords and 8,800 additional senses. Now that an index to the regional labels in these volumes is available (*Index* 1993), we can begin to see which states and regions loom large and which hardly loom at all in the distribution of that vast vocabulary. We can also see how distinct the regions are from one another, how much or how little continuity they have with their neighbors. In the context of LAVIS II, and because of the intrinsic interest, we can ask these questions particularly about the South.

The editors of *DARE* of course had to determine their regional labels in advance, so that they would be consistent in applying them as they wrote the individual entries. These regional labels were not arbitrary but were determined from sampling of the *DARE* material and from a century of previous studies of American dialects, especially the Linguistic Atlases. From 37 predetermined regional labels (Carver 1985:xxxii; *Index* 1993:xii–xv), and from all 50 states and the District of Columbia, the editors would in each case choose the label or combination of labels (with qualifiers) that best described the distribution of the word. Aided by the *Index*, we can now begin to find out how well these predetermined labels correspond with reality—reality being defined for our purposes as the tens of thousands of entries in those volumes, the mass of words that have been found to show regional variation. The accompanying tables show how the entries add up.

NUMBERS OF REGIONS

Where do these numbers come from? They are the results of thousands of individual decisions as the editors of *DARE* prepared the entries one by one. For the vocabulary elicited by the 1600-item *DARE* questionnaire, the editors had available to them lists and maps showing every one of the 1002 *DARE* communities throughout the nation where each term was attested (Carver 1985:xxiii). Additional evidence of regional distribution came from previous studies and *DARE*'s own reading program. Perhaps half of the evidence in the dictionary comes from the questionnaire and half from other sources.

It is not at all the case that every *DARE* entry or subentry has a regional label, and conversely, it is not the case that every entry or subentry has at most one regional label. There may be several different regional labels for a given entry—labels for different senses or different grammatical forms or even different pronunciations of a single entry. Furthermore, the limitation of the computer program used to make the *Index* means that not every instance of a regional label in an entry is recorded. Those labels that occur in the body of the entry rather than at the start are left out of the *Index*, as are those in the citations (*Index* 1993:viii).

But despite the uncertainty in exact numbers and the certainty of underreporting labels, much can be learned by the aggregate numbers of entries in the *Index*. And the very fact that the *DARE* editors were not trying to define dialect areas—that the numbers summarized in tables 1–6 are a wholly unintended byproduct of the editorial process—makes them especially interesting. In order to characterize the regional distribution of regional words, what regional labels do you need to use most?

The tables show a clear answer to this question. The areas labeled South and South Midland are by far the most frequently mentioned, and South leads them all. This means the deep South—the territory running from the eastern edge of Texas to the eastern edge of Maryland, while staying south of the northern boundaries of Louisiana, Mississippi, Alabama, and Georgia, and staying east of the western boundaries of South Carolina, North Carolina, Virginia, and Maryland. (For maps of these and the other *DARE* regions, see Carver 1985:xxxiii–xxxv.) As table 1 shows, this South is mentioned 1540 times in the *Index*—that is, the *Index* lists 1540 entries or senses in the first two volumes of *DARE* which include the regional label South. (To avoid prolixity, "entry" will henceforth be used to mean "entry or sense." Note that the counts of larger numbers are approximate.)

Table 1: Regions with more than 1000 entries

Region	Total	Exclusive[a]	Negative[b]	Exclusive with other regions (partial list)
South: eTX, c,sLA, c,sMS, c,sAL, c,sGA, FL, c,eSC, c,eNC, eVA, e,sMD	1540	316	33	+S Midl 851, Midl 151
South Midland: neOK, c,sMO, AR, nLA, sIL, sIN, sOH, KY, TN, nLA, nMS, nGA,sWV, wVA, wNC, wSC, nMD	1318	296	18	+South 851
Totals	2858	612	51	

[a] Exclusive: Labeled for that region (or part of that region) only.
[b] Negative: Labeled as *not* found in that region.

Next most prominent is the South's immediate neighbor, the South Midland, which begins to the west and north of the South proper; it extends as far west as northeastern Oklahoma and southwestern Missouri, as far north as the southernmost parts of Illinois, Indiana, and Ohio, and as far east as eastern Maryland. This South Midland is a regional label in 1318 entries in the first two volumes of *DARE*.

As the remaining tables make clear, no other label is used even half as much as South or South Midland. In other words, *DARE* very prominently displays the vocabulary of those two areas.

Or are these two prominent regions really just one? The argument that Midland is something of an artifact, and that what has been labeled Midland is generally an extension of South (or North), finds support in the figures here. (The argument was presented at length in Carver 1987, itself based on *DARE* materials, and was seconded, with statistical analysis and a convenient historical synopsis, in Davis and Houck 1992; but see Frazer in this volume.) While South and South Midland are included in regional labeling far more often than any other terms, they are not so often the exclusive regional labels for an entry. Only 316 times is a *DARE* entry labeled South and nothing else, and only 296 times is an entry exclusively labeled South Midland. If only exclusive labels are considered, South and South Midland have roughly the same degree of magnitude as the West, which is the exclusive label for 420 entries; New England, the exclusive label for 387; North, 321; Southwest, 222, and Northeast, 185 (table 2). By this measure, the South and South Midlands are merely equals among the prominent dialect regions of the country.

But what makes them again uniquely prominent is that the combination of South and South Midland is used as the sole label 851 times, twice as often as any other exclusive label. Of all the possible regions or combinations of regions to label an entry, South and South Midland is by far the most prevalent, the most real in terms of realizations.

The North Midland appears to be even less of a distinctive label than the South Midland. Only 8 of the 255 entries labeled North Midland have only that one regional label; 151 of them are labeled North as well. And the simple term Midland, attested 323 times, is exclusive only 76 of those times; it is conjoined with South almost exactly twice as often, 151 times to be exact.

LOW RECOGNITION

Perhaps just as striking as the instances of high numbers are those of the unexpectedly low. There was nothing to prevent Southern-related regions like Central Atlantic, Middle Atlantic, Atlantic, Southeast, the Ozarks, West Midland, Central, the Mississippi Valley, Inland South, and so on (table 3) from being mentioned hundreds of times—nothing, that is, except the absence of sufficient entries that could be characterized with those labels. It is surprising, for example, that the Ozarks with their fabled linguistic distinctiveness account for so few entries—just 32, and only 9 not in conjunction with some other region. Most of the Ozarks vocabulary is subsumed in the South Midland region.

Table 2: Regions with 100–700 entries

Region	Total	Exclusive[a]	Negative[b]	Exclusive with other regions (partial list)
North: WA, OR, nID, MT, nWY, ND, nSD, MN, nIA, WI, nIL, MI, nIN, nOH, nPA, NY, nNJ, Neng	624	321	11	+N Midl 151
West: wND, wSD, wNE, wKS, wOK, wTX, & all points west	599	420	15	
New England: CT, RI MA, VT, NH, ME	550	387	16	
Northeast: NEng, NY, nPA, NJ	332	185	24	
[c]**Midland:** NMidl, SMidl, DC	323	76	5	+South 151, North 15
Southwest: sCA, AZ, NM, OK, TX	259	222	0	
North Midland: NE, sSD, c,sIA, cIL, cIN cOH, nWV, c,sPA, nMD, nDE, sNJ	255	8	2	+North 151
[c]**South Atlantic:** FL, GA, SC, NC	188	81	8	
[c]**Appalachians:** neAL, nGA, wSC, eTN, wNC, eKY, WV, wVA, wMD, cPA	161	105	14	(sAppalachians 73)
[c]**Gulf States:** eTX, LA, MS, AL, FL	100	29	3	+S Atl 25
Totals	3391	1834	98	

[a] Exclusive: Labeled for that region (or part of that region) only.

[b] Negative: Labeled as *not* found in that region.

[c] Southern-related

Table 3: Southern-related regions with fewer than 80 entries

Region	Total	Exclusive[a]	Negative[b]	Exclusive with other regions (partial list)
Central Atlantic: sNJ, ePA, DE, eMD, DC, eVA	78	14	3	
Middle Atlantic MD, VA, NC, Sc	76	27	2	
Atlantic: ME, NH, VT, MA, RI, CT, NY, NJ, PA, DE, MD, DC, VA, NC, SC, GA, FL	65	36	6	
Southeast: MS, AL, TN, S Atl	51	40	3	
Ozarks: nwAR, swMO, neOK	32	9	0	+sAppalachians 13
West Midland: Midland except sNJ, sPA, DE, MD, DC	28	4	3	+South 5
Central: AR, OK, MO, KS, NE	27	2	1	
Lower Miss. Valley: LA, MS, AR, wTN, wKY, sMO, sIL	25	5	3	
Mississippi Valley: LA, MS, AR, wTN, wKY, MO, IL, IA, WI, MN	23	13	0	
Miss. River, East of	20	19	0	
Delmarva: DE, eMD, eVA	17	12	0	
East	14	12	0	
Inland South: MS, AL, TN, KY	13	2	1	
Miss.-Ohio Valleys: OH, KY, IN, IL, MO, IA, WI, MN	13	5	2	
Chesapeake Bay	9	8	0	
Ohio Valley	9	0	0	
Totals	500	208	24	

[a] Exclusive: Labeled for that region (or part of that region) only.
[b] Negative: Labeled as *not* found in that region.

The results are similar for non-Southern regions. There are few entries overall, and much fewer with exclusive labeling, for the North Central, Great Lakes, Pacific Northwest, Pacific, Inland North, North Atlantic, Northwest, and Upper Midwest, for example (table 4). Even apart from *DARE,* some of these areas have been intensively studied (e.g., Allen 1973–76), so it is not possible to account for the low numbers on grounds of insufficient material. The regional vocabulary of American English simply seems not to fall often into those patterns.

Even with 30,000 entries and senses now published in *DARE,* some labels scarcely have been used at all, as the bottom parts of tables 3 and 4 indicate. Among Southern-related regions (table 3), only 17 entries, 12 exclusively, are labeled for Delmarva; only 13, 2 exclusively, for the Inland South; only 13, 5 exclusively, for the Mississippi-Ohio Valleys. (Carver 1987:169 acknowledges the Inland South as "merely a minor subdivision of Southern speech.")

Table 4: Non-Southern regions with fewer than 80 entries

Region	Total	Exclusive[a]	Negative[b]
North Central: OH, KY, IN, IL, WI, MI	78	11	3
Great Lakes: MN, MI, WI, nIL, nIN, nOH, nwPA, nwNY	63	28	0
Pacific Northwest: nCA, OR, WA	56	39	0
Pacific: CA, OR, WA	55	30	8
Inland North: North except NEng	54	14	3
North Atlantic: NEng, seNY, nNJ	47	26	2
Northwest: WA, OR, ID (MT, WY)	47	23	3
Upper Midwest: ND, SD, NE, MN, IA	39	5	3
Rocky Mountains: wCO, UT, NV, WY, ID, MT	19	1	5
Plains States: KS, eCO, NE	12	5	2
Upper Mississippi Valley: nMO, c,nIL, IA, WI, MN	10	4	0
Desert Southwest: NM, AZ, seCA	8	8	0
Mississippi River, West of	5	4	0
Allegheny Mountains	1	0	1
Totals	494	198	30

[a] Exclusive: Labeled for that region (or part of that region) only.

[b] Negative: Labeled as *not* found in that region.

Among non-Southern regions (table 4), only 19 entries are labeled for the Rocky Mountains, only 1 exclusively; only 12 for the Plains States, 5 exclusively; only 10 for the Upper Mississippi Valley, 4 exclusively; and only 8 for the Desert Southwest, although all of those are exclusive. The Mississippi may link commerce, but it cuts across dialect regions, as indeed we would expect from the general north-south gradation of dialect in the United States.

Some of the lowest numbers among regional labels in tables 3 and 4 may be accounted for by their absence from the official list of *DARE* labels (Carver 1985:xxxii). So East of Mississippi River appears in just 20 entries and West of Mississippi River in just 5; East is in just 14 entries (and none after the letter D; the editors are systematically avoiding it now); Chesapeake Bay and Ohio Valley appear just 9 times each, while Allegheny Mountains is a nonce label, actually exclusionary, in the phrase 'east of Allegheny Mts'. Since these terms were not on the official list, it implies significance that they were used at all. If they had been on the list, they might have appeared more frequently.

Still, these unplanned exceptions aside, it remains striking that 24 of the 37 original regional labels are used in fewer than 80 *DARE* entries each, and that the 936 total occurrences of those 24 labels amount to considerably less than the 1540 of the South alone or the 1318 of the South Midland. Likewise, the 363 total exclusive labelings for those 24 less-used labels are dwarfed by the 851 for the combined South and South Midland.

Yet another kind of geographical distribution considered in *DARE* appears even less often in its entries. This is labeling having to do with terrain or population: 'urban', 'rural', 'coastal', and 'mountain'. Carver (1985:xxx–xxxi) discusses these and displays their distribution in a map. In actual *DARE* labels, however, these terms turn out to be extremely rare: 13 urban, 19 rural, 1 coastal, 0 mountain. The paucity of these labels suggests that contiguity is more significant than terrain, at least in the *DARE* vocabulary.[1]

STATE APPEARANCES

In addition to the larger regions, every one of the 50 states is named in a label at least once in the first two volumes of *DARE*. However, the states are not nearly as prominent as the more prominent of the regions; in numbers they match more closely the two dozen less frequently cited regions. This is perhaps not so surprising, since state boundaries are rarely linguistic ones, and entries characteristic of particular states are usually subsumed in larger regions.

Texas leads Southern states with mention in 125 total entries, and in exclusive labels Louisiana, with its distinctive French heritage, leads with 85. (Carver 1987:137–43 writes of the "Delta South layer" encompassing two-thirds of that state.) But balancing the perhaps expected prominence of Texas and Louisiana in table 5 is the unexpected insignificance, at the heart of the Deep South, of Mississippi and Alabama. And there are two border states, Delaware and Missouri, with even fewer mentions.

Of the non-Southern states (table 6), isolated Hawaii not surprisingly has both the greatest number of mentions and the greatest number of exclusive uses. California, perhaps surprisingly, is next most prominent; its 77 distinctive terms reflect the state's distinctive natural environment and inhabitants as well as its Spanish-language heritage. Pennsylvania owes its prominence in the list to the influence of Pennsylvania German (for which the *Index* has 71 entries). But far more typical are the states mentioned fewer than 10 times.

Overall, there are about four times as many regional labels as there are state labels. The ratio is slightly more than 4:1 for total labels, 7243 to 1613, and slightly less for exclusive labels, 2852 to 771. The South by itself has almost as many citations (1540) as all 50 states together (1613), and the South-South Midland combination has more exclusive occurrences (851) than those of all the states (771).

Table 5: Southern and nearby states

State	Total	Exclusive[a]	Negative[b]	Exclusive with other regions (partial list)
Texas	125	57	0	+LA 8, SW 8, OK 4, Sth-S Midl 4, Central 3, Sth 3
Louisiana (Plus 2 New Orleans)	110	85	0	+TX 8, MS 2
South Carolina (Plus 2 Charleston)	84	36	0	+S Atl 4, S Atl-Gulf 2, Gulf States 2
Virginia	71	32	0	+NC 6, MD 5, KY 2, NEng 2, S Atl 2
Kentucky	56	18	0	+TN 7, S Midl 6, VA 2
Florida (Plus 1 Palm Beach)	51	30	0	+GA 11, S Atl 2
Georgia	50	9	0	+SC 19, FL 11, S Atl 2
North Carolina	40	16	0	+VA 6, SC 3
Maryland (Plus 4 Baltimore)	36	12	1	+VA 5, PA 1, DE 1
Tennessee	20	5	0	+KY 7
Arkansas	17	2	0	+TX 1
West Virginia	14	4	1	+KY 1, PA 1
Mississippi	9	1	0	+LA 2
Alabama	8	3	0	
Delaware	5	0	0	+MD 1
Missouri	4	1	0	
District of Columbia	0	0	0	
Totals	700	311	2	
(Plus 9 for cities)				

[a] Exclusive: Labeled for that region (or part of that region) only.
[b] Negative: Labeled as *not* found in that region.

Table 6: Non-Southern states

State	Total	Exclusive[a]	Negative[b]	Exclusive with other regions (partial list)
Hawaii	133	127	0	+CA 3
California	123	77	0	+HI 3, OR 2, NV 2
Pennsylvania	113	49	2	+NY-NJ 6, NY 5
(Plus 1 Philadelphia)				
New York	87	25	0	+NEng 11, NJ-PA 6, PA 5, Neast 5, NJ 3, CT 2
(Plus 35 New York City, 2 Brooklyn)				(+Sth 2, Long Island 2)
Maine	66	40	0	+NEng 11, North 2
Massachusetts	44	29	0	+RI 4, NEng 4
(Plus 3 Nantucket, 2 Boston)				(+NEng 2)
Alaska	46	34	0	+NW 6, PacNW 3, N 2
Wisconsin	42	18	1	+MI 5, MI-MN 4, MN 2
New Jersey	33	10	0	+PA-NY 6, NY-NYC 4, PA 3
Michigan	30	8	1	+WI 5, WI-MN 4, scattered West 2
Ohio (Plus 1 Cincinnati)	27	6	0	+NEast 4, PA 2, IL-IN 2
Oklahoma	18	1	0	+TX 5, KS-TX 3
Rhode Island	15	2	0	+MA 4
Minnesota	14	1	0	+MI-WI 4, WI 2
Illinois (Plus 3 Chicago)	11	2	1	
Indiana	11	1	0	
Arizona	10	4	0	
Connecticut	10	4	0	+NY 2
Colorado	10	3	0	
Kansas	9	2	0	+OK-TX 3
North Dakota	9	0	0	
Utah	7	5	0	
Oregon	6	1	0	+CA 3
Washington	6	1	0	
New Mexico	5	2	0	
Vermont	4	2	0	
New Hampshire	4	1	0	
Nebraska	4	1	0	
Nevada	4	1	0	+CA 2
Wyoming	4	0	0	
Montana	3	1	0	
Iowa	2	1	0	
South Dakota	2	0	0	
Idaho	1	1	0	
Totals	913	460	5	
(Plus 47 for cities)				

[a] Exclusive: Labeled for that region (or part of that region) only.
[b] Negative: Labeled as *not* found in that region.

CAUTIONS

Are we to conclude, then, that the conjoined South-South Midland is indeed, by a factor of two, linguistically more prominent than any other single region; that this territory has more in the way of distinctive regional terminology than any other part of the country? Are we to conclude that, among the states, Texas and Louisiana are dialectally distinctive, while Alabama and Mississippi (not to mention Delaware and Missouri, and many other states outside of the South) blend inconspicuously into larger regions?

The numbers would indicate all that, but I must acknowledge some necessary cautions.

First, these numbers are necessarily preliminary, representing as they do less than half of the complete *DARE*. There is no reason to assume that the relative balance of regions will shift in later volumes, but it is possible to imagine anomalies, such as words from Hawaiian in Hawaii, or from Spanish in the Southwest, that might cluster at different letters of the alphabet and thus alter the final proportions.

Second, these labels are just for lexical items; they are not phonological or grammatical, although phonological and grammatical variants are labeled in some entries. There is no necessary concurrence between lexical variation and other kinds, though it stands to reason (and experience) that a linguistic community distinctive in one way might well be in another.

Third, the prominence of some regions and the insignificance of others could be in part an artifact of previous scholarship. Indisputably, some regions have been more thoroughly studied for their dialects than others. The South, in particular, has been intensively studied; for no other region is there a separate published bibliography (McMillan and Montgomery 1989, with nearly 3,000 entries), or for that matter conferences like LAVIS I and LAVIS II. Has there ever been a conference on Language Variety in the North?

Fourth, the numbers given here can be only approximate. For one thing, they do not differentiate among degrees of exclusivity, even though *DARE* does with its qualifiers 'chiefly' and 'especially' (Carver 1985:xxx–xxxii)—and occasional others like 'scattered'. More important, the restriction of the *Index* to what the computer program could retrieve in the usage labels (not in the entries) means that a considerable number of regional designations have necessarily been overlooked. Thus, for example, *copse* is not noted under North or North Midland in the *Index* because its designation 'scattered, but chiefly Nth, N Midl' is given in the middle of the citations. It would have been redundant to put this label at the start of the entry—but that meant the Index program did not pick it up.

Fifth, the labels do not distinguish degrees of prominence or frequency of use. A rare or obsolete word counts just as much as a widely used one, yet it has less impact on the region's sense of distinctiveness. Carver notes, for example (1987:240), that the *DARE* terms distinguishing southern California "have little currency and can be heard only occasionally," so it is not surprising that they create little sense of a distinctive dialect region.

And sixth, the vocabulary entered in *DARE,* like that of all dictionaries, is selective. The widely regional is better captured in *DARE* than the purely local, as one might expect from the "looser mesh" of communities surveyed compared to the Linguistic Atlases (Cassidy and Hall 1985–,I:xiii) and as attested in *DARE* volumes 1 and 2 by the relative paucity of individual state labels and the even rarer mention of cities. (As tables 5 and 6 show, New York is the only city with any appreciable number of indexed labels.) Those who turn to the *Index* to see what vocabulary distinguishes their state or locality are likely to be disappointed at the small number of entries. With its nationwide survey, *DARE* was assured of noticing most of the more broadly distributed regional vocabulary, but local items often fell through the net.

So there are reasons to doubt the reality of the picture these numbers present. But there are reasons to believe it, too. Evidence for the significance of these *Index* numbers is provided by the surprising variation in use of the regional and state labels available to the editors of *DARE.* As noted above, the Mississippi Valley, with its upper and lower branches, hardly manifests itself, despite arguments one could make a priori for its cultural importance. The Ozarks, known for distinctive speech, make a minimal showing in *DARE* volumes 1 and 2. Nor are North Central, the Inland North, or the Great Lakes particularly prominent. Among the states, would anyone have predicted Alabama and Mississippi to be so inconspicuous, compared to Georgia, South Carolina, and Florida?

The *Index* is like the Hubbell telescope when first launched into space: not yet entirely in focus but, despite a blurry lens, providing depth of vision much greater than previously possible. This is because *DARE,* the object at which it looks, is so much more substantial than previous studies of regional variation in vocabulary. No one claims that *DARE* records everything, but no one can dispute that *DARE* records many times more items than its predecessors.

There is also reasonable hope that, by the time the last volume of *DARE* is published with a final full version of the *Index,* the accuracy and completeness of that *Index* will be refined to a sharp focus, just as has been accomplished with the Hubbell. As one who is partly responsible for the current *Index,* I hope readers will not be shy in suggesting how the focus can be improved.

NOTE

1. Carver introduced these labels not with the expectation that they would be prominent in the dictionary but simply to alert the reader to distortions in the *DARE* map required by population density and crowding. For example, editor Joan Houston Hall points out (personal communication), there wasn't room on the *DARE* map's southern California coast for all the coastal southern California communities, so the detailed map on p. xxxi shows how some of them have been shifted inland. "Similarly, the symbol for mountains helps keep the reader aware that wSC should really be in line with wNC and nwGA. These weren't intended as labels." So perhaps it is impressive that they showed up at all.

DARE: Some Etymological Puzzles

Frederic G. Cassidy

The etymologies of words in dead languages are like other archeological remains. If they remain at all, they may be no more than shards which one attempts to fit together in some reasonable way on the assumption that before the vessel was broken the clay fragments together formed an *amphora* or a *kylix*—a usable, structured thing. The fragments of a language, individual words, can be treated following the same assumption: that they owe their forms to underlying rules, that if the history of their formation can be traced, these rules can become known, and known rules can then aid in tracing like formations. It is a cybernetic process. Our work in producing the *Dictionary of American Regional English* (*DARE*) has raised a number of puzzling questions, not all of which we have been able to solve. They illustrate some of the etymologists' problems. A number of them relating to the Southern United States are especially of interest.

DARE depends more heavily on direct field collecting than do other dictionaries. Over a five-year period eighty fieldworkers were sent out to 1002 communities in 50 States, using questionnaires with set questions. The fieldworkers had had training in phonetics and were expected whenever appropriate to transcribe in IPA characters the informants' replies. They also made tape-recorded interviews whenever the informants did not refuse. Even so, when it comes to editing entries for the dictionary, some responses remain uncertain. Is the transcription accurate? Did the fieldworker mishear or misrecord? Did the informant have a peculiar pronunciation? Did the word appear in the taped record?

Fade barn was one poser—what is a *fade barn*? Since the word was picked up in tobacco country, we guessed it might be the kind of barn—a curing barn—in which green tobacco leaves are hung to dry until they are ready to be stripped and made into "piles" for marketing. This seemed a reasonable guess. So Joan Hall queried Dennis Rogers, a columnist for the Raleigh *News and Observer*, who queried his readers. The response was instantaneous and unanimous: *fade barn* was the North Carolina farmer's pronunciation of *feed barn*, and everybody knows what *that* is. For *DARE*, the fieldworker's record was a "oncer"; the word did not appear on the audiotape, so it could not be checked that way. Our etymological guess died aborning, and *fade barn* did not make it into *DARE*.

One of our botanical puzzles, the *bettywood*, made it into Volume I, but the identity of the tree still eludes us. It is a story of frustrations. There are plenty of written occurrences of the *word* from 1786 forward, when it appears in survey books of Bourbon County, Kentucky, and in other documents. It is also still remembered by the older people of the region. But present-day botanists and foresters do not know it: it has evidently died out from official and scientific use. In the hope of finding a living *bettywood tree* known by that name, we sent our investigator, a native of that area, three times, to find a tree or the remains of one, for they had been used repeatedly as "corner trees" from which surveyors made their measurements. If we could get a piece of the wood, we thought, it could be identified at the U.S. Forest Products Laboratory in Madison. Our investigator got on the trail of several trees, but the original surveyors' trees had been cut down when the corner was incorporated into a public park. Then we heard of another certainly identified pair of trees and sought them out only to find that they had been cut down and bulldozed to make a car park for a motel. When it came time to go to press with Volume I, we had to satisfy ourselves with an unsolved puzzle. One possibility still is the genus name *Betula*, the birch, a tree which figures in much north European legend and folklore. In Irish this tree *Betula alba* is named *beith* or *beithe*. Could some Irish-speaking surveyor have brought it to Kentucky in the 18th century? Not impossible, but uncompelling. According to Cassidy's law, possibilities, no matter how many, do not constitute a probability. On *bettywood* we are left with the lesser likelihood of *buttonwood*, a common northeastern U.S. name for sycamore. We have not given up the hope of identifying the true bettywood tree and the correct etymology. Perhaps it may appear in the Supplement, Volume VI. Does anyone here personally know a genuine *bettywood* tree?

A different kind of problem is one that depends on the merging or blending of similar forms and meanings. This time we have clearly recorded evidence; the question is, which of the similar forms were actually blended. The phrases are *I have a mind to* and *I'm a mind to*—that is, one has a strong inward urging or impulsion or temptation to *do* something. *I have a mind to bat your ears in* or *I'm a mind to buy one of them contraptions*. The verbs *have* and *be* are in competition here. Starting as we normally do with standard-English assumptions or hidden prepossessions, we may assume that *have* is the "right" form, that the phrase is simply *have a mind to*, and that *I'm a mind to* is some sort of odd variant. What kind of variant? Perhaps the original form was *I am of a mind to*—properly standard—and the *of* dropped out and *I am* was condensed in normal pronunciation to *I'm*. Result: *I'm a mind to*. Then we check the phrase in Wright's [1898–1905] *English Dialect Dictionary* and find a single word *aminded* glossed as 'willing, disposed, inclined' with examples from seven counties of Southern and Southeastern England, the earliest dated 1876. This word could certainly have been brought over to the American colonies. The *-ed* was very commonly dropped colloquially—which would produce *amind* as in *I'm amind to*, with American examples from 1805 forward. No need to look for *have*. But how about what we took to be the present standard form *I have*—or *I've a mind to*? It turns out to be a separate phrase, similar in meaning but of quite different syntax and recorded later. The *Oxford English Dictionary* (*OED*) lists *minded* (verb, sense 5b), glossing it with 'have a mind to' as the modern English equivalent, but takes it to be a participial form when it is actually the noun *mind* plus *OED* -*ed* suffix-2. *To be minded to* is thus quite separate syntactically from *have a mind to*, and their etymologies are different. The *be* form has historical priority over the *have* form. Finally, could *of* in "be *of* a mind to" be a phonetic variant of *have*? Phonetically possible, but morphosyntactically not so since it comes only after *be*, not after *have*. What etymology do we finally come out with? We have to recognize two distinct phrases built around the word *mind*, as verb and noun: "I'm a mind to"—*am* + adjective *amind* + *to*, and a later *have* + *a* + *mind* + *to*. The senses are virtually the same, and both phrases may equally be broken by inserted adjectives: *good*, *great*, and others:

"I'm a good mind to—" or "I have a great mind to—." They not only differ as to syntax, and historically, but they also differ etymologically, as we have tortuously winkled it out.

The next word is *bobbasheely*. We first saw this in print in William Faulkner's *The Reivers*. It seemed a strange kind of word, but Faulkner knew his Mississippi folk speech (Brown 1976). Then it turned up in one of our field records from Texas in both noun and verb forms. Finally Joan Hall dug up the etymology: it is from Choctaw Indian *itibapishili*, meaning 'my brother' or, more literally, 'one who suckled at the same breast', what in English is a 'milk brother', in French 'frère de lait'. Adopted into American English, *bobbasheely* was used as a greeting among close friends. What is interesting is that in American English the noun has also become a verb. Faulkner uses it to mean 'to associate with or move along with someone in a friendly fashion'. It is still extant, a genuine loanword from Choctaw, of which there are not many. In it we have an etymology in the strict sense, the source or origin of the word itself.

Another word with Indian associations is *appaloosa*. Widely known for a type of horse developed in the West with mottled or blotched skin, *appaloosa* is also the name of a large spotted catfish of the lower Mississippi River country. Though the current form of the word is the same for both horse and fish, the areas of use are so far apart and the early recorded forms are so different that we felt it wise on etymological grounds to list the two separately in *DARE*. The appaloosa horse has been locally named *appaloose*, *appaloosus*, *appaloosy*, *appalouchi*, and *palouse*. The distinctive breed was developed by the Palouse Indians of the Palouse River area of southeastern Washington State, and this is clearly the tribal name. The spelling of the word sometimes shows French influence, possibly from the coureurs de bois and voyageurs who came early to the region. Final *-a* varying with final *-i* is parallel to the sound in *Missoura* and *Cincinnata*, as said by speakers of their regions, varying with *Missouri* and *Cincinnati*, except that in *appaloosa* the *-i* forms lost the contest. Influence has been suggested from French *pelouse*, a meadow. Though this brings up charming pictures of these mottled horses grazing happily in the great West, it is surely a false etymological trail. *Palouse* is an Indian tribal name.

As for the Gulf States catfish, that may be connected with the southern Louisiana *Opelousas* Indians, known from at least the 18th century, a small tribe ultimately absorbed into others. Hodge enters the name with initial *O*: *Opelousa*, but Schoolcraft chose initial *A*, which may show either accidental or intentional identification with the western *Palouse*. It is hard to guess which. The meaning of *Opelousa*, given as 'black above' (Hodge 1930:II.139/2), is puzzling for both the Indians and the mottled catfish. There may be a clue in the Choctaw word *apolusa* 'to be daubed'. Can these two tribal names, *Opelousas* and *Palouse*, be in some way connected? The tribes' living so far apart makes us suspect that the similarity of *Opelousas* and *Palouse* is accidental. On the other hand, Choctaw, originally a southeastern language, had a word *apolusa* meaning 'to be daubed', and from Choctaw was developed a trade jargon known as Mobilian (remember Mobile, Alabama), which became widespread in the south and was taken west. It is not impossible that this word *apolusa*, to be daubed, first applied to the mottled or spotted catfish, was taken into Mobilian Jargon, carried into the southwest and Palouse territory, and there applied to the conspicuously spotted horse, a breed for which the Palouse Indians are credited. Studies of Mobilian Jargon now in progress may shed some light on this question. Further evidence may perhaps linger in Spanish records of the Southwest, the Palouse Indians, and their horse-breeding activities. But for *DARE* I the etymological question had to remain open.

One of the most difficult phrases to trace to its source has been *dead cat on the line*. Not because of lack of evidence, or because it is little known: quite the contrary. We have been offered many explanations, some of them quite imaginative. But *cat* and *line* have so many different senses: which is the right one? The phrase became widespread, especially among Blacks, early in this century to mean that something underhanded or immoral was going on, producing a conspicuous stench. It was especially spread when used in a sermon of a black preacher, the Reverend Gates, which was so much admired that it was recorded on an old 78 r.p.m. record. The punch line—which I myself heard repeated by a black woman entertainer in New York City in the 1980s—is, "If a child don't favor its father some way, they's a dead cat on the line." *Favor*, of course, means 'resemble', and the *dead cat* is some other man, lying low.

This is certainly the most lively of the *dead cats* offered in various explanations, including some ingenious and some ingenuous ones. And as *cat* can be taken either literally or metaphorically, so can *line*. We have been assured that the line was a railroad line, and the cat was killed by a train. It is also understood as a cat which climbed the pole to a power line and was electrocuted. Or else the line is a telephone line, a party line, with someone listening in secretly. The secret listener is of course the dead cat on the line.

Sifting out the many explanations we were given, a number of which are presented in *DARE*, we finally considered the most plausible to be *cat* as a catfish and *line* as a trotline in a bayou or similar body of water. If someone sees a trotline with a dead catfish that has not been collected by the fisherman who owns it, there's literally a dead cat on the line, and that signals some kind of trouble back home. Also, the fish stinks. One white informant told me that his father was so taken with the Reverend Gates's use of the phrase, that he memorized the entire sermon from the phonograph record.

My final example is an expression that had a considerable vogue in sports broadcasting early in 1991: *Katie, bar the door*! There is no question of the meaning: it is a signal of alarm, accurately translated as 'All hell is about to break loose'. We have appealed for help in *NADS* (the newsletter of the American Dialect Society) and in *American Notes and Queries* but without much response. It seems pretty clearly to refer to the old story of the assassination in 1437 of King James I of Scotland. The King was in an outbuilding, unarmed, accompanied only by the Queen and her ladies among whom was Katherine Douglas. When the attack came, someone shouted, "Katie, bar the door!" But the murderers had removed the bar, so Katie Douglas thrust her arm through the staples and held on. The men were too strong for her, her arm was broken, and though the King defended himself, he was killed. However, the heroic deed won Katie the nickname of *Barlass*, the *lass* who *barred* the door, and her praise was sung throughout Scotland. Now, the etymological question. How did this phrase come to be used in the United States in the late 20th century? My best guess at present, based on no hard evidence but, I think, a reasonable surmise, is that *Katie bar the door* was a line, perhaps the refrain, of a popular song or ballad composed at the time of James's murder, that it was brought to America by Scottish immigrants, as so many ballads were, and that it lingered, most likely in Appalachia. Unfortunately, I have found no published form of this putative ballad, and if anyone knows it and can still sing it, he or she has not been found. Nevertheless, *Katie bar the door* has been in wide use for a long time. It is a reality, and the sense of it is exactly preserved in the form now used by sports figures and fans. It would require only one player or one sportscaster with Scottish roots to have revived it. Consider another well-known Southern phrase, which once had a popular vogue in the baseball world. "Sitting in the catbird seat" has been traced to Red Barber, a sports broadcaster of the 1930s and 1940s. It was later used in a short story by humorist James Thurber, who brought it to a wider audience. *Katie bar the door* may well have followed a similar route. I have come upon no competing explanation. But without some hard evidence, *this* particular scenario is inconclusive. I appeal once again to all with an interest in ballads or acquaintance with ballad singers.

The seven words and phrases I have discussed illustrate different etymological puzzles.

Fade barn was a casualty of field collecting, in which a response was misheard or misrecorded, with no way to check it. We had to reject it.

Bobbasheely was tracked down to Choctaw, and we feel quite confident of that.

Appaloosa is very likely Choctaw for the catfish, but for the mottled horse we are not sure. The two may be of the same source, as later evidence may show, but we separated them as two entries. They illustrate a problem of dealing with words of foreign languages not fully known.

Bettywood is still known, and it was once so commonplace that nobody, botanists, foresters, surveyors, took the trouble to identify it with a proper Latin binomial. We have not given up on it yet, but people who knew the tree are passing.

A mind to illustrates what happens to forms chiefly oral: they develop phonetic and syntactic variants; the variants tend to be confused or to merge; a standard form perhaps emerges. In this instance, we have to recognize both *I'm a mind to* and *I have a mind to*.

Dead cat on the line illustrates how, as it seems at present, a metaphorical sense can run away with the literal sense and almost mask it. The real catfish on a fishing line becomes an interloper, sexual or telephonic.

Finally, *Katie, bar the door*. The reconstruction I have offered, however plausible, does not produce an acceptable etymology. I hope that someone may still find us some hard evidence. Till then, it is still *etym. uncert.*

Expletives and Euphemisms in *DARE*: An Initial Look

Luanne von Schneidemesser

> The American people, once the most prudish on earth, took to a certain defiant looseness of speech during World War I and Prohibition. Today, after a second world war and threats of a third, words and phrases are encountered everywhere—on the air, on the screen, in the theaters, in the comic papers, in the newspapers, on the floor of Congress and even at the domestic hearth—that were reserved for use in saloons and bagnios a generation ago. (Mencken 1979:355)

This was Mencken's opinion of several decades ago, as reformulated by McDavid. Mencken goes on to state, "The palmy days of euphemism ran from the 1820s to the 80s. Bulls became *male cows, cow creatures* (more commonly *cow critters*), . . . and *to castrate* became *to change, to arrange,* or *to alter,* even on the farm" (357).

Have we come so far that we have overcome the use of euphemism for plain talk? No. Look only to our own area of education where we talk about deprived or at-risk children and late developers, or the government's inoperative statements, redistribution of wealth, or shared sacrifice. And of the terms mentioned above by Mencken from the 1820s to 1880s, the Dictionary of American Regional English[1] (DARE) has recorded all of them but *to arrange. Male cow* was given by 128 DARE informants, chiefly in the Midland region, but also in the South. *Cow critter* or *cow creature*, used chiefly in the South Midland, is termed old-fashioned. *To alter* was given by about 25% of 1,002 DARE informants, spread throughout the United States. And *to change* was given as a response by 27 DARE informants, chiefly in the South and southern Appalachians.

Regarding this topic of euphemisms, a query was recently made by a visitor to DARE which led to this paper: are Southerners more genteel in their use of language? Do they use fewer actual expletives, more euphemisms? While a rather general conception of Southern American English is that it is more relaxed and slower, this person extrapolated from the idea of gracious living and genteelness that indeed expletives would be used less in the South than among terse, rushed Northerners and historically rough and tough Westerners. While this is a much oversimplified view of the South, the idea of following up on the usage of expletives and euphemisms was intriguing.

Since DARE surveyed the whole country over a five-year period (1965–1970), there are data which allow investigation of this hypothesis, even though the information may not appear in the published or forthcoming volumes of the *Dictionary of American Regional English (DARE)*. The focus of this paper is twofold: first, to examine the extent of use geographically and according to social variables of the so-called four-letter words in the United States, as reflected in

DARE questionnaires for that time period, and to relate usage specifically in the South; secondly, to look at some euphemisms used for these terms, especially those more common in the South.

Allen Walker Read (1934:264) assessed the scholarly treatment of four-letter words:

> The obscene "four-letter words" of the English language are not cant or slang or dialect, but belong to the oldest and best established element in the English vocabulary. They are not even substandard, for they form part of the linguistic equipment of speakers of standard English. Yet they bear such a stigma that they are not even listed in the leading dictionaries of the language.

Although things have changed since 1934, the *Dictionary of American Regional English* has generally followed the tradition of not entering the common English expletives, albeit for different reasons than those of the dictionaries of that time period: DARE has not entered them because they *are* very common, standard terms, and standard terms fall outside of DARE's realm. Some of these terms in combination, such as *hellfire* and *hell's bells*, have been included, however. Also in the area of euphemisms, this topic offers an incredibly large number of lexical items to be studied, for Americans have been quite inventive in their use of both expletives and euphemisms. Mitford Mathews, in his *Dictionary of Americanisms*, for example, lists among others *blue blazes, dad-blasted, dad-gum, darnation, ding-busted, gee whitaker, gee whillikins, gee whiz, god-awful, goldarn, hell's bells, hell-bent, to give one hell,* and *thunderation*. Likewise, a large number of such responses are scattered throughout DARE's questionnaires.

As an initial study, this paper will of necessity confine itself to a limited number of terms. And from DARE's corpus, a limited number of questions will be used as source material, namely most of those from the last section of the questionnaire, section NN entitled "Exclamations." Some of these questions were excluded, such as those dealing with words for "hello" and "good-bye" or those said when one sneezes, since they yielded practically nothing for this study, but the remainder produced a high yield.[2]

Before turning to the use of expletives in the U.S., this study should present a quick summary of DARE's basic data: DARE has 1,002 completed questionnaires, done by 2,777 informants, so only somewhat over one-third of the informants answered any given section. Within a section of the questionnaire, the percentages of informants in each of DARE's social categories vary little from question to question, indicating that for the most part the same informants answered a whole section, as one would assume. That there are slight differences in these percentages stems in large part from the fact that the statistics given for each individual question are based on informants giving actual responses, excluding those informants who said no term was used in their area for the question or those who simply gave no response.[3] In the comparison of the whole of the United States to the South in the table below, the South is considered here in its broader sense, and as defined in Gastil (1975:174–204), not as in *DARE*; this corresponds roughly to *DARE*'s South and South Midland areas but using whole states only. (When discussing geographic use of terms, I will specify South, South Midland, and other regions as used in *DARE*.) These categories and the percentage of informants in each for section NN, are listed here for all DARE informants and for just those informants in the South:

Table: Percentages of informants by social category		
Social Category	*Percentages of Total*	
	U.S.	*South**
Community		
urban	6–7	0–1
large city	5–6	7–9
small city	19–21	18–20
village	39–40	32–36
rural	28–30	35–40
Age		
young (18–39)	12–14	13–16
middle-aged (40–59)	25–27	29–31
old (60+)	59–63	53–57
Education		
unknown	1	1
less than grade school	1–2	2–3
grade school	22–24	25–29
high school	42–43	38–40
college	31–32	29–33
Race		
white	93–94	89–90
black	6–7	10–11
Sex		
female	49–51	47–50
male	49–51	50–53
* *South* here is based on Gastil (1975:174–204).		

For the whole of the country, the largest range in section NN is 4 percentage points, while for the South alone it is 5. While there are some differences in the percentages of informants in each social category between the country as a whole and the South, they are not large. Blacks are represented by 10–11% in the South but 6–7% for the nation.

Corroborating Mencken's "defiant looseness of speech" mentioned above, Merryweather (1931:433) commented on the use of *hell*:

> We have come far from the day when bold people spoke of the infernal realm as *Hades*, timid ones, as *the other place*, and Mark Twain invented the facetious euphemism "hot as the hereafter." Today *hell* fills so large a place in the American vulgate that it will probably be worn out in a few years more, and will become obsolescent.

In that regard he needed to have had no fear. As DARE recorded in the latter half of the 1960s, it was alive and very well, as were many other expletives. Both profane and obscene terms, namely *damn, devil, god, lord, hell, christ, shit, jesus, bitch, bastard,* and *fuck* will be considered here.

DARE shows no basic regionality for these terms when looking at all occurrences in section NN, although *bitch* shows no usage in the Gulf States from Alabama through Texas. Of the expletives mentioned, *fuck* and *bastard* were given only 11 and 16 times respectively. *Bitch* was a response from 60 informants, *jesus* 90, and *shit* and *christ* from around 120. *Hell, lord,* and *god* were given by over 300 informants each, *devil* by over 500, and *damn* by 630.

Fuck and *bastard,* considered only briefly since the number of responses is so low, are by a large margin the two terms used the least by old informants: only 2 said *fuck* and 3 *bastard.* While half the responses of *bastard* came from mid-aged informants, 9 of 11 instances of *fuck* were from young; its respondents were also highly urban or from large cities and mostly college educated. And *fuck, shit,* and *bastard* in that order showed the highest usage by males.

Excluding these two terms with a low number of responses, almost none of the other terms shows much divergence in community size, amount of education, or race in their usage for the whole of the U.S. (*Shit* shows a 9% higher use by Blacks than expected.) Sex diverges in most cases, however: female use ranges from only 22% for *shit* up to 46% for *devil,* compared to the expected half; specifically, in order of increasing usage by females *shit,* then *bitch* 28%, *jesus, god, hell,* and *christ* 31–33%, *damn* 38%, *lord* 44%, and *devil.* Age shows varying degrees of divergence for these terms: old informants shied away from saying *shit* especially, with only 30% responding, not the 59–63% of old informants responding to all questions. This is followed at a distance by *bitch* 37% old, *jesus* 48%, *god* and *christ* 51%, *hell* 55%, *damn* 57%, up to *devil* and *lord* at 60 and 62%. The young and mid-aged groups both show their highest usage with *shit* and *bitch; lord* and *devil* fall within the expected range of age distribution for all groups, and *damn* and *hell* come very close.

Looking only at the informants in the South, how do they compare to the whole? About one-third of DARE's informants are in these states, and the percentage of informants in the South who responded *damn* and *god* corresponds to this, while Southerners account for 38–39% of the responses of *christ, devil, hell,* and *jesus,* and a high of 42% for *lord. Bastard* and *fuck,* on the other hand, low-response terms for the country as a whole, were represented even more sparsely in the South: 3 of 16 and 1 of 11 informants respectively (again, these two terms will be ignored in any comparisons here). *Bitch* accounts for only 23% of informants responding, *shit* for 30%. Use of profanities is higher than that of obscenities in the South.

And are the social categories similar in the South to those for the whole of the U.S.? Blacks, making up 10–11% of the Southern informants, account for 23% and 26% of the Southern responses of *shit* and *jesus* respectively.[4] *Christ* and *bitch* were used by more grade-school educated informants than expected and than in the country as a whole. And over 60% of the informants responding with *bitch* were rural compared to an expected 35–40%. (Over 90% of *bitch* responses were in the phrase *son of a bitch.* No other term was used so exclusively in one set phrase.)

Shit and especially *bitch* were the least used or most stigmatized terms by old informants and female informants for the country as a whole, and while this is also true for *shit* in the South for female informants, the terms are quite close to expected percentages of use by all old informants in the South, in order after *lord*, *devil*, and *damn*. *Bitch* also falls into this fourth spot for Southern female informants; they responded with it more readily than with *hell*, *god*, *christ*, *jesus*, or *shit*. And while the range of difference between the most and least frequently used terms by females or males was about the same for the U.S. and the South, age shows a different story: the range by old informants in the whole country covers a spread of more than 30 percentage points, while there is only a 16% spread in the South. At the low end, only 30% of the informants responding *shit* in the U.S. are old, whereas old informants in the South represent 42% of those responding with the least frequently used term, *god*. That is, in the South of the late 1960s, captured by the DARE questionnaire, there does not seem to be as strong an avoidance of some of these terms by people in DARE's age category *old* (60 or older) as in the country as a whole.

Going back to consideration of the entire U.S. informant pool, we can see that several phrases, when considered individually, may show a different picture. *Hell's bells*, for example, with only 13 informants, shows an older than overall age usage, quite a bit higher than that of all uses of *hell*, and 7 of the 13 using it are women, compared to only 32% for all responses of *hell*. *Hellfire*, given by only 7 informants, also shows high usage by old informants: 5 of 7, with no young informants. It is rural and male in usage as well. *What the hell* or *what in hell*, from 40 informants, showed a 40-60 female-male split but a usage of only 10% mid-aged but 80% old. *Holy hell*, on the other hand, was even lower than for all uses of *hell* in percentage of old informants, namely 39%, with 30% young, and showed less than a quarter of its usage from females.

Female usage of *jesus christ* is close to expected, while *jesus* by itself or *holy jesus* shows very low female usage. By age, young and mid-aged informants used *jesus christ* highly, the young used *holy jesus* somewhat more, but the old used *jesus* by itself more than would be expected when compared to overall *jesus* usage. The old use *holy christ* to a lesser extent than overall but the mid-aged use it heavily, and males almost exclusively. Similarly, *holy god*, with 13 informants, shows high mid-aged use and all but 1 informant a male, as well as heavy urban usage. Six of 7 informants using *holy shit* were also male, and 3 informants were young, 4 mid-aged, and none old. One can generalize that use of *holy* with one of these expletives seems to be a strongly male occurrence, and a mid-aged one, with less usage than expected by old informants, but for young informants the amount of usage of *holy* depends more on what word is following it.

Considering other phrases with *god*, two are noticeably higher in use by females than expected from overall use of *god*: *for god's sake* and *god almighty*. While *for god's sake* shows a higher use by old informants, *god almighty* shows a lower use than expected. And with 30% of the total, Blacks used it more than expected, as they did other expressions with *almighty*. *Swear to god* was given by only 38% old informants, while *my god* was used by 12 of 14 old informants, which ties in with use by more grade-school educated informants.

Great lord, with 12 responses, is used heavily by males and almost not at all by college educated informants. *Lord have mercy* is used heavily by Blacks, 6 of 14 informants.

Nine informants gave the expression *not by* (or *on*) *a damn sight*. Of these, 7 were male, and 6 were old, 3 mid-aged, no young. This expression was given by 1 informant in California, with all others in the North.[5]

As mentioned before, little regionality is demonstrated in the use of these expletives, but a few of the phrases containing them do show some regional usage. In addition to *not by a damn sight*, we find:

God almighty is more frequent in the South and South Midland, as shown on map 1. Specifically, *good god almighty*, marked on the map by a triangle, shows up only in the South, whereas most use of *great god almighty*, indicated by a square, is north of it.

Lord have mercy, seen in map 2, is South and South Midland in use. Map 3 shows the use of *great lord*, appearing in the South, the South Midland, and New England, albeit sparsely.

Hellfire, with only 7 informants, shown on map 4, is a South and South Midland term.

It has been shown here that overall usage of a term and its usage in certain phrases can be reflected by differences in the makeup of the people who use the terms. Should all usage of a term be lumped together for DARE's purposes? Perhaps. Perhaps not. But in this field of study more than in DARE's normal work much more comes into play than just the terms, although they themselves are complex enough. Merryweather (1931:434) describes the simple expression *O hell!*, as the "most soul-felt! With proper variation of the voice," he explains, "it may be made to express resignation, weariness, boredom, exasperation, consternation, rage, and probably other emotions." Indeed, if someone were to say "God bless it," would it be a real blessing or a curse? Much more would have to be recorded about the phrase, not just the phrase itself, before that could be determined. Already in the *Linguistic Atlas of New England* this problem was addressed: in the notes on map 599 one reads of the "verbal expressions (historical subjunctives) used as curses or imprecations" that

> some of them are rather strong (*damn, blast, rot, devil take it*), others relatively weak (*ding, blame, bother, rabbit*); but between the two extremes represented by *God damn your soul to hell!* . . . and *oh bother it!* . . . the order of these imprecations is too finely graded, too shifting and too uncertain to make any useful classification possible. Whether a given expression is felt as strong or as mild by an informant depends, of course, very largely on his personal background and habits. (Kurath 1939–43:map 599)

Although expletives generally show little regional usage, DARE does find that a number of euphemisms are regional. What euphemisms are Southern in usage? None of our most common, everyday terms are Southern, such as *darn, heck, son of a gun*, or *gee*, ones given by over 75% of DARE's informants. But *durn*, on map 5, a variant of *darn* with 226 responses, while scattered in DARE's data throughout the country except for New England, shows a clear concentration of use in the South and South Midland. Map 6 shows *dog* as a verb or participial adjective such as *dog it!* or *I'll be dogged* and as a noun in such phrases as *dog take it* or *dog bite it* being used almost only in the South and South Midland; 24% of these informants are black. *Doggone* (map 7) while even more widespread than *durn*, shows only a very slight margin of concentration in the South, South Midland, Upper Midwest, and Rocky Mountain states, but *daggone* (map 8), with only 28 informants to *doggone*'s 323, shows a somewhat similar but more confined pattern: it is chiefly in the Mid Atlantic states plus West Virginia and Kentucky, as well as the Dakotas, Montana, and Idaho. (And it is used much more by old informants.) *Dag* as a simplex is represented by 5 informants, all in the South and South Midland. *Dagnab*, on the other hand, has 8 of only 10 informants in the North and North Midland. *Dag* in its combined usage, with all occurrences shown on map 9, covers mainly the Mid Atlantic states, the South Midland area, and the Rocky Mountain states, similar to just *daggone*. There are no informants in the Gulf states or Georgia.

The concentration of the 113 responses of *dad* shown in map 10 is farther south: while there is a scattering of informants throughout the country, it is mainly a South and South Midland term, heaviest in these areas where *dag* is lacking. Considering its compounds, we see that *dad-burn* (map 11) has a similar region, as does *dad-blame* (map 12), although the scattering farther north and west has vanished in the latter. While the most frequent compound, *dad-gum*, with 47 informants, is also basically South and South Midland, it has almost no Mid Atlantic responses, but in the West the responses go as far as New Mexico and California (map 13).[6] *Dad-blast*, with only 7 informants, is not regional, and *dad-rat* appears mostly in the North and North Midland.[7]

Considering these Southern terms in light of social variables, *dad-gum* falls out pretty much as expected except for a higher than normal use by young informants. *Dad-blame* is used by slightly but not significantly more females, while the other *dad* terms show somewhat more male usage, up to 65% for *dad-burn*. *Dad-burn* is also used more by old informants, rural informants, and grade- and high-school educated ones.

Bull, in the sense 'boastful talk, nonsense', as plotted on map 14, includes only *bull*, not *bullshit* or its variants. Of the 270 informants 24% are young, 46% old; 64% are male.

Devilish (map 15), in response to the question "Something that keeps annoying you—for example, a fly that keeps buzzing around you: 'That _____ fly won't go away'," is South and South Midland in use, with 32% of the informants black. *Biscuit-eater*, as in "son of a _____," is also used in the South and South Midland, as seen in map 16, while the simplex *biscuit* is chiefly a Northern term.

Declare, in response to the NN questions including "Exclamations like 'I swear' or 'I vow'" is quite widespread, with a very slightly heavier concentration in the South and South Midland, as can be seen in map 17. Excluding that particular question, NN32 with its cue, however, shows that the geographical distribution of the remaining responses, while still somewhat scattered, is indeed chiefly South and South Midland (map 18).

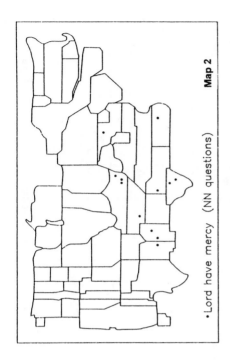

• God almighty (NN questions)

Map 1

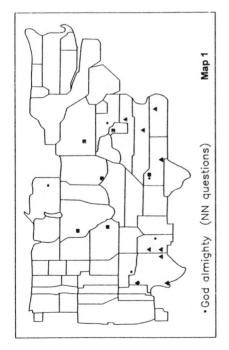

• great Lord (NN questions)

Map 3

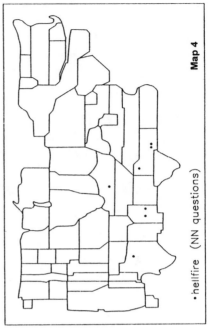

• Lord have mercy (NN questions)

Map 2

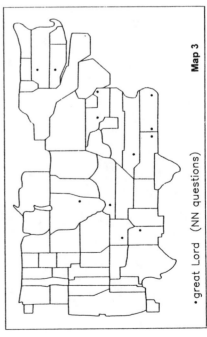

• hellfire (NN questions)

Map 4

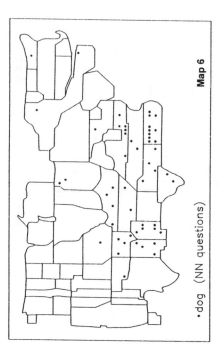

Map 5

• durn (NN questions)

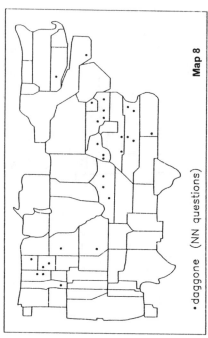

Map 6

• dog (NN questions)

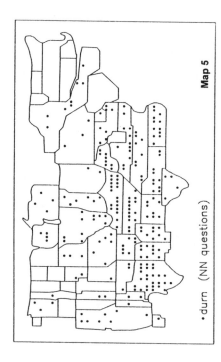

Map 7

• doggone (NN questions)

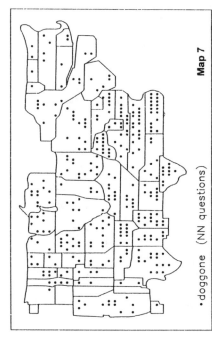

Map 8

• daggone (NN questions)

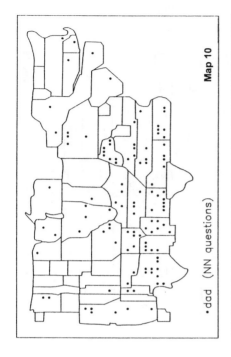

• dag (NN questions)

Map 9

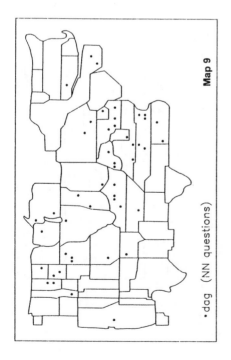

• dad (NN questions)

Map 10

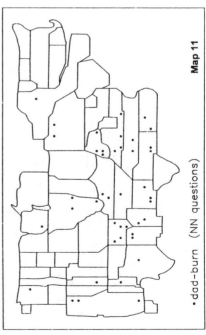

• dad-burn (NN questions)

Map 11

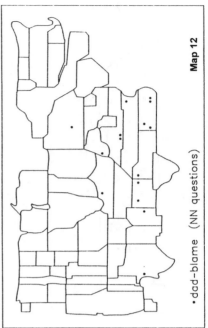

• dad-blame (NN questions)

Map 12

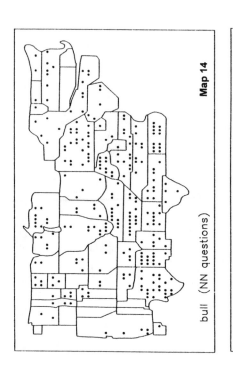

bull (NN questions)

Map 14

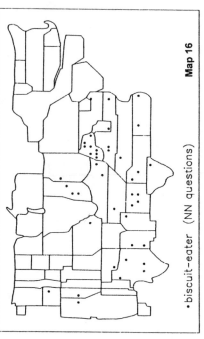

•biscuit-eater (NN questions)

Map 16

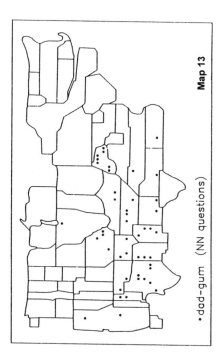

•dad-gum (NN questions)

Map 13

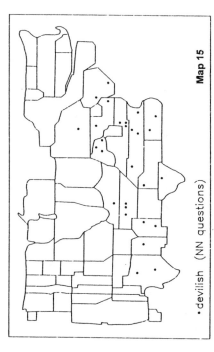

•devilish (NN questions)

Map 15

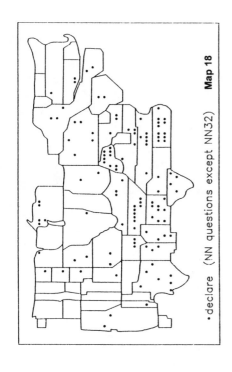

• declare (NN questions)   **Map 17**

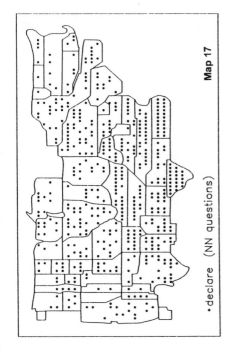

• torment (NN questions)   **Map 19**

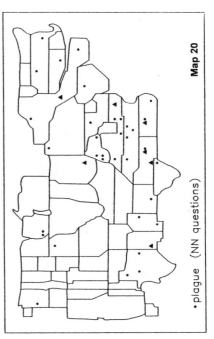

• declare (NN questions except NN32)   **Map 18**

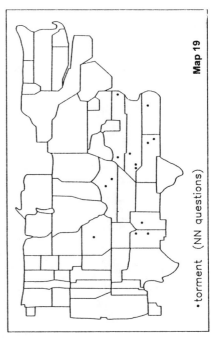

• plague (NN questions)   **Map 20**

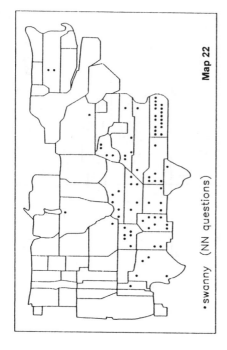

Map 21

•lordy (NN questions)

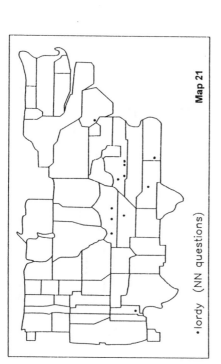

Map 22

•swanny (NN questions)

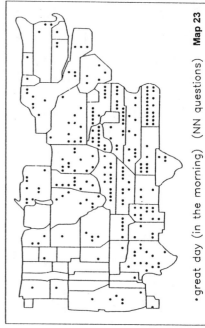

•great day (in the morning) (NN questions) **Map 23**

Foot shows 9 of 10 responses in the South and South Midland. Seven of these are female, all are high school or college educated. *Fudge*, on the other hand, is a Northern term.

Where informants in the North and North Midland used *gravy* in expressions like *good gravy* and *by gravy*, 7 informants in the South and South Midland responded *granny* or *grannies*; all 7 were old.

Milder words used for *hell* include *hellfire*, already mentioned, and *hello*, sometimes *hell-o* or *hello mary* (for *hail Mary*), given by 9 informants, 7 in the South and South Midland. In response to the question "Go to _____!" 14 informants responded *torment*, all in the South and South Midland (map 19). They were highly rural, most were mid-aged and grade-school educated, 4 were black. Of 6 informants responding *guinea* to the question, 4 were from Virginia and North Carolina, 1 each from Louisiana and Pennsylvania. All 6 were female, 5 college educated, and 5 old. And to the same question ("Go to _____!") 7 informants, 6 male, said *where it doesn't* [or *don't*] *snow*, from Georgia, Mississippi, Louisiana, and Texas; 1 informant from Alabama said *where it don't rain*.

Plague and *plagued* are used in the Atlantic and Gulf states, especially West Virginia and the Mid Atlantic states, as shown on map 20, in such phrases as "plague (take) it" or "that plagued fly." The occurrences of the variant pronunciation *plegged* are marked on the map with a triangle. Both of these show a higher than expected response by old informants.

Lordy (map 21), 12 informants, is used in the South and South Midland with the exception of the Gulf states. It is quite rural. *Swanny* (map 22) in the phrase "I swanny" is strictly South and South Midland and shows somewhat more use by younger informants than expected.

And finally, *great day* and *great day in the morning*, while widespread throughout the country, are used chiefly in the South and Midland, as well as in Pennsylvania and the eastern North Central states (map 23).

While displaying the usage of expletives and euphemisms in the South, some of these maps illustrate that the decision about the regionality of a certain term or expression may not be that clear-cut. One of the problems sometimes facing the DARE staff is when to declare a term regional. Is *bull* really regional? How about *doggone, declare,* or *great lord*? The DARE questionnaire material is considered together with all other written and oral material available at DARE to make the final decision in such cases. In many cases the additional material may clarify the situation; in almost no cases does it disagree with the questionnaire responses. And a comparison of the maps presented here also demonstrates that while the label South and South Midland basically refers to one geographical area, the exact extent of that area and the frequency of responses within it may differ widely.

Not only in determining exactly what terms are regional is there room for discussion, but also in assigning degree of strength of the expressions used, be they expletives or euphemisms, as mentioned above. To conclude this paper with even more questions, let us return to the original query of whether more genteel living in the South leads to more genteelness in the use of language, with fewer expletives and more euphemisms. Little can be said which is truly concrete. That there is little difference in the amount of usage of the more common expletives by females in the two populations may neutralize that argument. That *fuck*, *bastard*, and *bitch*, three terms commonly perceived as stronger expletives than several of the others discussed, were used less in the South than in the country as a whole would lend some credence to the idea; however, the discovery that some of these expletives are used much more among older people in the South than among older people in the country as a whole speaks against it. As others have also discovered, classifying and categorizing are difficult; this is not a question that can be solved simply by reporting usage alone: context, tone, intent, and a myriad of other factors should be considered.[8] And while it also cannot be said that Southerners have a larger inventory of euphemisms, they do indeed have an inventory of terms, as shown in this discussion, which they prefer, one used exclusively in the South or used more frequently by Southerners than by people in other sections of the United States.

NOTES

1. The Dictionary of American Regional English lexicographical project (DARE, producer of *DARE*, i.e., Cassidy and Hall 1985–) is supported in large part by grants from the National Endowment for the Humanities, the Andrew W. Mellon Foundation, and the National Science Foundation.

2. Specifically, questions NN1–3, 5, 6b, 10–12, 18, and 19 were not used; all other NN questions were. A text of these questions can be found in *DARE*, Volume I:1xxxi–1xxxii.

3. More exact definitions of the categories can be found in the prefatory matter in *DARE*, Volume I:lxxvi. A list of percentages for all DARE informants can be found in von Schneidemesser (1988:48), among other places. All percentages for the NN questions are within two percentage points of the overall DARE statistics.

4. Remember that usage of *shit* was also somewhat higher than expected by Blacks nationwide.

5. *Damnation*, which was not included in the conglomerate file of *damn*, is used almost equally by males and females but 14 of the 17 informants are old, the other 3 mid-aged.

6. *Gum* usage corresponds to that of *dad-gum*: of 54 informants using *gum*, 47 used *dad-gum*; 24 informants gave more than one response with *gum*.

7. *Rat* as a verb or imprecation is non-Southern.

8. See also, for example, Johnson 1991.

LAGS and *DARE*:
A Case of Mutualism
Joan H. Hall

In an essay published during Lyndon Johnson's presidency in 1967, Raven I. McDavid, Jr., remarked, "With a sub-Potomac accent now enunciating the national policies, the time is fair for examining what we know about Southern speech and what we need to learn" (1967:113). Now that there is yet another sub-Potomac speaker in the White House, it is appropriate to ask what we have learned in the intervening quarter century.

In his essay McDavid outlined some of the lexical and phonological features commonly thought of as Southern. He then pointed out, in his typically understated way, that despite careful investigations and scholarly treatises, "myths persist" (114). Judging by some of the recent newspaper articles (e.g., Broder 1992) attempting to prepare Americans for the "double-Bubba" administration (warning us to be ready for such phrases as *strut one's okra* and *not to know pea turkey*), it is only possible to conclude that myths *still* persist. Yet much progress has also been made.

In outlining his priorities for research in Southern speech those twenty-six years ago, McDavid emphasized the need to edit and publish the data that had been collected still a quarter century earlier for the Linguistic Atlas of the Middle and South Atlantic States (LAMSAS); to investigate the area from Missouri and Kentucky southward to Key West; to conduct a more intensive investigation of Appalachian speech; to carry out careful studies of Black speech; and to develop a liaison between these projects and the then-just-beginning Dictionary of American Regional English (DARE),[1] "so that investigators would not duplicate each other's work, and so that the greatest amount of data might be made available to all serious scholars" (118).

Which of these objectives have been realized? Certainly we know much more about the speech of African-Americans, both in the South and in Northern cities, than we did in 1967. Our knowledge of Appalachian speech has been enhanced by such studies as that by Wolfram and Christian (1976) in two counties of West Virginia and will be further bolstered by the work of the late Joseph Hall, being carried on by Michael Montgomery in his *Dictionary of Smoky Mountain English*. After a long, roller coaster history of support, the lexical data from LAMSAS are being computerized by Bill Kretzschmar and his staff.[2] The fieldwork gap from Missouri and Kentucky southward to Key West has been admirably filled by Lee Pederson and the staff of the Linguistic Atlas of the Gulf States (LAGS). And, I think it is fair to say, a good working relationship between those projects and DARE has indeed been established. So, given the recognition that our reach will always exceed our grasp, and that philosophical support for a project does not always translate into financial support as well, we have actually come quite a long way.

It is the relationship between LAGS and DARE that I will concentrate on in this paper, to illustrate a partly planned, partly serendipitous case of scholarly mutualism. A few months before LAVIS II, as I was thinking about the upcoming conference, my eye was caught by a crossword puzzle my fourth-grade son had brought home from his science class. The class had obviously been talking about relationships among organisms in the natural world, and the puzzle incorporated the concepts by including as three of the "across" words *parasitism*, *commensalism*, and *mutualism*. Not having thought about such concepts in quite a while, I was curious to see how the words were defined. For *parasitism*, the definition given in the puzzle read, "A relationship in which one organism benefits, while another is harmed"; for *commensalism*, "a relationship in which only one organism benefits, but the other is not harmed"; for *mutualism*, "a relationship in which each organism does something that benefits the other." All the words fit nicely in the puzzle, among such others as *ants*, *bees*, and *wasps* (illustrating successful social organizations) and *students* and *teachers*! (Who says we are not teaching moral values today?)

At the time that I saw the puzzle, I had recently been impressed by how useful the information in *LAGS* has been to the editors of *DARE*: we now routinely check the *Concordance* (Pederson, McDaniel, and Bassett 1986) whenever we have a word that is even remotely connected with the South. Sometimes it seems, with a rich source like this, we tend to devour it, using whatever is helpful, and move on. I thought about DARE's relationship to such data sources. I was not prompted to call it parasitism—we certainly were not harming any other organism—but I wondered about commensalism and mutualism. Was this a case in which DARE benefited while LAGS simply remained unharmed, or was there any way the LAGS project could actually benefit from DARE's voracious use of it?

The editing of *DARE* began back in 1975, at the same time that fieldwork for LAGS was well under way. While DARE had surveyed 2,777 people in 1,002 communities in fifty states, LAGS would ultimately include 1,121 informants from 699 communities in eight states. So the LAGS mesh was much finer, and could doubtless trap many items that would escape DARE's broader mesh. At the same time, since it covered a region that DARE had also covered, it would doubtless also confirm many of the same patterns we had found. While the investigative instruments were far from identical, there was enough overlap to provide substantiating evidence for hundreds if not eventually thousands of words; and, since the *LAGS Concordance* is bursting with other items not specifically targeted but elicited anyway, it is an excellent source for anecdotal evidence—the kind of unselfconscious, automatic use of words that practically guarantees their genuineness.

So—what have we found in using *LAGS*? We have found that the data from this micro-meshed survey substantiate to a very high degree the data from DARE's macro survey. This is true not only of broad regional patterns such as "South, South Midland," but also of those patterns restricted to areas within the Gulf Region, and those limited to a couple of states, or even one; it is true of racial, gender, and age distinctions; and it is true of those terms considered archaic or relics.[3]

Let us look first at a broad picture. Map 1 shows the distribution of DARE Informants who gave the term *French harp* for 'harmonica'.[4] This is a somewhat unusual distribution, with its paucity of evidence in Alabama, Florida, and Georgia and its abundance in the rest of the region, but the map still makes a convincing case for regionality. Based on this map and on our written quotations, we described this as "chiefly West Midland, Texas, Central."

Map 1

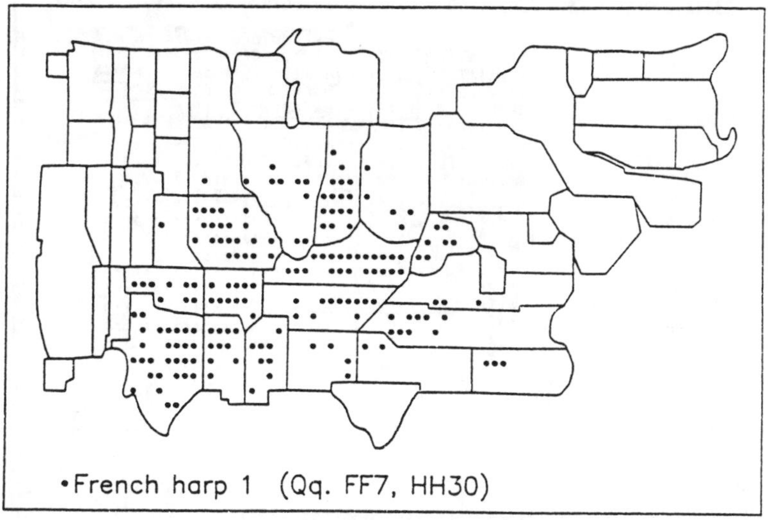

•French harp 1   (Qq. FF7, HH30)

From DICTIONARY OF AMERICAN REGIONAL ENGLISH, volume II, D–H edited by Frederic G. Cassidy and Joan Houston Hall. Copyright © 1991 by the President and Fellows of Harvard College. Reprinted by permission of Harvard University Press.

Fortunately, the *LAGS Concordance* was available by the time we were working on this term, so we consulted it and, after tracking informant numbers, discovered to our delight that a very similar pattern emerged from the LAGS data. Some time later, the fourth volume of *LAGS* (Pederson et al. 1986–1992), the *Regional Matrix*, was published and made easily available what we had earlier had to struggle to discern. As one can see on the LAGS map (map 2),[5] there is a strikingly similar empty area in Florida, south Georgia, and southern Alabama. This is precisely the kind of situation that validates DARE in terms of its initial selection of communities and the adequacy of its nationwide mesh.

A slightly different situation involved the term *dusk dark* and its variant *dust dark*, meaning 'dusk, twilight'. *DARE*'s map showed only 17 informants for *dusk dark* (plus three for *dust dark*), but we had numerous written quotes as well, from Florida, Alabama, Kentucky, South Carolina, Texas, Mississippi, and Arkansas. Taken together, this information justified the label "chiefly South." The *LAGS* material was slight because no precisely parallel question had been asked. But two similar questions did elicit the response *dusk dark* from six informants. Map 3 shows the DARE informants with dots, and the LAGS informants with superimposed *x*'s. What was particularly interesting here was that our variant *dust dark* (given by three informants, from Tennessee and Georgia) was also corroborated by a LAGS informant in southwest Georgia, reassuring us that this was indeed a legitimate variant and not a mishearing on the part of the fieldworker.

Map 2

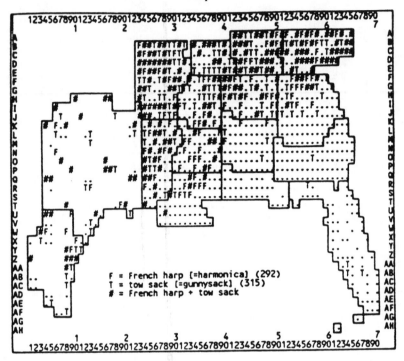

From LINGUISTIC ATLAS OF THE GULF STATES, volume IV, by Lee Pederson. Copyright © 1990 by the University of Georgia Press. Reprinted by permission.

The situation with the terms *dusky dark* and *dusty dark* (also meaning 'twilight') provides a nice parallel. As one can see by comparing maps 3 and 4, there is a slight but recognizable distinction between the regions—*dusk dark* has a southerly orientation, while *dusky dark* inclines toward a South Midland distribution. Again with the superimposed *x*'s on map 4, the LAGS informants show the same *relative* patterning as do the DARE informants and allow us to feel confident that our data are reliable.

DARE's ability to refine regional labels has also been facilitated by the information provided by LAGS. Take, for instance, the *DARE* map for *goober* (map 5). The term is surprisingly widespread throughout the country, given that it has been thought to be something of a Southern shibboleth. But the denser concentration of informants in the Southern part of the country caused us to describe this as "widespread, but chiefly South, Lower Mississippi Valley, Southwest."

Map 3

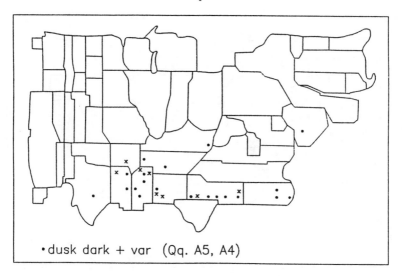

• dusk dark + var (Qq. A5, A4)

From DICTIONARY OF AMERICAN REGIONAL ENGLISH, volume II, D–H edited by Frederic G. Cassidy and Joan Houston Hall. Copyright © 1991 by the President and Fellows of Harvard College. Reprinted by permission of Harvard University Press.

Map 4

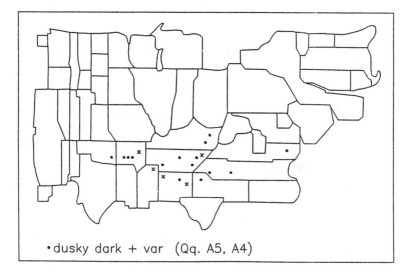

• dusky dark + var (Qq. A5, A4)

From DICTIONARY OF AMERICAN REGIONAL ENGLISH, volume II, D–H edited by Frederic G. Cassidy and Joan Houston Hall. Copyright © 1991 by the President and Fellows of Harvard College. Reprinted by permission of Harvard University Press.

Map 5

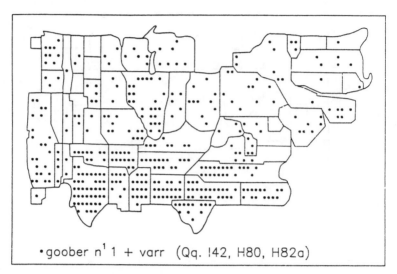

•goober n¹ 1 + varr (Qq. 142, H80, H82a)

Map 6

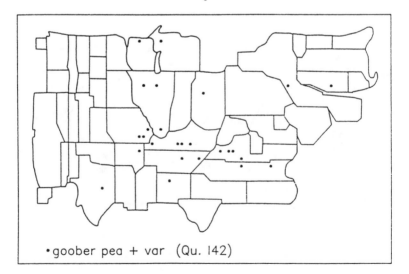

•goober pea + var (Qu. 142)

The question for DARE was not whether this was regional but how to deal with the variant *goober pea*. Our map (map 6) suggested a much more restricted distribution of this term. We were tempted to treat this as a separate entry and call it "chiefly South Midland" but wondered, given the scattering of other informants, whether this was legitimate, or whether basically it conformed to the larger pattern of *goober* and ought to be treated there. When we deciphered the LAGS information in the *Concordance*, there was no question: 24 of the 34 informants who said *goober pea* rather than *goober* were in Tennessee! We felt justified, then, in setting up *goober pea* as a separate entry with its own distinct regional distribution.

I mentioned earlier that LAGS is also useful in delimiting lexical distributions that are much narrower than that of the basic "Gulf Region." This has been particularly true of Louisiana French terms, since LAGS had a good sampling in southern Louisiana, while DARE's grid was broad enough that we couldn't treat that distinctive area as fully as we would have liked. It is satisfying, then, to get corroboration of our evidence for such French or French-derived terms as *banquette, choupique, coonass, fais dodo, filé, graton, jambalaya, lagniappe, pirogue,* and *sacalait*.

On the eastern edge of the region, corroboration of terms labeled "Gullah" in *DARE* has been less consistent than for Louisiana French. However, I realized as I checked *LAGS* against the *Index* (1993) to *DARE* for Gullah terms that most of our words so labeled are done so not on the basis of our own fieldwork, but on historical evidence. What the fieldwork from both projects indicates is that many Gullah terms have gone almost entirely out of use. Those African terms that have survived, such as *cooter, goober,* and *pinder,* have done so by "going national," or at least "going regional," in their escape into use by the dominant culture.

In the case of *joggling board,* 'a limber board suspended between two uprights and upon which one sits and bounces', the DARE evidence shows the term to be tightly localized to South Carolina and Georgia. *LAGS* provides confirmatory evidence of regionality, with 20 of 37 examples from Georgia. The question we are facing now with respect to the treatment of *joggling board* in Volume III of *DARE* is whether this tight regionality can be attributed to African influence, or whether we are simply dealing here with a phrase that is the sum of its English parts, and which only caught on as an entertainment phenomenon in a restricted area. Turner pointed out in *Africanisms in the Gullah Dialect* that in Wolof the word ['ɟɔgɑl] means 'to rise', and reported its use among Gullah speakers in the compound ['ɟɔgɑl bod] meaning 'rise-up board, seesaw' (195). A native Wolof speaker in Madison confirms that ['ɟʊgɒl] means 'to go up' and says that he would use the term ['ɟʊgɒl wɑ'čaɪ] 'up and down' for a seesaw. This information, as well as the congruence of this distributional pattern with others for which we can prove an African origin, suggests that the first element of *joggle board* or *joggling board* may well have originally been African, being reinforced by the homophony with English *joggle, joggling*.

Allen Walker Read (1992) published his discovery of a citation for *joggling board* that antedates by 23 years the citations in the *Dictionary of American English* and the *Dictionary of Americanisms*. Read came upon it in *American Photographs,* a book published in 1859 by Jane and Marian Turnbull, two English women who had traveled through the United States five years earlier. Describing what they had witnessed at a ball in Charleston, South Carolina, they recounted (1859, 2:100–101) with some amazement the extraordinary practice of sitting on a limber plank and bobbing up and down. In full dress! For fun, no less! This citation does not help etymologically, but it does push the evidence back to a time when such a simple sort of recreational device might have been in use on plantations, whence it escaped to the general populace, and even became acceptable entertainment at a ball.

The preceding examples, though miscellaneous and few, show some of the ways DARE has benefited from the tremendous collection of data in the LAGS publications and materials. I pondered earlier whether there could be some reciprocity in the relationship, whether DARE could prove useful to LAGS as well. I am happy to conclude that I think we have. I was gratified to hear from Lee Pederson that some of the definitions and illustrative quotations in DARE's first two volumes helped LAGS editors understand some of the unfamiliar terms from their fieldwork and determine appropriate headword spellings. *Coonass*, for instance, offered by 101 informants, chiefly in Louisiana, was not a term the scribes had heard, and *DARE* was able to corroborate the LAGS informants' use of it and provide an etymology as well.

Another way DARE can be helpful to LAGS has to do with the accessibility of LAGS data. The parts of *LAGS* that have been most useful to us—the *Concordance* (Pederson, McDaniel, and Bassett 1986) and the supporting *Basic Materials* (Pederson, Leas, Bailey, and Bassett 1981)—are available only on microfiche, and are appallingly expensive. We were fortunate that the University of Wisconsin Library was willing to purchase them, and doubly fortunate that they allow us to house them, so we can use them routinely. When we condense the information we find there and encapsulate it in a quote in *DARE*, we not only make it available to a wider audience but do much of the interpretation as well. Because our space constraints are much less stringent than those for other dictionaries, we have the liberty of citing many of the comments made by the informants. So, for instance, in our entry for *ill*, meaning 'vicious, bad-tempered; cross, fretful', we quote informants who provide such comments and context as "They're not ill at all—not mean, bad-tempered"; and "They're not as ill as the wasp and yellow-jacket"; and "The illest snake of all them—meanest." And, in our entry for *funky*, which DARE evidence had suggested should be labeled "especially among Black speakers," we were able to provide a summary of the comments given by LAGS informants: "Numerous informants report that *funky* refers to strong or offensive body odor, such as sexual odors or those of people who don't bathe often enough. A number of informants consider the word 'crude', 'not nice', or 'not polite'; several note that it is used especially by Blacks." Because many of these comments were in the *Basic Materials* and not the *Concordance*, our summarizing them should save other investigators a tremendous amount of time even if they do have access to the individual protocols.

A third way that DARE can prove useful to LAGS is to provide a wider context for its information. For instance, looking through the volume of *LAGS* matrix maps, one is impressed by the number of well-defined lexical distributions within the Gulf States. Pederson pointedly refrains from talking about dialect boundaries, but the evidence is there to be studied. Seeing maps of some tight clusterings in east Texas, Louisiana, or Florida, one might be tempted to look at similar patterns in north Georgia, Tennessee, or Arkansas and assume that they too represent well-defined, limited distributions. What is often the case, however, is that the tight clusters in these northern areas are really only the southernmost limits of a term that has a much wider distribution. The matrix map for *dip* (map 7), for instance, meaning 'a sweet topping', shows its occurrence chiefly in upper Georgia, east Tennessee, and Arkansas. The *DARE* map (map 8), however, shows the term to be "scattered, but chiefly North Central," with the most southerly informants coinciding with the northerly distribution in *LAGS*.

Map 7

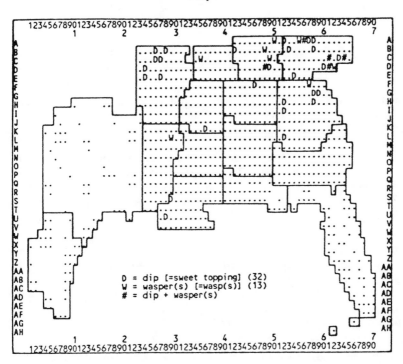

From LINGUISTIC ATLAS OF THE GULF STATES, volume IV, by Lee Pederson. Copyright © 1990 by the University of Georgia Press. Reprinted by permission.

Map 8

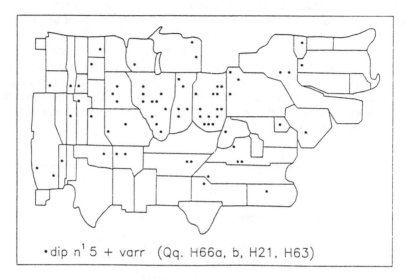

From DICTIONARY OF AMERICAN REGIONAL ENGLISH, volume II, D–H edited by Frederic G. Cassidy and Joan Houston Hall. Copyright © 1991 by the President and Fellows of Harvard College. Reprinted by permission of Harvard University Press.

Similarly, the LAGS informants who offered the term *snake feeder* for 'dragonfly' cluster nicely in east Tennessee (map 9). As the DARE map (map 10) shows, *snake feeder* has a strong Midland distribution, going just as far south as the *LAGS* informants. This doesn't alter the importance of the distribution within the Gulf States, but it does help put it in context. And it illustrates again how the two projects complement one another.

One last example will show once again how LAGS is useful to DARE and also illustrate a tool for data collecting that Raven McDavid could not have imagined a quarter century ago. My example focuses on the term *ice house*, which a DARE fieldworker picked up in Houston, Texas, meaning 'a convenience store'. We collected a second oral use from Dallas, and then found, in *Cuisine* magazine, this written citation from east Texas: "I would sprint down to the icehouse, palm a Moon Pie off the pastry rack, and slide a bottle of Yoo-Hoo from the melting ice . . . of the soda box" (Roberts 1984:15). We went straight to the *LAGS Concordance* and found three corroborating examples, all from San Antonio. So this was a nicely local term that certainly deserved inclusion in *DARE*. The editor who was working on this, Beth Simon, had recently signed on to the American Dialect Society e-mail bulletin board, and thought it would be worth sending out a query asking subscribers whether they too were familiar with this use. She did get more evidence for *ice house* meaning a convenience store, but she also discovered that the term had come to refer to a tavern as well. And implicit in people's explanations of *ice house* for a tavern was the understanding that an *ice house* was originally a place where ice was made and/or sold. A conversation with a friend from east Texas solidified this meaning. When I asked him about the tavern sense he replied,

> Oh, no. My community was dry, so we wouldn't have used it that way. But when I was growing up, the men who worked in the piney woods would stop at the ice house to get ice for their water barrels. If they didn't, their drinking water would be hot by the end of the day. The people at the ice house would cut it or chop it however you wanted it. They made the ice right there.

For those of us with Northern orientations, all of these senses were surprising, for to us an ice house is rather a rude but well insulated shelter designed to store blocks of ice cut from a farmer's pond. So our foray into fieldwork by e-mail resulted in three localized senses for what seemed at first a rather straightforward word.

While it is true that even a large-scale e-mail survey could never substitute for a traditional, systematic investigation such as LAGS, like the anecdotal evidence in the *LAGS Concordance* this e-mail chatter provides additional useful bits of evidence. I think we can view it as both lagniappe for the late 20th century and proof that the various investigators *are* communicating with one another.

Map 9

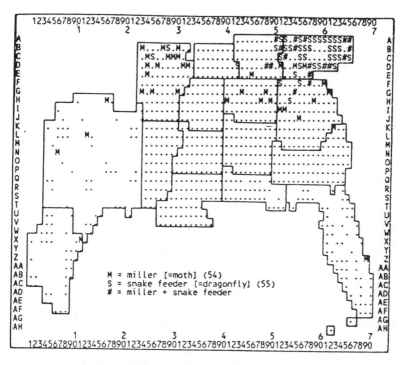

From LINGUISTIC ATLAS OF THE GULF STATES, volume IV, by Lee Pederson. Copyright © 1990 by the University of Georgia Press. Reprinted by permission.

Map 10

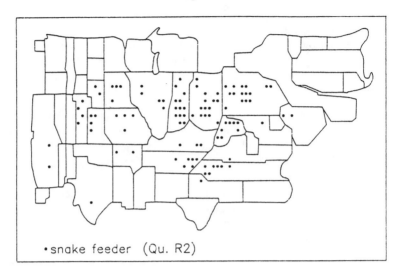

• snake feeder   (Qu. R2)

From DICTIONARY OF AMERICAN REGIONAL ENGLISH, volume II, D–H edited by Frederic G.
Cassidy and Joan Houston Hall. Copyright © 1991 by the President and Fellows of Harvard College.
Reprinted by permission of Harvard University Press.

NOTES

1. DARE (the dictionary project, producer of *DARE*, i.e., Cassidy and Hall 1985–) is
located at the University of Wisconsin-Madison and is funded in large part by grants from
the National Endowment for the Humanities (an independent federal agency), the Andrew
W. Mellon Foundation, the National Science Foundation, and from other private gifts.

2. To date, the only published materials from the LAMSAS project are the first two
fascicles of phonetic transcriptions (McDavid and O'Cain 1980) and the *Handbook*
(Kretzschmar et al. 1994). However, Kretzschmar has recently made the raw data available
through the Linguistic Atlas Web site (http://hyde.park.uga.edu). Funding for the
computerization of the data has once again been reduced severely; as of June 1996, about
15% of the data had been processed.

3. For more detail, see Hall (forthcoming).

4. The map used by DARE has been adjusted to reflect population density rather than
geographic area, while still retaining the basic shapes and relationships of the states. See pp.
xxiii–xxx of Vol. I of *DARE* for a full explanation. Maps 1, 3, 4, 5, 6, and 8 in this paper are
from Vol. II of *DARE*. Map 10 is from the as yet unpublished DARE files.

5. Maps 2, 7, and 9 are from that volume, pp. 309, 332, and 331 respectively. The LAGS
maps also retain the basic shapes and relationships of the Gulf States (Tennessee, Georgia,
Florida, Alabama, Mississippi, Louisiana, east Texas, and Arkansas), with outlines of the
sixteen LAGS "sectors" superimposed. For a full explanation, see the introduction to
Volume 4, *Regional Matrix* (Pederson et al. 1986–1992).

PART THREE

Methods of Sampling, Measurement, and Analysis

With the availability of large data sets and computer facilities to analyze them, research in Southern American English is rapidly becoming more statistically oriented. As Bailey (this volume) points out, although data-based research was a focus also of LAVIS I, the period following that conference has seen further development in sampling methods and analytical tools. The essays in this section especially emphasize methodology in the selection of populations, the measurement of linguistic features, and the representation of findings. They take advantage of new resources and use traditional resources in innovative ways.

Traditional dialect atlases, while useful in establishing a historical baseline, provide incomplete pictures of variation. Maps have always been a part of linguistic geography, but new kinds of maps are being introduced that not only show the areal distribution of features but also incorporate a variety of statistical techniques to display both performance and perception. In the essay that opens this section, Preston compiles nonlinguists' hand-drawn maps into computer-generated maps representing his respondents' perceptions of regional dialects.

The essays that follow by Frazer and by Lance and Faries show other ways of adding to the information provided by traditional atlases. Frazer's study of Illinois and Indiana compares surveys taken for the Linguistic Atlas of the North Central States (LANCS) with interview data gathered for the *Dictionary of American Regional English* (*DARE*). His research points out the necessity of combining lexical questionnaires with tape-recorded data. In their study of Missouri, Lance and Faries compare the traditional atlas technique of drawing isoglosses used in the Linguistic Atlas of the Middle and South Atlantic States (LAMSAS) and in LANCS with computerized maps showing county-by-county aggregate data.

In making comparisons with traditional atlas population samples, researchers are particularly attentive to methods of selecting respondents. Johnson, for example, recognizes that sampling procedures designed for traditional atlases that establish a historical baseline tend to overrepresent elderly, rural, less-educated, lifelong residents of an area. In her longitudinal study, by matching social characteristics of the 39 respondents interviewed for LAMSAS in the 1930s with those of the 39 respondents interviewed for her study in 1990, she is able to isolate rurality as a causal factor in lexical variation.

Quantifying the results of survey research can lead to a wide variety of statistically generated maps. Kretzschmar, who believes that traditional assumptions about dialects and speech communities have hindered efforts to specify relationships between language and space, illustrates how statistical methods can be used to determine whether the geographic dispersion of linguistic features is essentially random or significantly clustered or skewed. Wikle shows the advantages of using maps in representing complex relationships and in preserving linkages to the real world. He distinguishes between qualitative maps (using isoglosses) and quantitative maps and presents a number of useful techniques for displaying areal frequency data. Researchers agree that maps will continue to be an important research tool as survey methodologies become more and more refined.

One refinement in survey methodology has been the application of random-sampling procedures to the gathering of linguistic data. Tillery bases her research on random-sample telephone surveys of Texas and Oklahoma, surveys which provide the kind of data required for multidimensional modeling of spatial and social interactions. Tillery's statistical analysis reveals that nativity and attitude toward place are factors that should not be overlooked in explaining language variation.

New ways of looking at place are represented in work of Cukor-Avila and Davis, Smilowitz, and Neely. Cukor-Avila's "site study" emphasizes the site of language interaction as crucial to understanding speech participation. Using tape-recorded data gathered at the general store of a small community, Cukor-Avila explores the social and linguistic interactions within the community. Davis, Smilowitz, and Neely use statistical analysis based on "talking place maps" drawn by the adolescents in their study in order to investigate the association between talk and place

It is clear that no one type of data is sufficient to make reasonable analytical judgments. In evaluating the status of one construction, Wolfram uses grammaticality judgments, elicitation tasks, and semantic/pragmatic evaluations. His empirical evidence consists of both language production and responses to language samples. Labov and Ash use language samples ranging from spontaneous personal-experience narratives, to word lists, to computer-digitized syllables in word, phrase, and sentence contexts. They use speech samples not only from Birmingham but also from Philadelphia and Chicago in showing the importance of place in cross-dialectal comprehension.

Given the focus of LAVIS, all of the papers include Southerners among their population samples, but one cannot conclude that a feature or attitude is "Southern" without studying other regions as well. Thus, though the focus of these studies is regional, their conclusions and their methods should have broad application in the study of language variation.

The South: The Touchstone

Dennis R. Preston

INTRODUCTION

It has been said that Standard American English (SAE) is not what it is because of what it is but because of what it isn't. In a series of folk-linguistic investigations, I have shown that one of the most significant things SAE isn't is Southern United States English (SUSE). Here I review the findings, and the methodology behind them, which support this view of the special status of SUSE as a foil to SAE. A newer concern is the status of SUSE viewed internally. What do native speakers of SUSE believe about the provenance, differentiation, standardness, and agreeableness of their own variety? Are their patterns of identification and ranking of such matters similar to those obtained from Northern (Michigan, Detroit area) and Midland (southern Indiana, Louisville KY area) respondents, or do Southern raters have a different perception of and regard for their own (and other) varieties? Using data gathered from respondents who are themselves speakers of SUSE, I pay particular attention to the notion of linguistic insecurity and the degree to which (if any) Southern speakers themselves understand their special, albeit negative, contribution.

I begin with an account of how SAE has been defined in the past. A commonplace in United States linguistics is that every region supports its own standard variety; no one region is the locus (or source) of the standard. Historically, that is a fair assessment; no center of culture, economy, and government ever dominated. Therefore, the truth as represented in some linguistics textbooks is as Falk (1978:289) has it:

> In the United States there is no one regional dialect that serves as the model. What is considered standard English in New York City would not be considered standard in Fort Worth, Texas. Each region of the country has its own standard.

Although speakers can recognize, within their own local varieties, which forms are more standard (the usage of the best-educated speakers), it is not at all certain that they adhere to a cultural-linguistic relativism that allows them to admit that a standard exists in every region. More to the point, it is doubtful that nonlinguists in the United States believe that there is no region or area which is more (or less) standard than others. Falk's position is a confusion of sophisticated linguistic relativism, deriving from well-intentioned attempts to debunk notions of so-called primitive and deficient linguistic systems, with what she believes to be popular perception. The latter is the point which deserves investigation.

Other introductory texts use Broadcast English or propose a nonexistent variety:

> In America, Standard English is the form of the language used on the national media, especially in news programs. . . . (Akmajian, et al. 1979:181)

Several years ago there actually was an entire conference devoted to one subject: a precise definition of SAE. This convocation of scholars did not succeed in satisfying everyone as to what SAE should be. The best hint we can give you is to listen to national broadcasters (though nowadays some of these people may speak a regional dialect). (Fromkin and Rodman 1983:251)

From this it is clear that Fromkin and Rodman contrast the standard with regional varieties, though they earlier confuse the two notions:

... it is true that many words which are monosyllabic in Standard American are disyllabic in the Southern dialect: the word right, pronounced as [rayt] in the Midwest, New England, and the Middle Atlantic states and in British English, is pronounced [raət] in many parts of the South.[1] (1983:249)

Unintentionally, Fromkin and Rodman here come much closer to a folk linguistic description of a standard as their own prejudices peek through. SAE is exemplified in the Midwest, New England, and the Middle Atlantic states (and even in British English?) while the South has another variety (by implication, clearly not standard). Falk would have accused Fromkin and Rodman of regional prejudices (and she would be right), but a legitimate search for the source and locus of SAE will have to consider just such prejudices. What linguists believe about standards matters very little; what nonlinguists believe constitutes precisely that cognitive reality which needs to be described—one which takes speech community attitudes and perception (as well as performance) into account. In fact, it is pretty well agreed upon by sociolinguists that the notion *speech community* itself is better defined by the presence of shared norms of interpretation than by shared performance characteristics (Labov 1972b:158).

SAE cannot be characterized as a socioeconomic reality. If it could, why do Fromkin and Rodman make the mistake of contrasting regional vowels in the South (used by the most privileged and impeccably educated) with those of SAE? They commit the error of cloaking their personal folk beliefs in the mantle of linguistic expertise, confusing linguistic prejudice with scientific hypothesizing, when they assert that some Southern vowels, despite their use by educated and uneducated speakers alike, are regional and therefore not standard. In contrast, Langacker (1973:55) is self-conscious about his speculations: "British English enjoys special favor in the eyes of many Americans. Boston English is considered by many people to be more prestigious than Southern speech or Brooklynese."

To correct even introductory linguistics textbooks, research must be done which studies responses to varieties. Language attitude studies have explored just such dimensions of diversity, beginning by sampling attitudes towards different languages (Lambert et al. 1960) and moving on to different varieties of the same language (e.g., Tucker and Lambert 1969). Giles and his associates (summarized in Ryan and Giles 1982) have investigated a large number of such reactions (to taped voices) and have suggested a general pattern: speakers of regional varieties (where that suggests nonstandardness) find speakers of their own varieties warm, friendly, honest, sympathetic, and trustworthy, but often slow, unintelligent, and plodding; they often regard speakers of a superposed standard as cold, dishonest, and unsympathetic, but quick, intelligent, and ambitious. In short, to the extent that listeners find their own varieties less prestigious, they suffer from what Labov (1966) called "linguistic insecurity." One suspects that some of this insecurity has its direct source in speakers' awareness of the fact that the local variety does not serve extra-regionally. That is, it will not convince some outside listeners that the intelligence, education, and authority of the speaker or writer are high, and it will not, therefore, inspire confidence in the content of some messages. Of course, there are notable exceptions; information of the sort most likely to be delivered in a local or nonstandard variety (streetwise facts, farming information, sports calls and expressions, hunting and fishing facts) might, indeed, be seen as more trustworthy if delivered in a nonstandard variety, but the evaluation of other ("intellectual") characteristics of the speaker would not be improved.

Language attitude studies confirm, then, that regional varieties are not equal, even when only phonological features are contrasted (that is, when lexicon and grammar are not variables). Such studies help establish the folk linguistic base for another perspective on language varieties, an essential one for languages with no clear-cut standard model. What is lacking is an account of what speakers of various regions (and classes, and sexes, and ethnic groups, and ages, and so on) believe. While language attitude surveys hope to avoid the observer's paradox (Labov 1972b), which here includes the effect of awareness on respondents' evaluation and production of language, studies of an ethnographic nature seek to discover overt categories and definitions.

When speakers are presented with the task of identifying the areas of the United States where the most "correct" English is spoken, for example, how will they respond? If they are relativists like Falk, they will simply indicate that the task cannot be done, claiming that each area supports a standard. If, however, like Fromkin and Rodman, they have clear linguistic prejudices about the locus of SAE, they will readily rank areas of the country for language correctness, exhibiting a preference for Eastern and Midwestern over Southern speech. Additionally, if Langacker is right, preferences should emerge for speech that sounds British and for Boston speech over that of Brooklyn and the South.

Additionally, if the studies by Giles and his associates can be generalized to United States varieties, one might also expect to find that speakers who consider their accents "regional nonstandards" (i.e., who suffer from linguistic insecurity) will rank their home areas lower for correct speech than some other areas. On the other hand, since Giles and his associates found that there was a decided preference for the local area along affective dimensions (friendliness, honesty, and so on), one should find such a preference for the local area in a ranking task which asks where the most "pleasant" variety is spoken.

Such tasks are distinctly different from those found in typical language attitude surveys. In the latter, respondents check off attributes they assign to the speaker based on a short tape-recorded sample. A number of paired opposites (later factor analyzed to produce groups of terms with similar ratings) are presented to the respondents while each voice is played; they usually include such pairs as the following, placed at the extremes of a seven-point scale:

Friendly ___ ___ ___ ___ ___ ___ ___ Unfriendly

Such studies also often utilize a technique known as matched-guise, in which the same speaker (not detectable as the same by the respondents) provides samples of different varieties. Researchers claim that this technique allows for control of idiosyncratic qualities of voice.[2] These studies generally draw conclusions about attitudes toward regionally accented voices, but they do not, as a rule, ask the respondents where they thought each voice was from.[3] For example, research reporting that respondents from Detroit believe voices from Atlanta are "un-friendly" may accurately reflect response to the voice sample but may be misleading if 1) respondents did not recognize or misidentified the origin of the voice, or 2) respondents could not assign the voice to a specific area on their mental map. In short, folk linguistic considerations must be made a part of social psychological studies of language attitude.

METHODS

What follows is an excursion into the realm of one branch of folk linguistics (Hoenigswald 1966)—folk dialectology. This paper adds data collected from the United States South to earlier surveys of two regions of the United States: southern Indiana, an area suspected to be linguistically insecure, stemming from its association with caricaturistic South Midland ("hillbilly") speech; and southeastern Michigan, a typical Inland Northern speech community which should show little or no linguistic insecurity.[4] The research program reported here involves four tasks, which are discussed below in detail:

1) Respondents drew boundaries around areas where they believed the regional speech zones of the United States to be. Computerized summary maps from Indiana and Michigan respondents are contrasted below with individual hand-drawn maps from Southern respondents.[5]

2) Respondents ranked the fifty states on a scale of one to four (1 = "same," 2 = "a little different," 3 = "different," 4 = "unintelligibly different for the perceived degree of dialect difference from the home area.")[6]

3) Respondents ranked the fifty states, New York City, and Washington , D.C., on a scale of one to ten (1 = "least," 10 = "most") for "correct" and "pleasant" speech.[7]

4) Respondents listened to nine voices from sites on a north-to-south line down the middle of the United States (from Saginaw, Michigan, to Dothan, Alabama); the samples were all of male, well-educated, middle-aged speakers discussing nonspecialist topics. They were presented to the respondents in a scrambled order. Respondents were instructed to assign each voice to the site where they thought it belonged.

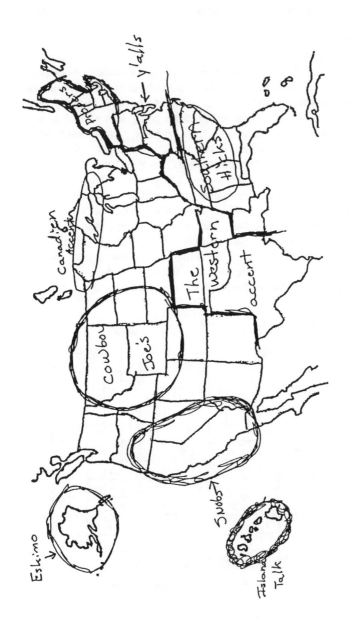

Figure 1: A southeastern Michigan hand-drawn map

Respondents were interviewed after they had performed tasks 1–4 to determine the etiology of their rankings, mappings, and identifications and to allow them to express other opinions about language distribution and status. Processing of these data is not yet complete and will be included only incidentally in what follows.[8]

Mental Maps of Dialect Areas

As indicated by the ordering of the above tasks, an important first task in determining dialect perceptions is to establish respondents' taxonomies of dialect areas. It will not do to assume that regions established by dialectologists form a cognitive set identical to that of lay speakers. A line map of the United States is given to respondents, who are asked to "draw boundaries around the areas where people speak differently and label the area and/or typical speakers from the area with the name(s) they ordinarily use to describe them." Since geographical knowledge is not being tested, respondents' questions about state locations are answered, and a detailed United States road map is available for them to consult.[9]

Figure 1 is a typical hand-drawn map from a southeastern Michigan respondent, and many of its characteristics will be shown below to be relevant to considerations of variety status and identification. Here, however, it is important to note that this map provides only a single respondent's view of where United States dialect boundaries are located. By tracing the outlines of the dialect areas onto a digitizing pad, however, it is possible to develop a more general picture.

Figure 2, which illustrates the maps of three hypothetical respondents, clarifies the procedure:

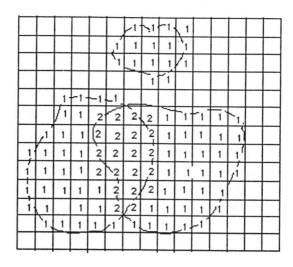

Figure 2: Three 'dialect region' outlines tallied in the computer record

Respondent #1 has drawn the more or less circular area to the left to outline a dialect region, and respondent #2 has indicated the same area in the partially overlapping circle to the right. The superimposed cell grid allows the computer to keep track of the number of times a cell has been included in a respondent's outline. A higher figure inside a cell indicates a greater number of respondents included it. It is possible, as we see in the small circular area outlined on the top, drawn by respondent #3, that there could be no agreement about an area (although one might question, in such a case, if the respondents were drawing the "same" area). In this case, the cells with a score of "2" represent the best agreement among these three respondents.

The generalizations which emerge from such considerations are not automatic. In all, 138 southeastern Michigan respondents drew some representation of the United States South, and their maps were subjected to the computer analysis outlined above. If we ask the computer to show us the entire territory of the South for which even one respondent included a cell, we get such an uninformative map as figure 3, an exaggeration most likely the result of one or two idiosyncratic drawings.

It is necessary, therefore, to seek other patterns of agreement. Figure 4 shows the area called "South" by both Indiana and Michigan respondents at a 50% level of agreement.

This procedure can be used to address some interesting questions. First, where is the core of a region? For 96% of Michigan respondents, as shown in figure 5, the heart of the South is to be found in southeastern Alabama. Second, do decreasing percentages of respondent agreement show regularly increasing concentric patterns of area outlining? Figure 6 shows that a regularly spaced series of concentric circles does not emerge from the Alabama heartland. Since some respondents drew outlines which overlapped with no part of an outline drawn by another respondent (as illustrated in figure 2), there cannot be 100% agreement. When a 91% reading is taken, a "tail" reaches to the coast, suggesting that although the heart of the South is in southeastern Alabama, its eastern and coastal ties are still significant for many respondents.

As demonstrated in figure 4, the difference between Michigan and Indiana perceptions of the South is not great. For both groups of respondents, the Southern speech area is a generally southeastern phenomenon; it includes none of Texas, little of Arkansas, and no more than one-half of Louisiana; Florida (more dramatically southern Florida for Michigan respondents) is obviously different. I believe it is easy to explain these exclusions. Texas and, less frequently, Louisiana are often singled out as separate speech areas, and Florida is often noted as a haven for Spanish-speakers and "Yankees" (see figures 7 and 8). Based on the study of the details of a number of individual hand-drawn maps which cannot be included here, I believe Arkansas is excluded due both to its "western" distance from the core and to the fact that the exclusion of Louisiana would have forced respondents to make an extra drawing effort to include it.

Figures 7 and 8 show all computer-generalized dialect areas in the continental United States drawn by at least 15% of the respondents for both Michigan (N=147) and Indiana (N=123). Outlines of the South are based on drawings by 138 Michigan

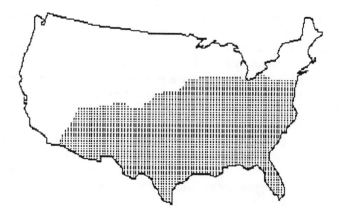

Figure 3: Southeastern Michigan respondents' computer-generalized map, showing where even one respondent outlined an area labeled 'South'.

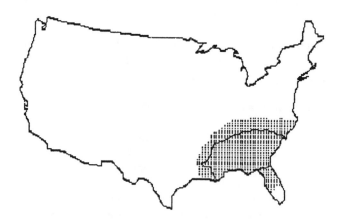

Figure 4: Indiana (outlined — 53 of 106) and Michigan (shaded — 69 of 138) respondents' generalizations at the 50% level of the United States 'South' dialect area

Figure 5: Michigan respondents' core South at the 96% (132 of 138)

agreement level

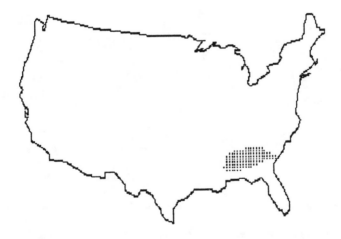

Figure 6: Michigan respondents' 91% (126 of 138) agreement for the South,

showing a coastal attachment

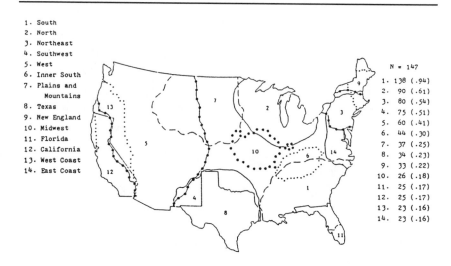

Figure 7: Generalized speech regions for southeastern Michigan respondents

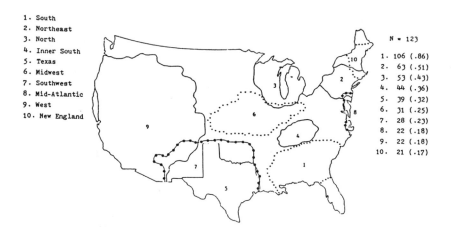

Figure 8: Generalized speech regions for southern Indiana respondents.

and 106 Indiana respondents. The South emerges as the most salient area: 94% of the Michigan respondents and 86% of the Indiana respondents drew a South. It is also interesting to note that for Michigan respondents the Outer South (or Southern Highland or Appalachian area) overlaps considerably a "deeper" South, while for Indiana respondents it is a separate zone. The second most salient area for the Michigan respondents was the North (actually a small Great Lakes area) at 61%.[10] A similar dramatic pattern exists for the Indiana data: their second next most frequently drawn area, the Northeast, was drawn by only 51% of the respondents. Michigan respondents see their entire state as uniquely in the Northern area (sharing space only with Wisconsin), while Indiana respondents put part of their state in the Midwest, part in the North, and, curiously, the part where they live, nowhere at all.

Data presented below will aid further in the interpretation of these generalized maps. Southern respondents' hand-drawn maps show a salient South which is essentially similar in shape to that of the Michigan and Indiana respondents. Of 163 maps drawn by Southern respondents, 96% outline a South.[11] I will present a number of these maps below when I discuss Northern and Southern caricatures of Southern speech. Like the Indiana and Michigan pattern, they show a Southeastern speech region which generally excludes Arkansas, Texas, and much of Louisiana and Florida and is drawn "deeper" by those who outline a South Midland, Appalachian, or, as it is much more frequently referred to in Southerners' maps, a "mountain" South.

From the very beginning of this research program (Preston 1982), it was clear that even the supposedly bias-free drawing project described above always results in overt expression and subtler hints that regional speech prejudice was at work. What is outlined as a dialect area by respondents reflects their folk understanding of *dialect* as "different speech," although the term *dialect* itself was scrupulously avoided in all the fieldwork. This being the case, it is not surprising, as figures 8 and 9 show, that the South is the most frequently drawn area and that the Northeast, which includes New York City, was often represented. These are, of course, precisely the areas referred to by Langacker as less prestigious—certainly not representatives of SAE. Research discussed below further develops this theme; for the moment, I will simply claim that evaluative notions of an area's speech, particularly those which are pejorative, enhance the area's salience as a distinct linguistic region.

Overt labels on maps also give a clear picture of what respondents believe about the South and other areas. Figures 9 and 10 display two Northern hand-drawn maps. The Michigan maps shown in figures 1 and 9 make clear that the Southern speech area is not one simply outlined as distinctive. In figure 1 the characterization is of "hicks" and in figure 9 of "hillbillies." The Michigan respondent who produced figure 1 apparently believes that local speech is so ordinary that it deserves no outline at all; the one who produced figure 9 calls the local area "midwestern english" and observes parenthetically that it is "normal." Here, however, it is important to note that although Indiana is in that larger "normal" circle, it is outlined as a subsection identified as having "its own expressions" and in which the "pronunciation is different." I refer to the special status of Indiana as I further develop its Southern ties (and its own futile attempts to deny them).

Figure 10, drawn by a Chicago respondent, makes these earlier "hillbilly" and "hick" labels even clearer: he notes that "Southern talk" is, quite simply, "the worst english in American." His "normal" talk is extremely localized in Chicago. Other interesting regional comments are the California label, "High Class Partying Slobs, a stuck up sound"; the New Jersey label, "Jerseyite Slang, always saying soda instead of pop"; and the Detroit label, "Black fro talk - because of the large % of Blacks."[12] Although I do not deal further with these interesting data here, it is clear

Figure 9: Michigan hand-drawn US dialect map

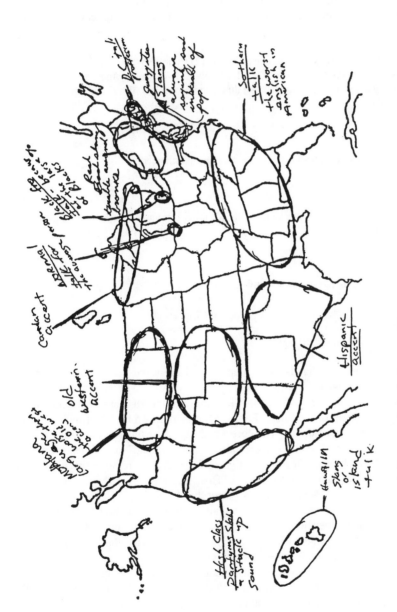

Figure 10: Chicago hand-drawn US dialect map

that, whatever the picture of other areas, the pejoration of the South by Northern respondents is consistent. As shown below, we do not need to rely on map labels to discover that Northerners make Southern speakers aware that their speech is held in low esteem. A displaced Southerner (C), who has moved to the Ann Arbor, Michigan, area, confesses when a fieldworker (M) asks if she can still "speak Southern":[13]

C: . . . I can't always do it on cue anymore. (2) ((mimics a Southern accent)) As y'all know, I came up from Texas when I was about twenty-one. And I talked like this. Probably not so bad, but I talked like this, you know I said "thi::s" and "tha::t" and all, those things.

M: Uh-huh.

C: And I had to learn rea:l fast how to talk like a Northerner?

M: Uh-huh.

C: Cause if I talked like this people ('ll, 'ld) think I'm the dumbest shit around. ((ends mimicry))

M: ((laughs))

C: So I learned to ta(h)lk li(h)ke a(h) Northerner
                              [
                              ((laughs)) Uh-hm.

C: ((rapidly)) Real fast. ((laughs))

Since Southerners' hand-drawn maps reveal the same general outline of the region as those drawn by Northerners and since the salience of the region in speech distinctiveness is as great, we must ask if these Southern maps reveal the same pejorative treatment of the South. Figure 11, a map drawn by a North Carolinian, would seem to reverse things. The core South (small as this representation has it) is characterized by "Southern Hospitality"; the "Upland" or "Outer South" is "Country As In Music" (a gloss designed, I believe, to remove the pejoration associated with the plain label "country"). "Boston & New York & New Jersey" are "Fast and Rude," and "Midwesterners"' speech is "Yak."

Southerners' maps much more often than Northerners' dichotomize North and South on a valued dimension, but accompanying labels do not make it clear that the evaluation is of language variety, although one could make that criticism of any number of labels used by Northerners as well (e.g., "hillbillies"). One map realizes this dichotomy directly in the assignment of "Them—the bad guys" to the Northeast and Great Lakes areas and "Us—the Good People" to a typically southeastern South. Another Southern map contrasts "Yankees" with "God's people." Figure 12 expresses in even more traditional language exactly what I suspect many of these North-South maps seek to express.

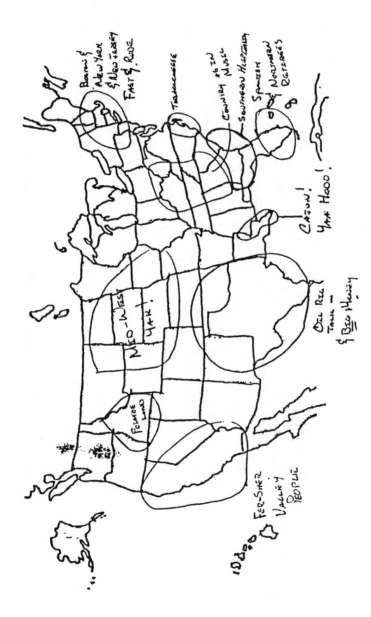

Figure 11: North Carolina hand-drawn dialect map

Figure 12: South Carolina hand-drawn US dialect map

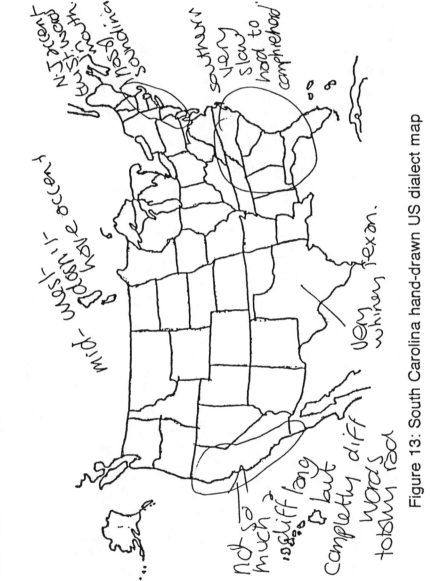

Figure 13: South Carolina hand-drawn US dialect map

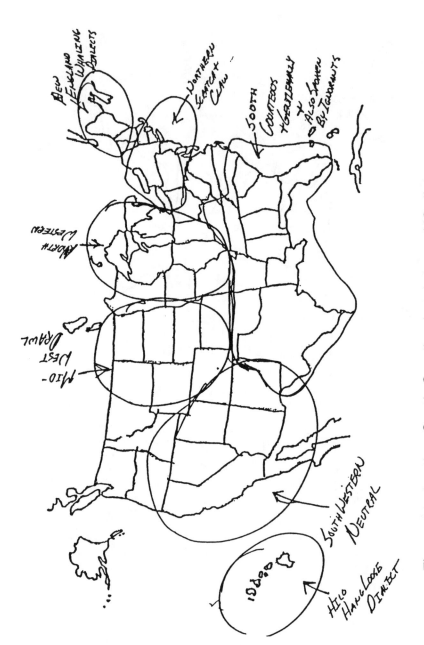

Figure 14: Another South Carolina hand-drawn US dialect map

There is no doubt that pride in local cultural values allows many Southerners to escape the self-hate or intense "linguistic insecurity" that so many of Labov's New York City respondents reported (1966), but negative valuation in Southern maps is not universally absent. Figure 13, for example, complains that Southern speech is "very slow hard to comprehend"[14] and that, except for a few caricaturistic labels, the rest of the United States is the "midwest" which "doesn't have accent." One might note, however, that comprehension (dealt with more extensively in the "degree of difference" task below) and rate are not the harshest criticisms that can be brought against a variety. Figure 14, although it continues the caricature of Northeastern speech ("Scratch and Claw") admits that Southern speech, although it may be "Courteous and Gentlemanly," is "Also Spoken By Ignorants," providing a counterexample to the notion that SUSE is one of the varieties of SAE.

Southerners are aware of Northern caricatures of Southern speech, and some Southerners have incorporated such negative caricatures into their own folk linguistic belief. Even for them, however, linguistic insecurity appears to be coupled with regional pride, particularly as even speech itself reflects certain cultural strengths ("gentlemanliness," "hospitality") or offers an excuse to outline a region with positive identities ("God's people") or contrast it with one which lacks positive identities (e.g., "Damn yankees"). Even among Southern respondents, however, there is a stereotype of "Midwestern" speech as being "accent free" or, as one respondent noted over a large Plains States area, as having "No Identity at all." Such labels on hand-drawn maps directly express the attitudes which underlie respondents' decisions to outline an area in the first place, but they are not easily quantified. Tasks 2–4 address this concern.

Degree of Dialect Difference
In the map-drawing task, unless a respondent refers specifically to comprehensibility or the degree of difference between one area and another, we cannot know the intensity of difference represented. Moreover, since some areas are not outlined at all, we have no information about them. Some of these deficiencies were overcome by having respondents rate each state for the degree of its difference from the local area as 1 (no difference), 2 (slightly different), 3 (different), and 4 (unintelligibly different). The mean score ratings were then divided into four groups: 1.00–1.75, 1.76–2.50, 2.51–3.25, 3.26–4.00.

Figure 15 shows that when Michigan raters evaluate degree of difference they perceive a larger local area than when they draw dialect maps. The "North" in figure 7 is a more circumscribed Michigan-Wisconsin area than the states rated "1" here, although that may be artificially imposed by the rating of entire states. In fact, all states rated "1" are at least partially included in the "North" in figure 7. This task reveals that Michigan respondents feel their speech to be closer to a large Western US group of States than to any other region, a fact not revealed in the hand-drawn maps

Here, however, it is the Michigan ratings of the South which are of interest. A much larger South than the one drawn in figure 7 emerges as a territory rated "3" (the same rating given the Northeast). Texas, Arkansas, Oklahoma, and Missouri (areas identified as separate speech areas, "Southwestern," or even "Midwestern")

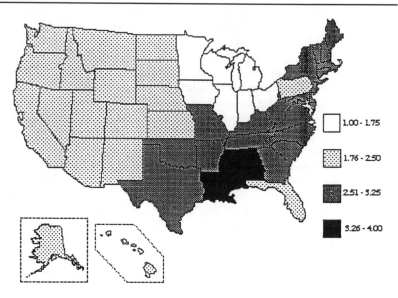

Figure 15: Degree of difference ratings for southeastern Michigan respondents

(N = 147)

are rated "3" along with obviously Southern states (e.g., Georgia and South Carolina). These differences, unlike those for the North outlined above, are not due to forced ratings of entire states, for Florida, for example, is excluded from this "3" rating. Only a core South (shifted a little to the West to include Louisiana) earns the "4" rating of unintelligibility. These ratings, unlike the map drawing, then, suggest that the Michigan raters are aware of a much wider area of influence of Southern speech, emanating from an unintelligible core. Even in the generally similarly rated Northeast there is no such "unintelligible" core.

Southern Indiana raters (figure 16) present a picture which is similar in some areas and strikingly different in others. Indiana respondents outline a strikingly smaller "1" area, one which includes only the laterally contiguous states of Ohio and Illinois, but, like Michigan raters, they also see the Northeast and the South as one degree more different from the large Western conglomerate of states (with the exception of Kentucky, right across the Ohio River from these raters).

More significantly, the Northeast is apparently the most different for these raters, for the "unintelligible" core, although small, is there in Massachusetts. Although they are from contiguous states, the Michigan and Indiana raters have different orientations to the Northeast and the South. The Northeast is "most" different for the Indiana raters, the South for the Michigan group. These findings coincide with traditional dialectology's affirmation that Michigan is, after all, an extension of western New England and upstate New York speech and that Southern speech influences are very strong in Indiana, particularly in the southern part of the state where this research was done.

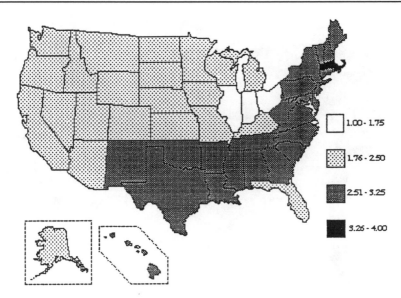

Figure 16: Mean degree of difference ratings for southern Indiana respondents

(N = 123)

Figure 17, the Southern raters' map of degree of difference, although more like the Indiana map in one important way, is different from the two earlier difference maps in a number of ways. Like Indiana raters, Southerners find the heart of major difference in the Northeast, but their zone of unintelligibility expands to include the entire Northeast and Wisconsin as well. Like Michigan raters, Southerners' zone of unintelligibility is larger than that of Indiana raters, suggesting that Indiana's "Midland" position is less likely to produce such radical evaluations.

Like Indiana raters, the Southerners have their own core zone of similarity (Georgia and South Carolina), but, unlike Indiana or Michigan raters, they have a secondary "local" zone surrounding this core. For these Southern raters, the large Western zone of states is lumped together as a "3." The two-level differentiation within the South seems to have promoted more distinctive ratings of all nonsouthern areas—the West, North, and Northeast. This "degree of difference" task adds information to generalizations from hand-drawn maps by providing a quantitative measure, but it does not let us know, for example, if two areas rated "3" are different along the same dimensions. I turn now to some more straightforwardly evaluative measures.

"Correct and Pleasant" Ratings

The data gathered in tasks 1 and 2 made it impossible to resist asking respondents to rate areas for their "correctness." Figures 18–20 show mean scores for the "correct" task from southeastern Michigan, southern Indiana, and the South.[15]

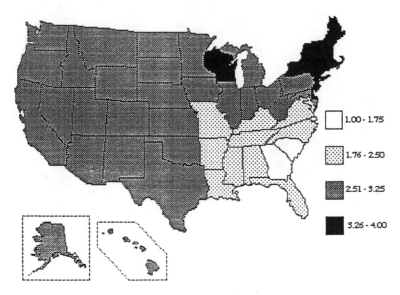

Figure 17: Mean degree of difference ratings for Southern respondents (N = 34)

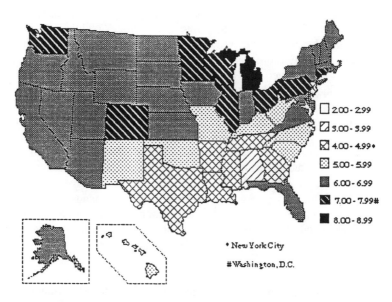

Figure 18: Mean scores of Michigan 'correctness' ratings

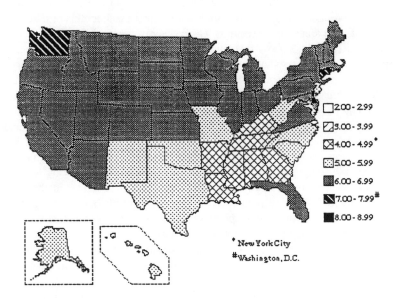

Figure 19: Mean scores of Indiana 'correctness' ratings

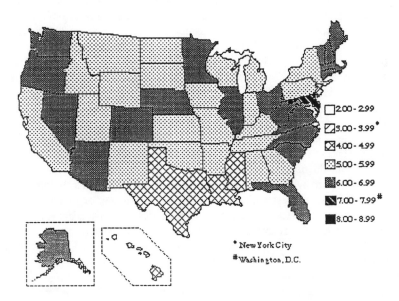

Figure 20: Mean scores of Southern 'correctness' ratings

Very few respondents complained about this task: the relativist position taken by Falk above was not that taken by the great majority of respondents. Although they often complained that they did not have information about this or that state, the ranking of most areas for correctness was for them a reasonable task.

Figures 18 and 19 show that for southeastern Michigan and southern Indiana respondents the areas associated with incorrect English are the South and New York City; they are the only areas which have mean scores within the range 4.00–4.99 (and for Michigan raters Alabama dips even into the 3.00–3.99 range). Langacker's assessment of what nonlinguists believe about correctness and Fromkin and Rodman's personal prejudices are upheld in this survey on at least two counts; the South and New York City (Langacker's "Brooklynese") are both rated low. In addition, areas which border on the South and New York City are given ratings in the 5.00–5.99 range, and their low ratings may be accounted for by noting their proximity to the lowest-rated areas. The other two sites falling in that range— Alaska (only for Indiana respondents) and Hawaii—must be interpreted differently. It is most likely that for many respondents the caricature of non-native speakers for these two regions may be very high. Unfamiliarity is an unlikely reason for the low rating since these respondents are just as likely to be unfamiliar with some of the plains and mountain states (e.g., Montana and Idaho) which fall in the 6.00–6.99 range.

Turning to the other end of the scale, predictions about linguistic insecurity seem to be borne out. Michigan raters, most strikingly, see themselves as the only state in the 8.00–8.99 range, exposing considerable linguistic self-confidence. Indiana respondents, however, rate themselves in the acceptable 6.00–6.99 range but clearly regard some other areas (Washington, D.C., Connecticut, Delaware, and Washington[16]) as superior. This lower ranking of the home area must indicate some (but not rampant) linguistic insecurity. They are clearly different from Michigan raters, who, apparently, see themselves as the only speakers of SAE in the United States. The Michigan ratings suggest at least one of the sources of the Indiana insecurity. Those raters allow surrounding states to bask in the warmth of Michigan's correctness. Wisconsin, Minnesota, Illinois, Ohio, and Pennsylvania (all nearby states) earned ratings in the 7.00–7.99 range. Indiana, however, which actually shares a land boundary with Michigan (as Illinois, Minnesota, and Pennsylvania do not), is rated one notch down, in the 6.00–6.99 range. Two interpretations are available. Indiana is seen by Michigan raters as belonging to that set of states farther west which earn ratings in that range, or, much more likely, Indiana is seen as a peculiarly northern outpost of Southern speech. It is surely that internal and external perception of Indiana as a site influenced by Southern varieties (an historically and descriptively accurate perception) which produces its linguistic insecurity. That Indiana respondents classify themselves along with Michigan, Illinois, Wisconsin, and other Great Lakes states in the 6.00–6.99 range in their own ratings may be interpreted as their attempt to align themselves with Northern rather than Southern varieties in order to escape the associations which form the basis of their insecurity. Further substantiation of this proposed dialect social climbing comes from their nonalignments. Their Kentucky neighbors are rated a full two steps lower for correctness, despite considerable linguistic similarity. On the other hand, the narrower range of ratings provided by the Indiana respondents (4.00–7.99) compared to the Michigan raters (3.00–8.99) might indicate a more democratic view of the distribution of correctness in general. That alternative but not necessarily contradictory interpretation requires investigation.

High ratings by both groups also include some of New England, which according to Langacker might be preferred. Unexpectedly, Washington, D.C., earns a high rating from both, an indication, perhaps, that the center of government is seen as an authority on matters linguistic. The West also emerges as a folk site for SAE for Indiana and Michigan respondents.

The Southern map of correctness (figure 20), like the comments on the hand-drawn maps, does not reveal a sweeping and unequivocal pattern of linguistic insecurity. In fact, some of these "southeastern Southerners" do not find themselves any less well-spoken than the southern Indiana respondents did, giving South and North Carolina, Virginia, and West Virginia ratings in the 6.00–6.99 range. Parts of the South rated one step down in the 5.00–5.99 range are just like the ratings for most of the country. New York City and New Jersey are the only big Northern losers, but those ratings are ubiquitous. The interesting zone of 4.00–4.99 incorrectness is the "western" South—Mississippi, Louisiana, and Texas, the latter two often excluded from the "true" South.

A comparison of the Indiana correctness map (figure 19) with the Indiana mental map of regional speech differences (figure 8) shows that, like degree of difference ratings, correctness evaluations do not necessarily change at the boundaries of perceived regional difference. While the low correctness ratings for the South, Outer South, and Southwest are very good matches between the two representations, the Midwest, North, West, New England, Northeast, and East Coast, all seen as distinct speech areas, differ little in their correctness ratings.

The Michigan map of perceived dialect areas (figure 7) shows little correspondence with the detailed levels of correctness in the Great Lakes area which emerged in the correctness ranking study (figure 18). Much of Indiana is lumped together with Michigan, Minnesota, Illinois, Wisconsin, and Ohio in a "North." On the other hand, the greater complexity of rankings in the Michigan correctness study is in general paralleled by a greater complexity of areal distribution in the hand-drawn map task. These responses might suggest that areas with less linguistic self-confidence (here Indiana) would show greater uniformity and consistency in perception.

This generalization is not supported, however, in the Southern correctness map (figure 20). There is little parallel between it and the Southern "difference" map (figure 17), and, although a computer generalization was not done, there is little support for this correctness rating map in the Southern hand-drawn maps (e.g., figures 1 and 11 through 14).

A factor analysis provides a more subtle way of grouping together those areas rated similarly. Figures 21 and 22 show the factor analysis of the correctness ratings from Michigan and Indiana.[17] Although the strongest factor group (#1) for both groups is the rather large western area to which both assigned high but not the highest ratings,[18] the second strongest factor group for both is the low-rated South, and, for Indiana residents, it reaches up to include the local area, rather strong proof that Indiana linguistic insecurity stems from associations with Southern speech. This same factor group is peculiarly divided for Michigan respondents; in addition to a small group of southern states, there is a continuum of New England, Mid Atlantic, and Great Lakes States in this category. Even these areas are broken up by a small number of idiosyncratic groups. These analyses suggest that the Indiana raters have a greater consistency in their perception of correctness as a geographical phenomenon. The third factor group for Indiana is a New England–Mid Atlantic stretch, the fourth a generally southwestern group of states, the fifth New York and New York City, and the sixth an interesting confirmation of the suggestion that Alaska and Hawaii might be rated lower on the basis of their being perceived as sites with a high concentration of non-native speakers. The inclusion of New Mexico in this factor group makes that interpretation plausible.[19]

These "correctness" ratings reveal the predicted differentiation between the Michigan secure and Indiana insecure raters and even more dramatically confirm the low prestige assigned Southern (and New York City) varieties. The task further confirms that it is association with Southern speech which gives Indiana its low external and internal regard. On the other hand, the more confused picture of Southern linguistic insecurity remains. These "southeastern" Southern raters were harsher on English in the United States in general, and, although they did not rate themselves high, they did not, as Indiana raters did, place several other areas higher than themselves.[20] On the other hand, they did locate a Southern region of incorrectness, but it was a "western" one which, with the exception of Mississippi, was often excluded from "core" Southern representations in the hand-drawn and degree of difference tasks.

Figures 23, 24, and 25 display the ratings of Michigan, Indiana, and Southern respondents respectively for "pleasant" speech. The suggestion by Giles and associates that local speech is affectively preferred, regardless of the evaluation of its "correctness," seems strongly confirmed, especially by the Indiana and Southern respondents. Only Indiana is rated in the 7.00–7.99 range for pleasantness, and the Southern raters place the entire Southeast in this high category but go on to elevate Alabama (the site where the ratings were done) to 8.00–8.99, a level paralleled only by Michigan's evaluation of its own correctness. The Michigan raters put only Washington, Colorado, and neighboring Minnesota in the same (7.00–7.99) range with their home site. These results suggest, further, that the preference for local norms along affective lines is stronger in areas where there is linguistic insecurity. At the other end, only a few areas are rated low by Indiana and Michigan respondents. New York City is the only site put in the 4.00–4.99 range by both Indiana and Michigan raters. More interestingly, the Southern respondents, similar to the Indiana and Michigan groups in the correctness task, are very different for this "pleasantness" task. The Michigan respondents continue to rate the South low, giving Alabama a score in the 4.00–4.99 range, but the Indiana raters, although they find the South incorrect, do not find it so unpleasant. In fact, New Hampshire, New Jersey, New York, and Delaware are a much larger pocket of unpleasant speech for Indiana respondents. For Michigan respondents, this Eastern unpleasantness is associated only with New York City and its immediate surroundings.

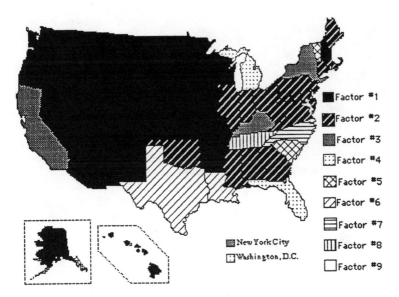

Figure 21: Factor analysis of Michigan 'correctness' ratings

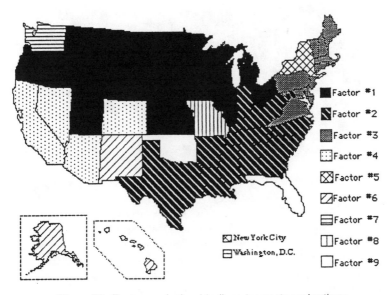

Figure 22: Factor analysis of Indiana 'correctness' ratings

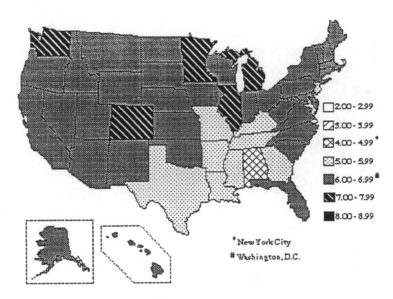

Figure 23: Michigan ratings of 'pleasant' speech

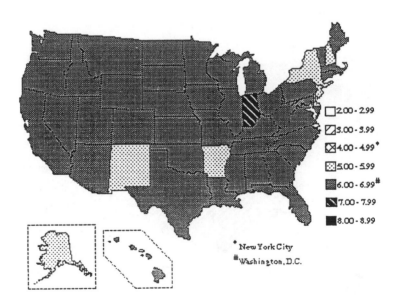

Figure 24: Indiana ratings of 'pleasant' speech

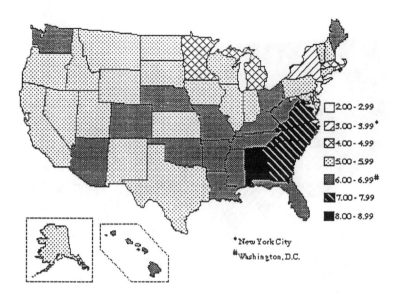

Figure 25: Southern ratings of 'pleasant' speech

Southern ratings of "unpleasantness" are much harsher. The only 2.00–2.99 mean rating of the entire series of studies shows up for New Jersey; New York City and New York State are given a 3.00–3.99; Massachusetts, Michigan, and Minnesota are assigned 4.00–4.99, a rating reserved by Michigan raters for only the "worst" Southern state (Alabama) and by Indiana raters uniquely for New York City.

Factor analyses of these pleasant ratings (figures 26 and 27) show that Indiana speakers do create a little pocket (along with Illinois) for themselves (figure 27, #6), but Michigan raters, more linguistically secure, extend the pleasant rating of their home site over the entire Great Lakes area (figure 26, #3). The factor groupings for both sets of respondents show a greater consistency and internal agreement than for the "correctness" tasks.

These "correct" and "pleasant" ratings provide final confirmation of the general patterns of linguistic security and insecurity outlined above. Areas with greater linguistic insecurity focus on regional solidarity (as expressed in "pleasantness") to express local identity. Areas with considerable security do not use local speech to express such identity, for its "uniqueness" is already taken up in the expression of status rather than solidarity matters.

Placement of Regional Voices

This last task may, at first, seem ill-placed in a folk linguistic setting, for it would seem to test only the acuity of a respondent in the detection of regionally different voices, but I believe that folk caricature expresses itself even here. This

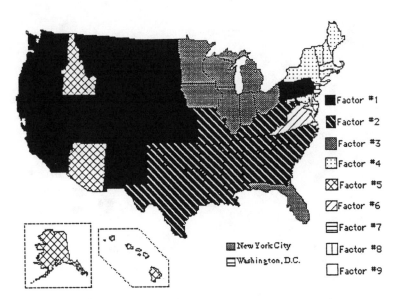

Figure 26: Factor analysis of Michigan 'pleasant' ratings

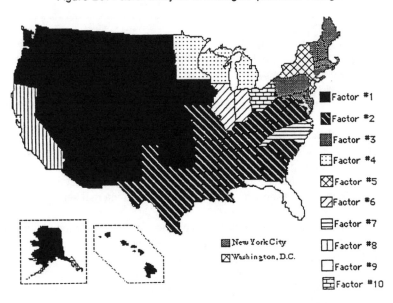

Figure 27: Factor analysis of Indiana 'pleasant' ratings

task asks how precisely respondents can place voice samples from different regions and how the boundaries which emerge from that task correspond to those already established in tasks 1–3. Figure 28 shows the sites at which recordings were made for the recognition test.

Figure 28: Home sites of nine voice samples

The voices (described above) were then played in no special order and the respondents were to associate each voice with a site. Assigning the sites the numbers one through nine (from south to north) allowed calculation of mean score for the task. For example, if a respondent said the voice from Saginaw, MI, was from South Bend, IN, the number "3" was tallied for that response. If each voice were recognized perfectly by each respondent, the scores would read simply, 1.00, 2.00, and so on from north to south. The actual scores are shown in the table below.

What is perhaps most striking is the fact that these nonlinguists were very good at arranging speech samples along a North-South dimension. If one assumes that a greater distance between mean scores indicates a greater distinctiveness heard between two samples, then a convention of calling a .50 or greater difference a "minor" boundary and a difference of 1.00 or greater a "major" one seems reasonable. Based on those calculations, a categorization of the respondents' areas of acoustic differentiation of United States dialects (along a midsection North-South dimension only, of course) is as represented in figures 29 and 30.

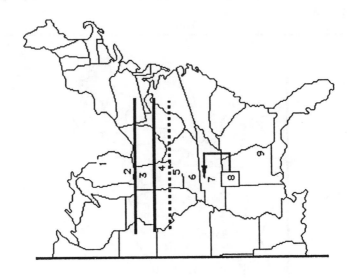

Figure 30: Indiana identification 'boundaries'

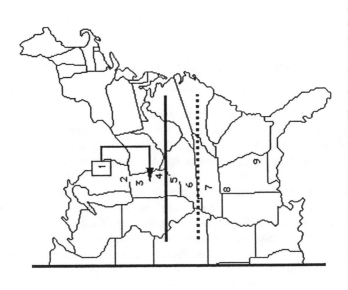

Figure 29: Michigan identification 'boundaries'

Table: Mean placement scores of the nine regional voices

Site	Assigned "correct" value	Mean Score Michigan	Indiana
1 Saginaw, MI	1	3.66	2.45
2 Coldwater, MI	2	3.05	2.63
3 South Bend, IN	3	3.46	3.75
4 Muncie, IN	4	4.13	5.09
5 New Albany, IN	5	5.27	5.83
6 Bowling Green, KY	6	5.52	6.06
7 Nashville, TN	7	6.22	6.38
8 Florence, AL	8	6.61	6.31
9 Dothan, AL	9	6.95	6.59

As figure 29 shows, the MI respondents distinguish a major boundary between a large northern territory which extends from their home state about half way through IN. This major boundary separates site #5 (the home site of the IN respondents) and everything farther south from this large northern area, lending further support to IN insecurity. The MI respondents also hear a minor boundary between sites #6 and #7, a division which would seem to distinguish between an "Appalachia" (or "South Midland") and a "Deep South."

In contrast, the IN respondents (figure 30) hear sharp subdivisions in the "North," placing major boundaries between sites #2 (Coldwater MI) and #3 (South Bend IN) and between #3 and #4 (Muncie IN), and a minor boundary between #4 and #5 (New Albany IN, their home site). IN respondents have placed their own region's voice in a large, undifferentiated "South." In what remains of this section, I shall compare these findings with those of the experiments already reported and with those of dialectologists.

The nine regional voices are typically described in terms of four major regions: 1) a "North" (or "Upper North"), 2) a "North Midland" (or "Lower North"), 3) a "South Midland" (or "Inner South," "Upper South," or often, inaccurately, "Appalachia"), and 4) a "South" (or "Lower," "Coastal," or "Deep South"). The following comparison considers two representations of this territory—one based exclusively on phonology, the other on general characteristics of dialect, although it is important to note that dialect vocabulary and grammar played no role in these identifications since the portions of the tape-recordings which were used for the task were specifically selected to exclude such features. Figure 31, based on Labov (1991), shows this four-part division in terms of 1) a "North," characterized by the "Northern Cities Shift" and extending from MI into about the upper one-fourth of IN; 2) a "North Midland," in which the low vowels [ɔ] and [ɑ] are merging and covering only about half of central IN; 3) a "South Midland," undergoing rapid, current change and extending from the lower third of IN through the northern third of TN; and 4) a "South," characterized by the "Southern Vowel Shift" and encompassing the rest of TN and all areas farther south (except FL). Our voices would be placed as follows:

Saginaw MI, Coldwater MI, South Bend IN	North
Muncie IN	North Midland
New Albany IN, Bowling Green KY	South Midland
Nashville TN	South Midland (south border)
Florence AL, Dothan AL	South

In our test, therefore, major boundary lines should have been heard between #3 and #4 and between #4 and #5. Ideally, at least minor boundaries should have been heard between #5 and #6 and between #6 and #7 (distinguishing the "transitional" or "border" nature of Nashville TN). Both the MI and IN identifications (figures 29 and 30, respectively) correspond to some degree with this schema. MI respondents do not distinguish a "North" from a "North Midland"—they include #4 (Muncie IN) in their larger "North." They do, however, hear the "North Midland"–"South Midland" distinction very strongly, placing their only major boundary there. This placement is consistent with Carver (1987), who suggests that the "South Midland" territory is actually an "Upper South," (but compare essays by Frazer and by Lance and Faries, this volume). The MI respondents also place a minor boundary between sites #6 (Bowling Green KY) and #7 (Nashville TN), the transitional area where the "South Midland" (or "Upper South") is thought to stop and the "South" (or "Lower South") begin, according to figure 31.

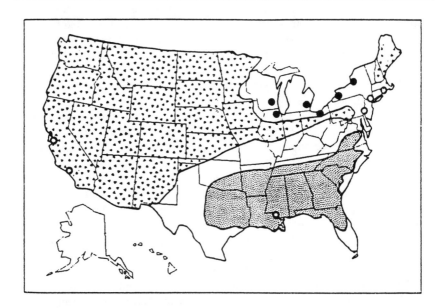

Figure 31: The 'three dialects of America' (Wolfram 1991:89)

The IN raters, on the other hand, make three distinctions (figure 30), but they do not completely fulfill the expectations of figure 31 either. First, they hear a "major" distinction between Coldwater MI (site #2) and South Bend IN (site #3) where, according to figure 30, there should be none. They are, however, exactly on target with a strong boundary between sites #3 and #4, strengthening the argument for a "North" versus "Midlands" distinction. That tendency would seem to be further supported, since they hear only a "weak" boundary between sites #4 and #5 (the traditional "North Midland"–"South Midland" distinction). In fact, however, their distinctions also support the absence of a "Midlands" territory, for their "South Midland" area (beginning at site #5) is not once subdivided (even with a minor boundary) from the "South." Moreover, their reversal of sites #7 and #8 makes their failure to make any southern subdivisions more difficult to interpret, although the very small difference in the means scores of sites #7 and #8 (.07) makes consideration of that point unnecessary.

MI raters see a division between the "South Midland" and the "South" but do not recognize the closer-to-home "North" versus "North Midland" split. Conversely, IN respondents separate the "North" from the "North Midland" (and add a "Far North" versus "Not-So-Far-North") but make no intermediate distinctions south of their home site.

Figure 32 shows a map prepared from a number of dialect studies reflecting phonological as well as lexical and grammatical criteria:

Figure 32: A 'conglomerate' of US dialect studies (Lance 1994)

The "A" line is a principal cutoff for "North," and it corresponds to what we have already seen above. The "D" line is also a major division, and it separates sites #4 and #5 exactly as figure 31 does. The "C" line is a weaker boundary and it separates sites #3 and #4 (also as figure 31 does). Although there are a number of minor dialect boundaries in the "Inner South," there is no major subdivision in the southern area except those separating areas "F" from "G" and "I" from "J" (limiting our attention to only those areas which include our sample voices). Based on this general picture, therefore, our voice samples should be stratified as follows:

Saginaw MI, Coldwater MI, South Bend IN	North of line "A"
Muncie IN	Between lines "C" and "D"
New Albany IN	South of "D," north of Ohio River
Bowling Green KY	South of "D," south of Ohio River
Nashville TN, Florence AL	Within area "G"
Dothan AL	Within areas "F" and "J"

These major boundary divisions create quite a different picture of the southern United States from that given in figure 31. This different picture, however, has only a little influence on what I have already said about the patterns of identification of these sample voices. The MI distinction between sites #6 and #7 is also supported in this representation, but, again, there is no justification for the IN placement of a boundary between sites #2 and #3.

In general, therefore, our respondents hear the right order of our north-to-south samples, but they sometimes do and sometimes do not "hear"greater distinctions at those boundaries discovered in the professional study of dialect differences.

How will these identifications supplement the information which has already been seen in the other quantitative studies? Figures 7 and 8 represent the composite of hand-drawn maps for MI and IN respectively.

For the MI respondents, the most noticeable correlation is the non-differentiation among voices #1, #2, #3, and #4 and the unity of that territory in the hand-drawn composite. All four sites fall within the area defined in figure 7 as "North," and no boundaries are heard by MI respondents in that area in the identification task. Figure 7 also shows that MI respondents have an "eastern tail" of their "Midwest" (area #10), but it falls between Muncie IN (site #4) and New Albany IN (site #5), encompassing neither. When the MI respondents produce a major boundary between these two areas, then, their hand-drawn composite is very supportive of that identification. One leaves the "North" and crosses the "eastern tail" of the "Midwest" between Muncie IN and New Albany IN.

On the other hand, New Albany IN does not quite fit into area #6 (the "Inner South" of figure 7) either, a fact which, as noted above, corresponds very well with, for example, Carver (1987). In figure 7, in fact, New Albany IN lies in a sort of trough between the "Midwest" and the "Inner South," but since the hand-drawn composite shows that there are two boundaries between New Albany IN and Muncie IN (to the north) and only one between New Albany IN and Bowling Green KY to the south, the identification task's major boundary between #4 and #5 strongly correlates with the hand-drawn task from a southern perspective as well.

Figure 7 shows an overlapping "Inner South" (area #6) and "South" (area #1). The remaining sample voices are distributed in that territory as follows:

Site #6 (Bowling Green KY) — Inner South (#6)
Site #7 (Nashville TN) — Inner South (#6) and South (#1)
Sites #8 and #9 (Florence AL and Dothan AL) — South (#1)

Only one of these boundaries (between sites #6 and #7) is supported, with a minor boundary, in the MI identification task.

The IN composite of hand-drawn maps (figure 8) shows a slightly different organization of the territory under consideration here. First, site #3 (South Bend IN) lies on a "dual boundary" (the southern limits of area #3—a "North," and the northern limits of area #6—a "Midwest"). Interestingly, although there is no support for it in professional studies, the IN respondents "heard" a major boundary between sites #2 and #3, just where their "North" and "Midwest" collide.

Muncie IN and New Albany IN also lie on a boundary in figure 8—the southern edge of the "Midwest" (area #6), an area separated from the "Inner South" (area #4) by a small trough or "empty" territory. In spite of the fact that the hand-drawn map puts the local area on the southern edge of the "Midwest" for IN respondents, they hear a difference (a minor boundary) between themselves and Muncie IN. Perhaps the following scenario can explain this discrepancy. When the map-drawing task is proposed, linguistic insecurity causes IN respondents to place themselves as far north as seems reasonable (the lower edge of a "Midwest"). The identification task does not invite such attention to insecurity, and the (accurate) distinction between "North Midland" (Muncie IN) and "South Midland" (New Albany IN) surfaces. The placement of sites #4 and #5 in the same area in the hand-drawn composite and their separation by a minor boundary in the identification task is the most striking discrepancy between these two measures for the IN respondents.

In the remaining southern territory, the IN hand-drawn composite shows a neat division between an Inner South (area #6) and a "South" (area #1), and the remaining voice samples are divided equally between them—Bowling Green KY and Nashville TN fall in the "Inner South," and Florence and Dothan AL fall in the "South." In the identification task, however, IN respondents mark no major or minor boundaries in this territory.

Since the "correct" and "pleasant" tasks and the "degree of difference" task used states for rankings, the comparison with the identification task will not be as productive, but I offer the few following comments.

In the "correctness" task (figure 18), the MI respondents indicate five gradations in the territory covered by the voice samples of the identification task. The home state is in the 8.00 range, IN 6.00, Kentucky 5.00, Tennessee 4.00, and Alabama 3.00. This would suggest the following subdivisions:

Saginaw and Coldwater MI
South Bend, Muncie, and New Albany IN
Bowling Green KY
Nashville TN
Florence and Dothan AL

In the identification task, however, only one MI boundary (the minor one between Bowling Green KY and Nashville TN) supports this division. The major boundary (between Muncie and New Albany IN) could not be represented in the correctness task at all (and is, perhaps, a good indication of the artificiality of the state-wide assessment required in that task). On the other hand, the displacement of the Saginaw MI voice (site #1) to a position between sites #3 and #4 (both in IN) ignores the considerable correctness distinction made by the same raters between MI and IN.

The IN correctness task, as figure 19 shows, reveals that IN raters make only two distinctions in the territory under consideration. All sites in MI and IN belong to a generally correct (6.00–6.99) northern area, and all sites to the south fall within the generally incorrect (4.00–4.99) region. Similarly, the IN identification task observes no major boundaries in the south (from sites #5 through #9), and that almost matches figure 19, except for the fact, of course, that these IN raters have put themselves (site #5) in the more correct "North" in this correctness task, the task which rather obviously promotes greatest attention to overt norms. Recall, however, that the factor analysis of IN correctness ratings—figure 22—teased out the IN relationship with the South. That more subtle measure parallels the IN classification of the local site as "Southern" in the identification task. Where IN raters make many identification distinctions (between sites #2 and #3, between #3 and #4, and between #4 and #5), however, there are none in the correctness task, although one could have occurred between sites #2 and #3 (MI and IN, respectively).

The MI "pleasant" task (figure 23) shows almost as many distinctions along the line of voice samples from the identification task as the "correct" task did. The only difference is that Kentucky and Tennessee (which are rated in different categories in the "correct" task, in keeping with the general MI tendency to rate states lower for correctness the farther south they are) are rated in the same (5.00–5.99) range in the "pleasant" task. The distinction in the identification task between Nashville TN and Bowling Green KY (supported by a minor boundary) is, therefore, not paralleled in the "pleasant" task for these respondents. The factor analysis of the "pleasant" task (figure 26) shows a two-way division between two strong factors: Factor Group #2, a "South," which contains the voices from sites #6 through #9; and Factor Group #3, a "North," which contains the remaining voices (including the southern IN site #5). The minor MI identification task boundary (between Bowling Green KY and Nashville TN) is not reflected in the factor analysis of these MI pleasant task data.

Results for the IN "pleasant" task (figure 24) show only two degrees—a "very pleasant" 7.00–7.99 for the home site and a "generally pleasant" 6.00–6.99 for everything to the north and the south. That classification is precisely paralleled in the major identification boundary between MI (site #2) and IN (site #3) to the north and would seem to cut IN off from surrounding territory exactly as the pleasant task did. It is interesting that all the IN major and minor identification boundaries fall within the state and that the state is isolated in the "pleasant" task. The IN factor analysis of the pleasant task (figure 27) is slightly more articulated than the mean score data from the pleasant task itself, and it divides the line of voices used in the identification task into three sets: MI voices (Factor Group #4), IN voices (Factor

Group #6), and all voices south of IN (Factor Group #2). This articulation again matches the strong IN identification boundary between Coldwater MI and South Bend IN.

Finally, the "degree of difference" ratings for MI respondents (figure 15) show a three-way division along the line of the stimulus voices: MI and IN voices are all "the same" (1.00–1.75), Kentucky and Tennessee voices are "very different" (2.51–3.25), and Alabama voices are "unintelligibly different" (3.26–4.00). In some ways this is a very close match to the MI identification scores. Recall that the MI respondents place no boundaries from site #1 (Saginaw MI) through site #4 (Muncie IN). Since site #5 (New Albany IN) is at the southern extreme of IN and since states were not subdivided in the "degree of difference" task, this large undifferentiated stretch in these two tasks is very similar. On the other hand, the minor boundary which MI respondents "heard" in the identification task is not paralleled in the "degree of difference" task, where, of course, it might have surfaced. Instead, the "degree of difference" task cuts Alabama off from Tennessee but suggests that Kentucky and Tennessee are similar.

IN responses to the "degree of difference" task (figure 16) also show three degrees of difference along the line represented in the stimulus voices for the identification task, but they are not organized in the same way. Although they rate the IN voice "the same" (1.00–1.75), IN respondents rate both MI, to the north, and Kentucky, to the south, as "slightly different" (1.76–2.50). They find both Tennessee and Alabama "very different" (2.51–3.25). Again the major boundary between IN (South Bend IN) and MI (Coldwater MI) in the identification task is reflected in another quantitative task. I cannot argue as I did above for the MI data, however, that the minor boundary between Muncie IN and New Albany IN in the identification task is reflected in the IN-Kentucky difference shown in the "degree of difference" task. Since these IN raters are from the southernmost part of the state and still reckon Kentucky "a little different," we must take them at their word. Doubtless, that is a reflection of the greater "overtness" of the "degree of difference" task and its ability to bring out the linguistic insecurity of these southern IN raters, manifested, as we have seen before, in their desire to cut themselves off from "southern" influences.

CONCLUSIONS

Southern United States English is clearly a variety with negative prestige. Northern speakers are prejudiced against Southern speech even along affective dimensions. There are substantial differences between the judgments of linguistically secure and linguistically insecure listeners regarding "pleasantness" and "correctness." There is some evidence that insecurity results in exaggerated isolation of the home area in affective evaluation and in exaggerated isolation from nearby "contaminating" areas in evaluations of correctness. Insecure areas also seem to be less harsh in evaluating correctness in general, although Labov reports the opposite tendency for stigmatized speakers' evaluation of others with similar features in his study of attitudes and production differences in New York City

(1966). Both secure and insecure areas agree, however, in assigning greater geographical salience to areas seen as incorrect.

The responses from rather than about the South, however, do not fit so neatly into this picture. When given the opportunity for self-loathing on correct speech ratings, Southerners do not express rampant insecurity (or they deflect it to another part of the South, as seen in figure 20). Nevertheless, they rate themselves very high for pleasantness, and assign Northerners, especially Northeasterners (particularly New Yorkers), the lowest mean ratings of any group in all tasks. Although there is both shame and pride in local speech, there is little grudging appreciation of Northeastern "standards" (as there was from both Michigan and Indiana raters); only a "national government" Washington, D.C., standard is admitted to by Southern raters. More data will have to come from below the Ohio River before we can hope to understand the complex currents of language valuation and status as seen from that point of view.

Most importantly, these several approaches have shown that correctness and related affective dimensions, at least in United States English, are notions which, for nonlinguists, have geographical significance. Though it is not easy to arrive at the folk perception held of such concepts, it is important to seek it out, for, at least for United States English, it represents a set of beliefs both strongly held and influential in the linguistic life of large and small speech communities. These data are being further analyzed for the consistency of general perceptions presented here with those of different age, sex, and status groups, and such subdivisions may have a great deal to say about the etiology of and change in the perception of language differences.

Such a multidimensional approach to what are ultimately folk linguistic questions provides a surer consideration of the limited data provided by language attitude surveys and from anecdotal and participant observer information. It serves, moreover, to help build a more complete and accurate picture of how speakers and listeners regard language use and variety within regions of their country. Most especially, it provides a means of eliciting responses to questions about language standards from the people who live in those regions.

NOTES

1. This pronunciation is, in fact, not disyllabic.

2. Of course, this begs the question of whether or not voice characteristics are associated with areal varieties. Since work by Esling and others (e.g., Esling 1981) suggests that vocal quality is connected to regional varieties, the matched-guise technique may not be as fail-safe as it was once thought to be. In addition, experiments in which one speaker has been said to represent accurately a large number of varieties (e.g., Giles 1970) are especially suspect; surely such performances capture only the grossest caricatures and are rife with inaccurate representations.

3. Milroy and McClenaghan (1977) is an exception.

4. The work reported on here for Michigan and Indiana was supported by a grant from the National Science Foundation. The respondents were subdivided into relatively well-balanced subgroups based on age, status, and gender, but in the findings reported here,

these groups are combined. Data collected from Appalachians and African-Americans in southeastern Michigan were excluded from the findings reported here; the Indiana respondents were all European-Americans.

5. Earlier applications of this methodology are reported on and summarized in Preston (1989a). More recent techniques developed by Preston and Howe (1987) allow computerized generalizations to be compiled from individual responses (e.g., Preston 1989b). Computer generalizations of Southern hand-drawn maps have not been produced.

6. One version of this technique is long-standing in dialect study (e.g., Daan and Blok 1970; Grootaers 1959; Kremer 1984; Rensink 1955; Weijnan 1968) and is reviewed in Preston (1989a); the revised version used here is reported in Preston (1989b).

7. Such ratings are common in other areas of cultural geography (e.g., Gould and White 1974). The version of this task used here is reported in Preston (1989b).

8. Niedzielski and Preston (under review) and Preston (in progress) contain fuller accounts of these more ethnographically oriented data; Preston (1993) contains some of these data specifically relevant to dialectology.

9. This procedure was first employed in Preston (1982), although hand-drawn mental maps had been used before (e.g., Gould and White 1974).

10. The Northeast is the third most salient area (54%) for the Michigan respondents.

11. I am indebted to Michael Montgomery for maps from Kentucky, Tennessee, North and South Carolina (the majority), Florida, Louisiana, Georgia, Alabama, Texas, Virginia, and West Virginia respondents. They represent both sexes, a considerable variety of social status and age groups, but only a few African-Americans.

12. Labels on hand-drawn maps are more thoroughly treated in Preston (1982).

13. These data are part of a more general National Science Foundation survey of folk linguistics in southeastern Michigan and are more fully treated in Niedzielski and Preston (under review). The discourse transcription conventions which are relevant here are the following:

    (( )) — transcriber comments
    (2) — pauses (in tenths of a second)
    (h) — "breathy" or "laughing" speech
    ? — rising intonation
    . — rise-fall ("final") intonation
    , — fall ("list") intonation
    [— point of overlap in above line
    : — vowel lengthening
    (x,y) — alternative interpretations of what was said

14. See Labov and Ash (this volume) on "local advantage."

15. The Southern sample consisted of 36 Auburn University students, principally from Alabama, Georgia (the majority), and South Carolina.

16. The 7.00–7.99 rating for Washington is a result of many respondents' not distinguishing it from Washington, D.C. In this task the states and areas were presented in an alphabetical list, not on a map.

17. Unfortunately, the smaller number of respondents did not allow a meaningful factor analysis of Southern data.

18. Oddly enough, New Hampshire and Delaware belong to this group in the Michigan responses.

19. The confusion of Washington and Washington, D.C., shows up even in the factor analysis (group #7).

20. Washington, D.C. (and adjoining Maryland), are, in fact, rated in the 7.00–7.99 range.

How Far North Is South?
A Critique of Carver's North-South Dialect Boundary

Timothy C. Frazer

On the map of popular imagination, the Ohio River has traditionally divided the United States into North and South. If we include as part of the South the "South Midland" of traditional dialectology, we would find some linguists like Dakin (1971) and Wood (1971) who agree with this popular concept, drawing the northern boundary for the South Midland dialect along the Ohio River. Other dialectologists, however, have found evidence of South Midland speech north of the river, especially in Indiana and Illinois (McDavid 1958; Frazer 1978, 1987). And in Missouri, somewhat west of the Ohio Valley but in latitudes far to the north of it, Lance and Faries (this volume) have also found a strong southern presence, farther north than the popular boundaries of the South.

The breadth and scholarly depth of Carver's *American Regional Dialects* give his conclusions a powerful stamp of authority. His American dialect maps are beginning to appear in standard texts on dialectology, and, for many students and laypersons, his conclusions may well preempt the debate on linguistic geography in the United States. In contrast to the research mentioned above, Carver's "North-South Divide" comes down on the side of popular imagination. North of the Ohio River is what Carver (1987:247) calls the "Lower North"; south of the river is the "Upper South" (Carver dismisses Kurath's 1949 delineation of the "Midland" dialect area, although his data do acknowledge a thin dialect layer which he calls "Midland.") In this paper, I examine the evidence for Carver's North-South boundary in terms of its apparent conflicts with my own conclusions and those of others.

The strongest argument against assigning all of Illinois and Indiana to the "North" (Carver does not include Missouri in his "North" area, but neither does he include any part of it in his "Upper South") is phonological. Chicagoans who venture south of Indianapolis in Indiana or Peoria in Illinois frequently remark on what they perceive to be the "Southern Accent" of the natives. And there is scholarly evidence for their perceptions. Habick (1980, 1991), for example, studied the speech of 20 adolescents in Farmer City, Illinois, a rural community 20 miles northwest of Champaign-Urbana, which is, according to Carver's maps, part of the "Lower North." Habick found ample evidence of what he called "Southern" speech, especially fronting of the mid- to upper-back vowels, a feature of Labov's (1991) Southern Vowel Shift.[1]

Within this "Northern" region, some southern pronunciation features seem to be increasing in frequency. Among Habick's Farmer City adolescents, fronting of back vowels involved more phonemes and appeared more frequently than in the parents' and grandparents' generations. Moreover, in a study of the speech of 50 residents of west-central Illinois, an area actually covered by Carver's *Upper* North boundary (emphasis mine), I found fronting of /au/, a phenomenon common to much of the South, to be higher among respondents who grew up during the Great Depression—almost twice as high as the generation born before 1910 (Frazer 1983b).

The geographical extent of the southern features in parts of Carver's "North" is shown in maps 1–3, which outline the northern limits of five southern pronunciation features: 1) fronting of /au/; 2) diphthongization of /u/ after alveolars; 3) glide shortening of /ai/; 4) diphthongization (with backing and/or rounding) of "open o"; and 5) ingliding of lax front vowels. Although they are not mapped here, I found the same contours, in Illinois at least, for other southern pronunciation features, including glide shortening of /oy/, front vowels upglided before /š/, /ʊ/ in *bulge* and final /i/ in *borrow* (Frazer 1987; see also Kurath and McDavid [1961] 1982).

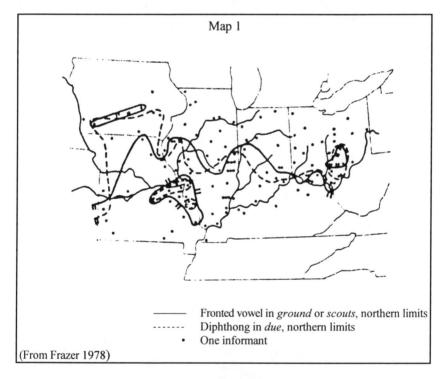

Map 1

——— Fronted vowel in *ground* or *scouts*, northern limits
- - - - Diphthong in *due*, northern limits
• One informant

(From Frazer 1978)

These maps, it should be noted, are based on the same set of interviews as Carver's maps, those performed for the Dictionary of American Regional English (DARE) between 1965 and 1970. But while Carver's maps are based on responses to the lexical questionnaire, maps 1–3 are based on taped readings of "Arthur the Rat."[2] A comparison of my maps to Carver's summary map (map 4) reveals the fundamental conflict: while my maps suggest a strong southern presence in much of southern Illinois and Indiana, much of Missouri, and parts of Ohio, Carver's shading of the "Lower North" and his attempt to affix a label to that region obscure this presence.

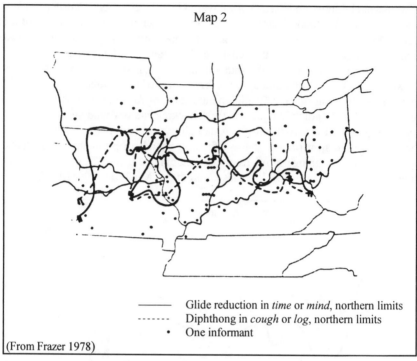

Map 2

——— Glide reduction in *time* or *mind*, northern limits
------- Diphthong in *cough* or *log*, northern limits
  •   One informant

(From Frazer 1978)

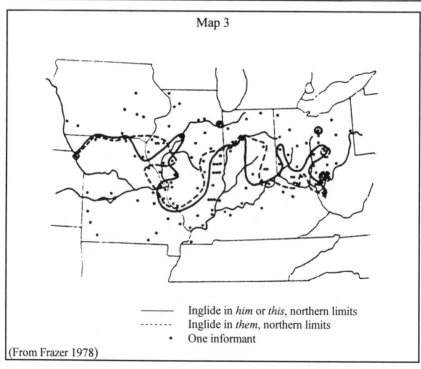

Map 3

——— Inglide in *him* or *this*, northern limits
------- Inglide in *them*, northern limits
  •   One informant

(From Frazer 1978)

Map 4: The major dialect regions summarized

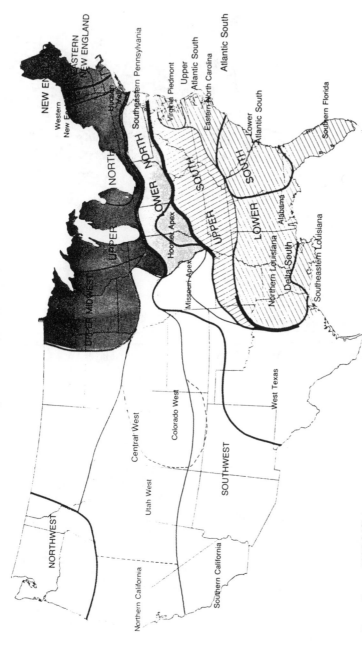

(From Carver 1987:248)

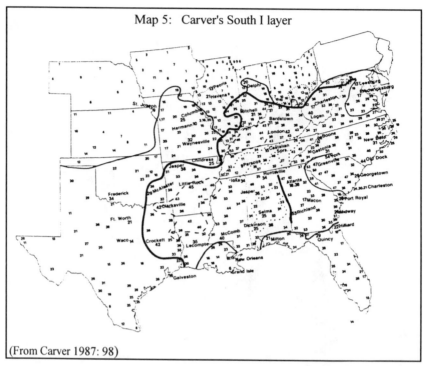

Map 5:   Carver's South I layer

(From Carver 1987: 98)

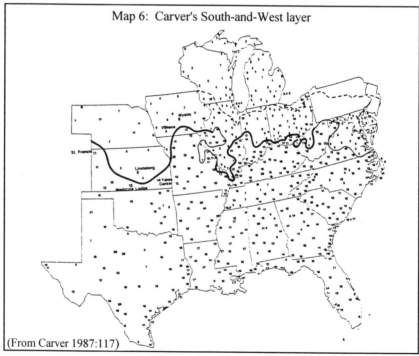

Map 6:   Carver's South-and-West layer

(From Carver 1987:117)

Moreover, this southern presence north of the Ohio is reinforced by some of Carver's own lexical data which appear on two of his other maps. The boundary for Carver's South I (map 5), representing 78 lexical isoglosses, follows closely the contours of my maps, except that southern Ohio and western Illinois do not fall within Carver's boundaries. An even closer resemblance comes from Carver's "South-and-West" map (map 6), which replicates the inclusion of western Illinois and southern Ohio. But Carver's South II map, whose boundaries cling to the Ohio River and the Missouri-Arkansas state line, appears to have been a stronger influence in determining Carver's North-South boundary, perhaps in part due to the 84 isoglosses on that map.

Do we have to choose between two realities here? I could argue that pronunciation boundaries ought to be given more weight, partly because pronunciation features are a more salient feature of normal discourse than is regional vocabulary. They are also a more integral part of systematic language.[3] But it is more productive to understand the differences between DARE and other databases. Four Illinois maps (maps 7–10) allow us to compare some DARE distributions with those from the Linguistic Atlas of the North Central States (LANCS) and also with checklist evidence from the LANCS collection.

Based on LANCS data, the map for *shucks* ('corn husks') illustrates one item which Carver (102) cites as a possible diagnostic feature, but for which the published DARE volumes provide no data. As the solid line on map 7 shows, *shucks* is common in southern and western Illinois. The LANCS checklist distribution, shown by broken lines, is similar, if a bit more widespread. The maps for *branch* ('small stream'), *firedogs* ('andirons'), and *Christmas Gift!* ('Christmas greeting') allow comparison with DARE findings. On these other three maps, DARE occurrences are shown by squares. *Branch*, in map 8, is one of Carver's South I terms. *Branch* shows a healthy isogloss presence in western Illinois among Atlas informants. But only six DARE informants gave *branch* in Illinois, and none of those six was in the disputed western part. The other two Illinois maps, for *firedogs/dog irons* (map 9) and *Christmas Gift!* (map 10), show similar discrepancies. Both of these South/South Midland terms appeared among western Illinois Atlas informants, as the solid lines in the western bulge of the state attest, but there are very few DARE squares for either item and none in western Illinois.

What are we to make of this difference between the Atlas and DARE surveys? One contributing factor is a time variable. As Carver himself notes, there is roughly a one-generation gap between the Atlas fieldwork and DARE. LANCS fieldwork began in 1939 for Illinois; the majority of the records were complete by 1952 and all by 1962. DARE fieldwork in Illinois took place from 1967 to 1970. Since the older LANCS records show southernisms like *firedog* and *Christmas gift!* present in western Illinois whereas they do not show up in DARE, it seems at least possible to infer that western Illinois's lexicon was at some point in history more southern than it is now—or was, at least, by the time of DARE's interviews.

A further analysis of several Illinois southernisms collected by LANCS at various times by Raven McDavid and Roger Shuy appears to support this hypothesis. These southernisms seem recessive when we compare the dates of LANCS field records on which they occur with the dates of those where the southernisms are less

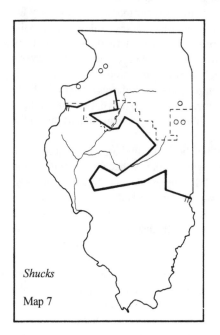

Shucks

Map 7

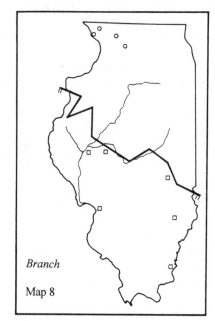

Branch

Map 8

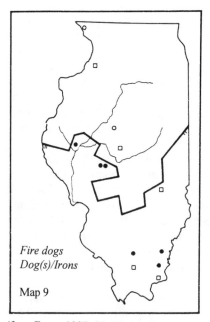

Fire dogs
Dog(s)/Irons

Map 9

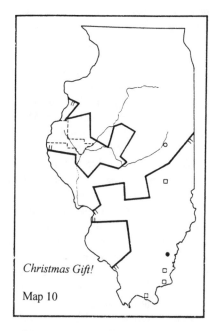

Christmas Gift!

Map 10

(from Frazer 1987: 80, 78, 81, 82)

frequent. *Fire dogs*, for example, appeared on 36% of McDavid's 1949–50 Illinois field records, but in none of Shuy's 1960–62 records. *Christmas Gift!* appeared in 47% of McDavid's records but in only 13% of Shuy's. Similar decreases between McDavid's and Shuy's records appear for *granny woman* ('midwife'), *corn dodger* ('corn-meal cake'), *hoe cake* ('corn-meal cake'), *mosquito hawk* ('dragonfly'), *lightbread* ('white bread'), *clabber cheese* ('cottage cheese'), and *snake doctor* ('dragonfly'), all terms which Carver used to define the "south" area, and all of which appear only rarely among DARE field records for Illinois (Frazer 1987). This limited survey also suggests that the pronunciation boundaries I drew for Illinois may be relics of a once-more-vigorous southern presence in western Illinois which was no longer as strongly in evidence by the time the DARE records were collected.

This hypothesis is further supported by McDonough County (IL) residents who submitted vocabulary checklists to the LANCS collection during the 1950s. Among these I found a higher proportion of southern vocabulary for respondents born between 1879 and 1890 than I did for respondents born after 1890 (Frazer 1983a). Again, southern lexicon receded with time. In terms of settlement history, this makes sense. In much of southern and western Illinois, southern settlers were the main source of the English-speaking population from the Revolution until about 1830; after the conclusion of the Black Hawk wars (1832) and the opening of the Erie Canal in New York State (1828), followed by increasing steam navigation on the Great Lakes, northern settlement became more of a factor. Moreover, much of the southern lexicon came from a folk culture virtually extinct, at least in Illinois: *lightbread* is rarely baked at home, and corn dodgers and hoecake vanished with the open hearth; granny women have given way to obstetricians, and *snake doctors* represent one of many species threatened by the widespread use of pesticides. Some of Carver's Northern terms, on the other hand, like *biffy* ('bathroom'; specifically, 'commode') and *bubbler* ('drinking fountain'), do not depend on a passing rural culture for their longevity.[4]

In contrast to lexicon, pronunciation does not depend on a continuing folk culture for the maintenance of regional features. Southern pronunciation remains as evidence of a strong southern presence throughout much of Illinois. All of this reminds us that, in isolation, vocabulary is something that must be used with caution in drawing dialect boundaries.

One remaining factor may also contribute to the differences between the southern lexicons of the Atlas and DARE. The DARE records for Illinois, especially western Illinois, where the differences between Carver's and my conclusions are sharpest, represent a more urban population than does the LANCS collection. LANCS collected 22 field records in western Illinois, of which only four are from large cities (Quad Cities [the Rock Island/Moline/Davenport, IA/ Bettendorf, IA urban area] and Peoria). This same area is represented in the DARE collection by only 7 records, of which three (Peoria, Quincy, Galesburg) are from cities with 50,000 or more in population. In other words, only about 18% of the LANCS sample for western Illinois is urban, but 43% of the DARE sample for the same area is urban. I have shown in several places (e.g., Frazer 1983b, 1987, 1993b) that in the lower Midwest, southern populations are more likely to be rural, northern populations urban. The greater urban bias of the DARE sample—at least for western Illinois—would also help to explain why Carver's evidence does not suggest much of a southern linguistic presence and why much of western Illinois is placed in Carver's North proper. It does not diminish the achievement of Carver's work—which I have been among the first to acknowledge—to remember that DARE was not designed as an atlas and that findings based on DARE data should be followed up by more intensive studies of the spaces between DARE communities. As this paper has shown, the southern presence north of the Ohio River is much stronger than DARE's lexical records would suggest, too much to allow places like central Illinois and Indiana to be considered part of the linguistic "North."

NOTES

Charles R. Frazer contributed to this and other work in ways he never imagined.

1. Habick and I both have found one southern pronunciation feature to be recessive: the diphthongization or tensing of front lax vowels before /š/. Why this feature should be recessive when other southern features are expanding their domains is a matter for further investigation.

2. One field interview that DARE planned for western Illinois was never completed. For this reason, I added to my map one reading of "Arthur" from McDonough County.

3. Labov's "The Three Dialects of English" (1991) argues that we should define dialects on the basis of systems rather than on inventories of features. Labov identifies the "South" by a vowel shift in which the high and mid-back vowels are fronted and the mid and high-front vowels are inglided. The "North" is identified by the "Northern Cities Shift" which raises and fronts /æ/ and /a/, with a parallel adjustment of vowels above and behind them. Something close to the traditional "Midland" participates in neither of these shifts but is marked by the low-back vowel merger which makes *cot* and *caught* into homophones.

4. But why did folk culture and folk vocabulary erode so much faster in Illinois than in Kentucky and Tennessee? I can't answer that question with anything more than an educated guess, but it's one I would bet the farm on. An important section of the Northwest Ordinance, which dictated the terms on which Illinois, Indiana, Ohio, Michigan, and Wisconsin could achieve statehood, set aside a portion of federal land in each of these states to finance public schools. Public education and literacy had a faster start, as a result, in Illinois than they would have had in Kentucky. And it does not seem much of a stretch to imagine that advancing literacy aided the erosion of folk vocabulary in favor of "book words."

In fact, portions of the North Central States took their time about taking advantage of the Northwest Ordinance's education provision. By 1860, for example, free public high schools had been created in every part of Illinois but the extreme southern tip covered by Carver's South I boundary. Perhaps that is one reason why this part of Illinois remains "more Southern," where LANCS records show *you-all* and perfective *done* surviving. I can't vouch as confidently for Indiana or Missouri, but it seems we at least need to investigate the possibility that some of the isogloss boundaries in this part of the U.S. may actually be, in part, education boundaries.

Regional Vocabulary in Missouri
Donald M. Lance and Rachel B. Faries

This article uses data from a word-geography dissertation of Missouri dialect (Faries 1967) in an attempt to answer a number of questions regarding dialect boundaries in Missouri: Can Missouri be divided into clearly delineated dialect regions? What patterns are discernible in areas of Missouri that were settled before 1830? Do South Midland usages predominate in the Ozarks? How is post–Civil War immigration from northern states reflected in the regional vocabulary of Missourians? What effect did 19th-century German immigration have on the distribution of regional dialect in Missouri? In what areas of the state are isoglosses most useful in determining dialect boundaries?

Faries' study is based on data from five master's theses written from 1952 to 1957, covering 37 counties,[1] and on data collected for the dissertation in 1965–1966 in the other 77 counties. St. Louis City was not included in the study. These investigations employed a checklist-questionnaire consisting of the 124 items (with 640 expressions) analyzed by Hans Kurath in *A Word Geography of the Eastern United States* (Kurath 1949). There were 700 informants, 43% women and 57% men; the average age was 75, so they were born between about 1860 and 1900. The fieldworkers made a special effort to select only informants who were lifelong residents of an older community of under 5,000 in population; the average amount of formal education of the informants was about eight years (Faries 1967).

In analyzing her data, Faries used the regional classifications that Kurath assigned to each term in chapter 2 of *Word Geography* (1949:figure 3). These regional divisions and classifications are also used in Atwood (1953:3) and in Kurath and McDavid (1961:map 2) and thus serve as a baseline for later studies that use questionnaires and techniques in the tradition established for the linguistic atlas of the United States and Canada (Kurath et al. 1939). In this essay, when we refer to regional terms, we will use the following abbreviations to indicate Kurath's (1949:figure 2) regional classifications: S = South, SM = South Midland, NM = North Midland, M = Midland, N = North, S+SM = South and South Midland, S+N = South and North, etc. In discussing the terms, Faries uses only the major divisions, with no reference to the minor subdivisions in the Eastern States (e.g., the Virginia Piedmont). See map 1 for the divisions established by Kurath.

In Faries' dissertation study, the area of Missouri with the largest number of regional terms was the Ozark Highland in combination with neighboring sections of the state, with a total of 48 terms in several patterns (158–59). The largest number of these terms (24) occurred in the Ozark Highland and the Mississippi Lowlands, a pattern shown in map 2, which displays traditional isoglosses for *redworm* 'fishing worm' (SM; Faries map 7, Kurath figures 28, 140 [henceforth F 7, K 28, 140]; n=72), *turn* 'amount of corn to be ground into meal' (S+SM; F 21, K 72; n=157), *plum peach* 'clingstone peach' (S+SM; F 27, K 128; n=100), *grass sack* 'burlap bag' (S; F2, K 71; n=42), and *johnny (house)* 'privy' (S+SM; F 20, K 55; n=35).

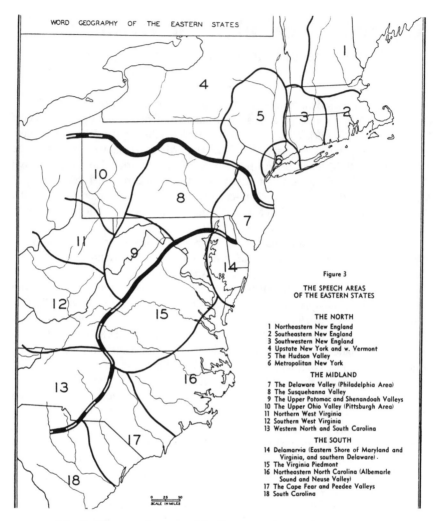

Map 1: The speech areas of the Eastern states (Kurath 1949:f3)

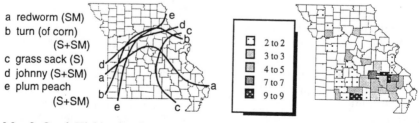

a redworm (SM)
b turn (of corn)
   (S+SM)
c grass sack (S)
d johnny (S+SM)
e plum peach
   (S+SM)

Map 2: Ozark Highland and
Mississippi Lowlands

Map 3: Ozark Highland

Twelve of these 48 terms were found in the Ozarks but not in the counties along the Mississippi, as we see in map 3,[2] which combines *laid out* (of school) (S+SM; F 38, K 158; n=34), *cookie* 'doughnut' (S; F 8, K 120; n=12), *scrich owl* (S+SM; F 25, K 136; n=25), *palings* 'picket fence' (S+M; F 9, K 63; n=20), *sugar orchard* 'maple grove' (N+M; F 45, K 145; n=35), and *milk gap* 'enclosed area where cows are milked' (SM; F 48, K 61; n=39).

A substantial number of the 48 terms occurred primarily in the Ozarks and/or southeast areas and north of the Missouri River as well. Some of these terms were found in as many as half of the counties in the three northern tiers. Some terms were found in the northeast but not in the northwest (map 4), and some in the northwest but not the northeast (map 5). Map 4 combines the terms *granny woman* 'midwife' (S+M; F 30, K 149; n=103), *paling fence* 'picket fence' (S+M; F 34, K 63; n=145), tow sack 'burlap bag' (S+SM; F 28, K 71; n=127), *batter cake* 'pancake' (S+SM; F 126, K 121; n=62), *worm fence* 'split-rail fence in a zig-zag pattern' (M; F 118, K 64; n=33), *midlin meat* 'salt pork' (S+SM; F 31, K 122; n=51), *plum peach* 'clingstone peach' (S+SM; F 27, K 128; n=100), and *fire board* 'mantel' (SM; F 68, K 27; n=68).

Map 5 combines *pile* (of hay) (S+NM; F 108, K 59; n=25), *hay cock* 'small pile of hay' (N+NM; F 98, K 58; n=46), (school) *turns out* (S+SM; F 50, K 155; n=193), *hot cake* (NM; F 18, K 121; n=90), *you'ns* (M; F 47, K 114; n=74), *sled* 'horse-drawn device for hauling rocks out of a field' (M; F 43, K p. 58; n=56), *low grounds* (S; F 19, K 91; n=26), *Piggoop!* 'call to pigs' (S+SM; F 49, K 104; n=105), *fish bait* (S+M; F 51, K 139; n=28), *Hommie!, Hommilie!* 'call to calves' (NM; F 69, K 102; n=31), *Co Boss(ie)!, Come Boss(ie)!* 'call to cows' (N; F 77, K 99; n=67), sick *to* the stomach (N; F 110, K 152; n=41).

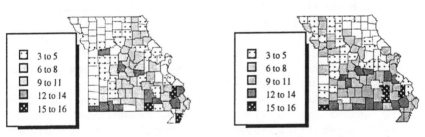

Map 4: Ozarks, Southeast, and Northeast

Map 5: Ozarks, Southeast, and Northwest

A smaller set of terms (19) was distributed primarily in the northern and western plains areas in Missouri. Of these terms, eight (42%) occur in the South and Midland areas in the Eastern states and the remainder in North and Midland areas (Faries 1967:160). This northern and western distribution is displayed in map 6, which combines *darning needle* 'dragonfly' (N; F 75, K 141; n=52), *grist* 'amount of corn to be ground' (N+NM; F 57, K 72; n=183), *wheel horse* 'horse on the left in plowing or hauling' (S+M; F 72, K 100; n=28), *Hoist!* 'call to cows during milking' (N+NM; F 73, K 101; n=33), (corn) *husks* (N+NM; F96, K134; n=101), (wooden) *pail* (S+SM; F 59, K 66; n=80), quarter *of* eleven (N+NM; F 62, K 44; n=105), *piece meal* 'small amount of food between meals' (SM; F 71, K 127; n=47), and *piece* 'piece meal' (NM; F 68, K 127; n=81).

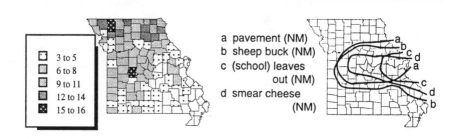

a pavement (NM)
b sheep buck (NM)
c (school) leaves out (NM)
d smear cheese (NM)

□ 3 to 5
□ 6 to 8
□ 9 to 11
▨ 12 to 14
▨ 15 to 16

Map 6: Northern and Western Plains   Map 7: German settlement area

Eight terms, of North Midland origin, are concentrated in the area southward along the Mississippi River from St. Louis to Perry County and westward up the Missouri River to Lafayette County. This pattern is displayed in map 7, combining *pavement* 'sidewalk' (NM; F 106, K 20; n=32), *sheep buck* (NM; F 105, K 95; n=40), (school) *leaves out* (NM; F 111, K 156; n=11), and *smear cheese* (NM; F 104, K 71; n=15). This area has a substantial German-American population (Faries 1967:170–71).

Faries found only 75 of the 640 Eastern dialect terms to be distributed in Missouri in patterns that lent themselves to the drawing of isoglosses; thus, the technique that Kurath found so useful in the East (1949:11–12) was not particularly productive in the Missouri study (Faries 1967:160–61). In addition to using traditional vocabulary, informants often added terms to the checklists (e.g., *lead troughs* 'device to carry off rain from a roof'; 7 instances) or used terms with meanings that were different from those listed by Kurath (e.g., *off horse* 'the horse on the left'; 18 instances), but Faries concluded that these 1053 responses were not sufficient evidence to indicate that Missouri is "a separate speech area wholly distinct from those of the Eastern States" (158). After examining her data from several points of view, Faries concluded that "the available evidence will hardly support the possibility that Missouri may be divided into separate speech areas [that] resemble the Eastern speech areas" (160).

Faries' original conclusion aside, close examination of her maps and tables suggests that with the aid of a computer one might be able to see patterns that merit further study. In the table below (using data from Faries' worksheets rather than those in tables in the dissertation), we see that the North provided the greatest number of individual items (103) and that the Midland and South + Midland areas in the East provided the highest frequencies of usage (11,308; 12,898). The combined North and North Midland area (N, NM, N+NM) provided Missouri with 211 terms (frequency: 15,015), whereas the combined South and South Midland area (S, SM, S+SM) provided only 128 terms (frequency: 10,111). These numbers include secondary responses.

The data displayed in maps 2–6 indicate that some terms with certain distributions in the East appear to have "changed allegiances" in Missouri—e.g., *hot cake* (NM) and *hay cock* (N+NM) patterning with South and South Midland terms in map 2, and *wheel horse* (S+M) and *piece meal* (SM) patterning with North and North Midland terms in map 6. In our analysis we had two options: reclassify certain terms on the basis of their Missouri distributions, or simply note the different areal distributions in Faries' and Kurath's studies and continue using the traditional labels as we analyzed the Missouri data. We preferred the latter option so that we could maintain consistent references to earlier studies in the East in which the same terms were elicited.

Table: Number of regional terms in Missouri		
	Expressions	*Total Occurrences*
North	103	3,833
North and North Midland	58	7,731
North and Midland	12	3,389
North and South Midland	1	662
North and South	30	1,467
Midland*	99	11,308
South	71	1,472
South and Midland	61	12,898
South and South Midland	55	7,800
South and North Midland	6	75
Totals	496	50,635
*Entire Midland	37	7,018
North Midland	50	3,451
South Midland	12	839

In order to examine the distribution of regional items more closely, we have displayed in maps 8–17 the county-by-county distributions of the data in the table. Because only three speakers were interviewed in two counties and as many as eight were interviewed in others, we have divided the number of items in each county by the number of speakers interviewed in the county so that the numbers in maps 8–17 represent the mean frequency per questionnaire. Below the maps we have also given abbreviations of Kurath's regional classifications, followed by the number of individual words in each category and the frequency totals. The shadings in these maps divide the 114 counties into approximate thirds: the widely dispersed dots and the light shading identify the counties in the lower two thirds of the frequency distribution, and the darker shadings identify the top third. Counties in the top 5–8% are indicated with the two darkest shadings.

Map 8 shows that the 103 terms ostensibly brought into the state from the North were used in all quarters of Missouri. In map 9 we see that many terms that were used in both the North (areas 1–4 in map 1) and the South (areas 14–18 in map 1) in the Eastern states were concentrated along the Missouri River and in the western half of the state. Terms of North Midland origin (especially areas 8 and 10 in map 1) were most heavily used in the northern and western counties and in the counties with German immigrant population (maps 10 and 11). Maps 12–14 indicate that the strongest Midland influence was in counties south of the Missouri River. Terms of South Midland origin (especially areas 11–13 in map 1) are concentrated in the Ozark Highland (maps 15 and 17). Terms from the South apparently had their greatest impact in the southeast and in the counties along the Missouri River in the middle of the state (maps 14–16).

The data displayed in maps 8–17 demonstrate why Faries did not feel comfortable with attempts to divide the state into clear dialectal regions; at the same time, however, the maps offer enough hints of regionality to tempt us to experiment with the data to search for ways of correlating immigration patterns with the Missouri distribution of dialect items that Kurath had found to be identifiably regional in the Eastern states. Maps 8 (N) and 16 (S), 10 (NM) and 17 (SM), 12 (N+M) and 14 (S+M), and 13 (N+NM) and 15 (S+SM) have complementary distributions, but the relatively high incidence of North, North Midland, and Midland terms in the eastern Ozarks and in the Southeast (maps 8, 10, 12, 13) suggests that the drawing of isoglosses in the state would obscure or oversimplify the complexity of the distribution of dialect terms in the state.

From shortly before the Louisiana Purchase in 1803 until about 1850, large numbers of immigrants came into Missouri from southern states, with Kentucky, Tennessee, Virginia, and North Carolina supplying the greatest numbers; from 1850 to 1890 large numbers came from northern states, especially Illinois, Indiana, Ohio, Pennsylvania, and New York. (See Faries 1967:23–29, citing Ellis 1929; Shoemaker 1927; Viles 1933; and Williams and Shoemaker 1930.) As land became available in the western Midwest (Missouri, Iowa, Kansas, Nebraska) in the 1840s and 1850s, immigrants came from areas that dialectologists have classified as North (New England, New York, New Jersey, northern Pennsylvania, the Great Lakes states), North Midland (most of Pennsylvania, the Middle Atlantic states, northern West Virginia, Ohio, Indiana, Illinois), South Midland (Appalachian and Blue Ridge areas), and South (the Coastal South and the Mississippi Delta). One would expect to find some evidence of South and South Midland as well as North and North Midland dialectal influence in the western Midwest, with North and North Midland usages more common in areas settled after midcentury.

In an effort to correlate settlement history and the distribution of regional dialect influence in the state, we devised formulas for deriving *indexes of regionality* by adding together the occurrences of all of Kurath's terms in Missouri. To determine the Index of "Southness" in Missouri, for instance, we added all of the dialect items classified as South in the table, half the total of the North plus South, half of the South plus South Midland, one third of the South plus Midland, and half of the South plus North Midland. The South Index for the entire state is 9,710. Analogous formulas were applied to the data to derive other regional indexes: North Index 9,893; South Midland Index 10,499; North Midland Index 11,993; Midland Index 25,171. These formulas show that the strongest influence on Missouri regional vocabulary is from the combined Midland areas. As well, we see that the Indexes for North and North Midland are larger than the South and South Midland Indexes.

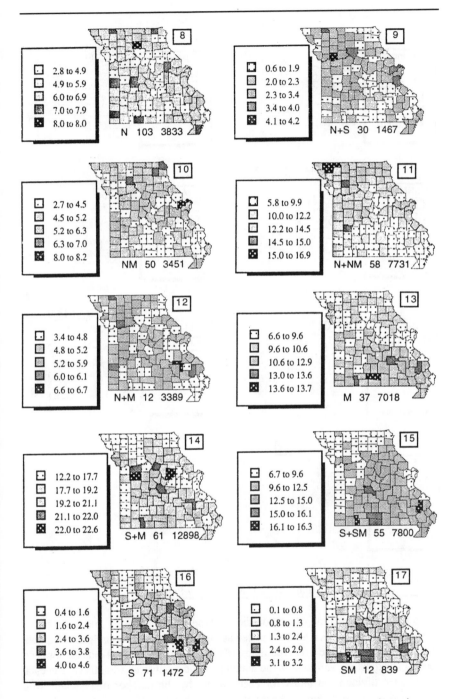

Maps 8–17: Aggregate regional usage, mean frequency per questionnaire

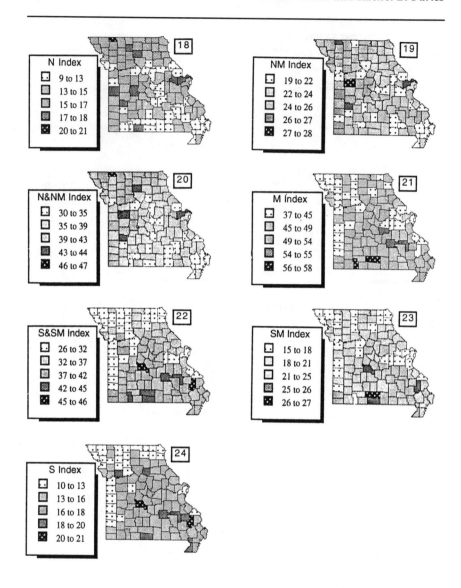

Maps 18–24: Regionality indexes

In order to determine which counties had the largest dialect influence from the geographical areas that Kurath designated as North, North Midland, South Midland, Midland, and South, we prepared maps 18–24 to display regional indexes for each county. To adjust for variation in the number of questionnaires administered in each county, we divided the index for each county by the number of residents who responded to questionnaires. The numbers in the legends of these maps imply that, hypothetically, on average, a respondent in a given county used a certain number of terms that originated in the Eastern regions indicated by the name of the Index. As in maps 8–17, the two lightest shadings represent approximately two thirds of the counties and the darker shadings the top third. These maps come closer to showing dialect regions within the state than maps 8–17, but there are still high North Midland indexes in the southeast in map 19 and high South indexes north of the Missouri River, as well as sporadic instances of counties that appear to be speech islands with a number of southern items in northern areas or vice versa. Except for maps 20 (N+NM) and 23 (SM), this procedure does not reveal cohesive areas where terms from particular areas of the East predominate in Missouri, but these maps have relatively fewer speech islands than do maps 8 (N), 9 (N+S), 10 (NM), 12 (N+M), and 13 (M).

In an attempt to determine why terms from northern and southern areas of the East are scattered throughout the state, we examined the 1870 and 1880 census data and the dates of the organization of the 115 counties in Missouri. We must remember that when Missouri was settled, the Americans who were moving to new lands in the west were neither Southerners nor Northerners, just Americans. Map 25 (adapted from Gerlach 1976:14) displays the expansion of American population from 1740 to 1800. By the 1760s, Americans were exploring the Great Lakes area, and settlers were making their way through Virginia and North Carolina into Tennessee and Kentucky. By the time Fort Harmer was established in southeastern Ohio in 1785, where the first Ohio town was to be settled three years later, at least 50,000 pioneers had claimed land in Tennessee, Kentucky, and Ohio (Meyer 1970:110).

The first group of Anglo-Americans to immigrate to what is now Missouri were Kentuckians who settled in New Madrid in 1789, the year after the founding of Marietta, Ohio (Meyer 1970:49–50). In 1795, fearing British encroachment into the territory, the Spanish Governor-General of Louisiana gave permission to allow additional Americans to settle west of the Mississippi (Meyer 1970:102). In 1797, Moses Austin, originally from Connecticut but at the time living in Virginia, received a land grant from Spain in the lead mining area that later became Washington County (Meyer 1970:74–75). In 1798, Daniel Boone, who was born in Pennsylvania, moved from Kentucky to St. Charles County, Missouri, and a group of North Carolinians settled southwest of Cape Girardeau (Gerlach 1976:17–18). Five years later, President Jefferson arranged for the purchase of the Louisiana Territory from France.

The migrations led by Boone and Austin represent a continuation of the pattern that McDavid describes as the route of settlers who migrated through Pennsylvania and thence across the Potomac and up the Shenandoah Valley between the Blue Ridge and Appalachian Mountains (McDavid 1958:500–508). Two of the three expansions of that stream of migration ultimately affected Missouri. One group turned westward and followed the Kanahwa Valley into western Virginia and Ohio. Another group continued in a southwestward direction to the Tennessee Valley. From this latter group were the explorers who found the Cumberland Gap and brought settlers into Tennessee, Kentucky, and Missouri. When we examine the map of American settlement before 1800, we can imagine two parallel thrusts of Midlanders driving a wedge out into the wilderness along the Ohio River and overland through Kentucky and Tennessee. We can see Kurath's areas 10 and 11 (map 1) feeding the northern half of the expansion and areas 12 and 13 expanding past the Appalachians. As we see in map 25, the earliest American immigrants into Missouri would have come overland through Kentucky and Tennessee or down the Ohio River.

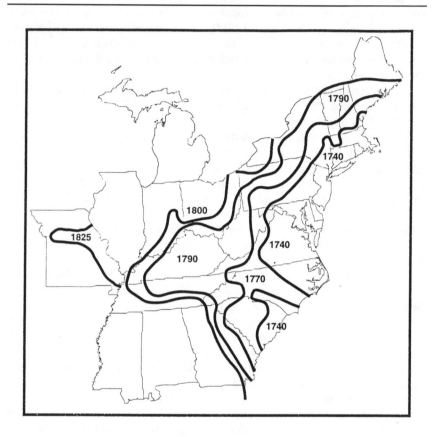

Map 25: Expansion of American population

At the time of the Louisiana Purchase in 1803, five territorial divisions along the Mississippi River had been set up by the Spanish governors (New Madrid, Cape Girardeau, Ste. Genevieve, St. Louis, St. Charles); the counties in map 26 kept their territorial names and are where the earliest French and Spanish colonists lived. The territory that now includes Missouri was explored by Marquette and Joliet in 1673, and in 1682 La Salle took possession in the name of Louis XIV of France. Later, as France experienced repeated losses in the French and Indian War with England (1754–1763), Louis XV secretly transferred Louisiana to his cousin Charles III of Spain in 1762, three months before losing the rest of the French territory in North America. Spain officially assumed control of the region in 1770 and divided the territory into Upper and Lower Louisiana. In 1800 Charles IV traded all of Louisiana to Napoleon for a portion of Italy, but the Spanish-appointed lieutenant-general remained in the Government House in St. Louis until the American military assumed control in March 1804.

In 1813 the area that had been settled by French lead miners was organized into a county, and by the time of statehood in 1821 twenty other counties had been organized along the Missouri and Mississippi Rivers and their tributaries. The origins of these early settlers help explain why dialect items of South and South Midland origin occur frequently in the central part of the state, as we shall see more clearly in later maps. In the first seventeen years of statehood, thirty-one additional counties were organized (map 27).

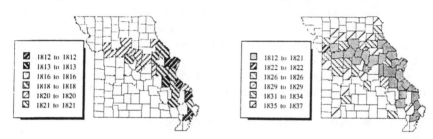

Map 26: Counties organized by 1821   Map 27: Counties organized by 1838

By the time of the War of 1812, the Native American population in Missouri was rather small. The Missouris moved northwest to the mouth of Platte River (Nebraska/Iowa) in 1798, and the Osage gave up their claims in the eastern part of the state in 1808. As Americans moved into the Midwest, several tribes were removed to Missouri: in 1789 the Delawares and Shawnees accepted the offer of Spanish governors to settle in the southwest part of the state, and in 1812 the U.S. government set aside a reservation in the southwest for the Kikapoos (Chapman 1983:120). By 1832, all Indian groups had agreed to move to present-day Kansas and Oklahoma, and in 1820, 1830, and 1836, by means of treaties and agreements, the federal government purchased the hunting rights of the Oto and Iowa Indians north and east of the Missouri River. Missouri annexed the northwest wedge of land known as the Platte Purchase in 1837 (Meyer 1970:138, 180–82), with American settlers moving into the Purchase in 1838, which is also the date of the Trail of Tears forced march of Cherokees across southern Missouri to Indian Territory.

By 1850 over two generations of Americans had migrated into the Midwest and Great Lakes states, building roads and railroads. These areas soon replaced the Southern states as sources for new population in Missouri and later Kansas. If we compare the shading in the counties in maps 27 and 28 with the locations of North and North Midland dialect usage in maps presented earlier, we see that these new counties were organized after the influx of immigration from the Great Lakes states. By midcentury, all but 17 of the present-day counties had been established.

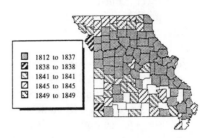

Map 28: Counties organized by 1850

The reports published in the 1870 and 1880 censuses list nativity statistics for each county in Missouri. The respondents for Faries' dissertation were born between 1860 and 1900, so these census data describe the Missouri population when the oldest of the respondents were children. In maps 14, 15, 16, 22, 23, and 24 we see South and South Midland terms concentrated along and north of the Missouri River. Maps 29 and 30 show that in the 1870 census over 6% of the residents in these counties were born in Kentucky or Virginia. Because the 1870 census was taken a full two generations after many of these counties were organized, one would expect the majority of the population to have been born in the state.

Map 31, indicating Missouri residents who were born in Tennessee (1870 census), demonstrates why there is a concentration of South Midland usage items in the Ozark Highland. Map 28 indicates that the counties in the Ozarks were among the last to be organized; the density of Tennessee-born residents (over 10% in 37 counties, in contrast to only 11 counties with over 10% Kentucky-born or Virginia-born residents in maps 29 and 30) also indicates recent immigration. Because most of the southern counties were not organized until after northern immigration had begun, it is not surprising to see several counties in the Ozarks with northern-born population in maps 32–35, nor to see sporadic concentrations of North and North Midland dialect items in southern counties, as we have seen in maps 8–12 and 18–20. The Illinois and Indiana natives who immigrated into southeastern Missouri (maps 32 and 34) probably came from the southern parts of these states that were originally settled by South Midlanders (see map 25).

We see in maps 6, 8, 10, 11, 12, 18, 19, and 20 that North and North Midland terms occur most frequently in counties in the northern and western plains of the state. We also see in maps 32–35 that more than 7% of the 1870 and 1880 residents in many of these counties were born in Midwestern states. The reports in the 1870 census publications included figures only for (northern) residents born in Ohio and Illinois, but by 1880 the percentage of immigrants from Iowa, Indiana, New York, and Pennsylvania had increased sufficiently to be included in the census reports— a reflection of changes in immigration trends.

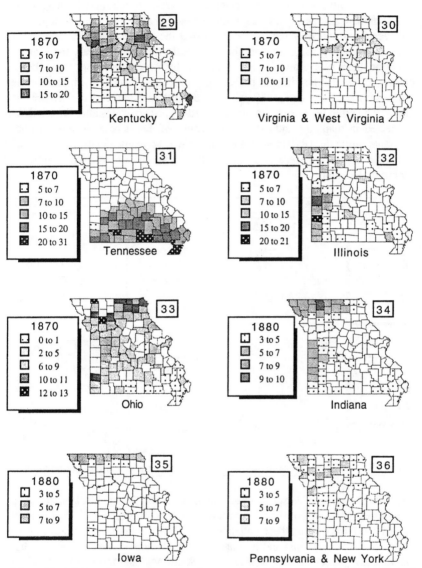

Maps 29–36: Immigration from Southern and Northern states (% of population)

Settlement of the northern counties was speeded up by the completion of the railroad from Hannibal to St. Joseph, 1851 to 1859. Historians also provide ample evidence that when Union troops were in western Missouri, they found the land and the climate desirable and decided to take advantage of the Homestead Act of 1862 that allowed settlers to acquire up to 160 acres of unappropriated public lands without cost (Viles 1933:167). By 1850 more immigrants were coming into

Missouri from Midwestern and Northern states than from the South, and after 1861 Southerners would have been reluctant to emigrate to Missouri because of the political climate associated with the requirement that all voting citizens sign a "test oath" verifying that they had never supported the Confederacy or the Southern cause (Meyer 1970:382). Thus, in the latter half of the 19th century the Southern population base was gradually being diluted by new immigrants from the old Northwest. We see this drop in percentages in maps 37 and 38, which represent Missourians in 1870 and 1880 who were born in Kentucky, Tennessee, and Virginia. The rapid increase in immigration from northern states after the Civil War is reflected in maps 39 and 40. The enormity of the increase in northern-born immigrants during the 1870s also helps explain why so many counties in the Ozarks and the Southeast that were organized in the 1850s have substantial numbers of northern dialect items.

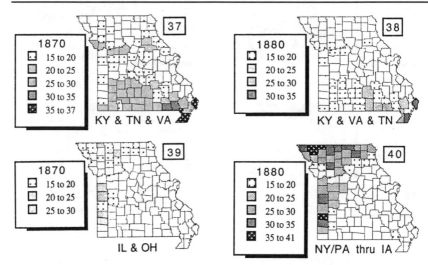

Maps 37–40: Immigration from the South and North (combined percentages)

In discussing map 7, we pointed out that certain North Midland terms are concentrated in the area of the state with substantial German immigrant population. In maps 8–11 we see that these counties have relatively high percentages of North and North Midland terms, and in maps 13, 14, 15, and 17 we see that they have relatively low percentages of Midland and South Midland terms. Map 41 shows these counties to have at least 5% German-immigrant population in the 1870 census. For more detailed discussions of the regional usage in German settlement areas in Illinois and Missouri, see Frazer (1978), Frazer (1979), Lance (1985), and Frazer (this volume).

As we have attempted in our maps to find coherent dialect regions in Missouri, we have had only moderate success so far. Maps 17 and 23 show that South Midland influence is predominant in the Ozarks, and maps 15 and 22 show a clear picture for combined South and South Midland influence. The South + South

Midland pattern in map 15 is mirrored fairly well in the North + North Midland pattern in map 11; however, we do not find such clear patterns for other pairs of regional designations.

Map 41: Immigration from German-speaking countries

Using information on settlement history and the geographical distribution of dialect items elicited in the fieldwork for the linguistic atlas of the United States, dialectologists generally divide the area east of the Mississippi River into North, North Midland, South Midland, and South, not just "North" and "South."[3] Nativity statistics in the census reports from 1850 to 1890 show that about four times as many Missouri residents were born in Midwestern and Upper South states (i.e., the Midland area) as in the other northern states and the Coastal South combined. Aggregate immigration during these four decades indicates that the number of Missouri immigrants from the North was approximately the same as the number from the Coastal South and that the aggregate immigration from the Midwest was about the same as that from the Upper South.

Using the hypothesis that immigrants from each of these four areas brought traditional dialect usages into Missouri, we used the regionality indexes in maps 18–24 to derive differential indexes for each county. For maps 42 and 43 we subtracted the North Index (map 18) from the South Index (map 24) and for maps 44 and 45 we subtracted the North Midland Index from the South Midland Index. The numbers in these maps indicate that, hypothetically, on average, respondents from the shaded counties in map 42 used more terms that Kurath found in Areas 14–18 (South) in map 1 than terms used in Areas 1–4 (North); many of these terms not only were used in the North but also were spread across two or three of these four areas in the Eastern States—i.e., South + South Midland, South + Midland, North + South, or South + North Midland. In map 43 terms classified as North, North + North Midland, North + Midland, South + North, and North + South Midland occur more frequently in the shaded counties than do the terms represented in map 42. Maps 44 and 45 compare the average number of items in each county that Kurath had found in South Midland areas in the Eastern states with those that he found in North Midland areas.

Because the general public thinks of "Northern" and "Southern" dialects, and not of "Midland" dialects (see Preston, this volume), we added together the Indexes of the two "Southern" areas (S and SM) and those of the two "Northern" areas (N and NM) and subtracted the latter from the former to see where the frequency of items with (General) Southern distributions in the East was larger than the frequency of those from (General) Northern areas, as we see in maps 46 and 47.

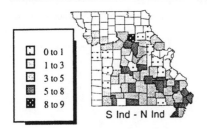

Map 42: Terms from the South more frequent than terms from the North

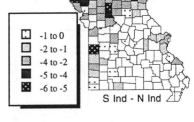

Map 43: Terms from the North more frequent than terms from the South

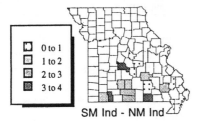

Map 44: Terms from S. Midland more frequent than terms from N. Midland

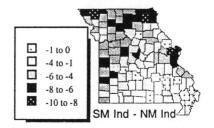

Map 45: Terms from N. Midland more frequent than terms from S. Midland

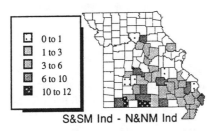

Map 46: Terms from Southern areas more frequent than terms from Northern areas

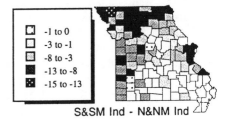

Map 47: Terms from Northern areas more frequent than terms from Southern areas

Heretofore we have had only moderate success in teasing out of our data coherent dialectal areas in the state. Maps 42, 44, and 46 appear to have more coherent patterns than we have seen in earlier maps, but we still can claim only modest success. In map 42, all of the counties with more terms from the South than from the North either had at least 15% Southern-born population in 1870 (map 37) or were settled before midcentury, in which latter case most of the population in 1870 would have been born in Missouri. In map 43, all but three of the counties with more terms from the North than from the South had at least 15% Northern-born population in 1880 (map 40). In map 44, however, we find South Midland terms are more frequent than North Midland terms in only 17 counties, with a maximum difference of 4. In map 45, we see that North Midland usage is more frequent by at least 4 terms in 14 other counties in southern Missouri that had more than 10% Tennessee-born residents in 1870. Maps 44 and 45 seem to raise more questions than they answer—particularly in regard to South Midland and Midland in general.

Maps 46 and 47 offer a picture that is somewhat satisfying but not entirely. General Southern terms are still more numerous in most of the Ozark Highland and in the area in central Missouri that has the historic name "Little Dixie" because it was initially settled by Southerners (see maps 26 and 37). However, when we compare map 46 with data in maps 14–17, it appears that immigration from North and North Midland areas has not just diluted but swamped the lexical base of General Southern dialect in much of the southern part of the state. If we refer to the relative numbers of terms from northern and southern regions in the table, we are not surprised.

Kurath (1949) uses "boldness rather than caution" in presenting evidence to support a "Midland" dialect division between the North and the South:

One fact of major importance seems to me to be fully established: *There is an extensive Midland speech area that lies between the traditionally recognized "Northern" and "Southern" areas.* This Midland area . . . corresponds to the Pennsylvania settlement area. (v; italics Kurath's)

But he is also tentative in some of his descriptions of the Midland area:

The Midland area extends westward to the Ozarks and beyond. West of Pennsylvania its northern boundary runs through the central part of Ohio, northern Indiana, and central Illinois. . . . (27)

The southern boundary of the Midland in Georgia and farther west is yet unknown. It probably runs somewhat to the north of the cotton lines. (27)

The Midland is not a uniform speech area, but it has a considerable body of words that sets it off from the North and the South. (27)

In his tables in chapter 2, Kurath lists Western North Carolina, West Virginia, and the Valley of Virginia as comprising the South Midland area (areas 11, 12, and 13 in map 1) and eastern Ohio, western Pennsylvania, central Pennsylvania, the Great Valley, and Delaware Bay as North Midland (areas 7–10), but he also points out that "all of northern West Virginia [area 11] is really a transition belt between the North Midland and the South Midland" (31). Atwood (1953) and Kurath and McDavid (1961) use the same geographical divisions in their analyses.

Because the Upper South (Appalachia to the Ozarks) is known for its unique folk expressions and other cultural patterns, one might expect to see much more South Midland influence in the traditional vocabulary in dialect studies, but Kurath found it not to be so:

Contrary to a widespread belief, the South Midland, comprising the Appalachians and the Blue Ridge south of the James River, has rather few unique

regional and local expressions. The great body of words that have been regarded
as peculiar to this region occur also either in the North Midland or in the
Southern area. (36)

It may well be that the South Midland . . . may have to be regarded in the end
as a subarea of the South rather than of the Midland; but it is here treated as a
part of the Midland. (37)

The preceding quotations are intended here as caveats to researchers rather than
as criticisms of Kurath's analysis of his data. He was confident in his interpretation
of the very large amount of data available to him but also recognized the need for
additional research:

Many details will in time find a new interpretation, but the correlation of speech
areas with settlement areas and trade areas is so striking that the major results
of this pioneer investigation will probably stand the test of critical examination
by future students of our language. (v)

He also recognized the fact that the area labeled "South Midland" was a secondary
settlement area, part of what he called "West Midland," "from western Pennsylvania to South Carolina" (30). Some terms were used frequently in the West Midland
area but had become relics east of the Susquehanna; as well, many innovations had
been introduced in West Midland usage as Americans and new immigrants
intermingled in the newly opened lands.

In the 1950s and 1960s, when someone planned a study like Faries', the only
reliable information base available for purposes of comparison and interpretation
was Kurath's *Word Geography* (1949), Atwood's *Verb Forms* (1953), Kurath and
McDavid's *Pronunciation of English in the Atlantic States* (1961), and scholarly
articles with preliminary analyses of portions of the Atlas data in the Eastern or
North Central States such as those of Marckwardt (1957), Allen (1958), and
McDavid (1958). In order to test Kurath's theory that "the main stock of the English
vocabulary of . . . later settlement areas is . . . clearly derived from the speech of the
earlier settlements on the Atlantic slope" (vi), it was necessary to use the terms in
Kurath's (1949) study, retaining the regional classifications that he assigned to
them.

Our goal in the present study was to examine Faries' dissertation data in several
ways in an attempt to find a means of determining the locations of dialect
boundaries within the state of Missouri. Faries found that isoglosses could be drawn
for many of Kurath's terms but that there were no convincing bundles of isoglosses
within the state that she could use in establishing dialect boundaries in the manner
of Kurath:

. . . [D]ialect boundaries can be established *only* by means of isoglosses. There
is no other scientific method of determining the boundaries of speech areas.
(Kurath 1949:v; emphasis ours)

Thus, we mapped the aggregate distribution of all traditional terms in Faries' study except for those that had generalized in the state (i.e., were used by more than 600 of the 700 respondents) but did not find a fully satisfying answer to the question posed in our opening sentence. Our quest certainly has not been futile because maps 42 and 46 come close to answering the question, though map 44 raises additional questions. Albert Cook has also found our approach to be very useful in analyzing data for the word geography of Kansas, which is now in manuscript form.

The settlement history of Missouri would not predict the heavy North Midland dominance shown in map 45. It seems to us that to a large extent maps 44 and 45 are adventitious artifacts of the nature of the data rather than precise representations of local language. Two categories in the frequency of data (see the table above) lead to a North Midland Index that is much larger than the South Midland Index. Most obvious is the ratio between the North Midland and South Midland: 3451:839. As well, our formulas assign 1/3 of the totals of South + Midland (12,898) and North + Midland (3,389) to each of the two subdivisions of Midland, thereby benefiting the North Midland Index much more than the South Midland Index. As we pointed out earlier, we had more than one option as we proceeded. We could have reassigned regional values to the data on the basis of their distribution within Missouri, regardless of their classification in the East, but that procedure would have obscured the relationship between settlement history and regional vocabulary. By retaining Kurath's classifications and forging ahead even though we knew that there are relatively few unique terms that characterize the South Midland area, we have been able to show the areas in the state where General Southern influence has remained strong as General Northern vocabulary spread across the state. Another approach would have been to administer more questionnaires in the 1980s or to have added questions to the survey, but those options were not realistic for several reasons, one of which renders all others irrelevant—the small number of living Missourians who were born between 1860 and 1900.

The other two early analyses of dialect in the Atlantic states also found the definition of Midland and South Midland to be problematic. Atwood points out that "as compared with the North and the South, the [Midland] area is more clearly marked by the absence of popular verb forms than by characteristic usages of its own" (39). He found that Southern forms "make up the largest body of items," many of which appeared to be "spreading" into the South Midland area, but "the question of whether some of these Southern-influence areas should be classed as Southern rather than Midland will be deferred until a more complete analysis of the Atlas materials can be carried out" (40). Kurath and McDavid (1961) point out that South Midland is "a linguistically graded area without any one dominant population center" (18) and conclude that

Although the dialect of the South Midland has hardly a single feature that does not occur either in the North Midland or the South, we must recognize it as a distinct regional type because of its unique configuration of phonemic, phonic, and incidental features. Historically, to be sure, it is a blend of Pennsylvanian and Southern features, graded from north to south. (19)

The preceding quotations indicate that our formulas *should* have given us the pictures they did. With so few unique features (vocabulary, verb forms, pronunciations) to characterize it, the "South Midland" cannot be easily defined by such devices as our formulas or by bundles of isoglosses, whether in Indiana, Illinois, Missouri, Kansas, or the San Joaquin Valley of California.

Now that the *Linguistic Atlas of the Gulf States* (Pederson et al. 1986–1992) has been published, researchers can look more closely at Kurath's speculation that "South Midland may have to be regarded in the end as a subarea of the South" (37), and additional data now available in the computer-based files of the linguistic atlases of the North Central States and Middle and South Atlantic States will enable researchers to address questions about the whole Midland area from the Atlantic to the Mississippi. It is likely that as Americans moved around the Great Lakes, across the Alleghenies and Appalachians, and across the South and along the Gulf of Mexico, many of the terms in Kurath's, and later Faries', study intermingled, shifting regional identity. Not until the Midland data in the linguistic atlases of the Gulf States, Middle and South Atlantic States, and North Central States have been examined in detail will it be possible to go much further in analyzing the Missouri data, or in deciding whether some or any of the Eastern terms should be reclassified in secondary settlement areas such as Ohio, tertiary settlement areas like Missouri, and quaternary settlement areas like Kansas.

We must keep in mind that our data represent the language of Missourians born between the Civil War and the turn of the century. Post-agrarian Missourians are no longer familiar with many of the regionally diagnostic terms that Kurath and Faries used in their studies. Population shifts from the 1920s to 1940 and since World War II have also changed the picture. Student questionnaires collected at Missouri during the 25 years since Faries' dissertation indicate that Missourians born since the atomic and during the computer age use very few of the regionally diagnostic terms that have been so important in classical American dialectology (see Faries and Lance 1993). Frazer (this volume) reports similar changes in Illinois. Even so, anecdotal evidence from comments made to the present authors indicates that, to outsiders, Missouri residents whose families have lived in the state for several generations sound more Southern than Northern. Though urbanization may have eroded some aspects of the Southern base in Missouri dialect, one can hear both the Southern Shift and the Northern Cities Shift in the speech of young Missourians (see Wolfram 1991:85–90 and Labov, this volume). We need new studies, but we also must keep fine-tuning our analyses of data from earlier investigations in order to have a better picture of what current generations are changing *from*.

NOTES

1. Bettie Bronson Shull, A survey of the vocabulary of eight western Missouri Valley counties (1953): Boone, Chariton, Clay, Cooper, Howard, Lafayette, Ray, and Saline counties. Erna E. Raithel, A survey of the vocabulary of eight west central Missouri counties (1954): Benton, Camden, Henry, Johnson, Miller, Moniteau, Morgan, and Pettis counties.

Rachel Bernice Faries, A survey of the vocabulary of seven northeast central Missouri counties (1954): Audrain, Lincoln, Marion, Monroe, Pike, Ralls, and Randolph counties. Jewell Mae Hoskins, A survey of the vocabulary of seven eastern Missouri Valley counties (1954): Callaway, Cole, Franklin, Gasconade, Montgomery, Osage, and Warren counties. Gordon Ray Sanders, A vocabulary survey of seven northeast Missouri counties (1957): Adair, Clark, Knox, Lewis, Macon, Scotland, and Shelby counties.

2. To make the shaded maps in this article, data were entered in the database of Microsoft Works for the Macintosh and county-by-county percentages were generated by the program. Then relevant data were imported as geographic data files in Atlas Pro to produce the maps that could be exported as PICT files and imported into a variety of word processing applications. The isogloss maps were made with MacDraw Pro, using a base map from Atlas Pro.

3. Since the publication of Carver's *American Regional Dialects: A Word Geography* in 1987, dialectologists have debated whether "Midland" is a viable dialect area (see Frazer, this volume). Some dialectologists also refer to the "Upper South" rather than to "South Midland," and in the *Linguistic Atlas of the Gulf States* Pederson et al. (1986–1992) have presented evidence of a "Piney Woods" dialect area in the South. Discussion of these and similar issues lies beyond the scope of this essay and are not directly relevant to a report based on 1960s research in Missouri whose procedures and analysis derived from Kurath's 1949 descriptions of regional vocabulary collected in the 1930s in the Eastern United States.

Geographical Influence on Lexical Choice: Changes in the 20th Century

Ellen Johnson

This paper examines the reasons rurality persists as an important factor in speech differences while the significance of region has decreased. It provides a summary of lexical variation associated with place of residence and a discussion of how patterns of variation have changed, along with historical evidence on cultural changes in the Southeast in the 20th century.[1]

The study is concerned with how speakers' place of residence influences their speech and how that influence has diminished in the last sixty years. It is based on a survey of 39 informants interviewed in Georgia, South Carolina, and North Carolina for the Linguistic Atlas of the Middle and South Atlantic States (LAMSAS) in the 1930s, and 39 additional informants interviewed in the same communities in 1990. (See the map, below, for locations of speakers.) Both sets of speakers responded to 150 questions designed to elicit lexical variants. The statistical analysis takes a particular word (e.g., *polecat* for 'skunk') and checks to see whether it is used more frequently by a particular group of people. Separate analyses were done for the 1930s and the 1990 speakers grouped by nonlinguistic variables.

The division chosen for informants by location is the familiar coastal, piedmont, and mountain configuration that stretches across the southeastern United States and has become associated with cultural characteristics as well as geological features. Speakers were assigned a region based on whether their county was located in the Coastal Plain (n=19), the Piedmont (n=13), or the Blue Ridge (n=7). Boundaries are those given by the U.S. Geological Survey on their map of "Fold and Thrust Belts of the United States" (1984, Reston, VA). Three counties were located partially in the coastal plain and partially in the piedmont—Baldwin Co., GA, Richland Co., SC, and Kershaw Co., SC—and these were assigned to the piedmont. All the other counties fell clearly within one region.

Informants in LAMSAS were grouped based on U.S. Census criteria into Urban (population greater than 2,500) and Rural categories. Thirty are rural in the 1930s data and only nine are urban. Five of the communities where informants live changed from rural to urban in the 55 intervening years between Guy Lowman's LAMSAS interviews and my own. Other differences in rurality between the two data sets appeared because I selected informants who were from a different part of the county than the LAMSAS informants. Two speakers came from more urban areas, while two came from more rural ones. Twenty-five of the second set of speakers are rural, and fourteen are urban.

One goal of the project was to chart the relative importance of the six non-linguistic variables and determine how their influence changed during the course of the century. The influence of region (here coastal, piedmont, or mountain) on speech declined considerably during the years between 1930 and 1990.

Map: Location of communities

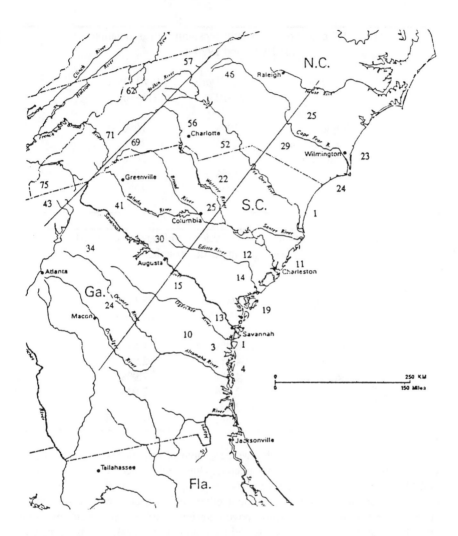

(Adapted from Kretzschmar et al. 1994)

Table 1 shows the percent of all associations significant at the .01 level that can be attributed to each of the nonlinguistic variables. Table 2 shows the percent of the total number of words that were tested from each data set that were associated with each variable.[2] Region accounted for 30% of the significant associations for the 1930s informants, but only 10% for the 1990 informants. Of the six variables studied—age, sex, race, education, region, and rurality—region was previously the most important and is now the least important. Rural versus urban residence is associated with 21% of the significant variation in the earlier set and 20% in the later set; thus, its influence has not declined in the same way as that of region of residence.

Table 1: Percent of all statistically significant associations
for 1930s and 1990 data

Variable	1930s Data (N=103)	1990 Data (N=70)
Region	30%	10%
Rurality	21%	20%
Education	19%	20%
Race	13%	20%
Age	10%	19%
Sex	7%	11%

Table 2: Percent of linguistic variables significantly associated
with each nonlinguistic variable

Variable	1930s Data (N=488)	1990 Data (N=484)
Region	6.4%	1.5%
Rurality	4.5%	2.9%
Education	4.1%	2.9%
Race	2.7%	2.9%
Age	2.1%	2.7%
Sex	1.4%	1.7%

This disparity in the effect of the two geographical variables is interesting when viewed from a language contact perspective. One would expect lexical differentiation to decrease with more contact between groups; that is, as speakers from the different groups interact more with one another, their speech would become more alike. A number of cultural factors have contributed to greater contact over the years between both regional groups and rural and urban speakers. These include changes in transportation, education, and communication, as well as the change from an agricultural to a market economy and corresponding urbanization. The influence of region has declined, as would be predicted, although the effect of rurality remains relatively strong. Cultural and psychological reasons for the differential behavior of the two variables of region and rurality will be discussed below.

In searching for an explanatory model for the changes in patterns of variation, Labov's concept of prestige (e.g., 1966) is one of the first to come to mind. Prestige is problematic as an explanatory mechanism of change, however, because different people subjectively view disparate models as prestigious. For example, in the

South, according to Reed 1986 (77), the regional social types with the greatest appeal to the white middle class are the "lady" (of aristocratic origin) and the "good old boy" (from yeoman farmers). Montgomery (this volume) notes that the prestige of the latter has become a nationwide phenomenon. Rather than viewing prestige, then, as the chief motivator of change, I have tried to discuss change in terms of language contact in the spirit of Milroy's model, of which he says, "The model is therefore less personalized than Labov's model appears to be: it is not so much about a kind of person as about the kind of links that exist between persons, and between groups of persons" (1992:175).

Change in the amount of variation attributable to particular variables and the diffusion of linguistic change is certainly related to the amount of contact between groups of speakers. Relying on contact alone to explain change cannot account for the differences in behavior of the variables of region and rurality, however, since social changes that bring people into contact with one another from different regions of the South also operate to bring city and country residents together. The different rates of decline are not easily explainable, then, in terms of contact but must be seen in the light of cultural conditions that enhance or undermine group loyalty. This brings up questions about social identity, a psychological construct similar to "covert prestige" (Trudgill 1974), that is, a feeling of identification with one's own group as opposed to other groups.

Cultural changes in the 20th century served to increase contact across geographical divisions and hence contributed to a decline in both region and rurality as variables affecting language. These forces include transportation and educational advances, industrialization, and the militarization of the nation that began with the First World War and was maintained at high levels, especially from World War II onward. After describing these changes, I will examine the causes of the greater decrease in the influence of region. One reason for this decrease can be found in the types of words associated with each variable. The other reason lies in a decline in differences between regions that are associated with ethnicity, religion, and class with no concomitant decline in conflict between urban and rural areas. Such conflicts between groups often result in an increased use of linguistic and other markers of identity.

Transportation technology has brought people together from different regions and from urban and rural areas. Most roads are paved today, highways link towns together, and Interstates 75, 85, 95, 20, 40, 77, 26, and 16 cross the area that was surveyed. All these were nonexistent when Guy Lowman traveled through the region in the 1930s. The availability of cars and roads has made travel outside of one's village, county, and state more common. Journalist Ralph McGill ([1963] 1992:12–13) recalls an interview circa 1947 with a centenarian in the mountains about the days when timber had to be floated down the rivers because there were no roads:

> I remember the ox-carts strainin' and creakin' and complainin' along the ridges. I think of men walking a hundred and sixty miles to Augusta—walked it myself a few times—and fetching back things they needed on their backs, or maybe packin' it in on a horse. Some drove oxen there. It took a couple of months to come and go. . . . Today, I don't know. What with all the radios a-squallin' and

all the useless goin' and comin' on the blacktop roads, I sometimes sit here and say to myself that maybe the oxen were the best after all. A feller sure didn't hitch up and go some place unless he needed to, or wanted to mighty bad.

Education has also led to increasing contact by providing the opportunity for a college education to larger numbers of young adults, though recently junior colleges and technical schools have sprung up near even the smallest cities, offering the possibility of schooling beyond high school that may not involve contact with speakers from other regions. Before such schools were widely available, however, college students in the South mostly moved away from home to attend either the large land-grant universities in their own states or the more elite Southern schools in their own or a neighboring state. Many contacts were made from outside the students' home counties, which, along with a more fluent command of Standard English, has certainly led to change in speech patterns. Labov and Ash (this volume) note the standardizing effects of college attendance on language patterns.

Economic changes have also served to increase contact between speakers of different dialects. Industrialists from other parts of the country, who had begun exploiting the mineral and human resources in the South in the 1880s, took advantage of the cheap labor available there. The jobs that were created were not tied to farmland; most were in larger towns or cities and thus required workers to move or commute. Textile mills were the most common industry in Georgia, South Carolina, and North Carolina, though in South Georgia pulpwood and naval stores developed as worn-out cotton lands were planted in pine, and many North Carolinians were employed in cigarette factories. Industries also contributed to the growth of towns and cities by bringing in managerial staff from outside the local area.[3] Wartime industries brought many people to the cities during World War II, and many returning soldiers were encouraged by the VHA to remain near the cities in the new suburban tract housing that sprang up after the war.

The military affected the mixture of the population in other ways, as well. Southern politicians have been especially adept at bringing federal dollars into the economy by the location of military bases in their home districts (witness Senator Sam Nunn's recent successes for Georgia, which stands to gain defense jobs even as the defense budget is being drastically reduced). While these are usually located outside of major cities, they have been instrumental in changing rural areas into urban ones, including some in this study, like Liberty County, Georgia, the location of the Army's Fort Stewart. Such bases have brought many non-natives into the local communities and provided loci for increasing linguistic contact. McDavid noted in 1948 that, "the presence in local military posts of many . . . servicemen with [constriction of /-r/ and] a more sophisticated line of conversation, has led many Southern girls to the conclusion that a person with constriction can be acceptable as a date . . ." (McDavid [1948] 1979:140). Of the 12 million Americans who entered the armed services during World War II, at least half spent time at a Southern base (Jubera 1990).

Not only are there disproportionately many military installations in the South, but there are more Southerners in the military. According to Jubera (1990), more than half of the nation's military payroll, including retirement, goes to Southerners.

Armies have always looked to the poorer classes and regions to provide recruits, and the South was for many years the poorest region of the United States, with few opportunities for secure employment outside of military service in some areas. *The Encyclopedia of Southern Culture* (Wilson and Ferris 1989, e.g., 3.461) blames the infamous Southern propensity for violence for the overrepresentation of the region in the armed forces. The men, and now women, who join up are immediately relocated with hundreds of other recruits from all over the country, speaking a variety of dialects. They invariably have a story to tell about an experience of linguistic awareness of peculiarities in their own speech (at least as perceived by others).

Thus dialect contact has contributed to a decline in importance for both geographic variables. Rurality is now more important than region, and an analysis of which vocabulary items are linked to which variables provides some evidence for why this is so. If there were a number of words specifically related to occupations only practiced in either rural or urban areas, for example, these lexical differences would likely remain regardless of the amount of contact between rural and urban residents. This is indeed the case, and differences based on material culture or lifestyles are reflected in the terms listed in table 3.[4] Fewer regionally marked variants seem to be of this type, i.e., words that refer to something that is more familiar to one group than another. Most of the terms that vary by region denote items that are found throughout the entire area. Terms for those referents that are not equally distributed are listed in table 4.[5]

Another possible explanation for the decrease in region-based variation without an equivalent decrease in rurality-based variation has to do with the greater proportion of terms denoting obsolete referents that were linked to the variable region, as shown in table 5, which gives the percent of terms linked to each variable that are obsolete or agricultural in reference. If geographical, social, or psychological distance has diminished so that new variants do not follow the same pattern of differences, variation by region should lessen as these words disappear from the vocabulary.

Table 3: Words associated with urban and rural groups due to cultural differences

Rural	*Urban*
lines (driving)	drawing room
doubletree (wagon)	dish towel
seed (cherry)	garden house (= privy)
loft (= attic)	toad
rail fence	trousers
shavs (buggy)	reins (riding)
polecat (= skunk)	frog
	firefly

Table 4: Words associated with regional groups due to geographical differences

Mountain (/Piedmont)	*Coastal (/Piedmont)*
sheepie (call)	sieva beans (= lima beans)
gully	kernel (peach)
seed (peach)	press peach
plum peach (= clingstone)	
chipmunk	

Table 5: Percent of questions exhibiting variation linked to social or regional variables that denote obsolete or agricultural referents

Rurality	*Education*	*Race*	*Sex*	*Age*	*Region*	*All Questions*
n=27	n=29	n=26	n=13	n=21	n=31	n=150
22%	24%	27%	31%	33%	42%	27%

Beyond differences in vocabulary favoring the retention of urban/rural distinctions, there are other factors that contribute to the new prominence of rurality over region. Each nonlinguistic variable represents multiple differences. Besides the major categorizing feature, other differences between groups may be encoded. For example, blacks typically have fewer years of education than whites; urban residents are typically younger and better educated than rural residents. The variable region includes differences in ethnicity and religion. The settlement history of the three regional categories, mountain, piedmont, and coastal, reveal these differences. They will be discussed here in terms of two distinct settlement areas and a transition zone.

The coastal areas were settled first; the dominant social group was Anglican from the south of England. Since the climate and soil were suitable for growing crops that were labor-intensive like cotton and rice, a plantation culture developed in this area, sustained by the importation of slaves from Africa. While lacking political or economic power to influence society, these forced laborers constituted the majority of the population in many areas, and their speech thus exerted an influence on the southern British dialects of the white settlers that it was originally modeled after (Schneider 1989; Feagin, this volume).

The mountain areas were settled much later, chiefly by Presbyterians and other evangelical groups that came from the north of England or from Scotland (some via Ireland). Some of these settlers went directly to the piedmont area upon arrival, taking the less fertile lands on the frontier not already claimed by the planters to the east. Others arrived after following the Shenandoah Valley down from original settlement areas on the Pennsylvania frontier. They represent a different culture from either of the two coastal groups. Cultural and linguistic differences attributable to these varying origins continue to this day according to both Fischer (1989) and Montgomery (1991b), though they have diminished over time, as evidenced by the results of this study.

The distribution of lexical items reflects these differences. Altogether, as shown in table 6, 24 variants were more common in the mountains and 14 along the coast.

Table 6: Mountain words and coastal words

Mountain Words

bawl (= moo)	milkgap (= cowpen)
paper poke (= bag)	bring a calf (= calve)
liver and lights (of a hog)	plum peach (= clingstone)
family pie (= cobbler)	red worm (= earthworm)
skillet	snake feeder (= dragonfly)
chipmunk	bawl (calf)
corn dodger	lot (hogs)
hull (beans)	gully
fireboard (= mantel)	soo-cow (call)
piggie (call)	soo-calf (call)
sheepie (call)	seed (peach)
tow sack (of burlap)	carriage (baby)

Coastal Words

mantelpiece	clabber (sour milk)
threatening (= clouding up)	chick (call)
sieva beans (= lima beans)	haslet (of hog)
spring frogs (= treefrogs)	kernel (peach)
relatives	press peach (= clingstone)
mosquito hawk (= dragonfly)	earthworm
cowpen	scholar (elementary age)

Cities in the upland areas were established only in the 19th century, while there have been large urban areas near the coast since the beginning of the colonial period. Charleston once attracted immigrants and travelers from all over Europe and was both multicultural and multilingual. The mountain areas, on the other hand exhibited a greater degree of cultural homogeneity and rurality. Although these characteristics lingered on until the earlier part of this century, they no longer are in evidence today. The foothills of the Appalachians are the newest exurbs for piedmont "Sun-Belt" cities like Atlanta and Charlotte. Tourists and retirees are moving in while natives either migrate or commute to neighboring urban areas to work. While a few coastal areas are growing, like the one near the submarine base in St. Marys, Georgia, many small towns in this geographic region have faced a drastic drop in population during the 20th century. Blacks, who contributed a great deal to ethnic distinctions between regions, have moved either to the North or to the industrial centers of the piedmont area. Thus, ethnic and religious groups are not now as segregated by region as they were historically. Meanwhile, current residents in these regions are becoming further removed from the distinct cultures of the original settlers. It may be that the strictly geographic component of region remains comparable to that of rurality. However, the ethnic/religious component of region, which was important in the earlier part of this century, is less viable today as a basis for linguistic differences.

Historically, there were more distinctions between the regions within the South than those reflecting the origins of their settlers in different parts of the British Isles and Africa. For many years, the wealthy planter class from the Low Country dominated the rest of the region economically, politically, and socially. Although Blacks were not allowed to vote, their numbers counted toward the political representation allotted to counties, giving the Whites of the plantation areas a disproportionate amount of power in the legislatures. Charleston's hegemony over the rest of South Carolina lasted until the middle of this century and is described in McDavid (1955), which also notes the hostility felt toward Charleston's elite by inland Upcountry residents. With the transfer of much of the region's power and wealth to larger cities in the piedmont and the decreasing economic importance of agriculture, this interregional rivalry has diminished. With the demise of this conflict, the need for distinguishing linguistic features to mark regional identity has diminished as well.

Whereas formerly region encompassed economic and political divisions, rurality now includes such distinctions. Items that vary by rurality are listed in table 7.

Table 7: Urban words and rural words

Urban Words

andirons	freestone (peach)
weatherboards	is the image of
clapboards	telltale (= tattletale)
cruller	trousers
toad	reins (riding)
frog	spring onions
(school) lets out	Idaho potatoes
spread (= bedspread)	new potatoes
living room	mutt
drawing room	changing (= clouding up)
dish towel	firefly
garden house (= privy)	

Rural Words

bedspread	(school) turns out
kope (call to horses)	rail fence
lines (driving)	doubletree (on wagon)
seed (cherry)	shavs (on buggy)
loft (= attic)	polecat (skunk)
weatherboarding	

Bartley (1990) notes that residents of urban/suburban areas (with the exception of depressed inner city neighborhoods) have higher incomes than those of rural areas and that rural-urban conflict has been a central feature of 20th-century Georgia politics. The 1993 session of the Georgia legislature bears this out, with the anti-Atlanta contingent undermining important budgetary allotments that were perceived as unduly benefiting the city. Bartley (1990:187) sums up such conflict in the latter part of the century:

> Planters, farmers, and small town dwellers watched the disintegration of their way of life with mounting horror and hostility. Their children moved away to the cities and many of their . . . communities wilted. Vast and impersonal social and intellectual changes as well as labor union organizers and black civil rights proponents challenged [their customs].
>
> . . . Grantham wrote: "Adverse economic and demographic forces have baffled and frustrated many rural people, exacerbating their fears of social change and their bitter hostility toward the city. Their declining economic and social status has made them more than ever the great conservators of the South's traditions."

In terms of group identity then, conflicts between urban and rural dwellers might lead to increased use of linguistic markers of loyalty to one's community. Hence, although rurality has declined in its influence on language due to more contact between urban and rural speakers, it has not declined as much as region has because the social divisions between urban and rural groups remain sharply delineated. Rurality retains its social component, while region does not. Though its influence is reduced in magnitude, rurality has become the primary geographical variable affecting language variation.

NOTES

1. The material in this paper is treated more fully in Johnson (1996). I acknowledge the insightful contributions of William A. Kretzschmar, Jr., although I myself remain responsible for any shortcomings.

2. To see which variables were most salient in determining use of particular lexical items, almost 500 words from each data set (1930s and 1990) were tested for a statistically significant link to each one using the Kruskal-Wallis statistic ($p < .01$). This is a nonparametric test based on rank rather than frequency. It is equivalent to the Wilcoxon Rank Sum Test, differing only in that it can compare scores for more than two groups.

3. McDavid ([1970] 1979) discusses at length the cultural and linguistic effects of industrialization and urbanization in the South, which put an end to the hegemony of the plantation aristocracy.

4. The selection of items for this table takes into account the relative wealth of urban dwellers compared to rural ones. So, for example, rural informants rarely wore *trousers*, even to church. Many wore their nicest pair of overalls, a term not included in the set for this linguistic variable. The list also follows the principle that familiarity with an item, hence more frequent use of the term denoting it, will favor the retention of traditional lexical variants. Borrowing occurs more easily in the less-common areas of the vocabulary, thus the urban use of *toad* or *frog* and *firefly* rather than the common *toad frog* and *lightning bug* and rural continuation of *polecat*.

5. Chipmunks, gullies, and sheep are not typically found in the coastal regions. Peaches are not grown in the mountain region, hence the generic *seed* for that part of a peach rather than *kernel* and *plum peach* in comparison to a more familiar fruit for the type that must be cut away from the seed. *Sieva bean* is a variant of *sewee bean*, apparently named for the coastal Sewee Indians, who became extinct shortly after colonists began arriving, though the exact relationship of this variety of lima bean to the tribe cannot be determined.

Generating Linguistic Feature Maps with Statistics

William A. Kretzschmar, Jr.

The first question about using statistical methods to make maps of linguistic features—words, grammar, pronunciations—is why. That question should be subdivided into two parts: first, why map single linguistic features separately; and second, why use statistics to do it? The answers lie in the changes over the past fifty years in survey methodology, in American demographics, in linguistic theory. I suggest just the outlines of a few answers here and then go on to the maps themselves.

On the Linguistic Atlas Project we are only beginning to react to the changed environment for study of language variation, but already I think we are able to show some interesting results. Our database, the Linguistic Atlas of the Middle and South Atlantic States (LAMSAS), was created in the 1930s and 1940s with survey methodology that is not ideal by modern standards. We are all familiar with the essential change in the ability of survey researchers to make predictions, as exemplified in the contrast between the great Dewey-Truman error of the earlier era and the present agreement that networks not announce election winners based on exit polling until after the actual voting has ended. The historical LAMSAS survey can be reconceived according to contemporary standards (Kretzschmar, McDavid, Lerud, and Johnson 1994) and so can provide an excellent database to test new assumptions and methods. We expect that our conclusions can be extended to new fieldwork, so that we can learn about American English using the same conceptual framework with data both from before the Second World War and from the present time. Traditional dialectology as it began in Europe and came to the United States contains assumptions, most often tacit, about the relatively settled, stable nature of regional populations, who were thought to constitute groups of dialect speakers. In reliance on those assumptions, creation of linguistic maps has traditionally concentrated on descriptive techniques (Kirk et al. 1985) or on qualitative interpretive maps (isoglosses, shadings; see Schneider 1988; Kretzschmar 1992a), including some which attempted generalizations about collections of features ("bundles" of isoglosses, e.g., Kurath 1949) or about systematic interrelations between features (e.g., Orton and Wright 1974; Speitel 1969). After the Second World War, those assumptions about stable populations were shattered in this country by several great migrations of people, of African-Americans and poor whites from the South to Northern urban centers, later of unemployed Northerners to the Sun Belt, and of everybody, all the time, to California. During the same period national telecommunications networks have emerged (though the effects of mass communications on linguistic change are incompletely understood; see Bailey, this volume), and the most highly educated portion of the population more and more has competed in national instead of regional marketplaces. Raven McDavid for many years commented on these movements, especially as they affected

Southern speakers, beginning in the 1940s (1946, 1948); he was known to describe his Atlas work as "salvage dialectology," in recognition that changing conditions had to supplant traditional assumptions (1979a).

Linguistic theory has not quite caught up to current conditions. In the 1960s, William Labov began a movement to accept empirical, most often quantitative, testimony for the generation of linguistic theory. His experiments and methods have made significant advances in many areas, not least in language change and phonology in addition to the nature of language variation. These advances have often been framed in terms of social classifications, which fit emerging conditions better than older regional categories. Up to the present, however, these studies have most often been more involved in generation of theory than in the measurement of variation across populations and thus have generally not taken advantage of modern wide-area survey methods. It is my impression, also, that the interest of many North American sociolinguists in the development of particular lines of theory has led them not to challenge some traditional assumptions, such as the existence of "speech communities"; Ash's (1992) discussion of mapping methods, for instance, cites as a model Moulton's 1960s structural maps of German phonology, still in the direct tradition of Weinreich (1954). There are, of course, notable challenges, like Le Page and Tabouret-Keller (1985) and development and application of social network theory by the Milroys (e.g., 1992) and Penelope Eckert (e.g., 1989b).

There have been attempts to bring more modern methods to regional studies. Serious counting of the presence of linguistic features at particular locations has occurred during the 1980s under the rubric of dialectometry (e.g., Kirk and Munroe 1989; Carver 1987 is in some ways similar, but see Kirk 1993b). These techniques establish some set of linguistic features and measure the number of features from the set that were elicited at any location, or otherwise associate frequencies of responses with locations, sometimes with considerable statistical sophistication. However, dialectometry typically does not consider the distribution of single features; that is, we do not know which particular items from the list of linguistic features are present at any given location. Schneider (1988:183) has termed this fact a "loss of relevant information"; it reflects the assumption that there are different dialects at different places, or that some definable "speech community" exists at each place, and that differences or relationships between the dialects can be revealed through the list of features. This is true of the designations "Southern accent" or "Southern dialect." Somewhat different are Walter Cichocki's work with dual scaling (e.g., 1989) and with dendrograms; the latter, in collaboration with Rose Mary Babitch, is somewhat like implicational scaling (Babitch and Lebrun 1989). In all of these methods, it seems to me that dialectometry concentrates on the places, and language is more a tool for the study of the cultural qualities of places than an end in itself.

I can now offer some reasons why we ought to try to make maps of linguistic features using statistical methods. Fundamentally, although times and conditions have changed, we still believe that there is such a thing as regional variation. We hear it around us and, although our perceptions may themselves be various and may lead to different kinds of judgments as Dennis Preston has told us (1989a and in this volume), our perception is sufficient cause to investigate the phenomenon. We want to specify the relationship between language and place, and I think we should prefer to do this without assumptions about "speech communities" or about the existence or status of linguistic systems called dialects. The plain fact is that we do not know much about how single linguistic features per se are distributed quantitatively across areas because our traditional assumptions about speech communities and linguistic systems have stopped us from objective investigation of the phenomena. There is a real chance to generate new theory by letting go of old assumptions, as demographic change now prompts us to do. We can reverse earlier practices and use geography as a tool in a new concentration on the facts of language. Such action can serve as a complement to other investigations that attempt to build on earlier assumptions. To that end, we ought to make the best use we can of established modern statistical and survey methods so that we can validate our findings.

Our new assumptions should be about area as area, and not about places as locations for speech communities. Area is two dimensional. We can think of the real landscape as a plane with the dimensions of longitude and latitude; we might see topographical features like mountains as sitting on the areal plane. In graphic terms, we plot area on the x and y axes, in cartographic terms on a North/South dimension and an East/West dimension. When we come to think of individual locations within an area, say the places at which a linguistic feature was elicited, we can think of those locations in dimensional terms: how far North or South, how far East or West. To do so is to think of the dispersion of the locations with respect to the area as a whole. For example, in figure 1, which shows responses to the LAMSAS question about 'improving weather' that contain *fair* (like *fair off*, *fairing off*, or *faired off*), it looks very much like the feature is more South than North. Figure 2 shows the more limited distribution of *fair off*.[1]

Another way of thinking about locations is with respect to each other, for instance to ask whether the places at which a linguistic feature was elicited seem to occur close to each other or whether they are widely separated. In such a case we are interested in local phenomena, in the arrangement of locations into clusters. In figure 1, it looks like the responses are clustered in Georgia, South Carolina, and eastern North Carolina, with a few more locations outside of that region.

In either case, we may ask ourselves whether the pattern of locations appears random or whether the pattern shows significant clustering or unequal dispersion. Answers to this sort of question are notoriously difficult by eye, and they really require measurement and appropriate statistical validation. If a statistical test cannot affirm significant clustering or dispersion, then we cannot rule out the null hypothesis of what is known as *complete spatial randomness*. If there are significant clusters or if the dispersion is significantly skewed, we are entitled to conclude that there is areal variation for the linguistic feature.

Figure 1

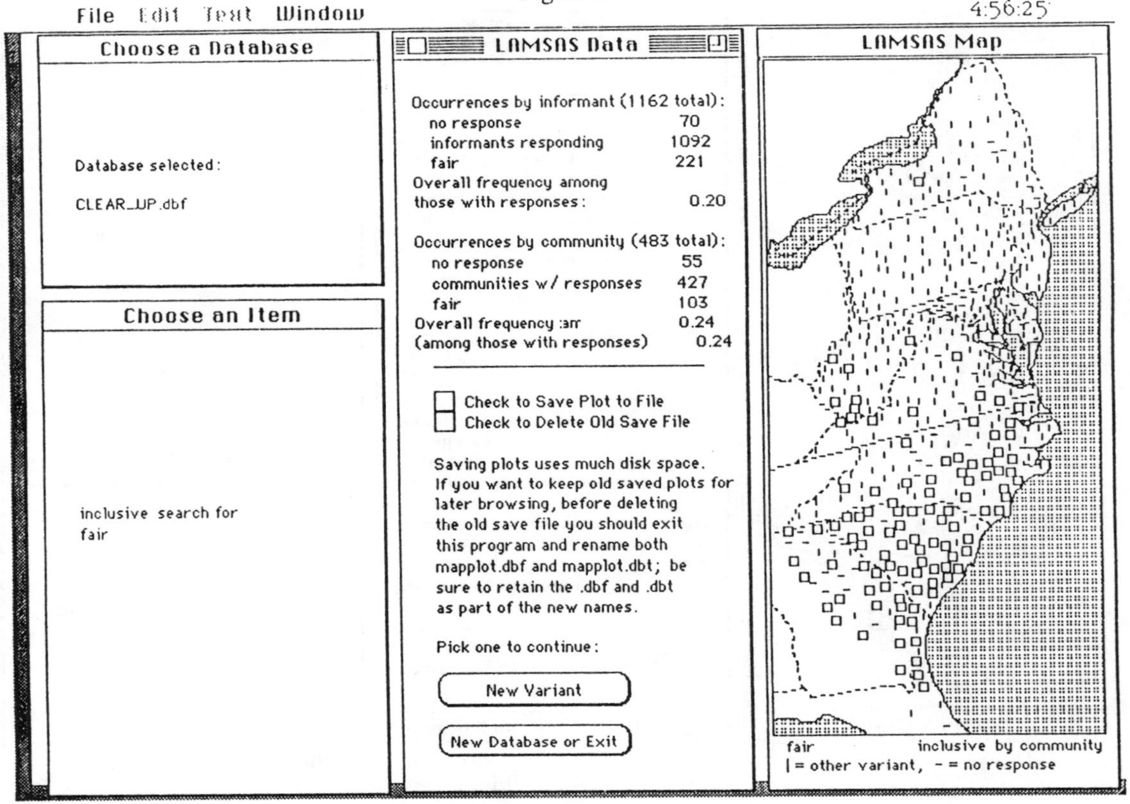

4:56:25

Choose a Database

Database selected:

CLEAR_UP.dbf

Choose an Item

inclusive search for
fair

LAMSAS Data

Occurrences by informant (1162 total):
no response   70
informants responding   1092
fair   221
Overall frequency among
those with responses: 0.20

Occurrences by community (483 total):
no response   55
communities w/ responses   427
fair   103
Overall frequency :among   0.24
(among those with responses)   0.24

☐ Check to Save Plot to File
☐ Check to Delete Old Save File

Saving plots uses much disk space.
If you want to keep old saved plots for
later browsing, before deleting
the old save file you should exit
this program and rename both
mapplot.dbf and mapplot.dbt; be
sure to retain the .dbf and .dbt
as part of the new names.

Pick one to continue:

[New Variant]

[New Database or Exit]

LAMSAS Map

fair   I = other variant, - = no response
          inclusive by community

Figure 2

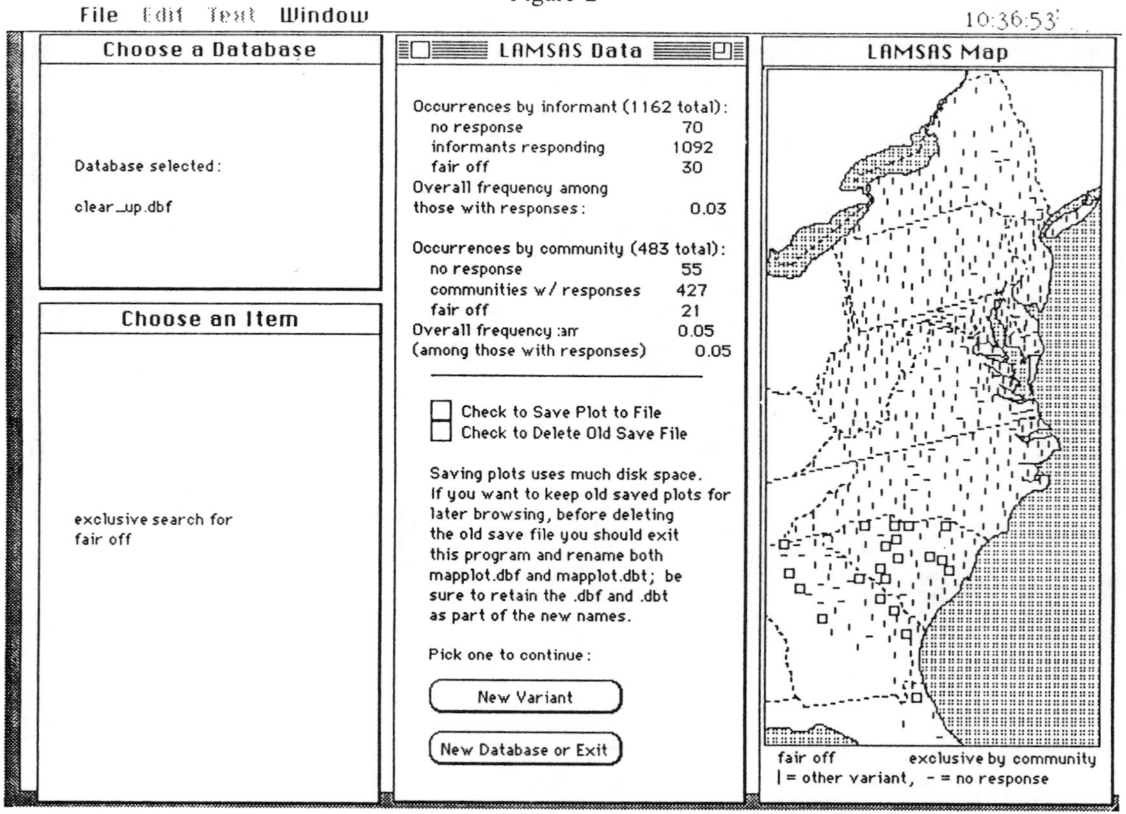

In 1989 Edgar Schneider and I introduced a technique to quantify the areal distribution of individual linguistic features from LAMSAS. We devised an 18-cell grid for the LAMSAS region (A1, 2, 3–F1, 2, 3 in figure 3a–c). The 18 cells gave us six North/South gradations (A–F) and three East/West gradations (1–3) for analysis by these two dimensions. As shown in figure 3a, we measured differences in frequency between the North/South bands and validated the significant North/South pattern (Schneider and Kretzschmar 1989) of *fairing off*. Figures 3b and 3c (Kretzschmar 1992a) illustrate a refinement of the cell-technique in which the statistical test consists of multiple comparisons of cell frequencies across common cell boundaries of the grid—33 in all. The marked cell boundaries are the ones found to be significant, which means that there is a significant change in how often the feature was elicited in the two cells across the boundary from each other.

Figure 3a: Regional distribution of *fairing off* with PROC FREQ, accumulated cells

```
                    SAS      11:30 Thursday, March 2, 1989   1
            TABLE OF REGION BY ITEM


        REGION      ITEM
        Frequency|
        Row Pct  |fairing |other  |
                 |off     |       |      Total
        ---------+--------+--------+
        A        |    0  |   193 |    193
                 | 0.00  | 100.00 |
        ---------+--------+--------+
        B        |    0  |   194 |    194
                 | 0.00  | 100.00 |
        ---------+--------+--------+
        C        |    1  |   189 |    190
                 | 0.53  |  99.47 |
        ---------+--------+--------+
        D        |   11  |   183 |    194
                 | 5.67  |  94.33 |
        ---------+--------+--------+
        E        |   46  |   150 |    196
                 | 23.47 |  76.53 |
        ---------+--------+--------+
        F        |   28  |   167 |    195
                 | 14.36 |  85.64 |
        ---------+--------+--------+
        Total         86     1076      1162

                    SAS      11:30 Thursday, March 2, 1989   4
            STATISTICS FOR TABLE OF REGION BY ITEM
        Statistic                    DF    Value      Prob
        -----------------------------------------------------
        Chi-Square                    5   132.499    0.000
        Likelihood Ratio Chi-Square   5   142.239    0.000
        Mantel-Haenszel Chi-Square    1    88.044    0.000
        Phi Coefficient                    0.338
        Contingency Coefficient            0.320
        Cramer's V                         0.338
        Sample Size = 1162
```

(Schneider and Kretzschmar 1989)

Figure 3b

Pail Boundary Segments (11)
(comparison of cell frequencies significant at p < .002)

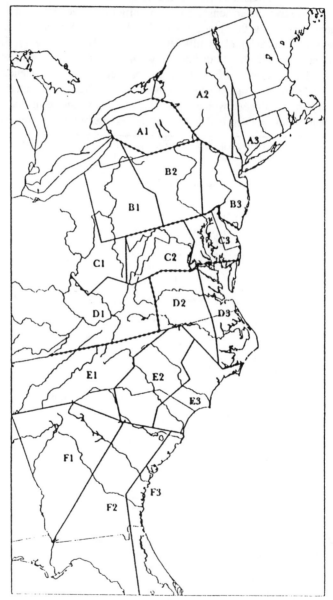

Figure 3c

Bucket (8 Northernmost) and *piggin* (3 Southernmost) Boundary Segments
(comparison of cell frequencies significant at p < .002)

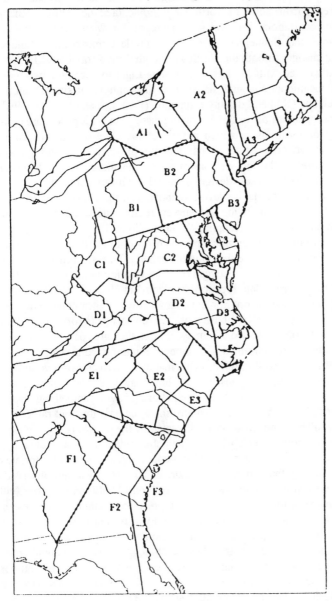

(Kretzschmar 1992a)

The multiple comparison method is able to reveal fairly gradual shifts in occurrence of a feature, here the decrease in the frequency of *pail* from the northernmost band to the central "C" band and then an increase from "C" to the areas further south. The *bucket* data in figure 3c also show a gradation, a decrease in occurrence from South to North; the *piggin* data at the bottom of that panel are more equivocal about direction of change. As for *fairing off*, in figure 4 (from Kretzschmar and Schneider 1996) the multiple comparison technique reveals significant changes to both the North and South from a core cell at E3.[2]

I have worked with Jay Lee and Deanna Light to introduce two more refined statistical techniques for analysis of areal distributions of single features: spatial autocorrelation (SA) and density estimation (DE). Lee and I (1991, 1993) offered the first description of the use of SA on linguistic data. This procedure considers the proximity of locations at which a feature was elicited and thus comments on clusters, or networks, of locations. The SA program illustrates graphically the nature of clusters and offers a means of statistical validation of such clustering. The original LAMSAS survey design included a uniform spread of representative informants; it is possible, however, to understand the LAMSAS survey as a set of data locations and to divide the survey region into a number of small areas corresponding to and "representing" data locations. The term *representative*, then, for us refers only to geographic space, not to political or other criteria. Each of these small areas would be the polygon, called a Thiessen polygon, that is created by drawing a line halfway between the data location at the center of the polygon and each neighboring data location. The communities can thus be reconceived as 483 Thiessen polygons, one for the data location of each community as digitized from the existing LAMSAS base map. As replacements for political boundaries, Thiessen polygons have two advantages. First, they are space exhaustive, whereas some counties were combined and some went unsampled in the LAMSAS survey. Second, they have well-defined, mathematically derived borders and established sets of neighboring polygons, unlike the irregular borders of counties and the uncertainty about what constitutes a neighboring county, something also true of the 18-cell grid. Figure 5 does not actually show the polygons but rather the network of about 1400 neighbor relationships created by the polygons.

Figure 6 shows which of those neighbor relations is activated by our *fair* responses; it also shows the result of join-count statistic, a test appropriate to binary data. We can say that a particular feature either was or was not observed at a data location; we can then count the number of "joins" between locations, either joins between places with different usage (the preferred method, here between a place where *fair* was elicited and a place where it was not) or joins between places with similar status. On the *fair* map, each location at which *fair* was elicited shows up as a nexus of line segments, where each segment is a potential join between neighboring locations; the map thus parallels figure 1 in that one can observe the density of the feature in different regions and one can see clustering in a more positive fashion. For the join-count statistic, however, we are interested in the number of joins that do not actually connect neighboring locations. The actual join count is compared against the count expected from the overall probability of occurrence of the feature (called "free sampling" or "sampling with replacement").

Figure 4: Regional and social distribution of *fairing off*
(Kretzschmar and Schneider 1996)

```
        *-----------*------*-------*
      /   A1      .  A2  .  A3  /
     /     -       .  -  .  -  |
    *......*.......*......*.....*
   /   B1  .   B2  .  B3      /
   |    -  .   -   .  -      /
   *....*....*...*...*......*    Total users:  88
   | C1 .  C2  .  C3      /     Percent of all informants:  8%
   |  - .   1  .  -      |
   *....*...*....*.......:*      *    end of boundary
   |   D1  .  D2 .  D3  |             between adjacent cells
   |    1  .  6  .  4   \     ...  non-significant boundary
   *........*....*---*-----*    ---  significant boundary
   |  E1   .  E2  .  E3   |          (p<.0025), or edge
   |   5   .  18 .  24   /          of survey area
   *........*....*...*----*
   |  F1   .  F2   .  F3 |     (*)  category significant (p<.01)
   |   9   .  14   .  6  |
   *----------*--------*----*
```

type:	I	II	III				sex:	F	M
	50	30	8					37	51
%	9	7	6				%	10	6

age:	-39	40	50	60	70	80+
	2	16	8	21	25	16
%	4	9	4	11	7	8

race:	B	W		comm.type:	F	R	U
	1	87			47	22	19
%	2	8		%	8	8	6

educ:	–	0	1	2	3	4	5	6
(*)	9	10	27	13	10	9	5	5
%	16	11	15	6	4	4	5	8

occup:	–	C	F	G	H	K	D
	1	2	39	0	2	29	1
%	4	7	7	0	17	10	4

	M	O	P	R	S	U	W
	8	0	4	0	1	0	1
%	8	0	9	0	6	0	8

Figure 5: Network of neighbor relations created by Thiessen polygons

JOIN COUNT STATISTICS

LAMSAS file name:
? █

Figure 6: Neighbor relations activated by *fair* responses

JOIN COUNT STATISTICS

Free Sampling:
    Z = -9.019835

Non-free Sampling:
    Z = -16.46497

Free sampling does not assume that the places where *fair* was elicited are necessarily the only places where it might be found, so that we must understand the observed overall probability as an estimate; this assumption matches the reality of LAMSAS sampling. The free sampling procedure is less likely than non-free sampling to render a significant result because of the estimated values in the calculation. Given the standard LAMSAS confidence level of $p < .01$ (Schneider and Kretzschmar 1989; Kretzschmar et al. 1994; Kretzschmar and Schneider 1996), z scores less than -2.33 indicate that there was significantly more clustering of responses than the null hypothesis of spatial randomness. The arrangement of *fair* responses has a z score of about -9, far greater than the confidence level demands. We can say, then, that *fair* responses are significant in both dispersion and arrangement. As figure 7 (from Kretzschmar 1992b) indicates, that is not unusual: in a test of the lexical variants from eleven separate LAMSAS questions, significant clustering occurred with more than half of those responses that did not have too few or too many responses for successful testing.

I will conclude by showing some of our latest attempts to make maps with statistics: density estimation (DE). Light (1992) offered the first description of the use of DE (using a function of discriminant analysis different from the multivariate dimensional analysis mentioned above) to show areal distributions for individual linguistic features. The SAS procedure makes plots that show the density of occurrence of the feature, show the probability the feature will occur in areas of the survey region, and predict comprehensively where a feature might be expected to occur. The general assumptions for density estimation are that, for any single response to a particular elicitation cue, there will be a set of points (the locations where informants lived) where the response was elicited (call it "set A") and another set where it was not (call it "set B"). Reasonable information exists about which of the whole set of 1162 informants were asked the question and which were not, and LAMSAS data files are so coded; set A and set B, for each test, are limited to those informants who were asked the question (typically well over 90% of the total). We expect points from set A to be intermixed with points from set B: we are interested in finding out whether a best-fit geographical boundary can be defined within which there is a significantly higher proportion of points from set A than expected. Currently, we can generate descriptive maps but cannot statistically validate significant clusters; we still rely on SA for validation.

There are two basic nonparametric statistics for density estimation: the kernel method and the nearest-neighbor method. Both are illustrated in figure 8, a map on which the 144 localities of LAMSAS informants are plotted with a grid overlay. For the kernel method, the program calculates the radius of a circle, which is then set around each informant location in turn. The density of occurrence of the target linguistic feature within the circle is then calculated. In figure 8, let us assume that the radius of the circle equals the length of one segment of the grid overlay; if an imaginary circle is then placed around each informant location in turn, the circles contain different numbers of other informants. A density of occurrence can be calculated for each circle, and all of those separate densities can then be put together to derive a map that shows changes in the density across the entire region. The nearest-neighbor method begins differently but ends the same way. The investigator gets to choose how many nearest neighbors will be calculated for each informant location. If we assume that we will be including the five nearest neighbors for each informant location, a look at figure 8 will show that the five nearest neighbors for any given location may include a greater or lesser amount of territory. When the program calculates how all of the separate densities can yield a map of areal density overall, the map assumes that different areas are associated with each informant location; under the kernel method the areas for each separate density are the same, but there are different numbers of informants included. We are now experimenting to see which method works better.

Figure 7: Results of Join Count Analysis (spatial autocorrelation)

Variants (=/equals) (c/contains)	Pres/Abs in 483 communs.	Z score >|2.33| sig @ p<.01	Variants (=/equals) (c/contains)	Pres/Abs in 483 communs.	Z score >|2.33| sig @ p<.01
andirons (8.3)			mantel (8.4)		
andiron c	302/181	-6.519	clock shelf =	19/464	-1.013
dog iron c	154/329	-6.821	fireboard c	97/386	-7.057
dogs =	50/433	-1.087	mantel =	345/138	-2.669
fire iron c	49/434	-0.583	mantel shelf =	38/445	-0.301
firedog c	182/301	-12.961	mantelboard c	42/441	-0.909
handiron c	85/398	-3.437	mantelpiece c	243/240	-11.318
			shelf =	94/389	-2.582
backlog (8.5)					
back stick =	69/414	-3.228	quarter of [the hour] (4.5)		
backlog c	400/83	-0.978	quarter of c	219/264	-9.355
chunk c	89/394	-2.012	quarter till c	213/270	-17.161
log =	173/310	-3.483	quarter to c	247/236	-13.111
stick =	35/448	-0.007			
			shades [for window] (9.4)		
clear up [weather] (5.4)			blinds =	164/319	-5.671
breaking c	74/409	-1.976	curtains =	196/287	-6.798
clearing =	114/369	-2.416	shades =	275/208	-8.151
clearing off =	219/264	-5.439	window blind c	104/379	-5.199
clearing up =	291/192	-2.089	window curtain c	70/413	-1.004
fairing off =	67/416	-3.882	window shade c	177/306	-3.466
			sofa (9.1)		
dresser (9.2)			bench c	81/402	-3.684
bureau c	427/56	-1.094	couch c	77/406	-1.879
chest c	148/335	-1.647	davenport c	28/455	-0.924
dresser c	186/297	-6.671	lounge c	157/326	-2.337
highboy c	17/466	-0.006	settee c	65/418	-3.297
			sofa =	426/57	-1.223
heavy rain (6.1)					
big rain =	74/409	-2.008	thunderstorm (6.2)		
cloudburst c	223/260	-4.247	electric storm c	76/407	-2.583
downpour c	227/256	-1.079	electrical storm c	31/452	-0.703
flood c	82/401	-2.662	storm =	76/407	-5.892
gully+ c	76/407	-2.079	thunder gust c	48/435	-2.759
hard rain =	118/365	-0.969	thundercloud c	76/407	-5.136
hard shower =	51/432	-0.003	thundershower c	176/307	-6.260
heavy rain =	133/350	-2.273	thundersqual c	35/448	-3.544
heavy shower =	38/445	-1.479	thunderstorm c	393/90	-1.107
pourdown c	59/424	-0.671			
half past [the hour] (4.4)					
half after c	82/401	-1.938			
half past c	435/48	-0.242			

(Kretzschmar 1992b)

Figure 8: Localities of LAMSAS informants in South Carolina

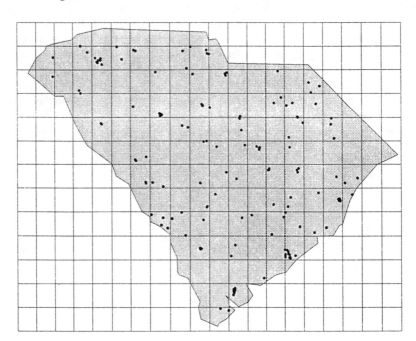

The differences in maps generated by the methods, and some of the pitfalls we still need to circumvent, can be shown from two items, *fairing off* and *dog irons* ('andirons'). Figure 9, with the kernel method, shows *fairing off* in a neat bull's-eye pattern centered on South Carolina; these are the estimated densities of occurrence of the feature (up to 4% or 5% at the densest point, so this is a low-frequency feature). The bull's-eye is characteristic of the kernel method, which has a "smoothing" coefficient that generates regular boundaries.[3] Figure 10 shows a slightly different prediction, the likelihood that *fairing off* will be found at different locations in the region; this map indicates a 50/50 chance of finding the form through South Carolina and Georgia—and a much higher likelihood in the ocean! Predictions outside the survey area are called "edge effects"; they occur because the program does not know that the longitude/latitude coordinates outside the survey area are not supposed to be included, and outside the survey area there is no data (no nonoccurrence of the feature) to restrain the prediction. The last *fairing off* map (figure 11) again shows something different, this time the binary prediction whether any grid location is likely, or is not likely, to have the form, that is, whether the probability generated on the previous map exceeds 50% for any given location. On this kind of map one can draw the equivalent of an isogloss, which I have done; *fairing off* has a good Piney Woods distribution.

Figure 9: SAS Plot of estimated densities for *fairing off*, contour plot of Y x X

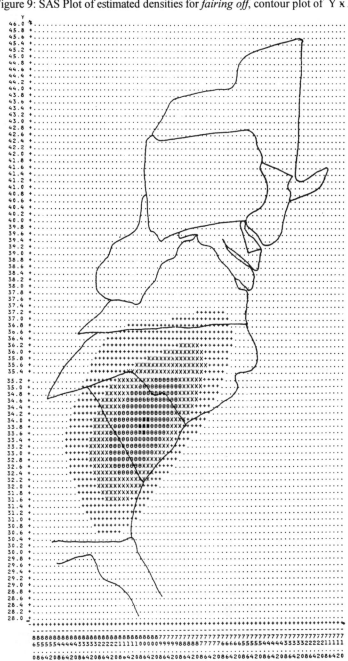

Symbols: ... = 0.00–0.01; ++ = 0.01–0.02; xx = 0.02–0.03; θθ = 0.03–0.04; ▮▮ = 0.04–0.05

Figure 10: SAS plot of posterior probabilities for *fairing off*, contour plot of Y x X

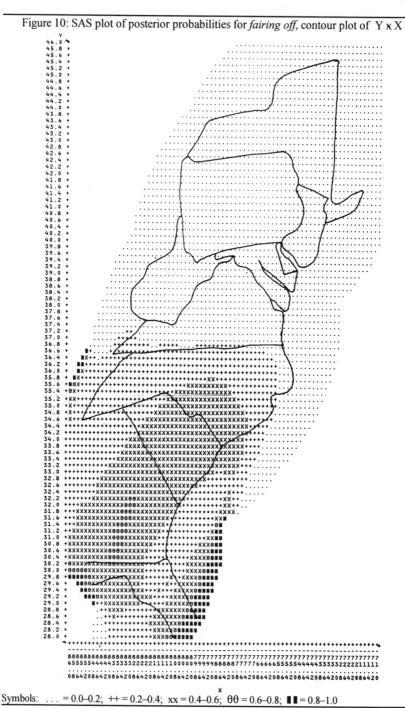

Symbols: ... = 0.0–0.2; ++ = 0.2–0.4; xx = 0.4–0.6; θθ = 0.6–0.8; ∎∎ = 0.8–1.0

Figure 11: SAS kernel method with R = 1 for *fairing off*, plot of Y x X

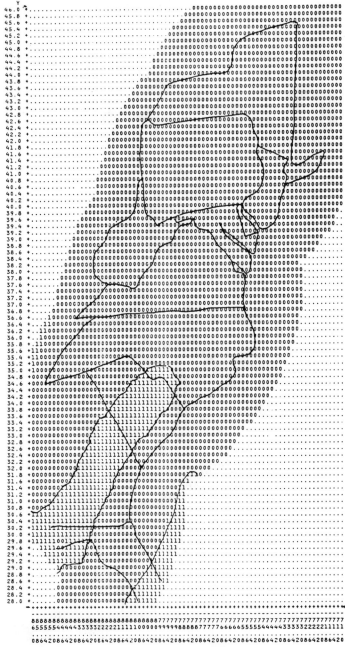

Symbol is value of _INTO_.

Figure 12: SAS plot of estimated densities for *dog irons*, plot of Y x X

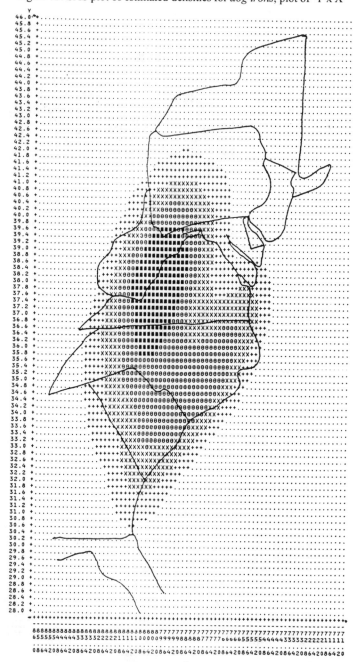

Symbols: . . . = 0.000–0.005; ++ = 0.005–0.010; xx = 0.010–0.015; θθ = 0.015–0.020; ∎∎ = 0.020–0.025

Figure 13: SAS plot of posterior probabilities for *dog irons*, contour plot of Y x X

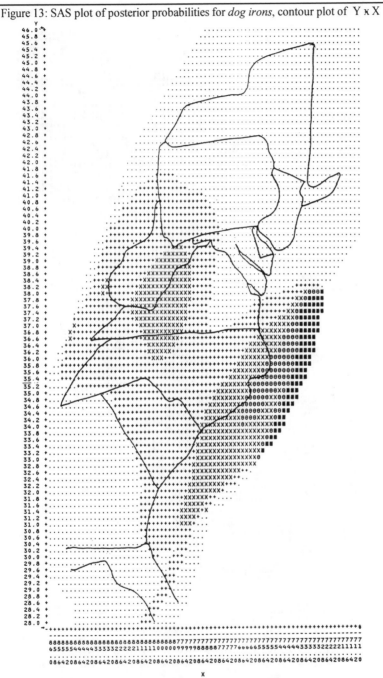

Symbols: . . . = 0.0–0.2; ++ = 0.2–0.4; xx = 0.4–0.6; θθ = 0.6–0.8; ▮▮ = 0.8–1.0

Figure 14: SAS kernel method with R = 1 for *dog irons*, plot of Y x X

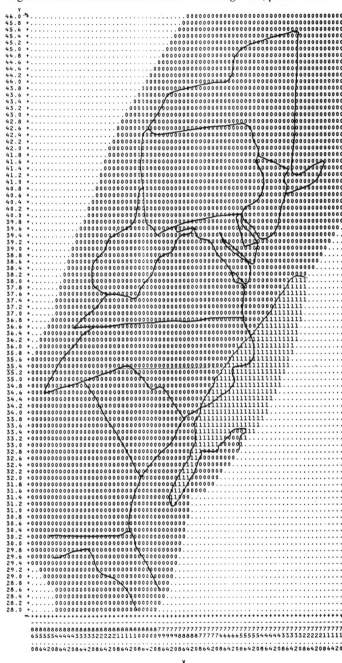

Symbol is value of _INTO_ .

Figure 15: SAS plot of posterior probabilities for *dog irons*, contour plot of Y x X

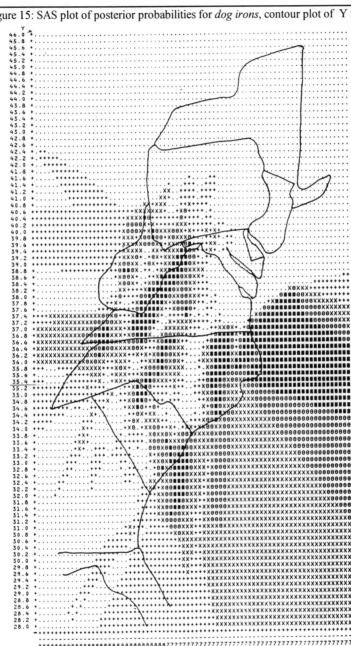

Symbols: . . . = 0.0–0.2; ++ = 0.2–0.4; xx = 0.4–0.6; θθ = 0.6–0.8; ▮▮ = 0.8–1.0

Figure 16: SAS nearest neighbors method with K = 5 run for *dog irons*, plot of Y x X

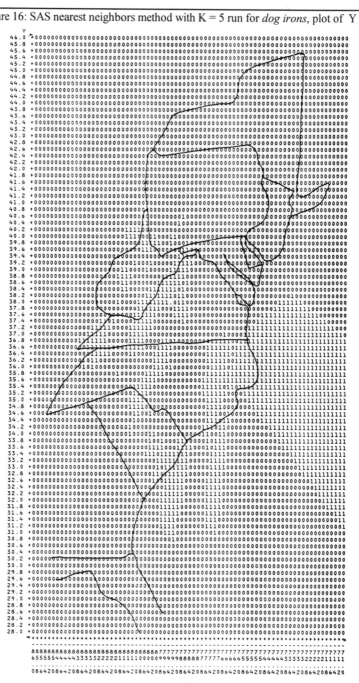

Symbol is value of _INTO_ .

Figure 17

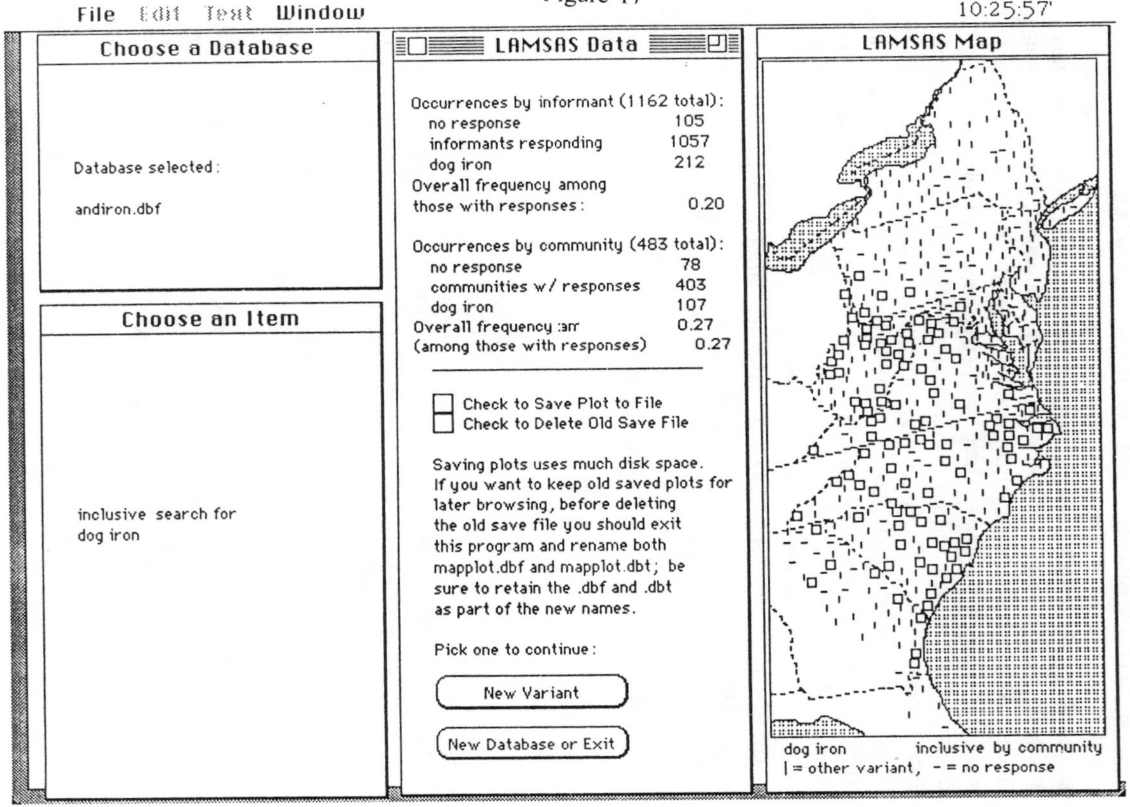

File Edit View Window

Choose a Database

Database selected:

andiron.dbf

Choose an Item

inclusive search for
dog iron

LAMSAS Data

Occurrences by informant (1162 total):

no response	105
informants responding	1057
dog iron	212

Overall frequency among
those with responses : 0.20

Occurrences by community (483 total):

no response	78
communities w/ responses	403
dog iron	107

Overall frequency :arr 0.27
(among those with responses) 0.27

☐ Check to Save Plot to File
☐ Check to Delete Old Save File

Saving plots uses much disk space.
If you want to keep old saved plots for
later browsing, before deleting
the old save file you should exit
this program and rename both
mapplot.dbf and mapplot.dbt; be
sure to retain the .dbf and .dbt
as part of the new names.

Pick one to continue :

New Variant

New Database or Exit

LAMSAS Map

dog iron   inclusive by community
! = other variant, - = no response

A similar kernel map for *dog irons*, figure 12, shows a mitten-shaped distribution of the feature for the density plot. The probability plot, figure 13, shows that the distribution is actually bimodal, in western Virginia and in eastern North Carolina. The binary prediction map, figure 14, shows only eastern North Carolina—and the Atlantic, again because of edge effects that make *dog irons* appear to be common in the ocean. The set is not really very satisfactory, not only because of the edge effects, but also because the smoothing coefficient tends to blur or hide small distributions. Better maps can be obtained with the nearest neighbor method. Although the density map is unenlightening, the probability maps tell a better story. Figure 15 shows three good-sized areas of high probability, one in eastern North Carolina and one on each side of the Blue Ridge Mountains. The binary probability map, figure 16, indicates the same fingers extending down from the top of the Shenandoah Valley (owing to the complexity of the distribution I have not drawn the boundary lines between the 1s and 0s). I would venture to say that none of us would have been able to form any such ideas about the distribution of the feature from the simple dot-plot of *dog iron* shown in figure 17.

These maps, I must emphasize, are experimental,[4] but we have hopes of good things from them. Even in this early state, it is fair to say that both dimensional studies and nondimensional SA and DE are useful for description and validation of single items. They are complementary techniques that address two different aspects of the areal distribution of linguistic features.

NOTES

1. An error in the version of the LAMSAS plot program used to make figures 1, 2, and 17 causes small mistakes in the counts of communities with and without responses.

2. Schneider and I have not forgotten social categories, and in fact we have attempted multivariate analyses, using both discriminant analysis and VARBRUL, and univariate analysis (Kretzschmar and Schneider 1996). North/South and East/West dimensional analysis is well-suited for multivariate studies where region is to be explicitly compared to social categories—but that topic is beyond my scope here. See Kretzschmar and Schneider (1996) for full discussion of social categories.

3. The state outlines are currently supplied with an overlay, not generated by the program; we are experimenting with ways of making the computer generate better presentations of results.

4. We are grateful to NSF for the chance to work on them.

Quantitative Mapping Techniques for Displaying Language Variation and Change

Tom Wikle

While many forms of graphic communication—tables, graphs, diagrams, photographs—can be used to represent complex relationships, only maps preserve linkages and measurable connections between spatial data and the real world. In fact, maps can be defined as diagrams that maintain the spatial association of selected objects on a landscape. As familiar tools, they can be used to assist us in the identification of unique spatial characteristics or distributions on landscapes.

Language, as a cultural phenomenon, lends itself to two basic types of cartographic representation: qualitative maps and quantitative thematic maps. Qualitative or location maps, such as those that employ isoglosses, focus on recording the spatial attribute of a linguistic feature. A single line drawn around a linguistic feature on such maps implies that a discrete separation exists between those areas having a linguistic feature and those without. In many circumstances, however, it is desirable for a linguist to know not only where a feature is found but also how its intensity varies over space. Quantitative maps can be used to represent the continuous distributions of linguistic features through map symbols representing a gradation of data values (see Kretzschmar, this volume). In addition to showing the intensity of a feature, quantitative maps may assist in the analysis of socio-demographic correlates of language usage or help to reveal the temporal dynamics of linguistic distributions. With recent developments in microcomputer technology, linguists can now take advantage of a wide variety of quantitative mapping procedures for analyzing and displaying linguistic data spatially. This paper explores the potential for applying these methods to reveal geographic relationships from linguistic survey information, while touching on some advantages and disadvantages of quantitative map types. Consideration is given to diverse data types and mapping objectives.

MAPPING DIALECT AREAS

As Kirk (1993a) notes, maps dealing with the structure of language have existed for little more than a century. The isogloss method, employing individual lines drawn around the outer limits of linguistic features to show their areal extent, is one of the oldest methods for mapping linguistic distributions and provides simple and unambiguous representations of linguistic landscapes. However, while groups of isoglosses can be useful indicators of dialect boundaries, the use of a line implies that a discrete boundary separates areas having a feature from areas that do not. Rarely are linguistic distributions so simple. Additionally, linguistic features are generally not uniformly distributed throughout geographic areas but are concentrated in core areas of high intensity. With increased distance from these core areas comes a gradual decrease in the presence of a feature until the feature no longer occurs. Selecting isogloss locations, therefore, involves positioning a line generalizing the presence or absence of a feature according to a minimum or threshold value. Thus, isoglosses should not be viewed as fixed boundaries but as transition zones where change from one linguistic form to another is assumed to be gradual. A more fundamental problem with isogloss maps is that they provide no clue concerning the internal structure of a linguistic distribution. Given their qualitative nature, isogloss maps are properly classified as general or locational maps since they show feature positions rather than the intensity of a distribution.

USE OF QUANTITATIVE MAPS

Interest in the role and function of linguistic maps has moved beyond simple representations of the location of linguistic items in favor of explaining the magnitude of their spatial variation (Kirk 1993a). Trudgill (1983) supports the use of quantitative maps as alternatives to location maps, suggesting that dialectologists should not be satisfied with maps that merely describe the spatial distribution of linguistic features, but should seek to develop maps that explain reasons for geographic patterns. Quantitative maps provide the possibility of addressing this shifting emphasis in dialectology.

Quantitative linguistic mapping can be applied to a number of problems such as identifying the intensity of a feature's presence, examining relationships between linguistic and nonlinguistic variables, and exploring spatial-temporal patterns of linguistic forms. Given their high information content, quantitative linguistic maps may involve significant amounts of data manipulation. Such processing can include the grouping of data into convenient reporting districts such as counties or zipcode areas and the selection of a method for classifying ordinal or ratio level data. The function and form of quantitative linguistic maps can vary from a simple and unambiguous overview of a distribution to more complicated representations of spatial or temporal associations between variables. Three families of quantitative maps may be used for uncovering the spatial structure of linguistic distributions: areal feature mapping, point mapping, and surface mapping.

AREAL FREQUENCY MAPPING

Areal frequency mapping uses survey data gathered and aggregated for pre-existing political or administrative areas such as counties, zip codes, or census tracts. Since enumeration areas are treated as single entities, values for areas are presented as areal averages. A number of large-scale linguistic projects such as *Linguistic Atlas of the Gulf States* utilize judgment sampling procedures for collecting data and present the results using areal frequency mapping. Others, such as a Phonological Survey of Texas (PST) and Labov's Lower East Side study, have applied random sampling procedures to survey work. However, while ideal for obtaining representative samples of populations for statistical analysis, simple random samples may present significant obstacles to areal frequency mapping. By including large numbers of respondents from densely populated areas, random samples often leave extensive regions with sparse populations unrepresented on maps, causing difficulty in the interpretation and analysis of distributions. As Bailey, Wikle, Tillery, and Sand (1993) suggest, stratified random samples can overcome mapping problems associated with simple random sampling by ensuring that a minimum number of respondents are included from all enumeration areas. As with random samples, stratified random samples are weighted towards population concentrations; however, a minimum number of responses are drawn from all enumeration areas, preventing the possibility of spatial gaps. Three types of maps most commonly used for displaying areal frequency data include choroplethic, bivariate choroplethic, and prism maps.

Choroplethic maps

The rationale for choroplethic map use, among the most popular methods for representing quantitative distributions, is that they are easily understood by most map readers. Shading or color patterns inside boundaries reflect each area's average value for the linguistic feature being represented. On black and white choroplethic maps, darker patterns indicate higher data values while lighter tones suggest lower values. A gradation of shading patterns or colors provides a visual indicator of the numerical values represented by each enumeration area and thus of the intensity at which a feature occurs.

Since patterns used on choroplethic maps cover enumeration areas uniformly, variation within individual areas cannot be represented. This may give inexperienced readers the false impression that the data distribution within enumeration areas is homogeneous. Despite this limitation, choroplethic maps such as figure 1 are well suited to comparing enumeration areas on multiple maps. A map reader can look for differences in the overall pattern represented, or single out a specific area for comparison. Methodologically, the choroplethic mapping approach is often used for a first look at data because it facilitates a quick and easy overview of a distribution.[1] Figure 1 represents the location of respondents in PST.[2]

Raw numbers are ordinarily not represented on choroplethic maps since the absolute quantity of a variable is a natural function of an area's size or population. Figure 2, which shows the absolute number of respondents to the Texas Poll who use the innovative form of lost (with /a/ as the vowel), illustrates how absolute numbers can be misleading (Bailey, Wikle, and Sand 1991). The map suggests that Houston, in southeast Texas, is as advanced as Dallas-Fort Worth in the use of this innovative feature. However, when percentages are used as in figure 3, Dallas-Fort Worth is clearly shown to be the more innovative area. Densities, ratios, or percentages are generally used in lieu of absolute numbers to avoid visual bias, which occurs unless the enumeration districts are nearly identical in terms of size and population.

As noted above, choroplethic maps generally express data using a limited number of data classes represented with a gradation of shading patterns or colors.

Figure 1: Location of respondents to PST

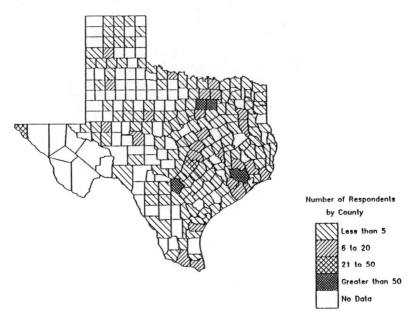

Figure 2: Number of respondents using the innovative form of *lost*

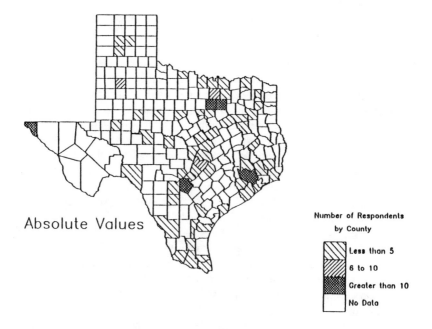

Figure 3: Percentage of respondents using the innovative form of *lost*

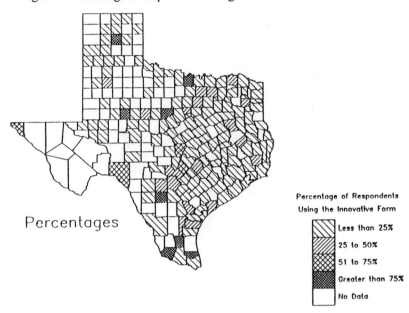

Percentages

Percentage of Respondents
Using the Innovative Form

Less than 25%

25 to 50%

51 to 75%

Greater than 75%

No Data

This is a form of symbolization that, like all forms of generalization, carries the potential for distortion. The number of class intervals used can affect the accuracy, usability, and legibility of a choroplethic map. Since classes are displayed instead of the original statistical data, the reader sees only those values that the cartographer chooses to emphasize. Although 16 methods commonly are used for categorizing data on simple choroplethic maps, possible methods of categorization are infinite (Tyner 1992). Classification methods may be chosen for a variety of reasons. The categories may reflect criteria outside the map or may be selected to remain consistent throughout a series of maps. The most desirable methods for class interval determination take into account the nature of the specific data distribution. Among simple classification methods that can easily be applied to linguistic data are quartiles, natural breaks, and standard deviations. Extreme caution must be used in the selection of class intervals, since classification can obscure or distort information. Figure 4 uses the quartile ranging method to display a weighted index of innovative features in PST using four categories, each having an equal number of data observations. The first quartile includes the first one-fourth of the observations from the bottom of the data array, the second includes the next one-quarter, and so on. Although the equal number of observations provides a balanced map, such distributions can mask variation in the data by subdividing naturally homogeneous categories (Monmonier 1977b). As a ranging method, the quartile procedure should be viewed as an ideal tool for a first look at areal frequency data.

Maps based on the natural breaks method, such as figure 5, are probably more suitable for calling attention to various internal characteristics of a distribution. The

Figure 4: Weighted index of innovative forms using quartile ranging

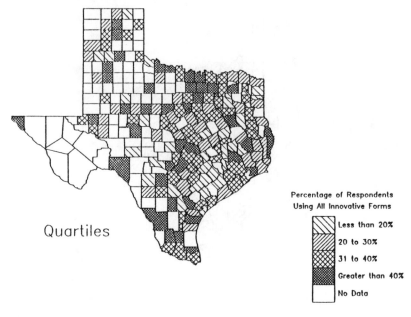

Figure 5: Weighted index of innovative forms using natural breaks ranging

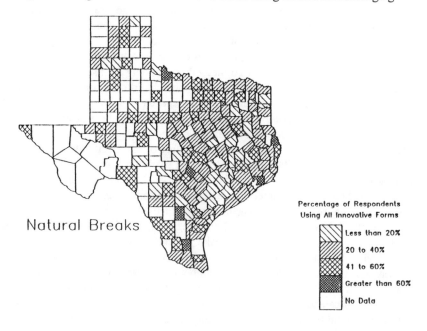

procedure requires that the observations be placed in order from highest to lowest to create a histogram. By identifying significant gaps in the data, the cartographer can determine data ranges based on visual inspection. A major criticism of this method is the subjectivity introduced into a procedure that should be as mechanical as possible. Thus, where natural breaks in a data distribution are not obvious, a less subjective ranging method may be more appropriate.

A third procedure for ranging data on choroplethic maps is the standard deviation method shown in figure 6. Standard deviation is a statistical measure of the dispersion of values around their mean. On a four-class map, the lowest class corresponds to observations greater than one standard deviation below the mean, the second class contains observations between the mean and one standard deviation below the mean, the third class includes observations between the mean and one standard deviation above the mean, and the highest class includes observations greater than one standard deviation above the mean. The standard deviation procedure allows internal characteristics of a distribution to be revealed without the subjectivity of the natural breaks method. This procedure is superior for representing normally distributed data but poor for displaying skewed data sets.

Figure 6: Weighted index of innovative forms using standard deviation ranging

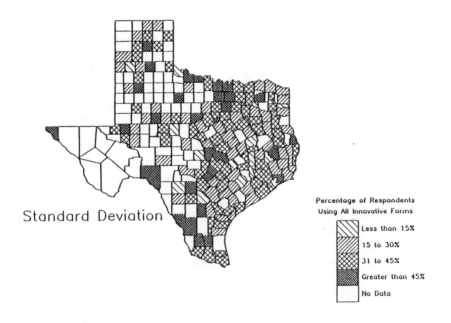

Derived indices can also be utilized for identifying the spatial patterns of language features. Bailey, Wikle and Sand (1991) used a weighted index for selecting class intervals on choroplethic maps of Texas to isolate the focal point of linguistic innovation. Derived indices, such as the one shown in figure 7, apply varying weights to linguistic changes according to how recent or general they are in order to identify linguistically innovative areas of the state. The index facilitates the mapping of an innovativeness score for each county in the sample. These procedures allow choroplethic mapping to be used for exploring the distribution of linguistic features, as well as for combinations of features and indices based on these features.

Figure 7: Derived cluster-weighted index of innovative forms

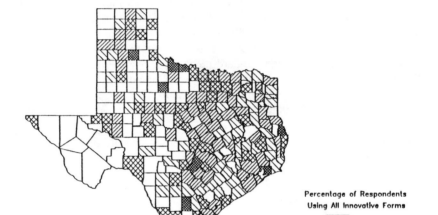

Percentage of Respondents
Using All Innovative Forms

Less than 30%
30 to 40%
41 to 50%
Greater than 50%
No Data

Bivariate choroplethic maps

One problem with simple choroplethic mapping is the difficulty in making comparisons of separate distribution maps to identify spatial association among variables. This problem can be addressed by examining two separate distributions on a single map. Carstensen (1986) notes that the bivariate map depicts complex statistical relationships better than any other choroplethic technique. Bivariate choroplethic maps, such as figure 8, which shows the relationship between Oklahoma's net migration and use of *might could* in a Survey of Oklahoma Dialects (SOD), allow the internal characteristics of separate distributions to be compared on a single, two-dimensional map.[3] Diagonal lines with a gradation of spacing can be used on black and white maps to represent data values with more closely spaced lines creating darker patterns to represent higher data values. The use of opposite slopes for diagonal lines representing the two variables forms a crosshatch pattern where similarity is high.

Figure 8: Bivariate map of relationship between net migration and use of *might could*

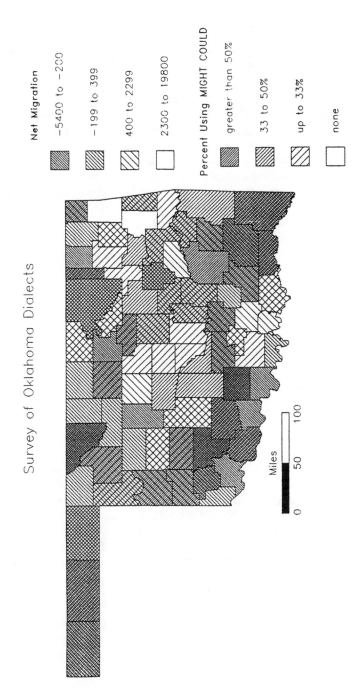

Survey of Oklahoma Dialects

Net Migration

-5400 to -200

-199 to 399

400 to 2299

2300 to 19800

Percent Using MIGHT COULD

greater than 50%

33 to 50%

up to 33%

Miles

0   50   100

On such bivariate maps similarity between variables is indicated by square boxes which form a dark pattern to indicate a positive relationship or a light pattern to suggest a negative relationship. Where the crosshatch pattern creates boxes with nearly equal sides, similarity between the variables is most pronounced. In contrast, elongated rectangles indicate the absence of similarity between the variables. Although some concentration is necessary for interpreting their complex patterns, bivariate maps can be extremely valuable for identifying spatial association.

The bivariate method can be used successfully to identify associations between a demographic variable and a linguistic feature over space. However, as Monmonier (1977a) cautions, extreme care must be exercised in the interpretation of correlation on bivariate choroplethic maps since the likelihood of an incorrect interpretation is high when the enumeration areas vary greatly in size. For example, it is possible for readers to ignore small enumeration areas and concentrate instead on trends within larger, more visible areas. Another problem relates to the level at which data are aggregated. Different types and degrees of spatial similarity may emerge, for example, depending on whether counties or five-digit zipcode areas are selected for map display. As Monmonier (1977a) points out, this effect may be more prominent where the data are not uniformly spread within the larger enumeration area.

Although bivariate mapping is a valuable method for highlighting spatial associations, care must be exercised in avoiding the assumption that correlation observed on the map can be applied to individual enumeration areas. The Pearson's correlation coefficient applies only to disaggregated data; under no circumstances should a relationship identified among areally aggregated data be applied to individuals. Bivariate choroplethic maps should therefore play a purely visual role to identify graphically similarity among variables.

Prism maps

Prism mapping, sometimes referred to as the "stepped statistical" procedure, is an areal frequency method that represents data values by varying the three-dimensional elevation of enumeration areas. Since the height of each area on a prism map represents value, the map can be considered equivalent to a three-dimensional bar graph. Areas with high average concentrations of a linguistic feature would appear as peaks, whereas areas without the feature would resemble lowlands. The three-dimensional attribute of prism maps is created by placing the reader's vantage point at an oblique viewing angle. Lines are removed behind prisms so that the diagram is perceived as a solid figure and maintains the three-dimensional effect. Figure 9 shows the relative number of respondents who used the innovative form of *lost* in PST.

Prism maps are most useful when applied to discontinuous data (geographical data with sharp breaks in the values among adjacent enumeration areas). As with all cartographic methods for depicting areal frequency data, prism mapping has limitations. One problem is the blocking of enumeration areas with low values by foreground regions having higher values. This issue can often be addressed by changing the vertical viewing position or the azimuth.[4] As a simple and unambiguous method for representing areal frequency data, the prism technique is most successful at representing the overall pattern of a linguistic distribution. However, the prism map's three-dimensional attribute makes it less suited for making comparisons between enumeration areas on a single map or among maps.

Figure 9: Prism map showing relative number of Phonological Survey of Texas respondents using innovative form of *lost*

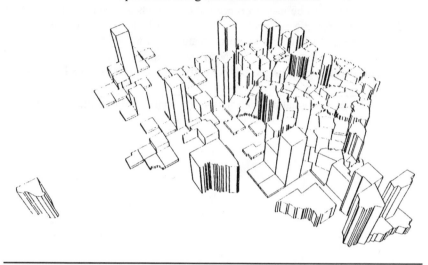

With the exception of prism maps, areal frequency maps are excellent tools for making comparisons among enumeration areas on single maps or for examining the similarity of enumeration area averages on multiple maps. The greatest criticism that can be leveled at the areal frequency family of maps is the unwarranted emphasis produced at enumeration area boundaries. Such abrupt changes rarely occur in reality. Areal frequency maps also suffer from an inability to represent spatial patterns within enumeration areas such as the clustering of data locations around metropolitan areas.

POINT MAPPING

Point maps play a variety of roles in representing spatial distributions. Graduated symbol maps that use symbols of varying sizes centered inside statistical areas or at discrete points are very easy to interpret. Such maps make use of symbol size to display ordinal or ratio level data. Another form of point map, the dot density method (see discussion that follows) is useful when the primary goal is to represent the clustering of a distribution. (See Kretzschmar, this volume.)

Graduated Symbol Maps

Graduated point symbols have long been used in thematic mapping and have been suggested as being among the most effective type of quantitative map (Meihoefer 1982). The method is based on a fundamentally simple idea. A symbol form is selected, such as a circle or square, and is varied in size according to the value of the feature represented. Symbols are placed either directly over a discrete point (such as a city), or in the geometric center of an enumeration area, allowing map readers to visualize distributions by examining the pattern of differently sized symbols. A variant of the graduated circle map, called the segmented graduated circle, or pie map, can be used to represent continuous and categorical variables simultaneously. Each pie can show a continuous variable, such as the percentage of survey respondents having a linguistic feature, and a categorical variable such as ethnicity. Figure 10, created with MapViewer, shows the innovative form of *night* and the percentage of native and nonnative respondents from PST.

Figure 10: Proportional pie map showing percentage of respondents using innovative form of *night*

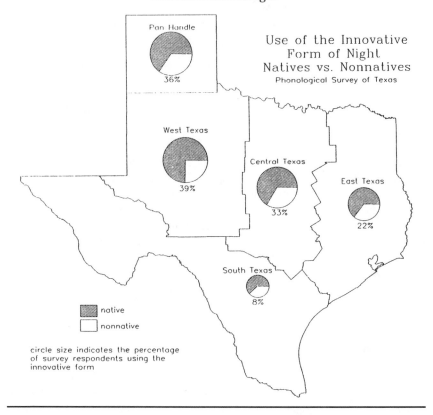

Dot density maps

Perhaps the most straightforward method of portraying linguistic distributions on maps is the dot distribution map where one dot represents a single survey respondent. Dot density mapping has been used for over a hundred years to display spatial distributions because of its simple rationale. Each dot shown on a dot map can represent a single item, although it is more common for a single dot to represent a group of items. In such cases the dot may be thought of as a spatial proxy because it represents a quantity that actually occupies geographic space. Information pertaining to the structure of the distribution is gained by visual inspection of the map.

Dot mapping by computer requires the use of data corresponding to a statistical area such as a five-digit zip code or census tract. All areas within an enumeration area are given equal weight since the mapping software randomizes the placement of dots within each area. An example of problems that can be produced by these random patterns can be illustrated by a dot density map of the U.S. population by state using the state as the data enumeration area. Although the computer would place the correct number of dots within each area, the dots would be spread randomly throughout each state, creating an unrealistic impression of the population distribution. For example, California might have more dots placed over the Mojave Desert than within Los Angeles County. The use of a smaller enumeration area such as a county, zip code, or census tract may solve this problem. Generally, the smaller the statistical area, the more accurate the placement of the dots. Figure 11, showing the location of SOD respondents, was created using the dot density option for Atlas*Graphics software. The improved accuracy in the clustering of dots within counties was achieved by utilizing five-digit zip codes as hidden enumeration areas inside county boundaries.

Figure 11: Dot density map showing location of respondents in SOD

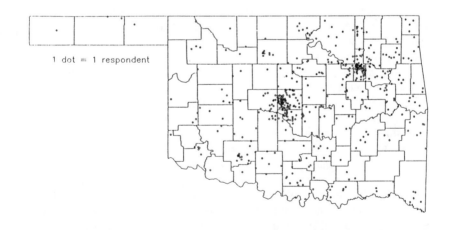

The simple and unambiguous representation of spatial information provided by the dot map has led to its widespread use. In addition, the dot method is particularly well suited for mapping distributions that are discontinuous in nature. However, dot maps are a poor choice if the primary purpose is to make statistical comparisons of enumeration areas on a single map or among maps. Precise numerical determinations are difficult since the counting of dots within areas is impractical. Another drawback is the potential for map readers to misinterpret relationships as one-to-one between dots and features, when in fact each dot represents a group of features. Nevertheless, despite the difficulty in using dot maps to determine data values corresponding to specific enumeration areas, they are extremely effective for showing spatial patterns without placing unwarranted emphasis on arbitrary boundaries.

SURFACE MAPPING

Most linguistic features are continuous in nature, occurring over space rather than at discrete points. If the data used in thematic mapping are thought of as having elevations relative to their magnitudes at certain locations, then linguistic phenomena can be conceived of as forming a continuous three-dimensional surface. Although speech patterns on landscapes cannot be seen, we can think of language distributions as statistical surfaces having peaks, pits, ridges, troughs, gentle lowlands, and high plateaus. Land surfaces are frequently represented in this way since they can be displayed in terms of latitude, longitude, and elevation. However, the abstract nature of social data makes the volumetric representation of linguistic data more difficult to grasp (Jenks 1963). A cartographer can represent such linguistic patterns as two-dimensional maps using lines connecting points of equal value or by using a three-dimensional perspective diagram.

Isoplethic maps

Isoplethic maps are planimetric (two-dimensional) representations of surfaces. Since enumeration areas are not displayed, the lines on such maps have a smooth appearance. The isoplethic technique requires that the mapped surface be continuous in nature rather than stepped. Linguistic data are well suited to this map type since language features occur over the earth's surface in continuous yet undulating frequencies.

Isoplethic maps use control points or points of known location and value in order to construct line symbols known as contours. The simplest method of establishing control points for isoplethic mapping involves placing a control point at the center of each enumeration area. In addition to latitude (x) and longitude (y) coordinates, each control point has a z-value in the form of a ratio or percentage corresponding to a linguistic feature. Microcomputer software packages such as SURFER can then be used to create a contour map from control points. As Peucker (1972) notes, a very important factor affecting the accuracy of an isoplethic map is the density of control points used. It is therefore desirable to use the smallest enumeration area possible.

Most microcomputer programs require a significant amount of preprocessing before isoline generation is possible. Primary interpolation involves the calculation of z-values at all locations on a fine-mesh grid. The primary interpolation stage may include a variety of mathematical models: inverse-distance weighted, planar, quadratic, or cubic (Dent 1990). Isolines are positioned with respect to the grid matrix during the secondary interpolation stage. Figure 12, created using the TOPO module of SURFER, shows the percentage of PST respondents using the innovative form of *night*. The difference between values represented by successive contours is called the isoline interval. Its selection is of critical importance because this value influences the perceived slope of the surface. The interval should be small enough so as not to miss significant variation in the surface without cramping the lines and producing a cluttered appearance.

Figure 12: Isoplethic map showing the percentage of respondents using the innovative form of *night*

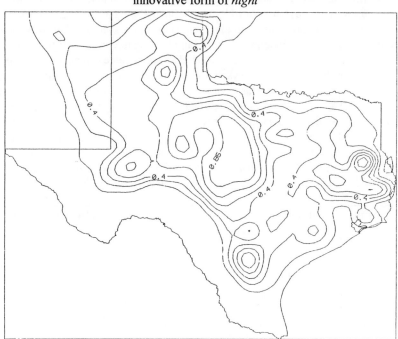

Although the curvature of lines used on isoplethic maps provides a graphic representation of the shape of a surface, it is not possible for the map reader to determine an exact value for every position on the map. Values must be estimated for points that are not located directly on a line. The accuracy of such estimates depends on the isoline interval and the variability of the surface.

In terms of map design, isoplethic mapping can be considered among the best methods for portraying quantitative information. The method facilitates the display of a linguistic pattern while allowing the reader to sample the approximate value for a specific location. Isoplethic maps are best suited to illustrating distributions where changes are relatively gradual. Abrupt distribution changes are not suited to isoplethic mapping and should be represented using a method more adapted to extreme spatial discontinuity such as the dot distribution or areal frequency methods. Some cartographers avoid isoplethic maps in favor of areal frequency methods such as the choroplethic because of the conceptual anxiety of using isoline interpolation where the precision of original data values has been lost.

Perspective diagrams

In recent years perspective diagrams, also called "fishnet maps," have become popular for creating three-dimensional models of surfaces. Continuous values on these imaginary landscapes create what is known as a statistical surface (Tyner 1992). According to Monmonier and Schnell (1988), perspective diagrams were not practical until surface plotting computer programs were developed in the late 1960s and 1970s. The computer interpolation routines used to create figure 13, which shows the relative percentage of respondents using the innovative form of night in PST, are similar to those employed by isoplethic mapping procedures used to create figure 12. Both require latitude and longitude coordinates and z-values representing the percentage of respondents having a linguistic feature at control points located in the center of enumeration areas. Subtle changes in value can be shown by peaks or ridges or by pits and valleys. Gradient is an important concept in surface mapping since statistical surfaces can show trends according to the direction and magnitude of a slope. The perspective diagram is especially useful for modeling the gradient of statistical surfaces representing linguistic features. One significant advantage of surface maps is their unique ability to represent the continuous nature of linguistic variation over space. However, a major challenge to the use of surface mapping in representing linguistic features is the problem of how to deal with data outliers that can cause subtle variations in a surface to be overlooked.[5]

Figure 13: Statistical surface map of Texas showing the relative percentage
of respondents using the innovative form of *night*

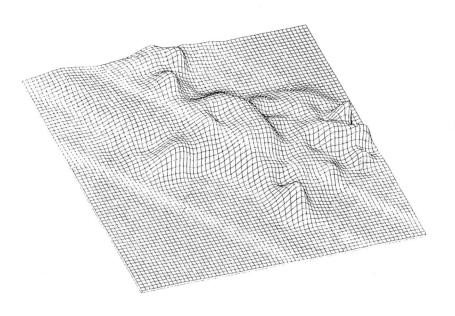

CONCLUSION

As Kirk (1993a) suggests, maps continue to serve as the principal tool of the linguistic geographer by facilitating the access, presentation, and explanation of linguistic data in a spatial format. As survey methodologies continue to be refined and as computers unveil new ways of analyzing and displaying linguistic data, the quantitative thematic map will play an increasingly important research role in the hypothesis testing cycle. Such spatial models of linguistic landscapes give linguists and geographers mechanisms for uncovering relationships and for experimenting with various analytical procedures or designs. In this way computer generated mapping procedures provide new methods for revealing the diversity of speech patterns on the landscape and introduce exciting possibilities for capturing the ephemeral nature of language variation.

NOTES

1. Atlas*Graphics software for IBM compatible computers was used to generate the choroplethic maps.

2. For a more complete description of PST see Bailey and Bernstein (1989), Bailey and Dyer (1992), and Bailey, Wikle, and Sand (1991).

3. For a description of SOD see Bailey, Wikle, Tillery, and Sand (1993).

4. This map was created using MapViewer software, which allows changes in the viewing azimuth (or compass direction), the height of the viewing position, and the distance of the observer from the map.

5. Smoothing algorithms appear to hold promise in solving such problems.

The Role of Social Processes in Language Variation and Change
Jan Tillery

INTRODUCTION

Traditionally, linguists have examined linguistic variation from two perspectives, that of dialect geography and that of sociolinguistics. Each field has developed distinct approaches for gathering and analyzing data and ultimately for explaining variation. On the one hand, dialect geographers, following Kurath and his predecessors in Europe, are concerned with the areal distribution of linguistic features and the dialect areas delineated by those distributions. In order to determine these distributions, dialect geographers typically lay out a grid of communities based on the settlement history of an area, select native informants whose roots in that community often go back three generations, and interview those informants with a detailed questionnaire which (in the United States anyway) links one atlas project with another. From these interviews, dialect geographers plot the spatial distribution of linguistic features and link that distribution to settlement history (Pederson 1972). Even allowing for changes in technology, recent dialect geography surveys are quite similar to those begun a half century earlier.

Sociolinguists, on the other hand, examine the distribution of linguistic variants among social groups and link variation to cleavages in social structure. In order to locate variation in the social structure, sociolinguists—following Labov (1966, 1972b), Milroy (1987a), and others—conduct either random sample surveys or in-depth community studies. Sociolinguists then correlate respondents' ethnicity, social class, age, and gender with linguistic features to explain the linguistic variation that they find. In many ways the methods of sociolinguists have become as fixed as those of dialect geographers. Social class, gender, and ethnicity have become as conventional as isoglosses. Wolfram's (1991) textbook on American dialects, which offers sections on social class, gender, and ethnicity as well as region as correlates for language variation, clearly shows how these variables have become fixed. While dialect geography and sociolinguistics continue to offer crucial insights into language variation, our research in Texas and Oklahoma suggests that neither approach provides a complete picture.

What the data from Texas and Oklahoma suggest is that factors not usually given prominence in either approach actually are as important in influencing variation as the traditional ones. Bernstein (1993, 1994), in her work on data from the Phonological Survey of Texas (PST), suggests that variation according to region, gender, and ethnicity account for a relatively small portion of the variation of that corpus, while our work in Oklahoma shows the impact of such features as rurality and nativity. In other words, the work in Texas and Oklahoma shows that we need to expand the set of explanatory categories used by dialect geographers and sociolinguists. This paper begins such an expansion by reporting on linguistic variation that occurs in the data from a Survey of Oklahoma Dialects (SOD).

Figure 1: Location of respondents in PST

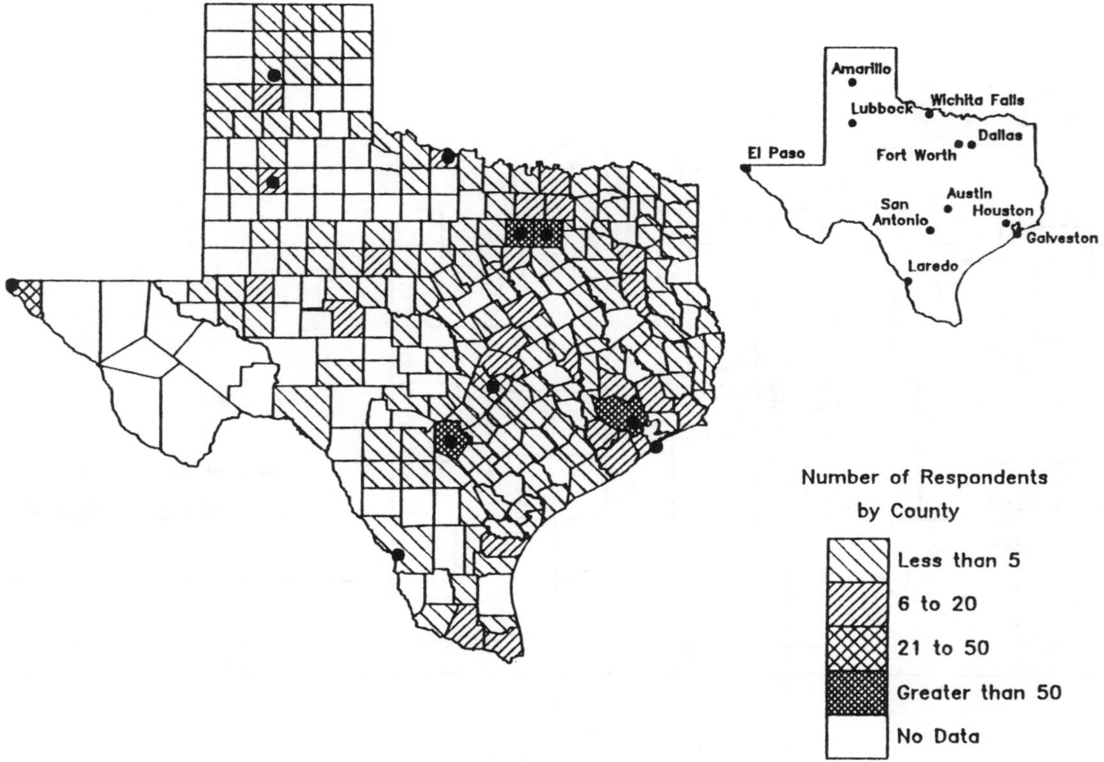

Number of Respondents
by County

Less than 5
6 to 20
21 to 50
Greater than 50
No Data

Amarillo
Lubbock
Wichita Falls
Dallas
Fort Worth
Austin
San Antonio
Houston
Galveston
Laredo
El Paso

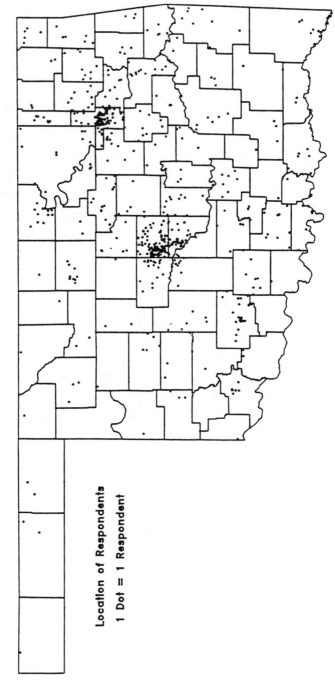

Figure 2: Location of Respondents in SOD

Location of Respondents
1 Dot = 1 Respondent

METHODS

The data used in this research come from three sources: a 1989 Phonological Survey of Texas (PST), a 1989 Grammatical Investigation of Texas Speech (GRITS), and a 1991 Survey of Oklahoma Dialects (SOD).[1] PST, GRITS, and SOD are all large-scale multifaceted investigations which include field and random sample telephone surveys of Texas and Oklahoma. The telephone surveys serve as the central component of each and provide the corpus of data for this paper. Figures 1 and 2 show the location of respondents of the telephone surveys in both states.

PST, GRITS, and SOD have been developed in an attempt to gather valid and reliable synchronic linguistic data to which a wide range of statistical and cartographic procedures can be applied.[2] For each respondent, these surveys elicit the standard demographic data—age, ethnicity, gender, occupation, levels of income, and education—for correlation with the linguistic variables. Figures 3–6 summarize the data for both states. A significant difference occurs in the ethnic makeup of both states as illustrated in figure 4. The Black and Hispanic populations are much greater in Texas than in Oklahoma, but the Oklahoma sample includes 6.9% Native Americans.

Another striking difference between the two, as figure 7 demonstrates, is the proportion of the population in large metro areas. Nearly half of the Texas respondents reside in metropolitan areas of over one million (Dallas/Ft. Worth, Houston, and San Antonio), while nearly three-quarters of the Oklahoma respondents reside in areas under 100,000. These differences are crucial for explaining the patterns of variation that occur in each state.

In addition, the Texas Poll, of which PST was a part, included a question asking respondents to rate Texas as a place to live. The correlation of responses to this question with the linguistic data suggested to us that affective factors might play an important role in explaining variation. For example, our analysis shows that the correlations between the use of monophthongal /aɪ/ and the standard social categories are confusing at the least; however, the use of monophthongal /aɪ/ and respondents' rating of Texas correlate strongly with one another. As figure 8 indicates, those respondents who rate Texas positively (excellent or good) as a place to live are much more likely to use monophthongal /aɪ/ before voiceless obstruents than those who rate the state as fair or poor. In other words, monophthongal /aɪ/ reflects a strong identity with the state (Bailey 1991; Tillery 1990; Tillery and Bailey forthcoming-a). Variation in the use of monophthongal /aɪ/, then, seems to be associated with a respondent's identity with place, a factor (or variable) not measured by most standard social categories. With this in mind, SOD was designed to explore the identity of respondents by gathering crucial information about respondents' perceptions of their regional, state, and local identities and their own status in relationship to them.

For example, we asked respondents how they would rate Oklahoma as a place to live and whether they view Oklahoma as a Southern, Midwestern, or Western state. Here, most Oklahomans, nearly 85%, rate the state favorably as a place to live (see figure 9), while over half consider the state midwestern, and one-third consider it to be southern as figure 10 shows.

Figure 3: % of total number of PST and SOD respondents by age group

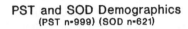
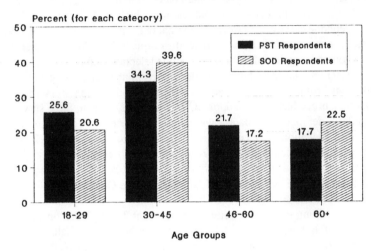

Figure 4: % of total number of PST and SOD respondents by ethnic groups

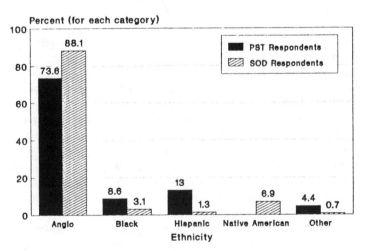

Figure 5: % of total number of PST and SOD respondents by gender

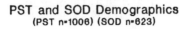

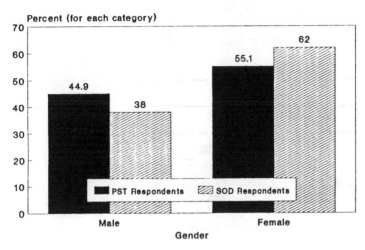

Figure 6: % of total number of PST and SOD respondents by education level

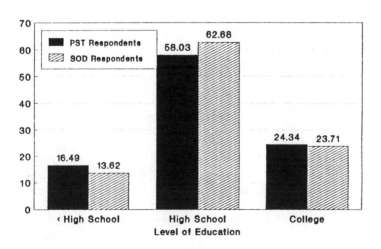

Figure 7: Urban/rural distribution of PST and SOD respondents

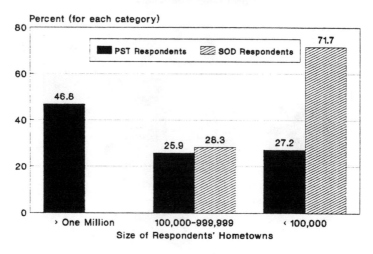

Figure 8: Correlation of monophthongal /aɪ/ in *night* with
respondents' rating of Texas

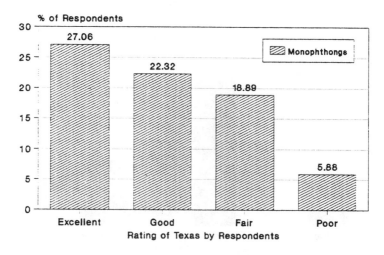

Figure 9: Rating of Oklahoma as a place to live

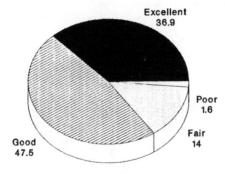

Percentage of Responses by Rank

Figure 10: Perception of Oklahoma's location

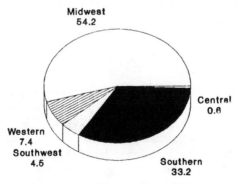

Percentage of Responses by Region

Following this question, respondents were asked to rank their neighborhoods as places to live. Figure 11 illustrates that Oklahomans rate their neighborhoods almost exactly as they rate the state, a consistency which demonstrates the strength of local identity in Oklahoma.

Figure 11: Neighborhood rating

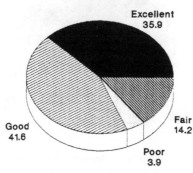

Excellent
35.9

Fair
14.2

Good
41.6

Poor
3.9

Percentage of Responses by Rank

We explored the effect of neighborhood in one other way as well. Respondents were asked how long they had resided in their current neighborhoods and the size of the communities where they had resided most of their lives. These elaborated measures go beyond nativity (length of residence in the state) and rurality (size of current residence) in that they enable us to assess the effect of the social process of mobility.

RESULTS

A comparison of the effects of standard social categories with the effects of the expanded measures of nativity and rurality demonstrates the importance of mobility on linguistic variation in Oklahoma. The distribution of linguistic variants across the categories of age, gender, occupation, income, education, and ethnicity accounts for only a small portion of the variation in the SOD data.

Table 1 presents all of the phonological variables in SOD, along with an indication of the statistical significance (using the chi square test) of their distribution according to standard sociolinguistic categories. Note that only three of the fourteen linguistic variables are affected significantly by at least three social factors. If age is eliminated, only fifteen of the 84 cells (less than 20%) are filled. Gender, occupation, and ethnicity are significant for only two features each, while income is significant for only three. Education, the category that affects the greatest number of linguistic features, influences only six, less than half of the phonological variables investigated in SOD. While standard social factors are sometimes important in explaining variation in Oklahoma, they do not tell the whole story. If we correlated only these six social variables with the phonological variables in SOD, we would have to conclude that much of the phonological variation in SOD is random.

Table 1: Statistical significance of correlation between social categories and SOD phonological variables

Variable		Social Category					
		Age	Gender	Occupation	Income	Education	Ethnicity
/j/	in *Tuesday*	—	—	—	—	—	—
/ʒ/	in *Thursday*	—	—	—	—	—	.01
/ə/	in *forty*	.05	—	—	—	—	.01
/æ/	in *thousand*	—	—	—	—	—	—
/ɚ/	in *wash*	.01	—	—	.05	—	—
/ɪ/	in *Wednesday*	—	—	—	—	.01	—
/ɪ/	in *pen*	—	—	—	—	.01	—
/a/	in *Friday*	—	—	—	—	—	—
/a/	in *time*	.01	—	.05	.01	.01	—
/a/	in *night*	—	—	—	—	.05	—
/ɪ/	in *field*	.01	—	—	—	—	—
/ɛ/	in *bale*	.01	.01	—	—	—	—
/u/	in *pool*	.01	—	—	.05	.01	—
/a/	in *hawk*	.01	.05	.05	—	.01	—

However, correlating phonological variables with the measures of nativity and rurality reveals that the variation is systematic, not random at all. Table 2 provides a striking contrast to table 1. Of the 56 cells in table 2, 25 (44%) are filled. In other words, nativity and rurality are significant factors over and over again. For three of the phonological features (intrusive [r] in *wash*, a high front vowel in *pen*, and a lax vowel in *pool*), all four of the demographic variables are statistically significant. At least two of the demographic variables are significant for five other features as well (a high front vowel in the first syllable of *Wednesday*, monophthongal /aɪ/ in *Friday*, *time*, and *night*, and an unrounded vowel in *hawk*). These demographic variables are not significant for only three features: the presence or absence of /j/ in *Tuesday* and unconstricted [r] in *Thursday* and *forty*. However, the latter two variables are ethnic features that occur almost exclusively among African-Americans. The presence or absence of /j/ in *Tuesday* represents an anomaly that correlates with none of the social variables investigated in SOD. What the data in tables 1 and 2 clearly show is that social class, ethnicity, and gender play relatively minor roles in variation in Oklahoma. The factors that seem to influence variation most in Oklahoma are how long respondents have lived in the state and in their neighborhoods and whether their communities are urban or rural.

While the data from PST and GRITS suggest that length of residence in the state is a key factor in linguistic variation in Texas, the data from SOD suggest that length of residence in a local neighborhood is more important in Oklahoma. For three of the five features in table 2 (intrusive [r] in *wash*, high front vowel in *pen*, and a lax vowel in *pool*), length of residence in one neighborhood is at least as significant as length of residence in the state. Moreover, for three variables (lax vowels in *field* and *bale* and an unround vowel in *hawk*), length of residence in the neighborhood is significant, while length of residence in the state is not. These distributions strongly suggest the importance of local identity in language variation in Oklahoma.

Table 2: Statistical significance of correlation between categories of nativity and rurality and SOD phonological variables

Linguistic Variable	Nativity	Years in Neighborhood	Rurality	Size of Longest Residence
/j/ in *Tuesday*	—	—	—	—
/ʒ/ in *Thursday*	—	—	—	—
/ə/ in *forty*	—	—	—	—
/æ/ in *thousand*	.05	—	—	—
/ɚ/ in *wash*	.05	.05	.05	.05
/ɪ/ in *Wednesday*	.01	—	.01	.01
/ɪ/ in *pen*	.01	.01	.01	.01
/a/ in *Friday*	—	—	.01	.01
/a/ in *time*	—	—	.01	.01
/a/ in *night*	—	—	.01	.01
/ɪ/ in *field*	—	.05	—	—
/ɛ/ in *bale*	—	.05	—	—
/u/ in *pool*	.05	.01	.01	.01
/a/ in *hawk*	—	.01	.01	—

Note: Nativity = length of residence in Oklahoma
      Rurality = size of place of current residence

Rurality is an equally important factor in language variation in Oklahoma. Rurality is statistically significant (again by chi square tests) for eight of the fourteen variables in table 2. Here, the size of the current community (not the community where respondents have lived the longest) seems to be the key. For example, in every instance that size of the place of longest residence is significant, size of current residence is also statistically significant. In fact, in the use of unround vowels in *hawk* size of current residence is significant while size of the place of longest residence is not. While the effects of nativity and rurality might seem to be unrelated, together they provide evidence on the most important social process of this century—the development of widespread geographic mobility.

Over the last hundred years (and especially the last fifty) the American South has been characterized by extensive movement from the country to the city. This urbanization paralleled migration from the South to the North between World War I and the 1960s and over the last twenty years paralleled migration from north to south as the Sunbelt became an important destination for business and industry, tourism, and retirement. When considered together the four variables of size of current residence, size of the place of longest residence, length of residence in the state, and length of residence in the local neighborhood allow us to measure respondents' participation in the processes of urbanization and migration. The chi square distributions in tables 1 and 2 above suggest that it is these processes of urbanization and migration, rather than cleavages in social structures, that motivate language variation and change in Oklahoma. The speech of those who have moved, whether from the country to the city or from state to state, tends to be different from the speech of those who have not.

While urbanization and migration are the chief correlates of language variation in Oklahoma, that is not necessarily the case everywhere. Table 3 illustrates this point. A chi square analysis of the correlation between the phonological variables in PST that appear also in SOD and the social variables of PST shows a much more complex interaction. Of the eight social variables in table 3, all but two significantly affect three or more phonological variables. While gender and income seem to have little influence on variation in Texas, occupation and education are about as influential as nativity and rurality. It is important to keep in mind here, however, that length of residence in Texas is the only measure of nativity in PST, while size of current residence is the only measure of rurality. More elaborate measures, like those done in Oklahoma, might provide different results. The effects of ethnicity are more widespread than any of these: ethnicity significantly affects six phonological variables. As the demographic comparison of Oklahoma and Texas above illustrates, Texas is an ethnically more complex state; linguistic variation in the state reflects that fact. The fact that a substantial number of Texans live in large metropolitan areas suggests that the state may be more complex socially than Oklahoma as well. Certainly the effects of occupation and education suggest that complexity. The important point here, though, is that the relative influence of social variables differs from one state to another and possibly one community to another.

Table 3: Statistical significance of correlation between social
and phonological variables in PST

Linguistic Variable		Age	Gender	Occ.	Social Variable Income	Educ.	Ethnic.	Nativity	Rurality
/j/	in *Tuesday*	.0001	—	—	—	.006	—	.04	.0001
/ə/	in *forty*	—	.05	—	—	—	.0001	—	—
/æ/	in *thousand*	—	—	—	—	—	.0001	—	—
/ɚ/	in *wash*	.0001	—	.01	—	—	—	—	—
/a/	in *night*	—	—	—	—	—	.01	—	—
/ɪ/	in *field*	.001	—	.0001	—	—	—	—	.002
/ɛ/	in *sale*	.0001	—	.001	.05	—	—	—	.03
/ʊ/	in *school*	.0001	—	.0001	—	—	.003	.001	.009
/a/	in *lost*	.0001	—	—	—	.04	.0001	.0001	—
/a/	in *walk*	.0001	—	—	—	.05	.0001	.0001	—

The work of Bernstein (1993) on data from PST points to an even more fundamental problem with the standard explanatory variables used in dialect geography and sociolinguistics. Bernstein looks not just at the statistical significance of social variables but at their interaction with one another and at the amount of variation that they actually explain. The results are enlightening. For example, a bivariate analysis of the Texas Poll data from PST shows that the five linguistic features in her cluster 1 are significantly affected by age, ethnicity, income, nativity, region of Texas, and rurality. Bernstein's multivariate analysis shows, however, that when interactions among factors are taken into account, only age and rurality have a significant effect. Moreover, these two factors only explain 25% of the observed variance in the sample.

Two surprising facts become clear from Bernstein's analysis. First, conventionally used social variables such as gender and social class contribute little to variation in the Texas Poll data, although ethnicity and region are powerful effects for some clusters. Age is the only factor which significantly affects all clusters. Second, we must look to variables such as nativity and rurality to fill in the explanatory gap. However, it is not enough simply to include nativity and rurality in our analyses. Rather we must be open to a wide range of social and demographic processes and not limit our analyses to standard categories that emerged from the early benchmark studies.

CONCLUSION

While gender, occupation, income, and ethnicity will remain important parts of the explanatory apparatus, those categories should not become the "be all and end all" of sociolinguistic analysis. By the same token, we should not be limited by the standard apparatus of dialect geography, i.e., standard isoglosses and dialect areas. Our research in Texas and Oklahoma suggests that spatial distribution of linguistic forms is often quantitative and that spatial distribution tends to interact with social factors in intricate ways to create complex linguistic landscapes (see Bailey, Wikle, and Tillery, 1992). To understand the interaction of the social with the spatial, we need multidimensional models that show those interactions.

With all of these social and spatial categories, we need to remember that they are only oblique indicators of social processes, such as migration and urbanization, that underlie those categories. In developing categories for sociolinguistic analyses, we need to seek those categories that are tied to social processes as directly as possible. Perhaps the most important thing our research in Texas and Oklahoma demonstrates, however, is that preconceptions limit discovery. What the data in Texas revealed with regard to the effects of respondents' identities to Texas on language variation was so dramatic that we expected a duplicate of that in Oklahoma. This did not occur. In the Oklahoma data, mobility is the key factor. Whatever motivation may lie behind linguistic variation elsewhere, one thing is certain—only the data know.

NOTES

1. PST, GRITS, and SOD have been funded by grants from the National Science Foundation (BNS-8812552, BNS-9009232, and BNS-9109695). I wish to thank Guy Bailey for his insights and suggestions during this study.

2. For in-depth discussions of the methodologies used in PST, GRITS, and SOD, see Bailey and Bernstein (1989); Bailey and Dyer (1992); Bailey, Wikle, and Sand (1991); Bailey, Wikle, Tillery, and Sand (1992); Bernstein (1994); and Tillery (1992).

An Ethnolinguistic Approach to the Study of Rural Southern AAVE

Patricia Cukor-Avila

ETHNOGRAPHIC RESEARCH

Central to the linguistic study of any community is a clear understanding of the relationship that exists between its inhabitants and the sites of linguistic interaction within that community, basically who talks to whom and where. In order to develop this understanding the linguist must also be an ethnographer, as it is only through participant observation that the linguist can truly observe the interaction between language and social life, or what Hymes (1964a) calls the "ethnography of speaking." Sociolinguistic research over the past two decades has benefited greatly from the combination of the qualitative methods of ethnographic analysis and the quantitative methods of linguistic analysis. Milroy (1987b) in Belfast, Eckert (1989a) in Detroit, Cheshire (1982) in Reading, Bortoni-Ricardo (1985) in Brazil, Edwards (1986) in Great Britain, and Gal (1979) and Lippi-Green (1989) in Austria are just a few who have successfully implemented participant observation in order to obtain what they feel is the most "naturalistic" data from the communities studied. Ethnographic description has also been the basis of more descriptive linguistic analysis, such as Blom and Gumperz's (1986) work on code-switching in Hemnesberget, Norway, and Schieffelin's (1990) study of the Kaluli and their language.

This paper offers a method for gathering large amounts of linguistic data in a context that preserves natural sociolinguistic interaction.[1] It does so by describing my research in Springville, Texas, over the past five years. By applying insights from ethnography to sociolinguistic fieldwork, I demonstrate how sociolinguists can shift the focus of study to the community itself, allowing the recording of people as they normally interact with each other on a daily basis and therefore the study of language as a "socially situated cultural form" (Saville-Troike 1989:3).

SPRINGVILLE

Springville is a small East-Central Texas town of fewer than 200 people.[2] It is an ideal laboratory for developing field methods because it is a stable, self-contained community whose social relationships are easily definable and whose sites of linguistic interaction are easily identified. Moreover, it provides an ideal laboratory for studying rural, insular varieties of African-American Vernacular English (AAVE) since it preserves almost intact the plantation system of social and economic organization that developed during slavery and persevered through the emergence of the tenant farming system. Although this system has disappeared in most places, it remains largely in place in Springville.

Most of the land in and around Springville is owned by Italian families who immigrated around the turn of the century. There are also some farms owned by non-Italian families who have been in the area for several generations. During its prime, Springville typified classic plantation culture; the population consisted of Whites and Blacks: white landowners and black field hands with a small segment of the population made up of white tenant farmers. It was the hub of the area's cotton industry and consequently a thriving community with a large population, three cotton gins, three stores, a cafe, two schools (one for the Blacks, one for the Whites), and it was a scheduled stop on the passenger train that ran between Wilson (some 15 miles SE) and Attmore (around 9 miles NE).³ Springville's prime lasted up until the end of the 1940s, after which it began to undergo rapid change both demographically and economically. It was not World War II that was responsible for this change but rather the advent of mechanized farm equipment, which reduced the need for manual labor in the fields. Many people were left without jobs and homes (as their homes were always provided for them by the owner of the farm where they worked), and consequently the population began to shift and to decrease rapidly as people moved to neighboring urban areas to seek employment. The Whites began their exodus in the late 1940s, and by the time farming had become completely mechanized in the early 1960s, Springville's white population had diminished drastically, and the black population had begun to decline too.

The factors behind this demographic shift are similar to what was happening in many other communities throughout the rural South during the post-WWII era. Even though the urban areas offered rural dwellers increased economic opportunities, these opportunities were reserved for Whites only. Racial discrimination was commonplace and hiring of Blacks was limited to menial jobs, such as janitorial positions in local cotton mills. Northern cities offered economic opportunities to Blacks, but making the journey north required a major change in lifestyle that not all southern Blacks were willing to make (Wright 1986; Kirby 1987).

It was during this period of population shift that Mexican immigrants, mainly undocumented workers, began to settle in and around Springville, offering local farmers a cheaper source of manual labor. They slowly replaced the Blacks who had previously worked in the fields, who now were either too old to do manual labor or who had found employment in service jobs in the surrounding communities. However, many black families continued to live in Springville in the few remaining tenant houses even though they no longer worked in the fields. The influx of Mexican field hands also served to alter the social status of the remaining black residents of Springville. Having been replaced in the fields by Mexicans, whom they viewed as having a lower social status within the community, young Blacks no longer perceived themselves to be on the bottom rung of the community's social ladder, and, therefore, were unwilling to work in the fields as their parents and grandparents had done.

Today, the Springville population is made up of approximately 50% Blacks, who live there year round, and 50% Hispanics, a substantial number of whom are migrant farm workers and therefore live there only seasonally. Life there revolves around three institutions: a general store/post office (offering soda, candy, snack items, beer, some staple items such as milk, bread, and cheese, household items such as laundry soap and paper products, and various other sundries); a beer joint located across the unpaved parking lot from the store; and the school, located about a block away, which serves around 60 students (depending on the migrant population), in grades 1–8 (high school students are bused to the county seat, about 9 miles away). During the time of my initial fieldwork there were only two white residents. One was an 82-year-old widow of a cotton farmer who moved to Springville in 1946. The other, whom I call Loretta, was born in 1920 and is a life-long resident of Springville and the owner of the general store. Her grandfather was a major landowner in and around Springville, and it was he who established and ran the general store and acted as postmaster. Two generations later, Loretta still runs the store, runs the post office (she has been postmistress for 30 years), and leases her land to other farmers in the area who raise cattle and farm cotton and maize.

But her role extends beyond this, and, in essence, it can be said that she represents the backbone of the community. During the height of the cotton culture (as it is called), there were tenant houses throughout the community, many of which were owned by Loretta's father. Now only a few remain, and they are all in ill repair. They are owned by Loretta, and every month the tenants, many of whom are former employees of Loretta's father, come to the general store to pay their rent as well as their electricity, gas, and telephone bills.[4] They also pay on their accounts, since many of the townspeople charge their purchases at the store and pay monthly installments (with interest) when they receive their checks the first of the month. Loretta extends them credit if needed and cashes their government checks. She also controls the local cemetery, where a plot costs $20. This situation is not unlike that of the migrant farm worker except that these people are not working in the fields— they either work for Loretta on her land or are employed by her to do various odd jobs around the store or on her property,[5] work seasonally as day laborers for other farmers in the area, work in service jobs in Attmore (population 5500) or Wilson (population 50,000), or are unemployed and on welfare.

METHODS

I began my research in Springville during the summer of 1988 when, for approximately six weeks, I made daily trips there which enabled me to become familiar with the community and life in the community, and in turn enabled the people of Springville to get to know me and to trust me. This initial six-week phase of my study proved very fruitful in that by spending the entire day there on a regular basis, I was able to record vast amounts of data encompassing a full range of this community's linguistic interaction. In order to maintain the connections I established in Springville during that summer, I have made subsequent trips there at least once each year since that time. Because of this, I have been able to widen the scope of my study to include longitudinal data on several "key" residents, which has in turn revealed evidence of linguistic change as the language of the adolescents of Springville has become more similar to the AAVE spoken by children in a neighboring city.[6]

My initial entry into the community was through Loretta's daughter, whom I knew from college. This is similar to the "friend of a friend" type of entry that Lesley Milroy used in Belfast; however, unlike Milroy, I was accompanied by this friend on my first day, which naturally included a visit to the store. She introduced me to the cashier, Vanessa, who later was to become my link with the rest of the community (see below).

Because the layout of the store provides people with a place to sit around and "shoot the breeze," and because there is a steady flow of traffic in and out throughout the day, especially on days when bad weather prevents workers from going to the fields, I decided to concentrate on the store as a site for the majority of my fieldwork. This strategy proved beneficial for many reasons. First, since I too was "hanging out" at the store, I was essentially participating in an established community activity. This provided me with numerous opportunities to both participate in and observe everyday linguistic interactions in and around the store. Second, since the store serves as the main setting for adult peer group conversations, I had access to and was able to record an important source of data on AAVE that has been noticeably absent from the literature. Third, and perhaps most important, I was able to formalize a strategy for recording speech at a site, the store, rather than focusing on individuals or contrived peer groups. Recording the linguistic interaction of a site rather than of individuals enabled me to change my role from that of audience to overhearer and even eavesdropper, thus substantially reducing the effects of what Labov (1972b) calls the Observer's Paradox (see Cukor-Avila and Bailey 1992, 1995).

The General Store

It is important to note that the general store is the focal point of Springville and that if the store were to close, it would significantly change the lifestyle and makeup of the town. Built in 1913, the store is the only one remaining in town. Since there is no home delivery and people must pick up their mail there, it is the principal site of community activity and linguistic interaction. Several of the older residents of Springville neither read nor write, and they depend on Loretta and Pam, a part-time post office employee, to pay their bills for them, read their mail to them, and explain their letters from the Social Security Office. Many of them do not have children or grandchildren they can trust to do these things for them. It is not uncommon to hear of Social Security checks being stolen and cashed by family members for drug money.

The store, while serving as the local hangout, also serves as the symbol of the rural (antiurban) values that many townspeople have. Since many residents do not have telephones, it provides a meeting place where they can see friends, gossip with the cashier or the woman who helps out in the post office, eat lunch, watch soap operas (there is a television strategically placed on an old bookshelf facing the entrance of the store),[7] or just wait around for someone to stop by and visit. I have observed and recorded countless conversations which serve to reaffirm local, rural values. These values, which are expressed throughout the interviews with community members, include such things as loyalty to the community, preference for relaxed, rural living as opposed to urban overcrowding and danger, and the friendliness and open honesty of rural people in general. These speech events tend to cement the interrelationships between people while at the same time buttressing the values of the Springville community.

Hanging out at the store every day enabled me to observe how people relate to each other both socially and linguistically at the single most important site in the community; that is, it enabled me to determine who talks to whom and under what circumstances. It became clear to me that the linguistic interaction townspeople had with Loretta differed considerably from their ways of communicating among themselves. Although all of their speech networks intersected in some ways, since they were all residents of Springville and the surrounding areas, they were certainly not all members of the same "speech participation groups."

Speech Participation Groups

Unlike social or communication networks (Milroy 1987b) which extend both in and out of a community and serve to explain linguistic variation based on the strength of those connections, speech participation groups are site-based within a community. Speech participation groups designate those people within a social network who are linguistic insiders and who are privy to the most intimate linguistic interaction. This intimacy manifests itself both in the subject matter and the speech code, for example in the sharing of gossip and in the shared use of the most intimate vernacular forms.

Since speech participation groups are centered at a specific site, it is the site that is the determining factor in the explanation of the speech relationships among interlocutors that exist at and around that site. The speech participation groups in Springville are composed of three types of members: 1) core members who are at the heart of the group and who interact on a regular basis at the site; 2) peripheral members who frequent the site but who do not always participate regularly in linguistic interactions with other members at the site; and 3) outliers, those people who rarely, if ever, visit the site but who are in close contact with those who do and consequently are able to share in the most intimate topics of conversation. Members of participation groups naturally interact both within and outside of their respective groups; however, the type of information shared is different in each case. "In-group" interaction occurs between two people from the same speech participation group who, for example, share gossip about another community member, either within or outside of their particular group. "Cross-group" interaction entails conversation between a member of Participation Group A and a member of Group B in which they might discuss an upcoming political election or a local school-related issue, but it never entails the gossip of "in-group" interaction.

Because few, if any, residents of Springville have telephones, they must come together to share community news and gossip. I have been able to ascertain the existence of two participation groups at the store: one centered around Vanessa, the cashier, and the other centered around Loretta, the town matriarch (see figure 1).

Figure 1: Speech participation groups at Springville's principal site
of linguistic interaction

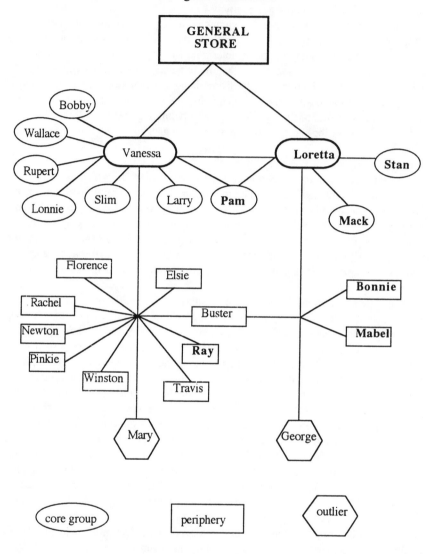

Names in **boldface** are community members who are not African-American.

Core Group Members

Vanessa was three years old when she came to Springville to live with Mary,
who was born in 1913 and never had any children of her own, though she has raised
several over the years. Vanessa dropped out of school after the tenth grade to run
away to Mississippi with a man she had met that summer. She returned home about
two months later, started dating someone else, and right before school was to start

she "came up pregnant." She left Springville for a short time during her pregnancy, but because she was homesick and had a bad relationship with her boyfriend, she decided to return. She has since had two other children with a man from Springville, Buster, who has worked for Loretta for over 25 years. The five of them live across the railroad tracks from the store in one of the "nicer" tenant houses belonging to Loretta. Although most of her friends left Springville years earlier, she has chosen to live, work, and raise her family there because she feels that things are much safer for them in Springville than in the neighboring urban areas.

At the time of our initial interview in 1988, Vanessa was 27 years old and had been working as a cashier at the store for almost three years. (She is no longer working there and has since completed her GED and is attending classes at a local Community College.) As can be seen in figure 1, Vanessa is the center of one of the core participation groups at the store. She knows everyone in the community, and because she is at the principal site of linguistic and social interaction six days a week from 8:30 to 4:30, she also knows all the Springville gossip.

The community members who make up this core group are those who spend all or much of their time at the store either because they work there, as in the case of Vanessa, Pam, who works part-time in the post office for Loretta (see below), and Larry who is also employed by Loretta to help out with odd jobs around the store, or because the store is a major part of their social lives. Such is the case with the other five members of this group who are store regulars, sometimes spending up to three and four hours at a time talking and gossiping with other core members or with peripheral members, as well as occasional "drop-ins" who hang out long enough to finish a soft drink or pick up their mail. Bobby, Slim, and Lonnie are all from a neighboring community about ten miles away. They often work together in and around the Springville area, making the store a regular stop for lunch, to buy soft drinks, or just to hang out. Rupert, who was born in 1916, moved to Springville from Georgia many years ago and lives with Mary, the woman who raised Vanessa. When in town, he usually spends a good part of the day either hanging out at the store or sitting on the front porch of the beer joint, the other major site of linguistic interaction in the community. Wallace is a retired brick layer who has spent all of his 75 years living in the Springville area. He has known Loretta and her family all his life.

Since I, too, was hanging out at the store every day, I was also privy to much of the "inside" talk amongst these core participants. Although I was technically an "outsider" to the community, my constant presence at the store, where I chose to hang around with them rather than with Loretta and her core group, and the fact that I had spent a lot of time with Vanessa and had gotten to know her quite well, facilitated my acceptance and subsequent trust by this group.

The only other person who spends as much time at the store as Vanessa is Loretta, the center of the other core group. While Vanessa's role as the central figure in her core group is due to the fact that she is at the heart of community information on a daily basis, Loretta's role is a direct result of her position in the community and the store. Her core group is made up of two employees, Stan and Pam, and a lifelong acquaintance, Mack, a major landowner in the area who is from neighboring Attmore. He, too, employs people from Springville to work on his land. He stops by the store every day at about the same time to pick up his mail and eat his lunch; however, he always sits either behind the counter with Stan or stands at the window of the post office in the back with Loretta.

Stan is a lifelong resident of neighboring Granger, and Loretta has known him all her life. He is retired and helps out at the store on busy days as a part-time cashier. Although he interacts regularly with Vanessa and members of her core group, their conversations are limited to topics such as the weather, politics, current events, and shared local gossip.[8] This type of gossip is different from the in-group gossip described earlier in that the topics are known by all members of the community, regardless of speech participation group membership.

Pam, who works part-time at the post office, was also born and raised in the area; in fact, she went to high school with Loretta's daughter, Bonnie. She is part of Loretta's core group because of their close working relationship, yet, interestingly enough, she is also part of Vanessa's core group, hanging out with them when she is not busy working. She is often the object of their teasing, which is one of the favorite pastimes of Bobby, Slim, and Lonnie. She is fully accepted by them and included in and often the source of "insider" gossip. Her unique relationship with both core groups at the store makes her, and not Vanessa, the probable link to "inside" community gossip for Loretta, although I suspect that Pam gives her an edited version. Notice that Vanessa and Loretta too are linked; however, their relationship is clearly not reciprocal in terms of shared information between each core group. Their link to each other is work related only.

Peripheral Group Members

The peripheral members of each core group are those people who visit the store frequently; however, they are not considered "store regulars." Even so, "inside" knowledge of the community is often shared between the peripheral and core members of Vanessa's group yet not between them and Loretta's group.

Like Vanessa, Rachel and Florence were also raised by Mary. Although neither of them lives in Springville year round, they keep abreast of local gossip and community business through their trips to the store and also through Vanessa.

Travis is in his early twenties and, at the time of our interview, was a junior at a university north of Dallas. Travis's family was living in one of the old tenant houses belonging to Loretta, so he was spending his summer vacation in Springville. He is unique in that he is the only young adult in town attending a university. Typically, people in Springville do not go to college, and many do not graduate from high school. Travis is unique in another aspect as well. Although he has left the rural, isolated life of Springville and is living in an urban university environment, he is still very much a part of the rural culture of Springville. In contrast to other teenagers and young adults living in Springville, who cannot wait to leave there and move to either a local urban area or even further away to Houston or Dallas, Travis commented to me that he much preferred the country over the city and that he would probably return to a rural area upon his graduation.

The summer of our interview Travis spent almost every afternoon sitting on the front porch of the beer joint talking with Pinkie, the woman who manages the beer joint, or Winston, a lifelong resident in his seventies who was raised on one of the larger Italian plantations in the area. Winston and some of the older residents hang out at the beer joint on a daily basis, passing through the store at least once or twice a day to pick up their mail and perhaps buy a soft drink.

Elsie, Florence's mother, moved to Springville over twenty years ago. Although she has never worked in the fields, she has worked on and off for Loretta cleaning houses. Elsie visits the store regularly to pick up her mail and to buy small items such as cigarettes and bread. She usually sits on the bench beside the wood stove where she reads her mail, watches television, and talks to whoever happens to be around.

Ray is the only Mexican-American resident who has a relationship to any participation group at the store. He, too, is a lifelong resident of Springville who makes his living in construction, often doing small repair jobs on the "rent houses" for Loretta. His trips to the store were never just for business; he would often hang out around the wood stove adding quite a lively tone to the group discussions.

Buster, Pinkie's brother and Vanessa's boyfriend, is linked to both groups; he is a peripheral member of Loretta's group because of employment (he has been working for her for 25 years), but he is definitely a member of Vanessa's group because of his relationship to her and to the other peripheral members of her group. He is in and out of the store all day long but rarely has time to stop and talk to core members because he is under the constant eye of his employer, Loretta.

There are only two peripheral members of Loretta's core group, Bonnie and Mabel. Bonnie, Loretta's only daughter, grew up and went to school in Springville. At one point several years ago, she and her second husband were working full-time at the store, where he was the accountant and she helped her mother with the other aspects of running the store. After their divorce, he moved to Wilson and she went back to pursue a master's degree. In 1988 she moved back to Springville and since that time has lived in her grandparents' old two-story plantation home, the largest home in town. At one time, this was a stately home where many formal parties were held; however, now it is in need of extensive structural and interior repairs. She works in Wilson and does not concern herself with store business anymore. Although she has lived most of her life in Springville and knows everyone in town, her relationship with most people there, especially those in Vanessa's core group, is superficial. She is very interested in community gossip but, without realizing it, usually receives an edited version. Mabel, the only other white resident in town, is an elderly widow of one of Springville's successful cotton farmers. She comes to the store to pick up her mail and on occasion will sit and visit with Loretta or Pam. She is "out of the loop" when it comes to shared community gossip; her conversations usually are about the weather, her grandchildren, or her health.

Outliers

The third type of group membership represented in figure 1 is that of "outlier." Outliers are those community members who are physically outside of store participation groups because they do not frequent the store yet still are linked to a particular core group because of their relationships with people who are either peripheral or core members.

Mary, the woman who raised Vanessa, rarely leaves her house because of ill health; however, she is in constant contact with Rupert, Vanessa, and Vanessa's three children, and from time to time with Wallace, Florence, and Rachel. Despite her absence from the store, she is well aware of everything that goes on in the community. She has lived in Springville for most of her adult life, has worked in various jobs as an overseer for Loretta's father, a seamstress, a maid, and a cook, and is still raising children for relatives and friends who have unsettled lives.

George has a long history of employment with Loretta's family; his father was their family cook and he was the overseer for the house and some of the hired hands. When his father passed away in the 1960s, George took over the cooking and continued to do so through the generations of Loretta's family up (until two years ago when he suffered a stroke and had to quit working). During the time I spent in Springville I saw him come to the store on only two occasions, staying only long enough to bring Loretta her noon meal. He spent his entire day either at Loretta's or Bonnie's house taking care of odd jobs and preparing their meals. (In fact when I wanted to interview him, I had to make arrangements through Loretta to make sure that he would not be taking too much time off work or else she would have to dock his pay.)

THE GENERAL STORE AND SPEECH PARTICIPATION GROUPS

Thus far I have established the store as an important element in the development of speech participation groups in Springville. Another factor in their development is the physical layout of the store itself, which is directly related to where conversations among and between group members take place. The post office is located in the back and is accessible by a back door to the store. Those people who come either to pick up mail or see Loretta usually enter from there. The front entrance leads directly to the soft drink cooler and the various food and sundry items and is also where the cash register is located. Even though there is a large porch attached to the front of the store, those people who are "store regulars" tend to hang out in the center of the store where there is a bench and a few old wooden chairs. During the summer months (in Texas that is approximately April through October), it is cooler inside because of a large floor fan that is constantly blowing air throughout the store. During the winter, people gather around the wood stove directly in front of the bench.[9] This is also where the TV is located.

Vanessa is usually behind the counter only when she is checking out a customer; otherwise she often sits on the counter or in a chair talking to whoever happens to be there, or she is watching TV. She is highly visible to anyone who enters the store. Loretta, on the other hand, is either in the small enclosed post office at the back of the store or she is busy working on her various accounts at a long built-in desk situated some two feet above the center area of the store. The only people who are allowed to either enter the post office or climb the two stairs to go behind the desk are Pam, the woman who works in the post office, and Bonnie, Loretta's daughter. Her desk is where she accepts payments on accounts and extends credit.

When she is at her desk she is actually in a position to look down on the rest of the store.

Thus, the physical layout of the store provides a symbolic representation of Loretta's power—there is almost always some type of physical barrier between her and those she interacts with, especially when she interacts with people outside of her participation group. She will occasionally participate in conversations as she is walking between the post office and her desk; however, she feels that she is too busy to take the time to stop and talk for any length of time. And when she enters or leaves the store, it is through a side entrance which has stairs that lead directly to where her car is parked.

THE CHILDREN OF SPRINGVILLE

In addition to the two adult speech participation groups, which are centered in and around the store, there are also the speech participation groups of the children of Springville. Their groups are not as easily defined as those of the adults for two main reasons. First, because their principal source of peer relationships, the Springville school, goes only as far as the eighth grade, most adolescents tend to seek and maintain friendships outside of the community, specifically in Attmore and Wilson. Second, and perhaps more importantly, there is no specific hangout in town for Springville youth. The store is where the adults hang out; children and teenagers will pass through to buy candy or a soft drink or perhaps to pick up the mail, but they never sit around there and gossip as the adults do. It is unusual to see groups of kids sitting around like the groups of adults at the store, since there is really no place in Springville where young people can go for entertainment (there are no malls, no movie theaters, no video game arcades, no places to rent videos, no organized team sports, and no playgrounds except at the school). During the summer months, the Springville school remains open, providing the only outlet for the younger generation: there are summer school classes, where many children are sent so that they do not get bored; and those who are old enough and qualify are able to work there and earn spending money. Some help out around town doing odd jobs for Loretta or following their fathers to work. Still others may spend several weeks or even the entire summer visiting relatives in nearby Wilson or as far as Dallas or Houston, where there is plenty to keep a child busy.

While the younger children in Springville appear to be content with their sheltered lifestyle, such is not the case with the preteens and teenagers. Those to whom I spoke were anxiously awaiting the short bus ride to Attmore, where they would attend high school, and none of them planned on staying in Springville after graduation; in fact, most of them were counting the days until they could leave their sleepy rural town and go live and work in an urban area. They identify with all aspects of urban culture—the dress, the music, the dances, and, most important, the language. They are very much aware of the way people talk in the "country" versus the "city." This was even the case some eighteen years ago when Vanessa was in high school; she and her Springville friends were referred to as "country bumpkins" by the kids in Attmore, who said that people from Springville "talk funny."

As Springville children grow up, they spend less time at home and more time in the surrounding urban areas, and, as a consequence, their social networks expand to extend outside of the community. Their speech participation groups are not centered in Springville; in fact, those adolescents who reject Springville culture the most do not even hang out with or date other kids from there.

LINGUISTIC EVIDENCE

Perhaps the greatest testimony for the adaptation of ethnographic methodology to the field of sociolinguistics is evidenced in the data itself. This is best illustrated through an example (figure 2), an argument between two members of Vanessa's participation group, Wallace and Florence. It was recorded during one of my routine visits to the general store. Unlike individual or group interviews, the site study provides the opportunity to experience and to record interactions between people in a community in the exact moment they are taking place. This is precisely the case with the argument transcribed below. Rather than relying on one participant's recollection, in the form of a narrative, of what transpired in the argument, the site study allows the fieldworker to record the argument as it unfolds. In this case, the fieldworker is not only privy to both sides of the argument but is also able to obtain firsthand knowledge of the intensity and emotions involved throughout the exchange. The speech recorded in a site study intense argument would be perhaps as close to the "deep" vernacular as a fieldworker could ethically obtain, even surpassing the type of data from Labov's (1972b) Context A situations. Extended participant observation and community interaction allows the fieldworker to be accepted in community activities, whatever they may be, at the various sites of linguistic interaction.

Figure 2: Argument at the General Store

(V, Vanessa; W, Wallace; FW, fieldworker; F, Florence)

V: Did he tell you about his girlfrien'?
W: What girlfrien'?
V: The one you got. [laughs]
W: I ain' got no girlfrien'. I ain't got . . . Did you find a girlfriend when you come over
      the other day? Who you foun' there?   5
FW: I found a guy there.
V: I'm gonna take her there an' show her. One of them.
W: Say what?
V: I'm gonna take her where they at. They ain' at the house.
W: You sure, you sure won't be taken nowhere.   10
FW: How many has he got?
W: I ain' got n'ere.
V: How many you tol' me this morning?
W: I ain' told you n'ere.
V: I think it was ten. [laughs]   15
W: Girl don't you let her never tell you that lie.
V: I tellin' Mr. Stan I gotta new, I'm, I gotta tell Mr. Stan I gotta new topic for his paper.
      Playboy Granger [V. and F. laugh]

W: [to V.] Don't be writin', sittin' up there writin' there.

FW: [FW thinks W.'s last comment was directed at her but it wasn't. In fact, W. doesn't   20
consider the FW as a participant in this conversation at this point. to W.] Oh no
I'm not. I'm just writin' your name on here.

W: [to V.] All right. Tell me somethin'. That's right.

V: Say Wallace, you don' wanna know how I know you a playboy, huh?

W: I ain' no playboy. I ain' never been no playboy. I tell 'em. I tell 'em right where   25
to head in an' head outta there. You hear me?

V: Huh?

W: I tell 'em right where, you know I will. I tell 'em right where to head in an' head outta there.

F: Yeah but that ain' excusin' all the womens you have.

W: I ain' got n'ere.   30

F: You oughta, you oughta tell her about your girlfrien's.

W: I ain' got no girlfriend. Don' want n'ere. I don' want no girlfriend.

F: Dependin' on who you tellin'. Tell it all.

W: I got Jesus Chris' for my friend.

F: You a hypocrite.   35

W: What are you?

F: A hypocrite.

W: That's what I figured.

F: Jus' like you an' I ain' ashamed to say it either.

W: That's right. I will go to church. You won'.   40

F: How you know I don'?

W: I, I ain' sees you up there. I been up there at church sometimes an' I ain' sees you there.

F: That ain' the only church people go to.

W: I been to several church. I haven' saw you.

F: I went this Sunday. I didn' see you.   45

W: I don' know where you, I don' where you went this Sunday 'cause I wasn' over here.

F: Think. Think.

W: I came over here.

F: Well think.

W: I don' know where you went to.   50

F: You still a hypocrite.

W: Ain' it Vanessa. You ain' nothin' but a hypocrite! That's all. [laughs]

FW: Now I don' want you two fightin'.

F: No, we ain' gonna fight. (overlaps with W.)

W: I ain' gonna fight. But I gonna go tell her.   55

F: [overlaps with W.] This is the way I would say it about anybody.

W: See I was in church all day yesterday. I was in church all day yesterday.

F: Jus' tell, tell the whole story.

W: She the one first brought the hypocrick up. She the one first brought that. 'Cause I
haven' never said nothin' about that.   60

F: I don' care if everybody know my business. I'd tell anybody.

W: Nobody. You ain' got no business. Ain' no Negro got no business. Only white folk
got business. I tell 'em all we ain' got no business. We got, jus' got 'rangement.

FW: Just got what?

W: Just got arrangement.   65

FW: Uh huh.

W: If we had business, we'd have some kind of factory or somethin'. That's business.

F: [overlaps W.] Why you s'pose you be tryin' to get me over there in business.

W: Arrangement jus' in the road. See what I mean? Did you get me Patricia?

FW: Uh huh.   70

W: All right.

F: She didn' get you straight. You know what Wallace? People like you, right, 'cause

W: you wanna, you wanna high side hypocrite me, I'll high side an' hypocrite you.
W: I ain' hypocrick you nothin'.
F: If you don' disrespect me, I won' disrespect you.   75
W: I respect you anyway I feel like I respect . . .
F: Jus' the way you sit over here in this store.
W: You the one brought the hypocrick up.
F: Jus' hush. Jus' the way you sit over here in this store an' you talk about me.
W: I ain' said a word about you.   80
F: . . . I gonna tell you exactly to your face what I want you to know 'cause so that
     way it won' sneak out behin' you. Jus' the way you sittin' there disrespectin'
     me and hypocritin' me . . . How many times have *you* tried to get me to come over to
     your house to be with you. Now you tell me! [V. laughs loudly in the background]
W: All right. I'll tell her.   85
F: Now I'm through with you. From now on, you don' say nothin' to me.
W: I'm through when I say [unintelligible].
F: You speak to me, an' smile at me if you want to an' keep on about your business.
     'Cause I do not play games.
W: I know all about your business 'cause. See I wasn' born, I wasn' born yesterday   90
     an' I wasn' born the day before.
F: [overlaps W.] I don' disrespect you. Ever since you get the age you is I always
     respected you. "Mr. Wallace How you doin'?" an' gone about my business.
W: Uh huh. Uh huh. That's right.
F: From now on if you wanna talk to me that way don' say anything to me at all.   95
     That's the way I really want you . . .
W: You first brought the hypocrick up. 'Cause I had never said anything.
F: At least I'm not ashamed of nothin' I do.
W: I'm not neither. I tell you 'fore your face, I ain' gonna get behin' your back.
F: That's the way I feel about it too. An' I'm through with you. I don' have nothin'   100
     to do . . .
W: Jus' like I tell her. Jus' what I got to tell her I tell her 'fore her face. I ain' gonna get
     behin' your back.
F: At least I don' Jesus an' sing an' Lord have mercy on my knees. Then turn aroun'
     five minutes later an' be a hypocrite.   105
W: That's right. That's right.

This example is an excerpt of a fifteen-minute argument recorded one afternoon while Wallace and I are at the general store. I have been talking with him for a while when Florence enters the store and starts talking to Vanessa. Wallace is interested in their conversation; apparently he is concerned that they are talking about him. His curiosity prompts Vanessa to tease him (line 1), but what she does not expect is that her harmless teasing will result in a full-blown argument between Florence and Wallace who apparently have a lot of bitter feelings between them. Here my role shifts among addressee, auditor, and overhearer according to the interaction between Wallace and Vanessa and Wallace and Florence; therefore, I have divided this example into two episodes, each of which delineates a change in my role as a participant.

In Episode I, lines 1–12, I am the addressee. Wallace and I have been hanging out in the store talking for about two hours. Florence then enters the store and Wallace's attention is diverted to Vanessa and Florence's conversation, which is taking place just out of his earshot. Vanessa's question in line 1, "Did he tell you about his girlfrien'?," perhaps one of the most important lines in this entire example, diverts his attention away from Florence and their problems by teasing him in front of me. (Up until that point I had no knowledge of Wallace's reputation. However, Vanessa and Florence both know that he does indeed have a reputation for "messing around" with women, especially young women). Line 1 also sets the stage for the events which unfold as the conversation becomes centralized around the topic of Wallace and women, which then ultimately leads to the argument between Florence and him.

Episode II, lines 13–106 (a portion of this episode), is where the majority of the argument takes place. Vanessa continues to tease Wallace about his girlfriends, and even though by doing so she is putting him in a potentially embarrassing situation, he neither appears to mind nor does he get angry with her. Up until this point Florence has been on the fringes of the conversation, but in line 29 she starts to say her piece and thus we see the beginning of the confrontation. She and Wallace go back and forth virtually uninterrupted from line 29 through line 105, practically the entire episode. There are, however, two instances when I attempt to break into the conversation but to no avail. The first is in line 53 when I start to get uncomfortable and try to calm Wallace and Florence down. They each briefly respond to my concerns and then go right back to their argument. The second, in line 64, is to ask Wallace to repeat his previous statement. He does so, and in an "aside" to me explains what he means (lines 65 and 67–69). He then goes right back to arguing with Florence whose sarcastic comment to him in line 68 actually overlaps the aside conversation between Wallace and me.

My role has taken a dramatic shift from Episode I, where I am the addressee, to Episode II, where I am an overhearer. I am seated next to Wallace throughout the argument; however, neither he nor Florence consider me a ratified participant in the conversation. They acknowledge my existence (lines 54–55, 65–71), but they do not let me have a role in the conversation. Even Vanessa's role in this segment has changed from addressee to overhearer as she stops teasing Wallace when Florence starts to argue with him.

What we can see by this chain of events is the natural, everyday flow of conversation, conversation not contrived by the fieldworker but controlled by the site and by the people interacting at that site. I am just like any other member of the community at the site; I can be a ratified participant in conversations as an addressee or auditor, yet within the same conversation, I can also be an overhearer.

CONCLUSION

The ethnolinguistic approach used in my study of Springville has proved beneficial in several ways. Extended participant observation in the community allowed me to identify the principal site of linguistic interaction, the general store. My observations are supplemented by numerous tape recordings which I have made over the course of my eight-year study. By placing the tape recorder with a sensitive microphone in a centrally located place, I was able to document the existence of speech participation groups which have developed around a site. The tape recorder, a staple for sociolinguistic interviews, also provides a supplement to the ethnographer's field notes; however, unlike these notes, the tape recorder can capture events that a human observer cannot. For example, my site study data contain numerous instances of overlapping conversations as well as a variety of speech events ranging from business transactions to arguments. Moreover, the tape recorder provides a permanent audio record of an event, allowing the fieldworker continually to reconstruct these recorded events, whereas field notes are a documentation of observations of an event at one point in time. The longitudinal nature of the study has also given me the opportunity to get to know several key residents of Springville, whom I was also able to record outside of the store, in their homes and at work, as well as at the principal sites of linguistic interaction. The result of this work is a documentary record of the linguistic activity of Springville residents that parallels the documentation of cultural activities in ethnography.

NOTES

This paper is dedicated to the people of Springville, Texas, who have so graciously spent time talking with me and letting me become a part of their lives, and without whom this research would not have been possible.

1. This project was partially funded by grants from the National Science Foundation (BNS-8812552) and The University of Michigan, Rackham Block Grant.

2. In an effort to maintain the privacy of my informants, I am using pseudonyms for the community and the towns in the surrounding area. I am also limiting demographic data to general descriptions, since a town of this size is easily recognizable to anyone familiar with this part of Texas.

3. Trains still pass through Springville several times a day on the two sets of tracks which run parallel to the highway; however, these carry cargo only.

4. Many Springville residents do not have telephones; consequently, they make and receive calls on the pay phone located outside the store.

5. Those people who work for Loretta are able to live rent-free in one of her houses if they choose. On my most recent trip to Springville, I learned that she had fired one of her hands and had subsequently told him to move out of his house or start paying rent of $50 per month.

6. See Cukor-Avila (1989, 1995) for examples of several features associated with urban AAVE which have recently become much more prevalent in the speech of Springville adolescents, especially those who have "urban connections." Features include zero copula, invariant be, the use of had + past as a simple past tense form, and absence of verbal -*s*.

7. Watching TV is not a prime reason for hanging out at the store, as almost all Springville residents have both televisions and VCRs in their homes.

8. Stan is an active member of the Democratic Party and is Springville's source for political news. Every year he makes sure all eligible townspeople are registered to vote.

9. See Clark (1944) for a detailed discussion of the role of the country store in small communities and how the layout of the typical country store was designed to promote the type of activities and conversations that were standard practice throughout the South.

Speaking Maps and Talking Worlds: Adolescent Language Usage in a New South Community

Boyd H. Davis, Michael Smilowitz, Leah Neely

What adolescents seem to do, more than anything else beyond eating or sleeping, is talk, and their talk often concerns themselves. They are highly self-referential beings; they are charting a universe of discourse, and the suns shift even as they talk about them. Friends, peer relationships, call them what you will, are necessary for the kinds of seemingly incessant conversations that adolescents have with each other. For example, Gottman and Mettetal (1986) claim that while "the most salient social process in middle childhood is successful negative-evaluation gossip," keyed to peer acceptance based on establishing "common ground" (197), adolescents have different bases for the conversations with friends. These are "characterized by the application of logic and psychological analysis to interpersonal events. The concern is with emotional self-understanding and self-disclosure. Honesty is a necessary concomitant. . . . Intimacy is only a secondary goal . . . maintained in the service of self-exploration. Self-disclosure does not have to be immediately reciprocated . . ." (215).[1]

Adolescent conversations are important, then, for several reasons: they are a principal means of socialization and of personal development, they allow adolescents to practice and internalize the language acts they think they will be called on to use, and they both allow and promote what others have called "acts of identity." It comes as no surprise to anyone having read Bloomfield (1933) or Whitney (1875), for example, to learn again that people—including early adolescents—often try to talk like those whom they admire. By analyzing the places that adolescents in a mid-South city and its surrounding county select as important for talking, this study demonstrates one approach for organizing adolescent talk.

The situation is more complex than we might have assumed. The investigation depends upon cross-disciplinary research and argues that the kinds of conversation, the kinds of register and dialect shift, even the ranges of literacy events we may expect to find when we do fieldwork with adolescents can be expected to vary in the various places that comprise the adolescent's network. In their early adolescence, humans expand their range, change their pathways, seek new landmarks. Each landmark points to a node in a network that shifts with age and territory, a context accompanied by a developing sense of history, by self-concept, and most of all, by other talkers.

CONCERNS UNDERLYING THE STUDY

Since 1980, when Davis began to collect mental maps of self-identified talking places first from American and later from Chinese adolescents, there have been several concerns and a single goal. The first concern is with the accuracy of the sample: that is, the representativeness of any given speaker or groups of speakers, and the validity and replicability of models used for the elicitation of speech and of the situational constraints affecting or revealed by interview data.

Landmark studies by linguists from several emerging schools (e.g., Labov 1966, 1972a, b; Gumperz and Hymes 1972; Hymes 1974; Wolfram 1969; Wolfram and Clarke 1971), studies conducted in the seventies by anthropologists (summarized by Bernard et al. 1984), and the first sets of studies by urban and cultural geographers all suggest that informant accuracy is a live concern. The adolescent population is voluble, volatile, and tricky to work with. Early adolescence is the part of life in which people move from late childhood—where Heath's *Ways with Words* pauses—to the high peak of puberty in midadolescence, where many studies including adolescents begin. Whether defined as an age or a stage, adolescence is filled with rapid change. The multiplicity of adolescence is exacerbated in circumstances of rapidly urbanizing New South cities within which traditional boundaries are fast disappearing. Some of these boundaries are geographic, others social. Indeed, the notion of community has become a slippery one. As Heath (1995:114) comments in her recent essay on ethnography in communities,

> As the twentieth century ends, membership in a community with no territorial basis or shared early socialization experience occurs at least as frequently as groupings that do bear these traditional features. . . . In earlier decades, individuals were drawn together through a sense of common history; now a sense of disparate present and diverging future leads to purposeful choices of language, norms and goals that separate many Americans from the primary group connections of former generations.

A second concern is keyed to perceptions of changes in mobility as well as changes in talking styles among the adolescents. A general description of how adolescents use language would need to discover and describe changes in their range, pathways, and landmarks and to see if and how these correlated with cross-cultural and cross-disciplinary studies of language use. Studies in social and developmental psychology, cognitive anthropology, environmental geography as well as linguistics have developed a variety of elicitative and interpretive models. For example, psychologists and geographers have experimented with neighborhood and community walks, a variety of mapping techniques (including beepers combined with diaries), and aerial photography, adding these to conventional surveys or interviews (see Bryant 1985; Larson and Richards 1991; Lynch 1977; Medrich et al. 1982; Van Vliet 1983; Wellman, Carrington, and Hall 1988).

Mobility has an additional twist in areas with cross-town busing. No single neighborhood has well-defined and exclusive boundaries keyed to a matching school. Discussions such as those by D'Andrade (1990) or Bernard et al. (1984) suggest that adolescents might individually present distorted data, keyed to their own perception of the world and their place within it (see also Briggs 1986). Mapping methods may provide researchers a basis for analyzing individual or group mobility and its variations against the maps that depict aggregate responses.

Enter the third concern: Can adolescents be presented with a minimal prompt and be expected to draw a meaningful map, in any way they liked, of the places that are important because these places are where they talk to people, and people talk to them? How will they furnish labels or identification of those places? One way to discover their norms, or at least their concepts of them, is to employ schematics—mental maps—that can be collapsed into a generalized model.

Assuming their use as an elicitation technique could be substantiated, it was hoped that the maps would provide a peek at an intersection between development and cognition. The underlying question is a simple one, though it has no simple answer: What do humans do with, to, and by means of language as they move from late childhood into high adolescence? How do they construct their worlds, and how are their worlds constructed, by language?

CONTEXTS AND PERSPECTIVES

The cliques, clubs, groups, or gangs that adolescents often form have been studied from a number of perspectives over the last decades. The focus has often been keyed to the interplay between socialization and education. Hollingshead's (1949) study of *Elmtown's Youth*, Seeley, Sim, and Loosley's (1956) *Crestwood Heights*, and Gordon's (1957) *The Social System of the High School* were extended both in Havighurst et al.'s (1962) *Growing Up in River City*, and in Coleman's (1961) *The Adolescent Society: The Social Life of the Teenager and Its Impact on Education*. Working out of the Chicago paradigm for examining social interaction, Coleman looked at ten schools in small towns, suburbs, small and large cities, focusing in Chapter VII on associational structures and their relationships to value-systems. Noting early sociometric processing of data in complex networks on Univac I, he commented: "The development of methods for quantitatively studying such structures as more than aggregates of individuals seems one of the most promising, and yet most difficult, methodological and theoretical tasks awaiting sociologists" (183n.5). Linguists and others have been searching ever since for ways to delineate and explain network structures.

As linguists moved further from traditional dialect study to the variation models initiated by Labov, Wolfram, and others in the early seventies, several major trends developed in the analysis of natural language usage. Historiographical studies appeared: Hymes and Fought (1981) updated their 1975 study of American structuralism; Montgomery and Bailey (1986), in the introduction to their volume of essays arising from LAVIS I, contextualized the study of language variety. As variation studies moved to include perspectives from creolists as well as statisticians, emphases began to shift as well. Sociolinguists fine-tuned the notion of variable rules and implicational scaling; anthropologists expanded the study of conversation as well as literacy within ethnolinguistic concerns.

An interesting trend has been a cross-disciplinary convergence of interest in mapping informational structures: in texts, in playgrounds, in cities, as well as in syntax. Whether we look back to the citation of the Univac in Coleman's (1961) study or at commentary citing Jackendoff's generative studies in Bickerton (1990), at social networks in Salzinger, Hammer, and Antrobus (1988) or at definition and construct in Wellman and Berkowitz (1988), we see new studies of space, time, analogy, and change, and of how these and humans are interrelated.

The use of maps as a way to look at both observed and self-reported behaviors, including the language of children and adolescents, also has changed. Downs and Stea (1977) surveyed the use of what was then called "cognitive mapping" by behavioral and urban geographers and environmental psychologists. Exploration of mental modeling ebbed and flowed, as scholars looking at the interplay between environment and the child or adolescent were often most interested in how actual movements corresponded with what their subjects drew or reported. This was particularly important for designs of playgrounds and play spaces, first as they surrounded expanding numbers of elementary schools during rapid population growth and then as spaces began to shrink with shifting patterns of urbanization.[2]

Definitions of community began to change as communities themselves were changing. Titles of two studies in volumes 2 and 4 of *Environment and Behavior* are suggestive: "Black Youths View Their Environment," by Ladd (1970); and "Images of Neighborhood and City among Black-, Anglo-, and Mexican-American Children," by Maurer and Baxter (1972), the same year that Blom and Gumperz published their analysis of "Social Meaning in Linguistic Structures: Code-Switching in Norway" and Labov's *Language in the Inner City* appeared. The concept of neighborhood established by McKenzie in his 1921 study of Columbus, Ohio (McKenzie [1923] 1970) expanded across several fields, evolving in several directions: compare, for example MacLeod's (1987) study of social contexts for language use by the Hallway Hangers and The Brothers, in *Ain't No Makin' It* with the network in Goodwin's (1990) *He-Said-She-Said*. The shapes of language maps were changing as well, in the offices of language dictionaries and atlases and in the kinds of graphics accompanying journal articles.

Metaphors for discussion of language change and language variation undergo change as well: the *topoi* of competence and performance have shifted to *topoi* involving new senses of speech and discourse networks, gender factors, maxims of conversation, politeness, social interaction, and negotiation. The intellectual traditions correlating community, network (especially in the sense of Milroy 1980) and education have been evolving to include these findings, particularly as major ethnographic analyses and work in symbolic anthropology informs them. Eckert's series of studies (1988, 1989a, b) interpreting high schoolers' uses of language draws on these themes, particularly in the context of work by Labov, by Heath, by Milroy, and by Varenne's series of interpretations of schooling and language (1982, 1983, 1986a). For example, Varenne's (1983) *American School Language* expanded his 1982 article: the issue is not so much that there are "jocks" and "freaks" in American high schools, or even that students use these words as labels in their social interaction—Coleman (1961) had noted similar categories—but his emphasis on the rhetoric these terms imply. In *Symbolizing America*, Varenne (1986b) moved to a full articulation of how symbolic anthropology can present action in culture using these verbs: "replicates," "improvises," "achieves," "ends/resolves," "reframes" and "opens up something new." "Finally, action in culture is told" (7). The focus on telling, on story and narration, on complex factors underlying negotiation can be seen, for example, not only in Goodwin's (1990) discussion of argument and socialization on a Philadelphia block or Johnstone's (1990) focus on narrative in *Stories, Community and Place*. Eckert's (1988, 1989a) conflation of categories such as "jock" in adolescent social networks with gender factors and with larger patterns of sound change leads us to Labov (1990). A number of the features that reveal the richness of adolescent language have begun to converge.

One feature that consistently surfaces in any examination of adolescent talk and other behaviors is friendship. The literature on friendship networks and their significance is immense and complicated. Varenne's work deals with different aspects of the signification of "friendship" and of American "friendliness"; see, too, Hewitt's (1986) *White Talk-Black Talk* as well as Goodwin's (1990) *He-Said-She-Said* and Gottman and Parker's (1986) *Conversations of Friends*. To review how friendship and space interact in childhood, compare Bryant's (1985) *The Neighborhood Walk* with Lynch's (1977) *Growing Up in Cities* and Weinstein and David's (1987) *Spaces for Children*. For a discussion and diagrams of friendship among the talkers whose language had first informed our notion of the inner city (Labov 1972a), see Teresa Labov (1981).

Just as there are all kinds of degrees of friendship and all kinds of ways to have an argument, so there are all kinds of ways to describe acts of identity: in terms, for example, of group socialization, or of human growth and development, or of roles and negotiations, conflict and compliments, all within increasingly complex networks of both dense and loose ties. What each of these has in common is discourse. For it is through language that we create and, as Ochs (1990) reminds us, index our world to ourselves and to others. And as we are newly-adolescent, moving away from childhood into the monster-ridden map of unknown adult territory, we signal and signify, index and negotiate our evolving acts of identity both figuratively (see Myers-Scotton's 1993 discussion of negotiation in code-switching) and literally. In early adolescence, our range, pathways and landmarks change; edges and boundaries shape-shift. Our navigation, like our growing awareness of our own pragmatics, abilities to recognize and negotiate our place in the world, varies and changes rapidly. The young adolescents in the enclaves, pockets, communities, and neighborhoods of the New South city have no time for nostalgia; their discourse shifts dialect and code and register to signify their emerging sense of self. Their task as young adolescents is to identify situations: to chart what seems unbounded spaces into places, nodes in their talking networks, defined by the faces that, more than buildings, offer them a reflected, sometimes a refracted world view.

DESIGN AND ANALYSIS

For three years (1980–83), the primary researcher went to each of the 21 junior high/middle schools in the consolidated city-county school system and solicited a talking-places map from students on each school's team. Principals at each junior high selected the 15-member school team prior to the initial visit during the first year of the study: a random sampling of 5 students at each grade level (grades 7, 8, and 9), balanced for gender, ethnicity, and ability groupings. Principals allowed a brief time each year to meet with the students, as they felt students ought to miss no more than a single class period per year to participate in the study.

The original design called for 15-person teams from each of 21 schools, which would have totalled 315 students. Due to absences on the specific day/time scheduled each year for the school visit, 280 students participated in the first year. Of that 280, 203 were still members of the study at its close, for a retention rate of 72.5%. However, because 10 schools elected to add in a total of 110 students to replace students promoted to high school, dropouts, and transfers, and because a number of students re-entered the project after the initial meeting and data collection at their school, 364 students had participated by the close of the study. A total of 773 pieces of written data were collected, of which 23 had to be discarded because of incomplete data (full name) furnished by the student. The data included 164 written house plans and 609 written maps; these included 204 maps drawn by the 68 students present all three years, 270 maps drawn by the 135 students participating for two years, 110 maps drawn by the 110 additional students, and 25 maps drawn by a cohort who presented oral descriptions in lieu of one set of written maps during year two. Of these 609 maps, 12 were discarded because of errors in data entry or missing demographic information, for a total of 597 maps (analyzed by grade, sex and ethnicity in table 2).

In addition to the written data, over 100 hours of tape recordings were collected: interviews with individual students, discussions with groups of students, and interviews which students conducted on their peers. One example, discussed later in this essay, is of a student talking to himself though intended for the interviewer's ears. An Appendix presents the set of maps drawn by "Phil Denton" as he moved through grades 7, 8, and 9.

Examination of the first 200 maps turned up 17 categories of places that students identified as important (see table 1). The full collection of maps was then coded for these categories. An initial hypothesis was that over the three years of the passage from late childhood to high adolescence, we would see first, the emergence of norms for range and specific location, and second that these norms would show significant correlation with gender, ethnicity, grade level, or a combination of these variables. A key concern was whether this mode of eliciting information could be quantified, could be substantiated, could be replicated. In other words, could we first trust the instrument as a way to expand conventional inventories of where and how people ascribe significance to talking in specific kinds of places? Next, if the maps would elicit reliable information, could they refine the ways we study language as it occurs in discourse community, speech community, or what Cukor-Avila (this volume) calls a participation group?

The data, depicted in table 2, on significant talking places were nominal, and coded as a yes-no answer: students either drew and labeled a place on their maps for a specific year or they didn't. The nominal data required nonparametric analysis. Cross tabulations of frequencies and chi-squares for each talking place against gender/ethnic/grade and against other talking places suggested that the presence or absence of places specifically designated as associated with one or more friends was robust. Given the literature on American adolescents and their social networks, it is not surprising to note that the presence of friends was a controlling factor.

Table 1: Talking place categories

Category	Description
mhome	the house, apartment, condominium, trailer, or other locale in which the adolescent lived with one or more adult care-givers
mp1pal	a specific location labeled by a friend's name, usually that friend's home or home-yard
mp2pals	locations labeled by 2 different friend-names
mp3pals	locations labeled by 3 different friend-names
mpmopals	locations labeled by 4–7 different friend-names
mpmanymo	locations labeled by > 7 friend-names
mpnigh	one or more locations labeled as, or indicating by proximity or other visual cues, a neighbor
mprel	one or more locations identified as a place where the speaker talked to relative(s); if the relative lived in a non-proximal relationship, the adolescent usually wrote an unprompted note about this on the map or talked about it on tape
mpchurch	location labeled as a church, temple, or other religious edifice; relative proximity to the home is usually indicated on the map
mpinsbl	a building that has sponsorship by or affiliation with some institution, such as a recreation center (in this area, these are sponsored by secular and religious organizations and agencies)
mpinsare	a named area that has sponsorship by or affiliation with some institution (e.g., a park, a field) (in this area, these are sponsored by secular and religious organizations and agencies)
mpfreepl	an area labeled on the map as being without official name, sponsorship, or affiliation, used for free play (e.g., a vacant lot, a wooded area)
mpconsto	a convenience store, franchise or otherwise
mpstore	a retail store that is not part of a regional or local shopping mall, though it may be part of a shopping "strip"
mpmall	a regional or local shopping mall, usually covered
mpfood	a fast-food outlet, franchise or otherwise
mplib	a branch of the city-county public library system

Table 2: Response distribution

	White						Black					
	Male			Female			Male			Female		
Grade:	7th	8th	9th	7th	8th	9th	7th	8th	9th	7th	8th	9th
N:	32	58	52	32	54	57	37	48	57	51	63	56
Location												
mhome	32	44	52	32	54	57	30	48	44	31	49	54
mp1pal	18	13	13	15	18	18	15	20	20	19	14	16
mp2pals	7	8	10	15	19	23	6	19	11	9	11	17
mp3pals	4	5	6	8	8	12	5	4	4	7	4	8.
mpmopals	1	6	8	9	5	7	1	5	1	4	3	3
mpmanymo	2	0	1	0	1	0	1	2	0	1	0	2
mpnigh	1	6	5	4	6	14	2	6	5	4	6	8
mprel	4	9	10	16	22	15	5	16	9	9	16	16
mpchurch	18	18	20	20	33	25	11	19	16	13	28	24
mpinsbl	9	16	14	13	25	20	5	13	17	10	19	13
mpinsare	14	23	16	14	24	14	10	35	8	11	26	14
mpfreepl	5	8	10	9	6	7	8	7	6	3	5	4
mpconsto	6	5	3	6	6	2	3	4	6	2	3	2
mpstore	12	12	11	11	19	12	9	20	14	9	15	15
mpmall	13	23	18	20	37	22	10	20	25	11	22	26
mpfood	11	8	13	13	29	24	5	14	13	4	15	22
mplib	8	8	7	4	16	9	10	7	13	6	10	6

Figure 1 presents percentages by sex and ethnicity for the category of Friends. The data are cumulative: that is, if an adolescent drew and labeled only one place on that year's map to signify a friend's home or talking place, it was coded as '1'; if the adolescent drew and labeled two Friends, it was coded as '2', and so on. Figure 1 collapses all three years of the project, displaying several features. Female adolescents, regardless of ethnicity, are more likely to identify a plurality of friend-places than are males; this correlates with reports such as Schlegel and Barry (1991), who examined 186 societies (for full bibliographical references to their sample and coding, see Barry and Schlegel 1980). They note that "the character of the adolescent peer group is shaped not only by the circumstances surrounding the group itself but also by the adult life that adolescents anticipate in the future" (Schlegel and Barry 1991:77); we will return to this aspect later. Schlegel and Barry comment that, in most societies, the principal companions of children are their parents or siblings, instead of other children. However, "when other children are the principal companions of the younger girl, adolescent girls are likely to have a high degree of contact with their peers. . . . For girls, but not for boys, there is continuity between childhood and adolescence in contact with age-mates. Boys' peer contact, like their contact with parents, appears to be determined more by what adolescent boys do than by patterns established in infancy or childhood" (168). Boys, apparently, spend more time with age-mates and "decouple" at an early age from the family (90); see the interpretation of directives, disputes and instigations, for example, in Goodwin's (1990) study of Maple Street.

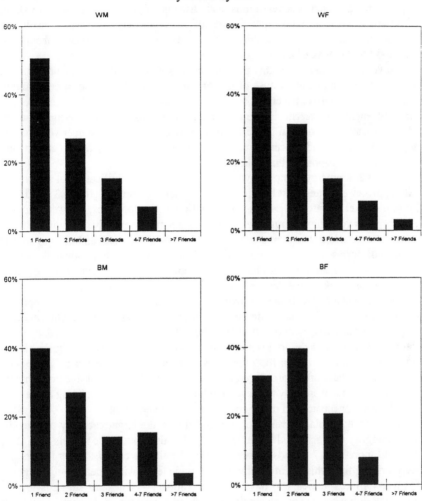

Figure 1
Friends as talking-places
by ethnic by sex

Goodwin's *He-Said-She-Said* closely examines interaction among Maple Street's children. Her definition of interaction can extend as well to the talking-places identified by the New South early adolescents and suggest why each category of place might have specific import: "Interaction thus constitutes a central place where members of a society collaboratively establish how relevant events are to be interpreted, and moreover use such displays of meaningfulness as a constitutive feature of the activities in which they engage" (1–2). She focused her investigation primarily on children aged 9–14 because children "fourteen and older generally interacted in couples. . . . Adolescents were frequently visiting in other neighborhoods, playing sports, working (generally at a local store), or sitting on the steps holding private conversations with friends of the opposite sex" (35). In Goodwin's study, as with other reports of same- and cross-sex relationships in adolescence, same-sex friendships hold sway during the passage from late childhood to the peak of adolescence.

However, one aspect of this present study is crucially different from most: it does not focus on one clubhouse or playground, one neighborhood or community, a sampling of suburbs or a cross-section of schools. Instead, it includes each of the kinds of enclave or territorial boundary typically chosen for a fine-tuned study, whether quantitative or qualitative. That is so we can begin to discover what norms might govern any adolescent's talk, what kinds of contexts might enfold any specific locus or topos for that talking.

Figures 2–4 portray comparative percentages for the identification of significant talking places analyzed first by sex (figure 2), then by ethnicity (figure 3), and then by grade level (figure 4). During the initial collection of maps, self-reporting of ethnicity was voluntary, though nearly every student chose to give this information, using the terms *white*, *black*, and *other*. Terms for Native American began to appear on school forms midway through the collection. Charlotte junior-high school populations in the early eighties had very low cohorts of students identified as other than *white* or *black*, so the data are analyzed only for those two cohorts.

The percentages are collapsed from maps of only those students who reported one or more Friends: it is a safe generalization to say that students who reported only Home and My School/Another School (which are not presented in these figures), but did not report Friend, also did not report any other talking places. Some of these reported in the interviews that they were expected to go straight home and stay there until parents returned, others said they did not live near anyone or anywhere, some were new to the area, others said they preferred being alone with the television or music, and many chose not to comment at all.

The 17 talking places were first correlated with the larger category of Friends. This category was achieved by lumping together the cumulative reports of 1, 2, 3, 4–7 and more than 7 friends, abbreviated on the figures as *pals*. What is immediately striking from this set of figures is that grade level, with a peak at eighth grade for many places, appears to have a heavier impact—or at least suggests greater variation—on what places are significant talking-places for adolescents than either sex or race. However, none of these three variables tells the whole tale when viewed alone. For example, female adolescents edge past their male counterparts for talking-contacts with multiple friends, for neighbors, relatives, and church, for institutionally sponsored areas, malls, and fast-food places: this suggests slightly different kinds of networks and network ties, and a movement (particularly with fast-food places) toward cross-sex conversation. Male adolescents talk with multiple friends but not as many; talk with almost as many neighbors but with a noticeably smaller number of relatives; edge past the females for institutionally sponsored areas, free-play areas, convenience and other stores but back off a bit from malls and fast-food outlets. One suspects that males might have a greater range, with similar landmarks for significant talking places that are fewer in number than those for females. But the differences are very slight. Differences are slight again with comparisons keyed to ethnicity: black adolescents in general identified a greater number of talking-place landmarks, with noticeable differences for church, institutionally sponsored buildings, malls, and fast-food outlets.

Figure 2
Percentage comparisons
by sex

■ ALL MALES ◉ ALL FEMALES

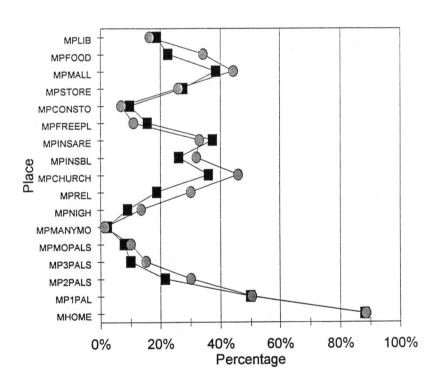

Figure 3
Percentage comparisons
by ethnic

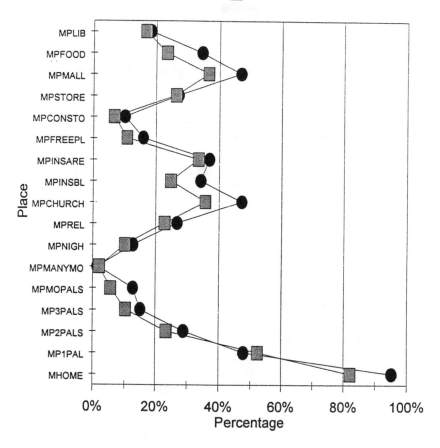

Figure 4
Percentage comparisons
by grade

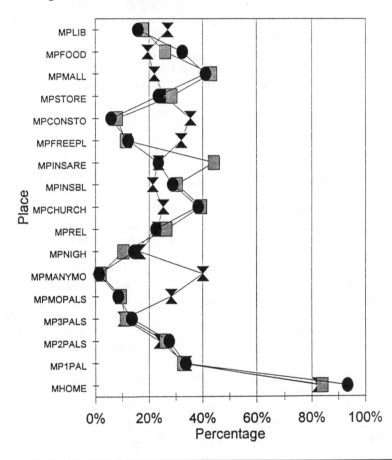

Where noticeable differences do surface, when controlling for a single variable, it is with the notion of grade level, which suggests that the concept of grade level carries sanction with the range of activities permitted or encouraged by care-givers. While students usually reported chronological age, we chose to perform the analysis by grade level for two reasons: first, due to uneven promotion/retention, there was a range of 18 months across each grade level; and second, student interviews consistently identified friends by grade level up until the time the friend either went to high school or got a driver's license. Seventh graders are more likely to identify talking with more than three friends as significant; they visit the convenience stores, find the free-play areas, edge out the others in their visits to the library branch. Eighth and ninth graders pattern in similar ways: they move away from the convenience store to the malls, shift away from free-play ranging to institutionally sponsored buildings, peak in the eighth grade for institutionally sponsored areas (the last surge in youth sports below the high school teams, perhaps). Ninth graders, like eighth graders, are beginning to limit the number of their talking-friends, and they nominate "home" more heavily than either of the other two grades. For example, collapsing the tokens for the five pals-categories into the larger category of Friend produces the array in table 3.

Table 3
Places for talking: Home compared to all friend locations, by grade level

Grade	Home	Friend
7th	92.2%	95.4%
8th	92.4%	72.8%
9th	96.3%	84.3%

Figures 5 and 6 present analyses of significant talking places controlled for sex and analyzed by grade and by ethnicity. Some isolated features stand out, and begin to explain some of the situational factors affecting where and to whom adolescents talk.

It is the black male eighth grader who nominates the institutionally sponsored area as heavily significant, the white male seventh grader who is finding church important for talk. Church is important to females as well but especially for eighth-grade white females and ninth-grade black females. And it is the black female seventh and eighth graders and all black males who are moving gradually away from home as a significant talking-place. We are beginning to get a clearer picture of the kinds of places adolescents value for talking.

Definitions of neighborhood and community change during the passage from late childhood through early adolescence and have, apparently, no single conditioning factor. When we go to certain places to collect data, those places might be stacked against us: that is, we might not be collecting fully representative data. How can we know—or rather, make a more informed guestimate?

Figure 5
Percentage comparisons of females
by ethnic by grade

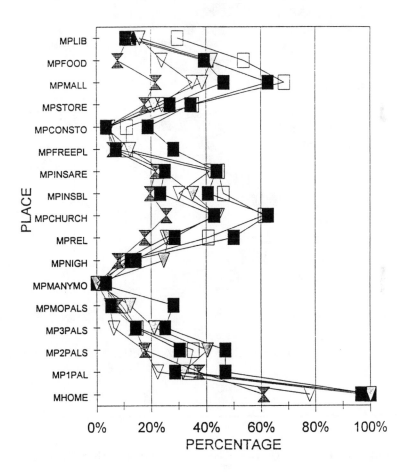

Figure 6
Percentage comparisons of males
by ethnic by grade

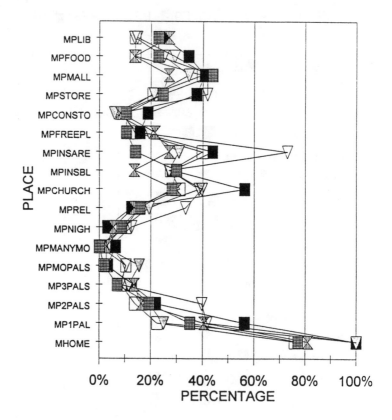

STRENGTH OF ASSOCIATIONS: PORTFOLIOS AND IMPLICATIONS

It is here, of course, that the concept of network, especially as illustrated by the Milroys (J. Milroy 1992; L. Milroy 1987a; Milroy and Milroy 1992), Cheshire (1982), and others, can be especially useful. One of the challenges in examining levels of language use from late childhood through early adolescence, at least in this New South urban area, is that adolescents' shifting mobility, their rapidly changing peer contacts, makes it difficult to see just what part "neighborhood" or "community" might play in accounting for some of the variation we find. Cross-town busing to schools, for example, meant that no single school in the early eighties could furnish a walk-in, live-by sample without careful review of demographic records for each school—and the principals of the 21 schools were not able to grant that kind of access. Moreover, it may be that the physically based concepts of neighborhood and community play less of a role during this age or stage: affiliation and alignment (see Goodwin and Goodwin 1990) may take precedence.

A junior-high student in this sprawling New South area may live in a subdivision or a suburb, an apartment or condominium complex, a particular clump of streets or blocks but attend school across the city via a bus that rolls through school-boundary maps that change as frequently as the rebuilding, realigning neighborhood core. As after-school play-time changes in quantity and quality, adolescents seek different places, different faces for their significant talk. The talking-world maps, the mental maps collected from the adolescents in this study, can be used as a needed alternative to neatly defined geographical locales because these maps identify not only the kinds of clusters in a city for an age group but also their multiplicity and their similarities. They provide broad-brush portraiture rather than close studies of variation (such as those by Cheshire 1982; Eder 1990; Canaan 1986; and especially Eckert 1988, 1989a, b).

One method for assessing the representativeness of patterns in the maps is shown by Cohen and Shinar (1985), who studied friendship networks and neighborhoods in Jerusalem. They were particularly interested in indices of attachment, network density, links between attachment, and the degree of localization of friendship networks. They used a semantic differential technique for obtaining "neighborhood image" and Cramer's V to measure strength of association between variables.

Likewise, the present study used Cramer's V, in this case to measure the likelihood of talking with friends at certain places, since the spaces they temporarily occupied to talk could be, as Brower (1980:179) notes, "cues for separate behavioral performances." Table 4 lists the 73 combinations of place (out of 81 total) that were significant for friends; that is, if students listed friends on their maps, they went to those places. Of those 73 combinations, 32 were also significant for grade level, 13 for sex alone (19 for sex and grade), and one for sex, ethnicity, and grade. Grade was not significant for any combinations with home, yard, or institutional building, or for most combinations of library-store-mall-fast foods. Grade was significant for combinations of institutionally sponsored area and building combinations with anything else, and gender was significant for combinations with church and with malls.

Table 4 prompts a look not only at changing definitions of neighborhood and community, but also at the notions of links and ties within networks. One implication here is that fieldworkers who want to survey, tape, interview, or check friendship/self-esteem or anything else with this particular age group may need to replicate their work in more than one setting to feel confident in their elicitation and interpretation of speech networks, strong or loose ties, and speech styles.

Table 4:　Strength of association among variables keyed to friendship
[*italics*= sex significant; CAPS = ethnicity significant; **bold** = grade significant ($p < .001$)]

Cramer's V	map-place	Cramer's V	map-place
.350	home	.191	**convstore+instarea+instbldg+**
.275	*church+home*		**library+store+mall**
.267	*home+neighbor's house*	.189	**church+instarea+instbldg**
.264	*home+convenience store*	.189	*FASTFOOD*
.260	*home+neighbor's house+*	.188	*church+instarea+instbldg*
	own yard	.187	library+mall
.259	home+own yard	.183	**church+instarea+instbldg+**
.248	home+free-play area		**library**
	(no name or sponsorship)	.178	**instarea+instbldg+library+**
.248	*mall*		**store**
.247	**church+instarea+instbldg+**	.178	instbldg+store
	library+store+mall+fastfood	.176	**convstore+store**
.236	store+mall	.175	**instarea+fastfood**
.233	store+fastfood	.172	**instarea**
.228	*church+home+relative*	.172	*church+relative*
.228	***church+store+mall***	.169	store+convstore
.227	store+mall+fastfood	.167	*instbldg+fastfood*
.224	*church+store*	.166	**church+instarea+instbldg+**
.221	*mall+fastfood*		**library+store+mall**
.221	home+yard+neighbor+free-play	.164	instbldg+library+store
.221	store	.157	**church+fastfood**
.220	**church+instarea+instbldg+**	.154	church+library
	library+store+mall	.152	library+fastfood
.219	**instarea+mall**	.150	**convstore+instarea+instbldg**
.216	instarea+instbldg+library+	.149	neighbor+freeplay
	store+mall+fastfood	.146	*church+instarea*
.215	**convstore+instarea+instbldg+**	.146	instarea+instbldg
	library+store+mall+fastfood	.142	instarea+library
.213	**convstore+mall**	.141	yard
.209	**church+instarea**	.140	**convstore+instarea+**
.207	*church+fastfood*		**instbldg+library**
.204	instbldg+mall	.139	instbldg
.203	instbldg+library+store+	.138	**instarea+fastfood**
	mall+fastfood	.137	neighbor+yard+fastfood
.202	*church*	.136	**home+relative**
.202	library+store+mall+fastfood	.136	*instarea +instbldg+freeplay*
.201	**instarea+store**	.135	**instarea+instbldg+library**
.199	library+store+mall	.134	instbldg+fastfood
.197	instbldg+library+store+mall	.131	convstore+instbldg
.196	**church+instarea+instbldg+**	.129	*relative*
	library+store	.128	*neighbor*
.194	home+neighbor+yard+	.112	instbldg+library
	freeplay+convstore	.109	*neighbor+yard*
.193	**instarea+instbldg+library+**		
	store+mall		

Wellman (1988) reminds us of the power of structured social relationships (31), claiming that the world "is composed of networks, not groups" (37). When he, Carrington, and Hall began to study East York in 1968, it did not fit standard sociological criteria for community: there were no physical signs, for example, of neighborhood life. "Community, like love, is where you find it. East Yorkers were finding it in ties, not in public places" (Wellman, Carrington, and Hall 1988:130). Instead of looking at community defined by neighborhood, they looked at community defined by networks—which ties and networks fostered "sociable relations, interpersonal support, informal social control, and a sense of personal identity . . ." (131). Their focus has been not on the study of boundaries or gatekeepers, but on the notion of significant ties. In East York, people spend a lot of time interacting with a few people they are not close to and have less frequent contact with their close and intimate ties—the operation of their personal communities is within the homes and hidden from public view. The adolescents in this study may be like Poe's Purloined Letter: the operation of their personal communities, being openly displayed, is not always seen as they develop ties. Will these ties be multistranded or specialized, in the kinds of "diversified portfolios" (171) they may need to operate in the adult world? Developing those portfolios, out of their talking places, is one of their tasks.

The kinds of variation we may expect to find in an adolescent's portfolio will be illustrated later in this section by two segments from the tape-recorded interviews which accompanied the collections of the maps. All of the interviews were school-based, as it was neither permitted nor feasible to follow each adolescent to the variety of places indicated on the maps. At the schools, the following kinds of speech were recorded: interviews with individual students about their maps and about perceived differences between "neighborhood" and "community"; group discussions with school teams about "neighborhood," "community," and ways they recognized language differences in each other and in themselves; and interviews by students of other students, with no adult present, on out-of-school literacy events.

The two segments chosen as illustrations of adolescents' variation are from a junior high school at the northern end of the county. Here, rural, suburban, and small-town students are joined by students bused in from city neighborhoods. The first transcript, Turner's talk to himself, though intended for the interviewer's ear, shows little shifting of phonological or morphological markers from the kinds of speech he quotes and even replicates from his mother. We can infer that the data-collector may have been interesting to Turner but was not important, as the collector was not part of any of the associations in his social networks, had little or no standing in his worldview, and was not perceived as having a language variety desirable for emulation. He also presented little variation in his interview of another student, who was in his grade level and from his personal network of friends at the school. The friend he discussed, however, was apparently someone to emulate, and emulation began to surface in the kinds of shifting he displayed in the group discussion taped earlier that day. We may infer that this group included a network to which he aspired, and with at least some of whom he wanted to achieve the kind of social relationships discussed by Wellman, Carrington, and Hall (1988).

As early adolescents are sanctioned to have a wider range, developmentally, as they become even more conscious of peer and other networks, they are also cognitively ready to perform other complicated tasks, one of which is to move away from spaces that are indeterminate and keyed initially to home location. This movement is apparently important for their self-definition. They peer eagerly, constantly, into the reflections of that identity through the reactions of others to their talk. For it is by their talk that they so often negotiate their temporary and possibly modify their permanent identities, identifying and trying on styles. You may recall the ephemeris, as studied by biologists as well as anthropologists: the minute ways by which the honeybee or the bird realigns its journey and reports its range and landmarks to others of its group. The developmental passage from late childhood to high adolescence for humans is ephemeral; their experimentation with style and register is ephemeral as well. And what they notice seems to be incremental, developmentally and cognitively cued, and very interesting in terms of pragmatics. At each "place," the early adolescent is now able to store, access, retrieve a complex template that is keyed to—and can be used to produce—minute distinctions in phonology, morphology, lexicon, and syntax in terms of discourse cues, situational constraints, and pragmatic concerns. At these places, in contact with the faces—real or projected—they call up complex schema which include what Myers-Scotton (1993) calls acts of negotiation in a variety of speech acts.

Myers-Scotton's claim is that "each linguistical variety used in CS [code-switching] has socio-psychological associations, making it indexical of a rights-and-obligations set . . . derived from salient situational features . . . and relevant cultural values" (1993:7). Like Auer (1988) and others, Myers-Scotton wants the constructs of situational and metaphorical switching, based on Blom and Gumperz (1972), to be on a continuum that would allow us to "exploit the possibility of linguistic choices in order to convey intentional meaning of a socio-pragmatic nature" (57). Her markedness model, and its cognitively based markedness metric would be part of a speaker's competence (79–80), establishing criteria for sets of rights-and-obligations "derived from whatever situational features are salient for the community for that interaction type" (84). Code choices are then indexical, not symbolic (86). The model, keyed to community norms, establishes principles of negotiation (to index the set of rights and obligations in speech interactions) and of virtuosity, which allows the speaker to switch, to carry on, and to accommodate the participation of others (148). Myers-Scotton adds that identities are tied to what you use and how you use it, and may change with context and topic (104).

As they pass from early to high adolescence, young people become self-conscious about styles and shifts and negotiations, and in that sense we may say that their development of self-awareness is a key factor in their learning to decipher and exploit a number of pragmatic cues which they will use both now and later. The two figures that follow display an overview of volunteered information, from the tape-recorded individual and group interviews, about what features some adolescents notice in the speech of other adolescents (figure 7) and the cues that trigger their awareness of speech or register shifts that they themselves initiate (figure 8).

Figure 7: What adolescents acknowledge noticing about their own shifting

What they notice	*Who notices*
country vs city "accents"	7–9, schools ringing perimeter or who have a sizable bused-in cohort of "rural" speakers
voice change (for males)	7–8 males, low SES
clothing as signal	all report this
"diction": prosody	8–9; f and m, random, but noticers all in advanced classes <SESxtestingxparent OR marked as "popular" by a) peer naming/labeling; b) realignment of prosody, lexicon, insertion of consonants and possible modifications of /aɪ/ during group interaction tapings
"diction": lexical choice	7–9: when mentioned by 7s, usually the only marker acknowledged
who speakers talk to and/or companions	8–9, m/f, random; keyed to location and repertoire by 10th graders; how-hard-to-break-in signals
topics	8–9, f primarily; keyed to situation [locus and speakers] expanded by fs in 10th grade, attending prestige school and self/group-identified as "popular"
lexicon: terms and profanity	7–9, m and f, all
paralinguistic: e.g., carriage, movements, eye movement, attitude, confidence, dominance	8–9, slightly more m; 10, more f. Correlates with who-they-talk-to, situations, companions, locations

Figure 8: Registers in contact—Reading each other as a text

The Adolescent's Hierarchy of Interpretation/Projection
Read down: from known/given/shared to inferable

macro-cues
    location
    dress
    paralinguistic cues
    companions
        "known" information about popularity of speaker within in-group
rhetorical-cues
    situation
    topic
    presence/absence of lexical signals (e.g., profanity or in-group words as "key")
conversation-cues (negotiable)
    prosody (which can include or lead into shifting)
    topic-shift distance cues
        degree-of-referentiality to in-group persons
    politeness and power signals at lex. level keyed to discourse topic and conversationalists
micro-cues (negotiable)
    morphological and/or phonological signals for city/country, attitude, in-group, power . . .

The shifts that adolescents make can range from phonological through syntactic and lexical, hence pragmatic, levels (see Figures 9 and 10). The tapes of speakers at this school displayed variation in shortened and lengthened glides for /aɪ/ (in *I*, *five*, *ninth*); present- and past-tense markings; markers used to signal features such as reference, topic, and social distance; and politeness phenomena. Figures 9 and 10 contextualize what adolescents acknowledged in taped interviews about their own and others' shifting, and what they seem to be doing as they interpret the discourse situation in which they find themselves. Figures 9 and 10 present two snippets from Turner's talk which suggest further substantiation of Myers-Scotton's markedness model. In these, so that we may focus on Turner's realignments, his staging, his negotiation to be part of the group in the second transcript, we have minimized uses of spelling, to suggest pronunciation.

Figure 9: Turner talks to himself

[BD . . . I'll go get my phone call. And when you get tired of talking, punch it off. You know how to work it.]

Um. Well, I like the way he uh teach me. He teach me. And he a good friend to me, you know. He takes me to the basketball games and stuff. And I met him,

well, why she was asking me

  **What you doing in the C-booth?

Talking on a tape recorder, doing a project.

  **A project?

Um. And I was, uh [door shuts] and I was, uh, well, how I meet him, you know, I was, I was, I lived beside him and, and he got a cousin named Huddy Jay, Hudley Jay I mean, and, and that's my, my uncle too. So I just, I just wanted to be his friend so bad because me and him was almost close cousin, you know. Might be, a little teensie bit. You know. And I just, I think I just like him. And I like him pretty good. Yeah. And he's alright to me. But, some people I just don't like. Hate to say it, but some people I just don't like. Like this uh, it was a, you know, like these people in Atlanta. I don't know about them or not, but they came in the park. And they got this almost, they was chasing this girl name Vanessa, and, and she, and they was chasing me, and she went around her house and then she, they would have caught her and got her in the car. I don't know what she, probably would have killed her. And she went in this door, this lady name Miz Craig, and that was save. I said, ain't that a shame, they out here. Then my momma talk to um, "Y'all be careful, just don't go, don't go in the front yard, don't go, if you're gonna go in the back way." I said "OK, Momma." She kept on telling us that. Every day. "Go in the back yard. Go in the back yard." And you know we hear a lot up there. They said that they was gonna keep um on the, keep on the watch of them. They wasn't gonna put it on the news because they trying to catch them. Things like that. You know. But I be on the watch-out so. And they just catch me, they just have to catch me, you know. But I try not to let them catch me. [door opens. BD: OK. . . .]

Figure 10: Turner's talk in group discussion

5	the ninth, tenth
10	[name]
42	I'm going to the game. I already got a ticket.
44	All right
201	It's like, you know, it's not like me just, you know, sort of associating, you know, wearing clothes. Just, you know, the way they act, too. Like they don't care. When they're around you, they—you know—they can just walk around, you know, be dominant to anything.
255	Well, we're down here in the country almost, most of us
265	Sort of like some schools. I know one school, you know, up in Charlotte, where McDonald's is just right across the street. You want to go eat there, they just arrange you to go there, eat, and come back.
290	We try to have, uh, you know, standards, you know, good-natured, but maybe have a dress code, where you have to wear ties or something.
410	Not really
447	Decide if you want to work or not
481	The way it seems to me, it just seems like private schools are just, just for smart people almost, you know. That's the way it seems to me. You know, like its just a separate school for smart people
502	But they all just seem to be, you know, growing up fascinated by this. That's the way it seem to me.
539	You gotta pay to go in a private school, right?
581	In our school, you have the doors when you go into the bathroom are off
585	Now I haven't seen any that bad
614	I thought, you know, once you get up to Nxx[school name], you know, the atmosphere would change a great deal. But you know, since I've been up there, when I've been up there the past week or so, you know, it seems the same. People are still friendly. I still thought it, you know, would be different.
669	One thing is, at another school, they always say "We gonna get you!" But seventh grade, it wasn't nothing at all. If you have a big school and you all alone, you know that's, that's a pretty sad feeling, you know, you all alone in a big school, walking by yourself.
675	Say, like you're new—from another school, or something.

Turner often speaks the variety of AAVE spoken in his neighborhood and, if his falsetto mimicry of his mother's speech can be trusted, of his family. He habitually simplifies consonant clusters and deletes the copula, for example, in his interviews of another student [not shown] and his reminiscences. The glide on his /aɪ/ lengthens and shortens according to the situation he is in, which includes its purpose or function, its topic, and the other peers. A phonetic transcription suggested that he was varying his glides and reinserting final consonants in clusters affecting subject-verb concord and plurals. As shown in the transcript of his participation in the group discussion (figure 10), he expands his use of the copula in contractions (l. 201), increases his variety of hedges (l. 481) and elaboration within informational discourse (ll. 265, 290; see Biber 1988), and otherwise signals his awareness of levels of formality. He is busy establishing an identity that lets him participate in a full-group, site-specific contact, moving toward the more prestigious forms exhibited by some of the group members known to be popular, known to be the sun around which, for this hour, he revolves. The other members of the group were black and white, male and female: his prosody began to resemble Kevin's, a black male athlete from a citified subdivision, and he realigned his /aɪ/ and chimed into conversational turns established by cheerleader and student-council representative, Jonelle.

Like every adolescent in the study, Turner had more than one kind of talk, and from his experience—recorded in part by his series of maps—he had noticed ways to negotiate a variety of identities, some of which he would maintain. As with the other adolescents, each place on each map was a crystallization of significant talk, a nexus for code, register, or style shifting, a possible site for literacy, a complex, multidimensional schematic. It may be that the passage from late childhood to high adolescence is a second stage of acquisition for humans which replicates, extends, and moves to the forefront the importance of pragmatics (see Ochs 1990). At the very least, the study suggests that teachers working with junior high students need greater awareness of the multiple tasks, the multiplicity of negotiations that Turner and all the other adolescents bring to class, in order to decide how best to reach them, using language to meet theirs.

Turner modifies his speech as spaces and faces, keyed to important associations, shift in his own mind. It is likely that the places drawn on his maps, and on the full collection of maps, will have similar distinctiveness. His situationally cued shifts, where locus fuses with topos, suggest confirmation of the mapping technique used for elicitation. The minimal prompt apparently is successful as an elicitation device and as a prompt for interviews. The frequency analyses, extended by the strength of association indicated by Cramer's V show that students, when asked to report, will do so in a way that produces a fairly generalizable representation, adequately representative of the speech habits of a particular community of children and adolescents.

CONCLUSION

The elicitation of talking places and the subsequent analysis of that type of data provides a useful tool for understanding adolescent talk. Their maps establish that adolescents do organize and construct a social world made up of places in geographically disparate locations, a network with loose ties. The neighborhood, as a locale where many adolescent speech practices occur, may change, disappear, or blur its boundaries, but it is replaced by a nexus of social groupings and activities that exist, sometimes in places clearly understood to be spatial and literal and sometimes not. The patterns and the correlations suggest that the maps compare well to other techniques for obtaining self-reported data. When studied against the interviews, the distinctive locales of the maps do, in fact, imply and correspond to different language patterns and practices for the adolescents collaborating in this study.

Each individual map is a story, the skeleton of adolescent narratives about themselves. In the aggregate, the technique provides insight into the unique practices and patterns of a particular language community and can be depended on to provide an accurate representation of the places speakers go for talk. As such, talking-world maps occupy a place in the analysis of language.

NOTES

1. This series of claims fits well with the kinds of classifications established by D'Andrade and Wish, in which they review a number of theories and conflate them into a series of 12 speech acts (1985:246).

2. See Altman and Wohlwill (1978), particularly Siegel, Kirasic, and Kasil (1978) on cognitive maps. For an extensive discussion of behavioral geography, see Golledge and Stimson (1987).

APPENDIX: Talking Places Maps

These maps were drawn by "Phil Denton" during 1981–83, his 7th, 8th, and 9th grade years. The map for 7th grade includes Phil's response to two writing prompts which were asked each year; this information has been deleted from the figures for maps 2 and 3. The first prompt, to the left of the map, asked students for their nicknames; two characteristics they thought others noticed; three typical daily activities; two characteristics they wished others would notice; and their full legal names. The second prompt asked students to identify persons whom they might consult to discuss an important or troubling issue. The leftmost column contains names or categories for people of the same age; the middle column contains names or categories for older people; the rightmost column contains names of people the students might wish to emulate.

Phil lived near UNCC (University of North Carolina-Charlotte) and occasionally used its outdoor sports facilities; McD is McDonald's; Godfather's is the name of a pizza franchise. JT and West are nicknames for public schools. The maps were scanned, their additional information deleted and their contrast enhanced by Maria Domoto, UNCC Japan Center Director.

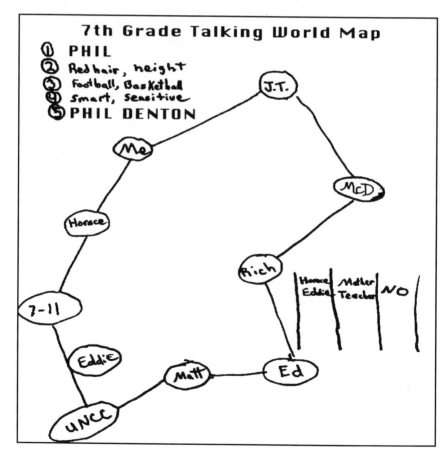

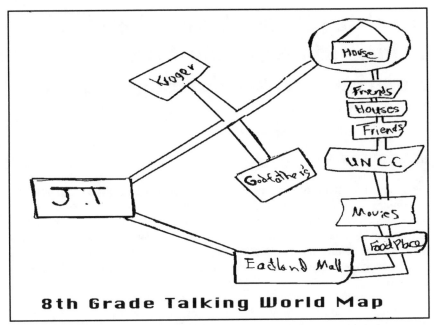

8th Grade Talking World Map

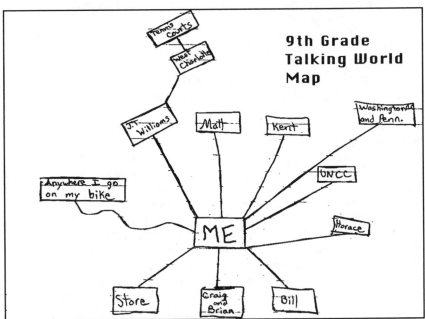

9th Grade Talking World Map

Resolving Dialect Status: Levels of Evidence in Assessing African-American Vernacular English Forms

Walt Wolfram

INTRODUCTION

Although the status of African-American Vernacular English (AAVE) has been scrutinized over the past three decades, a surprising number of issues remain unresolved. The overall diachronic and synchronic status of AAVE in relation to other varieties remains in dispute, as does the function of particular structures associated with this variety. In attempting to sort out the status of AAVE, the classic structures continue to be re-examined and new structures have been uncovered.

It is somewhat surprising that structures might continue to emerge in a variety as thoroughly studied as AAVE, but there are a number of explanations for this descriptive situation, including innovation, differential methods of data collection, structural infrequency, and structural obscurity, or camouflaging. Thus, in a recent investigation of a previously undescribed structure of AAVE, I concluded that these explanations converged to account for some aspects of the construction NP_i *call* NP_i V*ing*—in sentences such as *They call theyselves/themselves dancing* or *I call myself dancing*—that were unique to this variety (Wolfram 1994).

At first glance, it might appear that the microscopic focus on a restricted construction such as NP_i *call* NP_i V*ing* is little more than a search for a dialect needle in a language haystack, or the latest version of the dialect collector's mad pursuit of elusive dialect forms to fill up the language diversity archives. Upon closer investigation, however, the consideration of forms such as NP_i *call* NP_i V*ing* is critical to general sociolinguistic issues and to the status of AAVE. For general sociolinguistics, the examination of these forms is essential for understanding (1) the nature, direction, and explanation of language change and its manifestation in language variation; (2) the adequacy of linguistic and sociolinguistic field methods, including where and how we obtain data; and (3) the nature of ethnolinguistic marking, that is, the role that particular language structures play in establishing ethnic identity. For the study of AAVE specifically, the NP_i *call* NP_i V*ing* construction relates to (1) levels of similarity and differentiation in AAVE and comparable vernacular varieties; (2) the direction of change in AAVE, including its convergence and/or divergence with European-American varieties; and (3) issues of transparency and opaqueness in the realization of AAVE structures.

The construction NP_i *call* NP_i V*ing* is a paradigm case of a relatively insignificant dialect structure which has important implications for the establishment of evidence and the nature of argumentation about the status of dialect forms. This is especially true since my original description of this form (Wolfram 1994) has met with some skepticism, particularly with respect to my claim that some dimensions of this form are presently unique to AAVE. Some dialectologists have reported informally that certain European-Americans in some regions under particular circumstances may use this form. These are, of course, exactly the kinds of comments we confronted in the earlier stages of studying the relation of African-American and European-American varieties in the 1960s and 1970s (e.g., Wolfram 1969; Labov 1972a; Wolfram and Fasold 1974). Certainly, the careful study of some of these forms in the ensuing decades showed that sociolinguistic affinity was a matter far more involved than the "he-said-she-said" approach to dialect data (e.g., Wolfram 1974; Fasold et al. 1987; Butters 1989; Bailey and Maynor 1987).

In the following sections, I would like to set forth a claim about the status of NP$_i$ *call* NP$_i$ V*ing* as explicitly as possible and then review the types of evidence that support this claim. My focus is on explicitness in formulating dialect hypotheses and the nature of evidence and argumentation in confirming or rejecting a particular hypothesis about the status of a construction. In the long run, the principled consideration of evidence is more essential than the specific conclusion we arrive at about the status of NP$_i$ *call* NP$_i$ V*ing*. Furthermore, knowing how to carry out an impartial sociolinguistic argument seems more important than declaring the winner in the dispute over a particular form.

THE CLAIM

There are several aspects to the claim about the status of NP$_i$ *call* NP$_i$ V*ing* in AAVE, including hypotheses that are directly testable in an experimental framework and hypotheses that must be evaluated on the basis of naturalistic data. One part of the claim about the status of NP$_i$ *call* NP$_i$ V*ing* involves its structural and semantic/pragmatic status; and, as such, its validity is subject to the traditional kinds of syntactic and semantic/pragmatic argumentation that are offered about the structural status of forms. Since much of this argumentation was presented in my original discussion of NP$_i$ *call* NP$_i$ V*ing* (Wolfram 1994), I shall simply summarize my conclusions about its descriptive status. The second part of the claim involves the sociolinguistic status of NP$_i$ *call* NP$_i$ V*ing* as a potential AAVE structure. Since this is the part of my original hypothesis that has been met with the most skepticism, evidence for this conclusion will be highlighted in this presentation. As we shall see, there are dimensions that are quite open to verification through replication, particularly with reference to controlled experimental frames. The last part of the claim involves an interpretation about the sociolinguistic status of NP$_i$ *call* NP$_i$ V*ing* as an ethnic marker. This dimension has a more explanatory sociolinguistic objective in that it strives to show how such a form may be obscured as an AAVE structure. It is a rather modest attempt to strive toward a more explanatory-based sociolinguistics.

The explicit claim for which we shall attempt to provide evidence is as follows: **The form NP$_i$ *call* NP$_i$ V*ing* in sentences such as *They call theyselves/themselves dancing* or *I call myself dancing* constitutes a paradigmatic expansion of the XP small clause complement which functions as a counterfactual proposition** involving a personal co-indexed referent. Its use in this structural context appears to be distinct in AAVE from small clause complements of *call* found in some comparable European-American varieties. The peculiar uses of NP_i *call* NP_i V*ing* in AAVE, however, may be obscured or "camouflaged" on the basis of a generalized counterfactual semantic/pragmatic reading of *call* + small clause XP construction that is shared by AAVE and comparable European-American varieties.

Structurally, the verb *call* is part of a limited class of verbs, including verbs such as *consider, imagine, let* and so forth, that take an NP direct object complement; at the same time, the surface object NP stands in a predicative relation with a following small clause NP, AP, PP, or VP. Given the fact that small clauses are of the canonical form [NP XP], we might expect four major types of small clause complements with verbs: nominal small clauses; adjectival small clauses; prepositional small clauses; and verbal small clauses divisible into infinitival, gerundive, and participial clauses based on the morphological characteristics of the head V of the predicate VP. One of the very noticeable characteristics of verbs taking small clause complements is their apparent subcategorization restrictions (Stowell 1981:259). For example, a verb such as *imagine* in (1) is fairly extensive in its range of XP complements, a verb like *let* in (2) is quite restricted, and a verb such as *call* in (3) seems to fit somewhere in between.

(1) (a) I can't imagine him serious about life. (AP)
    (b) I can't imagine him a teacher. (NP)
    (c) I can't imagine him in a suit. (PP)
    (d) I can't imagine him lying about inhaling. (V_{ing})
    (e) I can't imagine him dominated by everybody. (V_{en})

(2) (a) *I won't let you unhappy. (AP)
    (b) *I won't let you a complete fool. (NP)
    (c) I won't let you out of the house. (PP)
    (d) *I won't let you going home. (V_{ing})
    (e) I won't let you go home. (V)
    (f) *I won't let you taken advantage of. (V_{en})

(3) (a) He called her intelligent. (AP)
    (b) She called him a fool. (NP)
    (c) ?I called him in trouble. (PP)
    (d) *I called him lying about inhaling. (V_{ing})
    (e) ?I called him dominated by everybody. (V_{en})

Given the lexically based subcategorization which serves as the basis for the restriction of small clause complements, we might expect dialectal variation in the range of small clause complements for particular verbs. This seems to be a reasonable basis for explaining the apparent syntactic expansion of *call* with V*ing* in AAVE, just as it is a reasonable basis for explaining other cases of dialect variation that exist in verb + small clause complements. It is interesting to note that Radford (1988:359), in illustrating the apparent idiosyncratic range of verb + small clause complement constructions, includes several examples of dialectally sensitive complements without noticing this dialect sensitivity. For example, he observes that a noun clause complement with the verb *imagine* is ungrammatical in his British English dialect (e.g., **I can't imagine you a policeman*), but this complement is quite acceptable in many American English dialects. Within this paradigm of selective subcategorization for verb + small clause complements, it seems quite reasonable to expect dialect variation in the small clause complements with *call*, as we have here for AAVE.

The co-indexed subject and object of such sentences is restricted to [+Personal], with the understanding that this feature includes humans and some nonhuman animates assigned experiencer attributes metaphorically, such as domesticated pets. Thus, sentences with personal pronouns such as (4) are acceptable whereas sentences such as (5), with the nonpersonal pronoun *it*, apparently are not.

(4) Look at the dog, he calls himself watching T.V.
(5) *Look at the dog, it calls itself watching T.V.

In this regard, the pronoun selection shows the type of restriction that Christian (1991) found for the personal dative. That is, a construction like (6a) is acceptable but not (6b).

(6) (a) The dog got him a bone.
     (b) *The dog got it a bone. (from Christian 1991)

Although I claim that many European-American varieties do not typically use the co-indexed NP$_i$ *call* NP$_i$ V*ing* construction (as opposed to well-documented use of the NP$_i$ *call* NP$_i$ NP/AP/PP construction as in *He calls himself a professor*), they do use a subset of V*ing* complements; however, the surface object NP is quite restricted to constructions of the type indicated in (7). Noticeably absent from these are [+Personal] NPs.

(7) (a) Look at that, they call that dancing.
     (b) She calls it dancing.
     (c) They call the twist dancing.
     (d) They call the war horrifying.

Examples such as (4), (5), and (7) suggest that "personal" aspect of *call* with small clause V*ing* is the distinguishing characteristic of dialectal *call* rather than the V*ing* complements per se, which, in turn, suggests that the thematic assignment of small clause NP predication is different in these varieties.

ADMISSIBLE EVIDENCE

There are two primary types of data that provide evidence for the status of linguistic forms: (1) the observation of naturally occurring speech in its everyday context, including a full range of speech situations and events, and (2) the elicitation of judgments about speech, ranging from the direct elicitation of linguistic intuitions to a variety of elicitation tasks that reveal structural functions and relations more indirectly. While these two methodological approaches to data have sometimes been considered antithetical and a source of conflict between so-called contextual and abstract linguistics, there is an important sense in which they should be viewed as complementary rather than competitive (Wolfram 1986). As we shall see, an authentic understanding of the dialectal status of NP$_i$ *call* NP$_i$ V*ing* reveals the true complementarity of these data sets.

OBSERVATIONAL EVIDENCE FOR THE DIALECTAL STATUS OF NP$_i$ *CALL* NP$_i$ V*ING*

The observational basis for the claim that NP$_i$ *call* NP$_i$ V*ing* is a structure of AAVE comes from a collection of examples that spans almost three decades of fieldwork in a variety of vernacular dialects, including several different projects involving AAVE speakers. Examples obtained from traditional sociolinguistic interviews have been supplemented by informal observation in an African-American community in Washington, D.C., for over two decades. The following examples illustrate real time (from 1965 through 1992) and apparent time span (from present-day teenagers to speakers currently in their 60s) as well as regional range (from speakers born in Mississippi and South Carolina to speakers born in Baltimore and Washington). Example (8d), which comes from informal observation of everyday conversation rather than a sociolinguistic interview, also indicates that this construction is hardly limited to vernacular speakers, since this speaker is a middle-class speech and language pathologist who fastidiously avoids the use of any socially stigmatized features of AAVE.

(8) (a) Well, I see 'em sittin' down on the floo', out there in the yard, they's countin' one another's toes. Now what they be doin' that fo' I don't know. . . . They be doin' that kind of game, and when they get through, somebody got to do some runnin'. I don't know what it('d) be, what *they be calls theyself doin'*. (47-year-old African-American male, Subject 506: Detroit Dialect Study 1965; Shuy, Wolfram, and Riley 1967)

     (b) The pots and pans was supposed to be a little better than the bus job anyway. He already . . . *So he call himself,* I guess, *really putting me back*, cause, see, if you working pots and pans, you in that kitchen where all the heat and the sweat, . . . I mean, the water, steam, and stuff, you know, you really . . . that's a messy job, they call it. (61-year-old African-American male, born in South Carolina; after-dinner conversation/interview with subject's wife, Walt Wolfram, and Marge Wolfram, Washington, D.C., 1992)

     (c) We got a little skit together. We got nothin' together. *I don't know what we call(ed) ourself doin'.* I forgot. I know it wadn't nothin' that we shoulda got up there and said we as a group did. (teenage African-American female, Washington, D.C., native; conversation between several teenagers and networked indigenous interviewer, 1986)

     (d) He referred to me as an old lady. And *he called himself defending me.* (October 21, 1992, mid-50s, middle-class African-American career

> speech and language pathologist, Baltimore City Public Schools, during a special interest discussion group with fellow SLPs in the school administration building)

Although we conducted hundreds of interviews with European-American speakers in various regions of the North and South in different sociolinguistic projects (e.g., Shuy, Wolfram, and Riley 1967; Wolfram 1974: Wolfram and Christian 1976; Christian, Wolfram, and Dube 1989), I have found no attestations of NP_i *call* NP_i V*ing* among these speakers. This does not, of course, mean that European-Americans may never use this construction since it is admittedly quite rare in single-subject interviews. Other dialectologists (e.g., Guy Bailey, personal communication) have offered selected attestations among European-American speakers; and the *Dictionary of American Regional English* (*DARE*) implies that the structure is not unique to AAVE. While several of the *DARE* citations are from obvious AAVE speakers, others are apparently European-American speakers, as illustrated below:

call oneself v phr
1944 Wentworth ADD 91 WV, "What do you call yourself a-doing'?" = What do you think you're doing? What are you doing? What do you say you're doing there? . . . "I call myself making better gravy" = (I think that) my gravy making is improving. **1950** Faulkner *Stories* 27 **MS**, A seventy-year-old man, with both feet and one knee, too, already in the grave, squatting all night on a hill and calling himself listening to a fox race that he couldn't even hear unless they had come right up onto the same log he was setting on and bayed into his ear trumpet. **1977** Smitherman *Talkin* 258 [Black], *Call yo'self,* to assume to be doing something, to intend to do a thing, as in "I call myself having this dinner ready on time," or "Girl, what you call yo'self doing?" (*DARE* 1985:519)

While my own observational data suggest that NP_i *call* NP_i V*ing* is linked uniquely to AAVE, attestations such as those found in *DARE*, along with the informal observations offered by reputable, honest dialectologists cannot simply be dismissed cavalierly. Certainly, some of our early descriptions of AAVE (e.g., Wolfram and Fasold 1974) were premature in identifying unique AAVE structures without sufficient background knowledge of comparable Southern-based European American varieties. Thus, our early descriptions of AAVE suffered from a confining Northern bias at the same time that we accused traditional dialectology of suffering from a restrictive anecdotal bias in its approach to AAVE. The evidence from observational data is suggestive but certainly not as conclusive as we might hope for in establishing NP_i *call* NP_i V*ing* as a unique AAVE construction.

BEYOND OBSERVATION IN THE ESTABLISHMENT OF EVIDENCE

As important as data based on the observation of ordinary language in interview or naturalistic settings may be, it is still only one kind of data. Sociolinguists have ascribed primary status to this type of data, but it must be recognized that there are limitations to observational data. Notwithstanding all the ingenuity and refinements of the methods available for collecting spontaneous speech data, there are at least three types of situations where we need more or different kinds of information than the data collected solely from spontaneous speech samples: (1) situations where forms critical for analysis are infrequent in natural conversation, (2) situations in which performance issues in spontaneous conversation may cloud issues related to the description of structures, and (3) occasions where particular hypotheses about structural relations are dependent on judgments or intuitions about structures that go beyond observational adequacy, such as those involving cross-lectal language knowledge (Wolfram 1986).

As Labov (1973) has pointed out, there are a number of different levels on which forms may be evaluated in terms of their cross-lectal status. Some of the dimensions critical for the assessment of cross-lectal language knowledge clearly extend beyond usage per se. Following are the six questions Labov claims to be critical with respect to the evaluation of forms across dialects:

1) Do speakers recognize the structure as grammatical for some native speakers of English?
2) Do speakers evaluate its social significance (e.g., social/ethnic/regional status, stylistic/register status)?
3) Can it be interpreted in neutral and unfavorable contexts?
4) Can the meaning be recognized in isolation?
5) Can the use of the structure be predicted in a range of syntactic, semantic/pragmatic contexts?
6) Can the structure be used productively? (adapted from Labov 1973)

These questions provide a convenient guideline for evaluating some of the important issues about the status of NP_i *call* NP_i V*ing* as an AAVE form. Furthermore, answers to some of these questions can only be obtained by going beyond the traditional limits of ordinary conversation.

The first question we may ask about NP_i *call* NP_i V*ing* is whether it is recognized cross-dialectally as a grammatical form. In its most simple interpretation, this question can be reduced to a straightforward grammaticality judgment. Thus far, I have accumulated data on grammaticality judgments in three different settings: from African-American and European-American speakers conveniently sampled in the Baltimore-Washington area; from speakers in Raleigh, North Carolina; and from a sample of speakers in Philadelphia, Pennsylvania. While the sample from Philadelphia is limited, it is important since it involves the type of replication that is important for the establishment of evidence. The judgments reported in table 1 represent conventional grammaticality judgments by a set of European-American and African-American subjects for two typical NP_i *call* NP_i V*ing* sentences. Speakers were simply asked to make decontextualized grammaticality judgments on the acceptability of these sentences. In the table, "OK" means the sentences were judged as well-formed, grammatical sentences and "*" as ill-formed or ungrammatical.

Table 1: Grammaticality judgments for NP$_i$ *call* NP$_i$ V*ing* sentences, European-American and African-American responses in the Baltimore-Washington area

	African-American		European-American	
	OK	*	OK	*
They call themselves going to school/	16	7	1	22
She calls herself combing her hair				
	73.4%	26.6%	4.3%	95.7%

The differential response patterns of European-American and African-American subjects to these two sentences are obvious, with the vast majority of African-American subjects accepting the form as grammatical and practically all (22 of 23) European-American subjects rejecting it as ungrammatical.

A related grammaticality judgment task was given to an undergraduate English grammar class at North Carolina State University in the spring of 1993. In this instance, the judgments for three sentences related to *call* and its complements were embedded in a general grammaticality judgment task that included a number of other sentence types (there were 20 sentences in all). Included in the task was a sentence representing NP$_i$ *call* NP$_i$ V*ing* (*She called herself doing the exercise*), one which used a non-co-indexed pronoun in the small clause complement (*She called him doing the exercise*), and one with a small clause complement with an NP predicate (*She called him a weirdo*). As we shall see, there is some question as to whether the construction requires co-indexing as a part of its structural specification. The inclusion of a sentence of the NP$_i$ *call* NP$_i$ + NP type (*She called him a weirdo*) allows us to compare the construction under review with a structure we hypothesize to be shared by African-American and European-American speakers. Respondents to this task are divided into native Northern European-Americans, native Southern European-Americans, and African-Americans. Unfortunately, there was only one African-American in the class, a native of the Washington, D.C., area. Results for the 34 students in the class are given in table 2.

Table 2: Grammaticality judgments for three different complements of *call* Response from an English grammar class at North Carolina State University

	Northern Euro.-Am.		Southern Euro.-Am.		African-American	
	OK	*	OK	*	OK	*
She called herself doing the exercise	0	7	0	26	1	0
She called him doing the exercise	0	7	0	26	0	1
She called him a weirdo	7	0	26	0	1	0

The results of this judgment task are amazingly categorical. All of the Northern and Southern European-American subjects rejected the NP$_i$ *call* NP$_i$ V*ing* sentence as ungrammatical, while the single African-American subject judged it grammatical. All subjects, including the African-American, rejected the nonreflexive construction with V*ing* as ungrammatical while judging the predicate nominal complement as grammatical. The latter result is quite predictable from our hypothesis that this construction is shared across American English dialects.

The task reported in table 2 was replicated by Bill Reynolds for a limited group of speakers in Philadelphia; his results are given in table 3.

Table 3: Grammaticality judgments for three different complements of *call* Responses from the replication of the task in Philadelphia

	Northern European-American		African-American	
	OK	*	OK	*
She called herself doing the exercise	0	7	2	1
She called him doing the exercise	0	7	1	2
She called him a weirdo	7	0	3	0

The evidence from decontextualized grammaticality judgments seems very straightforward in the responses accumulated thus far in Washington and Baltimore, North Carolina, and Philadelphia. The evidence in response to Labov's initial question, "Do speakers recognize the structure as grammatical for some native speakers of English?" certainly seems to point to the conclusion that there are differences in the grammatical status of NP_i *call* NP_i V*ing* in AAVE and some European-American dialects, including some Southern-based varieties.

As mentioned previously, I personally have not encountered examples of NP_i *call* NP_i V*ing* in any of my sociolinguistic surveys involving European-American speakers. However, this is a rather infrequent structure to begin with, and I have never attempted to directly elicit this form. To see if it was possible to elicit the use of this form by European-Americans, I thus constructed an elicitation task that I administered to 23 European-American and 23 African-American subjects. The frame I used, given in (9), may be referred to as a *modeled productivity frame* since it provides a model and then attempts to get subjects to follow the model in providing different forms.

(9) I am interested in understanding how sentences such as *They call themselves going to school* or *She calls herself combing her hair* are used in some dialects. . . .
   Think of three different ways you might complete the following expression.
   He calls himself_____

The responses of subjects to this frame are given in table 4. Two types of summary figures are given for the responses. In the first column, the number of subjects who gave at least one sentence of the type NP_i *call* NP_i V*ing* is given for each group. In the second column, the number of NP_i *call* NP_i V*ing* constructions out of the total responses is calculated. This figure is given since the instruction requested three different sentence completions for the *He calls himself____* frame.

Table 4: Production of NP$_i$ *call* NP$_i$ V*ing* vs. other XPs
for European-American and African-American subjects

Ethnic Group	No. Speakers Producing NP$_i$ *call* NP$_i$ V*ing*		No. NP$_i$ *call* NP$_i$ V*ing* Constructions	
African-American	14/23	60.9 %	31/67	46.3 %
European-American	2/23	8.7 %	2/69	6.9 %
	$\chi^2 = 13.80; p < .001$		$\chi^2 = 34.78; p < .001$	

The evidence from modeled productivity again shows a significant difference between the responses of the African-American and European-American speakers in Washington and Baltimore. We thus see that the answer to Labov's question six, "Can the structure be used productively?" points to a contrast between AAVE and other American English varieties.

A more subtle question in the use of *call* complements with V*ing* concerns the possibility of using this construction with nonreflexive referents. Up to this point, we have only presented examples of personal *call* V*ing* involving anaphors because we have only directly observed examples of this type. Is the small clause complement limited to anaphors or is this an accidental gap? The question is whether or not sentences such as (10a,b), with pronominals and *r* expressions in the surface object NP slot, are permissible.

(10) (a) ?The men call her dancing.
      (b) ?The mother call(s) the child walking.

The status of such sentences is not a trivial question, as it relates to consider-ations of grammaticality and pragmaticality and, in turn, to the notion of idio-maticity. Furthermore, it directly addresses questions three ("Can it be interpreted in neutral and unfavorable contexts?") and five ("Can the use of the structure be predicted in a range of syntactic, semantic/pragmatic contexts?") in Labov's inventory of diagnostic questions about the cross-dialectal status of structures.

Informal, direct probing of decontextualized sentences such as (10) (e.g., "Can you say, 'The men call her dancing'?") met with categorical rejection by respondents who were admitted users of NP$_i$ *call* NP$_i$ V*ing*; however, it is difficult to determine the basis for this restriction. In order to determine if, in fact, this was an accidental gap, I constructed the scenario illustrated in (11) to determine if non-anaphors could occur as the object NP. This forced test attempted to elicit pronominals while maintaining the conventional counterfactual reading of the *call* construction with anaphors.

(11) Testing for non-anaphoric reference

      (a) Suppose a little child was just beginning to walk, and his proud mother wanted to think that he was walking even though he wasn't.

Choose just one of the sentences to describe what might be said. Remember, you can   only choose one sentence for the description.
1. Look at that, he calls himself walking.
2. Look at that, she calls him walking.

(b) Suppose that Melinda, a poor judge of dancing, thinks that the people on the dance floor are actually not dancing very well at all. . . .
1. She calls them dancing.
2. They call themselves dancing.

(c) Suppose a woman who has a dog would like to think that the dog is listening to her when, in fact, he is not listening at all. . . .
1. Look at that, he calls himself listening.
2. Look at that, she calls him listening.

The scenarios were constructed to provide a context in which a pronominal or *r*-expression may reasonably occur in the surface object–small clause subject slot. For example, in a sentence like (11a), it is the mother who is making the claim about walking, not the child. To attribute the claim to the child would, in a sense, force a reading different from the one explicitly presented in the scenario, thus suggesting a syntactically restricted item, a kind of idiom. If, on the other hand, respondents are quite willing to select the non-co-indexed object, then it suggests that the inventory of examples limited to co-indexing may simply be a non-significant syntactic gap in the data. The elicitation task was administered to a limited set of self-reported users of NP_i *call* NP_i V*ing* in Washington and Baltimore and a group of European-American nonusers in Washington, D.C., and Raleigh, North Carolina. The results are reported in table 5.

Table 5: Responses to pronoun selection task in (11)

Question	AAE Speakers		EAE Speakers			
	Refl.	Non-Refl.	Refl.	Non-Refl.	χ^2	p
(a)	19	4	12	11	4.846	.05
(b)	16	7	6	17	8.712	.01
(c)	18	5	5	18	14.696	.001

The results show that African-American users clearly favor a co-indexed referent reading despite the contextualized scenario suggesting otherwise. The results suggest that the co-indexed selection is, in fact, a genuine restriction of this construction. This kind of restriction is a typical characteristic of idiomaticity, as syntactic options are restricted along with semantic-pragmatic specialization.

The European-American speakers' responses differ significantly from their African-American counterparts (as indicated by the application of χ^2 test of significance to the nominal results), but the level of accurate referent identity does not match the level we might expect in the typical reference identity task. In fact, for the first scenario, approximately half of the European-American subjects chose a co-indexed reading despite the fact that the context suggested that it was the mother, not the child, who claimed that the child could walk. Other things being equal, we would expect more accurate deictic referencing by respondents. There is a sense, then, that the differences between groups, while significant, are more gradient than categorical. We return to this issue after discussing the semantic-pragmatic aspects of this construction.

EVIDENCE FOR CAMOUFLAGING

The evidence from observation and elicitation accumulated thus far certainly point to some cross-dialectal differences for NP_i *call* NP_i V*ing*. The empirical data offered in relation to some of the critical questions about its status point to obvious structural differences as an AAVE construction when compared with other varieties of English. In fact, the differences appear so obvious that we might wonder about the basis for the controversy about this form. Before dismissing the controversy over its status as a simple case of mistaken identity, however, it is important to examine more closely the semantic/pragmatic function of this form. In its unmarked semantic-pragmatic context, it functions as a weak type of counterfactual. Its generalized reading is that the activity of small clause proposition is projected as nonauthentic according to the speaker's evaluative standards. This reading is succinctly illustrated by the exchange in (12), which took place after an African-American woman made a comment about a man who was doing an out-of-date dance step.

(12)   S: . . . and he called hisself dancing.
      WW: What do mean by that?
        S: He thinks he can dance, but he can't. I'll have to show him how to dance. When you call yourself doing, you don't know what you're doing. (Mid-30s African-American female, lifetime D.C. resident).

Many of the occurrences of *call* collected recently involve the evaluation of behavior that is sensitive to cultural differences (e.g., dancing, eating, talking, etc.); in fact, this use may be gaining specialized cultural significance within the present-day African-American community, although the construction has certainly been around for some time. Our earlier attestations from the 60s do not focus on this theme nearly as much as our later ones.

The generalized counterfactual reading of this construction is certainly not unique to African-American English. Clearly, European-Americans share in this reading, presumably by analogy with the unmarked counterfactual reading of NP_i *call* NP_i XP constructions. Thus, when the T.V. character Murphy Brown uttered the statement reported in (13) to a colleague in the newsroom, she was clearly implying that her colleague was posturing rather than behaving like a genuine journalist.

(13) . . . and you call yourself a journalist (Murphy Brown, Jan. 27, 1992)

Evidence of this type clearly links the semantic-pragmatic function NP_i *call* NP_i XP in other varieties of English and the African-American use of NP_i *call* NP_i V*ing*. It is interesting to note that responses by European-Americans to items such as (14) and (15), included as part of a general questionnaire on this form (see Appendix, this essay), illustrate the similarity of the semantic-pragmatic reading for African-American and European-American speakers.

(14) Q: Suppose somebody said, "She calls herself combing her hair." How would her hair look?
      S: Not as good as the comber assumes, certainly.

(15) Q: Suppose somebody said, "He calls himself dressing." How would he be dressing?
      A: Poorly according to the speaker.

There is obvious convergence in the semantic-pragmatic reading of NP_i *call* NP_i V*ing* among African-Americans and European-Americans with respect to its counterfactual reading.

Whereas the unmarked semantic-pragmatic reading of the small clause complement in NP_i *call* NP_i V*ing* is counterfactual, it is important to examine a conversational routine in which the negative reading of *call* is clearly canceled through a special kind of "flouting" (Levinson 1983). In this routine, Speaker A questions Speaker B with the statement in (16), which functions as an indirect accusatory speech act.

(16) What do you call yourself doing?

In this specialized context, a felicitous denial of the accusation is accomplished by flouting the obvious negative implicature. Thus, a response to (16) such as *I call myself eating my lunch* is now to be taken as a statement of actual behavior rather than one with the traditional reading that focuses on the discrepancy between pretext and 'authentic' activity. To support my interpretation of this conversational routine, I constructed the structured elicitation task given in (17) and gave the frame to a group of admitted African-American NP_i *call* NP_i V*ing* users and a group of European-American nonusers who rejected this construction as ungrammatical in a decontextualized sentence grammaticality task. The typical African-American and European-American responses are given in (18) and (19).

(17) Suppose you were minding your own business eating your lunch. A friend comes in and says to you, "What do you call yourself doing?" What would you say? Try to use, "I call myself . . ." in your answer.

(18) Typical African-American Responses:
      (a) I call myself eating lunch.
      (b) I call myself minding mine.
      (c) I call myself minding my ownself's business and leaving yours alone.
      (d) I call myself eating my lunch before you came in and disturbed me.

(19) Typical European-American Responses:
    (a) I call myself eating.
    (b) I call myself eating lunch and minding my own business.
    (c) I call myself enjoying my food.
    (d) I call myself woofing down this sandwich.

Again, we see a shared African-American and European-American semantic-pragmatic reading, despite the fact that our European-American speakers apparently do not use NP$_i$ *call* NP$_i$ V*ing* constructions.

The evidence we have accumulated about the semantic-pragmatic reading of NP$_i$ *call* NP$_i$ V*ing* constructions clearly suggests that there is convergence in the responses of African-Americans and European-Americans despite the structural unfamiliarity of European-Americans to the form. Thus, Labov's questions relating to its semantic-pragmatic relations (e.g., question three, "Can it be interpreted in neutral and unfavorable contexts?" and question four, "Can the meaning be recognized in isolation?" and the semantic-pragmatic part of question five, "Can the use of the structure be predicted in a range of syntactic, semantic/pragmatic contexts?") show comparable responses by African-Americans and European-Americans.

We have now established that NP$_i$ *call* NP$_i$ V*ing* shows structural contrast for African-American and European-American speakers at the same time that it shows semantic-pragmatic similarity. The evidence for the coexistence of semantic-pragmatic convergence and structural divergence is the point where we may appeal to the explanation of camouflaging to understand the cross-dialectal status of NP$_i$ *call* NP$_i$ V*ing*. As found in descriptive accounts of AAVE, camouflaging refers to forms that, on the surface, appear structurally identical to acrolectal forms while maintaining some unique functions. The two prime examples of camouflaged forms in the descriptive literature of AAVE are so-called "indignant *come*" with complement V*ing* clauses (Spears 1982), as in (20a), and aspectual *steady* (Baugh 1984), as exemplified in (21a). The analogous acrolectal structural forms that provide the disguise for (20a) and (21a) are given in (20b) and (21b) respectively.

(20) (a) They come talking that trash about him. (from Spears 1982)
    (b) They came running when they heard the news.

(21) (a) They steady working on the project. (from Baugh 1984)
    (b) They work steadily.

The case of *call* discussed here seems to be somewhat different from the classic cases of camouflaged forms while sharing some common traits with these forms. For one, it involves a slight expansion of the XP within a small clause complement, a shift that is very understandable in terms of the canonical paradigm of small clause phrases.

Furthermore, there is a common semantic-pragmatic reading that unites the reading of NP$_i$ *call* NP$_i$ V*ing* constructions and the counterfactual reading of NP$_i$ *call* NP$_i$ NP/AP small clause constructions in other varieties of English (such as

Walt Wolfram calls himself a linguist.) This semantic-pragmatic commonality, in fact, seems to contribute a great deal to the camouflaging, since it provides a ready semantic reading for an analogical syntactic expansion that might seem obtrusive otherwise. In other words, the common semantic-pragmatic counterfactual reading operates as a distractor for the syntactic extension.

In the limited descriptions of AAVE camouflaging offered thus far, it is the syntactic similarity that disguises the semantic uniqueness of a form. There seems adequate reason to conclude that semantic-pragmatic similarity may just as easily help disguise reasonable syntactic extensions such as this one, or at least provide an impetus for a kind of syntactic editing that allows these constructions to pass through the acrolect filter without much sociolinguistic fanfare.

Our discussion of camouflaging here shows that it is not as unilateral and unidimensional as set forth in previous discussions. There are, in fact, several different dimensions that need to be recognized with respect to camouflaged forms. As noted above, the basis of camouflaging may be syntactic, in which case a syntactic similarity disguises a unique semantic-pragmatic function, as in the classic cases offered by Spears (1982) and Baugh (1984), or the basis may be semantic-pragmatic, in which case a common semantic-pragmatic reading disguises a syntactic difference, as in the case of NP$_i$ *call* NP$_i$ V*ing*. The generalization of *ain't* for *didn't* in AAVE sentences such as (22a) by analogy with the model of (22b,c), where *ain't* corresponds to *have+not* (22b) or be+*not* (22c), respectively, seems to be another case of semantic-pragmatic commonality disguising syntactic expansion in AAVE. In this case, however, the distractor is a nonstandard rather than a standard form.

(22) (a) She *ain't* go to the store.
        (b) She *ain't* got none.
        (c) She *ain't* here now.

There may also be directional changes in camouflaging. For example, the change leading to the obscured differences may derive from expansion of an earlier, more restricted, construction, or it may be the result of retraction from a more expansive pattern. *Call* is appropriately classified as an expansion since it appears to fill out the XP small clause paradigm. On the other hand, I would hypothesize a form such as *tell say* illustrated from the Natalie Maynor interview in (23) as a case of retraction from a proto-form of serial verbs drastically reduced in decreolization (Holm 1988:185).

(23) ... once a white lady got up and **told** us **said**, "Now y'all colored people," she **say**, "I'm getting up to tell y'all that the government got something going," **say**, "and if you don't mind losing your home when you die, your peoples won't have nothing. But I want to let you know, hold your home." **Say**, "When they want to renew your home, don't do it."
       (Tape 4A: American English Speech Recording Collection, The Center for Applied Linguistics; 80+ native African-American female, rural Mississippi, courtesy of Natalie Maynor)

While it may be reasonable to posit a creole base for the development of *say* use as a complementizer in AAVE, it is untenable to posit NP$_i$ *call* NP$_i$ V*ing* from this same source; participles are more likely a product of post-creole development and expansion.

Finally, there may be differences in the social marking of camouflaged forms. NP$_i$ *call* NP$_i$ V*ing* is not socially marked. In fact, this construction has been documented among African-Americans who otherwise avoid any use of the traditionally stigmatized forms of AAVE (see example 8d above). Camouflaging thus might occur based on either a Standard English or a vernacular model. The logical possibilities in terms of the different dimensions of camouflaging are summarized in the figure below:

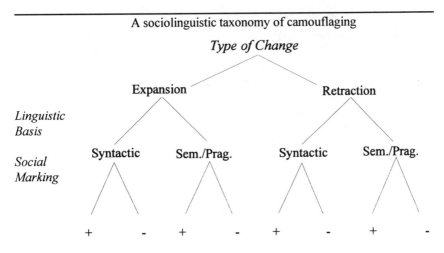

A sociolinguistic taxonomy of camouflaging

The camouflaging of dialect forms may derive from several different sources and wear several types of sociolinguistic masks. Furthermore, explanations for camouflaging involve an appeal to structural, functional, and sociolinguistic bases, showing a tender balance between language organization and language behavior. In this respect, our discussion of the bases of camouflaging with respect to NP$_i$ *call* NP$_i$ V*ing* is a modest start toward understanding the authentic sociolinguistic nature and role of this phenomenon.

CONCLUSION

We have seen that there are a number of different levels of language knowledge that must be considered in assessing the status of a dialect form. While the simple, anecdotal observation of forms across dialects is certainly one of these levels, cross-dialect knowledge goes considerably beyond that point. Questions of grammaticality, productivity, and semantic-pragmatic interpretation must all be a part of the assessment process. But these questions need not simply be matters of conjecture and speculation. As seen in our discussion of NP$_i$ *call* NP$_i$ V*ing*, testable hypotheses can be made explicit and empirical evidence appealed to in order to confirm or disconfirm these hypotheses. In this respect, I have presented my claim, my evidence, my argument, my conclusion, and my explanation. I am ready to argue about the dialect status of this form, but I demand more than anecdotes as evidence. Indeed, dialectology has much to gain and nothing to lose from paying rigorous attention to the nature of evidence and principled argumentation in the cross-dialectal consideration of forms.

NOTE

I am thankful to Guy Bailey, Patricia Cukor-Avila, Ralph W. Fasold, Barbara Fennell, Joan Hall, Bill Reynolds, and Natalie Schilling-Estes for discussions in the preparation of this article. I am also grateful to Bill Reynolds for replicating some of my structured elicitation sets in Philadelphia.

APPENDIX: Questionnaire on *Call*

I am interested in understanding how sentences such as *They call themselves going to school* or *She calls herself combing her hair* are used and interpreted in some dialects. I would appreciate it if you could answer the following questions about this form.

Have you ever heard anyone use this expression?   ___Yes ___No
Would you ever use this expression yourself?   ___Yes ___No

Think of three different ways **you** might complete the following sentences.
a. He calls himself . . .
     1.
     2.
     3.

Suppose a person said, "He calls himself acting bad." Would acting bad be considered something positive or negative?

Suppose a person said, "He calls himself acting foolish." Would acting foolish be considered something good or bad?

Suppose somebody said, "She calls herself combing her hair." How would her hair look?

Suppose somebody said, "He calls himself dressing." How would he be dressing?
Suppose a little child was just beginning to walk, and his proud mother wanted to think that he was walking even though he wasn't. Choose just one of the sentences to describe what might be said. Remember, you can only choose one sentence for the description.
    1. Look at that! He calls himself walking.
    2. Look at that! She calls him walking.

Suppose that Melinda, who is a very poor judge of dancing, thinks that people on the dance floor are dancing great when they are actually not dancing well at all. Choose just one of the following sentences to describe this situation. Remember, you can only choose one sentence for the description.
    1. Melinda calls them dancing.
    2. They call themselves dancing.

Suppose a woman who has a dog would like to think that he is listening to her when, in fact, he is not listening at all. Choose one of the following sentences to describe this situation. Remember, you can only choose one sentence.
    1. Look at that, he calls himself listening.
    2. Look at that, she calls him listening.

Suppose you were minding your own business eating your lunch. A friend comes in and says to you, "What do you call yourself doing?" What would you say to the friend? Use "I call myself . . ." in your answer, even if you don't normally use it in your speech.

Understanding Birmingham
William Labov and Sharon Ash

This report is concerned with Southern English, in particular, the Southern vowel system that is the most prominent feature of its regional identification.[1] The focus will not simply be on how Southerners speak, but rather how they use and understand their own vowel system in performing the primary linguistic task: the coding and decoding of information. Though the inquiry begins with the problem of how others understand Southern speech, the major concern will be how Southerners understand themselves.

1. THE DIVERGENCE OF AMERICAN ENGLISH

The research we are drawing on here forms part of the continuing investigation at the Linguistics Laboratory at the University of Pennsylvania of the increasing diversity of American English. It begins with the main finding of our research, one that violates the most commonsense expectation of how language works and is supposed to work. In spite of the intense exposure of the American population to a national media with a convergent network standard of pronunciation, sound change continues actively in all urban dialects that have been studied, so that the local accents of Boston, New York, Philadelphia, Atlanta, Buffalo, Detroit, Chicago, and San Francisco are more different from each other than at any time in the past (Labov 1966, 1980b; Labov, Yaeger, and Steiner 1972; Laferriere 1977; Callary 1975; Eckert 1986, 1991b; Moonwomon 1987). Though the first findings dealt with sound change in Eastern cities, it is now clear that it is equally true of Northern, Western and Southern dialects. As Guy Bailey's research group has shown, many features of Southern States English (SSE) which were assumed to be the inheritance of the 19th century are actually a part of this ongoing diversification, recent creations of the 20th century (Bailey and Ross 1992).

1.1. Regional Patterns
The sound changes responsible for this diversity operate below the level of social awareness, as changes from below, but they do not produce an unlimited diversity of local patterns. Instead, we find broad regional patterns of similar structures, which advance in parallel directions under a few basic organizing principles. "The Three Dialects of English" (Labov 1991) shows how the major sound shifts in American English—and to some extent British English—can be organized into three different phonological patterns, operating under the same general linguistic principles, but moving in opposite directions. These are the Northern Cities Shift of the Northern dialect area, the Low Back Merger found generally in Canada and the West, and the Southern Shift, which will be the focus here.

1.2. The Cognitive Consequences of Linguistic Diversity

The concern of this report will not be the phonetic and phonological diversification itself, but rather its cognitive consequences. Most of the material will be drawn from the results of the research project on Cross Dialectal Comprehension at the Linguistics Laboratory at Penn (CDC). This research examined the capacities of speakers of various dialects to understand and interpret the advanced forms of other dialects that are undergoing transformation in directions opposite to their own. The three target cities that were first selected are Birmingham, exemplifying the Southern Shift, Chicago, a leading exponent of the Northern Cities Shift, and Philadelphia, a city that is basically Southern but is reversing some areas of phonology in the Northern direction. In this paper, we will examine the ability of local listeners of these three cities to decode and interpret advanced forms of Birmingham speech.

In a first approach to the development of a general theory of linguistic change, Weinreich, Labov, and Herzog argued that it had not yet been demonstrated that there was a loss of communicative efficiency in the course of language change in progress (1968). However, the first CDC studies showed that sound changes did in fact interfere with communication, as many 19th-century historical linguists had believed (Muller 1861; Whitney 1867). In a number of different experiments, speakers using advanced forms of new sound changes were understood worse by subjects from other regions than by fellow residents of their own cities. But it is also true that local subjects have difficulties similar to those of outsiders: the local advantage is surprisingly small in many cases, and local subjects did not do as well in the various experiments as we thought they would. Speakers and subjects were drawn from the same social groups, and in the experiments, people often failed to understand pronunciations that were common coin in their everyday life. We began to wonder if there was a defect in the experimental method—that perhaps we were failing to detect knowledge that people really had. The analysis of a second series of experiments with Birmingham subjects to be presented here will make some progress towards correcting that impression of incompetence. It will appear that subjects are not so far out of touch with their surroundings as we first thought and can draw upon the knowledge they have gained growing up in their own community.

2. PRINCIPLES AND PATTERNS OF CHAIN SHIFTING

Many of the sound changes that diversify American English involve consonants, particularly the vocalization of liquids and the devoicing of obstruents. But the most striking changes continue to be rotations and mergers in the stressed vowel systems. To understand these patterns, it is necessary to review the general principles that govern chain shifting.

Vowel movements are governed by three principles, which were first stated by Sweet (1888) but generalized for chain shifting in Labov, Yaeger, and Steiner (1972):

In chain shifts,
  I. Long or tense nuclei rise.
  II. Short or lax nuclei fall.
  III. Back nuclei move to the front.

When these principles operate in modern English, they follow principles of organization that are particular to the Germanic, Baltic, and Slavic languages. The phonological space in which sound changes operate is distinguished by peripheral and nonperipheral paths in both the front and back regions. Tense or long vowels rise along the peripheral path, and lax or short vowels fall along the nonperipheral path.[2]

Figure 1: Peripheral and nonperipheral paths in the phonological space of modern Germanic languages

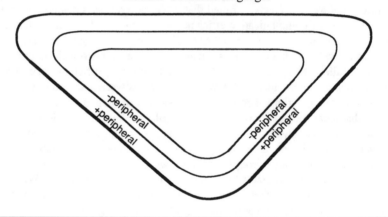

2.1. The Peripheral-Nonperipheral Contrast

It is now clear that the tense/lax phonetic distinction corresponding to location on the peripheral and nonperipheral tracks is sufficient to maintain a distinction between vowels and prevent merger. But the perceptual correlates of this distinction are relatively weak. The phonetic distinction between a tense nucleus on the peripheral track and a lax nucleus along the nonperipheral track is hard for most people to hear without instrumental assistance; this includes phoneticians as well as lay speakers. Whereas most dialect atlases distinguish 16 levels of height, they register only 3 distinctions along the front-back dimension. The four levels of height distinguished by the symbols [i, e, ɛ, æ] can each be amplified by a raising and lowering diacritic (subscript periods or up-arrows for raising, cedillas, subscript commas or down-arrows for lowering). In atlases we sometimes see these diacritics doubled or parenthesized, indicating intermediate degrees of raising and lowering. On the other hand, three degrees of fronting and backing are indicated by such symbols as [e, з, ɔ]; when these are modified by fronting or backing diacritics, they usually indicate a discrete shift from front to center or back. Thus [ö] is a front [o], [ü] is a front [u], and [ʉ] is a central [u]. The + and - subscripts permitted by IPA for advancement and retraction are rarely applied; when they are applied, they are applied primarily to low vowels.

Our studies of Southern States vowel systems show a radical difference between production and perception. The distinction between peripheral and nonperipheral location plays a crucial role in controlling the phonetic organization of the Southern Shift from a productive viewpoint. But from a perceptual view, moderately large differences along the F2, front-back, or the peripherality dimension may be disregarded by listeners who are attempting to assign phonemic status to a given sound.

2.2. The Initial Positions for Modern Changes in Progress

For a comparative view of the various sound changes now taking place in the stressed vowel systems of American English, we need a starting point that is neutral, relative to all of them. The base that we need must incorporate the output of the Great Vowel Shift, which was completed for all American English, with full diphthongization of ME ī and ū.[3] In addition, it must register the diphthongization of the long high and mid vowels. Though in many dialects, the nuclei of these vowels are still located on the peripheral track, this diphthongization sets the stage for the mechanism of the Southern Shift.[4] The base must also preserve all distinctions that appear to have been maintained in the period of original settlement: long and short open o, open and closed o before /r/, short and long distinctions before liquids and nasals, and front short vowels before intervocalic /r/. It must maintain the distinction between the back /uw/ that is the output of the Great Vowel Shift and the fronted or diphthongal /iw/ that combines the reflexes of the ME diphthong **ew** and French-derived **ui**. Short /o/, even when unrounded to [ɑ], will be distinct from long /ah/ in *father, calm*, and *pa*. On the other hand, it must not show any distinctions among the high and mid short vowels /i, e, u, ʌ/ before syllable final /r/. We will refer to this representation as the *initial position* of the American English vowel system, displayed in table 1.

Table 1: The initial positions of American English vowels

Short		Front Upgliding		Back Upgliding		Ingliding	
i	u	iy		iw	uw	ih	uh
e	ʌ	ey	oy		ow	eh	oh/ɔh
æ	o		ay		aw	æh	ah

The units in table 1 will be cited in the slash notation, i.e., /i, e, u/, but they are not to be understood as representing phonemes of any given dialect. Rather they represent *word classes*, the lexical set defined by the occurrence of a particular vowel in each member of the set. The description of changes in progress which follows requires the use of this diachronic unit as the point of reference for synchronic description. The word class /i/ is the set of current English words that contain the historical reflexes of ME short **i** plus all the words that have since joined that class and share a common history with it: not only *bit, ship, written*, etc., but also *kid* and *skit*. Our studies of the Birmingham dialect will show that all of these short /i/ words display a common phonetic development, the shift of the lax short [ɪ] to a tense ingliding [i:ə]. All vowels involved in change in progress will be seen to have departed in one way or another from their initial positions indicated by table 1, following the general principles of chain shifting, and frequently locked into patterns of correlated changes with other vowels. Vowels that remain in the initial position will, as a rule, be identified as *stable vowels* in that dialect, though in the course of a century or so, vowels can also move from the initial position to a new position and remain stable there.[5] Stable vowels normally show a globular distribution around their means; vowels involved in change in progress usually show long elliptical distributions with a long axis in the direction of the change. Those tokens located near the extreme end of the ellipse, in the direction that the change is progressing, will be called *advanced vowels*.

2.3. The Southern Shift

There are two major patterns of correlated vowel shifts found in modern English vowel systems: the Southern Shift and the Northern Cities Shift. The first of these, the focus of attention here, is the dominant form of chain shifting throughout the English speaking world.[6] The Southern Shift is essentially a continuation of the Great Vowel Shift, following the general principles of chain shifting in a pattern that duplicates many of the 16th-century movements. Yet it does not repeat the Great Vowel Shift, since the initial position of the vowel system now shows the upgliding diphthongs /iy, ey, uw, ow/ in place of the Early Modern English long monophthongs /i:, e:, o:, u:/. The unidirectional principles of vowel shifting produce the patterns of figure 2.

Figure 2: Schematic diagram of the Southern Shift

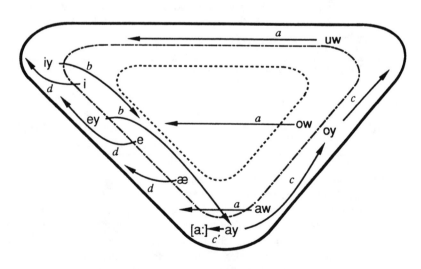

The Southern Shift of figure 2 is composed of four subsets of vowel movements, which include both chain shifts and parallel shifts. The first component is *Vw fronting*; this appears to be the oldest and the most widespread aspect of the Southern Shift. It consists of the parallel fronting of the nuclei of the back upgliding long vowels /uw/, /ow/ and /aw/, marked *a* on figure 2. In some versions of the Southern Shift, the nuclei of /uw/ and /ow/ are unrounded, while in others, they retain their rounded character. In some versions, the glide target remains [u], while in others, it is fronted from [u] to [ü]. In some dialects, /ow/ is lowered more than fronted, so that it forms a chain shift with /aw/ (as in London English; see Labov, Yaeger, and Steiner 1972; Labov 1991). In a wide range of Southern Shift dialects, including the Southern States, short /u/ is fronted along with /uw/, but the short vowel that corresponds most closely to the nucleus of /ow/, /ʌ/, is not included in this sound shift.[7]

The second component of the Southern Shift is the *Vy chain shift* that develops further the nucleus-glide differentiation of the tense mid vowels following the Great Vowel Shift. The lax nuclei of the front upgliding diphthongs /iy/ and /ey/ fall along the nonperipheral track on trajectories marked *b* on figure 2. At the bottom of this series is the position occupied by /ay/, the reflex of ME ī produced by the Great Vowel Shift. One version of the Southern Shift follows the path *c*: the nucleus of /ay/ becomes tense, and continues the chain shift, moving up and to the back along the peripheral track. The nucleus of /oy/ moves at the same time to high position along the back peripheral path. This tensing and raising of /ay/ and /oy/ is the most common version of the Vy shift; it is found in Southern England, Australia, Philadelphia, and the Outer Banks of North Carolina. The alternate path, marked *c′*, is found primarily in the Southern United States: /ay/ is monophthongized and slightly fronted.[8] This monophthongization removes /ay/ from the path of /ey/ as effectively as the shift to the back, and the nucleus of /ey/ can fall to the same degree of opening as the nucleus of /ay/ without becoming confused with it.

The third set of changes characteristic of the Southern Shift is *Vh raising*. This is a backing and raising of the low and mid ingliding vowels, parallel to the *c* component of the *Vy* chain shift, and is most frequent before /r/.[9] In combination with *Vw fronting,* this forms the most common types of chain shifting, discussed in Martinet (1955), found throughout Western Europe. We frequently find /ah/ → /oh/ → [uə] as well as /ahr/→ /ohr/ → /uhr/ and /ay/→ /oy/→ [uy]. But in the Southern Shift, the fronting and monophthongization of /ay/ at *c′* bleeds the *c* chain shift. Furthermore, the "long open o" class that is ingliding in other dialects shows a back upglide in many areas of the Southern States, and the nucleus remains in about the same position as the nucleus of short open o.[10]

The fourth set of vowel shifts characteristic of the Southern Shift is *short vowel tensing:* a movement of the short vowels in the opposite direction from the Vy shift. While the lax nuclei of /iy/ and /ey/ fall along the nonperipheral track, the short nuclei /i, e, æ/ become tense; that is, they move to the peripheral track and shift upwards towards the peripheral high and mid positions formerly occupied by the long vowels, along the paths marked *d* on figure 2.[11] In most other versions of the Southern Shift (Southern England, Australia, South Africa) these vowels remain short; in the Southern States, they are lengthened and develop inglides.[12] When they do so, they become members of the ingliding set /ih, eh, æh/ of table 1 and become identified with the small vowel classes of *idea, yeah,* and *salve*; in non-rhotic dialects, they also merge with the large vowel classes of *beer* and *bear.*

The central feature of this complex set of changes is the Vy shift, the lowering of the lax nuclei of /iy/ and /ey/. Accordingly, the Southern Shift is most advanced today in those regions where the Great Vowel Shift has developed to its fullest extent. The initiating position for the modern Southern Shift shows the reflexes of ME ē and æ as diphthongs /iy/ and /ey/ with a lax nucleus, and ME ī as an /ay/ with a low central nucleus. In Great Britain, the modern Southern Shift reaches its most extreme form in Southern England: London, Birmingham, Berkshire and the home counties, Norfolk, Essex, Kent and Southampton. Outside of Great Britain, the Southern Shift is the organizing force in the vowel systems of South Africa, Australia and New Zealand. In the United States, the Southern Shift dominates the vowel systems of the dialect areas identified by Kurath and McDavid as the Upper and Lower South, the Gulf States, eastern and central Texas, and the South Midland, but affects Philadelphia and many areas of the North Midland as well (Labov 1991).

The main focus of this paper will be on the vowel system of Birmingham, Alabama. Before displaying the Southern Shift in its Birmingham version, it may be helpful to place the Birmingham system in a wider perspective by presenting two other exemplars of this general pattern in widely separated areas of the Southern States, in fact, from the two geographic endpoints of the region that could be considered the Southern United States. Figure 3 shows the vowel system of Monty O'Neil, a shrimp-boat captain from Wanchese, in the Outer Banks of North Carolina, interviewed in 1969 at the age of 31. As in all of the diagrams to follow, this is a display of the formant positions of the nuclei of stressed vowels, using a linear scale of F2 on the horizontal axis and F1 on the vertical axis. Some vowel classes are shown with mean values only, in small bold circles. Other vowel classes are displayed with individual vowels surrounded by ellipses, with the words labeled for the most advanced and least advanced tokens.

The vowel system of Monty O'Neil shows Vw fronting of /uw/, /ow/ and /aw/ to a center or front of center position. As usual, /uw/ is in advance of /ow/. The glide targets, not shown here, are directed frontward, towards the location of [ü], at an F2 of about 1900 Hz. The Vy shift locates nuclei of /iy/ and /ey/ in non-peripheral position; they show a moderate degree of lowering. The nucleus of /ay/ has moved along the path *c* of figure 2 and ranges from low back to mid back position,[13] while /oy/ has moved up to high position. The parallel chain shifts /ah/ → /oh/ and /ahr/ → /ohr/ are both in evidence.

Short vowel tensing in the Outer Banks shows the characteristic reversal of position relative to the originally long vowels /iy/ and /ey/. In figure 3, /i/ is in high front position, and /e/ in mid front position. These vowels begin at the position of cardinal [i] and [e] and glide towards the center. The most extreme forms are found in monosyllabic words with initial velars and palatals, *kids* and *ship,* while the least extreme forms are polysyllables such as *seven.*

Figure 3: The Southern Shift in the vowel system of Monty O'Neil, 31, Wanchese, N.C. [1969]

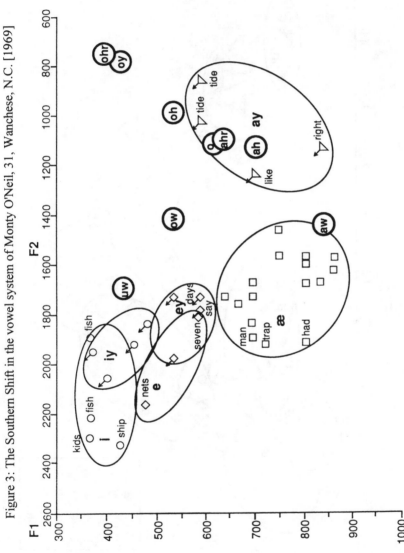

Figure 4: The Southern Shift in the vowel system of Jerry Thrasher, 20, Leakey, Texas [1969]

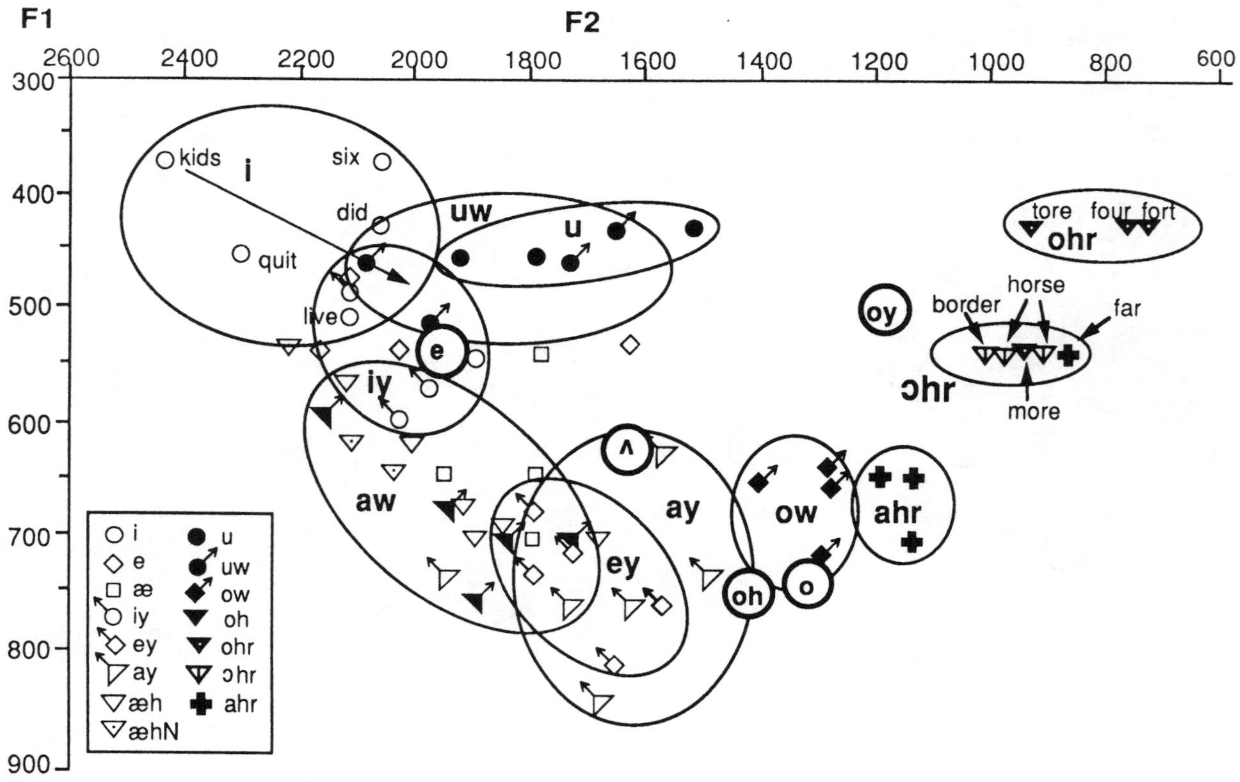

At the western end of the Southern States is Leakey, Texas, a small town in the south central portion of the state. Figure 4 shows the vowel system of Jerry Thrasher from Leakey, who was interviewed in 1969 at the age of 20. We observe that Vw fronting carries /uw/ and /u/ to a high front position but that the nucleus of /ow/ has moved down to a low back nonperipheral position.[14] In the Vy chain shift, /iy/ and /ey/ have fallen along the nonperipheral track to a further extent than we observed in figure 3. The nuclei of /ey/ have reached low central position, as low as any vowel in the system, and overlap completely the range of /ay/, which is consistently monophthongal. Since /ay/ has not moved up, but follows path c' of figure 2, it is not surprising that /oy/ remains in mid back position. On the other hand, Vh raising in the Southern Shift appears in the back chain shift of /ahr/ → /ɔhr/ → /ohr/ → [uÿ].[15]

The short vowel tensing in figure 4 shows the characteristic reversal in relation to the nuclei of the long vowels. /i/ is in high front position; again, the most extreme token shows an initial velar in the same word: *kids.* The inglide of this token is indicated by a solid arrow. The less fronted forms of /i/ are all forms that show expected centralization through their phonetic environment: a following consonant cluster (*six*), auxiliary status (*did*), and an initial /l/ (*live*).

3. THE BIRMINGHAM VOWEL SYSTEM

Birmingham, Alabama, was selected as one of the three target cities for the CDC project, along with Philadelphia and Chicago. As a first step in the CDC experiment, Ash carried out a series of interviews with youth in city-oriented universities, where a high percentage of locally raised students are to be found. In Birmingham, the local university selected was the University of Alabama at Birmingham (UAB).[16] Ash interviewed 8 students at UAB between Feb. 29 and March 2, 1988.[17] In December 1990, she interviewed 7 students at Fultondale High School, in a white, lower-middle-class area.

When studies of dialects are carried out at major nationally oriented universities like Yale, Cornell, Berkeley, or the University of Chicago, the results are bound to be confusing and reinforce the common stereotype that local dialects are weakening and disappearing. At such universities the local students are a minority and are usually oriented towards national norms in occupational goals and linguistic behavior. This is not the case at city universities where the majority of students are from local neighborhoods, look for jobs in local areas, and remain in the city. Furthermore, at city universities many students are from upwardly mobile families and are often the first generation to get a college education. They represent that stratum of the upper working class and lower middle class which is in the forefront of linguistic change in progress, the culturally dominant group of *local* society.

As noted above, the Birmingham subjects came from the University of Alabama at Birmingham. In Chicago, we selected the University of Illinois at Chicago Circle. And in Philadelphia, we drew subjects from Spring Garden College, Drexel University, and from Temple University. In the second series of CDC experiments, we drew subjects from local high schools in Birmingham and Chicago who supplied students to these universities: Fultondale High School for Birmingham and Mother Guerin High School for Chicago.

Let us now consider the vowel systems of two Birmingham speakers drawn from this population who provided the stimuli for the CDC experiments: Wendy P. and Melanie O., who were 18 and 24 respectively when they were interviewed at UAB by Ash in 1988. Figure 5 shows the mean formant positions for the stressed vowel nuclei of Wendy P.[18] The dashed arrows show the direction and extent of the sound changes that make up the Southern Shift, lettered in conformity with figure 2. The starting point of the arrows are the approximate phonetic positions of English vowels indicated by the notation of table 1, the output of the Great Vowel Shift and 17th–18th century diphthongization of the long vowels, the initiating positions for modern sound changes. Vw fronting, *a*, is found in an extreme form: /uw, u, ow, aw/ have all reached front nonperipheral position, and /aw/ has begun the rise to mid position parallel with /æ/, the next step in the Southern Shift. The Vy chain shift, *b*, has moved /ey/ downward to a low front nonperipheral position; /iy/ is lowered to a lesser degree behind it. The third member of the Vy series, /ay/ follows the path *c'*: it is generally monophthongal, but not notably fronted. In contrast, /oy/ has shifted to high position. The /ahr/ → /ohr/ chain shift marked *c* follows the same pattern as in Texas. Note that the mean of /ɔhr/ is distinctly lower and more central than /ohr/. Finally, short vowel tensing, *d* is quite active: /i/ and /e/ move up to peripheral high and mid positions, and the mean of /æ/ moves to a peripheral upper low position as well. Both /i/ and /e/ show the reversal of nucleus position with /iy/ and /ey/ which characterizes the most advanced forms of the Southern Shift, more extreme in the case of /e/. Furthermore, the mean of /e/ is quite close to the mean of /i/; the consequences of this encroachment will be seen below.

The second Birmingham speaker, Melanie O., shows the more conservative system of figure 6.[19] Vw fronting is more moderate, except for /aw/, which is in low front peripheral position. The Vy chain shift has not operated to move the nuclei of /iy/ and /ey/ to a nonperipheral position, although /ey/ has shifted downward to low position. As in figure 5 for Wendy P., /ay/ remains in low central position, and again, /oy/ is raised to high position, without any pressure from an upward movement of /ay/. Finally, we see that /i/ and /e/ are both shifted upward to positions that are relatively higher than /iy/ and /ey/, without moving to the peripheral track. Thus the Southern Shift reversal of the relative heights of /e/ and /ey/ are present but not the reversal of peripherality. This is characteristic of more conservative realizations of the Southern Shift.

Figure 7 shows the mean vowel positions of Alison K., a high school student from Fultondale, interviewed by Ash at the age of 16 in 1990.[20] Here we see a display of the Southern Shift as advanced as, and in some respects more extreme than, that of Wendy P.[21] Vw fronting *a* has operated on /uw, u, ow, aw/. Of these the most advanced element is /uw/, which is in high front peripheral position, as front as /i/. The Vy chain shift *b*, has affected both /iy/ and /ey/, and has lowered /ey/ to a low central position, slightly front of center. As also shown in figure 7, /ay/ remains low central and has become completely monophthongal; /ahr/ has shifted to mid back position, but /ohr/ shows no corresponding upward movement. Finally, we see the tensing of the short vowels; in *d* there is a clear shift of /i/ and /e/ to the peripheral track. Though /e/ does not show as much raising as in figure 5, /i/ has moved upward to high front position.

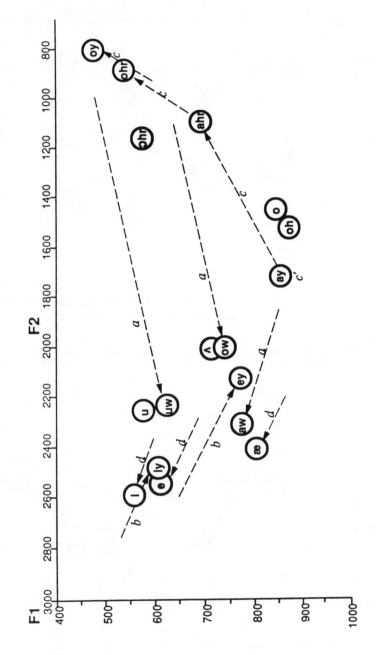

Figure 5: Mean formant positions of nuclei of stressed vowels of Wendy P., 18, UAB, Birmingham [1988]

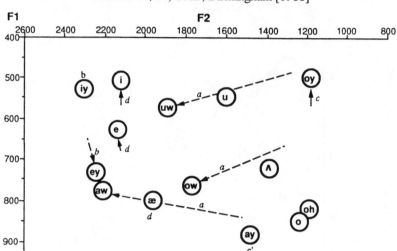

Figure 6: Mean formant positions of nuclei of stressed vowels of
Melanie O., 24, UAB, Birmingham [1988]

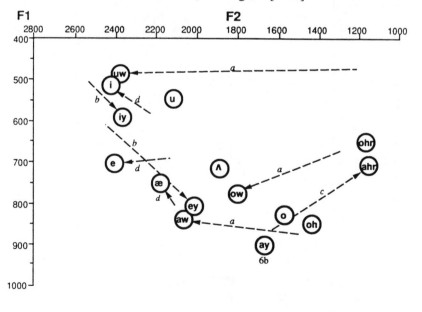

Figure 7: Mean formant positions of stressed vowels of Alison K., 16,
Fultondale H.S., Birmingham [1990]

The critical elements of the Southern Shift for cross-dialectal comprehension are the reversal of the positions of the nuclei of the front short and long vowels. Any occurrence of /i/ as [iə] and /e/ as [eə] may lead to misunderstanding when, for one reason or another, the glide is shortened or eliminated: in rapid speech, in polysyllables, or before consonants that tend to absorb glides. It is therefore important to examine the /i/ and /e/ distributions more closely in order to determine the range of variation and to see to what extent these vowels consistently reverse the expected relations with /iy/ and /ey/. In all cases, there are some phonetic environments that act uniformly: initial velars, following palatals and apicals lead to higher and fronter nuclei, while following velars and labials tend to produce lower and more central vowels. These effects are largely the constant effects of co-articulation. The crucial factors for studying change in progress are those that affect the time available for the vowel to reach its target. These are the degree of stress (reflected in greater or lesser duration) and the presence of following syllables or following consonant clusters which shorten the nucleus and prevent it from reaching its most extreme position. Function words tend to exhibit reduced stress and shorter durations. Thus if sound change is moving a vowel towards a high front position, polysyllables and function words will cluster in a low central position; if the vowel is moving towards the center, they will be left in peripheral position.

Figures 8a–d show the detailed structure of the Vy chain shift and short vowel tensing in the vowel system of Wendy P. These diagrams label each word in the distribution, display the mean values, and show the direction of any glides that are actually realized in the acoustic signal.[22] Figure 8a displays the relations of /i/ and /iy/, showing how their relations are inverted from the initial position. The mean F1/F2 values are shown in bold circles and the main distributions of /i/ and /iy/ are enclosed in ellipses. Short /i/ nuclei are located with open circles, and /iy/ nuclei by solid circles. In addition, the /iy/ words are labeled with bold characters.

Since the presence of glides and their directions are essential elements in the dynamics of the Southern Shift, each vowel was examined acoustically and impressionistically for the presence and direction of glides. In figures 8a–c, front upglides towards [i] are indicated by arrows pointing to upper left, while arrows pointing to lower right indicate inglides towards schwa. The absence of an arrow attached to any symbol indicates a monophthongal pronunciation.

Two subsets in the /i/ word class are not included in the calculation of the means in figures 8a. At upper right are three pronunciations of the word *live* (in small caps) all with F2 values markedly lower than the rest of the distribution.[23] At lower right are three /i/ words before velar nasals (underlined); these are shifted outside of the normal distribution and are best classified as allophones of /æy/.

Differences in the mean values of the /i/ and /iy/ formants are shown in the table at lower left: The F1 difference of -124 Hertz and the F2 difference of 274 Hz, indicating a reversal of the relative positions of /i/ and /iy/ in the initial position, are both significant (p < .005). But the distribution of the tokens shows that the reversal of /i/ and /iy/ is greater than indicated by these figures. Within the /i/ ellipse, simple monosyllables like *kid* and *hit* occur at the most advanced position at upper left, some with distinct inglides. The less advanced forms at the lower right of the ellipse, lower and more central, consist entirely of words with complex codas and additional syllables (*sitting, system, didn't*).[24] The centralizing influence of a following liquid syllable, as in *middle*, is enough to place this word well within the /iy/ distribution. None of the less-advanced forms show phonetic inglides.

The /iy/ forms in figure 8a show the opposite tendency in the distribution of monosyllables and polysyllables. The most advanced forms are in the main distribution at lower right, where we find seven words with /iy/ with a simple coda and no following syllables (*neat, each, Denise, fifteen, eighteen*) and only two words with following syllables (*teenager, beatin'*). A smaller set of words remains in the high front position, enclosed by a smaller ellipse at upper left. These are all polysyllables (*reason, people, evenings*).[25] Thus it seems clear that in this realization of the Southern Shift, the main targets of /i/ and /iy/ are reversed and moving in opposite directions, while there is less differentiation in nuclei of shorter durations.[26] The main body of /iy/ words all have distinct front upglides, while two of the three less-advanced forms are monophthongal.

Figure 8b shows the corresponding situation for /e/ and /ey/. The /e/ tokens are indicated by open diamonds, the /ey/ tokens by solid diamonds, with the direction of glides again indicated by arrows. The reversal of the two vowels from the initial position is clear: there is no overlap in the distributions, and the means are significantly different along both dimensions. The /e/ nuclei show a wide elliptical range from front to back. At extreme left are words with a following front nasal (*entry, again, anything, N*); words with following complex codas (*end, best*) are shifted further back, and polysyllables even more so (*general, center, better*). Again, the effect of a following liquid syllable in *center* and *better* can move the token well outside the main distribution. About half of the more-advanced monosyllables show inglides, while none of the less-advanced forms do.[27] On the other hand, all of the /ey/ tokens show distinct front upglides.

The most advanced tokens of the /ey/ words, at lower right, are again monosyllables, but in this case, the least-advanced forms are also monosyllables, since the effect of a following voiceless consonant limits the lowering and backing of /ey/ (*hate, eight, State, make*).[28] Interestingly, the most extreme backing is found before nasal consonants, the reverse of the situation with /i/ and /e/, where F2 values before front nasals are generally higher than with other environments. In figure 8a, /iy/ before /n/ shows a parallel lowering, where three words with *teen* are among the most advanced. The effect of following nasal consonants in lowering words in the Vy class is apparently quite consistent in Birmingham, since we also find it in the most extreme tokens of other speakers.[29]

Figure 8c shows the detailed distribution of /ay/, /o/, and /oh/ for Wendy P. Again, arrows are used to indicate the glides that are phonetically realized. All /ay/ nuclei are indicated by an empty triangle pointing to upper left. Words that are completely monophthongal show no arrows; a weak or reduced glide (Thomas and Bailey 1991) is shown by a small arrow, and the normal front upglide by a full-sized arrow.[30] Nuclei in words in the short /o/ class are shown as bold squares; these do not normally show glides. Words in the /oh/ class are indicated by solid diamonds, with back upglides shown by arrows pointing to upper left, and inglides by arrows pointing to lower right. The overall distributions of /o/ and /oh/ are enclosed in ellipses, except for the two eccentric function words *got* and *gone*.

Figure 8a: Distributions of /i/ and /iy/ in the vowel system of Wendy P., Birmingham

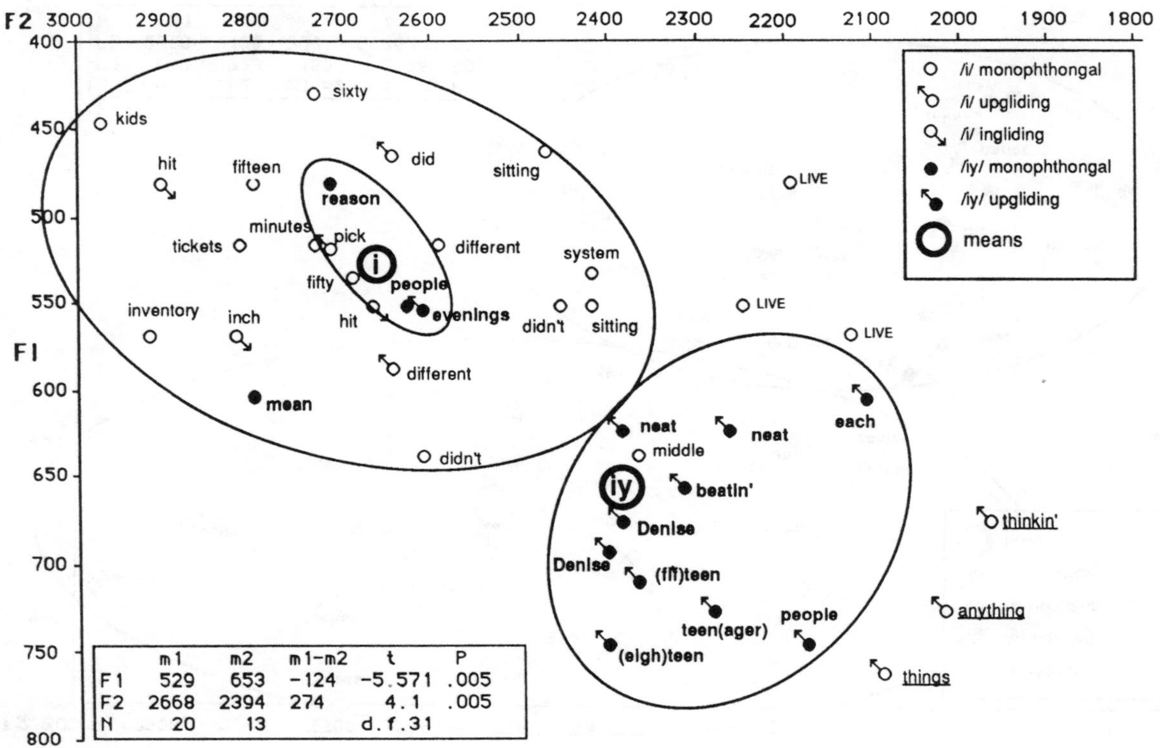

	m1	m2	m1-m2	t	P
F1	529	653	-124	-5.571	.005
F2	2668	2394	274	4.1	.005
N	20	13		d.f.31	

Figure 8b. Distributions of /e/ and /ey/ in the vowel system of Wendy P., Birmingham

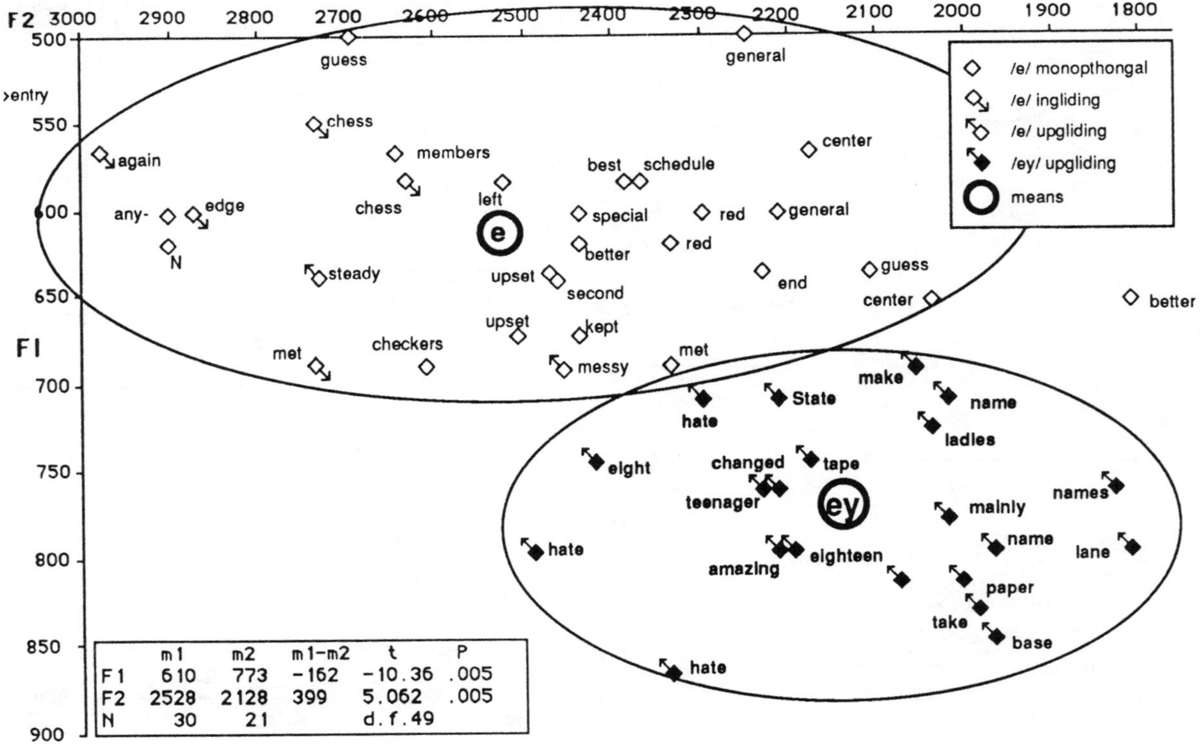

Figure 8c: Distributions of /ay, o, oh/ in the vowel system of Wendy P., Birmingham

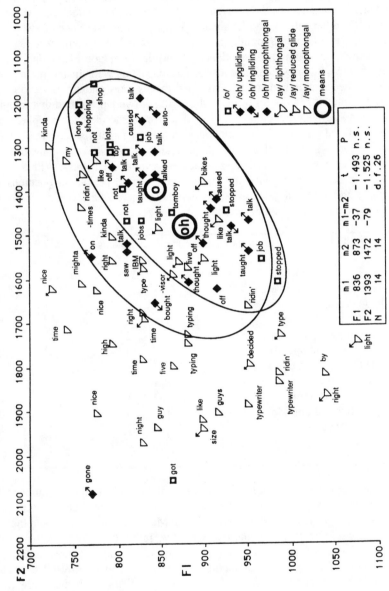

The overlapping distributions of these three vowels makes the presence of glides an essential condition for their distinctiveness. Whenever a distinct front upglide is present for /ay/, it will be differentiated from both /o/ and /oh/, but this is only true in 6 of the 36 /ay/ tokens; 9 more vowels show reduced glides. The crucial question is the distribution of these glides in relation to the overlapping areas of the nucleus. Table 2 shows the distribution of glides for /ay/ within and without the region of overlap with /o/ and /oh/, before voiceless consonants and elsewhere. The great majority of the full upglides are found before voiceless consonants, as is well established for Southern States dialects. Outside the region of overlap, we find mostly monophthongs before voiceless consonants as well. Inside the region of overlap, the situation is reversed, and 7 of 8 tokens show glides.[31] If we look more closely at the distribution of forms in the region of overlap, we find that full glides are associated with /ay/ before /k/ (*like, bikes*), closer to the back peripheral area, while reduced glides and monophthongs are more characteristic of /ay/ before /t/ (*light, right*), with higher F2 values. In general, most of the overlapping tokens are found in the more centralized areas associated with reduced stress. With full stress before voiceless consonants, the nuclei shift to more peripheral positions with stronger glides, yielding the distinctive allophones in low back position before /k/, and in low central position before /t/.

Table 2: Distribution of glides for the /ay/ tokens of Wendy P.

	Before voiceless consonants	*Elsewhere*
Outside the region of overlap with /o/ and /oh/		
monophthongs	8	9
reduced upglide	2	1
full front upglide	3	2
Within the region of overlap with /o/ and /oh/		
monophthongs	1	6
reduced upglide	4	3
front upglide	3	0
	21	21

The overlap of /o/ and /oh/ in the position of the nuclei is almost complete. The general understanding in the dialectology of the Southern States is that /oh/ is differentiated by its back upglide (Kurath and McDavid 1961) and would therefore most properly be shown as the phoneme /ow/ rather than the ingliding notation /oh/.[32] Fourteen of the 22 tokens of /oh/ show back upglides, 2 show inglides, and 7 are monophthongs. The monophthongs are not found in polysyllables but in simple stressed monosyllables: *off, saw, talk, talked, long.* Whether these vowels are distinguished from /o/ and monosyllabic /ay/, and how, remains to be seen.[33]

Figure 8d shows the distributions of tokens for the system as a whole.[34] Bold ellipses mark the front upgliding series. The front peripheral area is dominated by the more advanced distributions of the three short front vowels /i, e, æ/. The allophone of /æ/ before front nasals /m/ and /n/ (not shown in figure 8a) is located in a much higher position than the main distribution, as in many other dialects (Labov, Yaeger, and Steiner 1972). As noted above, there is considerable overlap of /i/ and /e/ and of /o/ and /oh/. The overlap of the nuclei of /æ/ and /ey/ is not a significant issue for comprehension, since as figure 8b shows, all /ey/ show distinct front upglides. The overlap of the nuclei of /uw/, /iy/, and /ey/ might seem to be easily resolved by the glides. However, the back upglide indicated by /uw, ow, aw/ is fronted to [ü] in many Southern dialects, including Birmingham, and it has been shown that the distinction between a [ü] glide and an [i] glide is not very reliable.[35] Even when differences based on glide direction operate distinctively in fully stressed, monosyllabic position, the overlap of nuclei may produce a loss of distinctiveness in less-stressed occurrences in polysyllables.

On figure 8d are located four tokens spoken by Wendy P. which appear as stimuli in the experiments on cross-dialectal comprehension to be discussed below.

Figure 9 shows a similar situation for Alison K. Individual vowels are shown for ten vowels—/i, e, æ, ey, ay, uw, ow, o, oy, aw/—and mean values for the rest. As the legend shows, the symbols used here are the same as those in figures 3 and 4, where the figures with arrows indicate the general word class of upgliding vowels, irrespective of whether a glide is realized phonetically. The reversal of the initial positions of /i/ and /iy/, /e/ and /ey/ are quite clear (only the mean value of /iy/ is shown). The most advanced tokens of /i/ are the monosyllables *king* and *gym*, while among the least advanced are the polysyllable *bigger*, function words *did* and *this*, and the word *sixth* with a three-consonant coda. Among the /e/ words, the frontest are monosyllables that end in nasals;[36] but among the /ey/ words, the lowest and most central words are two monosyllables ending in nasals, *main* and *same*.

For Alison K., the shift of /uw/ to high front position leads to a complete overlap of the positions of the nuclei of /uw/ and /i/. The /ay/ nuclei are in low central position, but some tokens are further back, overlapping with the nuclei of /o/ and /oh/, which show similar mean values. The nuclei of /aw/ are realized as [æ] and are well to the front of /ay/. The back chain shift before /r/ is evident in the mid back position of /ahr/, but /ohr/ remains in upper mid position, instead of appearing in high position as with Wendy P.

These three speakers illustrate the way in which the Southern Shift is implemented in the Birmingham speech community and the range of variation found among younger women speakers. The other 12 people interviewed by Ash in Birmingham in 1988 and 1990 showed patterns similar to these.

Figure 8d: Overlapping ranges in the vowel system of Wendy P., Birmingham, with Gating items

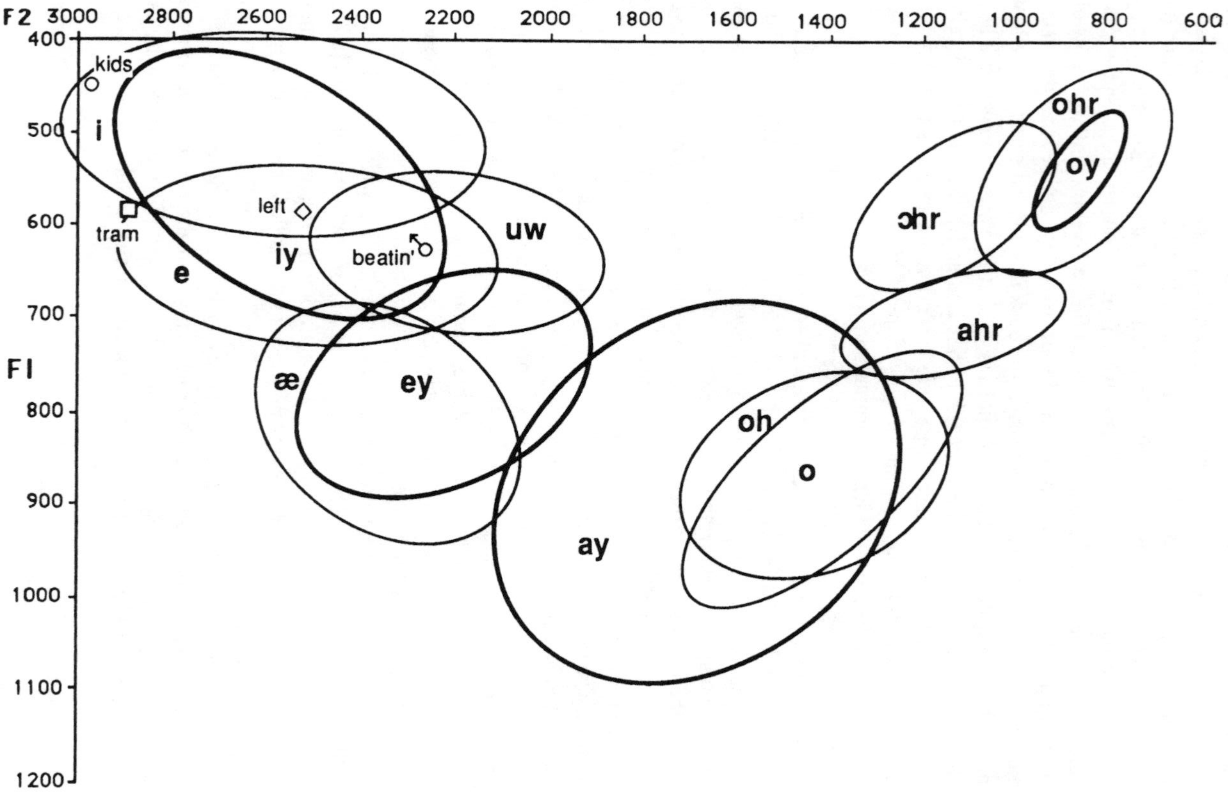

Figure 9: Vowel system of Alison K. with distributions of short front and front upgliding nuclei

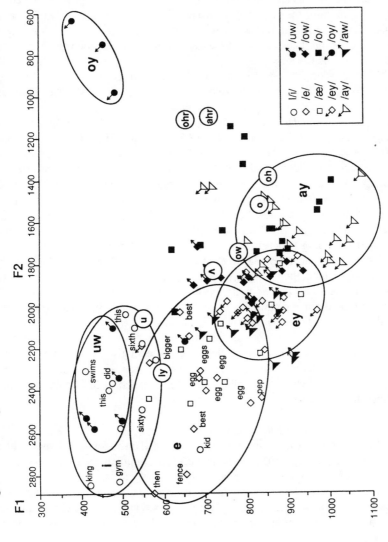

4. COMPREHENSION OF THE BIRMINGHAM VOWEL SYSTEM

We can now turn to the question of how people from Birmingham and elsewhere understand the vowel system outlined above: that is, how well do they assign these phonetic tokens to the correct phonemic categories in their interpretations of words, phrases, and sentences of the language. For this purpose we will draw upon the work on cross-dialectal comprehension—that is, the CDC project, which was designed to examine the cognitive correlates of the increasing diversity of American English dialects. In what follows we will be reporting the joint work of the research group as a whole: besides ourselves, Robin Sabino, Julie Roberts, Tom Veatch, Mark Karan, and Corey Miller.

The findings on the comprehension of Birmingham speech are drawn from three of the experimental approaches used by the CDC project. All three built upon stimuli drawn from recordings of speakers from Philadelphia, Chicago, and Birmingham. As noted above, we selected the most advanced exponents of the local changes in progress: young women from 16 to 25, upwardly mobile, from recently arrived ethnic groups, who were central figures in their local social networks but also connected to wider social networks by multiple links.[37] In these interviews we focused upon spontaneous narratives of personal experience, which have been found in the past to come closest to the vernacular of everyday speech. The first of the experimental approaches, the *Extended Decoding* series, will not be considered here in detail but provided the basic problem that the others addressed. In the Extended Decoding experiments, listeners were asked to repeat back, word for word, the text of narratives played to them in overlapping sections. Whenever they failed to understand, the passages were replayed as many times as they liked. There was no time pressure, and no writing tasks were involved. The results showed that even in these optimal conditions, there were many clearly pronounced words that could not be deciphered by listeners, even when the surrounding context seemed to provide all of the information needed to infer what was meant by the speaker. It appeared that when some listeners clearly identified a given vowel as a member of a word class different from the one intended, it was very difficult for them to change this identification to another one when it failed to fit into any reasonable interpretation.

4.1. Controlled Vowel Identification

This series of experiments was essentially a dialect-controlled replay of the Peterson and Barney (1952) experiment. The stimuli were recordings of two speakers from each target city reading a list of 14 words in the /k__d/ context: *kid, ked, cad, cod, cud, could, keyed, cade, cooed, code, cawed, kide, cowed, coid.*[38] Subjects heard randomized blocks of words—from only one dialect at a time—and were asked to identify the vowel by selecting the item from a fixed number of choices.

Figure 10 shows the overall rate of success for three groups of college students listening to the Birmingham productions of the 14 vowels.[39] The graph gives some idea of the difficulty that speakers of other dialects have in dealing with the phonology of Birmingham, even in the relatively formal, carefully articulated style of speech that is used in reading lists of words. The vertical axis represents the mean percent correct for subjects from the three target cities, and the horizontal axis shows the fourteen vowels. A wide range of variation appears. There is no problem for /iy/, short /i/, and /oy/, but the low vowels /ay, o, oh/ are close to the 50% success level, /æ/ and /aw/ are in the 60–70% range, and short /e/ is extremely low. The Birmingham subjects show a local advantage for all of the difficult items, but that advantage is surprisingly small. In particular, Birmingham listeners have the same type of problem with short /e/ that everyone else does. While three times as many Birmingham subjects identify it correctly as do subjects from Chicago and Philadelphia, the success rate in Birmingham is still only 25%.

Figure 10: Mean correct identifications of l4 Birmingham vowels in Controlled Vowel Identification experiment by listeners from three cities

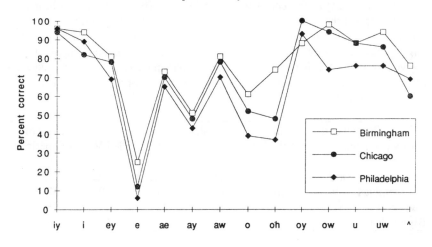

The factors responsible for the pattern of figure 10 will be apparent from the following array of phonetic transcriptions of six word-list items for the three cities.

	kid	*ked*	*cad*	*kide*	*cod*	*cawed*
Philadelphia	[kɪd]	[kɛd]	[kæd]	[kɑˈd]	[kɑd]	[ko̞əd]
Chicago	[kɪ̯d]	[kʌˤd]	[kɛˤəd]	[kaˈd]	[kad]	[kɒd]
Birmingham	[ki̯əd]	[ke̞əd]	[kæd]	[kad]	[kɒd]	[kɒɣd]

The word list pronunciation of *ked* by the two Birmingham speakers showed extreme raising and is shifted in the opposite direction from Chicago *ked*, which is highly centralized. For Wendy P. in particular, *ked* is very close to the level of *kid*. The overlap of /e/ and /i/ was observed quite clearly in figure 8d: in particular, /e/ after initial velars and palatals is raised well into the /i/ area.[40] The /ay/ diphthong was [kad] for one of the Birmingham speakers: monophthongal, somewhat fronted and relatively short; for the other speaker (Melanie O.), who used both monophthongs and diphthongs in spontaneous speech, the word list pronunciation was a clear diphthong. Birmingham *cod* is quite far back for both speakers, in low back rounded position, at the opposite end of the low vowel spectrum from Chicago, which has an extremely fronted short **o**. Birmingham *cawed* has a nucleus in the same low back position but with a following unrounded vocalized glide that sounds like an /l/ to listeners from other areas.

Table 3 shows the percent correct identification of the six vowels in the Controlled Vowel experiments. There was little difficulty in identifying /i/: the inglide in Birmingham [ki̯əd] prevented its identification with /iy/. But only 6% of the Philadelphia speakers and 12% of the Chicago speakers heard the Birmingham version of *ked* as [ke̯əd] as /ked/: the majority of the rest heard it as /kid/. The levels of identification of *cad* were relatively high and uniform for all three dialects, but *cod* again posed serious problems. Only a minority of Philadelphians heard Birmingham [kɒd] as the *cod* it was intended for. The rest tended to hear it as *cawed*, and half the listeners from Chicago showed the same tendency. A similar problem was found in identifying the Birmingham pronunciation of *cawed*. The back upglide resembles a vocalized /l/ for most speakers from Philadelphia (where the vocalization of /l/ is much more frequent than in Chicago). Thus the skewing of *ked*, *cod*, and *cawed* away from the phonetic norms of the other dialects led a majority of them to a wrong identification.

Table 3: Percent correct identification by listeners from the three target cities of six words pronounced by Birmingham speakers in the Controlled Vowel Experiment

	kid	ked	cad	kide	cod	cawed
Philadelphia	89	06	65	43	39	37
Chicago	82	12	70	48	52	48
Birmingham	94	25	73	51	61	74

In the case of *kide*, all three groups have a success rate of about 50%. Almost all of the correct judgments were for the diphthongal token of *kide* produced by Melanie O. The overwhelming majority of listeners, in Birmingham and elsewhere, failed to recognize the Birmingham production of *kide* as [kad] as the /kayd/ that it was intended for. Here Birmingham shows a local advantage over Chicago and Philadelphia in identifying controlled vowels, but the advantage is not a large one. For the [ke̯əd] pronunciation of *ked*, and the monophthongal pronunciation of *kide*, fully 75% of the Birmingham college students failed to recognize the production of their own classmates. The pronunciations that they were listening to were not at all strange to them; it should be emphasized that the speakers who produced the experimental stimuli were drawn from the same classes as those who listened to them at UAB. This is not an easy result to interpret, and it raises the principal problem that we will try to resolve in what follows: Birmingham listeners have almost as much difficulty as outsiders in understanding the most advanced forms of the local dialect pattern, even though it is the form of speech that they hear most often in everyday life.

The Controlled Vowel Identification experiment is not a test of listeners' ability to decipher the most advanced vowel tokens. What it does measure is listeners' ability to understand the relatively conservative vowels that are the product of careful style. Yet comprehension of these tokens was still quite limited. In the Gating experiments to be discussed below, subjects heard much more advanced tokens of the Southern Shift.

4.2. The Gating Experiments

The third series of experiments, the Gating Experiments, was designed to examine the contribution of variable amounts of contextual information to listeners' ability to decipher the phonemic category intended by the speaker of advanced tokens of sound changes in progress in the three target cities. The stimuli were extracted from the interviews carried out by Ash in 1988 and 1990 with speakers drawn from the target population. Extracts from spontaneous speech were digitized and entered into a design that allowed us to examine subjects' relative success in identifying the sounds with minimal context, a small amount of context, or an extended sentential context. Subjects first heard a block of 18 single syllables and were asked to write down for each one what word or syllable they thought was said. Then they heard the same 18 items in the context of a short phrase and were asked again to write down what they thought was said in a column adjacent to that of the first set of responses. Finally, a second answer sheet was distributed on which was printed the entire set of 18 sentences with a blank for the phrase context of the second part. The block of 18 items was played again, this time with the full sentence, and subjects were asked to fill in the blanks.

Two series of Gating experiments were carried out in the three target cities. This report will focus on the second series, involving not only subjects from local universities, but also from local high schools in Chicago and Birmingham. In this series, subjects were told for each block of 18 sentences that they would be hearing speakers from that target city. Appendix A gives all of the Birmingham items for the Gating Experiments along with the instructions for the administration of the study.

As a whole, the studies of Cross-Dialectal Comprehension were designed to discover the cognitive consequences of the continued development of local sound changes. The results of all experiments, including the Gating Experiments, show that the consequences for comprehension are severe. The rotation of vowels by the Northern Cities Shift and the Southern Shift create great difficulties in decoding, not only for isolated words, but to a surprising degree in contexts where the contribution of syntax, semantics, and pragmatics might easily have been adequate to overcome the effects of sound change. This finding echoed the initial results of the Extended Decoding Experiment. In every Gating series, a consistent local advantage was found, indicating that the changes in progress had made it harder for people from Chicago and Philadelphia to understand the dialect of Birmingham. But in many cases, this local advantage was small. Listeners from each target city had grave difficulties in understanding the advanced tokens from their own city, even when they were spoken by members of their own local group. The discussion of the Gating Experiments in Birmingham will show how the difficulty in comprehension is rooted in the specifics of the Southern Shift and how the phonology of Birmingham has become, to some extent, incomprehensible to those with contrasting phonological systems. At the same time, we will confront the problem of why the local advantage was not absolute—why local subjects had difficulty in identifying the speech that they heard around them every day. The first part of this analysis will compare the results for the three target cities, using the most comparable groups of subjects, the white college students (Birmingham, 29; Chicago, 60; Philadelphia, 30). The differences between these groups and the African-American, Hispanic, and Asian groups will be considered in section 4.2.3.

4.2.1. Comparison of Subjects from the Three Target Cities

Let us begin by examining the effect of the first component of the Southern Shift: the Vw fronting of back vowels. Item 1 of Gating series II involved the fronting of /uw/ in *group*:[41]

(1) If you want to see *a diversified* [gre$_\perp^\text{ü}$p], sit in the UAB cafeteria.

This sentence was spoken by Melanie O., whose mean formant positions for stressed vowels are shown in figure 6. In that display, the mean of her fronted /uw/ is fronted and lowered to a lower high or upper mid position. Under the influence of the initial obstruent-liquid onset of *group*, the nucleus falls to the lowest point of the distribution, since such onsets have a very strong effect in lowering F1 and F2 (Labov, Yaeger and Steiner 1972, ch. 3; Labov 1994). The glide is also fronted to the position of [ü]. As a result, the vowel in isolation is assigned by most listeners to /ey/, transcribed as *grape, grade, great,* and *grey.* Figure 11a shows the percent correct in word, phrase, and sentence context for white college students from Philadelphia, Chicago, and Birmingham.[42] The local advantage of Birmingham is clear. None of the out-of-state judges heard the token correctly in word context, but 28% of the Birmingham speakers did. In phrase context, 90% of the local judges identified the word *group* correctly, but less than half of the nonlocal judges did. In the sentence context, none of the local judges made an error, but almost 20% of the nonlocal judges did. This pattern is typical of the results in general. If we compare the Controlled Vowel Identification results and the word context results of the Gating experiments to the phrase and sentence context of the Gating experiments, it appears that the greatest local advantage is not absolute identification out of context but rather the ability to use a limited context to reach a correct conclusion.

In figure 11a, Chicago and Philadelphia appear to be equally matched in their ability to identify the fronted /uw/ in *group*. If we turn to the converse view and examine the tendency to misidentify /uw/ as /ey/, a different picture emerges. Figure 11b shows that in the word context almost all of the listeners from Philadelphia and Chicago made this error but almost half of the local listeners did not. In the phrase context, Chicago and Philadelphia are sharply differentiated: 43% of the Chicago listeners persisted in hearing fronted /uw/ as /ey/ in the phrase context.

Figure 11a: Percent correct identification of fronted and lowered /uw/
in *diversified GROUP* by target city

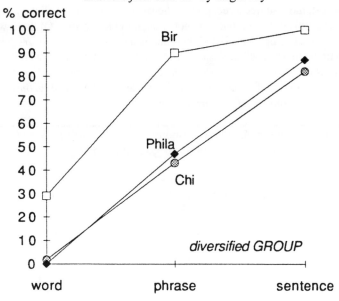

Figure 11b: Percent identification as /ey/ of fronted and lowered /uw/
in *diversified GROUP* by target city

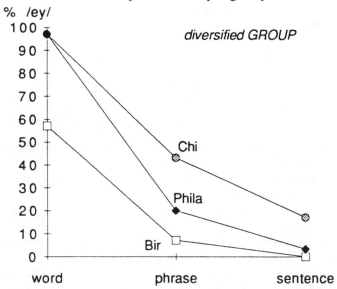

Table 4 is a breakdown of these persistent errors. Of the 60 subjects, 56 heard /ey/ in the word context; of these, ⅔ were the word *great* and ⅓ *grape*. In the phrase context, most subjects recognized the word *diversified.* In slightly more than half the cases, this context alone was not enough to yield *group.* Of those who first wrote *great,* 4 gave up, 7 persisted with the meaningless phrase *diversified great,* 4 shifted to the more sensible *diversified grade,* 4 others came up with the slightly less likely *diversified grain* or *diversified grape,* and almost half recorded the correct word. In the full context of the sentence, the word *group* becomes inescapable, and almost everyone hears it that way.

Table 4: Word and phrase responses for *a diversified GROUP*
of Chicago white college students [n=60]

Word					*Phrase*					
	great	grape	grave	gray	grade	grain	other	0	group	Total
great	7	2			4	2	2	4	17	38
grape		4			3			2	7	16
grave			1							1
gray				1						1
other	1								1	2
group									1	1
0									1	1
Total										60

Now let us consider a token spoken by Wendy P. that exemplifies the Vy chain shift, shown as (2):

(2) No, *he started* [be¹tn] *me*, and then he said, "I let you win!"

The F1/F2 position of this token is shown on figure 8d. It is a typical realization of her /iy/, lying in the center of the /iy/ distribution and on the upper edge of both the /ey/ and /æ/ ranges. From a phonetic point of view, it has a mid nucleus, not a high one, and in isolation, it sounds like a clear example of [e¹]. Figure 12a shows the percent correct recognition of *beatin'* for the three target cities. In isolation, none of the subject groups shows any tendency to recognize this as /iy/. The predominant judgment for all listeners is that the word intended as *beatin'* is *baby.* But given the phrase context, over half the Birmingham subjects hear a phrase with the morpheme *beat*; if not *He started beating me,* then *He's already beat me,* and in the sentence context almost all get it right. The Chicago and Philadelphia subjects lag far behind. Figure 12b shows the converse: the tendency for judges to abandon the phonetically cued /ey/ judgment. Again, the local advantage appears in the fact that Birmingham listeners drop the /ey/ reading rapidly, the others much more slowly. Listeners from Philadelphia and Chicago find it difficult to accept an /iy/ reading and frequently make sense out of the phrase with *He started dating me,* or *debating me.*[Editors' note: see Cassidy, this volume, on confusion of *fade* and *feed* by DARE workers who could not intuit *feed* as the target lexeme.]

Figure 12a: Percent correct identification of centralized and lowered /iy/
in *started BEATIN'* by target city

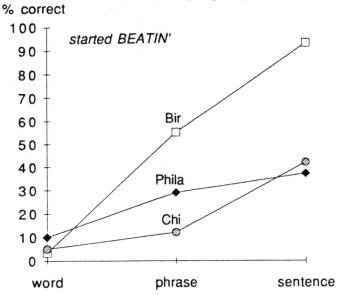

Figure 12b: Percent identification as /ey/ of centralized and lowered /iy/
in *started BEATIN'* by target city

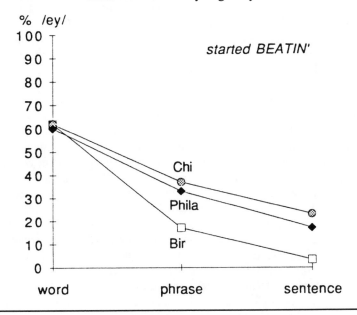

In this detailed view of error patterns, the Birmingham responses to items (1) and (2) are not difficult to understand. The vowel systems of figures 5–9 show that /iy/ is most commonly found with a high nucleus, and it is only the more advanced tokens in the use of some speakers which are as low as [e^{I}]. It is therefore not unreasonable for Birmingham listeners to identify the sound as /ey/, and given the infrequency of *baitin'*, hear the word as *baby* or *bacon*. In the phrase context, they have the double advantage of (1) familiarity with the prosodic and morphophonemic features of Birmingham speech, and (2) the awareness that vowels as low as [e^{I}] are used for /iy/. Birmingham listeners are thus able to retrieve *beatin'* much faster than listeners from other dialect areas. Another way of stating the effect represented by the steeper slopes of the Birmingham lines in figures 12a, b is that the effects of context and local membership are not independent; there is an interaction of these two effects on comprehension such that the acceleration of recognition with increasing context is greater for local listeners than nonlocal.

An even more dramatic example of the local advantage in using context is found in another Vy chain shift item shown in (3), which shows the lowering of /ey/ along the nonperipheral front track delineated in figures 5–9. The vowel nucleus of *weight* may be written as a centralized and lowered [ɛ] or as a fronted [ɐ]:

(3) She's on a [wɐ^{ɪ}t] *watchers* diet now, so she eats a lot of cottage cheese.

This is one of a class of items in the Gating series that was selected to provide maximum information in the phrase. When the second element of compounds like *double-decker* and *weight-watchers* is supplied, there is very little choice in the identification of the first element. The only factor that can retard the subject's correct transcription is the disbelief that the nucleus of the first word can have the value that it does. Figure 13a shows that only 10% of the Birmingham listeners identified the isolated [wɐ^{ɪ} t] as *wait* or *weight*, and practically none of the nonlocal people did. In the phrase context, there is a sudden conversion of the judgments of the Birmingham group to 97% *weight* responses, but Chicago and Philadelphia show only 80 and 70% respectively, in spite of the compelling character of this compound.

In the word context, [wɐ^{ɪ}t] is identified most often as *white, wipe,* or *like*. For Birmingham, this would be the most reasonable choice, since as we have seen there is an overlap of the F1 and F2 positions of /ey/ and /ay/ and the diphthongal form of /ay/ before voiceless consonants is much more common than before voiced consonants, especially at higher educational levels (Kurath and McDavid 1961). Figure 13b shows the rate at which the three different groups abandon this phonetically based judgment under the influence of the *weight-watchers* context. The Birmingham subjects begin with a higher rate of /ay/ responses and fall below the other groups in the phrase context. In so doing, the Birmingham subjects demonstrate their greater familiarity with the fact that there are two possible phonemic interpretations of [wɐ^{ɪ}t] as /wayt/ or /weyt/.

The next item is from the third element of the Vy chain shift, the monophthongization of /ay/—in this case, again before voiceless obstruents. In (4), the item *works* [naːts] occurs in a sentence context along with another item, [stɪl] *plant*, to be considered below.

Figure 13a: Percent correct identification of centralized and lowered /ey/ in *WEIGHT-watchers* by target city

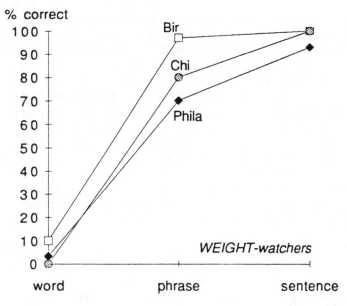

Figure 13b: Percent identification as /ay/ of centralized and lowered /ey/ in *WEIGHT-watchers* by target city

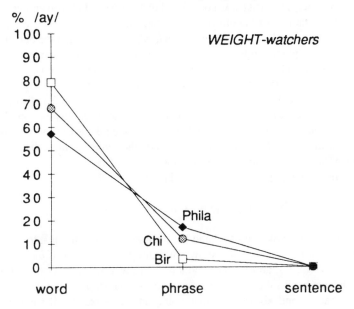

(4) *If he works* [naːts] at the [stɪl] *plant,* then he'll come in and sleep a couple of hours, then go work all day.

The nucleus of *nights* is the most open vowel of the system and quite long. We would therefore expect a higher recognition rate than we found for the relatively short monophthong in *kide* in the Controlled Vowel Identification series, where the success rate was close to zero. Figure 14a shows that this is the case; the success rate for the identification of the vowel in *works* [naːts] is about 50% in the word context for Birmingham subjects. This does not mean that all of these listeners wrote *nights.* Since the [t] is weakly articulated, 8 of the 29 supplied *nice,* 1 *nine,* and 2 *nights.* From the point of view of this inquiry, these are all successful recognition of the fact that [aː] is a common form of the nucleus of /ay/. The most common competing phonemic identification is /o/. If the rest of the word context is correctly identified, this yields *knots,* and 6 of the 29 Birmingham subjects gave this form, along with *nods* (6), *knobs* (3) and *not* (1). Figure 14b shows that there is the same pattern of local advantage in the abandonment of this competing choice as in figure 13b: the Birmingham subjects begin with more /o/ and switch to less in the phrase context.

Despite this continued evidence for the interaction of context and locality, it must be recognized that the effect is surprisingly small for this item. In the case of *weight watchers,* the phonetic facts show that /ey/ and /ay/ are equally likely choices. But it is generally considered that the nucleus of monophthongized /ay/ is a central vowel, well front of /o/. This fact was cited by Sledd (1966) as evidence for the existence of a tenth phonemic entity in American English. The center-back contrast of [nats] vs. [nɑts] was considered distinctive and played an important role in the abandonment of the effort to fit American phonology into a system of nine vowel nuclei, with the three low nuclei /æ/, /a/, /ɔ/. But though the nucleus of item (4) is squarely placed in low central position, we have to recognize that 16 of the 41 tokens of Wendy P.'s /ay/ were within the /o/ area, and the situation is the same for Alison K., as figure 9 shows. Thus the fact that 50% of the Birmingham subjects produced a word with short /o/ as an interpretation of [nats] indicates that the opposition of /a/ and /ɑ/ is not a rock-solid phonemic distinction. Listeners' behavior seems to reflect their knowledge that *some* tokens of monophthongal /ay/ overlap with /o/ and do not therefore rely upon the center vs. back distinction, even though no tokens of /o/ are as front as most tokens of /ay/.

The next item, (5), shows /ay/ in final position:

(5) *I did not* [baːːʔ] any kind of Hawaiian print.

This sentence is spoken by Melanie O.; the nucleus is located just to the front and below the mean value for /ay/ shown in figure 6. The vowel of *buy* is extra long (almost 400 msec), an extended monophthong with no change in quality. At the end, Melanie begins the next word *any* with a glottal stop, so that the segmentation of *buy* had to end abruptly at that point, and as a result, all subjects heard a consonantal coda for this word.

Figure 14a: Percent correct identification of monophthongal /ay/
in *works NIGHTS* by target city

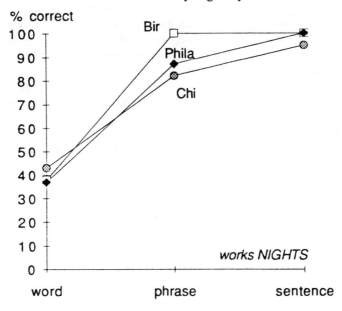

Figure 14b: Percent identification as /o/ of monophthongal /ay/
in *works NIGHTS* by target city

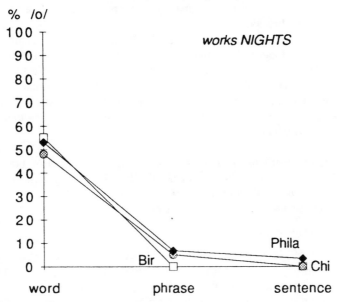

Table 5 shows the actual transcriptions by the Birmingham subjects in the word context. The most common identifications were with /oh/: *bought, thought,* in addition to /o/: *got, bot, bod,* with only one *bite,* which is the only possible word that accounts for the central location of the vowel nucleus. However, we must bear in mind that for all three of the Birmingham speakers considered, the distributions of /ay/, /o/, and /oh/ overlap, so that the same asymmetrical situation prevails as for item (4). Some tokens of /ay/ produced by Melanie O. are as far front as 1650 Hz, but others are as far back as 1250 Hz. Though no tokens of /o/ or /oh/ are as far front as the nucleus of [ba::], many tokens of /ay/ are as far back as *bought* or *bodice.*

Table 5: Transcriptions of *I did not* [ba::ʔ] in the word context by Birmingham white subjects [n=29]

/ay/	bite	1
/oh/	thought	6
	bought	7
/o/	bot	2
	bod	1
	got	5
other	but	1
	ha	1
	that	1
blank		3

Figure 15a shows that for Birmingham subjects there is no local advantage in the correct identification of [ba::ʔ] in the word context. But in the phrase context, an absolute local advantage appears: the 100% value for Birmingham leaves the others far behind. Figure 15b compares the three groups for the elimination of these /o, oh/ readings with context. In the phrase context, the rise in correct identification does not complement the fall of the /o, oh/ identifications since many of the Chicago and Philadelphia subjects were puzzled by the phrase and left their entries blank. Again, there is a cross-over pattern, with Birmingham falling to 0% and the other groups remaining at about 10% /o, oh/.

These results seem to show a severe limitation in the ability of Birmingham subjects to use their knowledge of the monophthongal character of /buy/, and they throw doubts upon the distinctive character of long low central [a:]. The next item will help to illuminate this situation.

Sentence (6) was also spoken by Melanie O.

(6) And I *knew the* [ga::].

The nucleus of [ga::] is almost identical with [ba::ʔ], and the length is about the same: 400 msec. But this item was selected to represent free vowels in true final position, and there is no glottal stop following. Figure 16a shows a very different situation from figure 15a. The overall rate of correct identification is much higher. In the word context, Birmingham listeners show a rate of correct response of 66% for [ga::], as compared to 3% for [ba::ʔ]. Here the local advantage is entirely confined to the word level. Figure 16b shows Birmingham subjects displaying their sensitivity to the central character of the nucleus of [ga::], with a percentage of /o/ or /oh/ in the word context that is less than half of that shown by Chicago or Philadelphia. This is not so much an interaction of context and locality as a straightforward superiority in phonetic interpretation.

We can conclude that sensitivity to the central location of the nucleus of monophthongal /ay/ emerges only when the phonetic context shows no contrary indications. In the word context, subjects were instructed to identify a "word or a syllable."[43] When they heard [ba::ʔ], the length appears to have been too great to allow them to interpret the word as *bite*, and only one subject responded with the form; *buy it*, which was given in the phrase context, did not appear as an answer in the word context since it is two words. Since there is no word *bot*, most subjects decided on *bought* or *thought*, without taking the difference in vowel quality into account. Without context, no one came to the conclusion that the word was *buy*. But [ga::], without the complication of the glottal stop, was recognized immediately by two-thirds of the Birmingham subjects. The question remains as to why the remaining one-third did not recognize it; we will return to this problem later.

We now turn to another component of the Southern Shift: short vowel tensing. In the Controlled Vowel Identification, it was clear that the nucleus of *ked* had been advanced even beyond the point of cardinal [e], and we would expect this to cause considerable confusion. Though *ked* rarely occurs in speech, we do find the corresponding /i/ form *kid* in figures 4 and 5. Item (7) focuses on this element of the short vowel tensing component in a sentence spoken by Wendy P.

(7) I was always with a *bunch of* [ki:ədz]

This token appears on figures 8a and 8d as the highest and frontest token in Wendy P.'s /i/ distribution. Due to the extreme character of this item, the response difference between the Birmingham subjects and others is striking. Figure 17a shows that listeners from Birmingham have no difficulty in recognizing [ki:ədz] in isolation as *kids*, but those from Chicago and Philadelphia reach only 60% and 40% levels respectively. The high front position of the vowel is the most influential in determining what phoneme nonlocal subjects hear: *keys* is supplied by 11 of the 90 nonlocal subjects, along with other forms such as *kief* and *piece* that suggest a simple /iy/ nucleus. But there are also quite a few forms that reflect the perception of the inglide of figure 8a: *he is* (1), *he has* (1), *peers* (3), and *P.S.* (4). Figure 17b shows the rate of abandonment of these /iy/ responses by the three target groups: the Birmingham record is flat at 0%, while the nonlocal groups show a marked rate of /iy/ response even in the phrase context.

The long ingliding developments of /i, e, æ/, which can be identified phonemically as /ih, eh, æh/, are perhaps prototypical instances of the "Southern drawl" (Feagin 1987). The second item characteristic of the short vowel tensing displays this characteristic in the most extreme fashion. Short *a* in *tram* is tensed and lengthened to a considerable degree, the nucleus rising to an extreme front, upper mid position.

(8) Last time I went to Albuquerque it was in March, and there was snow, and we *rode the* [treˌːʲəm].

Figure 15a: Percent correct identification of monophthongal /ay/
in *I did not BUY* by target city

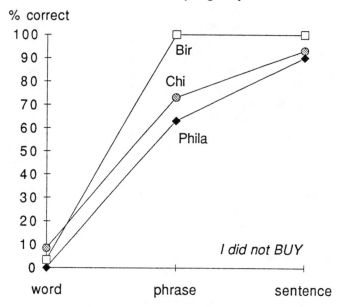

Figure 15b: Percent identification as /o/ or /oh/ of monophthongal /ay/
in *I did not BUY* by target city

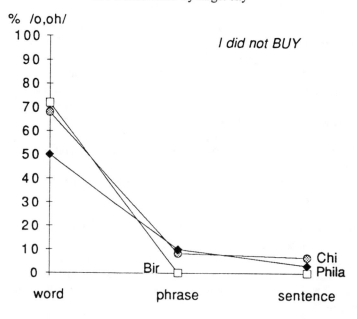

Figure 16a: Percent correct identification of monophthongal /ay/
in *knew the GUY* by target city

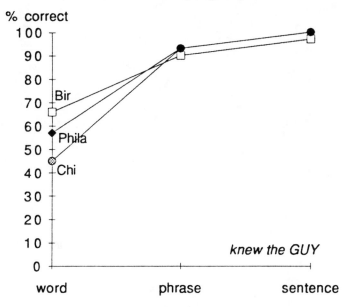

Figure 16b: Percent identification as /o/ or /oh/ of monophthongal /ay/
in *knew the GUY* by target city

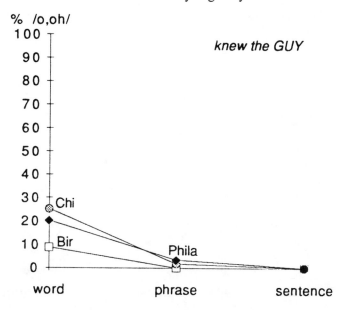

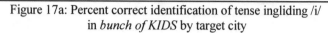

Figure 17a: Percent correct identification of tense ingliding /i/
in *bunch of KIDS* by target city

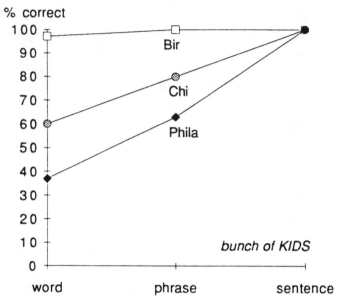

Figure 17b: Percent identification as /iy/ of tense ingliding /i/
in *bunch of KIDS* by target city

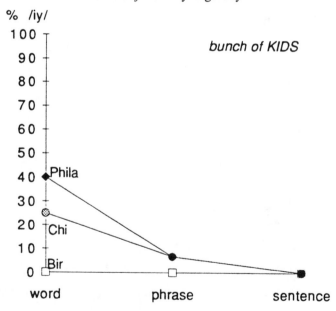

Tram is located on figure 8d in the middle of the most advanced short /i/ and /e/ distributions, as one of the small set of tensed /æ/ words before nasals, considerably advanced beyond others in the word class. A low amplitude palatal glide is heard between the nucleus and the centering inglide. The overall success rate of figure 18a shows a pattern somewhat different from what has preceded. The interaction of context and locality is extreme: Birmingham subjects go from a very low rate of recognition to a very high one, while the other two groups of subjects show only a moderate increase from their midrange positions. The reason for this eccentric pattern will become more evident when we examine the fate of the leading competitors of the correct word *tram*. For Birmingham, this is *trim*, as shown in figure 18b. The fact that 76% of the Birmingham subjects identified [tre̞:ʲəm] as *trim* shows that it had an unusually high nucleus even for that community. Of course, *rode the trim* does not make sense, and the frequency of *trim* declines rapidly, disappearing completely in the sentence context. On the other hand, *trim* was a minor element in the Chicago responses and rare in Philadelphia, indicating that these listeners did not associate /i/ with a tense and ingliding form. The other leading competitor is supported by the development of the [j] glide between nucleus and glide, creating a triphthong. Figure 18c shows that in the word context, there is a sizable frequency of *train* responses, which are reinforced in the context of the phrase *rode the ___*. At this point, the influence of lexical familiarity may emerge. Subjects presumably differ in their knowledge of the word *tram*. It seems likely that the pattern of figure 18c is the result of this differential knowledge: those who have not traveled outside of their local areas and do not know the word in this context shift to *train*.

Figure 18a: Percent correct identification of tense ingliding and drawled /æ/ in *rode the TRAM* by target city

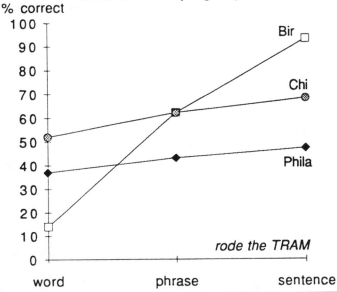

Figure 18b: Percent identification as /i/ in *trim* of tense ingliding and drawled /æ/ in *rode the TRAM* by target city

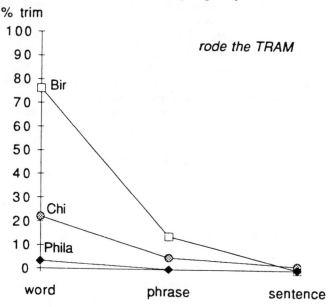

Figure 18c: Percent identification as /ey/ in *train* of tense ingliding and drawled /æ/ in *rode the TRAM* by target city

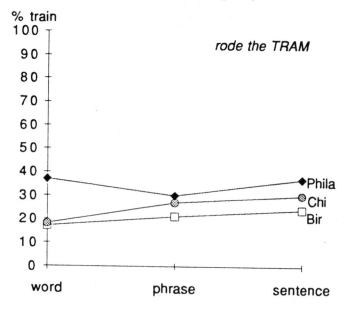

The eight Gating items of figures 11–18 show that different components of the Southern Shift have different cognitive consequences. The strongest local advantage is found with the tensing of short vowels. This is the pattern that appears to be the least salient in atlas transcriptions and in popular dialect writings, and it is only with instrumental measurements that the full extent of the fronting and raising of the /i, e, æ/ nuclei can be realized. The next strongest advantage is in the fronting of Vw, where a moderate effect appears for *diversified group*. In the Vy chain shift, an advantage almost as large appears for the lowering of /iy/ and /ey/ in *started beatin'* and *weight watchers*. The smallest local advantage appears in the monophthongization of /ay/ in *works nights, did not buy,* and *knew the guy*. Here the distinctive central position of the monophthongal [a:] nucleus appears to be recognized only under the most favorable conditions.

Two other items in the Gating series concerned features of the Birmingham dialect that are not involved in the Southern Shift. One is the monophthongization of /oy/ before /l/:

(9) Everybody says that only *children are* [spɔ::ld].

The vowel here is long, as long as the /ay/ items of (5) and (6), and perfectly monophthongal. Figure 19 shows that this yields the most extreme form of local advantage that we have seen yet. In the word context, all Birmingham subjects immediately identify *spoiled*, a result that holds for every Birmingham group examined so far: black and white, high school and college, in the first and second series of Gating experiments, a total of 112 Birmingham subjects. Other groups show only a moderate level of recognition in the word context. The phrase context gives rapid recognition, since the phrase *children are spoiled* is a common one, but still the nonlocal groups do not reach 100% until the full sentence is given. In evaluating the absolute success of the Birmingham listeners with [spɔ::ld], it is important to note that the onsets and codas of this syllable are articulated very clearly. It should also be borne in mind that for most Northern speakers, the diphthong /oy/ is the most clearly articulated diphthong of all, with a glide that moves from all the way from the back to a high front target. For /ay/ and /aw/, the extent of the glide trajectory varies considerably, and with reduced stress in some environments, monophthongization is common. Before /l/, the rigidly diphthongal character of /oy/ for Chicago and Philadelphia contrasts with its routine monophthongization in the South.

Finally, we have one case of a merger: the collapse of /i/ and /iy/ in lax position before /l/, which appears in item (4) above in [stɪl] plant. The vowel here is a short, nonperipheral [ɪ] in the position most commonly identified with /i/ in the majority of dialects. The merger of /i/ and /iy/ before /l/ is an ongoing change that has been traced in other parts of the United States as well: Utah (Labov, Yaeger, and Steiner 1972; Di Paolo 1988; Di Paolo and Faber 1990), Texas (Tillery and Kerr 1989; Bailey, Wikle, Tillery, and Sand 1991). Our Birmingham studies show that the merger is also represented among the speakers we interviewed. Since the vowel is [ɪ] rather than [i], it seems reasonable for speakers to identify the word as *still*, which is the predominant response (along with *silk* and *stiff*). Yet if the merger were a matter of common linguistic knowledge, and if it were deeply entrenched in the linguistic system, we might expect 50% *still* and 50% *steel*. If the merger is not complete, then it is only reasonable to guess that [stɪl] is *still*.[44]

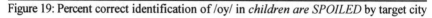

Figure 19: Percent correct identification of /oy/ in *children are SPOILED* by target city

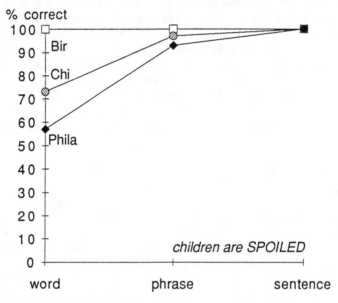

As in the case of the vowel rotations, it requires a certain amount of context to recognize that the intended word is actually *steel*. Figure 20a shows that given the context of __ *plant,* local subjects rapidly replace *still* with *steel*, far outpacing the nonlocal groups. Since *still plant* is not an impossible construction, some Birmingham subjects retain this reading until the sentence construct is reached.

Figure 20b shows /i/ responses. Here again, Birmingham listeners do far better than the other groups. Chicago and Philadelphia actually increase the number of /i/ responses in the phrase context, at the expense of other vowels and blank responses, and begin to converge on *steel* only in the full context. It follows that their awareness of a merger of /il/ and /iyl/ is minimal.

Figure 20a: Percent correct identification of lowered and laxed /iy/ in *STEEL plant* by target city

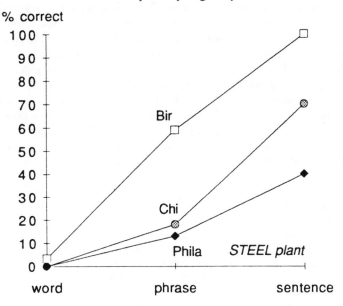

Figure 20b: Percent identification as /i/ of lowered and laxed /iy/ in *STEEL plant* by target city

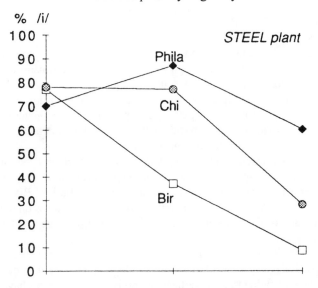

4.2.2. Differentiation of High School and College Subjects

So far, we have been treating Birmingham in terms of the responses of a single group of 29 white college students at UAB, building upon the results of an initial series of experiments with 37 students of similar background from the same university in the first series of Gating experiments in 1988. As noted above, the 1990 experiments also obtained Gating responses from 45 students at Fultondale High School. This is a public school located in the town of Fultondale, just north of Birmingham, and closely associated with it.[45] In the 1990 census, Birmingham proper had a population of 265,968, with 36% white and 63% black; Fultondale had a population of 6,400, with 98% white and 1.7% black. The median house value in Fultondale is $58,600, considerably higher than that of Birmingham and equal to that of several neighboring suburbs. The social backgrounds of the students are reflected in their listings of their parents' occupations:

Fathers:
professional	2	(minister)
management	5	
small business	3	(contractor)
white collar	11	(salesperson, teacher, inspector, technician)
skilled trades	8	(plumber, mechanic, machinist)
factory	2	(iron worker, plant worker)

Mothers:
professional	3	(nurse, accountant)
white collar	15	(secretary, salesperson, bank employee, florist)
unskilled	3	(lunchroom worker, restaurant worker, crossing guard)
homemaker	6	

The students' own aspirations point to a pattern of upward social mobility. All but three indicated that they intended to go to college, and a great many were aiming at professional jobs: lawyer, doctor, nurse, singer, etc. On the whole, we can characterize Fultondale High School as located in a predominantly white, lower-middle-class town oriented to a pattern of upward mobility in terms of both education and employment. This is basically the same pattern that marks the college students at UAB who formed the first group we examined.

In Chicago, Ash carried out a comparable study in Mother Theodore Guerin High School, where responses to the Gating experiments were provided by 38 students. Guerin High School is located in the Chicago suburb of River Grove, a community of a little less than 10,000. With a group of other towns on the northern and western edge of Chicago, it forms a solid enclave of white residents with a small percentage of Asians.[46]

Most of the students at Guerin High School live in Chicago, but some live in the suburbs. A good majority are said to go on to college, and in one class of 24, all but 2 said they were planning to go to college themselves. Their parents have the same types of occupations as the parents of the Fultondale HS students: nurse, policeman, field engineer, secretary, real estate agent, salesperson, mail carrier, seamstress, machinist, sales, butcher.

Figure 21 compares the responses of high school and college subjects from Birmingham and Chicago to item (1), *diversified* [gre̜ᵘp]. In both cases, college students have a sizable advantage in the phrase and sentence contexts, though not in the word context. In other words, they are no more skilled at identifying the /uw/ vowel, but they are better at using context to draw the right conclusion.[47]

Figure 21: Percent correct identification of fronted and lowered /uw/
in *diversified GROUP* by city and educational level

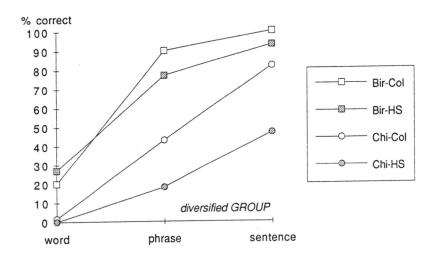

Figure 22a shows comparable data for item (3), *weight-watchers*. The Birmingham high school students have a distinct advantage in the word context—23% as against 10% for college students—but, again, a sharper upward slope for the college students appears for both Birmingham and Chicago. The differences between high school and college are not significant, but they suggest that the increasing skill at disambiguation in the phrase context may be independent of vocabulary, since the compound *weight-watchers* would seem to be equally available to all.

Figure 22b reverses the view and examines the tendency to interpret [wɒᵗt] as containing /ay/: *white, wipe, bite,* etc. by educational level. A striking difference appears between the Fultondale High School students and the other three groups. In figure 22a, the high school students showed a local advantage in the word context, but the great majority did not succeed in recognizing [wɒᵗt] as *weight*. Figure 22b shows that the Fultondale students did not fall into the opposing error of identifying [wɒᵗt] as *white* in the isolated word contexts; only 20% did so, as opposed to 74% of the UAB college students.

Figure 22a: Percent correct identification of centralized and lowered /ey/ in
WEIGHT-watchers by city and educational level

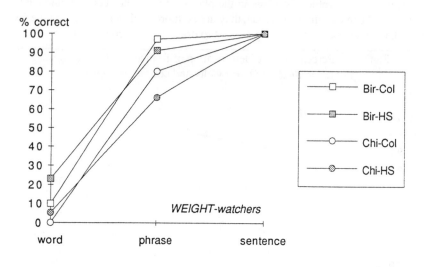

Figure 22b: Percent identification as /ay/ of centralized and lowered /ey/ in
WEIGHT-watchers by city and educational level

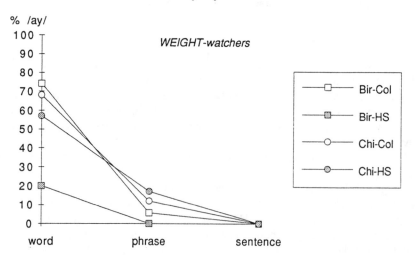

How can we account for this difference between high school and college? Figure 23 shows the complete array of responses to [wɒˤt] in the word context for UAB and Fultondale. While Fultondale responses were evenly spread over a wide range, with only a slight preference for /ey/ and /ay/, the majority of their responses are scattered almost at random. On the other hand, the college students' responses are heavily concentrated in /ay/. We infer that they are much more prone to be influenced by national norms and hear much more nonlocal speech. Although they may use open /ey/ vowels themselves, they are more prone to identify [wɒˤt] as *white* when they hear it in isolation.

Figures 22a and 22b show that in spite of this preference for /ay/ in isolation, the college students' knowledge of the Birmingham system comes into play as soon as context is supplied. The downward slope of the Birmingham college students is sharper than that of the Chicago college students and much steeper than that of the Chicago high school students. These small effects are not significant and are only interesting because they repeat in many other cases, indicating the joint effects of education and local familiarity.

The ability of the Birmingham college students to use the phrase context effectively is maximized in the case of item (4), *works* [na:ts]. Figure 24 shows that they outperform the Birmingham high school students and both Chicago groups, going from 38% correct in the word context to 100% in the phrase context; the white Birmingham high school students do not do better than Chicago subjects here. Furthermore, Chicago college subjects have no advantage over Chicago high school subjects in this case, where there is no problem of unfamiliar vocabulary. The advantage of the Birmingham college students is an interaction between ability to use context and linguistic knowledge of the variable.

Our previous investigation shows that item (6), *knew the* [ga::], provides the best insight into the subjects' ability to interpret the long monophthong [a:] as the Birmingham realization of /ay/.[48] In the comparison of the three target cities, we raised the question as to why the Birmingham college students, though superior to Chicago and Philadelphia, were still far from 100% in their ability to recognize [ga:] as *guy*. This is puzzling for several reasons. First, there is no competing form; if [ga:] is not *guy,* there is no reasonable alternative: there is no [gæ:], [gɑ:], or [gʌ:]. Second, the long monophthong appears to be the dominant form in the everyday speech of these subjects.[49] Figure 25 displays the wide range of abilities of the various groups to recognize the simple monosyllable [ga:] in the word context. The Fultondale students give the near-perfect performance that restores our confidence in the reality of the Birmingham vernacular and the perceptual abilities of Birmingham speakers. The Birmingham college students are at an intermediate position in the word context, though they join the high school students at the phrase and sentence context. In this case, the superiority of the high school students over the college students is significant at the .02 level. The inability of 11 of the 29 UAB students to recognize [ga:] can only be ascribed to interference from competing norms in the college environment. Even though they were told that the words and phrases in this series were spoken by someone from Birmingham, they could not seem to find their way back to the obvious vernacular interpretation. Three wrote *ga* or *gah,* two *gone,* two *God,* and four left the space blank.

Figure 23: Distribution of vowel nuclei in responses to centralized and lowered
/ey/ in *WEIGHT* in the word context for UAB and Fultondale subjects

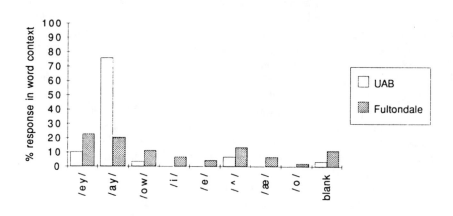

Figure 24: Percent correct identification of monophthongal /ay/ in
works NIGHTS by city and educational level

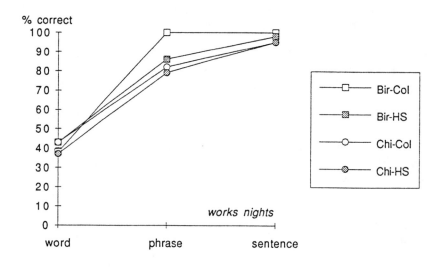

Figure 25: Percent correct identification of monophthongal /ay/ in
knew the GUY by city and educational level

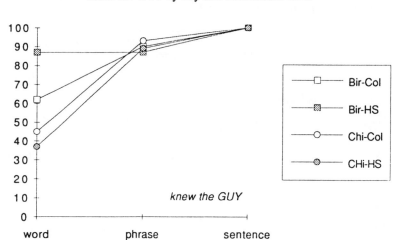

We have already seen that item (8), *rode the* [tre̞ːʲəm] produces patterns different from any of the other items because of the extreme drawl and break into two syllables and the problem of lexical recognition of *tram*. Figure 26a compares college and high school groups in Birmingham and Chicago for success in identifying this word. Only the Birmingham college group shows a steep increase in recognition with expanding context. The others show a fairly flat profile, and the Chicago high school group actually falls close to zero with expanding context.

Figure 26b shows that the identification of [tre̞ːʲəm] with *trim* is strongest for the Birmingham college group but that they abandon this identification more quickly than the Birmingham high school students. Finally, figure 26c shows the *train* responses. All of the groups show a low level without much increase with expanding context, except for the Chicago high school group. Their rate of identification of [tre̞ːʲəm] with *train* is 40%, much higher than the others, and it rises steeply almost to 100%.

Limited familiarity with the word *tram* does not square with the relatively high scores in the word context in figure 26a, particularly for the Chicago college subjects. This is because "correct" in the word context means the correct vowel, not the correct word. Many of the correct answers in this column of figure 26a are the word *tramp,* a response which disappears rapidly when the context *rode the____* appears.

The explanation for this pattern seems to come from two different directions. The identification of [tre̞ːʲəm] with *trim* may correspond to an ongoing development of short vowel tensing among Birmingham college students which is more extreme than elsewhere. But the major factor operating here is the unfamiliarity of subjects with the word *tram*, which is responsible for the categorical adoption of *we rode the train* by the Chicago high school group. The combined effect of less common lexical forms and most advanced phonetic forms is what is responsible for many of the failures of communication in everyday life, as shown in the CDC study of natural misunderstandings (Labov 1989b).

Figure 26a: Percent correct identification of tense ingliding and drawled /æ/ in *rode the TRAM* by city and educational level

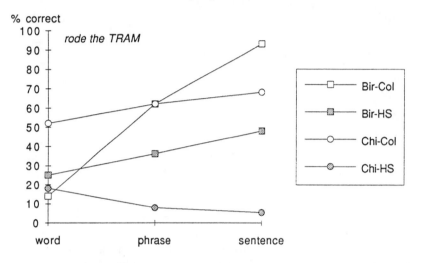

Figure 26b: Percent identification as /i/ in *trim* of tense ingliding and drawled /æ/ in *rode the TRAM* by city and educational level

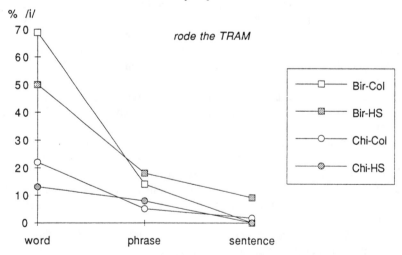

Figure 26c: Percent identification as /ey/ in *train* of tense ingliding and drawled /æ/ in *rode the TRAM* by city and educational level

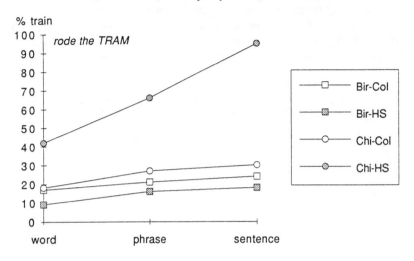

Finally, we return to the merger of /i/ and /iy/ before /l/, as exemplified in item (4) as [stɪl] *plant*. The results for educational groups appear in figure 27, which again shows the interaction between local membership and context: both Birmingham groups show a steeper rise of recognition of the merger in the phrase context, and this effect is stronger for the college group.

The steeper slope of recognition with expanding context is characteristic of the local college groups. It appears in figures 21 (*diversified group)*, figure 22 (*weight-watchers*), figure 24 (*works nights*), figure 26 (*rode the tram*) and figure 27 (*steel plant*). The only case where the slope for the Birmingham college group is not the greatest is figure 25 (*knew the guy*), where the high school group begins close to 100% in the word context and all groups attain the same success rate in the phrase context. To a lesser extent, the same tendency appears when we compare the Chicago college subjects with the high school subjects. In figures 21, 22, and 27 this effect is clear; it is obscured in figures 24 and 25. In figure 26 the effect is exaggerated for the Chicago groups by the high school group's ignorance of the word *train*. There are no reverse cases where college students show a shallower slope of increasing recognition with expanding context. This ability to use context to interpret phonetic forms appears not only in the search for the correct interpretation but in the ability to eliminate incorrect interpretations that are more probable from the phonetic standpoint. The use of context to recognize advanced, vernacular, and unexpected forms in speech appears to be accelerated by two factors. First, college students show an increased ability to interpret ambiguous linguistic signals, an effect that appears in a wide range of different experiments. This may simply be due to increased age and experience, or the educational process, or a combination of both. Second, high school students are better able to identify Southern vernacular forms in isolation than college students. This appears in figure 21 (*diversified group*), figure 22 (*weight-watchers*), figure 25 (*knew the guy*), and figure 26 (*rode the tram*).[50] In other cases, there is no discernible difference between the college and high school groups. Again, there are no cases where the reverse appears: where college students are better able to identify forms out of context.

Figure 27: Percent correct identification of lowered and laxed /iy/ in
STEEL plant by city and educational level

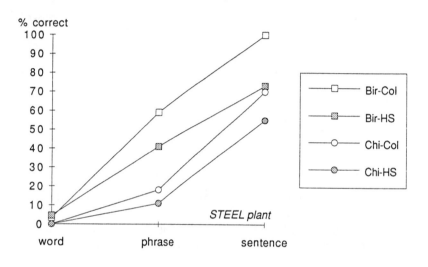

4.2.3. Comparison of Racial and Ethnic Groups

So far, we have been considering only the responses of the white college respondents. The second series of Gating experiments at UAB included 7 African-American students. Though this is a small group, the comparison with the 29 white students shows a consistent pattern and is reinforced by the results with 27 African-American subjects in the first Gating series. The second Gating series at the University of Illinois at Chicago Circle included 35 members of nonmainstream ethnic groups besides the 60 white students studied. We have the following distribution of racial and ethnic groups for comparison (with abbreviations to be used in the figures):

Birmingham white	Bir-Wh	29
Birmingham African-American	Bir-AA	7
Chicago white	Chi-Wh	60
Chicago African-American	Chi-AA	7
Chicago Asian	Chi-Asian	12
Chicago Hispanic (English dominant)	Chi-His(E)	8
Chicago Hispanic (Spanish dominant)	Chi-His(S)	7

Figure 28 shows the characteristic pattern that differentiates these six groups for item (1), *diversified group*. At the phrase and sentence contexts, it is clear that:

a) The white Birmingham group shows the greatest rate of recognition, followed by the African-American Birmingham group.
b) These are followed by the Chicago whites and Asians.
c) Performance by the African-American and English-dominant Hispanic speakers is next.
d) The lowest recognition rates are shown by the native Spanish speakers.

In addition, we can see that both Hispanic groups show relatively little gain in the sentence context and that the Hispanic groups occupy the lowest rank at that point. Looking more narrowly at the word context, it appears that the Birmingham African-American group has the highest recognition rates but that the Birmingham white group shows a steeper rise in recognition with the phrase context.

Figure 28: Percent correct identification of fronted and lowered /uw/ in *diversified GROUP* by city, race, and ethnicity

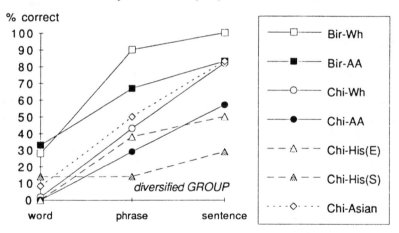

Let us examine other elements of the Vy shift to see if these patterns persist. Figure 29 shows the recognition rates for these six groups reacting to item (3) *weight-watchers*. The phrase context shows almost the identical ordering as in figure 28, though the high rate of information provided in the phrase context brings all groups very close together, and in the sentence context they all coalesce at 100%. However, there is a considerable spread in the word context, where we observe that both the Birmingham and Chicago African-American groups have a higher recognition rate than any other group, at 33% and 29%. Here the African-American subjects have the same relation to the white subjects as the Birmingham high school group has to the Birmingham college group. They show a higher recognition rate in the word context, but the white group shows a steeper increase and achieves a higher rate in the phrase context.

Figure 29: Percent correct identification of centralized and lowered /ey/ in *WEIGHT-watchers* by city, race, and ethnicity

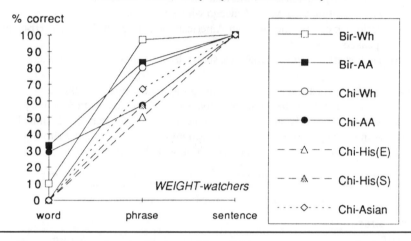

The regularities found with items (1) and (3) are not preserved for item (2), *started beatin'*. Figure 30 shows that all groups begin with a recognition rate close to zero; in the phrase context, only the Birmingham white group shows any sizable success, while the others remain at zero or close to zero. In the sentence context, the African-American Birmingham group emerges with a 67% recognition rate. The Chicago African-American group is particularly low, and we can infer that the lowering of /iy/ in the Vy chain shift is not as salient as the lowering of /ey/.

Figure 30: Percent correct identification of centralized and lowered /iy/ in *started BEATIN'* by city, race, and ethnicity

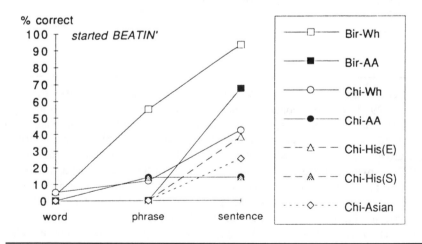

When we turn to the monophthongization of /ay/, the regularities of figures 28 and 29 reappear in figure 31. Item (5), *I did not buy*, was seen before to show very low recognition rates in the word context with a rapid increase to close to 100% in the phrase context. Here again we see that the Birmingham white group shows the steepest slope from word to phrase context. We also see that both of the African-American groups have the highest scores in the word context. Again, the Chicago Spanish speakers have the overall lowest rates of recognition, but the other Chicago groups do better in the phrase context than the Chicago white speakers.

Figure 31: Percent correct identification of monophthongal /ay/ in *I did not BUY* by city, race, and ethnicity

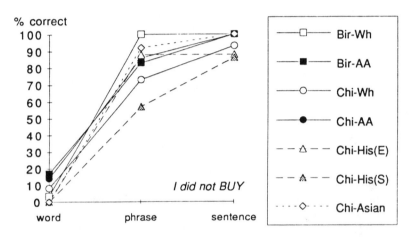

As we have seen, item (6), *knew the guy*, provides the best view of listeners' capacity to identify monophthongal /ay/ in isolation. Figure 32 shows a wide spread of recognition rates in the word context, from 0% for the Spanish speakers to 83 and 86% for the two African-American groups. Here the advantage of the African-American subjects over others is again comparable to the advantage of the high school students from Fultondale. Next come the Birmingham and Chicago white groups, then the English-dominant Hispanic speakers, the Asians, and finally the Spanish speakers. Though all show a sizable increase in recognition in the phrase context, there is no room for them to surpass the level set by the African-American groups, which reaches 100% in the phrase context.

Since many of these groups are small, the differences between any two of them do not reach statistical significance. However, the differentiation of the seven ethnic groups as a whole is highly significant, with a chi-square of 151. But the important fact is that a fairly intricate set of relationships are replicated in many different tests.

Figure 32: Percent correct identification of monophthongal /ay/ in
I knew the GUY by city, race, and ethnicity

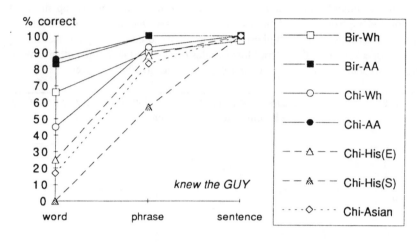

Finally, figure 33 reviews ethnic differences in recognition of *steel plant* in item
(4). Only the two Birmingham groups show any recognition of /iy/ in the phrase
context, and here is one example where the African-American subjects show higher
rates at this point. We conclude that the merger is not at all salient in Chicago.

Figure 33: Percent correct identification of lowered and laxed /iy/ in
STEEL plant by city, race, and ethnicity

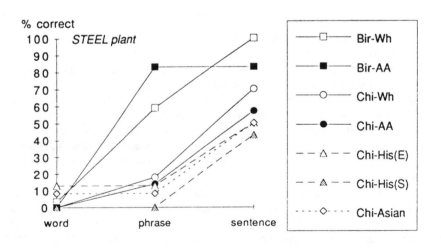

4.2.4. Sex Differences in Recognition

Since sexual differentiation plays a major role in the development of linguistic change, and women have been found to be more sensitive than men to prestige and stigma attached to linguistic variables, it is only natural to ask if there are any differences between the sexes in the recognition of Birmingham variables. The main group of white subjects from UAB consists of 15 women and 14 men; the main group of white subjects from Chicago consists of 38 women and 22 men. Comparison of these subgroups across all items shows no significant or consistent differences. Figure 34, showing sex differences for item (6), *knew the guy,* is typical of these results: males and females follow almost identical paths from word to phrase to sentence. This is particularly striking because other studies of the merger of high vowels before /l/ show that women are consistently in advance of men in this sound change (Tillery and Kerr 1989; Di Paolo 1988). But in this, as in other cases, there are no significant differences in recognition rates between the sexes.

Figure 34: Percent correct identification of lowered and laxed /iy/
in *STEEL plant* by city and sex

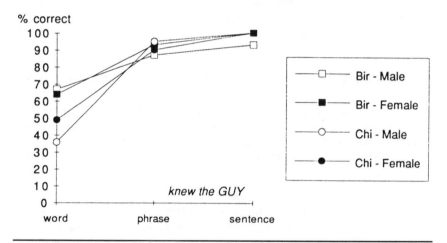

4.3. Differentiation of the Elements of the Southern Shift

In these recognition experiments, not all of the elements of the Southern Shift are recognized at the same rate or with the same patterns of social differentiation. Differences in the results of the Gating experiments are due to the amount of information provided by context in the different items (which was deliberately varied across items) and to the influence of the phonetic environment and the lexical contrasts available in that phonetic frame. Overall results also point to differences in the salience of components of the Southern Shift, and these in turn suggest differences in the development of the Shift over time.

The most salient and recognizable feature of the Southern Shift is the monophthongization of /ay/, as we would assume from popular stereotypes and imitations of Southern speech. The Gating experiments show relatively high rates of recognition in word context before a voiceless stop (*works nights*, figure 14a) and finally (*knew the guy*, figure 16a). The high recognition rates for *guy* are no doubt related to the absence of any lexical alternatives in the /g__/ framework, but this is not true for *nights*, where *knots* was available and frequently given. The salience of /ay/ for both local and nonlocal subjects is evident from the fact that all groups showed at least 40% recognition in isolation. The absolute success of Birmingham subjects in recognizing *spoiled* shows a parallel salience of the monophthongization of /oy/. Part of the reason for the recognizability of these variants is their relatively discrete character compared to other elements of the Southern shift; a purely monophthongal /ay/ is the recognizable terminal point of the sound change. At the same time, we found evidence that the central location of the monophthongized nucleus is not a sufficient cue to enable listeners to differentiate *knots* from *nights* and *bought* from *bite*.

Other elements of the Vy chain shift are less salient. The lowering of /iy/ in *beatin'* (figure 12a) and of /ey/ in *weight* (figure 13a) both show rates of recognition close to zero in the word context. In the case of *beatin'*, the only available lexical alternative is *baitin'*, which is considerably less common; yet comparatively few subjects perceived the lowered vowel as a form of /iy/ in this context. The fronting of /uw/ in *group* (figure 11a) is somewhat better recognized by Birmingham speakers, but nonlocal subjects had no success with this item in the word context.[51]

5. GENERAL FINDINGS ON CROSS-DIALECTAL COMPREHENSION

This study of the comprehension of Birmingham dialect is a part of the CDC inquiry into the cognitive consequences of the sound changes that are continuing to differentiate the dialects of American English. The findings in Birmingham, consistent with the studies of Chicago, Philadelphia, and Pittsburgh, can be summed up as six generalizations:

1) There is a consistent local advantage in the recognition of advanced forms of the local vernacular. The Controlled Vowel Identification experiments show that there are no significant differences among dialects in the recognition rates of stable vowels but a strong local advantage in the recognition of advanced forms. Gating experiments that focus on the advanced forms consistently report a local advantage in the phrase context. For the most advanced cases, the mutual intelligibility of the phonologies of different dialects is seriously impaired by the results of sound change.

2) Local subjects show the same pattern of difficulties in recognizing advanced forms of their own dialect as speakers from other dialects do. Controlled Vowel Identification results show the same ordering of recognition for local as for nonlocal subjects, and in Gating experiments, the local advantage is small or nonexistent in the word context.

3) Words heard in isolation are most generally identified with less advanced forms of the local dialect or with initial positions in preference to more advanced forms of the local dialect.

4) Local advantage in recognition is most consistently shown by an interaction between locality and context: local listeners show a greater ability to use context to correct the erroneous identifications that follow from tendency 3) above than nonlocal listeners.
5) The ability to use context to correct erroneous phonetic identifications is most highly developed by subjects in the white (mainstream) college group.
6) The ability to recognize advanced forms of the local dialect in isolation is greater among high school students than college students and greater among African-American subjects than white subjects.

The ability to use context to correct erroneous identifications may be thought of as a repair strategy that responds to the problems of ambiguity and overlap created by sound change within the community as well as the results of sound changes moving in opposite directions across communities. Studies of natural misunderstandings show that such repair strategies are needed in many situations that have nothing to do with sound change or dialect differences. But when a phonological system is operating most efficiently, with less overlap and ambiguity, the need for such correction will be less. This is shown clearly when the vowels being tested for recognition are close to initial positions. The true test of the efficiency of a phonological system is therefore the recognition of sounds with minimal context, as in the Controlled Vowel Identification experiments or the word context of the Gating experiments. In this context, we have found an advantage for high school students over college students and black subjects over white subjects in the identification of vernacular forms. This means that the advanced forms are incorporated into the phonological systems of those subjects in a more consistent way and that their systems operate more efficiently when confronted with such advanced forms. Conversely, these subjects may be seen as less conscious of the national norms that affect the judgments of others.

There is a striking parallel between the responses of African-American college students and high school students in the word context. Figure 35 shows the similarity of UAB African-American students and Fultondale students compared to the UAB white students for an item with a low rate of recognition in the word context: *weight-watchers.* Figure 36 makes the same comparison for *knew the guy*, with a high rate of word recognition. In both cases, the UAB African-American students and the Fultondale students show less difficulty in recognizing the advanced form than the UAB white students, and their patterns are quite similar.

How can we account for the similar patterns of these two groups? It seems likely that they are both inserted into local social networks more consistently than the white UAB students. Conversely, one may say that they have less interference from speakers of other dialects. This can only be speculation without a sociolinguistic study of Birmingham, and it rests primarily on inferences drawn from the study of social networks in Philadelphia.

It has appeared consistently that listeners raised in Philadelphia are considerably less able to understand Birmingham phonology than are listeners raised in Chicago. Chief exceptions are the fronting of /uw/, which is well established in Philadelphia but has only recently begun to occur in Chicago, and the merger of /i/ and /iy/ before /l/, which is not found in either Philadelphia or Chicago. The advantage of

Figure 35: Percent correct identification of centralized and lowered /ey/ in
WEIGHT-watchers by education and race in Birmingham

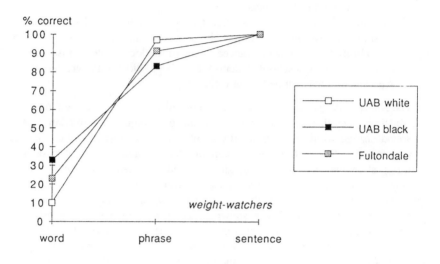

Figure 36: Percent correct identification of monophthongal /ay/ in *knew the GUY*
by education and race in Birmingham

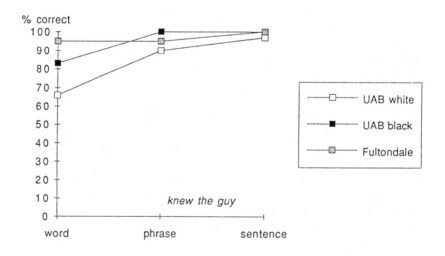

Chicago is entirely understandable in light of north-south patterns of migration in the U.S. The massive movements from southern rural areas to northern cities followed this axis. The African-American population of Philadelphia and New York has close family ties with North Carolina, South Carolina, and Georgia, and a comparable relationship exists between Chicago and Mississippi and Alabama. Similar patterns of migration are followed by the white migrants to the Northern Cities, and the Mississippi River is the major channel of linguistic influence from south to north.[52] The Chicago community as a whole therefore shows a greater capacity to recognize Birmingham pronunciations than Philadelphia does. But if the small sample in the Gating Series II is representative, we can say that the sensitivity of the Birmingham African-American community to the Birmingham vernacular is not mirrored in Chicago. The only instance where the Chicago African-American group showed a higher level of recognition than the white group was the most salient item, the monophthongization of *guy*. For changes that appear to be the most recent, like the merger of /i/ and /iy/ before /l/, the Chicago subjects show little capacity to recognize what is happening.

On the whole, the differences in cross-dialectal comprehension that we have recorded here do not appear to be the result of differences in the general decoding skills or linguistic abilities of the various groups, but rather the interactions of different phonological systems and different degrees of exposure to national norms.

NOTES

1. The research reported in this essay forms part of the project on Cross-Dialectal Comprehension, supported by the National Science Foundation under grants to the University of Pennsylvania. We are indebted to the NSF for its financial support, and to our colleagues on the research project: Mark Karan, Corey Miller, Julie Roberts, Robin Sabino, and Tom Veatch. The Gating experiments that are the chief focus of this report were carried out by Ash, who did the largest part of the interviewing, test administration, and analysis involved. Veatch was the principal person involved in design and preparation of the stimuli for the first series of experiments and is largely responsible for the success of the experimental method.

2. Labov (chapter 8, 1994) shows that this statement of the principles of chain shifting can be further simplified in a view of phonological space that is based on articulatory rather than acoustic positions. In this framework, there is no high back corner occupied by [u], but a continuous transition from low back [ɑ] to high front [i]. The three principles of chain shifting can then be reduced to a single principle that tense nuclei become less open along a peripheral path, and lax nuclei become more open along a nonperipheral path. This view of phonological space is particularly well suited to SSE, where the wholesale fronting of high back vowels leaves the high back corner unoccupied, even in acoustic measures.

3. This is of course not true for Scots English and many North English dialects, where diphthongization of ME ū has never taken place. It is also possible that the centralized nuclei for /aw/ found in Canada, Virginia, and Martha's Vineyard, MA, do not represent new retrograde movements but relics of an incomplete lowering of the diphthong that was the output of the Great Vowel Shift.

4. Again, there are many American dialects that do not show marked diphthongization of these vowels, particularly in the case of /iy/ and /uw/. There are in fact a number of areas of American English where pure monophthongs have been attested in free position, particularly in Eastern Pennsylvania (Kurath and McDavid 1961) and the North Central States (Allen 1976). But these seem to be developments that followed the original settlement, under the influence of a new and dominant German and Scandinavian population.

5. This is the case with Philadelphia /ahr/, which moved from low central to lower mid back position, where it is now stable and constant for all age levels and social groups. It also happens that a vowel that appears to be stable in the initial position will have arrived there after an earlier sound change and a second retrograde movement that returned it to where it started from. This is the case with Philadelphia /ey/ in closed syllables.

6. Not to be identified with SSE, the Southern Shift is a term that refers to the variety of dialects spoken in the Southern United States but is found in the whole range of dialects in Southern England, Australia, New Zealand, South Africa, and the Mid-Atlantic United States, as noted below.

7. In a number of South Midland dialects, /ʌ/ is raised in a chain shift with /u/, with unrounding of both vowels, /ʌ/ → /u/ → [ɨ].

8. Thomas and Bailey (1991) argue that a better term is "glide shortening," since a small diphthongal movement remains in many cases. While such a truncated glide is found in many instances, the Birmingham dialect we are discussing here shows characteristic monophthongal steady states for /ay/ in free position. See figure 8c below.

9. Vhr vowels show the lowest F2 values and define the outer periphery.

10. In this respect, the underlying forms of SSE antedate the initial position. SSE reflects an earlier pronunciation that is shown in the orthography of *hawk, law, caught* and is generalized to tensed short o words *on, lost,* etc.

11. The behavior of /æ/ in the Southern States is not as regular as that of /i/ and /e/; it intersects with the more general tensing and raising of the short **a** class and in many areas shows a variety of different divisions of this class into tense and lax members.

12. In LAMSAS representations of the short vowels, the nuclei are consistently shown as lax [ɪ, ɛ], with a following inglide (Kurath and McDavid 1961). Instrumental studies of speakers from widely separated areas of the Southern States (Atlanta, Anniston, Bluefields, Knoxville, Birmingham, and the Outer Banks of North Carolina) show that this notation understates the reversal of the positions of the nuclei of the originally short and long vowels. While many tokens of the front short vowels do show nuclei in nonperipheral position, the more advanced, emphatic tokens characteristic of the spontaneous speech of vernacular speakers are found along a fronted path that contrasts clearly with the lax nuclei of the originally long vowels, and approximates the quality of cardinal [i, e] (Labov, Yaeger, and Steiner 1972; Labov 1991).

13. This backing and raising of /ay/ is the most well known feature of the Outer Banks dialect, which has given rise to the label of "Hoi Toiders" (Labov, Yaeger, and Steiner 1972; Wolfram 1993b).

14. This low position of /ow/ is characteristic of London English as well. Note that /ow/ then assumes the position formerly held by /aw/, which is extremely front and tense. Instead of the parallel movement indicated in figures 2 and 3, these vowels form a chain shift.

15. The distinction between /ohr/ and /ɔhr/ gives this chain shift a third member. However, there is some indication that the distinction is weakening. Figure 4 shows that three members of the /ohr/ class are in high back position, but *more* is grouped with /ɔhr/. Furthermore, a token of /ahr/ is also found in the /ɔhr/ class, which is not unexpected since the merger of /ahr/ and /ɔhr/ is widespread in Texas.

16. We are much indebted to Ed Battistella for the indispensable help he gave us in this entire enterprise at UAB.

17. Since the stimuli were drawn from the UAB interviews, they were recorded so as to obtain the best possible signal-to-noise ratio in the field. A Nagra tape recorder operating at 7 ½″ per second was used with a Sennheiser 415 condenser microphone.

18. Wendy P. lives at home with her mother and also held a part-time job as a data entry clerk. Her mother is a hospital cashier who was raised in Birmingham; her grandmother lived in Tifton, Georgia, up to the age of five and then moved to Birmingham. Wendy attended high school there and was raised in the Fultondale section of Birmingham (see below). Her language background is entirely English.

19. Melanie O., a 24-year-old English major at UAB, was interviewed in 1988. Her parents both grew up in Alabama, and Melanie lived in the Homewood section of Birmingham all her life. The racial balance of the high school she attended was, according to her estimate, 40% black and 60% white. Her mother is an accountant and her father a warehouse supervisor at Alabama Power. Melanie studied Spanish in school; otherwise, her language background is entirely English.

20. Alison K.'s parents are both natives of Birmingham. Her mother is a housewife and her father does body repair; she plans to be an obstetrical nurse. Her language background is entirely English.

21. The phonetic patterns of these three students should not in themselves be taken as evidence for change in progress. Unlike the studies of Chicago and Philadelphia, the exploratory studies in Birmingham and other Southern cities are synchronic in character, without any systematic sampling of age groups or real-time comparisons. Thomas and Bailey (1993) present real-time evidence on the development of Southern vowel systems using phonograph recordings which show that these systems are involved in change in progress and that 19th-century systems were missing many of the phenomena of the Southern Shift outlined here.

22. For the best comparison of short and long vowels, only checked words are shown, since the short vowels do not have any free tokens. In many dialects, vowels in free position show more extreme forms of the Southern Shift than vowels in checked position, but this is not the case in Birmingham, where the checked forms actually show an equal or greater advancement of the sound changes concerned.

23. Vowels before syllable final /l/ are always excluded from mean calculations, since they usually have radically lower F2 values than the rest. Initial /l/ does not always have as great an influence on the nucleus as the consistent effect shown in figure 8a. Southern States syllable initial /l/ is clearer than in Northern dialects, but the /li/ allophone contrasts here with a much fronter set of /i/ tokens than found elsewhere.

24. If we divide all /i/ tokens into those which occur above the mean (further towards the upper left extremity of the ellipse) and below the mean (further towards the lower right extremity), we have the following:

	above the mean	below the mean
final syllables	5	0
nonfinal syllables	6	8

The probability of this distribution by Fisher's Exact Test is .04.

25. The distributions of words with and without following syllables in the two subsets show a probability of .07 by Fisher's Exact Test.

26. It is particularly notable that for /iy/, vowels with longer, more highly stressed nuclei move away from the periphery towards more central positions, since this is contrary to the common assumption that preferred target positions are generally more peripheral under a general tendency to maximize distances between vowels (Liljencrants and Lindblom 1972). A similar situation is analyzed in detail for London English (Labov 1991).

27. Two /e/ words show front upglides: *messy* and *steady*.

28. The distribution shows some exceptions, like *base* and *take*. There are 8 words ending in voiceless consonants less advanced than the mean (more closed), and 2 more advanced; of the 11 words ending in voiced consonants, the proportions are 4 and 7. Fisher's Exact Test for this distribution shows a probability of .05.

29. For Melanie O., there is a great gap between *eight* and *April*, in mid front position, and *cake* and *plain*, in lower mid central position. The low position of *plain* might be attributed to the effect of initial /pl/, but for Alison K., the most extreme forms are *main* and *same*.

30. The distribution of glides follows the expected pattern of conditioning by following voiceless consonants:

Following Segment	monophthong	reduced glide	full glide
voiceless consonant	10	7	5
voiced oral consonant	4	3	
nasal consonant	5		
none	7		

31. A chi-square test shows that this contrast of vowels before voiceless consonants, within and without the region of overlap, is significant at the .05 level.

32. In fact, it is the presence of a back upglide that allows us to classify words such as *on* and *off* as members of the /oh/ class rather than /o/.

33. The absence of glides for this class may be parallel to the phenomenon reported by Feagin in Anniston, Alabama (1993). Feagin reports that young, upper-middle-class speakers in Anniston are showing an ongoing merger of /o/ and /oh/ as a result of their abandonment of the back upglide.

34. For the sake of clarity, several vowels that are not crucially involved in the discussions of cross-dialectal comprehension to follow are omitted, including /aw/ and /ow/.

35. Experiments reported in Labov, Yaeger and Steiner (1972) show that the fronted glides of Eastern North Carolina are frequently mistaken for front unrounded glides by speakers of other dialects, so that *house* is heard as *highest*, *true* as *tree*.

36. Alison K. does not have a complete merger of /i/ and /e/ before nasals. Brown (1990) shows that this merger is far from complete in the Southern States and represents a change still in progress.

37. This characterization of the most advanced speakers of local dialects is drawn from the results of the project on Linguistic Change and Variation in Philadelphia, designed to locate the social position of the innovators of sound change (Labov 1980b, 1994).

38. Fourteen words were used instead of ten as in the Peterson-Barney experiment, since it was essential to include the diphthongs. The frame /k__d/ was preferred to the Peterson-Barney /h__d/ frame, since it yielded more familiar words and fewer artificial ones. The mid-central vowel /ɚ/ in *heard* or *curd* was not included here because a pilot study yielded zero errors in identification.

39. The Controlled Vowel Identification series was carried out in 1988, along with the first series of Gating Experiments. The subjects were all college students, drawn from the University of Alabama at Birmingham, the University of Illinois at Chicago Circle, and in Philadelphia, Drexel and Temple Universities.

40. Although merger of /i/ and /e/ before nasals is a well-known phenomenon of Southern speech (Brown 1990), such an overlap of /i/ and /e/ before oral consonants has not been reported before, to the best of our knowledge.

41. In (1) and all following examples, the extract used in the word context will be shown in phonetic notation; the surrounding material used in the phrase context will be shown in italics, and the full extract used in the third, sentence context, will be shown in normal type.

42. In scoring the responses to the Gating Experiment, a response in the word context is counted as correct if the intended vowel phoneme was given; in the phrase and sentence contexts, the intended word or an inflectional form of it was required for a response to be counted as correct.

43. Some subjects did write nonsense words like *ga* and *gah*, but this was never a sizable percentage. When they could not find a word, most subjects left the space blank.

44. The situation shows a certain degree of parallelism with the monophthongization of /ay/, though there we have no reason to believe that the overlap is leading to merger at present.

45. In filling out their residence histories, a number of students in Fultondale wrote "Birmingham (Fultondale)." The 45 subjects at Fultondale included 3 African-American students, but they were not grouped separately and are included in the Fultondale results.

46. In the four adjacent communities of River Grove, Elmwood Park, Franklin Park, and Melrose Park, the census shows only 241 African-Americans.

47. It is possible that the difference between high school and college is due to the fact that the context is a fairly learned word, *diversified*. High school students have a great deal of difficulty with this word, showing spellings like *divesifed, diversivied, deiversi, deviseified, devesifity, dercied*, etc. But the difference between high school and college students is not significant in this respect.

48. Bear in mind that item (5), *I did not* [ba::ʔ], has the artifact of a glottal stop in the word context and is not easily recognized in that context as the word *buy*. Item (5) does illustrate the capacity of Birmingham speakers to use context more rapidly than others to identify the word; in this respect, Birmingham high school and college students are alike, though the high school students show a higher level of recognition.

49. Thomas and Bailey (1991) show that the monophthongization of /ay/ is an ongoing and gradual process and that the forms used by most middle-aged members of the speech community show shortened glides rather than pure monophthongs. They propose that the process is *glide shortening* rather than *monophthongization*. In any case, for this generation of college and high school students, the process is complete, and the form [ga:] cannot be considered an advanced form phonetically, comparable to [greᵘp], [wɛᵈt] or [kiəds].

50. Of these three effects, only figure 25 shows a result that is significant.

51. Since the Philadelphia system shares with Birmingham a well-established fronting of /uw/, one might expect Philadelphians to have done better than Chicagoans, but the only difference that did appear was a more rapid abandonment of /ey/ responses in figure 11b. The factor responsible here may be the lowering of the nucleus rather than its fronting.

52. This effect appears clearly in the study of the words for submarine sandwich. The New Orleans term *po' boy* has spread along the Gulf coast and up the Mississippi to Tennessee, Illinois, and Chicago (Labov 1988).

References

This bibliography excludes references identified as "personal communication" (p.c.). Duplicate-year entries are cited as *a* or *b* throughout the volume.

Adam, Lucien. 1882. *Les classifications, l'objet, la méthode, les conclusions de la linguistique*. Paris.

Akmajian, Adrian, Richard A. Demers & Robert M. Harnish. 1979. *Linguistics: An introduction to language and communication*. Cambridge, MA: MIT Press.

Algeo, John. 1993. *DARE* in the classroom. In *Language variation in North American English: Research and teaching*, ed. by A. Wayne Glowka and Donald M. Lance, 140–43. New York: Modern Language Association.

Allen, Harold B. 1958. Minor dialect areas of the Upper Midwest. Publication of the American Dialect Society (PADS) 30:3–16.

Allen, Harold B. 1973–1976. *The linguistic atlas of the Upper Midwest in three volumes*. Minneapolis: University of Minnesota Press.

Alleyne, Mervyn. 1971. Acculturation and the cultural matrix of creolization. In Hymes (ed.), 169–86.

Alleyne, Mervyn C. 1980. *Comparative Afro-American: An historical-comparative study of English-based Afro-American dialects of the New World*. Ann Arbor: Karoma Publishers.

Allsopp, Richard. forthcoming. *Concise dictionary of Caribbean English usage*. Oxford: Oxford University Press.

Altman, Irwin, & Joachim Wohlwill (eds.). 1978. *Children and the environment*. Vol. 3 of *Human behavior and environment*. NY: Plenum Press.

Alvarez Nazario, Manuel. 1974. *El elemento afronegroide en el español de Puerto Rico*. 2d ed. San Juan, PR: Instituto de Cultura Puertorriqueño.

Ancelet, Barry Jean. 1988. A perspective on teaching the "problem language" in Louisiana. *The French Review* 61:345–56.

Anshen, Frank. 1969. *Speech variation among Negroes in a small southern community*. New York University dissertation.

Anshen, Frank. 1970. A sociolinguistic analysis of a sound change. *Language Sciences* 9:20–21.

Arceneaux, Jean. 1991. Nouvelles en français sur radio free acadie. *Feux follets* 1:2–3.

Arends, Jacques. 1995a. Demographic factors in the formation of Sranan. In Arends (ed.), 233–77.

Arends, Jacques (ed.). 1995b. *The early stages of creolization*. Philadelphia: John Benjamins.

Ash, Sharon. 1992. New ways of mapping phonological variation. Paper presented at NWAVE-XXI, Ann Arbor.

Atwood, E. Bagby. 1953. *A survey of verb forms in the Eastern United States*. Ann Arbor: University of Michigan Press.

Auer, J. C. P. 1988. A conversation analytic approach to code-switching and transfer. In *Codeswitching: anthropological and sociolinguistic perspectives*, ed. by Monica Heller, 187–213. Berlin: Mouton de Gruyter.

Babitch, Rose Mary, & Eric Lebrun. 1989. Dialectometry as computerized agglomerative hierarchical classification analysis. *Journal of English Linguistics* 22:83–90.

Baggioni, Daniel. 1988. L'histoire de la créolistique et ses rapports à l'histoire de l'anthropologie: de Lucien Adam (1883) à Louis Hjelmslev (1938). *Etudes Créoles* 11:82–93.

Bailey, Charles-James N. n.d. *Southern states phonetics*. ms.

Bailey, Charles-James N. 1973. *Variation and linguistic theory*. Washington, DC: Center for Applied Linguistics.

Bailey, Charles-James N. 1978. *System of English intonation with gradient models*. Bloomington: Indiana University Linguistics Club.

Bailey, Charles-James N. 1982. *On the yin and yang nature of language*. Ann Arbor: Karoma Press.

Bailey, Charles-James N. 1985. *English phonetic transcription*. Dallas: Summer Institute of Linguistics/University of Texas at Arlington.

Bailey, Charles-James N. 1996. Old and new views on language history and language relationships. In *Essays on time-based linguistic analysis* (reprinted essays by Bailey), 244–88. Oxford: Clarendon Press.

Bailey, Charles-James N., & Karl Maroldt. 1977. The French lineage of English. In Meisel (ed.), 21–53.

Bailey, Guy. 1989. Sociolinguistic constraints on language change and the evolution of *are* in Early Modern English. *Standardizing English: Essays in the history of language change in honor of John Hunt Fisher*, ed. by Joseph B. Trahern, Jr., 158–72. Knoxville: University of Tennessee Press.

Bailey, Guy. 1991. Directions of change in Texas English. *Journal of American Culture* 14:125–34.

Bailey, Guy. 1993. A perspective on African American English. In *American dialect research*, ed. by Dennis Preston, 287–318. Amsterdam: John Benjamins.

Bailey, Guy, & Cynthia Bernstein. 1989. Methodology for a phonological survey of Texas. *Journal of English Linguistics* 22:6–16.

Bailey, Guy, & Margie Dyer. 1992. An approach to sampling in dialectology. *American Speech* 67:1–18.

Bailey, Guy, & Natalie Maynor. 1987. Decreolization? *Language in Society* 16:449–74.

Bailey, Guy, & Natalie Maynor. 1989. The divergence controversy. *American Speech* 64:12–39.

Bailey, Guy, Natalie Maynor & Patricia Cukor-Avila. 1989. Variation in subject-verb concord in Early Modern English. *Language Variation and Change* 1:285–300.

Bailey, Guy, Natalie Maynor & Patricia Cukor-Avila (eds.). 1991. *The emergence of black English: Text and commentary*. Creole Language Library, No. 8. Philadelphia: John Benjamins.

Bailey, Guy, & Garry Ross. 1988. The shape of the superstrate. *English World-Wide* 9:193–212.

Bailey, Guy, & Garry Ross. 1992. The evolution of a vernacular. In *History of Englishes: New methods and interpretations in historical linguistics*, ed. by Matti Rissanen, Ossi Ihalainen, Terttu Nevalainen & Irma Taavitsainen, 519–31. Berlin: Mouton de Gruyter.

Bailey, Guy, & Clyde Smith, Jr. 1992. Southern American English in Brazil, no? *SECOL Review* 16:71–89.

Bailey, Guy, Tom Wikle & Lori Sand. 1991. The focus of linguistic innovation in Texas. *English World-Wide* 12:195–214.

Bailey, Guy, Tom Wikle & Jan Tillery. 1992. The concept of a linguistic landscape. Paper presented at the Southeastern Conference on Linguistics (SECOL), Gainesville, FL.

Bailey, Guy, Tom Wikle, Jan Tillery & Lori Sand. 1991. The apparent time construct. *Language Variation and Change* 3:241–64.

Bailey, Guy, Tom Wikle, Jan Tillery & Lori Sand. 1992. Using apparent time data to chart linguistic diffusion. Paper presented at NWAVE-XXI, Ann Arbor, MI.

Bailey, Guy, Tom Wikle, Jan Tillery & Lori Sand. 1993. Some patterns of linguistic diffusion. *Language Variation and Change* 5:359–90.

Bailey, Nina. V. 1930. *Pitch and time variations in certain American dialects.* Iowa State University thesis.

Baker, Philip. 1984. Agglutinated French articles in creole French: Their evolutionary significance. *Te Reo* 27:89–129.

Baker, Philip. 1990. Off target? *Journal of Pidgin and Creole Languages* 5:107–19.

Baker, Philip. 1993. Assessing the African contribution to French-based creoles. In Mufwene with Condon (eds.), 123–55.

Baker, Philip, & Chris Corne. 1986. Universals, substrata and the Indian Ocean creoles. In Muysken & Smith (eds.), 163–83.

Bakhtin, Mikhail M. 1982. *Rabelais and his world.* Trans. Helene Iswolsky. Cambridge: MIT Press.

Ballance, Alton. 1989. *Ocracokers.* Chapel Hill: University of North Carolina Press.

Barry, Herbert, & Alice Schlegel. 1980. *Cross-cultural samples and codes.* University of Pittsburgh Press.

Bartley, Numan V. 1990. *The Creation of modern Georgia.* 2d ed. Athens: University of Georgia Press.

Bateson, Gregory. 1972. *Steps to an ecology of mind.* NY: Ballantine.

Baugh, John. 1980. A reexamination of the Black English copula. In Labov (ed.), 83–106.

Baugh, John. 1983. *Black street speech: Its history, structure, and survival.* Austin: University of Texas Press.

Baugh, John. 1984. Steady: Progressive aspect in Black English Vernacular. *American Speech* 59:1–12.

Bayley, Robert. 1991. Variation theory and second language learning: Linguistic and social constraints on interlanguage tense marking. Stanford University dissertation.

Bayley, Robert. 1994. Consonant cluster reduction in Tejano English. *Language Variation and Change* 6:303–26.

Becker, A. L. 1984. The linguistics of particularity: Interpreting superordination in a Javanese text. *Proceedings of the Berkeley Linguistics Society, 10th Annual Meeting,* ed. by Claudia Brugman & Monica Macaulay (with Amy Dahlstrom, Michele Emanatian, Birch Moonwomon & Catherine O'Connor), 425–36. Berkeley, CA: Berkeley Linguistics Society.

Becker, A. L. 1988. Language in particular: A lecture. In Tannen (ed.), 17–35.

Becker, A. L. 1994. Repetition and otherness: An essay. *Repetition in discourse: Interdisciplinary perspectives*, vol. 2, ed. by Barbara Johnstone, 162–75. Norwood, NJ: Ablex.

Bell, Allan. 1984. Language style as audience design. *Language in Society* 13:145–204.

Bender, Harold H. 1936. The origin of *ain't. Word Study* 11:2–3.

Bennett, John. 1908 & 1909. Gullah: A Negro patois. *South Atlantic Quarterly* 7:332–347, 8:39–52.

Bernard, H. Russell, Peter Killworth, David Kronenfeld & Lee Sailer. 1984. The problem of informant accuracy: the validity of retrospective data. *Annual Review of Anthropology* 13:494–517.

Bernstein, Cynthia. 1993. Measuring social causes of phonological variation in Texas. *American Speech* 68:227–40.

Bernstein, Cynthia. 1994. A phonological survey of Texas: Cluster analysis of Texas poll data. *ZDL-Beiheft 76: Proceedings of international congress of dialectologists*, Bamberg 1990, vol. 3, ed. by Wolfgang Viereck, 39–51. Stuttgart: Franz Steiner Verlag.

Biber, Douglas. 1988. *Variation and change across speech and writing*. Cambridge: Cambridge University Press.

Bickerstaffe, Isaac. 1768. *The padlock: a comic opera*. London.

Bickerstaffe, Isaac. [1795] 1962. The padlock: a comic opera. *Early American Imprints*, ed. by Clifford K. Shipton. Worcester, MA: Readex Microprint.

Bickerstaffe, Isaac. [1805] 1967. The padlock: a comic opera. *Early American Imprints*, ed. by Clifford K. Shipton. Worcester, MA: Readex Microprint.

Bickerton, Derek. 1974. Creolization, linguistic universals, natural semantax and the brain. *University of Hawaii Working Papers in Linguistics* 6.3:125–41.

Bickerton, Derek. 1975. *Dynamics of a creole system*. NY: Cambridge University Press.

Bickerton, Derek. 1981. *Roots of language*. Ann Arbor: Karoma Press.

Bickerton, Derek. 1984. The language bioprogram hypothesis. *The Behavioral and Brain Sciences* 7:173–221.

Bickerton, Derek. 1988. Creole languages and the bioprogram. In *Linguistics: The Cambridge survey*, vol. 2, ed. by Frederick J. Newmeyer, 268–84. Cambridge: Cambridge University Press.

Bickerton, Derek. 1989. The lexical learning hypothesis and the pidgin-creole cycle. In Pütz & Dirven (eds.), 11–31.

Bickerton, Derek. 1990. *Language and species*. University of Chicago.

Bickerton, Derek. 1992. The creole key to the black box of language. In *Thirty years of linguistic evolution: Studies in honor of René Dirven on the occasion of his sixtieth birthday*, ed. by Martin Pütz, 97–108. Philadelphia: John Benjamins.

Bickerton, Derek. 1996. The origins of variation in Guyanese. In Gregory R. Guy, Crawford Feagin, John Baugh & Deborah Schiffrin (eds.), 311–28.

Bilby, Kenneth M. 1993. Latent intervocalic liquids in Aluku: Links to the phonological past of a Maroon Creole. In Byrne & Holm (eds.), 25–35.

Blanton, Mackie J. V. 1989. New Orleans English. In Wilson & Ferris (eds.), 780–81.

Blom, Jan-Petter, & John J. Gumperz. 1972. Social meaning in linguistic structures: Code-switching in Norway. In Gumperz & Hymes (eds.), 407–34.

Bloomfield, Leonard. 1933. *Language*. NY: Holt, Rinehart & Winston.

Blyth, Carl. 1993. Lexical aspects of language attrition. Paper presented at Ateliers Créole et Français Cadien, University of Southwestern Lousiana.

Bortoni-Ricardo, Stella Maris. 1985. *The urbanization of rural dialect speakers: a sociolinguistic study in Brazil*. NY: Cambridge University Press.

Botkin, Benjamin A. 1945. *Lay My Burden Down: A Folk History of Slavery*. Chicago: University of Chicago Press.

Boyette, Dora S. 1951. *Variation pronunciations from Rockingham County, North Carolina, 1829–1860*. Chapel Hill: University of North Carolina thesis.

Braun, Friederike. 1988. *Terms of address: Problems of patterns and usage in various languages and cultures*. Berlin: Mouton de Gruyter.

Brewer, Jeutonne P. 1973. Subject concord of *Be* in early Black English. *American Speech* 48:5–21.

Brewer, Jeutonne P. 1974. The verb "be" in early Black English: A study based on the WPA Ex-Slave narratives. University of North Carolina at Chapel Hill dissertation.

Brewer, Jeutonne P. 1979. Non-agreeing *am* and invariant *be* in early Black English. *SECOL Bulletin* 3:81–100.

Brewer, Jeutonne P. 1980. The WPA slave narratives as linguistic data. *Orbis: Bulletin international de documentation linguistique* 29:19–33.

Brewer, Jeutonne P. 1986a. Camouflaged forms in early Black English: Evidence from the WPA ex-slave narratives. In *Proceedings of the Society for Caribbean Linguistics*, vol. 1, ed. by Lawrence Carrington, 1–19. St. Augustine, Trinidad, West Indies: University of the West Indies.

Brewer, Jeutonne P. 1986b. Durative marker or hypercorrection? The case of *-s* in the WPA Ex-Slave narratives. In Montgomery & Bailey (eds.), 131–48.

Brewer, Jeutonne P. 1991. Songs, sermons, and life-stories: The legacy of the ex-slave narratives. In Bailey, Maynor & Cukor-Avila (eds.), 155–71.

Briggs, Charles. 1986. *Learning how to ask*. Cambridge University Press.

Broder, John. 1992. On Inauguration Day, look for Clinton strutting his okra. *Sacramento Bee* (final ed.), Nov. 19, A/2.

Brooks, Cleanth. 1935. *The relation of the Alabama-Georgia dialect to the provincial dialects of Great Britain*. Baton Rouge: Louisiana State University Press.

Brooks, Cleanth. 1985. *The language of the American South*. Athens: University of Georgia Press.

Brousseau, Anne-Marie. 1994. The phonology of Haitian Creole, French, and Fongbè. Paper presented at the MIT Symposium on the Role of Relexification in Creole Genesis: The Case of Haitian Creole, Cambridge, MA.

Brower, Sidney. 1980. Territory in urban settings. In *Environment and culture*, vol. 4 of *Human behavior and environment*, ed. by Irwin Altman, Amos Rapaport & Joachim Wohlwill, 179–207.

Brown, Becky. 1986. Cajun/English code switching: A test of formal models. In Sankoff (ed.), 399–406.

Brown, Becky. 1993. The social consequences of writing Louisiana French. *Language in Society* 22:67–101.

Brown, Calvin S. 1976. *A glossary of Faulkner's South*. New Haven: Yale University Press.

Brown, Penelope, & Stephen Levinson. 1987. *Politeness: Some universals in language use.* Cambridge: Cambridge University Press.

Brown, Roger, & Marguerite Ford. 1964. Address in American English. In Hymes (ed.), 243–44.

Brown, Roger, & Albert Gilman. 1960. The pronouns of power and solidarity. *Style in language*, ed. by Thomas Sebeok, 253–76. Cambridge, MA: MIT Press.

Brown, T. Allston. 1870. *History of the American stage.* NY.

Brown, Vivian. 1990. The social and linguistic history of a merger: /ɪ/ and /ɛ/ before nasals in Southern American English. Texas A&M University dissertation.

Brown, Vivian. 1991. Evolution of the merger of /ɪ/ and /ɛ/ before nasals in Tennessee. *American Speech* 66: 303–15.

Brown, Vivian. 1993. Relative pronouns in the Civil War veterans questionnaires: The limits of written corpora. Paper presented at the Southeastern Conference on Linguistics (SECOL), Auburn, AL.

Bruner, Jerome. 1986. *Actual minds, possible worlds.* Cambridge, MA: Harvard University Press.

Bryant, Brenda K. 1985. *The neighborhood walk: Sources of support in middle childhood.* Vol. 50, No. 3 (No. 210) of Monographs of the Society for Research in Child Development. Chicago: Child Development Publications, the University of Chicago Press.

Burwell, Letitia M. 1895. *A girl's life in Virginia before the war.* NY.

Butters, Ronald R. 1989. *The death of Black English: Divergence and convergence in black and white vernaculars.* Frankfurt am Main: Peter Lang.

Butters, Ronald R. 1995. What did Cary Grant know about "going gay" and when did he know it? On the development of the popular term *gay* 'homosexual'. Paper presented at the meeting of the Dictionary Society of North America, Cleveland, OH.

Butters, Ronald R., & Ruth A. Nix. 1986. The English of Blacks in Wilmington, North Carolina. In Montgomery & Bailey (eds.), 254–63.

Byrd I, William. 1977. *The correspondence of the three William Byrds of Westover, Virginia, 1684–1776.* vol. 1, ed. by Marion Trilling. Charlottesville: Virginia Historical Society & University of Virginia Press.

Byrne, Francis, & John Holm (eds.). 1993. *Atlantic meets Pacific: A global view of pidginization and creolization.* Philadelphia: John Benjamins.

Callary, R. E. 1975. Phonological change and the development of an urban dialect in Illinois. *Language in Society* 4:155–70.

Canaan, Joyce. 1986. Why a 'slut' is a 'slut': Cautionary tales of middle-class teenage girls' morality. In Varenne 1986 (ed.), 184–208.

Caress, Jay. 1979. *Hank Williams: Country music's tragic king.* NY: Stein & Day.

Carpenter, Ronald H. 1990. The statistical profile of language behavior with machiavellian intent or while experiencing caution and avoiding self-incrimination. *Annals of the New York Academy of Sciences*, 606:5–18

Carrington, Lawrence. D. (ed.). 1983. *Studies in Caribbean language.* Augustine, Trinidad: Society for Caribbean Linguistics.

Carstensen, Laurence W. 1986. Bivariate mapping: The effects of axis scaling. *The American Cartographer* 13.1:27–42.

Carter, Hazel. 1979. Evidence for the survival of African prosodies in West Indian creoles. Occasional paper number 13. St. Augustine, Trinidad: Society for Caribbean linguistics.

Carter, Hazel. 1982. The tonal system of Jamaican English. Paper presented at the Fourth Biennial Conference for Caribbean Linguistics, Paramaribo, Suriname.

Carter, Hazel. 1987. Suprasegmentals in Guyanese: Some African comparisons. In Gilbert (ed.), 213–63.

Carter, Hazel. 1993. Vowel length in Afro-American: Development or retention? In Mufwene with Condon (eds.), 328–45.

Carver, Craig M. 1985. The *DARE* map and regional labels. In *DARE*, vol. I, xxiii-xxxv.

Carver, Craig M. 1987. *American regional dialects: A word geography.* Ann Arbor: University of Michigan Press.

Cassidy, Frederic G. 1978. Gullah and Jamaican Creole—the African connection. *Georgetown University round table on languages and linguistics*, 621–29. Washington, DC: Georgetown University Press.

Cassidy, Frederic G. 1983. Sources of the African element in Gullah. In Carrington (ed.), 75–81.

Cassidy, Frederic G. 1986. Some similarities between Gullah and Caribbean creoles. In Montgomery & Bailey (eds.), 30–37.

Cassidy, Frederic G., & Joan Houston Hall (eds.). 1985–. *Dictionary of American regional English.* Cambridge: Belknap Press of Harvard University Press.

Cassidy, Frederic G., & Robert B. LePage. 1967. *Dictionary of Jamaican English.* Cambridge: Cambridge University Press.

Cervantes, Miguel de. [1613] 1982. El celoso extremeño. *Novelas ejemplares*, II, ed. by Juan B. Avale-Arce, 173–221. Madrid: Clasicos Castalia.

Cervantes, Miguel de. [1640] 1900. *Exemplary novels.* Trans. by Don Diego Puede-Ser [James Mabbe]. Ed. by S. W. Orson. London: Gibbings & Co.

Chafe, Wallace. 1980. The deployment of consciousness in the production of a narrative. In *The pear stories: Cognitive, cultural, and linguistic aspects of narrative production*, ed. by Wallace Chafe, 1–50. Norwood, NJ: Ablex.

Chafe, Wallace. 1987. Cognitive constraints on information flow. In *Coherence and grounding in discourse*, ed. by Russell Tomlin, 21–51. Philadelphia: John Benjamins.

Chambers, J. K. 1992. Dialect acquisition. *Language* 68:673–705.

Chapman, Carl. 1983. *Indians and archaeology of Missouri.* Rev. ed. Columbia: University of Missouri Press.

Chastellux, François Jean, Marquis de. 1787. *Travels in North America in the years 1780, 1781, and 1782 . . . translated from the French by an English gentleman who resided in America at that period.* 2 vols. London.

Chaudenson, Robert. 1979. *Les créoles français.* Paris: Fernand Nathan.

Chaudenson, Robert. 1989. *Créoles et enseignment du français.* Paris: L'Harmattan.

Chaudenson, Robert. 1992. *Des îles, des hommes, des langues: langues créoles—cultures créoles.* Paris: L'Harmattan.

Cheshire, Jenny. 1982. *Variation in an English dialect: a sociolinguistic study.* NY: Cambridge University Press.

Ching, Marvin K. L. 1982. The question intonation in assertions. *American Speech* 57:95–107.

Ching, Marvin K. L. 1988. Ma'am and sir: Modes of mitigation and politeness in the southern United States. In *Methods in dialectology*, ed. by Alan R. Thomas, 20–45. Philadelphia: Multilingual Matters.

Chomsky, Noam, & Morris Halle. 1968. *The sound pattern of English.* New York: Harper & Row.

Christian, Donna. 1991. The personal dative in Appalachian English. In *Dialects of English: Studies in grammatical variation*, ed. by Peter Trudgill & Jack K. Chambers, 11–19. NY: Longman.

Christian, Donna, Walt Wolfram & Nanjo Dube. 1988. *Variation and change in geographically isolated communities: Appalachian English and Ozark English.* Publication of the American Dialect Society (PADS) 74. Tuscaloosa: University of Alabama Press.

Cichocki, Wladyslaw. 1989. An application of dual scaling in dialectometry. *Journal of English Linguistics* 22:91–6.

Clapp, William M. 1853. *Record of the Boston stage.* Boston.

Clark, Thomas D. 1944. *Pills, petticoats and plows: The Southern country store.* New York: Bobbs-Merril.

Clark, Thomas D. 1956. *Travelers in the old south: A bibliography.* 3 vols. Norman, OK: University of Oklahoma Press.

Clinton, Catherine. 1980. The plantation mistress: Another side of southern slavery, 1780–1835. Princeton University dissertation.

Clinton, Catherine. 1982. *The Plantation mistress: Woman's world in the old south.* NY: Pantheon.

Cohen, Yehoshua S., & Amnon Shinar. 1985. *Neighborhoods and friendship networks.* University of Chicago Department of Geography, Research Paper No. 215.

Coleman, James Samuel. 1961. *The adolescent society: The social life of the teenager and its impact on education.* NY: Freepress of Glencoe.

Collymore, Frank A. 1970. *Notes for a glossary of words and phrases of Barbadian dialect.* 4th ed. Bridgetown, Barbados: Advocate.

Comrie, Bernard. 1976. *Aspect: An introduction to the study of verbal aspect and related problems.* Cambridge: Cambridge University Press.

Conklin, Nancy Faires, & Margaret A. Lourie. 1983. *A host of tongues: Language communities in the United States.* NY: Free Press.

Conron, John (ed.). 1973. *The American landscape: A critical anthology of prose and poetry.* NY: Oxford University Press.

Conwell, Marilyn J., & Alphonse Juilland. 1963. *Louisiana French grammar.* The Hague: Mouton.

Cook, Albert B. n.d. A word geography of Kansas. ms.

Cooper, Vincent. 1979. Basilectal creole, decreolization and autonomous language change in St. Kitts-Nevis. Princeton University dissertation.

Craigie, William A. 1938. Dialect in literature. *Essays by Divers Hands* 17:69–91.

Craigie, Sir William A., & James R. Hulbert (eds.). 1938. *Dictionary of American English on historical principles.* Chicago: University of Chicago Press.

Crane, L. Ben. 1977. The social stratification of /aɪ/ in Tuscaloosa, Alabama. In Shores & Hines (eds.), 180–200.

Crum, Mason. 1940. *Gullah: Negro life in the Carolina Sea Islands.* Durham, NC: Duke University Press.

Cukor-Avila, Patricia. 1989. The urbanization of rural BEV. Paper presented at the Southeastern Conference on Linguistics (SECOL), Norfolk, VA.

Cukor-Avila, Patricia. 1995. The evolution of AAVE in a rural Texas community: An ethnolinguistic study. University of Michigan dissertation.

Cukor-Avila, Patricia, & Guy Bailey. 1992. Sociocultural contexts of style. Paper presented at NWAVE-XXI, Ann Arbor, MI.

Cukor-Avila, Patricia, & Guy Bailey. 1995. An approach to sociolinguistic fieldwork: African American English in a Texas community. *English World-Wide* 16:21–36.

Cunningham, Irma Aloyce Ewing. 1970. A syntactic analysis of Sea Island Creole "Gullah." University of Michigan dissertation.

Curtin, Philip D. 1969. *The Atlantic slave trade: A census.* Madison: University of Wisconsin Press.

Curtin, Philip D. 1975. *Economic change in precolonial Africa: Senegambia in the era of the slave trade.* 2 vols. Madison, WI: University of Wisconsin Press.

Cusic, Don (ed.). 1993. *Hank Williams: The complete lyrics.* NY: St. Martin's Press.

Daan J., & D. P. Blok. 1970. *Von randstad tot landrand.* Bijdragen en Mededelingen der Dialecten Commissie van de Koninklijke Nederlandse Akademie van Wetenschappen te Amsterdam, XXXVII. Amsterdam: N. V. Noord, Hollandsche Uitgevers Maatschappij.

Dakin, Robert. 1971. South midland speech in the old Northwest. *Journal of English Linguistics* 5:31–48.

Damon, S. Foster. 1934. The Negro in early American songsters. *The Papers of the Bibliographical Society of America* 28:132–63.

D'Andrade, Roy. 1990. Some propositions about the relations between culture and human cognition. In Stigler, Shweder & Herdt (eds.), 65–128.

D'Andrade, Roy, & Myron Wish. 1985. Speech act theory in quantitative research on interpersonal behavior. *Discourse Processes* 8:229–59.

DARE. See Cassidy & Hall 1985–.

Davis, Boyd H. 1986. The talking world map: Eliciting Southern adolescent language. In Montgomery & Bailey (eds.), 359–64.

Davis, Lawrence M. 1971. *A study of Appalachian speech in a northern urban setting.* Final report. National center for Educational Research & Development, Washington. Eric Document 061 205.

Davis, Lawrence M., & Charles L. Houck. 1992. Is there a Midland dialect area?—again. *American Speech* 67:61–70.

Dawsey, Cyrus B., & James M. Dawsey (eds.). 1995. *The Confederados: Old south immigrants in Brazil.* Tuscaloosa: University of Alabama Press.

D'Costa, Jean, & Barbara Lalla. 1989. *Voices in exile: Jamaican texts of the 18th and 19th centuries.* Tuscaloosa: University of Alabama Press.

Debien, Gabriel. 1961. Les origines des esclaves aux Antilles. *Bulletin de l'Institut Français d'Afrique Noir,* séries B, 23.

DeCamp, David. 1960. Four Jamaican Creole texts. In *Jamaican Creole,* ed. by R. B. LePage, 127–179. London: Macmillan.

Denning, Keith et al. (eds.). 1987. *Variation in language: NWAV-XV at Stanford.* Stanford, CA: Department of Linguistics, Stanford University.

Dent, Borden. 1990. *Cartography: Thematic map design.* Dubuque, Iowa: Wm. C. Brown Publishers.

Devonish, Hubert. 1989. *Talking in tones: A study of tone in Afro-European creole languages.* London: Karia Press and Christ Church, Barbados: Caribbean Academic Publications.

Dibdin, Charles. 1803. *The professional life of Mr. Dibdin.* Vols. 1–4. London.

Dillard, J. L. 1972. *Black English: Its history and usage in the United States.* NY: Random House.

Dillard, J. L. 1975a. *All-American English: A history of the English language in America.* NY: Random House.

Dillard, J. L. (ed.). 1975b. *Perspectives on Black English.* The Hague: Mouton & Co.

Dillard, J. L. 1977. *Lexicon of Black English.* NY: The Seabury Press.

Dillard, J. L. 1993. The value (linguistic and philological) of the WPA ex-slave narratives. In Mufwene with Condon (eds.), 222–31.

Di Paolo, Marianna. 1986. A study of double modals in Texas English. University of Texas at Austin dissertation.

Di Paolo, Marianna. 1988. Pronunciation and categorization in sound change. In Ferrara et al. (eds.), 84–92.

Di Paolo, Marianna, & Alice Faber. 1990. Phonation differences and the phonetic content of the tense-lax contrast in Utah English. *Language Variation and Change* 2:155–204.

Ditchy, Jay K. (first published anon.). [1901] 1932. *Les Acadiens louisianais et leur parler.* Paris.

Dorian, Nancy C. 1994. Purism versus compromise in language revitalization and language revival. *Language in Society* 23:479–94.

Dorrill, George T. 1986a. Black and white speech in the South: Evidence from the Linguistic Atlas of the Middle and South Atlantic States. *Bamberger Beiträge zur Englischen Sprachwissenschaft* 19. NY: Peter Lang.

Dorrill, George T. 1986b. A comparison of stressed vowels of black and white speakers in the South. In Montgomery & Bailey (eds.), 149–57.

Dow, James R. (ed.). 1991. *Language and ethnicity: Focusschrift in honor of Joshua A. Fishman on the occasion of his 65th birthday*, vol. 2. Philadelphia: John Benjamins.

Downer, James W. 1958. Features of New England rustic pronunciation in James Russell Lowell's *The Biglow Papers.* University of Michigan dissertation.

Downs, Roger, & David Stea. 1977. *Maps in minds: Reflections on cognitive mapping.* NY: Harper & Row.

Drapeau, Lynn. 1993. Language birth: An alternative to language death. In *Proceedings of the XVth International Congress of Linguists, Québec, Université Laval, 9–14 August 1992*, vol. 4, ed. by André Crochetièr et al., 141–44. Sainte-Foy: Les Presser de l'Université Laval.

DuBois, Marguerite-Marie. 1960. *Dictionnaire moderne français-anglais.* Paris: Librairie Larousse.

Dunlap, William. 1832. *A history of the American theater.* NY.

Duranti, Alessandro. 1992. Language in context and language as context: the Samoan respect vocabulary. In Duranti & Goodwin (eds.), 77–99.

Duranti, Alessandro, & Charles Goodwin (eds.). 1992. *Rethinking context*. Cambridge: Cambridge University Press.

Eckert, Penelope. 1986. The roles of high school social structure in phonological change. Paper presented at the Chicago Linguistic Society.

Eckert, Penelope. 1988. Adolescent social structure and the spread of linguistic change. *Language in Society* 17:183–207.

Eckert, Penelope. 1989a. *Jocks and burnouts: Social categories and identity in the high school*. NY: Teachers College Press.

Eckert, Penelope. 1989b. The whole woman: sex and gender differences in variation. *Language Variation and Change* 1:245–67.

Eckert, Penelope (ed.). 1991a. *New ways of analyzing sound change*. NY: Academic Press.

Eckert, Penelope. 1991b. Social polarization and the choice of linguistic variants. In Eckert (ed.), 213–32.

Eder, Donna. 1990. Serious and playful disputes: variation in conflict talk among female adolescents. In Grimshaw (ed.), 67–84.

Edwards, John R. 1982. Language attitudes and their implications among English speakers. In Ryan & Giles (eds.), 20–33.

Edwards, Viv. 1986. *Language in a black community*. San Diego: College Hill Press.

Edwards, Walter F. 1992. Sociolinguistic behavior in a Detroit inner-city black neighborhood. *Language in Society* 21:93–116.

Eliason, Norman. 1956. *Tarheel talk: An historical study of the English language in North Carolina to 1860*. Chapel Hill: University of North Carolina Press.

Ellis, James Fernando. 1929. *The influence of environment on the settlement of Missouri*. St. Louis: Webster Publishing Company.

Ellison, Ralph. 1952. *Invisible man*. NY: Vintage.

Elvas narrative of DeSoto in Arkansas. [{1542} 1939] 1986. In *Authentic voices: Arkansas culture 1541–1860*, ed. by Sarah Fountain, 3–17. Conway: University of Central Arkansas Press.

Emeneau, Murray B. 1964. India as a linguistic area. In Hymes (ed.), 642–50.

Enninger, Werner. 1991. Linguistic markers of anabaptist ethnicity through four centuries. In Dow (ed.), 23–60.

Erickson, Frederick, & Jeffrey Shultz. 1982. *The counselor as gatekeeper: Social interaction in interviews*. NY: Academic Press.

Ervin-Tripp, Susan. 1972. On sociolinguistic rules: Alternation and co-occurrence. In Gumperz & Hymes (eds.), 213–50.

Escott, Colin. 1993. Pamphlet accompanying the *Health & Happiness Shows* audio recording. Mercury 314 517 862–2.

Escott, Colin. 1994. *Hank Williams: The biography*. Boston: Little, Brown.

Esling, John H. 1981. Methods in voice quality research in dialect surveys. In *Methods/Méthodes IV*, ed. by Henry J. Warkentyne, 126–38. Victoria, BC: Department of Linguistics, University of Victoria.

Etter-Lewis, Gwendolyn. 1991a. Black women's life stories: Reclaiming self in narrative texts. In *Women's words: The feminist practice of oral history*, ed. by Sherna Berger Gluck & Daphne Patai, 43–58. NY: Routledge.

Etter-Lewis, Gwendolyn. 1991b. Standing up and speaking out: African American women's narrative legacy. *Discourse and Society* 2:425–37.

Etter-Lewis, Gwendolyn. 1993. *My soul is my own: Oral narratives of African American women in the professions.* NY: Routledge.

Falk, Julia. 1978. *Linguistics and language: A survey of basic concepts and implications.* 2d ed. NY: Wiley.

Faries, Rachel B. 1967. A word geography of Missouri. University of Missouri dissertation.

Faries, Rachel B., & Donald M. Lance. 1993. *Regional variation in Missouri.* In Frazer (ed.), 245–56.

Fasold, Ralph. 1972. *Tense marking in early Black English: A linguistic and social analysis.* Washington, DC: Center for Applied Linguistics.

Fasold, Ralph. 1976. One hundred years from syntax to phonology. In *Papers from the parasession on diachronic syntax*, ed. by Sanford B. Steever, Carol A. Walker & Salikoko S. Mufwene, 79–87. Chicago: Chicago Linguistic Society.

Fasold, Ralph. 1990. *The sociolinguistics of language.* Cambridge: Basil Blackwell.

Fasold, Ralph, & Yoshiko Nakano. 1996. Contraction and deletion in Vernacular Black English: Creole history and relationship to Euro-American English. In Guy, Feagin, Baugh & Schiffrin (eds.), 373–95.

Fasold, Ralph W., William Labov, Fay Boyd Vaughn-Cooke, Guy Bailey, Walt Wolfram, Arthur K. Spears & John Rickford. 1987. Are black and white vernaculars diverging? Papers from the NWAVE-XIV panel discussion. *American Speech* 62.1.

Faust, Drew Gilpin. 1988. *The creation of Confederate nationalism: Ideology and identity in the Civil War South.* Baton Rouge: Louisiana State University Press.

Feagin, Crawford. 1979. *Variation and change in Alabama English: A sociolinguistic study of the white community.* Washington, DC: Georgetown University Press.

Feagin, Crawford. 1985. A new approach to variation in the southern drawl: A sociolinguistic analysis of Alabama talk. Paper presented at the annual meeting of the American Dialect Society, Seattle, WA.

Feagin, Crawford. 1987. A closer look at the Southern drawl. In Denning et al. (eds.), 137–50.

Feagin, Crawford. 1990. The dynamics of a sound change in Southern States English: From R-less to R-ful in three generations. In *Development and diversity: Linguistic variation across time and space*, ed. by Jerold A. Edmondson, Crawford Feagin & Peter Mühlhäusler, 29–146. Dallas: Summer Institute of Linguistics/University of Texas at Arlington.

Feagin, Crawford. 1993. A new merger of /o/ and /oh/. Paper presented at NWAVE-XXIII, Ottawa, Canada.

Feagin, Crawford. 1996. Peaks and glides in Southern States short-a. In Gregory R. Guy, Crawford Feagin, John Baugh & Deborah Schiffrin (eds.), 136–60.

Ferrara, Kathleen, Becky Brown, Keith Walters & John Baugh (eds.). 1988. *Linguistic change and contact: Proceedings of the sixteenth annual conference on New Ways of Analyzing Variation.* Austin: University of Texas, Department of Linguistics.

Fields, Linda. 1992. *Early Bajan: creole or non-creole?* Paper presented at the Ninth Biennial Conference of the Society for Caribbean Linguistics, Cave Hill, Barbados.

Finegan, Edward. 1992. Style and standardization in England: 1700–1900. In *English in its social contexts: Essays in historical sociolinguistics*, ed. by Tim William Machan & Charles T. Scott, 102–30. NY: Oxford University Press.

Fischer, David Hackett. 1989. *Albion's seed: Four British folkways in America*. Oxford: Oxford University Press.

Fogel, Robert William, & Stanley L. Engerman. 1974. *Time on the cross: The economics of American negro slavery*, 2 vols. Boston: Little, Brown.

Foote, Horton. 1989. *Three screenplays*. NY: Grove Weidenfeld.

Foster, Charles. 1971. *The representation of Negro dialect in Charles W. Chesnutt's The conjure woman*. Publication of the American Dialect Society (PADS) 55. Tuscaloosa: University of Alabama Press.

Fox-Genovese, Elizabeth. 1988. *Within the plantation household: Black and white women of the old south*. Chapel Hill: University of North Carolina Press.

Frazer, Timothy C. 1978. South midland pronunciation in the north central states. *American Speech* 53:40–48.

Frazer, Timothy C. 1979. The speech island of the American Bottoms: A problem in social history. *American Speech* 54:185–93.

Frazer, Timothy C. 1983a. Cultural assimilation in the post-frontier era. *Midwestern Journal of Language and Folklore* 9.1:5–23.

Frazer, Timothy C. 1983b. South change and social structure in a rural community. *Language in Society* 12:313–28.

Frazer, Timothy C. 1987. *Midland Illinois dialect patterns*. Publication of the American Dialect Society (PADS) 73. Tuscaloosa: University of Alabama Press.

Frazer, Timothy C. (ed.). 1993a. *Heartland English*. Tuscaloosa: University of Alabama Press.

Frazer, Timothy C. 1993b. The language of Yankee cultural imperialism: Pioneer ideology and "General American." In Frazer (ed.), 59–66.

Friedrich, Paul. 1972. Social context and semantic feature: The Russian pronominal usage. In Gumperz & Hymes (eds.), 301–24.

Fromkin, Victoria, & Robert Rodman. 1983. *An introduction to language*. 3d ed. NY: Holt, Rinehart & Winston.

G. M. 1831. South Carolina. *New England Magazine* 1:249–50.

Gal, Susan. 1979. *Language shift: Social determinants of linguistic change in bilingual Austria*. NY: Academic Press.

Galloway, Patricia, & Phillip P. Boucher (eds.). 1992. *Proceedings of the fifteenth meeting of the French Colonial Historical Society*. Lanham, MD: University Press of America.

Gastil, Raymond D. 1975. *Cultural regions of the United States*. Seattle: University of Washington Press.

Genovese, Eugene. 1974. *Roll Jordan, roll: The world the slaves made*. NY: Pantheon Books.

Gerlach, Russel L. 1976. *Immigrants in the Ozarks: A study in ethnic geography*. Columbia: University of Missouri Press.

Gilbert, Glenn. (ed.). 1986. *Pidgin and creole languages; Essays in memory of John E. Reinecke*. Honolulu: University of Hawaii Press.

Gilbert, Glenn, & Alicia Spiegel. 1996. The non-appearance of postvocalic R in the English-based New World Creoles: A case of "favored syncretism." Paper presented at the annual meeting of the Society of Pidgin and Creole Languages, San Diego, CA.

Giles, Howard. 1970. Evaluative reactions to accents. *Educational Review* 22:211–27.

Giles, Howard. 1973. Accent mobility: A model and some data. *Anthropological Linguistics* 15:87–105.

Giles, Howard, & Richard Powesland. 1975. *Speech style and social evaluation*. NY: Academic Press.

Giles, Howard, Donald M. Taylor, Wallace Lambert & Richard Bourhis. 1973. Towards a theory of interpersonal accommodation through language: Some Canadian data. *Language in Society* 2:177–92.

Gilman, Charles. 1985 Proto-Creole /r/. In *Diversity and development in English-related creoles*, ed. by Ian Hancock, 33–43. Ann Arbor: Karoma Press.

Gilman, Charles. 1986. African areal characteristics: Sprachbund, not substrate? *Journal of Pidgin and Creole Linguistics* 1:33–50.

Gilpin, William. [1860] 1973. The central gold region. Excerpted in *The American landscape: A critical anthology of prose and poetry*, ed. by John Conron, 372–77. NY: Oxford.

Giroux, Robert. 1971. Introduction. In *Flannery O'Connor, the complete stories*, vii-xvii. NY: Farrar.

Goffman, Erving. 1959. *The presentation of self in everyday life*. Garden City, NY: Doubleday Anchor Books.

Goffman, Erving. 1974. *Frame analysis: An essay in the organization of experience*. NY: Harper & Row.

Golledge, Reginald, & Robert J. Stimson. 1987. *Analytical behavioral geography*. NY: Croom Helm.

Gonzales, Ambrose E. 1892. *Silhouettes*. Columbia, SC: The State Newspaper.

Gonzales, Ambrose E. 1922. *The black border: Gullah stories of the Carolina Coast (with a glossary)*. Columbia, SC: The State Printing Company.

Gonzales, Ambrose E. 1924a. *The captain: Stories of the black border*. Columbia, SC: The State Printing Company.

Gonzales, Ambrose E. 1924b. *Laguerre: A gascon of the black border*. Columbia, SC: The State Printing Company.

Gonzalez, Andrew, FSC. 1991. Cebuano and Tagalog: Ethnic rivalry redivivus. In Dow (ed.), 111–29.

González, Gustavo. 1988. Chicano English. In *Chicano speech in the bilingual classroom*, ed. by Dennis J. Bixler-Marquez & Jacob Ornstein-Galicia, 71–82. NY: Peter Lang.

Goodwin, Charles, & Marjorie Goodwin. 1990. Interstitial argument. In Grimshaw (ed.), 85–117.

Goodwin, Marjorie. 1990. *He-said-she-said: Talk as social organization among black children*. Bloomington: Indiana University Press.

Gordon, Wayne. 1957. *The social system of the high school*. Glencoe, IL: The Free Press.

Gore, Al. 1992. *Earth in the balance: Ecology and the human spirit*. Boston: Houghton.

Gorman, James. 1993. Like, Uptalk? *New York Times Magazine*. August 15:14–16.

Gottman, John, & Gwendolyn Mettetal. 1986. Speculations about social and affective development: Friendship and acquaintance through adolescence. In Gottman & Parker (eds.), 192–237.

Gottman, John, & Jeffrey Parker. 1986. *Conversations of friends: Speculations on affective development*. Cambridge: Cambridge University Press.

Gould, Peter, & Rodney White. 1974. *Mental maps*. Harmondsworth, Middlesex: Penguin.

Gregersen, Edgar A. 1977. *Language in Africa: An introductory survey*. NY: Gordon & Breach.

Grimshaw, Allen D. (ed.). 1990. *Conflict talk: Sociolinguistic investigations of arguments in conversations*. Cambridge: Cambridge University Press.

Griolet, Patrick. 1986. *Mots de Louisiane*. Göteborg: Acta Universitatis Gothoburgensis.

Grootaers, Willem A. 1959. Origin and nature of the subjective boundaries of dialects. *Orbis* 8:355–84.

Gumperz, John J. 1982a. *Discourse strategies*. Cambridge: Cambridge University Press.

Gumperz, John J. (ed.). 1982b. *Language and social identity*. Cambridge: Cambridge University Press.

Gumperz, John J. 1992. Contextualization and understanding: Rethinking context. In Duranti & Goodwin (eds.), 229–52.

Gumperz, John, & Dell Hymes (eds.). 1972. *Directions in sociolinguistics: The ethnography of communication*. NY: Holt, Rinehart, & Winston.

Guy, Gregory R. 1980. Variation in the group and the individual: The case of final stop deletion. In Labov (ed.), 1–36.

Guy, Gregory. 1981a. Linguistic variation in Brazilian Portuguese: Aspects of the phonology, syntax, and language history. University of Pennsylvania dissertation.

Guy, Gregory. 1981b. Parallel variability in American dialects of Spanish and Portuguese. In *Variation omnibus*, ed. by David Sankoff & Henrietta Cedergren, 85–96. Edmonton: Linguistic Research.

Guy, Gregory R. 1988. Advanced VARBRUL analysis. In Ferrara et al. (eds.), 124–36.

Guy, Gregory R. 1991a. Contextual conditioning in variable phonology. *Language Variation and Change* 3:223–39.

Guy, Gregory R. 1991b. Explanation in variable phonology: An exponential model of morphological constraints. *Language Variation and Change* 3:1–22.

Guy, Gregory R., & Sally Boyd. 1990. The development of a morphological class. *Language Variation and Change* 2:1–18.

Guy, Gregory R., Crawford Feagin, John Baugh & Deborah Schiffrin (eds.). 1996. *Towards a social science of language: Papers in honor of William Labov*, vol. 1. Philadelphia: John Benjamins.

Guy, Gregory, Barbara Horvath, J. Vonwiller, E. Daisley & I. Rogers. 1986. An intonational change in progress in Australian English. *Language in Society* 15:23–51.

Habick, Timothy. 1980. Sound change in Farmer City. University of Illinois dissertation.

Habick, Timothy. 1991. Burnouts vs. rednecks. In Eckert (ed.), 185–212.

Hall, B. C., & C. T. Wood. 1992. *Big muddy: Down the Mississippi through America's heartland.* NY: Dutton.

Hall, Gwendolyn Midlo. 1992a. *Africans in colonial Louisiana: The development of Afro-creole culture in the eighteenth century.* Baton Rouge: Louisiana State University Press.

Hall, Gwendolyn Midlo. 1992b. The 1795 slave conspiracy on Pointe Coupée: Impact of the French Revolution. In Galloway & Boucher (eds.), 130–41.

Hall, Joan H. forthcoming. Packaging LAGS for DARE. In Montgomery & Nunnally (eds.).

Hall, Joan H., Nick Doane & Dick Ringler (eds.). 1992. *Old English and new: Studies in language and linguistics in honor of Frederic G. Cassidy.* NY: Garland.

Hall, Joseph Sargent. 1942. *The phonetics of Great Smoky Mountain speech.* American Speech Monograph 4. NY: Columbia University Press.

Hallowell, A. I. 1955. The self and its behavioral environment. In *Culture and experience,* ed. by A. I. Hallowell, 75–110. Philadelphia: University of Pennsylvania Press.

Hancock, Ian F. 1969. A provisional comparison of the English-based Atlantic creoles. *African Language Review* 8:7–72.

Hancock, Ian F. 1986a. On the classification of Afro-Seminole creole. In Montgomery & Bailey (eds.), 85–101.

Hancock, Ian F. 1986b. A preliminary classification of the Anglophone Atlantic creoles. In Gilbert (ed.), 264–333.

Hancock, Ian F. 1994. Componentiality and the creole matrix: The southwest English contribution. In *The crucible of Carolina: Essays in the development of Gullah language and culture,* ed. by Michael Montgomery, 95–114. Athens: University of Georgia Press.

Hannah, Dawn. 1995. Samaná English copula and the linguistic history of AAVE. Paper presented at NWAVE-XXIV, Philadelphia, PA.

Harris, Joel Chandler. 1883. *Nights with Uncle Remus: Myths and legends of the old plantation.* Boston.

Harris, John. 1986. Expanding the superstrate: Habitual aspect markers in Atlantic Englishes. *English World-Wide* 7:171–99.

Hartford, Beverly S. 1975. The English of Mexican-American adolescents in Gary, Indiana. University of Texas at Austin dissertation.

Haskell, Ann Sullivan. 1964. The representation of Gullah-influenced dialect in 20th century South Carolina prose, 1922–30. University of Pennsylvania dissertation.

Hasselmo, Nils. 1970. Code-switching and modes of speaking. In *Texas studies in bilingualism,* ed. by Glenn G. Gilbert, 179–210. Berlin: de Gruyter.

Haugen, Einar. 1956. *Bilingualism in the Americas: A bibliography and research guide.* Publication of the American Dialect Society (PADS) 26. Tuscaloosa: University of Alabama Press.

Havighurst, Robert J., Paul H. Bowman, Gordon P. Liddle, Charles V. Matthews & James V. Pierce. 1962. *Growing up in River City.* NY: John Wiley (for the University of Chicago).

Hawkins, Opal. 1982. Southern linguistic variation as revealed through overseers' letters, 1829–1858. University of North Carolina at Chapel Hill dissertation.

Heath, Shirley Brice. 1983. *Ways with words: Language, life, and work in communities and classrooms.* Cambridge: Cambridge University Press.

Heath, Shirley Brice. 1995. Ethnography in Communities. In *Handbook of research on multicultural education*, ed. by James Banks & Cherry McGee-Banks, 114–28. NY: Macmillan.

Hemphill, William Edwin, Marvin Wilson Schlegel & Sadie Ethel Engelberg. 1957. *Cavalier commonwealth.* NY: McGraw-Hill.

Henrie, Samuel Nyal, Jr. 1969. A study of verb phrases used by five year old nonstandard negro English speaking children. University of California at Berkeley dissertation.

Herold, Ruth. 1990. Mechanisms of merger: The implementation and distribution of the low back merger in Eastern Pennsylvania. University of Pennsylvania dissertation.

Herskovits, Melville. 1941. *The myth of the negro past.* NY: Harper.

Hewitt, Roger. 1986. *White talk-black talk: Interracial friendship and communication amongst adolescents.* Cambridge: Cambridge University Press.

Hill, Archibald A. [1940] 1971. Early Loss of [r] before dentals. In Williamson & Burke (eds.), 88–100.

Hill, Archibald A. 1965. The tainted *ain't* once more. *College English* 26:298–303.

Hill, Jane H., & Kenneth C. Hill. 1986. *Speaking Mexicano.* Tucson: University of Arizona Press.

Hill, West T. 1971. *The theater in early Kentucky, 1790–1820.* Lexington: University of Kentucky Press.

Hobson, Fred C. 1983. *Tell about the South: The southern rage to explain.* Baton Rouge: Louisiana State University Press.

Hodge, Frederick Webb. 1930. *Handbook of American Indians.* Smithsonian Institution, Bureau of American Ethnology, Bulletin 30.

Hoenigswald, Henry. 1966. A proposal for the study of folk-linguistics. In *Sociolinguistics*, ed. by William F. Bright, 16–26. The Hague: Mouton.

Hollingshead, August B. 1949. *Elmtown's youth.* NY: Wiley.

Holm, John. 1978. The creole English of Nicaragua's Miskito Coast: Its sociolinguistic history and a comparative study of its lexicon and syntax. University of London dissertation.

Holm, John. 1980. African features in white Bahamian English. *English World-Wide* 1:45–65.

Holm, John. (ed.). 1983a. *Central American English.* Heidelberg: Groos.

Holm, John. 1983b. On the relationship of Gullah and Bahamian. *American Speech* 58:303–18.

Holm, John. 1984. Variability of the copula in Black English and its Creole kin. *American Speech* 59:291–309.

Holm, John. 1988/89. *Pidgins and creoles*, 2 vols. Cambridge: Cambridge University Press.

Holm, John. 1991. The Atlantic creoles and the language of the ex-slave recordings. In Bailey, Maynor & Cukor-Avila (eds.), 231–48.

Holm, John. 1992. A theoretical model for semi-creolization. Paper presented to the Ninth Biennial Conference of the Society for Caribbean Linguistics, Cave Hill, Barbados.

Holm, John. 1993. Phonological features common to some West African and Atlantic Creole languages. In Mufwene with Condon (eds.), 317–27.

Holm, John A., with Alison W. Shilling. 1982. *Dictionary of Bahamian English.* Cold Spring, NY: Lexik House.

Hoole, W. Stanley. 1946. *The ante-bellum Charleston theater.* Tuscaloosa: University of Alabama Press.

Hopkins, Tometro. 1992. Aspects of the study of Afro-Creole: Gullah and Afro-Cuban. Indiana University dissertation.

Howren, Robert. 1962. The speech of Ocracoke, North Carolina. *American Speech* 37:163–75.

Huffines, Marion Lois. 1991. Pennsylvania German: 'Do they love it in their hearts?' In Dow (ed.), 9–22.

Hutton, Laurence. 1891. *Curiosities of the American stage.* NY.

Hymes, Dell. 1964a. Introduction: Toward ethnographies of communication. *American Anthropologist* 66:12–25.

Hymes, Dell (ed.). 1964b. *Language in culture and society.* NY: Harper & Row.

Hymes, Dell (ed.). 1971. *Pidginization and creolization of languages.* Cambridge: Cambridge University Press.

Hymes, Dell. 1974. *Foundations in sociolinguistics: An ethnographic approach.* University of Pennsylvania Press.

Hymes, Dell, & John Fought (eds.). 1981. *American structuralism.* The Hague: Mouton Publishers.

Index by region, usage, and etymology to the Dictionary of American regional English, *volumes I and II.* 1993. Prepared by the staff of DARE. Preface by Allan Metcalf, introduction by Luanne von Schneidemesser. Publication of the American Dialect Society (PADS) 77. Tuscaloosa: University of Alabama Press.

Ireland, Joseph N. [1866–67] 1966. *Records of the New York stage from 1750–1860.* NY: Benjamin Blom.

Ives, Sumner. [1950] 1971. A theory of literary dialect. In Williamson & Burke (eds.), 145–77.

Ives, Sumner. 1954. *The phonology of the Uncle Remus stories.* Publication of the American Dialect Society (PADS) 22. Tuscaloosa: University of Alabama Press.

Ives, Sumner. 1955. Dialect differentiation in the stories of Joel Chandler Harris. *American literature* 17:88–96.

Jaffe, Hilda. 1965. The speech of the central coast of North Carolina: The Carteret County version of the Banks "brogue." Michigan State University dissertation.

Jaffe, Hilda. 1973. *The speech of the central coast of North Carolina: The Carteret County version of the Banks "brogue."* Publication of the American Dialect Society (PADS) 60. Tuscaloosa: University of Alabama Press.

Jakobson, Roman. [1931] 1962. Über die phonologischen Sprachbünde. *Travaux du Cercle Linguistique de Prague 4.* Reprinted in *Roman Jakobson selected writings I: Phonological studies,* 137–143. The Hague: Mouton.

Jakobson, Roman. [1974] 1987. A glance at the development of semiotics. In *Language in literature,* ed. by Krystyna Pomorska & Stephen Rudy, 436–54. Cambridge, MA: Belknap.

Jenks, George. 1963. Generalization in statistical mapping. *Annual of the Association of American Geographers* 53.1:15–26.

Jespersen, Otto. 1922. *Language: Its nature, development and origin.* NY: W.W. Norton & Co.

Johnson, Ellen. 1996. *Lexical change and variation in the Southeastern United States in the twentieth century.* Tuscaloosa: University of Alabama Press.

Johnson, Guy. 1930. *Folk culture on St. Helena Island, South Carolina.* Chapel Hill: University of North Carolina Press.

Johnson, Jean L. 1991. A comparative ethnography of linguistic taboo: Profanity and obscenity among American undergraduate college women. Indiana University of Pennsylvania dissertation.

Johnstone, Barbara. 1990. *Stories, community, and place: Narratives from middle America.* Bloomington: Indiana University Press.

Johnstone, Barbara. 1996. *The linguistic individual: Self-expression in language and linguistics.* New York: Oxford University Press.

Jones, Hugh. [1724] 1956. *The present state of Virginia.* Chapel Hill: Virginia Historical Society & University of North Carolina Press.

Jones-Jackson, Patricia A. 1978. The status of Gullah: An investigation of convergent processes. University of Michigan dissertation.

Jones-Jackson, Patricia. 1986. *On the status of Gullah on the sea islands.* In Montgomery & Bailey (eds.), 63–72.

Joyner, Charles. 1984. *Down by the riverside: A South Carolina slave community.* Urbana: University of Illinois Press.

Joyner, Charles. 1989. *Remember me: Slave life in coastal Georgia.* Atlanta: Georgia Humanities Council.

Joyner, Charles. 1991. One people: Creating an integrated culture in a segregated society, 1526–1990. In *The meaning of South Carolina history: Essays in honor of George C. Rogers, Jr.*, ed. by David R. Chesnutt & Clyde N. Wilson, 214–44. Columbia, SC: University of South Carolina Press.

Jubera, Drew. 1990. The military hitch. *The Atlanta Journal*, Sept. 16.

Kenstowicz, Michael, & Charles Kisseberth. 1979. *Generative phonology: Description and theory.* NY: Academic Press.

Kerswill, Paul. 1994. *Dialects converging: Rural speech in urban Norway.* Oxford: Clarendon Press.

Kerswill, Paul. 1995. Children, adolescents and language change. *Reading Working Papers in Linguistics* 2:201–22.

Killingsworth, M. Jimmie, & Jacqueline Palmer. 1992. *Ecospeak: Rhetoric and environmental politics in America.* Carbondale: Southern Illinois University Press.

King, Edward. [1879] 1972. *The great South.* Baton Rouge: Louisiana State University Press.

King, Ruth. 1991. Acadian French and linguistic theory. *Journal of the Atlantic Provinces Linguistic Association* 13:35–46.

Kiparsky, Paul. 1972. Explanation in phonology. In *Goals of linguistic theory*, ed. by S. Peters, 189–227. Englewood Cliffs, NJ: Prentice Hall.

Kiparsky, Paul. 1982. Lexical morphology and phonology. In *Linguistics in the morning calm*, ed. by I. S. Yang, 3–91. Seoul: Hanshin.

Kirby, Jack Temple. 1987. *Rural worlds lost: The American south 1920–1960.* Baton Rouge: Louisiana State University Press.

Kirk, John M. 1993a. Linguistic maps. *Encyclopedia of language and linguistics*, 10 vols. Oxford: Pergamon Press.

Kirk, John M. 1993b. *Mapping the American linguistic south*. Paper presented at Language Variety in the South II, Auburn, AL.

Kirk, John, Stewart Sanderson & J. D. A. Widdowson. 1985. Introduction. In *Studies in linguistic geography*, ed. by Kirk, Sanderson & Widdowson, 1–34. London: Croom Helm.

Kirk, John, & G. Munroe. 1989. A method for dialectometry. *Journal of English Linguistics* 22:97–110.

Klingberg, Frank J. [1941] 1975. *An appraisal of the Negro in colonial South Carolina: A study in Americanization*. Philadelphia: Porcupine Press.

Klingler, Thomas A. 1992. A descriptive study of the creole speech of Pointe Coupee Parish, Louisiana with focus on the lexicon. Indiana University dissertation.

Knight, Henry Cogswell [a.k.a. Arthur Singleton]. 1824. *Letters from the south and west*. Boston.

Kochman, Thomas. 1981. *Black and white styles in conflict*. Chicago: University of Chicago Press.

Krapp, George Philip. 1924. The English of the Negro. *The American Mercury* 2:190–95.

Krapp, George P. [1925] 1960. *The English language in America*. NY: F. Ungar Publishing Co.

Krapp, George P. 1926. The psychology of dialect writing. *The Bookman* 63:522–27.

Kremer, Ludger. 1984. Die Niederländisch-Deutsch Staatsgrenze als subjective Dialektgrenze. *Nedersaksiche Studies* 7:76–83.

Kretzschmar, William A., Jr. (ed.). 1979. *Dialects in culture: Essays in general dialectology by Raven I. McDavid, Jr.* Tuscaloosa: University of Alabama Press.

Kretzschmar, William A., Jr. 1992a. Isoglosses and predictive modeling. *American Speech* 67:227–49.

Kretzschmar, William A., Jr. 1992b. Quantitative methods in a qualitative paradigm. Paper presented at NWAVE-XXI, Ann Arbor, Michigan.

Kretzschmar, William A., Jr., & Jay Lee. 1991. Quantitative methods for word geography. Paper presented at NWAVE-XX, Washington, DC.

Kretzschmar, William A., Jr., & Jay Lee. 1993. Spatial analysis of linguistic data with GIS functions. *International Journal of GIS* 7:541–60.

Kretzschmar, William A., Jr., Virginia G. McDavid, Theodore K. Lerud & Ellen Johnson (eds.). 1994. *Handbook of the linguistic atlas of the middle and south Atlantic states*. Chicago: University of Chicago Press.

Kretzschmar, William A., Jr., & Edgar W. Schneider. 1996. *Introduction to quantitative analysis of linguistic survey data: An atlas by the numbers*. Thousand Oaks, CA: Sage Publications.

Kretzschmar, William A., Jr., Edgar W. Schneider & Ellen Johnson (eds.). 1989. Computer methods in dialectology. *Journal of English Linguistics* 22.1.

Kurath, Hans (ed.). 1939–43. *The linguistic atlas of New England*. 3 vols. Providence: Brown University Press.

Kurath, Hans. 1949. *A word geography of the eastern United States*. Ann Arbor: University of Michigan Press.

Kurath, Hans. 1972. *Studies in area linguistics*. Bloomington: Indiana University Press.

Kurath, Hans, Marcus L. Hansen, Julia Bloch & Bernard Bloch. 1939. *Handbook of the linguistic geography of New England*. Providence: Brown University Press.

Kurath, Hans, & Raven I. McDavid, Jr. [1961] 1982. *The pronunciation of English in the Atlantic States*. Ann Arbor: University of Michigan Press. Reprinted Tuscaloosa: University of Alabama Press.

Labov, Teresa. 1981. Social structure and peer terminology in a black adolescent gang. *Language and Society* 12:391–421.

Labov, William. 1963. The social motivation of a sound change. *Word* 19:273–309.

Labov, William. 1966. *The social stratification of English in New York City*. Washington, DC: Center for Applied Linguistics.

Labov, William. 1972a. *Language in the inner city: Studies in the Black English Vernacular*. Philadelphia: University of Pennsylvania Press.

Labov, William. 1972b. *Sociolinguistic patterns*. Philadelphia: University of Pennsylvania Press.

Labov, William. 1973. Where do grammars stop? In *Sociolinguistics: Current trends and prospects*, ed. by Roger W. Shuy, Charles-James N. Bailey & Einar Haugen, 43–88. *Georgetown University round table on languages and linguistics*. Washington, DC: Georgetown University Press.

Labov, William (ed.). 1980a. *Locating language in time and space*. NY: Academic Press.

Labov, William. 1980b. The social origins of sound change. In Labov (ed.), 251–66.

Labov, William. 1982. Objectivity and commitment in linguistic science: The case of the Black English trial in Ann Arbor. *Language in Society* 11:165–201.

Labov, William. 1988. Lexical competition in the short order cuisine. Paper presented at the annual meeting of the American Dialect Society, New Orleans, LA.

Labov, William. 1989a. The child as linguistic historian. *Language Variation and Change* 1:85–97.

Labov, William. 1989b. The limitations of context. *Chicago Linguistic Society* 25, Part 2, 171–200.

Labov, William. 1990. The intersection of sex and social class in the course of linguistic change. *Language Variation and Change* 2:205–54.

Labov, William. 1991. The three dialects of English. In Eckert (ed.), 1–44.

Labov, William. 1994. *Principles of linguistic change*, vol. 1. Oxford: Blackwell Publishers.

Labov, William, Paul Cohen, Clarence Robins & John Lewis. 1968. *A study of the non-standard English of Negro and Puerto Rican speakers in New York City*. Cooperative Research Project #3288. Washington: Office of Education, Department of Health, Education & Welfare.

Labov, William, & Wendell Harris. 1986. De facto segregation of black and white vernaculars. In Sankoff (ed.), 1–24.

Labov, William, Mark Karan & Corey Miller. 1991. Near-mergers and the suspension of phonemic contrast. *Language Variation and Change* 3:33–74.

Labov, William, Malcah Yaeger & Richard Steiner. 1972. *A quantitative study of sound change in progress*. 2 vols. Philadelphia: U.S. Regional Survey.

Ladd, Frances. 1970. Black youths view their environment: neighborhood maps. *Environment and Behavior* 2:74–99.

Ladefoged, Peter. 1964. *A phonetic study of West African languages.* Cambridge: Cambridge University Press.

Laferriere, Martha. 1977. Boston short a: Social variation as historical residue. In *Studies in language variation: Semantics, syntax, phonology, pragmatics, social situations and ethnographic approaches,* ed. by Ralph W. Fasold & Roger W. Schuy, 100–107. Washington, DC: Georgetown University Press.

LAGS. See Pederson et al. 1986–1991.

Lakoff, Robin Tolmach, & Deborah Tannen. 1984. Conversational strategy and metastrategy in a pragmatic theory: The example of scenes from a marriage. *Semiotica* 49.3/4:323–46.

Lalla, Barbara, & Jean D'Costa. 1990. *Language in exile: Three hundred years of Jamaican Creole.* Tuscaloosa: University of Alabama Press.

Lambert, Wallace, E. R. Hodgson, R. C. Gardner & S. Fillenbaum. 1960. Evaluational reactions to spoken languages. *Journal of Abnormal and Social Psychology* 60:44–51.

Lance, Donald M. [1985] 1993. Dialect features in the English of Missouri Germans. In Frazer (ed.), 187–97.

Lance, Donald M. 1994. Variation in American English. In *American pronunciation* by John Samuel Kenyon, expanded 12th ed., ed. by Lance, 333–56. Ann Arbor: George Wahr.

Langacker, Ronald W. 1973. *Language and its structure: Some fundamental linguistic concepts.* 2d ed. NY: Harcourt Brace Jovanovich.

Larison, C. W. [1883] 1969. *Silvia Dubois, (now 116 yers old.): A biografy of the slav who whipt her mistres and gand her fredom.* NY: Negro Universities Press.

Larson, Reed, & Maryse H. Richards. 1991. Daily companionship in late childhood and early adolescence: Changing developmental contexts. *Child Development* 62:284–300.

Latrobe, Benjamin Henry. [1796] 1977. *The Virginia journals of Benjamin Henry Latrobe, 1795–8.* New Haven: Maryland Historical Society/Yale University Press.

Lawton, David. 1963. Suprasegmental phenomena in Jamaican Creole. Michigan State University dissertation.

Lawton, David. 1968. The implications of tone for Jamaican Creole. *Anthropological Linguistics* 10.6:22–26.

Lawton, David. 1982. English in the Caribbean. In *English as a world language,* ed. by R. W. Bailey & M. Gorlach, 251–80. Ann Arbor: University of Michigan Press.

Lawton, David. 1984. Tone structure and function in Jamaican Creole. Paper presented at the fifth biannual meeting of the Society for Caribbean Linguistics, Kingston, Jamaica.

Lefebvre, Claire. 1986. Relexification in creole genesis revisited: The case of Haitian Creole. In Muysken & Smith (eds.), 279–300.

Legman, G. 1941. The language of homosexuality: An American glossary. Appendix to *Sex variants: A study of homosexual patterns,* by George William Henry, 1149–79. NY/London: Hoeber.

Lehiste, Ilse. 1988. *Lectures on language contact.* Cambridge, MA: MIT Press.

Lemotte, Justin G. T. 1985. *New Orleans talkin': A guide to Yat, Cajun and some Creole.* New Orleans: Channel Press.

Le Page, Robert B., & Andrée Tabouret-Keller. l985. *Acts of identity.* Cambridge: Cambridge University Press.

Levine, Lewis, & Harry Crockett. [1968] 1971. Speech variation in a Piedmont Community. In Williamson & Burke (eds.), 437–60.

Levinson, Stephen C. 1983. *Pragmatics.* Cambridge: Cambridge University Press.

Lévi-Strauss, Claude. 1966. *The savage mind.* London: Weidenfeld & Nicholson.

Liebling, A. J. 1980. Preface to Toole.

Light, Deanna. 1992. Quantitative analysis of areal linguistic data. Paper presented at the annual meeting of the Modern Language Association, New York.

Lighter, Jonathan E. 1994–. *Historical dictionary of American slang.* NY: Random House.

Liljencrants, J., & Lindblom, B. 1972. Numerical simulation of vowel quality systems: The role of perceptual contrast. *Language* 48:839–62.

Lippi-Green, Rosina. 1989. Social network integration and language change in progress in a rural Alpine village. *Language in Society* 18:213–34.

Lipski, John M. 1978. Code-switching and the problem of bilingual competence. In Paradis (ed.), 250–64.

Loman, Bengt. 1967. *Conversations in a Negro American dialect.* Washington, DC: Center for Applied Linguistics.

Loman, Bengt. 1975. Prosodic patterns in a Negro American dialect. In *Style and text: Studies presented to Nils Erik Enkvist,* ed. by Håkan Ringbom et al., 219–42. Stockholm: Sprakforlaget Skriptor.

Lomax, John A. 1937. Field experience with recording machines. *Southern Folklore Quarterly* 1:57–60.

Lyman, Tim. 1978. Introduction to Matthews, i-v.

Lynch, Kevin. 1977. *Growing up in cities.* Cambridge, MA: MIT Press.

McCollie-Lewis, Cynthia. 1994. The genesis of African-American English: Sociolinguistic insights from Virginia (1619–1700). Paper presented at the annual meeting of the Society for Pidgin and Creole Linguistics, Boston.

McDavid, Raven I., Jr. 1941. *Ain't I* and *aren't I. Language* 17:7–59.

McDavid, Raven I., Jr. 1946. Dialect geography and social science problems. *Social Forces* 25:168–72.

McDavid, Raven I., Jr. 1948. Postvocalic /-r/ in South Carolina: A social analysis. *American Speech* 23:194–203. Reprinted 1964 in Hymes (ed.), 473–80; 1978 in *A pluralistic nation,* ed. by Margaret A. Lourie & Nancy Conklin Faires, 178–86, Massachusetts: Newbury House; 1979 in Kretzschmar (ed.), 136–42.

McDavid, Raven I., Jr. [1955] 1979. The position of the Charleston dialect. In Kretzschmar (ed.), 272–81.

McDavid, Raven I., Jr. 1958. The dialects of American English. Ch. 9 in W. Nelson Francis, *The Structure of American English,* 480–543. NY: Ronald Press.

McDavid, Raven I., Jr. 1967. Needed research in Southern dialects. In *Perspectives on the South: Agenda for research,* ed. by Edgar T. Thompson, 113–24. Durham, NC: Duke University Press.

McDavid, Raven I., Jr. [1970] 1979. Changing patterns of southern dialects. In Kretzschmar (ed.), 295–308.

McDavid, Raven I., Jr. 1979a. The linguistic atlas of the North-Central States: A work of salvage dialectology. *Philologica Praguensia* 22:98–101.

McDavid, Raven I., Jr. 1979b. Review of Labov 1972b. *American Speech* 54:291–304.

McDavid, Raven I., Jr., & Virginia McDavid. [1951] 1971. The relationship of the speech of American Negroes to the speech of Whites. *American Speech 21: 3–17.* Reprinted in *Black-White speech relationships*, ed. by Walt Wolfram & Nona H. Clarke, 16–40. Washington, DC: Center for Applied Linguistics.

McDavid, Raven I., Jr., & Raymond K. O'Cain. 1980. *Linguistic atlas of the Middle and South Atlantic States. Fascicles 1,2.* Chicago: University of Chicago Press.

McDonnell, Lawrence T. 1993. Work, culture, and society in the slave South—1790–1861. In *Black and white cutural interaction in the antebellum South*, ed. by Ted Ownsby, 125–47. Jackson: University Press of Mississippi.

McGill, Ralph. [1963] 1992. *The South and the Southerner.* Athens, GA: University of Georgia Press.

McGowan, James T. 1976. Creation of a slave society: Louisiana plantations in the eighteenth century. University of Rochester dissertation.

McKenzie, Roderick Duncan. [1923] 1970. *The neighborhood: A study of local life in the city of Columbus, Ohio.* NY: Arno Press.

McLemore, Cynthia. 1990. Intonation as communicative strategy in a Texas sorority. Paper presented at NWAVE-XIX, Philadelphia, PA.

McLemore, Cynthia. 1991a. The pragmatic interpretation of English intonation: Sorority speech. University of Texas at Austin dissertation.

McLemore, Cynthia. 1991b. Situated symbols. Paper presented at the meeting of the American Association for Applied Linguistics, Vancouver, Canada.

MacLeod, Jay. 1987. *Ain't no makin' it: Leveled aspirations in a low income neighborhood.* Boulder: Westview Press.

McLeod-Porter, Delma. 1991. Gender, ethnicity, and narrative: A linguistic and rhetorical analysis of adolescents' personal experience stories. Texas A&M University dissertation.

McMillan, James B. 1971. *Annotated bibliography of Southern American English.* Coral Gables, FL: University of Miami Press.

McMillan, James B., & Michael B. Montgomery. 1989. *Annotated bibliography of Southern American English.* [Updated and expanded.] Tuscaloosa: University of Alabama Press.

McWhorter, John H. 1992. Substratal influence in Saramaccan serial verb constructions. *Journal of Pidgin and Creole Languages* 7:1–53.

McWhorter, John. 1996. Tracing the birthplace of the Atlantic-based creoles: Inductions from Surinam. Paper presented at the annual meeting of the Society for Pidgin and Creole Linguistics, San Diego, CA.

Malmstrom, Jean, & Annabel Ashley. 1963. *Dialects, U.S.A.* Champaign, IL: National Council of Teachers of English.

Marckwardt, Albert H. 1957. *Principal and subsidiary dialect areas in the North Central States.* Publication of the American Dialect Society (PADS) 27. Tuscaloosa: University of Alabama Press.

Marshall, Margaret M. 1989. The origins of Creole French in Louisiana. *Regional Dimensions* 8:23–40.

Martinet, André. 1955. *Économie des changements phonétiques.* Berne: Francke.

Marx, Leo. 1963. *The machine in the garden: Technology and the pastoral ideal in America.* NY: Oxford University Press.

Mathews, Mitford M. 1948. *Some sources of Southernisms.* Tuscaloosa: University of Alabama Press.

Mathews, Mitford M. (ed.). 1951. *Dictionary of Americanisms on historical principles.* 2 vols. Chicago: University of Chicago Press.

Matthews, Bunny. 1978. *F'sure: Actual dialogue heard on the streets of New Orleans.* New Orleans: Neetof Press.

Maurer, Robert, & James C. Baxter. 1972. Images of neighborhood and city among Black-, Anglo- and Mexican-American children. *Environment and Behavior* 4:351–88.

Maynor, Natalie. 1988. Written records of spoken language: How reliable are they? In *Methods in dialectology: Proceedings of the sixth international conference held at the University College of North Wales, 3–7 August 1987,* ed. by Alan R. Thomas, 109–20. Philadelphia: Multilingual Matters.

Maynor, Natalie. 1991. The WPA slave narratives revisited. Review of Schneider 1989. *American Speech* 66:82–86.

Medrich, Elliott, Judith Roizen, Victor Rubin & Stuart Buckley. 1982. *The serious business of growing up: A study of children's lives outside school.* Berkeley: University of California Press.

Megenney, William. W. 1978. *A Bahian heritage: An ethnolinguistic study of African influences on Bahian Portuguese.* Chapel Hill: University of North Carolina Press.

Meihoefer, Hans-Joachim. 1982. The utility of the circle as an effective cartographic symbol. *The Canadian Cartographer* 6.2:105–17.

Meisel, Jürgen M. (ed.). 1977. *Langues en contact/pidgins/creoles/languages in contact.* Tübingen: Gunter Narr.

Mencken, H. L. 1979. *The American language.* 4th ed., ed. by R. McDavid, Jr. NY: Alfred A. Knopf.

Menz, Florian. 1989. Manipulation strategies in newspapers: A program for critical linguistics. In *Language, power and ideology: Studies in political discourse,* ed. by Ruth Wodak, 227–49. Philadelphia: John Benjamins.

Mercier, Alfred. 1880. Etude sur la langue créole en Louisiane. *Comptes rendus de l'Athénée Louisianais* 5:378–83.

Meredith, James. 1966. *Three years in Mississippi.* Cincinnati: Meredith Publishing Company.

Merryweather, L.W. 1931. Hell in American speech. *American Speech* 6:433–35.

Meyer, Duane. 1970. *The heritage of Missouri: A history.* St. Louis: State Publishing.

Mille, Katherine Wyly. 1990. A historical analysis of tense-mood-aspect in Gullah Creole: A case of stable variation. University of South Carolina dissertation.

Milroy, James. 1992. *Linguistic variation and change: On the historical sociolinguistics of English.* Oxford: Basil Blackwell.

Milroy, Lesley. 1980. *Language and social networks.* London: Basil Blackwell.

Milroy, Lesley. 1987a. *Language and social networks.* 2d ed. Oxford: Basil Blackwell.

Milroy, Lesley. 1987b. *Observing and analysing natural language.* Oxford: Basil Blackwell.

Milroy, Lesley, & P. McClenaghan. 1977. Stereotyped reactions to four educated accents in Ulster. *Belfast Working Papers in Language and Linguistics* 2.4:1–11.

Milroy, Lesley, & James Milroy. 1992. Social network and social class: Toward an integrated sociolinguistic model. *Language in Society* 21:1–26.

Monmonier, Mark. 1977a. *Maps, distortion, and meaning*. Association of American Geographers, Commission on College Geography Publications, Resource Paper No. 75-4.

Monmonier, Mark. 1977b. Viewing azimuth and map clarity. *Annals of the Association of American Geographers* 68.2:180–95.

Monmonier, Mark, & George A. Schnell. 1988. *Map appreciation*. Englewood Cliffs, NJ: Prentice Hall.

Montgomery, Michael. 1989. Exploring the roots of Appalachian English. *English World-Wide* 10:227–78.

Montgomery, Michael. 1990. The evolution of verb concord in Scotch-Irish English. Paper presented at NWAVE-XIX, Philadelphia, PA.

Montgomery, Michael. 1991a. The linguistic value of the ex-slave recordings. In Bailey, Maynor & Cukor-Avila (eds.), 173–89.

Montgomery, Michael. 1991b. The roots of Appalachian English: Scotch-Irish or British Southern? *Journal of the Appalachian Studies Association* 3:177–91.

Montgomery, Michael. 1992. The diversity of Appalachian English. Paper presented at the Appalachian Studies Association meeting, Asheville, NC.

Montgomery, Michael. 1993a. Review article: The Linguistic Atlas of the Gulf States. *American Speech* 68:263–318.

Montgomery, Michael. 1993b. The Southern accent—alive and well. *Southern Cultures* 1:47–64.

Montgomery, Michael. 1995. The linguistic value of Ulster emigrant letters. *Ulster Folklife* 41:26–41.

Montgomery, Michael B. forthcoming. *Dictionary of Smoky Mountain English*.

Montgomery, Michael, & Guy Bailey (eds.). 1986. *Language variety in the South: Perspectives in black and white*. Tuscaloosa: University of Alabama Press.

Montgomery, Michael, & Stacey Epting. 1990. The acquisition of Southern American English. Paper presented at the Southeastern Conference on Linguistics, Lander College.

Montgomery, Michael, Janet Fuller & Sharon DeMarse. 1993. "The black men has wives and sweet harts [and third person plural -s] jest like the white men": Evidence for verbal -s from written documents on nineteenth-century African American Speech. *Language Variation and Change* 5:335–54.

Montgomery, Michael, & Cecil Ataide Melo. 1990. The phonology of the lost cause: The English of the Confederados in Brazil. *English World-Wide* 11:195–216.

Montgomery, Michael, & Stephen J. Nagle. 1994. Double modals in Scotland and the Southern United States: Trans-Atlantic inheritance or independent development? *Folia Linguistica Historica* 14:91–107.

Montgomery, Michael, & Thomas Nunnally. forthcoming. *Linguistic studies from the Gulf States and beyond*. Tuscaloosa: University of Alabama Press.

Montgomery, Michael, & Philip S. Robinson. 1992. Ulster English as Janus: Language contact across the North Atlantic and across the Irish Sea. Paper presented at the Societas Linguistica Europaea, Galway, Ireland. Forthcoming in

Linguistic Contact across the North Atlantic, ed. by Sture Ureland. Tubingen: Max Niemeyer.

Moody, Anne. 1969. *Coming of age in Mississippi*. NY: Dell.

Moonwomon, Birch. 1987. Truly awesome: (O) in California English. In Denning et al. (eds.), 325–36.

Morgan, Lucia. 1960. The speech of Ocracoke, North Carolina: Some observations. *Southern Speech Journal* 25:314–22.

Mufwene, Salikoko S. 1985. The linguistic significance of African proper names in Gullah. *New West Indian Guide* 59:146–66.

Mufwene, Salikoko S. 1986. Number delimitation in Gullah. *American Speech* 61:33–60.

Mufwene, Salikoko S. 1987. Review of Montgomery & Bailey 1986. *Journal of Pidgin and Creole Languages* 2:93–110.

Mufwene, Salikoko S. 1989. For the record let us get some facts straight. (A reply to Derek Bickerton's letter.) *The Carrier Pidgin* 17.2/3:6–7.

Mufwene, Salikoko S. 1991a. Is Gullah decreolizing? A comparison of a speech sample of the 1930s with a sample of the 1980s. In Bailey, Maynor & Cukor-Avila (eds.), 213–30.

Mufwene, Salikoko S. 1991b. Review of *Grammatical relations in a radical creole*, by Francis Byrne. *SECOL Review* 13:200–206.

Mufwene, Salikoko S. 1991c. Some reasons why Gullah is not dying yet. *English World-Wide* 12:215–43.

Mufwene, Salikoko S. 1992. Africanisms in Gullah: A re-examination of the issues. In Hall, Doane & Ringler (eds.), 156–82.

Mufwene, Salikoko S. 1992. A propos de substrat et superstrat dans la genèse des créoles: les vrais et les faux problèmes. *Etudes créoles* 15:135–49.

Mufwene, Salikoko S. 1994. On decreolization: The case of Gullah. In *Language, loyalty, and identity in creole situations*, ed. by Marcyliena Morgan, 63–99. Los Angeles: Center for African-American Studies.

Mufwene, Salikoko S. 1996a. Creole genesis: A population genetics perspective. In *Caribbean language issues old and new*, ed. by Pauline Christie, 163–96. Kingston, Jamaica: The Press University of West Indies.

Mufwene, Salikoko S. 1996b. The Founder Principle in creole genesis. *Diachronica* 13:83–134.

Mufwene, Salikoko S., & Charles Gilman. 1987. How African is Gullah and why? *American Speech* 62:120–39.

Mufwene, Salikoko S., with Nancy Condon (eds.). 1993. *Africanisms in Afro-American language varieties*. Athens, GA: University of Georgia Press.

Mühlhäusler, Peter. 1986. *Pidgin and creole linguistics*. Oxford: Blackwell.

Muller, Max. 1861. *Lectures on the science of language, delivered at the royal Institution of Great Britain in April, May and June, 1861*. First Series. London.

Muysken, Pieter, & Norval Smith (eds.). 1986. *Substrata versus universals in creole genesis*. Philadelpina: John Benjamins.

Myers-Scotton, Carol. 1993. *Social motivations for code-switching: Evidence from Africa*. Oxford: Oxford University Press.

Myhill, John. 1988. Post-vocalic /r/ as an index of integration into the BEV speech community. *American Speech* 63:203–13.

Naipaul, V. S. 1989. *A turn in the South*. NY: Alfred Knopf.

Nathan, Hans. 1962. *Dan Emmett and the rise of early Negro minstrelsy*. Norman: University of Oklahoma Press.

Neilson, Melany. 1989. *Even Mississippi*. Tuscaloosa: University of Alabama Press.

Neu, Helen. 1980. Ranking of constraints on /-t/d/a deletion in American English: A statistical analysis. In Labov (ed.), 37–54.

Neumann, Ingrid. 1985. *Le créole de Breaux Bridge, Louisiane: Etude morphosyntaxique, textes, vocabulaire*. Hamburg: Helmut Buske.

Neumann-Holzschuh, Ingrid. 1987. *Textes anciens en créole louisianais*. Hamburg: Helmut Buske.

Nichols, Patricia C. 1976. Linguistic change in Gullah: Sex, age, and mobility. Stanford University dissertation.

Nichols, Patricia C. 1986. Prepositions in black and white English of coastal South Carolina. In Montgomery & Bailey (eds.), 73–84.

Nichols, Patricia C. 1989. Language contact and shift in colonial South Carolina. Paper presented at ICHL IX, Rutgers University, NJ.

Nichols, Patricia C. 1991. Verbal patterns of black and white speakers of coastal South Carolina. In *Verb phrase patterns in Black English and creole*, ed. by Walter F. Edwards & Don Winford, 114–28. Detroit: Wayne State University Press.

Niedzielski, Nancy, & Dennis R. Preston. under review. *Folk linguistics: An ethnographic study of language beliefs in southeastern Michigan*.

Nketia, J. H. Kwabena. 1971. The linguistic aspect of style in African languages. In *Current trends in linguistics 7: Linguistics in Sub-Saharan Africa*, ed. by Thomas A. Sebeok, Jack Berry, Joseph H. Greenberg, David W. Crabb & Paul Schachter, 733–57. The Hague: Mouton.

Nugent, Maria Skinner. [1839] 1934. *Lady Nugent's Journal: Jamaica one hundred and thirty years ago*, ed. by Frank Cundall. Reprinted from a journal kept by Maria, Lady Nugent, from 1801 to 1815. London: Institute of Jamaica/West India Committee.

Ochs, Elinor. 1990. Indexicality and socialization. In Stigler, Shweder & Herdt (eds.), 287–308.

Ochs, Elinor. 1992. *Indexing gender*. In Duranti & Goodwin (eds.), 335–58.

O'Connor, Flannery. [1957] 1969. *Mystery and manners: Occasional prose, selected and edited by Sally and Robert Fitzgerald*. (Expanded ed.) NY: Farrar, Straus & Giroux.

Odell, George C. D. 1927. *Annals of the New York stage*, vols. 1–2. NY: Columbia University Press.

Odland, John. 1988. *Spatial autocorrelation*. Beverly Hills, CA: Sage Publications.

Oomen, Ursula. 1985. 'I tell you just like I been know it'—Die Entwicklung einer kreolischen Konstruktion im Black English. In *Anglistentag 1984*, ed. by Manfred Pfister, 105–15. Giessen: Hoffmann.

Oomen, Ursula, & Monika Lissewski. 1989. Pronoun variation in South Carolinian "early Black English." In Pütz & Dirven (eds.), 109–33.

Orton, Harold, & Nathalia Wright. 1974. *A word geography of England*. London: Seminar.

Oxford English Dictionary. 1933. 2nd ed. 1989. Oxford: Clarendon Press.

Paradis, Michael (ed.). 1978. *Aspects of bilingualism*. Columbia, SC: Hornbeam Press.

Pardoe, T. Earl. 1937. A historical and phonetic study of Negro Dialect. Louisiana State University dissertation.

Parkinson, Dilworth. 1985. *Constructing the social context of communication: Terms of address in Egyptian Arabic*. New York: Mouton de Gruyter

Patrick, John. 1953. *Savannah's pioneer theater from its origins to 1810*. Athens: University of Georgia Press.

Patrick, Peter L. 1991. Creoles at the intersection of variable processes: -t,d deletion and past-marking in the Jamaican mesolect. *Language Variation and Change* 3:171–90.

Payne, Arvilla. 1976. The acquisition of the phonological system of a second dialect. University of Pennsylvania dissertation.

Payne, Arvilla. 1980. Factors controlling the acquisition of the Philadelphia dialect by out-of-state children. In Labov (ed.), 143–78.

Pederson, Lee. 1966. Negro speech in *The adventures of Huckleberry Finn. Mark Twain Journal* 13:1–4.

Pederson, Lee. 1968. Mark Twain's Missouri dialects: Marion County phonemics. *American Speech* 42: 261–78.

Pederson, Lee. 1972. An introduction to the LAGS project. In *A manual for dialect research in the southern states*, ed. by L. Pederson, R. McDavid, C. Foster & C. Billiard, 1–31. Atlanta: Georgia State University. [2nd ed., Tuscaloosa: University of Alabama Press, 1974.]

Pederson, Lee. 1993. A southern phonology. *SECOL Review* 17:36–54

Pederson, Lee, et al. (eds.). 1986–1992. *Linguistic atlas of the Gulf States*. 7 vols. [Vol. 1: *Handbook for the Linguistic Atlas of the Gulf States*; Vol. 2: *General Index for the Linguistic Atlas of the Gulf States*; Vol. 3: *Technical Index for the Linguistic Atlas of the Gulf States*; Vol. 4: *Regional Matrix for the Linguistic Atlas of the Gulf States*; Vol. 5: *Regional Pattern for the Linguistic Atlas of the Gulf States*; Vol. 6: *Social Matrix for the Linguistic Atlas of the Gulf States*; Vol. 7: *Social Pattern for the Linguistic Atlas of the Gulf States*]. Athens: University of Georgia Press.

Pederson, Lee, Susan Leas, Guy H. Bailey & Marvin H. Bassett (eds.). 1981. *Linguistic atlas of the gulf states: The basic materials*. Ann Arbor, MI: University Microfilms.

Pederson, Lee, Susan Leas McDaniel & Marvin H. Bassett (eds.). 1986. *Linguistic atlas of the gulf states: A concordance of basic materials*. Ann Arbor, MI: University Microfilms.

Penfield, Joyce. 1984. Prosodic patterns: Some hypotheses and findings from fieldwork. In *Form and function in Chicano English*, ed. by Jacob Ornstein-Galicia, 49–59. Rowley, MA: Newbury.

Penfield, Joyce, & Jacob L. Ornstein-Galicia. 1985. *Chicano English: An ethnic contact dialect*. Amsterdam: John Benjamins.

Perkins, David. 1992. *Is literary history possible?* Baltimore: Johns Hopkins.

Peterson, Gordon E., & Harold L. Barney. 1952. Control methods used in a study of the vowels. *JASA* 24:175–84.

Peucker, Thomas K. 1972. *Computer cartography*. Commission on College Geography Resource Paper No. 17. Washington, DC: Association of American Geographers.

Picone, Michael D. 1994a. Lexicogenesis and language vitality. *Word* 45:261–85.

Picone, Michael D. 1994b. Code-intermediate phenomena in Louisiana French. *Papers from the thirtieth regional meeting of the Chicago Linguistic Society*, vol. 1, ed. by Katharine Beals et al., 320–34.

Pitts, Walter. 1986. Contrastive use of verbal -z in slave narratives. In *Diversity and diachrony*, ed. by David Sankoff, 73–82. Philadelphia: Benjamins.

Polanyi, Livia. 1985. *Telling the American story: A structural and cultural analysis of conversational storytelling*. Norwood, NJ: Ablex.

Pollock, T. C. 1933. *The Philadelphia theatre in the eighteenth century*. Philadelphia: University of Pennsylvania Press.

Poplack, Shana. 1980. Sometimes I'll start a sentence in English y termino en español: Towards a typology of code-switching. *Linguistics* 18:581–618.

Poplack, Shana. 1981. Syntactic structure and the social function of code-switching. In *Latino language and communicative behavior*, ed. by Richard P. Durán, 169–84. Norwood, NJ: Ablex.

Poplack, Shana. 1988. Language status and language accommodation along a linguistic border. In *Language spread and language policy: Issues, implications, and case studies*, ed. by Peter H. Lowenberg, 90–118. Georgetown University Round Table on Language and Linguistics 1987. Washington, DC: Georgetown University Press.

Poplack, Shana. 1989. Statut de langue et accommodation langagière le long d'une frontière linguistique. In *Le français canadien parlé hor Québec: Aperçu sociolinguistique*, ed. by Raymond Mougeon & Edouard Beniak, 127–151. Québec: Les Presses de l'Université Laval.

Poplack, Shana, & David Sankoff. 1984. Borrowing: The synchrony of integration. *Linguistics* 22:99–135.

Poplack, Shana, & David Sankoff. 1987. The Philadelphia story in the Spanish Caribbean. *American Speech* 62:291–314.

Poplack, Shana, David Sankoff & Christopher Miller. 1988. The social correlates and linguistic processes of lexical borrowing and assimilation. *Linguistics* 26:47–104.

Poplack, Shana, & Sali Tagliamonte. 1991a. African American English in the diaspora: Evidence from old-line Nova Scotians. *Language Variation and Change* 3:301–39. [Reprinted in *Focus on Canada*, ed. by Sandra Clarke, 109–50. Amsterdam: John Benjamins.]

Poplack, Shana, & Sali Tagliamonte. 1991b. There's no tense like the present: verbal -s inflection in early Black English. In Bailey, Maynor & Cukor-Avila (eds.), 275–324.

Poplack, Shana, Susan Wheeler & Anneli Westwood. 1987. Distinguishing language contact phenomena: Evidence from Finnish-English bilingualism. In *The Nordic languages and modern linguistics, 6*, ed. by Pirikko Lilius & Mirja Saari, 33–56. Helsinki: University of Helsinki Press.

Postman, Neil. 1992. *Technopoly: The surrender of culture to technology*. NY: Knopf.

Preston, Dennis R. 1982. Perceptual dialectology: Mental maps of United States dialects from a Hawaiian perspective. *University of Hawaii Working Papers in Linguistics* 14:5–49.

Preston, Dennis R. 1985. The Li'l Abner Syndrome: Written representations of speech. *American Speech* 60:328–36.

Preston, Dennis R. 1986. Five visions of America. *Language in Society* 15:221–40.

Preston, Dennis R. 1989a. *Perceptual dialectology*. Dordrecht, Netherlands: Foris.

Preston, Dennis R. 1989b. Standard English spoken here: The geographical loci of linguistic norms. In *Status and function of language and language varieties*, ed. by Ulrich Ammon, 324–54. NY: Walter de Gruyter.

Preston, Dennis R. 1993. Folk dialectology. In *American dialect research*, ed. by Preston, 333–77. Philadelphia: John Benjamins.

Preston, Dennis R. In progress: Folk views of language variety in the United States: A study of the folk perceptions of regional and prescriptive varieties of English in the United States.

Preston, Dennis R., & George M. Howe. 1987. Computerized generalizations of mental dialect maps. In Denning et al. (eds.), 361–78.

Pütz, Martin, & René Dirven (eds.). 1989. *Wheels within wheels: Papers of the Duisburg symposium on pidgin and creole languages*. Frankfurt am Main: Verlag Peter Lang.

Pyrnelle, Louise-Clarke. [1882] 1910. *Diddie, Dumps, and Tot, or Plantation Child-Life*. NY: Grosset & Dunlap.

Quinn, Arthur H. 1943. *A history of the American drama from the beginning to the Civil War*. 2d ed. NY: Appleton Century-Crofts.

Rabinow, Paul, & William M. Sullivan (eds.). 1979. *Interpretive social science: A reader*. Berkeley: University of California Press.

Radford, Andrew. 1988. *Transformational grammar*. Cambridge: Cambridge University Press.

Rand, David, & David Sankoff. 1990. *GoldVarb 2.0: Program and documentation*. Montreal: Centre de recherches mathématiques.

Rankin, Hugh F. 1960. *The theater in colonial America*. Chapel Hill: University of North Carolina Press.

Rawick, George P. (ed.). 1972–1979. *The American Slave: A Composite Autobiography*. 19 vols. Westport, CT: Greenwood Press.

Rawson, Hugh. 1981. *A dictionary of euphemism and other doubletalk*. NY: Crown Publishers.

Read, Allen Walker. 1934. An obscenity symbol. *American Speech* 9:264–78.

Read, Allen Walker. 1939. The speech of Negroes in colonial America. *Journal of Negro History* 24:247–58.

Read, Allen Walker. 1992. The use of travelers' evidence in historical lexicography. In Hall, Doane & Ringler (eds.), 254–63.

Reed, John Shelton. 1986. *Southern folk plain and fancy: Native white social types*. Athens: University of Georgia Press.

Reinecke, John. 1971. Tay Boi: Notes on the Pidgin French of Vietnam. In Hymes (ed.), 47–56.

Reinecke, John E., Stanley M. Tsuzaki, David DeCamp, Ian F. Hancock & R. E. Wood (eds.). 1975. *A bibliography of pidgin and creole languages*. Honolulu: University of Hawaii Press.

Rensink, W. G. 1955: Dialectindeling naar opgaven van medewerkers. *Mededelingen der centrale commissie voor onderzoek van het nederlandse volkseigen* 7:20–3.

Ricard, Ulysses S., Jr. 1992. The Pointe Coupée slave conspiracy of 1791. In Galloway & Boucher (eds.), 116–29.

Richardson, Gina. 1984. Can *y'all* function as a singular pronoun in Southern dialect? *American Speech* 59:51–59.

Rickford, John R. 1972. "Sounding" black or "sounding" white: A preliminary acoustic investigation of a folk-hypothesis. ms.

Rickford, John R. 1974. The insights of the mesolect. In *Pidgins and creoles: Current trends and prospects*, ed. by David DeCamp & Ian F. Hancock, 92–117. Washington, DC: Georgetown University Press.

Rickford, John R. 1977. The question of prior creolization in Black English. In *Pidgin and creole linguistics*, ed. by Albert Valdman, 190–221. Bloomington: Indiana University Press.

Rickford, John R. 1986a. Social contact and linguistic diffusion. *Language* 62:245–90.

Rickford, John R. 1986b. Some principles for the study of black and white speech in the South. In Montgomery & Bailey (eds.), 38–62.

Rickford, John R. 1987. *Dimensions of a creole continuum: History, texts, and linguistic analysis of Guyanese Creole*. Stanford: Stanford University Press.

Rickford, John R. 1991. Representativeness and reliability of the ex-slave materials, with special reference to Wallace Quarterman's recordings and transcript. In Bailey, Maynor & Cukor-Avila (eds.), 191–212.

Rickford, John R. 1992. Grammatical variation and divergence in Vernacular Black English. In *Internal and external factors in syntactic change*, ed. by M. Gerritsen & D. Stein, 175–200. The Hague: Mouton de Gruyter.

Rickford, John R. 1993. Phonological features in Afro-American pidgins and creoles and their diachronic significance. Comments on the papers by Holm & Carter. In Mufwene with Condon (eds.), 346–63.

Rickford, John R. 1995. AAVE and the Creole Hypothesis: Reflections on the state of the issue. Paper presented at NWAVE-XXIV, Philadelphia, PA.

Rickford, John R. 1996. Copula variability in Jamaican Creole texts and African American Vernacular English: A reanalysis of DeCamp's texts. In Guy, Feagin, Baugh & Schiffrin (eds.), 357–72.

Rickford, John R., & Jerome S. Handler. 1994. Textual evidence on the nature of early Barbadian speech, 1676–1835. *Journal of Pidgin and Creole Languages* 9:221–56.

Rissel, D. 1989. Sex, attitudes, and the assibilation of /r/ among young people in San Luis Potosi, Mexico. *Language Variation and Change* 1:269–84.

Roberts, Julie. 1993. The acquisition of new and vigorous sound changes by Philadelphia children. Paper presented at NWAVE-XXII, Ottawa, Ontario.

Roberts, Julie. 1994. Acquisition of variable rules: (/-t,d/) deletion and (ing) production in preschool children. University of Pennsylvania dissertation.

Roberts, Peter. 1992. The fabric of Barbadian language. Paper presented to the Ninth Biennial Conference of the Society for Caribbean Linguistics, Cave Hill, Barbados.

Roberts, Wade. 1984. A pie and a hoo. *Cuisine* 13:10–15ff.

Robin, Charles C., Jr. [1966] 1984. *Voyage to Louisiana, 1803–1805*. Trans. Stuart O. Landry. New Orleans: Pelican Publishing Co.

Rosen, Harold. 1988. The autobiographical impulse. In Tannen (ed.), 69–88.

Rousseau, Pascale, & David Sankoff. 1978. Advances in variable rule methodology.

Linguistic variation: Models and methods, ed. by David Sankoff, 57–69. NY: Academic Press.

Ryan, Ellen B., & Howard Giles. 1982: *Attitudes towards language variation*. London: Arnold.

Ryan, James S. 1973. Black is white on the Bay Islands. *University of Michigan Papers in Linguistics* 1.2:128–39.

Sabino, Robin. 1990. Towards a phonology of Negerhollands: An analysis of phonological variation. University of Pennsylvania dissertation.

Sabino, Robin. 1993a. The moving target: Taking advantage of a heterogenous superstrate. Paper delivered at the International Conference of Americanists, New Orleans, LA.

Sabino, Robin. 1993b. On onsets: Explaining Negerhollands initial clusters. In Byrne & Holm (eds.), 37–44.

Salzinger, Suzanne, Muriel Hammer & John Antrobus. 1988. From crib to college: An overview of studies of the social networks of children, adolescents and college students. In *Social networks of children, adolescents and college students*, ed. by Suzanne Salzinger, Muriel Hammer & John Antrobus, 1–16. Hillsdale, NJ: Erlbaum.

Sankoff, David (ed.). 1986. *Diversity and diachrony*. Philadelphia: John Benjamins.

Santa Ana, Otto A. 1991. Phonetic simplification processes in the English of the barrio: A cross-generational sociolinguistic study of the Chicanos of Los Angeles. University of Pennsylvania dissertation.

Santa Ana, Otto A. 1992. Chicano English evidence for the exponential hypothesis: A variable rule pervades lexical phonology. *Language Variation and Change* 4:275–88.

Sapir, Edward. 1968. Communication. In *Selected writings of Edward Sapir in language, culture and personality*, ed. by David G. Mandelbaum, 104–9. Berkeley & Los Angeles: University of California Press.

Saville-Troike, Muriel. 1989. *The ethnography of communication*. 2d ed. NY: Basil Blackwell.

Schafer, Roy. 1981. Narration in the psychoanalytic dialogue. In *On narrative*, ed. by W. J. T. Mitchell, 25–49. Chicago: University of Chicago Press.

Schegloff, Emanuel A. 1979. Identification and recognition in telephone conversational openings. In *Everyday language: Studies in ethnomethodology*, ed. by George Psathas, 23–77. NY: Irvington Publishers.

Schieffelin, Bambi. 1990. *The give and take of everyday life: Language socialization of Kaluli children*. NY: Cambridge University Press.

Schiffrin, Deborah. 1987. *Discourse markers*. Cambridge: Cambridge University Press.

Schilling-Estes, Natalie, & Walt Wolfram. 1994. Convergent explanation and alternative regularization patterns: *Were/weren't* leveling in a vernacular English variety. *Language Variation and Change* 6:273–302.

Schlegel, Alice, & Herbert Barry. 1991. *Adolescence: An anthropological inquiry*. Macmillan: Free Press.

Schneider, Edgar W. 1981. Morphologische und syntaktische Variablen in amerikanischen early black English. *Bamberger Beiträge zur Englischen Sprachwissenschaft*, 10. Frankfurt am Main: Peter Lang.

Schneider, Edgar W. 1983a. The diachronic development of the Black English perfective auxiliary phrase. *Journal of English Linguistics* 16:55–64.

Schneider, Edgar W. 1983b. The origin of the verbal -s in Black English. *American Speech* 58:99–113.

Schneider, Edgar W. 1988. Qualitative vs. quantitative methods of area delimitation in dialectology. *Journal of English Linguistics* 21:175–212.

Schneider, Edgar W. 1989. *American earlier Black English: Morphological and syntactic variables.* Tuscaloosa: University of Alabama Press.

Schneider, Edgar W. 1990a. Appalachian mountain vocabulary: Its character, sources, and distinctiveness. Paper read at the International Conference on Dialectology, Bamberg, Germany.

Schneider, Edgar W. 1990b. The cline of creoleness in English-oriented creoles and semi-creoles of the Caribbean. *English World-Wide* 11:79–113.

Schneider, Edgar W. 1994. Review of Bailey, Maynor & Cukor-Avila (eds.) 1991. *American Speech* 69:191–6.

Schneider, Edgar W., & William A. Kretzschmar, Jr. 1989. LAMSAS goes SASsy: Statistical methods and linguistic atlas data. *Journal of English Linguistics* 22:129–41.

Schoolcraft, Henry Rowe. 1851–57. *Information respecting the Indian tribes of the United States.* Philadelphia.

Scott, Jerrie. 1986. Mixed dialects in the composition classroom. In Montgomery & Bailey (eds.), 333–47.

Seeley, John R., R. Alexander Sim & Elizabeth W. Loosley. 1956. *Crestwood Heights: A study of the culture of suburban life.* NY: Basic Books.

Seilhamer, George O. 1888–1891. *The history of the American theatre.* 3 vols. Philadelphia.

Selkirk, Elisabeth O. 1982. The syllable. In *The structure of phonological representations,* part II, ed. by Harry van der Hulst & Norval Smith, 337–83. Dordrecht, Netherlands: Foris Publications.

Shaffer, David. 1978. The place of codeswitching in linguistic contacts. In Paradis (ed.), 265–75.

Shen, Xiaonan Susan. 1988. Ability of learning the prosody of an intonational language—French—by speakers of a tonal language—Chinese. In Ferrara et al. (eds.), 326–35.

Shockley, Martin. 1977. *The Richmond stage 1784–1812.* Charlottesville, VA: University Press of Virginia.

Shoemaker, Floyd C. 1927. *A history of Missouri and Missourians.* Columbia, MO: Lucas Brothers.

Shores, David L. 1984. The stressed vowels of the speech of Tangier Island, Virginia. *Journal of English Linguistics* 17:37–56.

Shores, David L. 1991. Outer Banks dialect. In Wilson & Ferris (eds.), 662–3.

Shores, David L., & Carole P. Hines (eds.). 1977. *Papers in Language Variation.* Tuscaloosa: University of Alabama Press.

Shuy, Roger W., Walt Wolfram & William C. Riley. 1967. *Linguistic correlates of social stratification in Detroit speech.* USOE Final Report No. 6-1347.

Siegel, Alexander, Kathleen Kirasic & Robert W. Kasil, Jr. 1978. Stalking the elusive cognitive map: The development of children's representations of geographic space.

In Altman & Wohlwill (eds.), 223–58.

Simpkins, Karen L. 1969. *Terminology used in selected local settings*. Chapel Hill: University of North Carolina thesis.

Singh, Rajendra, & Pieter Muysken. 1995. Wanted: A debate in pidgin/creole phonology. *Journal of Pidgin and Creole Languages* 10:157–69.

Singler, John V. 1984. Variation in tense-aspect-modality in Liberian English. UCLA dissertation.

Singler, John V. 1986. Short note. *Journal of Pidgin and Creole Languages*. 1:141–45.

Singler, John V. 1989. Plural marking in Liberian Settler English. *American Speech* 64:40–64.

Singler, John V. (ed.). 1990. *Pidgin and creole tense-mood-aspect systems*. Philadelphia: John Benjamins.

Singler, John V. 1991. Liberian Settler English and the ex-slave recordings: A comparative study. In Bailey, Maynor & Cukor-Avila (eds.), 249–74.

Singler, John V. 1995. The demographics of creole genesis in the Caribbean: A comparison of Martinique and Haiti. In Arends (ed.), 203–32.

Sledd, James H. 1966. Breaking, umlaut, and the Southern drawl. *Language* 42:18-41.

Sledge, Mailande Cheney. 1991. Roles and relationships of women, children and the family in our shared heritage. Paper presented at Reflections on the Black Belt: A Shared Heritage. Alabama Rural Heritage Center, Thomaston, AL.

Smith, Raoul Lawrence. 1977. *The Gullah dialect and the Gullah-influenced writings of Ambrose Elliott Gonzales*. Clemson, SC: Clemson University thesis.

Smith, Reed. 1926a. The black border series: Review of Gonzales. *American Speech* 1:559–62.

Smith, Reed. 1926b. *Gullah*. Columbia: Bureau of Publications, University of South Carolina.

Sobel, Mechal. 1987. *The world they made together: Black and white values in eighteenth century Virginia*. Princeton: Princeton University Press.

Spears, Arthur. 1982. The semi-auxiliary *come* in Black English Vernacular. *Language* 58:850–72.

Speitel, Hans Henning. 1969. An areal typology of isoglosses near the Scottish-English border. *Zeitschrift für Dialektologie und Linguistik* 36:49–66.

Spruill, Julia Cherry. [1938] 1972. *Women's life and work in the southern colonies*. NY: Norton.

Stein, Gertrude. [1938] 1969. *Picasso*. NY: Bantam.

Stephenson, Edward A. 1968. The beginnings of the loss of postvocalic /r/ in North Carolina. *Journal of English Linguistics* 2:57–77. [Reprinted 1977 in Shores & Hines (eds.), 73–92.]

Stevens, Martin. 1954. The derivation of *ain't*. *American Speech* 29:196–201.

Stewart, William A. 1970. Historical and structural bases for the recognition of Negro dialect. In *Georgetown University round table on languages and linguistics*, ed. by James Alatis, 239–47. Washington, DC: Georgetown University Press.

Stewart, William A. [1968] 1975a. Continuity and change in American Negro dialect. *The Florida FL Reporter* 6.1. Reprinted in Dillard (ed.), 233–47.

Stewart, William A. [1967] 1975b. Sociolinguistic factors in the history of American Negro dialects. *The Florida FL Reporter* 5.2. Reprinted in Dillard (ed.), 222–32.

Stewart, William A. 1988. Whence the nominal dual in Gullah? *CUNYForum: Papers in linguistics* 14:211–8.

Stigler, James, Richard A. Shweder & Gilbert H. Herdt (eds.). 1990. *Cultural psychology: Essays on comparative human development*. Cambridge: Cambridge University Press.

Stone, George W. (ed.). 1962. *The London stage 1660–1800*. Carbondale, IL: Southern Illinois University Press.

Stowell, Timothy. 1981. Origins of Phrase Structure. University of Massachusetts dissertation.

Sutcliffe, David. 1982. Verbal patterns of a Jamaican speaker: Syntax and tonality in JMC. Paper presented at the Fourth Bienniel Conference on Caribbean Linguistics, Paramaribo, Suriname.

Sweet, Henry. 1888. *A history of English sounds*. Oxford.

Sylvain, Suzanne. 1936. *Le créole haïtien: Morphologie et syntaxe*. Wettern, Belgium: Imprimerie De Meester; Port-au-Prince: Chez l'auteur.

Tagliamonte, Sali, & Shana Poplack. 1988. How Black English past got to the present: Evidence from Samaná. *Language in Society* 17:513–33.

Talbot, Michael. 1991. *The holographic universe*. NY: HarperCollins.

Tannen, Deborah. 1981. New York Jewish conversational style. *International Journal of the Sociology of Language* 30:133–49.

Tannen, Deborah. 1984. *Conversational style: Analyzing talk among friends*. Norwood, NJ: Ablex.

Tannen, Deborah (ed.). 1988. *Linguistics in context: Connecting observation and understanding*. Norwood, NJ: Ablex.

Tarone, Elaine E. 1972. Aspects of intonation in vernacular white and black English speech. University of Washington dissertation.

Tarone, Elaine E. 1973. Aspects of intonation in Black English. *American Speech* 48:29–36.

Thomas, Erik, & Guy Bailey. 1991. A phonetic description of Southern American monophthongal /ay/. Paper presented at NWAVE-XX, Washington, DC.

Thomas, Erik, & Guy Bailey. 1993. The evolution of some Southern vowel systems. Paper presented at Language Variety in the South II, Auburn, AL.

Thomason, Sarah Grey, & Terrence Kaufman. 1988. *Language contact, creolization and genetic linguistics*. Berkeley & Los Angeles: University of California Press.

Thurgood, Graham. 1996. Language contact and the direction of internal drift: The development of tones and registers in Chamic. *Language* 72:1–31.

Tillery, Jan. 1990. Language and identity in Oklahoma. Paper presented at the Southeastern Conference on Linguistics (SECOL), Atlanta, GA.

Tillery, Jan. 1992. The locus of language variation in Oklahoma. Oklahoma State University dissertation.

Tillery, Jan, & Guy Bailey. forthcoming-a. The social status of two southernisms. *Journal of English Linguistics*.

Tillery, Jan, & Guy Bailey. forthcoming-b. *Yall* in Oklahoma. *American Speech*.

Tillery, Jan, & Grace Kerr. 1989. The merger of tense and lax vowels before /l/. Paper presented at NWAVE-XVIII, Durham, NC.

Toole, John Kennedy. 1980. *A confederacy of dunces*. Baton Rouge: Louisiana State University Press.

Trudgill, Peter. 1972. Sex, covert prestige, and linguistic change in the urban English of Norwich. *Language in Society* 1:171–98.

Trudgill, Peter. 1974. *The social differentiation of English in Norfolk*. Cambridge: Cambridge University Press.

Trudgill, Peter. 1983. *On dialect*. NY: New York University Press.

Trudgill, Peter. 1986. *Dialects in contact*. Oxford: Basil Blackwell.

Trudgill, Peter. 1990. *The dialects of England*. Cambridge: Basil Blackwell.

Tucker, G. Richard, & Wallace E. Lambert. 1969: White and Negro listeners' reaction to various American English dialects. *Social Forces* 47:463–68.

Turnbull, Jane M. E., & Marion Turnbull. 1859. *American photographs*. 2 vols. London.

Turner, Lorenzo Dow. 1949. *Africanisms in the Gullah dialect*. Chicago: Chicago University Press.

Twain, Mark. [1883] 1945. *Life on the Mississippi*. NY: Bantam.

Tyler, Andrea, & Catherine E. Davies. 1990. Cross-linguistic communication missteps. *Text* 10.4:385–411.

Tyner, Judith. 1992. *Introduction to thematic cartography*. Englewood Cliffs, NJ: Prentice Hall.

U.S. Bureau of the Census. 1860. *The eighth census*. Prepared by Joseph C. G. Kennedy. Washington: Government Printing Office.

U.S. Bureau of the Census. [1870] 1976. A compendium of the ninth census. Comp. by Francis A. Walker. Washington, DC: Government Printing Office. NY: Arno Press.

U.S. Department of Commerce. 1990. U.S. census of population and housing. Tape File 1A: Tennessee: Table detailed race. CD-ROM. Washington: Government Printing Office.

U.S. Geological Survey. 1984. *Fold and thrust belts of the United States*. Reston, VA.

Valdman, Albert. 1977. Créolisation sans pidgin: Le système des déterminants du nom dans les parlers franco-créoles. In Meisel (ed.), 105–136.

Valdman, Albert. 1983. Creolization and second language acquisition. In *Pidginization and creolization as language acquisition*, ed. by Roger Andersen, 212–34. Rowley, MA: Newbury House.

Valls, Lito. 1981. *What a pisatarcle! A dictionary of Virgin Islands Creole*. St. John, USVI: n.p.

Van Vliet, Willem., 1983. Exploring the fourth environment: An examination of the home range of city and suburban teenagers. *Environment and Behavior* 15:567–79.

VanWagenen, Sterling (producer). 1985. *The Trip to Bountiful*. A Filmdallas I and Bountiful Film Partners Production, distributed by Island Pictures.

Varenne, Hervé. 1982. Jocks and freaks: The symbolic structure of the expression of social interaction among American senior high school students. In *Doing the ethnography of schooling*, ed. by George Spindler, 210–35. New York: Holt, Rinehart & Winston.

Varenne, Hervé. 1983. *American school language: culturally patterned conflicts in a suburban high school*. NY: Irvington Publishers.

Varenne, Hervé. 1986a. "Drop in Anytime": Community and authenticity in American everyday life. In Varenne 1986b, 209–28.

Varenne, Hervé (ed.). 1986b. *Symbolizing America*. University of Nebraska Press.

Ver Steeg, Clarence L. 1975. *The origins of a Southern mosaic: Studies of early Carolina and Georgia*. Athens: University of Georgia Press.

Viereck, Wolfgang. 1988. Invariant *be* in an unnoticed source of American Black English. *American Speech* 63:291–303.

Viereck, Wolfgang. 1989. In need of more evidence on American Black English: The ex-slave narratives revisited. *Neuphilologischen Mitteilungen* 92:247–62.

Viles, Jonas. 1933. *A history of Missouri for high schools*. NY: The Macmillan Company.

Vinson, Julien. 1882. Créole. *Dictionnaire des sciences anthropologiques et ethnologiques*. Paris.

von Schneidemesser, Luanne. 1988. The foundations of the *Dictionary of American Regional English*. *Lexicographica* 4:34–59.

Wallace, David Duncan. 1961. *South Carolina: A short history: 1520–1948*. Columbia, SC: University of South Carolina Press.

Walser, Richard. 1955. Negro dialect in eighteenth century American drama. *American Speech* 30:269–76.

Warner-Lewis, Maureen. 1996. *Trinidad Yoruba: From mother tongue to memory*. Tuscaloosa: The University of Alabama Press.

Webster, Noah. [1789] 1951. *Dissertations on the English Language*. Gainesville, FL: Scholars' Facsimiles & Reprints.

Weijnen, A. 1968. Zum wert subjektiver Dialektgrenzen. *Lingua* 21:594–96.

Weinreich, Uriel. 1953. *Languages in contact*. The Hague: Mouton.

Weinreich, Uriel. [1954] 1986. Is structural dialectology possible? In *Dialect and language variation*, ed. by Harold Allen & Michael Linn, 20–34. Orlando: Academic Press.

Weinreich, Uriel, William Labov & Marvin Herzog. 1968. Empirical foundations for a theory of language change. In *Directions for historical linguistics*, ed. by W. Lehmann & Y. Malkiel, 97–195. Austin: University of Texas Press.

Weinstein, Carol Simon, & Thomas G. David (eds.). 1987. *Spaces for children: The built environment and child development*. NY: Plenum.

Wellman, Barry P. 1988. Structural analysis: from method and metaphor to theory and substance. In Wellman & Berkowitz (eds.), 19–61.

Wellman, Barry P., & Stephen B. Berkowitz (eds.). 1988. *Social structures: A network approach*. Cambridge University Press.

Wellman, Barry P., P. J. Carrington & A. Hall. 1988. Networks as personal communities. In Wellman & Berkowitz (eds.), 130–184.

Wells, John C. 1982. *Accents of English*, vol. 3. Cambridge: Cambridge University Press.

Welmers, William E. 1973. *African language structures*. Berkeley: University of California Press.

Welty, Eudora. [1941] 1980. Petrified man. In *Major American short stories*, ed. by A. Walton Litz, 519–30. NY: Oxford.

Westermann, Dietrich, & Ida C. Ward. 1933. *Practical phonetics for students of African languages*. London: Oxford University Press.

Westermann, Dietrich, & M. A. Bryan. 1952. *The languages of West Africa: Handbook of African languages*, Part II. London: International African Institute/Oxford University Press.

White, Hayden. 1973. *Metahistory: The historical imagination in nineteenth-century Europe*. Baltimore: Johns Hopkins.

Whitney, William Dwight. 1867. *Language and the study of language*. NY.

Whitney, William Dwight. [1875] 1979. *The life and growth of language*. NY: Dover Publications.

Willard, E. Payson. 1936. The origin of *ain't*. *Word Study* 11:2–3.

Willard, George O. 1891. *History of the Providence stage*. Providence.

Williams, Elizabeth Joan. 1953. *The grammar of plantation overseers' letters, Rockingham County*. Chapel Hill: University of North Carolina thesis.

Williams, Glyn. 1992. *Sociolinguistics: A sociological critique*. London: Routledge.

Williams, John G. l895. A study in Gullah English. *The Charleston (SC) Sunday News* (Feb. 10). ms. in University of South Carolina Library.

Williams, Roger. 1980. *Sing a sad song: The life of Hank Williams*. 2d ed. Urbana: University of Illinois Press.

Williams, Selase W. 1993. *Substantive Africanisms at the end of the African linguistic diaspora*. In Mufwene with Condon (eds.), 406–22.

Williams, Walter, & Floyd Calvin Shoemaker. 1930. *Missouri: Mother of the West*. Chicago: The American Historical Society.

Williamson, Juanita. 1968. *A phonological and morphological study of the speech of the negro in Memphis, Tennessee*. Publication of the American Dialect Society (PADS) 50. Tuscaloosa: University of Alabama Press.

Williamson, Juanita, & Virginia Burke (eds.). 1971. *A various language: Perspectives on American Dialect*. NY: Holt, Rinehart & Winston.

Willis, Eola. 1924. *The Charleston stage in the XVIII century*. Columbia, SC: State Co.

Wilmeth, Thomas L. 1992. "You hope to learn": Flem's self-empowerment through silence in Faulkner's Snopes trilogy. *SECOL Review* 16:165–78.

Wilson, Charles Reagan, & William Ferris (eds.). 1989. *Encyclopedia of Southern culture*. Chapel Hill: University of North Carolina Press.

Winford, Donald. 1992. Back to the past: The BEV/creole connection re-visited. *Language Variation and Change* 4:311–57.

Wolfram, Walt. 1969. *A sociolinguistic description of Detroit Negro speech*. Washington, DC: Center for Applied Linguistics.

Wolfram, Walt. 1974. The relationship of white Southern speech to Vernacular Black English. *Language* 50:498–527.

Wolfram, Walt. 1986. Good data in a bad situation: Eliciting vernacular structures. In *The Fergusonian impact: In honor of Charles A. Ferguson on the occasion of his 65th birthday*, vol. 2, ed. by Joshua A. Fishman, Andree Tabouret-Keller, Michale Clyne, Bh. Krishnamurti & Mohamed Abdulazizi, 3–22. The Hague: Mouton de Gruyter.

Wolfram, Walt. 1990. Re-examining Vernacular Black English. Review article of Schneider 1989 and Butters 1989. *Language* 66:121–33.

Wolfram, Walt. 1991. *Dialects and American English*. Englewood Cliffs, NJ: Prentice-Hall.

Wolfram, Walt. 1992. A proactive role for speech-language pathologists in sociolinguistic education. *Ethnotes* 2.4:2–10.

Wolfram, Walt. 1993a. Ethical considerations in language awareness programs. *Issues in Applied Linguistics* 4.2:225–55.

Wolfram, Walt. 1993b. The sociolinguistic vacation: Continuity and change in "quaint" island communities. Paper presented at NWAVE-XXIII, Ottawa, Canada.

Wolfram, Walt. 1994. On the sociolinguistic significance of obscure dialect structures: The NP_i call NP_i Ving construction in African American Vernacular English. *American Speech* 69:339–60.

Wolfram, Walt, & Donna Christian. 1976. *Appalachian speech.* Washington, DC: Center for Applied Linguistics.

Wolfram, Walt, & Nona H. Clarke. 1971. *Black-White speech relationships.* Washington, DC: Center for Applied Linguistics.

Wolfram, Walt, & Ralph Fasold. 1974. *The study of social dialects in American English.* Englewood Cliffs, NJ: Prentice-Hall.

Wong, Sau-ling Cynthia. 1988. The language situation of Chinese Americans. *Language diversity: Problem or resource?*, ed. by Sandra Lee McKay & Sau-ling Cynthia Wong, 193–228. NY: Newbury House.

Wood, Gordon R. 1967. *Sub-regional speech variations in vocabulary, grammar, and pronunciation.* Cooperative research project no. 3046. Final report. Edwardsville: Southern Illinois University.

Wood, Gordon. 1971. *Vocabulary change: A study in variation in regional words in eight of the southern states.* Carbondale: Southern Illinois University Press.

Wood, Peter H. 1974. *Black majority: Negroes in colonial South Carolina from 1670 through the Stono Rebellion.* NY: Alfred A. Knopf.

Wood, Peter H. 1989. The changing population of the colonial South: An overview by race and region, 1685–1790. In *Powhatan's Mantle: Indians in the colonial Southeast*, ed. by Peter H. Wood, Gregory A. Waselkov & M. Thomas Hatley, 35–103. Lincoln: University of Nebraska Press.

Woolard, Kathryn A. 1991. Linkages of language and ethnic identity: Changes in Barcelona, 1980–1987. In Dow (ed.), 61–81.

Wright, Gavin. 1986. *Old South, new South: Revolutions in the southern economy since the Civil War.* NY: Basic Books.

Wright, Joseph. 1898–1905. *The English dialect dictionary.* London.

Wright, Richard Louis. 1976. Language standards and communicative style in the black church. University of Texas at Austin dissertation.

Wright, Richardson. 1937. *Revels in Jamaica 1682–1838.* NY: Dodd, Mead & Co.

Wyld, Henry Cecil. 1920. *A history of modern colloquial English.* Oxford: Basil Blackwell.

Yansen, C. A. 1975. *Random remarks on creoles.* Margate: Thanet Press.

Yetman, Norman K. 1967. The background of the slave narrative collection. *American Quarterly* 19:534–43.

Yoon, Keumsil Kim. 1992. New perspective on intrasentential code-switching: A study of Korean-English switching. *Applied Psycholinguistics* 13:433–49.

Contributors

Sharon Ash, University of Pennsylvania

Guy Bailey, University of Nevada, Las Vegas

Robert Bayley, University of Texas at San Antonio

Jeutonne P. Brewer, University of North Carolina at Greensboro

Ronald R. Butters, Duke University

Frederic G. Cassidy, Dictionary of American Regional English

Marvin K. L. Ching, University of Memphis

Felice Anne Coles, University of Mississippi

Marianne Cooley, University of Houston

Chris Craig, North Carolina State University

Patricia Cukor-Avila, University of North Texas

Catherine E. Davies, University of Alabama at Tuscaloosa

Boyd H. Davis, University of North Carolina at Charlotte

Walter F. Edwards, Wayne State University

Rachel B. Faries, Alton, Illinois

Crawford Feagin, Arlington, Virginia

Timothy C. Frazer, Western Illinois University

Joan H. Hall, Dictionary of American Regional English

Kirk Hazen, North Carolina State University

Ellen Johnson, Western Kentucky University

Barbara Johnstone, Texas A&M University

Tom Klingler, Tulane University

William A. Kretzschmar, Jr., University of Georgia

Hsiang-te Kung, University of Memphis

William Labov, University of Pennsylvania

Donald M. Lance, University of Missouri at Columbia

Natalie Maynor, Mississippi State University

Allan Metcalf, MacMurray College

Katherine Wyly Mille, University of North Carolina at Greensboro

Michael Montgomery, University of South Carolina

Salikoko S. Mufwene, University of Chicago

Leah Neely, University of North Carolina at Charlotte

Michael D. Picone, University of Alabama at Tuscaloosa

Dennis R. Preston, Michigan State University

Natalie Schilling-Estes, North Carolina State University

Edgar W. Schneider, Universität Regensburg

Michael Smilowitz, University of North Carolina at Charlotte

Bruce Southard, East Carolina University

William C. Taylor, Talladega College

Jan Tillery, University of Nevada at Las Vegas

Luanne von Schneidemesser, Dictionary of American Regional English

Joan Weatherly, University of Memphis

Tom Wikle, Oklahoma State University

Thomas L. Wilmeth, Concordia University

Walt Wolfram, North Carolina State University

Index